THE COMPLETE

FAR SIDE

VOLUME ONE
January 1980–June 1984

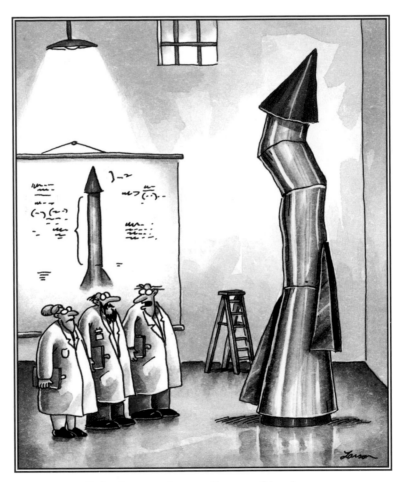

"It's time we face reality, my friends. ...
We're not exactly rocket scientists."

THE COMPLETE FAR SIDE

VOLUME ONE
January 1980–June 1984

Gary Larson

Andrews McMeel Publishing

an Andrews McMeel Universal company
Kansas City Sydney London

For information, write Andrews McMeel Publishing
a division of Andrews McMeel Universal
1130 Walnut Street, Kansas City, Missouri 64106.

First Paperback Edition
First Printing, November 2014
Ninth Printing, December 2021
ISBN: 978-1-4494-6004-4

The Library of Congress has cataloged the hardcover edition as follows:

Larson, Gary.
   [Far Side]
   The Complete Far Side / Gary Larson.
      p. cm.
"Presents every Far Side cartoon ever syndicated. More than 4,000 cartoons,
1,100 which have never been published in a book, are included in this
two-volume, slipcased treasure trove"--CIP text.
   ISBN 0-7407-2113-5
   1. American wit and humor, Pictorial. 2. Caricatures and
cartoons--United States--History--20th century. I. Title.

NC1429.L32A4 2003
741.5′973--dc21

                    2003045301

Produced by Lionheart Books, Ltd.
3522 Ashford Dunwoody Rd. N.E. #229
Atlanta, Georgia 30319

Designed by Michael Reagan
Printed and bound through Asia Pacific Offset
Volume One, page 1 painting by Jerry Tiritilli

CONTENTS

Volume One

FOREWORD
By Steve Martin

Different Beginnings for Gary Larson Essay

I am sorry to report, given the occasion of this very important publication, that many of the scenes depicted in this book are actually false. Several years ago I began to suspect the veracity of a few of the events portrayed by Larson. "Wait a minute," I thought. "A chicken couldn't confess to murdering Old MacDonald: Old MacDonald was a *fictitious* character." It was a small thought that grew to a big one: Was Gary Larson just making a lot of this stuff up? Though many believe that chickens talk, does it necessarily follow that likewise so do ducks and dogs?

Gary Larson came to my house last weekend, and I was surprised to find that he is an insect. All this time I figured him for a bear or a little fat kid, but when he walked across my ceiling and hid in the drapes, I knew ...

An Open Letter to Gary

Dear Gary,

Life does not come with little frames around it. Life is not topsy-turvy and surreal. Life is hard and it's not really funny when you make light of it. Have you ever read Schopenhauer? He thinks that death ...

I suppose Mr. Larson and others like him think it's funny to depict young boys standing on top of a flattened dog. This attempt at "humor" actually teaches and encourages young boys to stand on top of flattened dogs. In fact, though I am not a young boy, I myself was tempted to stand on top of a flattened dog. But you know what? There are no flattened dogs where I live. There are, however, hundreds of cats who, though not flattened, are actually quite thin, and if laid on their side, would qualify as flattened. I'll guarantee that standing on them was not funny. Not really funny, not har-de-har-har funny, just mildly funny.

Gary Larson is the greatest living cartoonist OOPS sorry, Gary—make that greatest beheaded cartoonist ...

Gary Larson, born Garyisovich Larsonoffsky, the third son of a farmer and a duck, raised in Peking, swore when he saw his family being taken away and bean-fried by two pandas that he would move to the United States and make enough money so that one day he could return in triumph, though when he did make enough money, he thought, "Actually I'd prefer to lose all my money and return in defeat."

Many Larson scholars like to cite panel 108, caption 16, as proof of the existence of a deity. However, the exact nature of the deity is contradicted by several other panels. Scholars working at the Institute of Talking Dogs offer panel 247, with its image of two men standing on white clouds of heaven talking out of earshot of the deity, as proof of Larson's *theory of semi-omniscience*. In another panel depicting heaven, the newly deceased are issued harps, indicating a *benevolent un-musical mover*. However, the two men in the previous panel do not have harps, they have a gun. So how does a supreme being regarded as a *benevolent un-musical mover* fit into the *theory of semi-omniscience*, especially when the devil, who is handing out accordions, is revealed to be a blithe humorist (panel 42, caption 16)?

I'll bet Gary Larson's neighbors would say that Gary is very quiet:

"He kept to himself, never bothered anybody."

"And how did you feel when you found out he wrote *The Far Side*?"

"I was shocked. He seemed like such a nice guy."

Questions I would like to ask Gary Larson:

Who are you currently dating?

What's coming up in the future for a Gary Larson?

Are you crazy and nutty at home?

If you were in a strict foreign country run by zealots, and they demanded that you renounce your belief that humans can deflate like balloons and fly around the room, would you recant, escape, or die while being squeezed by red-hot pincers?

Hey Gary, what do you think?

Steve

Introduction

by Jake Morrissey

"Well, this started off innocently enough . . ."
—Gary Larson

My favorite Gary Larsons were never published. For the better part of a decade they sat at the bottom of a desk drawer, crammed into a tattered white envelope, forgotten by me and, no doubt, by Gary. I rediscovered them by chance one afternoon as I rifled through a drawer looking for something unrelated to *The Far Side.* The contents slipped out of the envelope and fell into my hand. It took a moment for me to recognize them and to realize what small wonders they are.

Wonders the size of a Post-it note.

Some of the most revealing work Gary Larson ever produced as a cartoonist can be found in the brief notes he stuck to his cartoons just before he sent them to Universal Press Syndicate, where I worked as his editor for the last 10 years

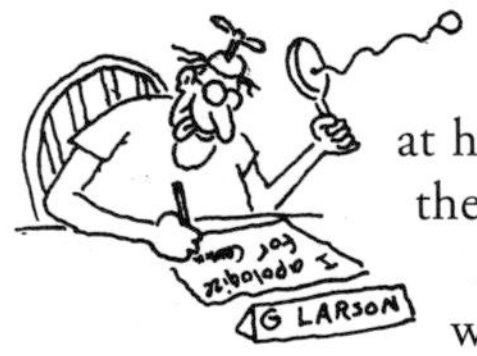
G LARSON

that he drew *The Far Side.* Every week, as his deadline loomed and the Federal Express driver hovered expectantly at his door, Gary would dash off last-minute comments about the cartoons he was sending me. Some of the notes suggested how he thought a caption could be improved; others wondered if a drawing would reproduce satisfactorily in newspapers. A couple even questioned whether a cartoon was funny at all. They were pithy, astute, and self-deprecating, but what I like best about them now is the insight they offer into the process of creating *The Far Side.* In a way, they are a peek behind the curtain.

I can offer no reasonable explanation for why I kept these notes—they certainly weren't written for the ages. I know I didn't keep all of them; usually I threw them away. But one day as Gary and I were talking on the phone, instead of throwing the note into the wastebasket, I stuffed it into a spare envelope. And so a habit was born.

"I have no idea why I drew this or what it means,
but compared to the ***next*** *cartoon, it's very normal."*

Rereading Gary's notes, I am struck by how open he is to his own creativity, how willing he is to be guided by it. Several mention that his initial ideas for cartoons turned into (pupated?) panels that differed markedly from their inspiration. What continues to interest me about Gary Larson the cartoonist is *how* his methods differ from those of his peers. Many cartoonists begin with a gag, a punch line, and write toward it. Gary begins with the seed of an idea, which often doesn't feel traditionally funny, and then tends it a bit to see what takes root. What's so exceptional about *The Far Side* is that sometimes what sprouts isn't what anyone expects, least of all Gary: He plants what he thinks is a carrot and it turns out to be cabbage. It is this sense of not quite knowing how something will come out that makes *The Far Side* subversively exhilarating.

Cows ring doorbells. Monsters' eyes reflect in rearview mirrors. Praying mantises bicker over who devoured whose mate. Surprise may be a part of all humor, but in *The Far Side,* surprise, even astonishment, is the norm.

"Jake: Your version was the best of all. (Damn it!)"

Editing Gary's work can be tricky: "Improving" a vision as idiosyncratic as his without his input isn't easy, though there were editors who thought it was. "Just take the word out, nobody will get the damn thing anyway," a newspaper editor once said to me when he called to complain about the language in a *Far Side* caption. What the editor didn't understand—or didn't care to understand—was how hard Gary works to get his art and his language just right. And I always kept in mind that readers turn to *The Far Side* for Gary's view of the universe, not mine, so my job was to help him find in himself the best work he was capable of.

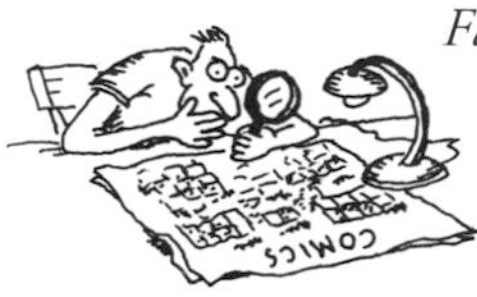
COMICS

Early on, we settled into a working rhythm that served us well. Every Monday morning I received the next week's cartoons from Gary, and after going over them on my own I would call him. We would then discuss each cartoon, addressing the points he raised in the notes he attached, editing language or modifying art when we agreed it was necessary. He always knew where the true humor was in each panel—sometimes the best part of a cartoon was the reaction on a character's face, for example—and he knew when to stop fiddling with it, which some cartoonists can't do.

Gary is a rigorous, even ruthless, editor of his own work, writing and rewriting his captions so the flow of the words matches the cartoon's art and tone. He understands that the heart of a successful cartoon lies in the writing. Good writing can save bad art, but good art can never save bad writing. That is why Gary willingly reworked captions word by word to get them right. If you spend any time at all analyzing *Far Side* captions, you'll see that removing a word can ruin the rhythm and dilute the humor. We once had six different phone conversations in one day about a single word in a caption. (No, I won't tell you which cartoon; I invoke the cartoonist-editor privilege.)

His intriguing use of language also had unexpected benefits: Helping to decide the correct spelling of *luposlipaphobia* was a lot of fun for someone who likes to play with language. Saying the word aloud still makes me smile.

Finding the right order for the *Far Side* cartoons over the course of a week was as important as finding the right language in the captions. We tried to pace the cartoons based on our own admittedly idiosyncratic view of newspaper readership. We opened the week on Monday with what we thought was the funniest cartoon. Tuesday's was usually a little less strong, but Wednesday's had to be the second funniest, since newspapers in North America usually ran their coupons and food advertisements in that day's edition, which generally meant a fatter newspaper and a wider-than-normal readership. Thursday's cartoon was more often than not one of the week's strange cartoons, while Friday's and Saturday's were usually the oddest of the group—the ones we weren't

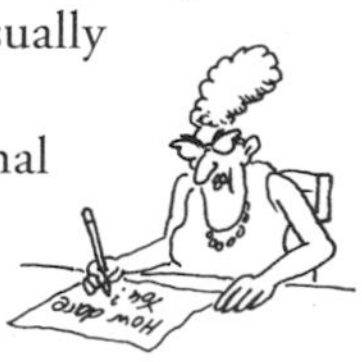
How dare you

quite sure people would get but which we liked anyway. (The Sunday cartoons were another matter entirely.)

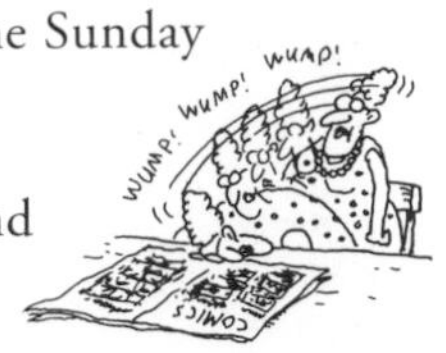
WUMP!
WUMP!
WUMP!
COMICS

I make no claim that this was the most effective way to publish *The Far Side;* no doubt there are people who will find this system bizarre. But it suited us and *The Far Side,* since it seemed to mimic its readers' tastes and sensibilities.

"For the life of me, I can't pronounce let alone spell the word know[n] to every trumpet player. Omnisure? Ambrochure? Oxzfyghzx? What is it?"

But still the questions came—sometimes before the cartoons were even published. In the days before the common use of the Internet, I was the one who hunted down the correct spellings of words that Gary wanted to use in his cartoons, words such as "embouchure," and more unusual phrases or names, such as "Puddin' Tame." I spent hours on the telephone over the years asking experts and librarians to give me the correct spellings of the strange words that popped up in *The Far Side.* I did not usually tell them why I was calling. I did once, but I flustered a librarian at the Kansas City Public Library so much that she told me to hang up and call the reference desk again. "I can't help someone I don't understand," she said, sounding a trifle panicked at the mere thought of *The Far Side.*

"Not sure about the spelling of Honah-Lee. More importantly, this is a little obtuse. Do you get it, and did you get it right away? This is a test. Do not attempt to ask someon[e] else."

As all cartoonists do, Gary draws inspiration from personal experience: his interests, his childhood memories, the world he sees on his way to play basketball. He is sensitive to the fact that his readers may have a different view of life, so we often discussed whether they would understand a particular cartoon and find it funny. A line from *Puff, the Magic Dragon,* for example: Would the millions of people around the world who read *The Far Side* recognize the references? As Gary's audience grew, so did the number of head-scratchers, those readers who didn't quite understand *The Far Side* every day. So some cartoons became a judgment call: Should we release a cartoon that not everyone would understand, or use one that more people might understand but that might not be as funny? More often than not, funny won out. So I became the guy who could explain every *Far Side* cartoon. I know that the praying mantis standing atop a gramophone in one cartoon is the only insect that can cock its head at the same angle as the RCA Victor dog could in the classic "His Master's Voice" pose. And I am one of the few people outside Seattle and the cafés of Italy who knew what a "latte" was before Starbucks made it a ubiquitous part of the coffee experience. I fielded dozens of calls and letters from puzzled readers who thought that the cowboy who asked, "Latte, Jed?" was proposing a bizarre sexual frolic.

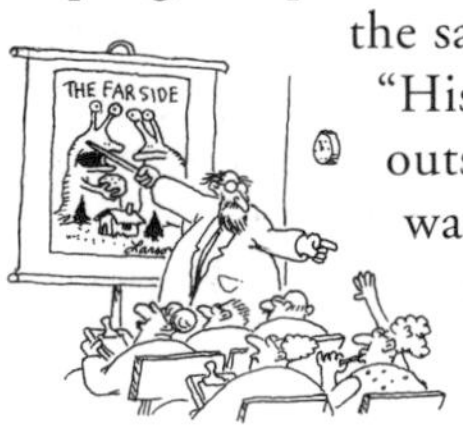
THE FAR SIDE

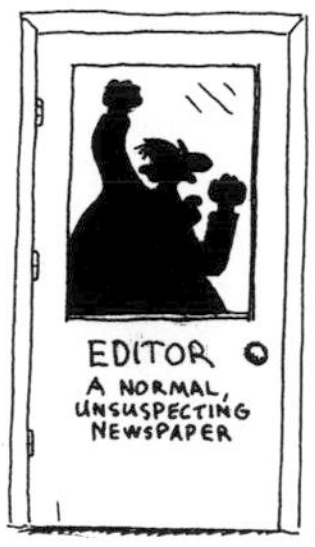
EDITOR
A NORMAL, UNSUSPECTING NEWSPAPER

A week did not go by that I was not asked—by an editor, by a reader, by the media—to explain a particular *Far Side* cartoon. When I did, I invariably heard one of two reactions: a moment of silence at the other end of the phone and then a sudden "Aaaah, *now* I get it," or a perturbed, "That's the joke? That's not funny." I tried to explain to those disappointed souls that a cartoon usually isn't funny when it has to be explained to you.

"Would you mind responding to this guy on my behalf? I would just say you shared his comments with me, and that I offered my apologies for causing him any anger or concern ... and does he know how many dead babies it takes to—oh, forget the last part."

The thornier problems were those readers who understood a *Far Side* cartoon but didn't like what they read and felt the need to express their indignation. Because Gary wants his work to speak for itself and was never comfortable discussing it, I was the first line of complaint for anyone who was offended by a *Far Side* cartoon. I became adroit at replying to a litany of protests about the cartoon: How it was anti-dog, anti-cat, and anti-God; how it was pro-torture, pro-Satan, and pro-violence against animals. None of this was true, of course, as I tried over and over to explain. I came to understand that what bothered people most about *The Far Side* was that they couldn't predict where Gary would find his humor, and that can be disturbing. It always amused me that the cartoons that generated the most irate comments from people who found them reprehensible and morally bankrupt were exactly the same ones that other people indicated were their favorites.

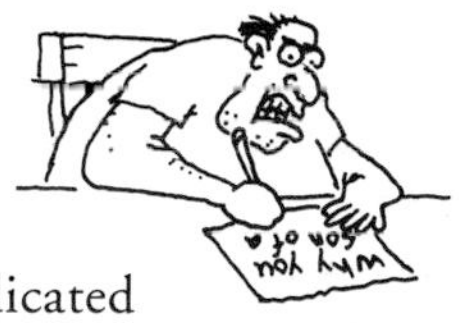

"Originally, what made this thing funny to me, was the fact we couldn't see the tarantula—suggesting where the hell is it? I still think that's what makes this effective. Yet, last-minute stuff, I drew this one, big, hairy leg, making the humor less 'sophisticated,' I think, but maybe a more direct line to the funny bone? (It could easily be whited out at your end.) This would be a good question in the HATs. (Humor Aptitude Tests—I got 680.)"

As painstaking as Gary is with his writing, he is just as careful about making his artwork unambiguous. Though he is the first to admit that his drawing style isn't sophisticated, it shares a certain minimalist charm with the likes of classics such as *Krazy Kat.* Like *Krazy Kat,* the art of *The Far Side* is simple, even naive, but it's comfortably free of the self-conscious, archcartooniness that characterizes so many comic strips. *The Far Side* doesn't look slick or processed because it isn't—because Gary never wanted it to look that way.

His choice of subject matter is just as personal. One of the more interesting subsets of *The Far Side* are the cartoons about cartooning itself. Several characters from other comic strips have appeared in *The Far Side,* notably Charlie Brown, Lucy, Garfield, and even Mark Trail, but I've always found the cartoons about the form more interesting. The characters understand they are in a cartoon and that they are being watched. This conceit makes fun of the idea of *being* a cartoon, an unusual conceit for newspaper comics pages when these first appeared. Over the years Gary has used this technique sparingly but to great effect. And the idea stayed with him: The final two *Far Side* cartoons that appeared on January 1, 1995, were both about cartooning and Gary's role as a cartoonist.

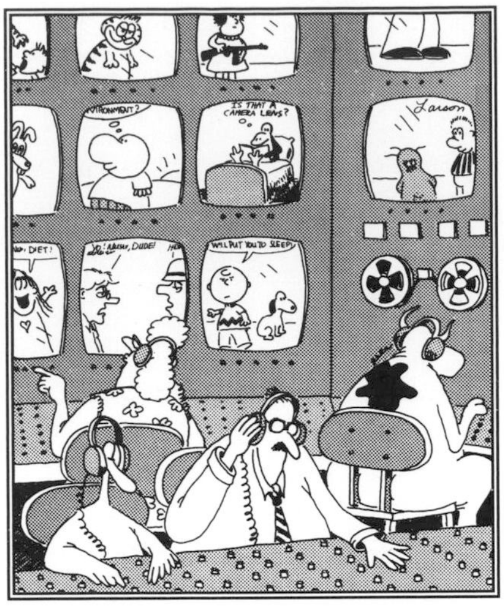
Larson
At *The Far Side*'s spy center

Sometimes I am asked if I think these are the "best" *Far Side* cartoons. I do admit to having a special affection for several others. One mad-scientist cartoon mentions a "Dr. Morrissey" who creates a hideous beast with the nine heads of the Brady Bunch. In another, Gary resorted to his version of "the dog ate my homework" to explain why that week's batch of cartoons was one short. He submitted a panel of an angry truck driver shaking his fist at an oblivious driver who had just cut him off. The caption reads: "Suddenly, Jake realized there was nothing funny about this cartoon. 'Maybe,' he murmured to himself, *'That's* what's funny.' (However, a replacement cartoon would arrive on his desk Tuesday and he would breathe a tremendous sigh of relief.)"

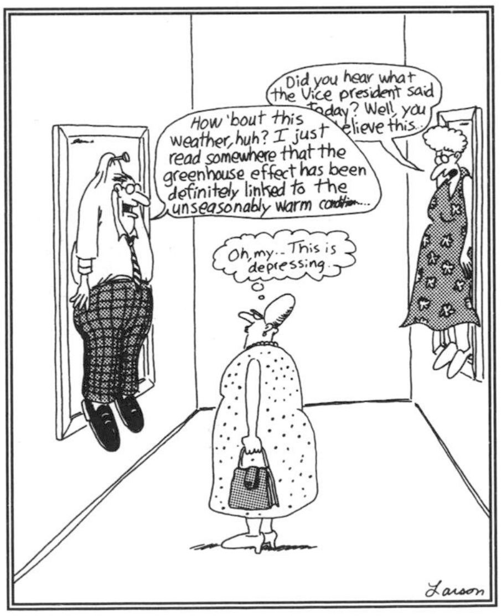
Did you hear what the Vice president said today? Well, you lieve this...
How 'bout this weather, huh? I just read somewhere that the greenhouse effect has been definitely linked to the unseasonably warm condition...
Oh, my.. This is depressing.
Larson
The art of conversation

Finally, there is a simple cartoon whose most interesting characteristic is its genesis. On Halloween night 1989, I sat on a wide windowsill in an apartment in New York City that Gary and his wife had rented while he was on sabbatical. As we talked, Gary said suddenly, "You just gave me an idea for a cartoon. It's the first idea I've had since I've been on sabbatical." Several months later, after he had returned to drawing *The Far Side,* Gary submitted a panel in which

a woman was standing in front of a man hanging in a picture frame who was prattling on about the weather. The woman is thinking, "Oh, my ... This is depressing." The cartoon's caption is "The art of conversation."

The cartoon doesn't cast me in the most flattering light, I know, but that's not something I dwell on. I prefer to think of it as an object lesson in understanding that ideas for cartoons can come from anywhere if you know where to look.

Being a cartoonist can be very solitary: just you and the Bristol board in front of you. And it's not that easy. Anyone who thinks he can get rich by producing something funny that's read every day over soggy cornflakes should buy a lottery ticket instead. There are a limited number of comic strip slots in newspapers, and many of them are filled by cartoons drawn by old men and have been around for decades. (The Web is changing this, but for many cartoonists, the newspaper is still the venue of choice.) Imagine that the only bookstore in town has a selection of just two dozen titles, some of them 70 years old, and you have a fairly accurate idea of what cartoon syndication is like: It's a very competitive business. The odds are stacked against you.

But sometimes, when newspaper editors take a chance and readers aren't looking that carefully, something a little innovative can sneak in. Day by day, panel by panel, a cartoonist with a different point of view that's clear and fresh and impertinent catches people unaware, engaging them in unexpected ways and prompting them to think a little about the world around them. A connection is forged. Gary Larson and *The Far Side* did that.

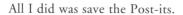

"If by chance worse comes to worse and you don't hear from me—please just use your own judgment as far as selecting one version over another, one word over another, or repairing any of my usual grammatical errors. In other words, make me funny, Jake."

I never made Gary Larson funny. No one did. What he created over 15 years came from someplace unique within him, a universe all his own. That is why *The Far Side* still seems fresh, still seems rare, years after the cartoons were first drawn.

CARTOON POLICE
HUMORCIDE

All I did was save the Post-its.

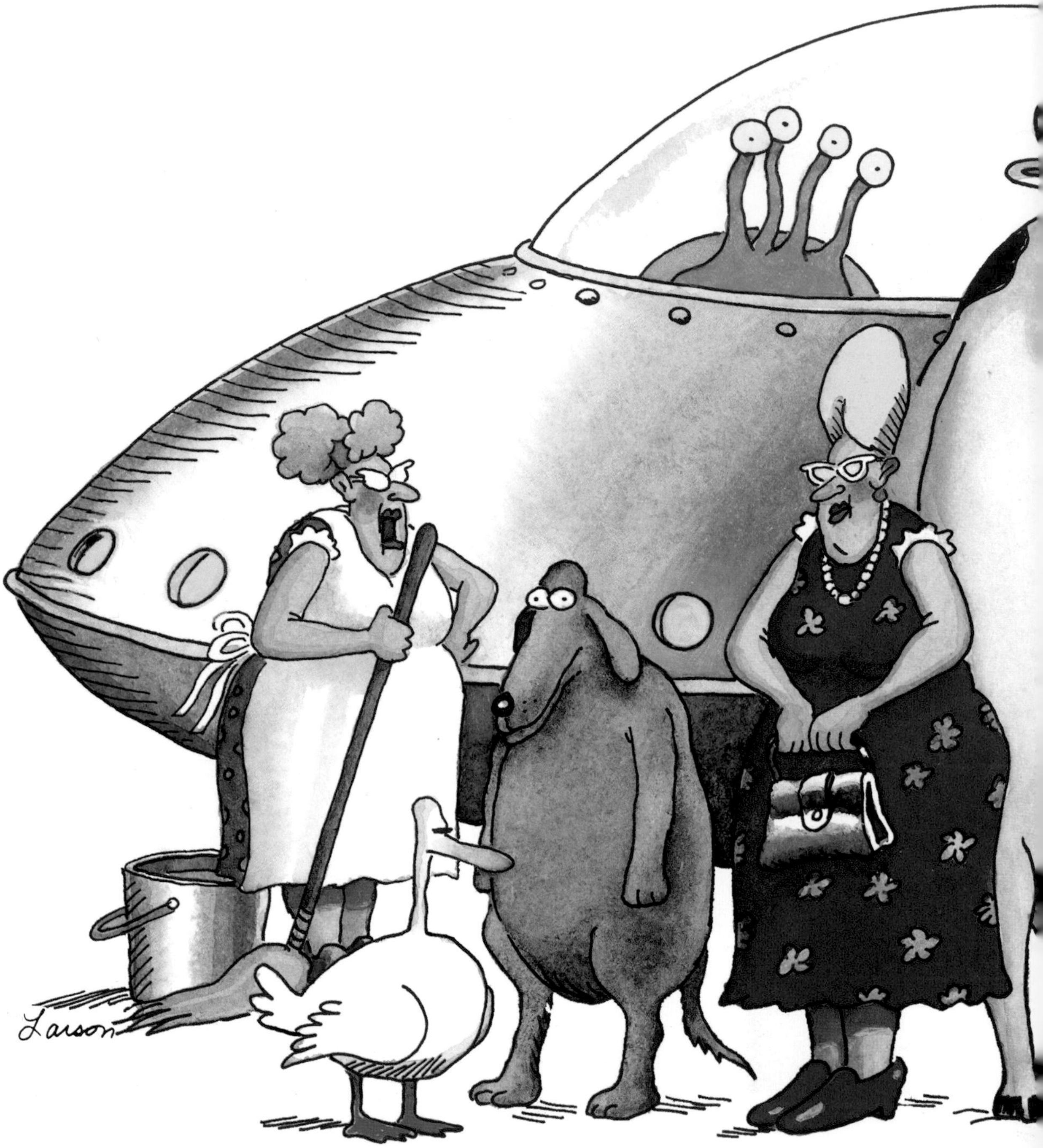
Larson

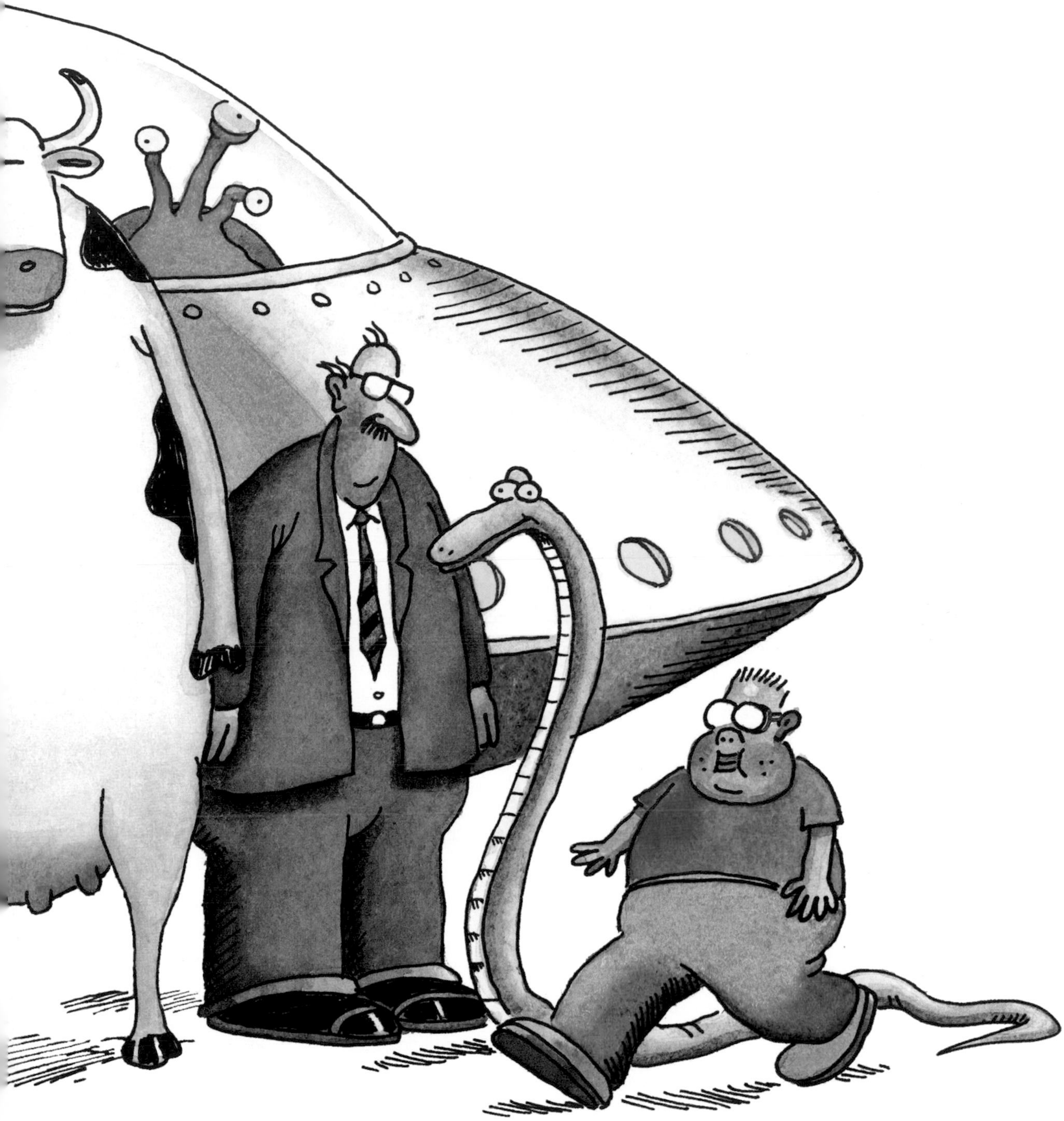

Preface

You know I'm nervous.

As I write, it's been almost seven years since I hung up my eraser. (For the record, an eraser was the most essential tool I owned.) And this is the first time, ever, that I have reviewed my own work in its entirety. I must tell you: I have seen things.

To begin with, I stumbled across a couple small mysteries herein: One cartoon appears twice, years apart, but with different captions. I have no idea what happened there, except that I strongly suspect chaos theory was involved. And another I unwittingly drew twice—again, several years apart. (No wonder I had this eerie sensation the thing was practically drawing itself.) I'm not going to identify any of the above offenders; I'm banking on you just saying "déjà vu" a couple times and moving on.

Now, that covers four cartoons—as for the remaining 4,333.

In hindsight, I realize it probably wasn't a great idea to base any cartoon on some news event, fad, expression, person, movie, TV show, or commercial that was destined to fade from everyone's memory before my ink was dry. Of course, time eventually erodes all humor, which is why you no longer hear the one about the Visigoth and the Hittite, or that old Neanderthal favorite, "Why did the Archaeopteryx cross the road?" (Actually, that last one still works for me.)

And then there are those cartoons that trigger something a friend of mine calls the What-the? Reflex. This reflex is entirely involuntary, much like the way a dead frog's leg can be made to kick with the proper stimulus. You'll see a cartoon, and "What the?" will simply burst from your voice box. (I love biology.)

Of course, there are a number of other reflexes that could be discussed (the more upsetting My God! Reflex is sure to strike on occasion), and I'm obviously hopeful that laughter is included among them. But there is only one more I wish to mention, and one I hope you encounter only rarely. Because this is the bad one. This is the one that any credible cartoonist truly fears. And it is this: the silent yawn. It seems innocuous enough, perhaps even preferred to the My God! Reflex. It is not. It is death. To bore someone—to fail to engage them on some level, good or bad (and you hope it's good), to fail to give something to them that sticks to their bones—even if they wish you hadn't—that is simply a creative effort that tanked. It's a frog's leg that not only won't kick, it won't even twitch. It's just going to lie there, cold and still. I beg you, please: Quit poking the damn thing and just move on. I'm sure a good, solid "What the?" is just around the corner.

Yes, I'm definitely nervous.

However, let me quickly add, I don't mean to sound defensive, or somehow distancing myself from anything in this book. Quite the contrary. Despite the experiments that somehow went awry, I'm actually proud of this body of work. I'm ready to hand it in. (And, if nothing else, the other cartoonists will never call me "Skinny Books" again.)

So why, I have to ask myself, am I nervous? Well, I think it has something to do with what the cartoonist Richard Guindon once said to me when I was first starting out. We were discussing our shared, iron-clad rule of never accepting cartoon ideas from others, and Richard said, "It's like having someone write in your diary." It's an apt analogy. As I look over my 14 years of *Far Side* cartoons, what I really see are my daily "entries," my musings, my little experiments in ink. Every one of these cartoons is just something that drifted into my head when I was alone with my thoughts. And, for better or worse, I "jotted" them down. It was only later, when perhaps I received an angry letter from someone, that it struck me: Hey! Someone's been reading my diary!

Enough of my blabbering. What's done is done. I'll get out of your way. But maybe it would be helpful if I told you this: My drafting table, where I drew *The Far Side* for most of my career, faced a window that overlooked a beautiful garden; beyond the garden was a lake, and beyond the lake Mount Rainier rose majestically into the Washington sky.

I worked at night.

—Gary Larson

The Larson brothers, California (1957)   *Photo by Gary's mom*

Acknowledgments

Someone once told me that no one has ever realized their goal in life without someone else having opened that first door for them. I believe it's true. (Even Jeremiah Johnson got that old geezer to show him the "ways" of the mountain.)

My Door Opener was Stan Arnold, the General Manager of Chronicle Features Syndicate. I met Stan in the summer of 1979, and in the space of about 20 minutes, while sitting in his office, I went from Gary Larson the Confused to Gary Larson the Confusing Cartoonist. (I guess Stan must have seen something in me, sort of like the way a horse trainer might recognize qualities in a two-year-old, despite the dull expression on its face.) When Stan passed away a few years ago, it was a contemplative time for me as I recalled the man who, well—there's no other way to put it—changed my life.

But if Stan Arnold opened the door to my cartooning career, I had a slew of folks who strove to keep it from swinging back shut on me.

Stuart Dodds was the lone and intrepid salesperson who first ventured forth with *The Far Side,* knocking on the office doors of newspaper editors, presenting my work, and braving their occasional shock and indignation. Believe me, in the heyday of *Nancy* and *Blondie,* what Stuart did took some chutzpah. (I've long suspected he pitched *The Far Side* wearing one of those big nose and glasses disguise.) If there was some kind of Purple Heart for syndicate salespeople, Stuart would be plastered with them.

Similarly, I must deeply thank those newspapers that did not recoil when they first saw my work. Indeed, a handful even embraced it. When you draw a cartoon that may, for example, show a nerdy kid walking toward the front of his class for "show 'n' tell," carrying a jar with a human head in it, then you definitely need some folks around you who aren't afraid to shake things up a little, or at least willing to look the other way once in a while. During the first year or two that I was drawing, these papers essentially paid my rent and kept me in ink.

And on the subject of ink, I suppose I know a little something about drawing, but when it later came to painting my work, I sat on the bench and watched as a number of artists made wonderful, often inspired, contributions to my work. I am extremely grateful to them all, but I must specifically mention Donna Oatney, the alpha artist who created the lion's share of watercolors within these three volumes. If anyone ever came close to having a mind-meld with me, it was Donna. (Frankly, I think this was starting to worry her.)

My long-time editor at Universal Press Syndicate was the invaluable Jake Morrissey. And let me say this about editors in general: Not having a good one is like doing brain surgery with a butter knife—you can do it, but you're always paranoid the other surgeons are rolling their eyes when you're not looking. What a relief to have someone standing next to you hand you a sharp scalpel and just say, "Cut that thing, Gary! Right there! Cut it, damn you!" Thanks, Jake.

In team sports, they refer to some athletes as the "Go-To Guy." In my world, that person was Tom Thornton, the president of Andrews McMeel Publishing. Always the trusted voice of calm and reason, Tom often guided me through the Valley of Nuts, where I believe I had a tendency to sometimes linger. Moreover, you hold in your hands a book for which virtually nothing was spared when it came to quality. That's not a rollover decision for any publisher, but I've always had a playbook with just one page in it, which simply says, "Get the ball into Tom's hands."

I cannot adequately thank my wife, Toni, for her unwavering support. Even with the help of a reliable editor, it takes someone who truly cares about you, someone who can look at something you've worked really hard on, and then, with eyes full of love, gaze into your own and softly say, "That's not funny."

My sincere gratitude is extended to this book's main editors, Dorothy O'Brien and Chris Schillig, for their collective advice and feedback, and also to author/editor John Yow, for his own helpful insights. Also, my thanks go to Charles Wheeler, who created the inspired database that allowed us all (especially the designer) to maneuver through thousands of images and make innumerable decisions on the crafting of the book.

Early on in the planning process, someone at my publisher warned me that there was no avoiding some screwup or two in the final product. Too many layers to this thing, they said, and the glitch gnomes are always out in force. Probably true, but I immediately decided to haul out my secret weapon: a human microscope who is fondly known around here as Kate "The Eye" Gentry. You can stand outside The Eye's office when she's proofreading and hear those glitch gnomes scream for their lives. It's a lovely sound.

Now rumor has it that this book's designer and guiding force, Michael Reagan (not the son of a former president; the son of a ship fitter), having wrestled for three years with this project's enormous complexities (and one Mother Hen cartoonist), may have gone insane just as *The Complete Far Side* went to press. But I hope you'll agree, Michael went out in glory. (And should the rumor prove true, I certainly intend to swing by on occasion and express my deep thanks to him during visiting hours.)

And finally, of course, I must thank you. I found myself so often in hot water when my work crossed some invisible line, I intermittently thought, "Well, that was fun while it lasted." The Humor Police, it seems, are always hovering around; I just didn't know you were out there as well. Boy, did you guys save my butt on more than one occasion. My gratitude knows no bounds.

I would also like to thank Jeremiah Johnson.

Production Note

It all started simply enough: I received a call from Tom Thornton, the president of Andrews McMeel, in November of 2000, asking if I would be interested in working on the final *Far Side* book. It would include everything Gary had done during the 14 years *The Far Side* was in syndication, over 4,300 cartoons. I was a big fan so it was not a difficult decision.

I had never met Gary, so we set up a meeting a few weeks later to initiate a relationship that, as we both realized, would need to work effectively for the next three years. After all, this would be Gary's legacy book, and he was very serious about having it done right. In person, I found Gary to be surprisingly shy and modest; he does not try to impress you with his brilliance or overwhelm you with his ego. However, under that low-key, mild-mannered appearance is indeed a man of steel. Gary is ferocious in guarding against mediocrity and a perfectionist about his art. We have had endless discussions and generated a zillion e-mails about things like commas, italics, em dashes, and word choice—and that was just for the captions. When it came to reproducing the drawings or creating new ones—those black lines that make up the world Gary lives in—well, suffice it to say that Gary is unrelenting when it comes to making his work as good as it can be. (You can probably see why it did not stay simple for very long.)

But who can blame him? *The Far Side* was unique; there has never been anything quite like it, before or since. Maybe the timing was right. The first *Far Side* cartoon appeared in 1980, the year we elected Ronald Reagan. And over the next 14 years, a steady diet of hilarious abnormality was maybe just what the world needed. Or maybe a steady diet of bizarre genius was simply what the comics page needed—a riotous upheaval in a land where change comes glacially slow.

For whatever reason, *The Far Side* rocked the world. It became a cultural phenomenon. People didn't simply read *The Far Side;* they reacted to it, often with strange passion. On that first visit to Seattle, I was flabbergasted when Toni, Gary's wife, showed me a room full of boxes filled with letters that Gary and his publisher had received over the years. A room full. A lot of it was fan mail, of course, but there was an amazing amount of hate mail, much of it suggesting that Gary was a very sick person and should be put away, or at the very least barred from the comics page.

Not surprisingly, given the odd animals, insects, microbes, aliens, and humans that populate the panel, there were also thousands of letters from readers pointing out some mistake or other. Another large category consisted of letters from people who generally liked *The Far Side* but felt that in the case of a specific cartoon, Gary had gone too far and had offended them. In other words, as long as he poked fun at someone else, Gary's work was great. Looking back through all the cartoons, I've concluded that over the years he has been very evenhanded and managed to offend nearly every group.

But more than that, of course, what the letters show is that Gary engaged his readers—perhaps more than any cartoonist before or since. The response he stirred in the heart and mind of his audience—whether outrage, dismay, wonder, or hilarity—constitutes the necessary other half of the *Far Side* experience.

One last thing: You will probably notice that we organized the book in chronological order, but not rigidly. In the end, this is a book about images and at times the design overruled a strict chronology.

I hope you enjoy your journey into *The Far Side* as much as I have. Buckle up—it's going to be a wild ride.

—*Michael Reagan*

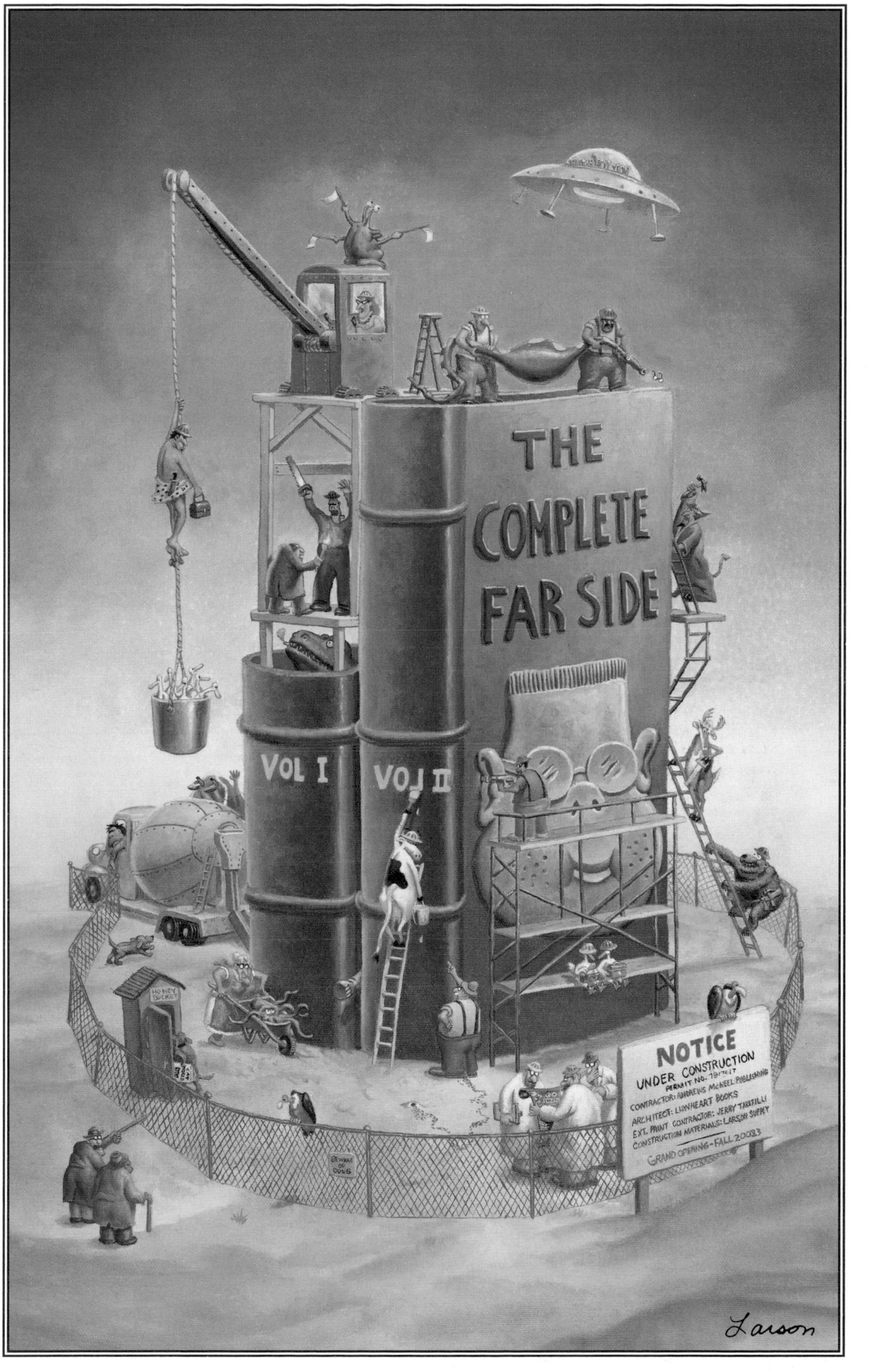
THE COMPLETE FAR SIDE
VOL I
VOL II
NOTICE
UNDER CONSTRUCTION
PERMIT NO.
CONTRACTOR: ANDREWS McMEEL PUBLISHING
ARCHITECT: LIONHEART BOOKS
EXT. PAINT CONTRACTOR: JERRY TARTILLI
CONSTRUCTION MATERIALS: LARSON SUPPLY
GRAND OPENING–FALL 20083
Larson

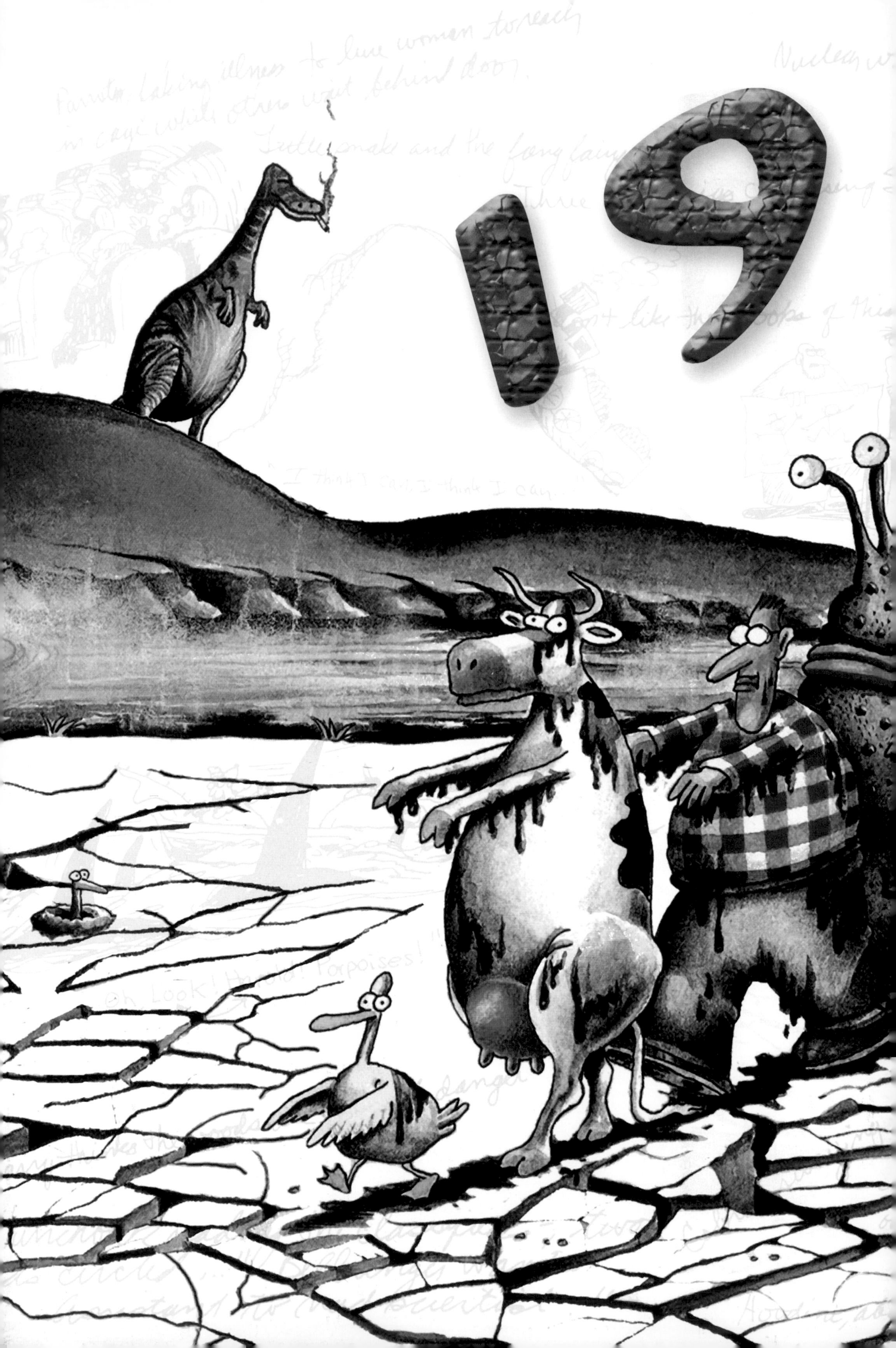
19

80

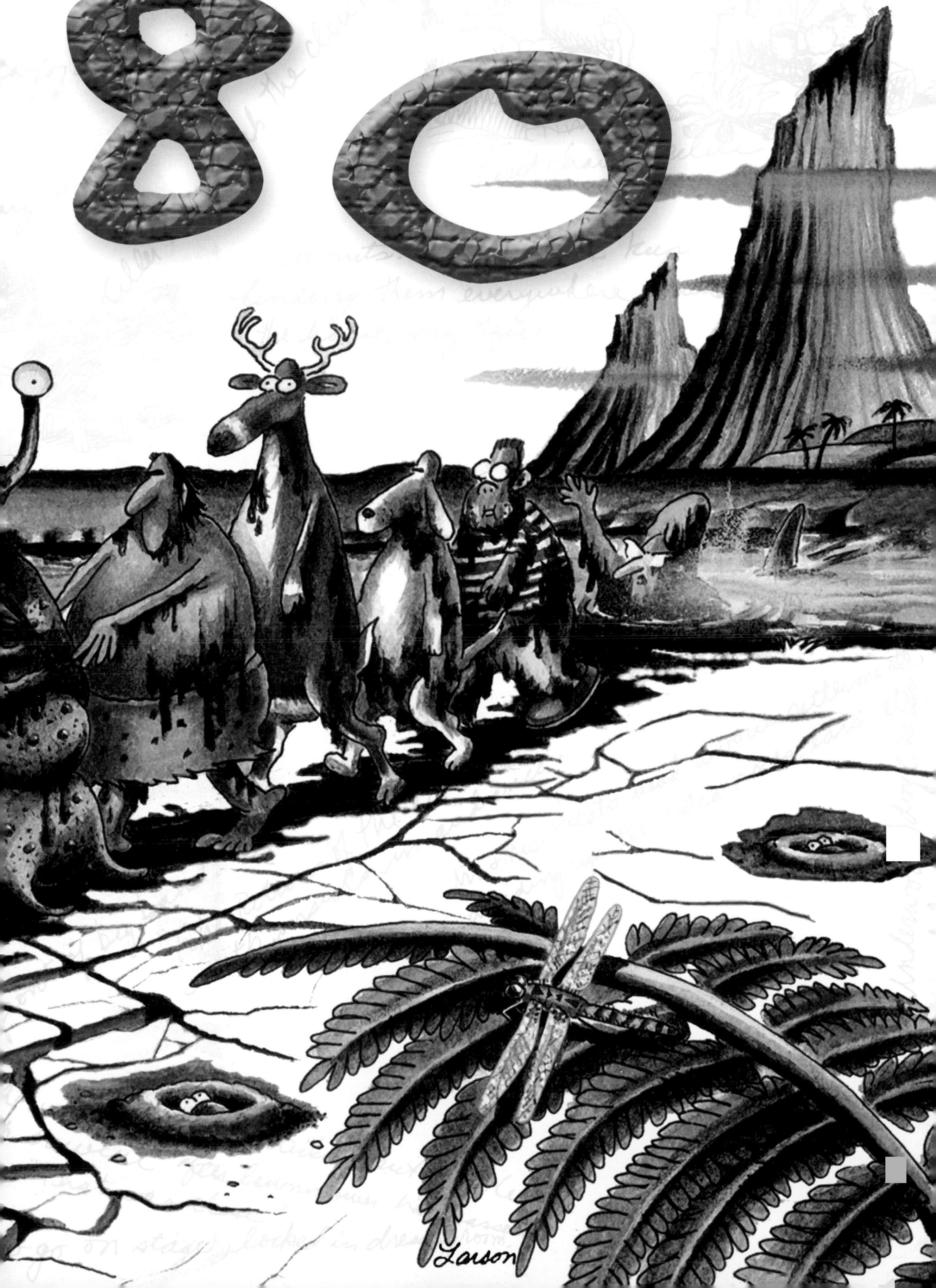
Larson

On Dorothy Parker, Gorilla Masks, and a Very Close Call

A few months before *The Far Side* made its formal debut, I was sitting in the San Francisco office of my editor-to-be, Stan Arnold, the head honcho at Chronicle Features Syndicate. And Stan, studying my meager portfolio, suddenly asked me if I would consider doing a strip. (Comic, not the dance.)

I was terrified. *The Far Side* comic strip? I had a single-image brain; I drew single-image cartoons. My primary influences had been Gahan Wilson and B. Kliban, both masters of the panel form who also spoke to my own sense of humor. There were a handful of others: George Booth, Edward Gorey, and the indisputable Charles Atlas of dark humor, Charles Addams. Nary a strip cartoonist in the bunch. I was doomed.

When it came to strips, for me, there was really only Don Martin of *Mad* magazine. Martin was not only a god to a lot of kids of my generation, he was a cartoonist's cartoonist. (Not only were his ideas often hysterical, the guy could just plain *draw*.) And I was no Don Martin. For that matter, I wasn't even Gary Larson; I was just an eager-to-please lump of self-doubt sitting in some editor's office.

Truth is, I've always been sort of in awe of comic strips. I used to think, How do those guys do it? As a kid, I always had a fondness for *Alley Oop,* and later on I consistently enjoyed the work of a couple of my contemporaries, Bill Watterson *(Calvin and Hobbes)* and Berkeley Breathed *(Bloom County)*. But I could never get inside the *heads* of strip cartoonists, even the ones I liked. Clearly, I was wired differently.

I haven't reflected on any of this until now, but I believe I may have come up with a theory—just a theory—on why, for me, a single-panel cartoon was so natural, while the thought of drawing and writing a strip struck terror in my heart. As it seems so much does in life, it boils down to this: the way I was raised.

Imagine your own father sitting at the Algonquin Round Table, surrounded by that famous group of New York intellectuals. Would he most likely attempt to use his verbal alacrity and facile mind to impress and entertain everyone? Or would he find a quiet moment and simply lean over and ask Dorothy Parker to pull his finger? (Sorry, Dad, but I know the answer to this one.)

In short, the Larson Round Table was not a place where sharp dialogue and witticisms abounded. They happened, of course, and I hasten to add that wit was especially my mother's strong suit. But in reality you didn't fear a verbal put-down as much as you feared someone slipping a small invertebrate into your glass of milk while your head was turned. It wasn't a witty retort that ensured your survival; it was good peripheral vision.

What I'm clumsily trying to say here is that, like the famous folks who once lunched at the Algonquin, most strip cartoonists (in my opinion, at least) approach their work from an appreciation of wit. And wit, of course, is the reflection of an agile and creative mind. Or, as my dictionary says, "a talent for banter." What's relevant to me, as a cartoonist, is what that implies: If you're striving to be witty, then you need banter, and if you need banter, you need a strip. You need characters like a sit-com needs them, talking to one another, setting things up, leading to that rimshot in the last panel when something clever or unexpected is said. (Okay, I know there are exceptions to any formula; I'm just firing some broadsides here.)

Wit, I think, grows out of a conscious desire to make someone else laugh, to be entertaining, to be liked. (I mean, why else make the effort?) A sense of humor, on the other hand, has to do with what makes *us* laugh. It's that largely unconscious, reactionary "funny bone" we all possess (well, most of us, anyway), and it struggles to exercise any self-control. (All of us, I'm sure, have a memory of trying not to laugh at a time we sensed was inappropriate.) The two undoubtedly overlap, but my gut tells me these are different animals leading separate lives, except when they might run into each other at some water hole in our brains. (Note: Never see a neurologist who uses this kind of terminology.)

Our sense of humor obviously didn't "burst" on the scene one day; it's been carved into our respective brains during all our formative years, eventually becoming as much a part of us as our eye color. Wit, on the other hand, is living in the moment. It's out on the dance floor, twirling, kicking, showing its moves—everyone's watching, either in admiration or embarrassment. Sense of humor is lurking in the shadows, secretly hoping that Wit falls into the punch bowl.

I'm not out on that dance floor. I'm a lurker. I draw—and draw from—my family's sense of humor. If you would allow me any talent, it's simply this: I can, for whatever reason, reach down into my own brain, feel around in all the mush, find and extract something from my persona, and then graft it onto an idea. I guess it's a Little Jack Horner kind of thing, only I fully admit it was not always a plum I pulled out—there are things down there I probably should have jerked my hand away from as soon as I made contact. Too late now.

Physical comedy—especially if it contained psychological overtones, such as those old chestnuts fear and humiliation—pervaded our home like a poltergeist. Around any corner, in any room, humor lurked, waiting to pounce. Not "Stooge" humor, I assure you. Research, observation, psychology, biology—these were the tools, usually applied with deathly nuance, that one used in the quest to amuse oneself. For me, it was all *Far Side* boot camp. Study your prey, approach carefully, savor the moment, and then strike. (Truthfully, I was more often the "prey" in these training exercises, but I nonetheless could appreciate the skill involved.)

A single drawing is all I ever needed. I rarely required a series of panels to set up a "gag" or a punch line. In fact, I never thought in terms of punch lines and gags. I never thought of myself as a "joke writer" with a drawing attached. Maybe that's what I was doing, in some people's minds. But to me, *The Far Side* was more of an attitude, a distillation of life that came from growing up in a family that had a deep, sincere appreciation for the many uses of a good gorilla mask. (It was kept on the shelf in the coat closet, for quick access.)

For me, that little rectangle I drew in was the equivalent of a canvas. I needed to stare at it for a while and try to "see" as much as I could before things began. The thought of storyboarding an idea just sounded like a lot of work, and it flat out didn't interest me. (Besides, I could never get the characters to look exactly the same from one little box to the next.)

Back to my meeting with Stan. (God, have I digressed.)

So I'm sitting there in his office, sweating. And he was going on, explaining about the strengths that comic strips held over panels. "People like to see characters they recognize," he said. It was the old familiarity-breeds-fondness thing. Strips engage the reader in a more intimate way, like an old friend who comes by to visit every day or so. And that leads to reader loyalty. Single-panel cartoons are like strangers that suddenly appear on your doorstep. No one flings open their door for strangers. However, if you look out and see good ol' Charlie Brown, it's like, why sure—open the door! C'mon in, Charlie! … Hey, wait! Quick! … Shut the door! There's a damn cow out there!

So once you've got your character established in the hearts and minds of readers, it's not a good idea to run him over with a truck a few weeks later. Whoa! I was not going to be good at developing a character. I was not going to be good at developing a strip. I was not going to be good at telling a joke in visual form. I was hit and run. My ever-changing characters got crunched, speared, shot, beheaded, eaten, stuffed, poisoned, and run over about twice a week. (Tastefully, of course.)

And yet another layer was added to the discussion when Stan said that strips were easier to *sell*. This was, I assumed, a big one. Newspapers, he said, really weren't thrilled with single-panel cartoons. Strips are easy to format on a comics page; single panels just throw the whole design out of whack. My cartoons might be funny, he encouraged, but couldn't I just transfer my sense of humor over to a strip format? (Maybe that's when I should have asked him to pull my finger.)

Well, I sat there in Stan's office, listening to him describe the virtues of a strip, the headaches with a panel. I didn't say much (certainly nothing "witty"). Stan, I recall, wasn't really even looking at me; he was just flipping through my portfolio, talking about the wonders of comic strips, while clearly feeling me out about developing one strong, returning character. I just listened, smiling on the outside, dying on the inside.

And then, out of the blue, he said, "Well, let's just go ahead and do it your way." And that's the last time a comic strip was ever discussed. Believe me, I never felt such a whoosh of relief.

On December 31, 1979, *The Far Side*—a single-panel cartoon—was launched. I was crunching, spearing, shooting, beheading, eating, stuffing, poisoning, and running over my own characters within a week.

Tastefully, of course.

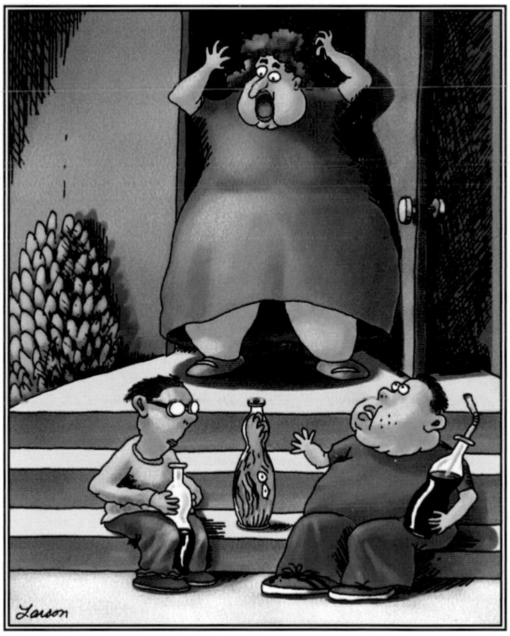
Larson

"Gee, Mom! Andy was just showing us how far he could suck his lip into the bottle!"

1/1/80

Larson

"Yes. ... They're quite strange during the larval stage."

1/2/80

Larson

"Of course I never eat the shells."

1/3/80

Larson

1/5/80

AN ARK!
AN ARK, YOU FOOL!
Larson

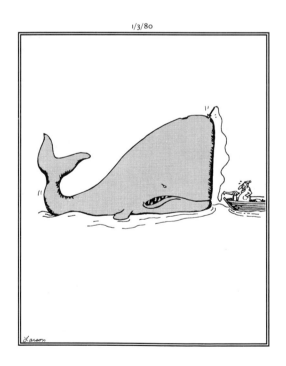

1/8/80

"Egad! We must find some means of
discarding the hideous thing!"

1/10/80

"Bring back his ear."

1/11/80

"Polly wanna cracker. ... Polly wanna cracker. ...
Pretty bird. ... HARRY! DON'T SHOOT! ...
Pretty bird."

1/12/80

"Egad! ... What a hideous creature!"

January 1980

1/14/80

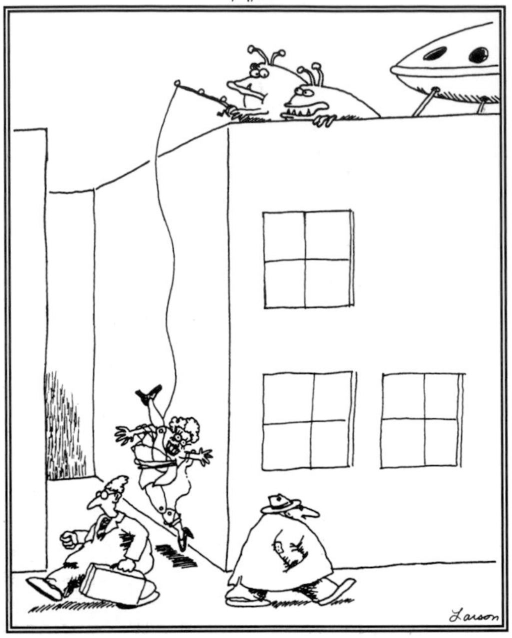

"Something's wrong. ... Reel up and check the bait."

1/15/80

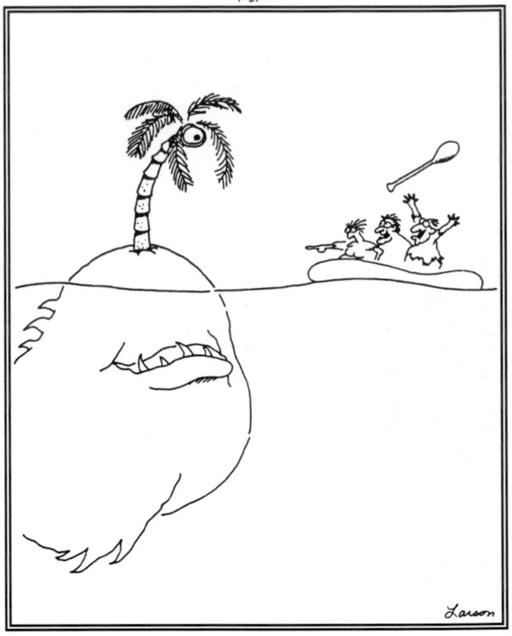

1/16/80

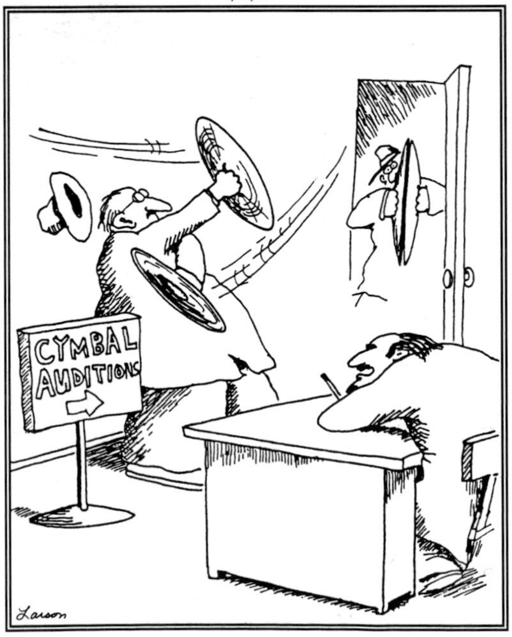
CYMBAL
AUDITIONS

"Next!"

1/17/80

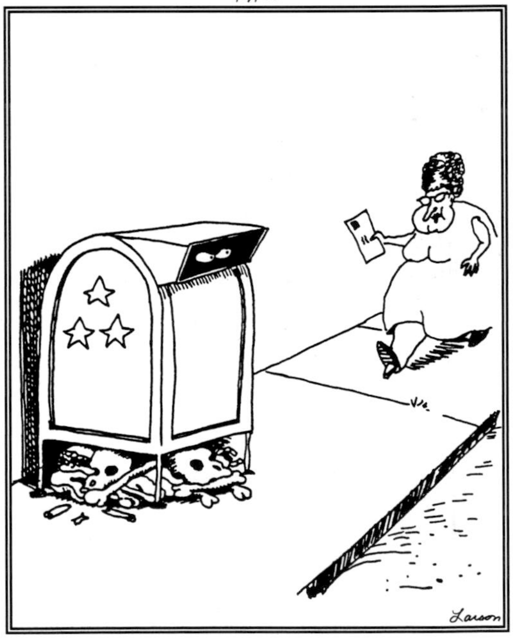

1/18/80

Larson

"And so I ask the jury—is that the face of a mass murderer?"

1/21/80

Larson

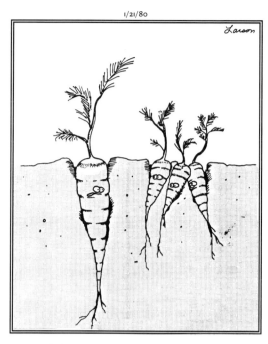

"... And then the creatures yanked him out of the ground, skinned him alive, boiled him, and ate him. The end. *Now go to sleep!*"

1/22/80

BEWARE OF DOG
Larson

1/23/80

Larson

January 1980

1/24/80

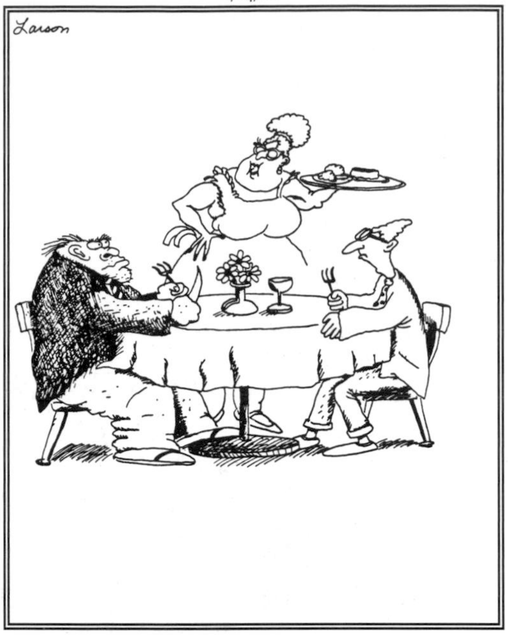

"All right, let's see ... which one's the 'Viva la Vegetarian' and which one's the 'Prime Rib Papa'?"

1/28/80

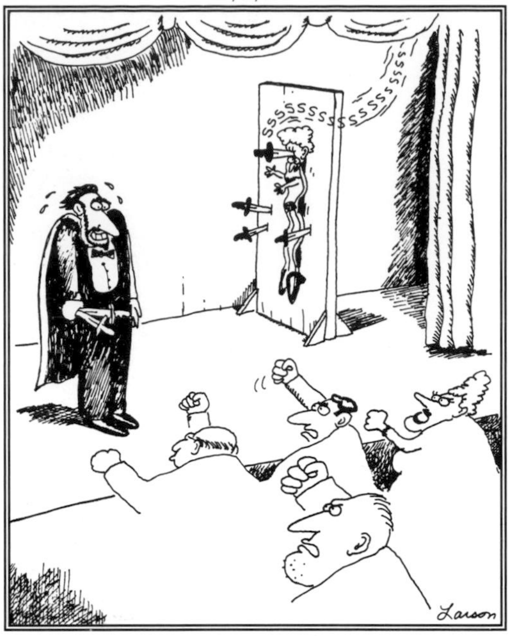

1/25/80

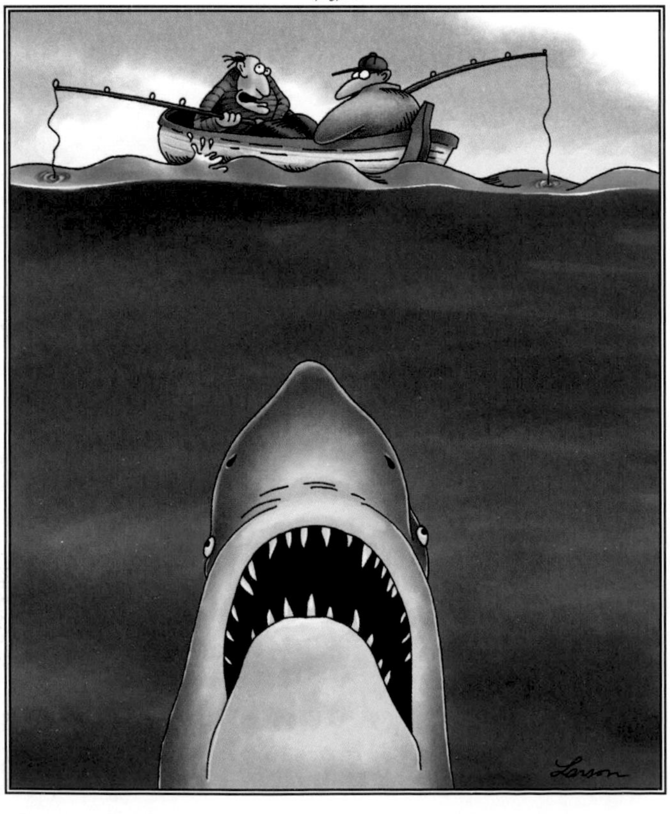

"There it goes again ... that eerie music."

1/30/80

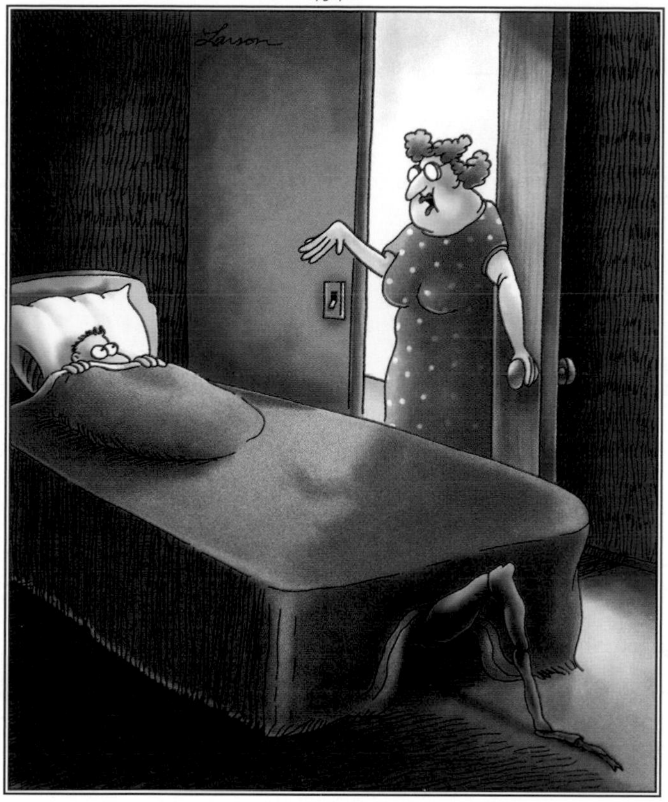
Larson

"Nighty-night, dear, sleep tight ... and don't let the bedbugs bite."

1/29/80

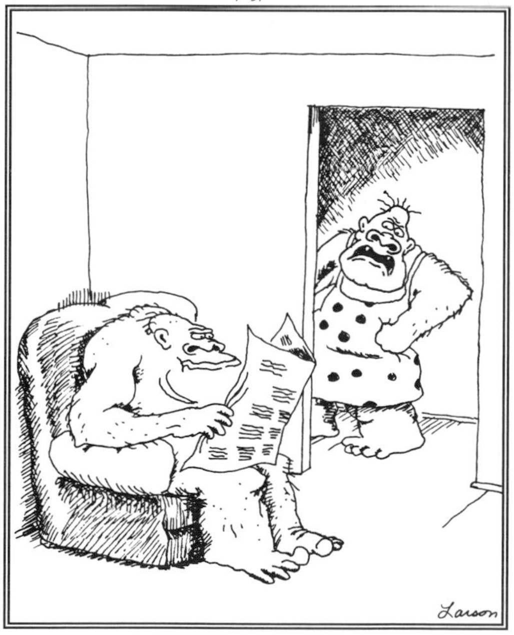
Larson

"And don't you flare your nostrils at me, either!"

1/31/80

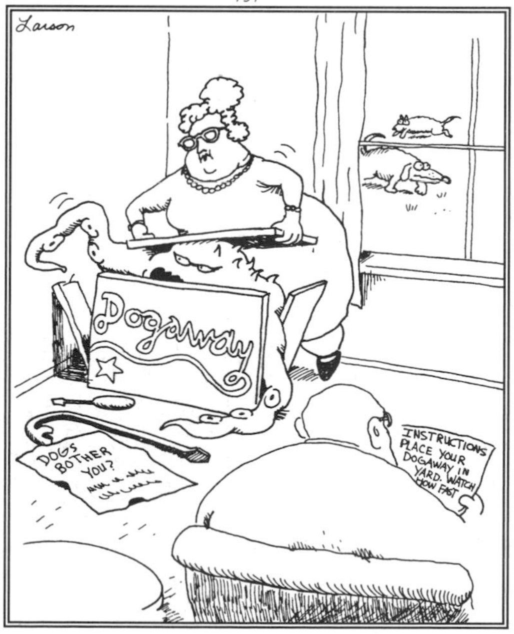
Larson
Dogaway
DOGS BOTHER YOU?
INSTRUCTIONS PLACE YOUR DOGAWAY IN YARD. WATCH HOW FAST

February 1980

2/5/80

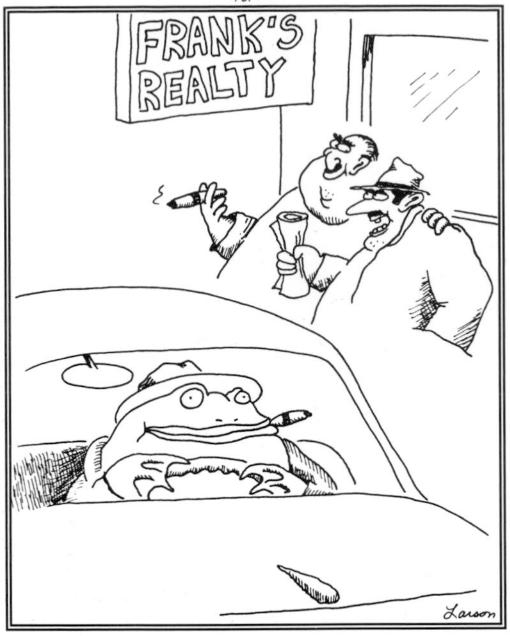
FRANK'S
REALTY

"Well, another sucker just bought twenty acres of swampland."

2/1/80

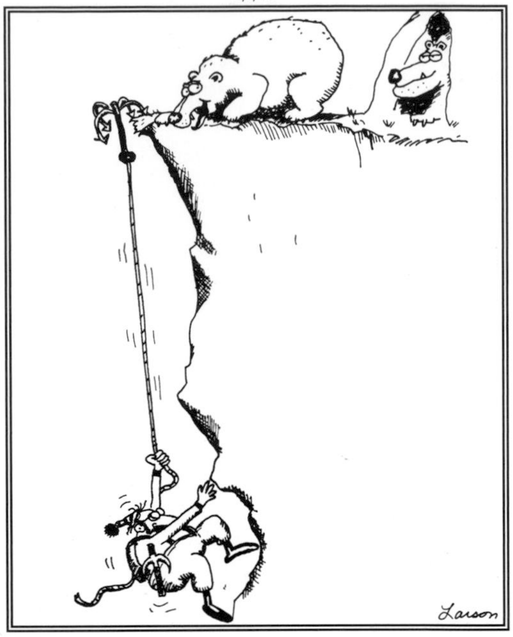

"We'll be eating in tonight."

2/4/80

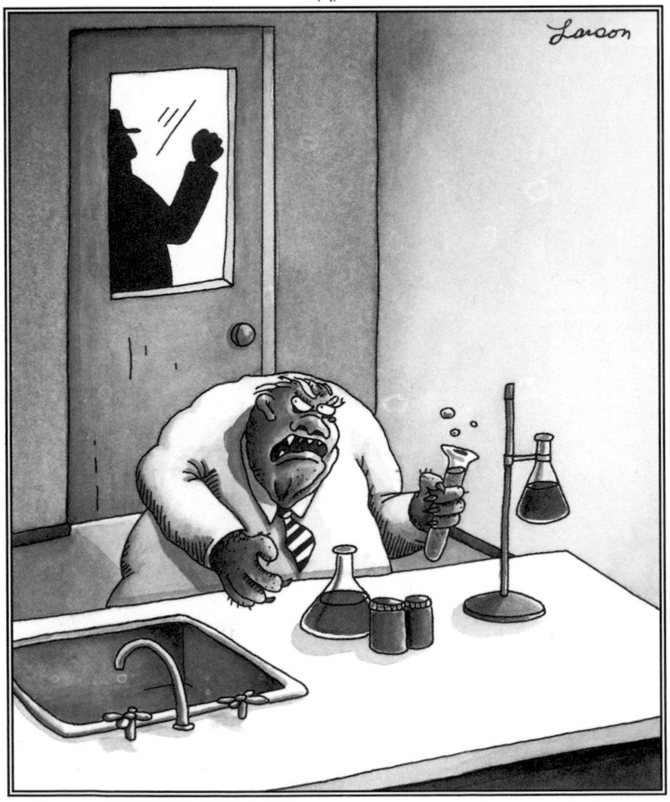

"Hang on! I'm changing!"

2/6/80

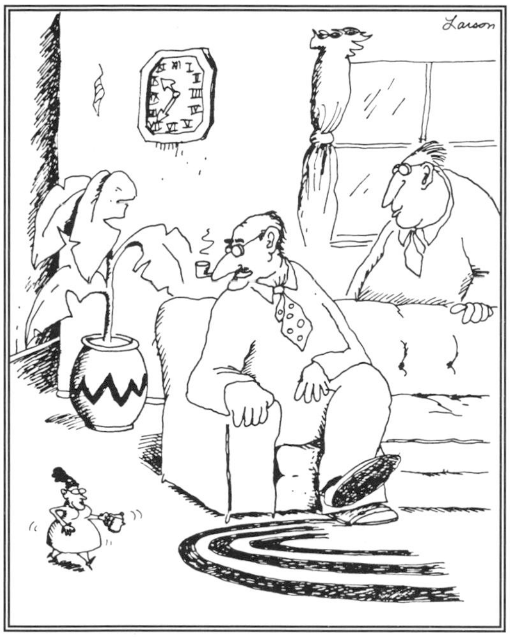
Larson

"... and this must be the little woman."

2/7/80

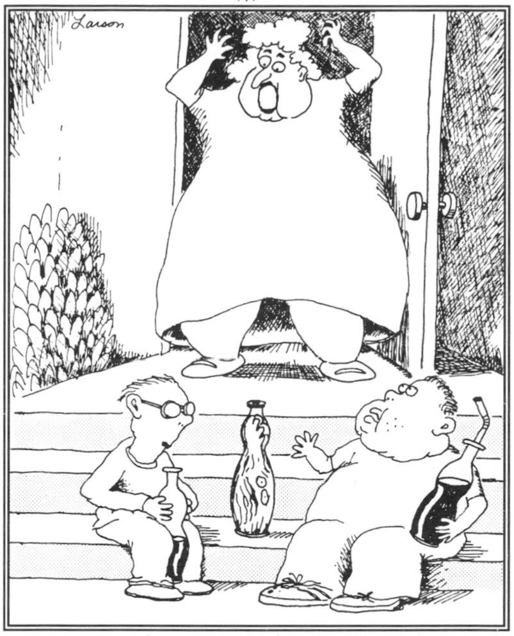
Larson

"Gee, Mom! Andy was just showing us how far he could suck his lip into the bottle!"

2/8/80

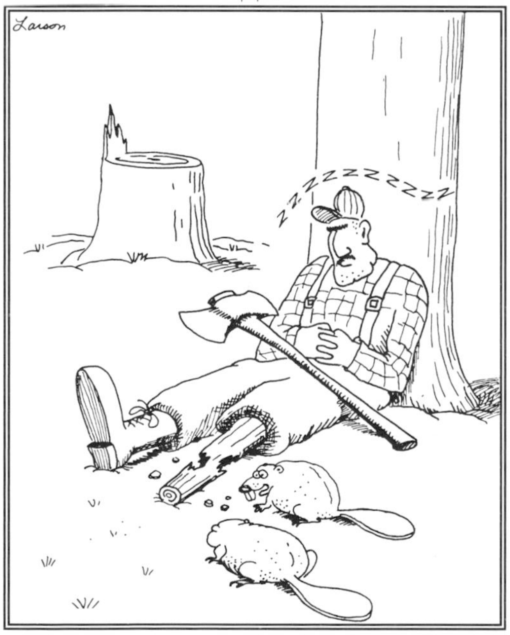
Larson

"Hey! They're edible! ... This changes everything!"

2/9/80

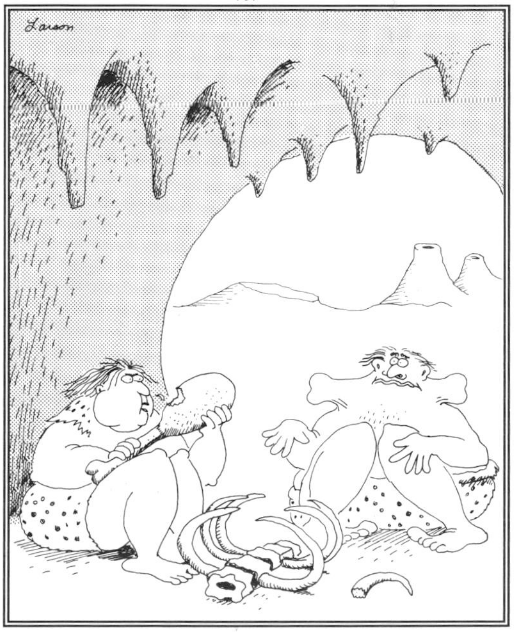
Larson

"I told you to watch for bones."

2/11/80

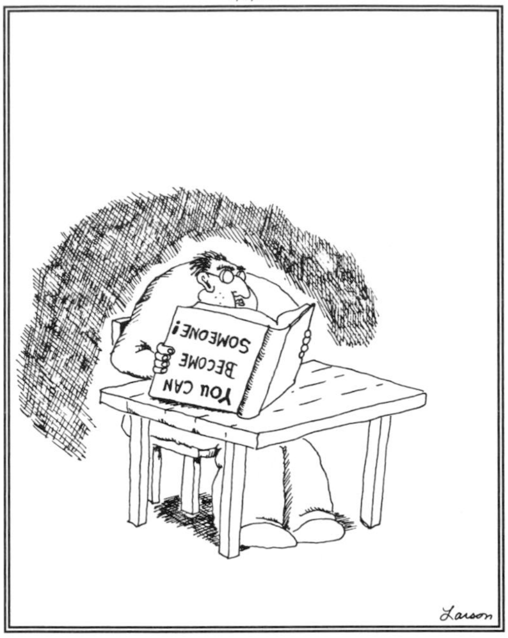
YOU CAN
BECOME
SOMEONE!

2/12/80

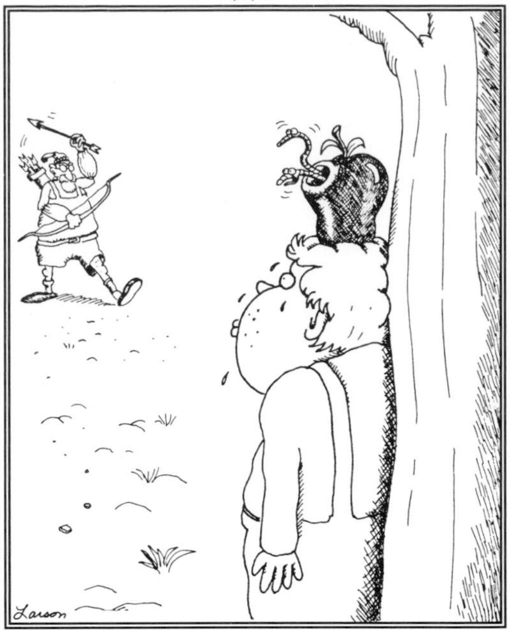

"But what if he hits the apple?"

2/13/80

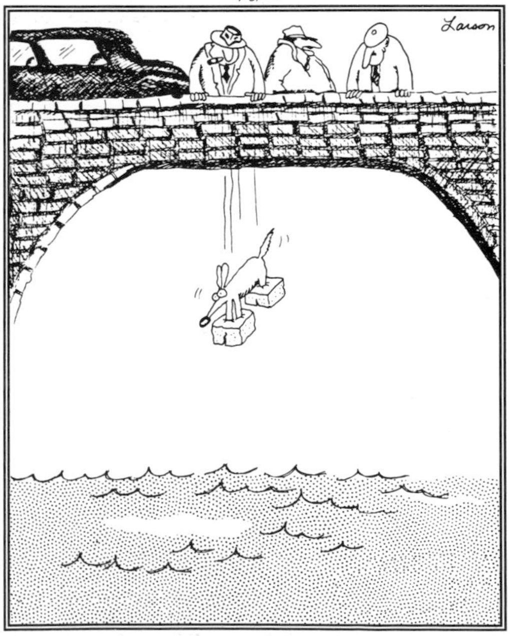

"He bit the Godfather."

2/14/80

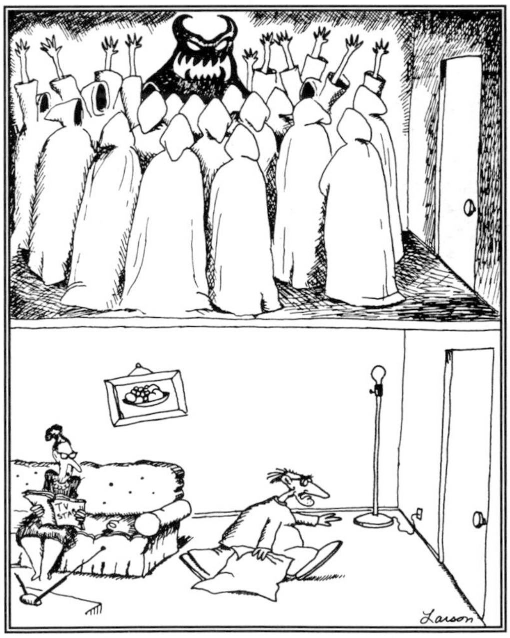

"That does it! ... I'm going to go up there and give those people *hell!*"

2/19/80

"'H,' please ... for *both* of us."

2/15/80

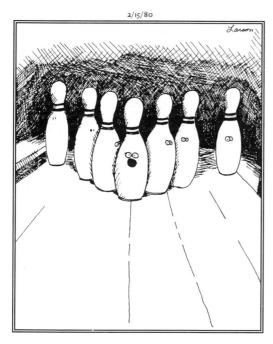

"My God! ... Here it comes again!"

2/18/80

"Old McDonald *had* a farm, eeyi-eeyi-yo ..."

"Mother was right—you're nothing but an old goat."

"Incredible you say? But true, ladies and gentlemen! ... *He has only one head!*"

"Excuse me, but must you smoke that foul thing around here?"

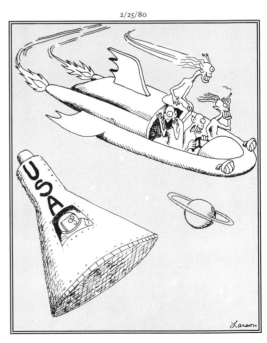

"GET A ZORB!"

2/26/80

"He's makin' a fool of us, Bart."

2/27/80

2/28/80

"And I tell ya ... the next trail drive I sign
onto, I'm readin' the fine print!"

2/29/80

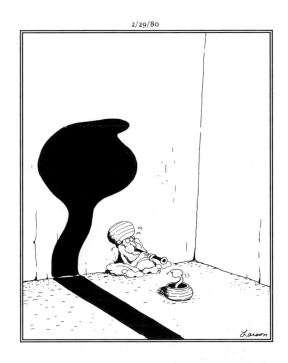

3/3/80

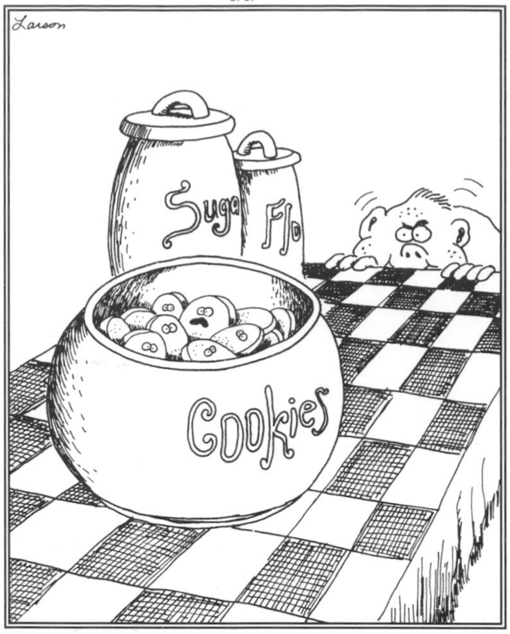
Sugar
Flo
Cookies
Larson

"It's back!"

3/4/80

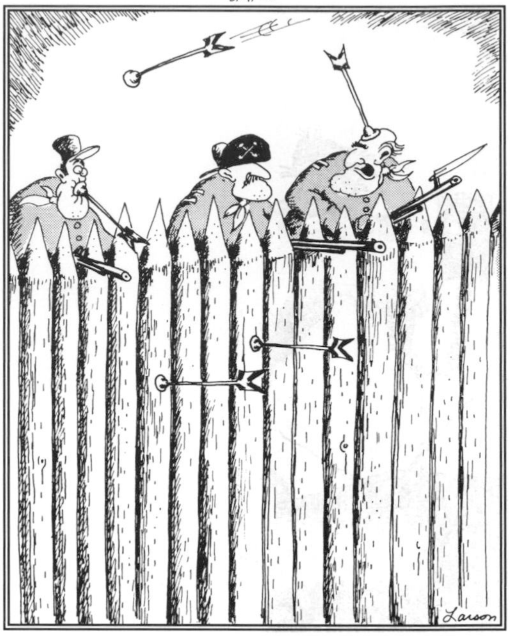
Larson

"Gad! ... Not *these* Indians again!"

3/5/80

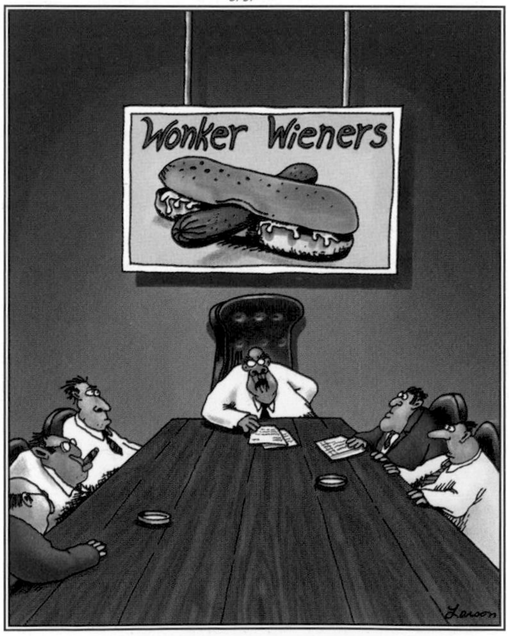
Wonker Wieners
Larson

"And so I've reached the conclusion, gentlemen, that the Wonker Wiener Company is riddled with incompetence."

3/7/80

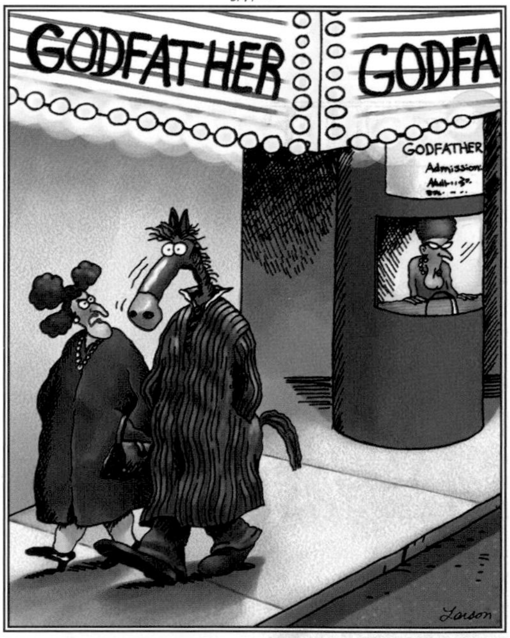
GODFATHER
GODFA
GODFATHER
Admission
Larson

"Get a hold of yourself! ... It was only a movie, for crying out loud!"

3/12/80

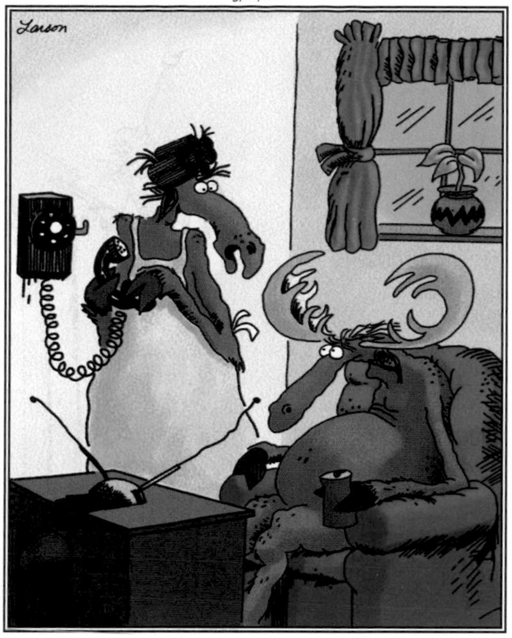
Larson

"It's the call of the wild."

3/13/80

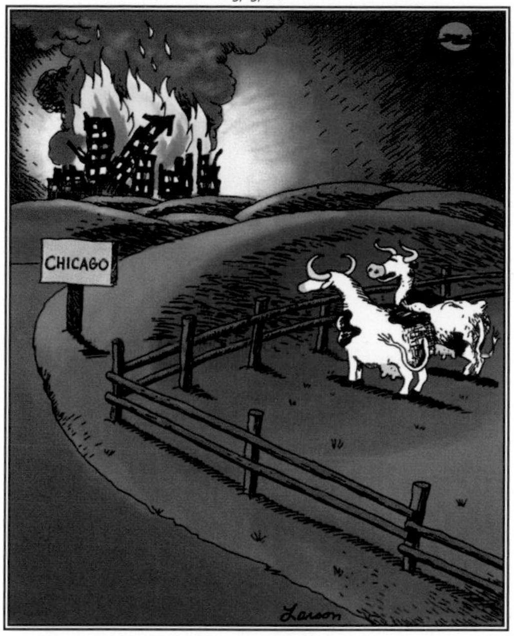
CHICAGO
Larson

"It seems that agent 6373 has accomplished her mission."

3/11/80

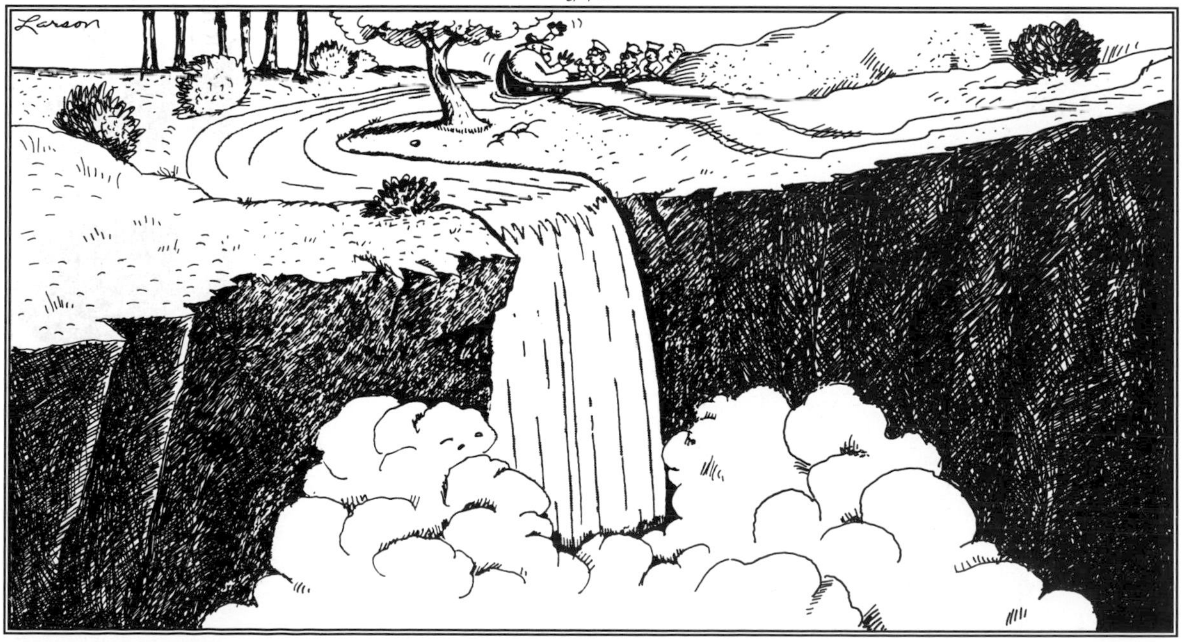
Larson

"... and then the second group comes in—'row, row, row your boat'..."

3/6/80

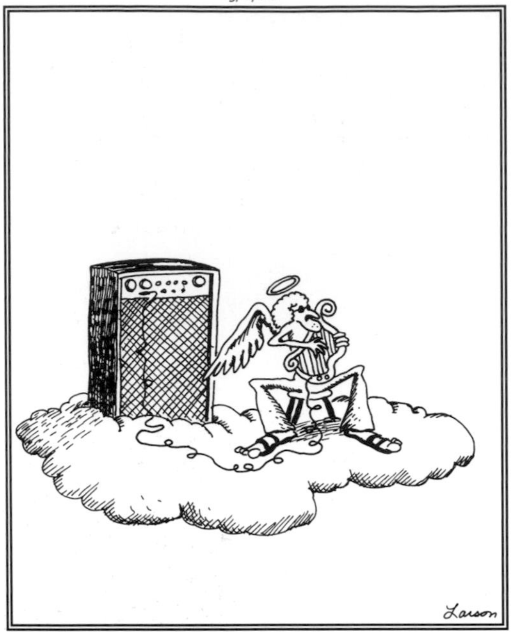
Larson

3/10/80

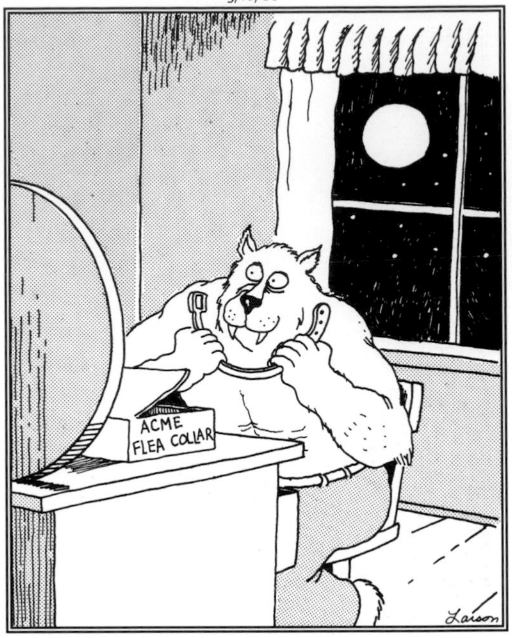
ACME
FLEA COLLAR
Larson

3/14/80

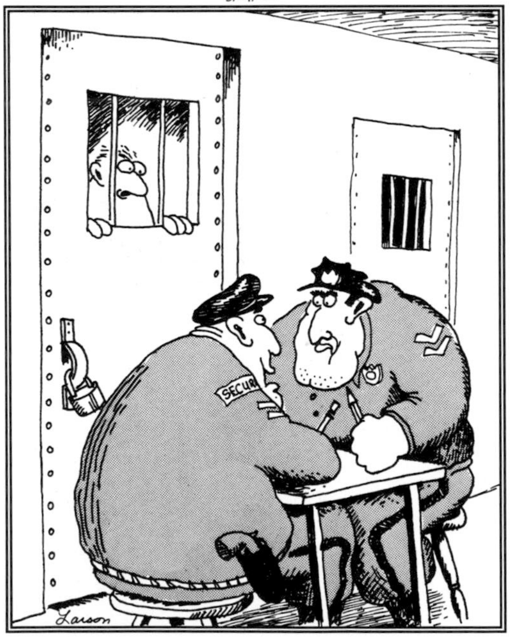
Larson

"HANGMAN! ... You lose!"

3/17/80

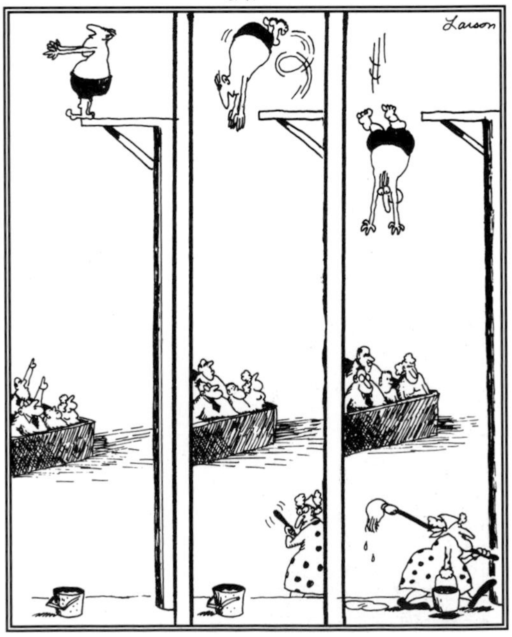
Larson

3/18/80

"*Now* you've done it!"

3/20/80

"We just listed it. ... Some young punks vandalized the place and cooked the owner."

3/21/80

"C'mon! You'll miss the fun! ... All the lemmings are going down to the beach!"

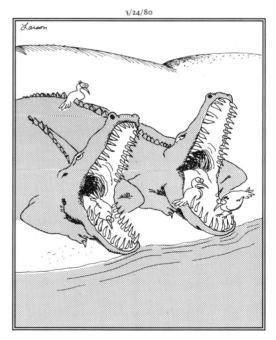

3/24/80

"Food's okay ... I just can't get used to the atmosphere."

3/25/80

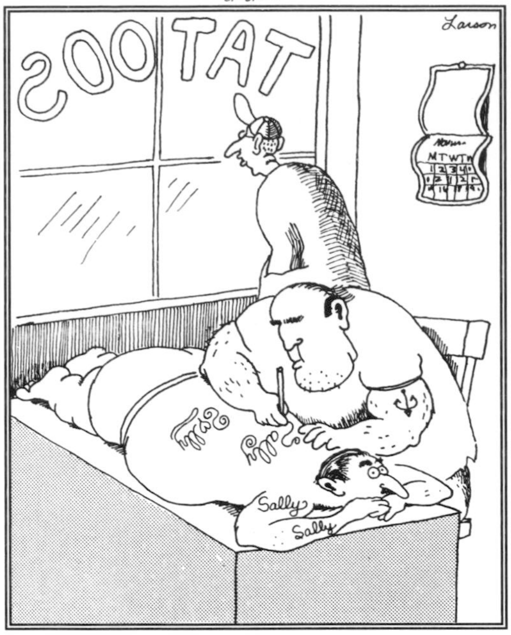
Larson
Sally
Sally

"Say, Ernie ... that looks like Sally across the street. ... And she's with some guy."

3/26/80

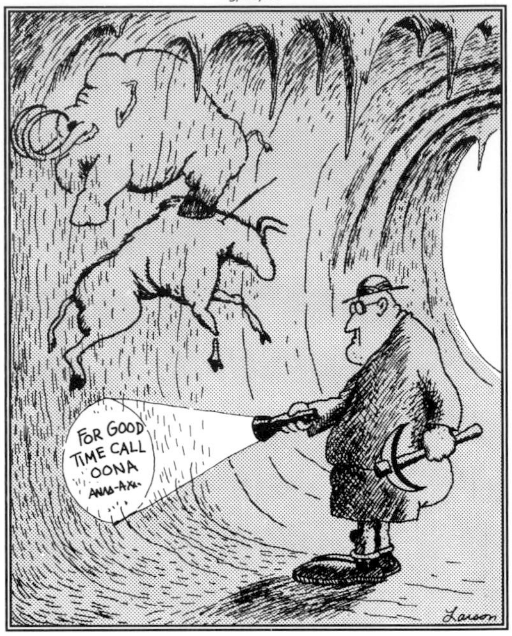
FOR GOOD TIME CALL OONA
Larson

3/19/80

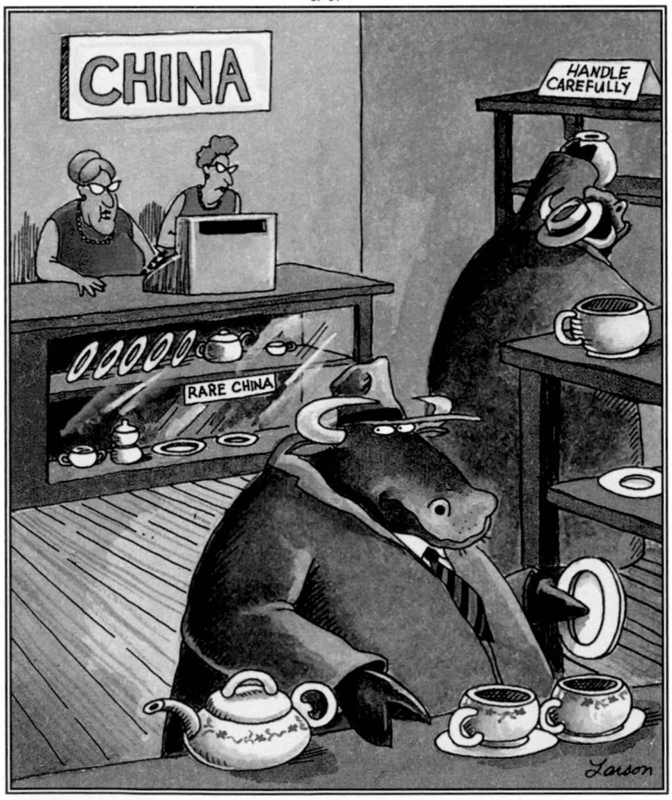
CHINA
HANDLE CAREFULLY
RARE CHINA
Larson

"I got a bad feeling about this, Harriet."

3/28/80

WARNING -
EYEGLASS
TESTING
AREA
2
Larson

3/27/80

Larson

"Egad! ... Another flat!"

3/31/80

Larson
CAMELOT
NEW
&
USED

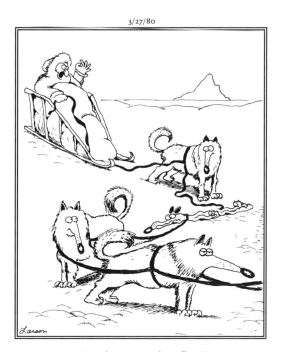

April 1980

4/1/80

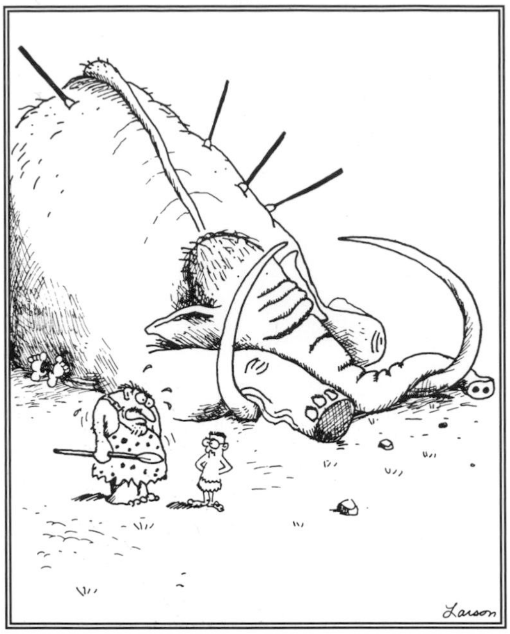
Larson

"I don't care if you don't like it! ... By God, you're gonna eat it!"

4/2/80

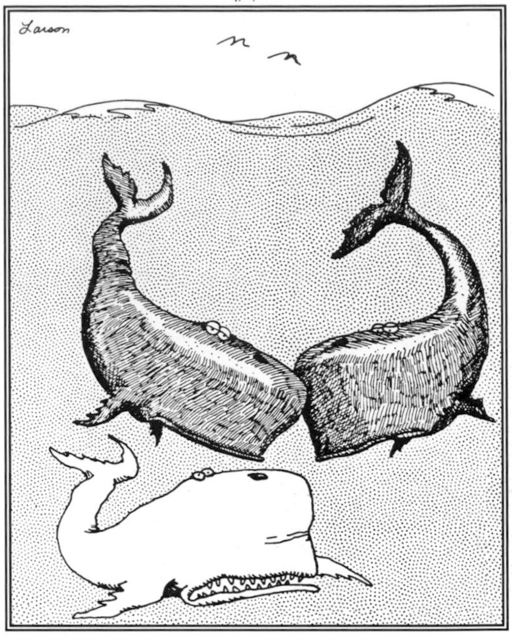
Larson

"I tell you he's up there! ... Those wild, sunken eyes! That horrid wooden leg! ... And he's looking for *me!*"

4/3/80

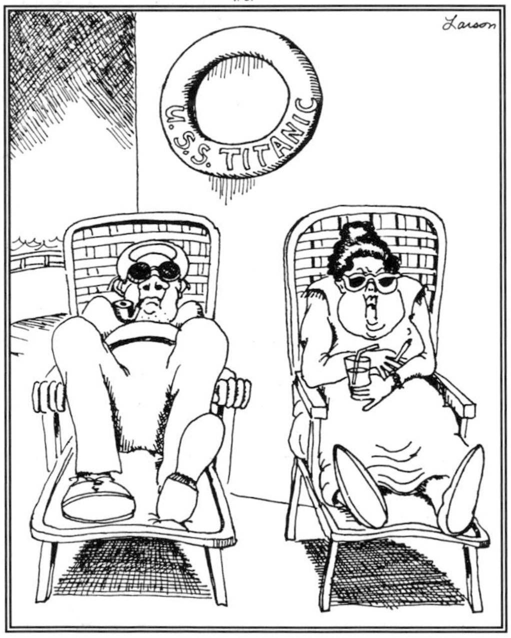
Larson
U.S.S. TITANIC

"Lousy food ... crummy service ... dinky cabins ... and that's only the tip of the iceberg!"

4/4/80

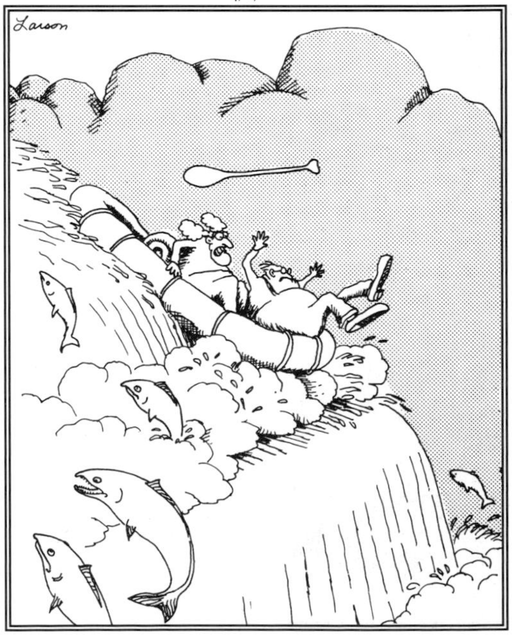
Larson

"I doubt if *they'll* ever reach the spawning grounds."

April 1980

4/7/80

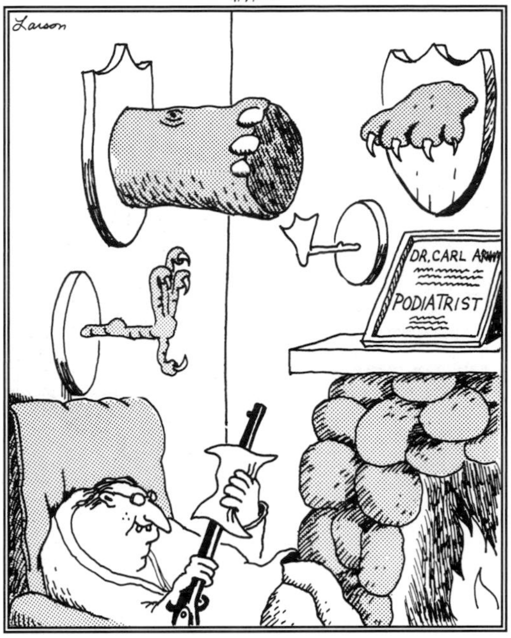
Larson
DR. CARL
PODIATRIST

4/8/80

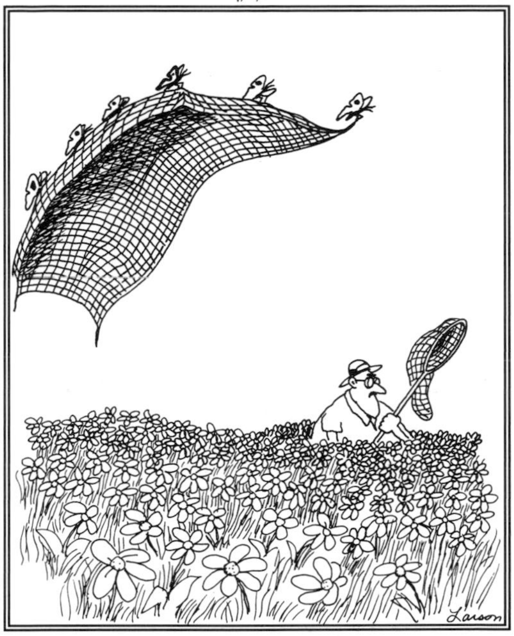
Larson

4/9/80

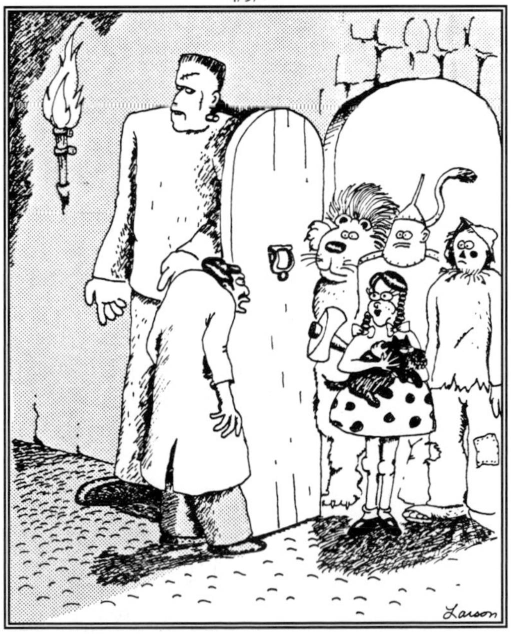
Larson

"I'm sorry ... try the wizard up the road. I just used my last heart and brain."

4/10/80

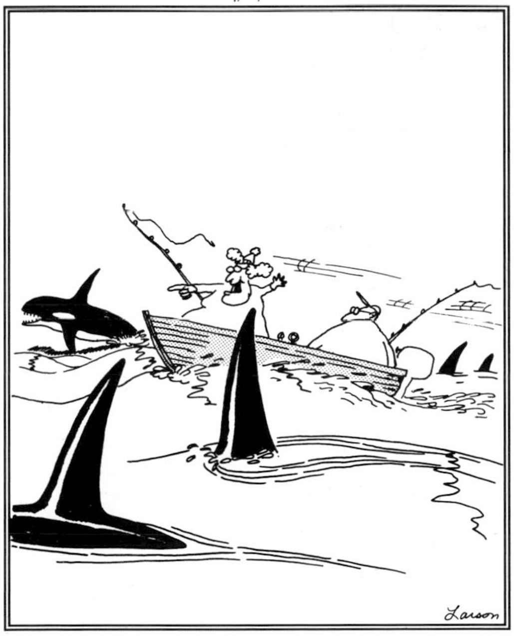
Larson

"Oh, Harold! Look! Porpoises!"

4/11/80

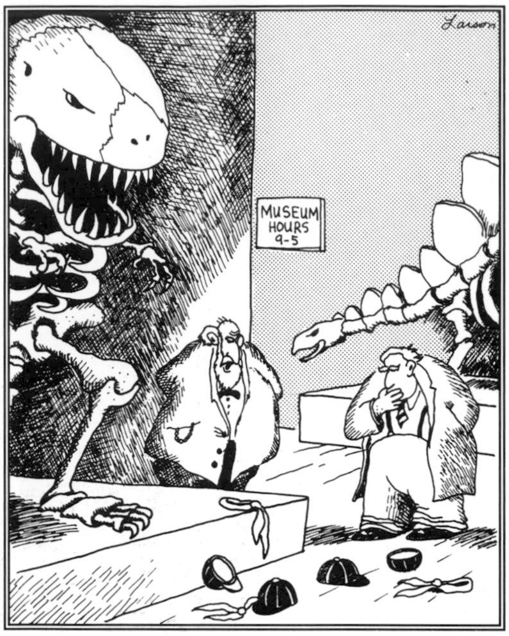
Larson
MUSEUM HOURS 9-5

"Most peculiar, Sidney ... another scattering of Cub Scout attire."

4/14/80

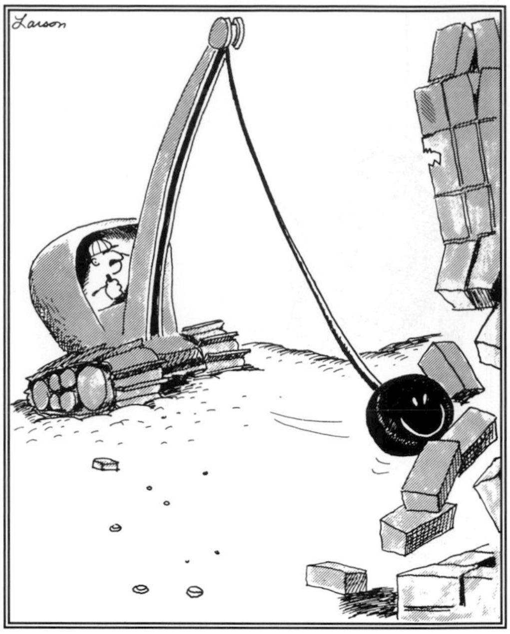
Larson

4/15/80

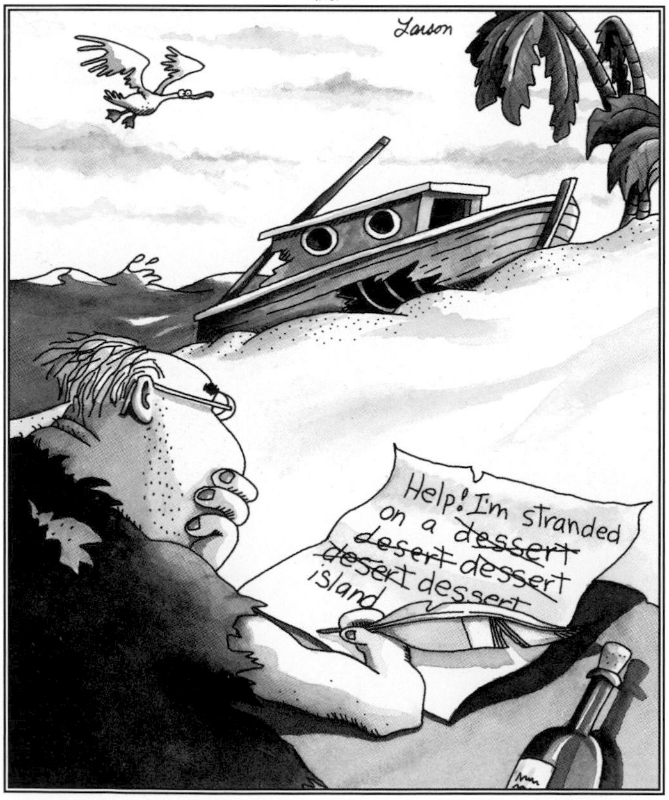
Larson
Help! I'm stranded
on a ~~dessert~~
~~desert~~ ~~dessert~~
~~desert~~ ~~dessert~~
island

4/16/80

"I can't believe it! ... I was just
talking to him yesterday!"

4/17/80

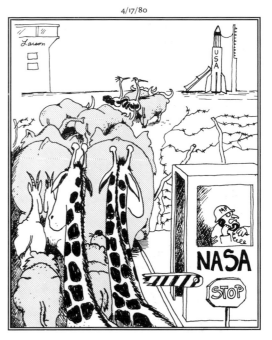

"Something big's going down, sir! ... They're
heading your way now!"

4/28/80

4/18/80

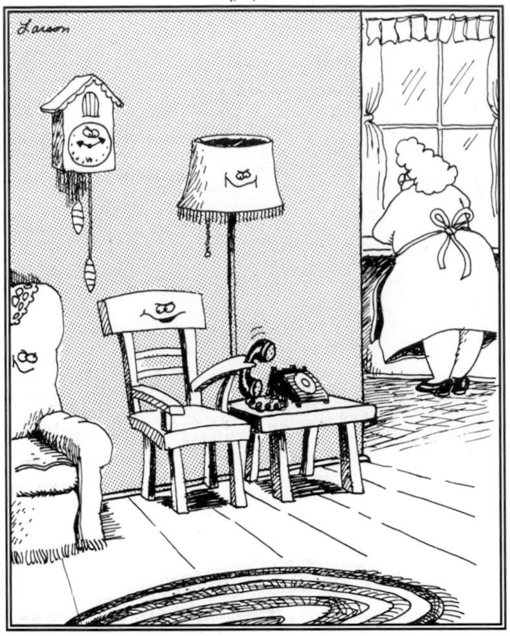
Larson

"Okay, the sanatorium's on its way over ... all we gotta do now is start talking to her."

4/21/80

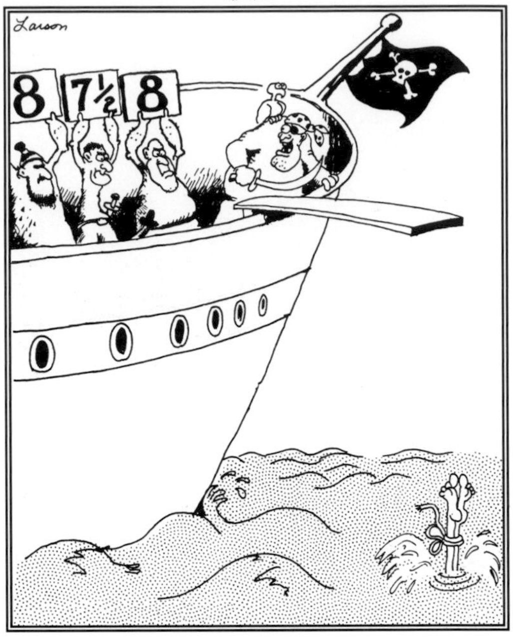
Larson
8
7½
8

4/22/80

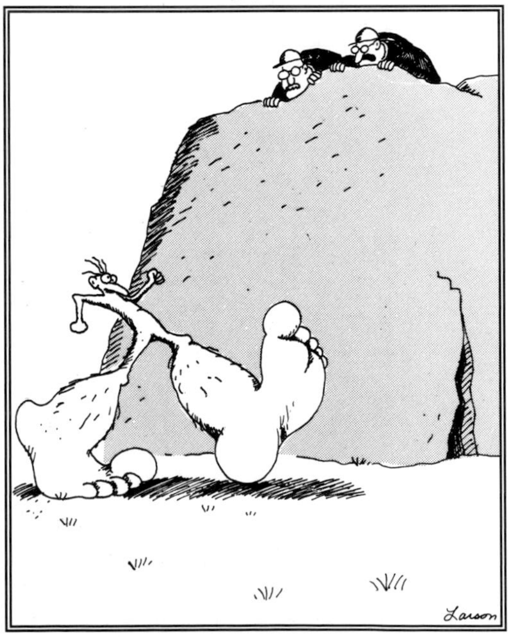
Larson

"It certainly has taken the romance out of the Bigfoot mystery."

4/23/80

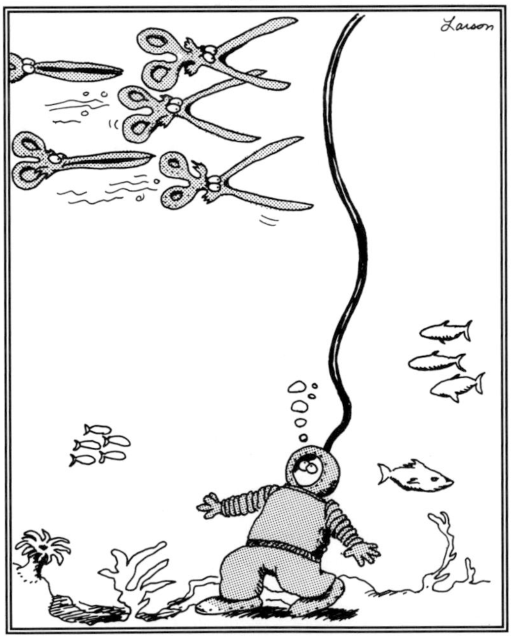
Larson

4/24/80

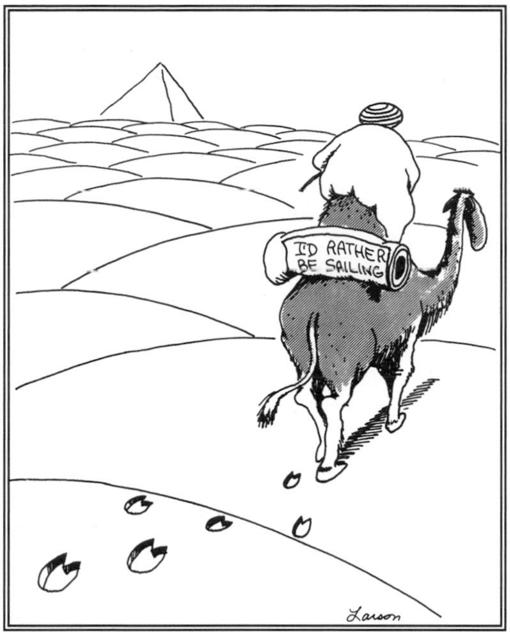
I'D RATHER BE SAILING
Larson

4/25/80

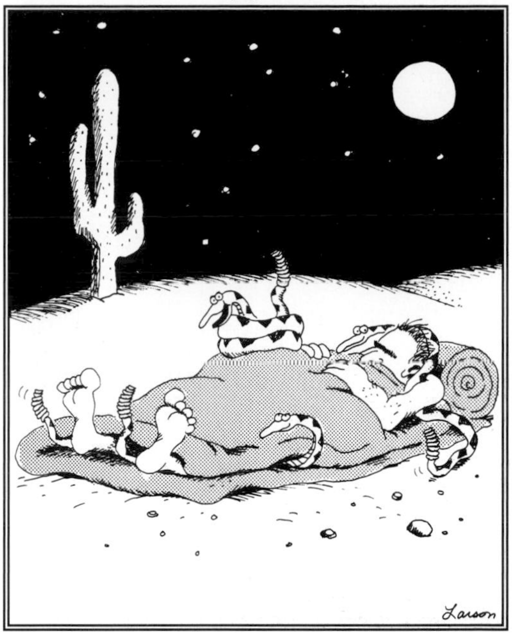
Larson

"Okay ... on the count of three, everybody rattles."

4/29/80

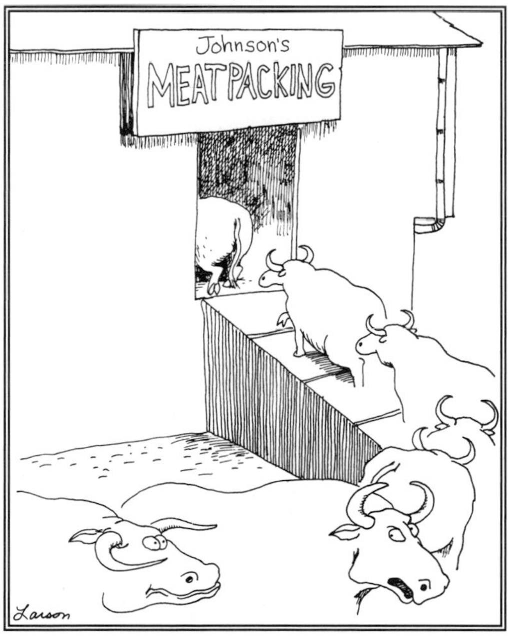
Johnson's
MEATPACKING
Larson

"Just look at this line! ... They'll never get me to come back here again!"

4/30/80

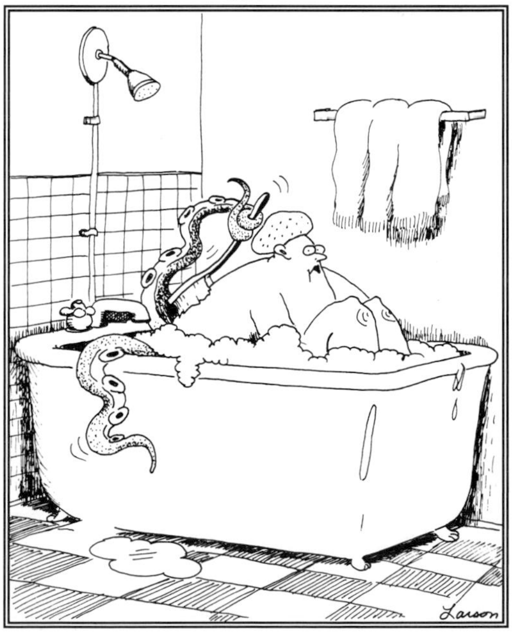
Larson

5/5/80

"We've got the murder weapon and the motive ...
now if we can just establish time of death."

5/1/80

"So! The little sweethearts were going to
carve their initials on me, eh?"

5/2/80

"All right. Run along and play ... and stay
away from those tar pits!"

May 1980

5/6/80

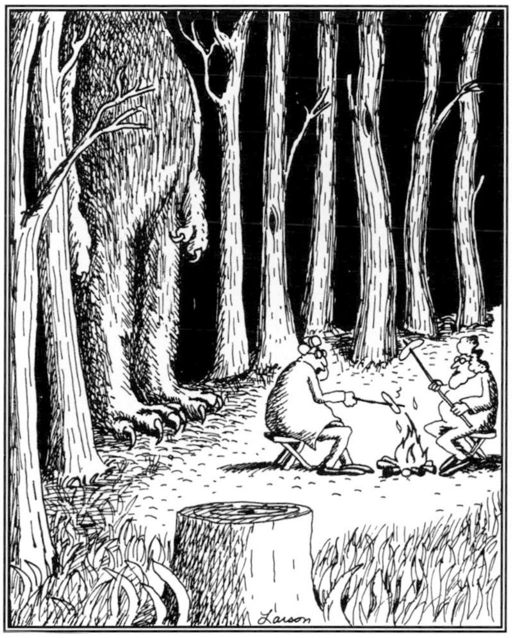
Larson

"Thank God! Those blasted crickets have finally stopped!"

5/7/80

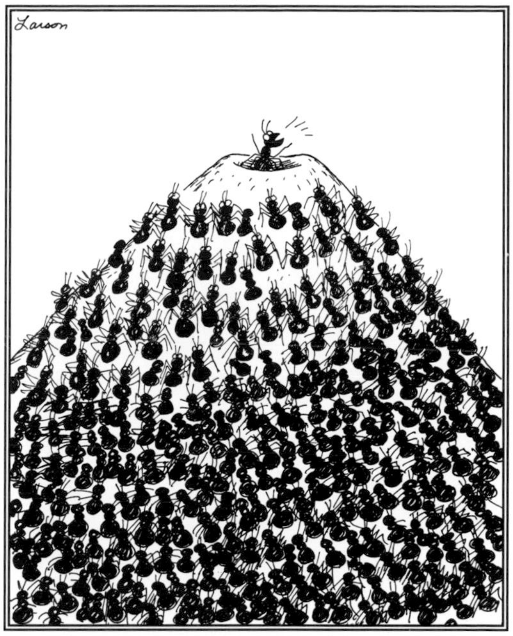
Larson

"And remember ... ask *not* what your anthill can do for you, but what you can do for your anthill."

5/9/80

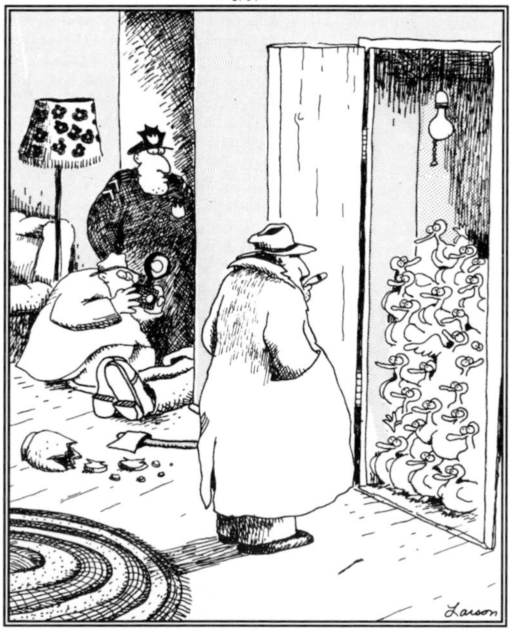
Larson

"Ahhh ... the plot thickens."

5/10/80

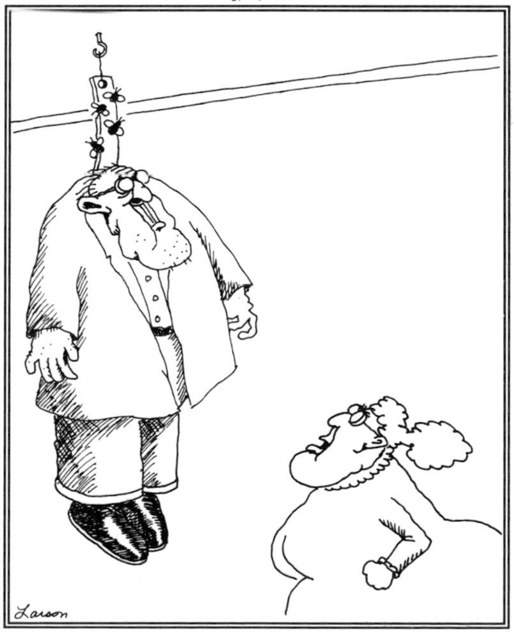
Larson

"So! You've been buzzing around the living room again, haven't you?"

5/8/80

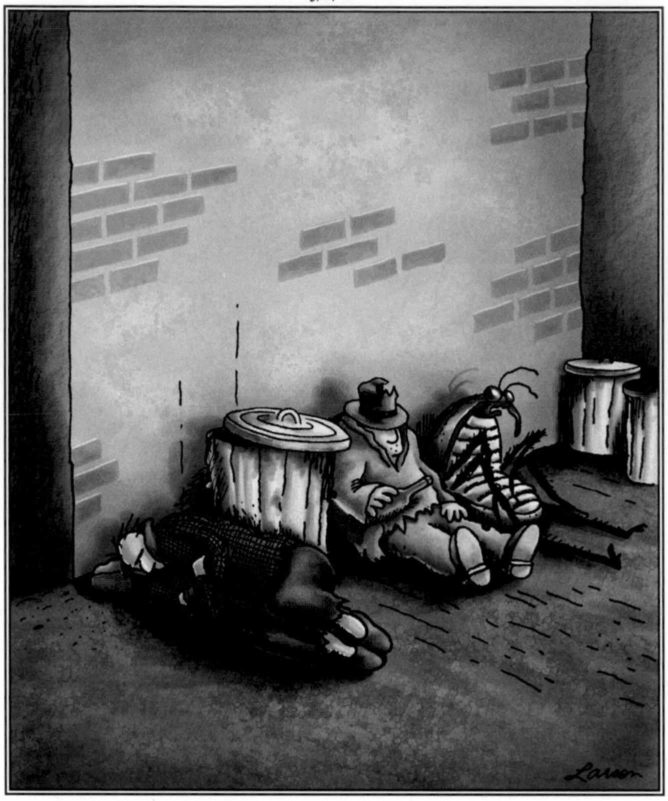

"I used to be somebody ... big executive ... my own company ... and then one day someone yelled, 'Hey! He's just a big cockroach!'"

5/13/80

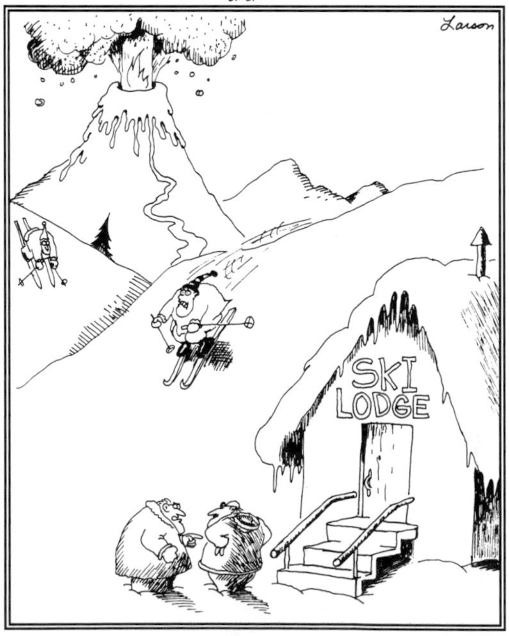
SKI LODGE

"Me? This year it was *your* turn to go up and sacrifice the goat!"

5/14/80

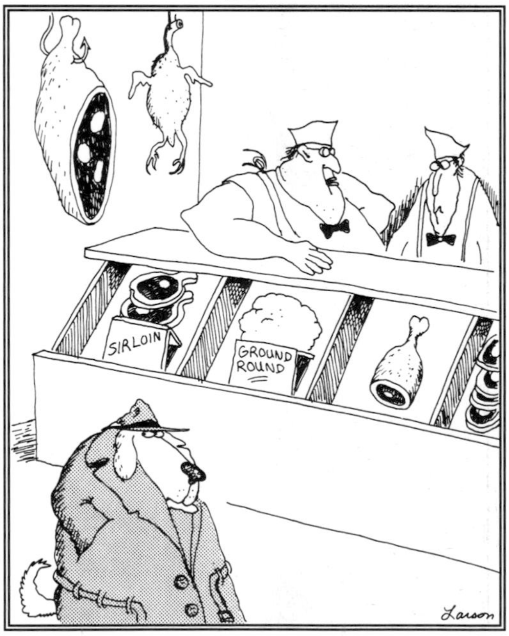
SIRLOIN
GROUND ROUND

"Keep your eye on that guy. ... He hasn't said or bought a thing for over an hour."

5/15/80

Larson

5/17/80

Larson

5/12/80

HAPPY BIRTHDAY SMO
Larson

"Can I look now?"

5/16/80

Larson

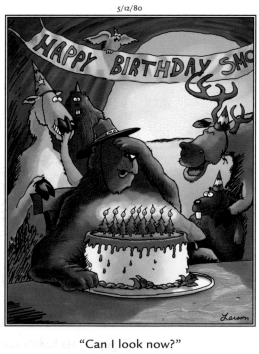

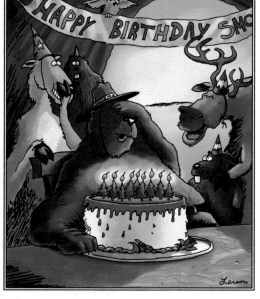

5/19/80

DON'T WALK
PUSH BUTTON FOR SIGNAL
CITY ELECTRIC
Larson

"This is the place, all right ... and it looks like it's been stuck on 'Don't Walk' for some time."

5/20/80

Larson
POLICE

"Well, well, well—what do we have here? ... I do believe it's a broken taillight."

5/21/80

SEKRET
Larson

"Okay—those that want to call our new club 'The Buccaneers' raise their ... Hey! Who's the wise guy that keeps cracking his knuckles?"

5/22/80

Larson

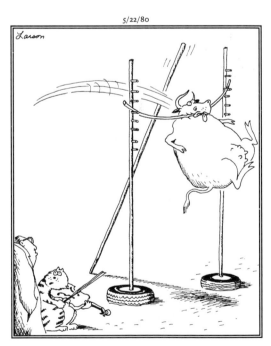

"We've still got a couple of years to go before we're ready for the moon."

5/23/80

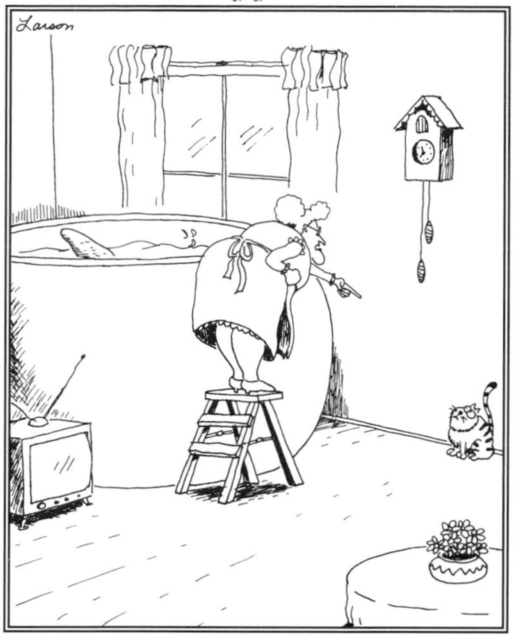
Larson

"And remember—I don't want to catch you bothering the fish!"

5/24/80

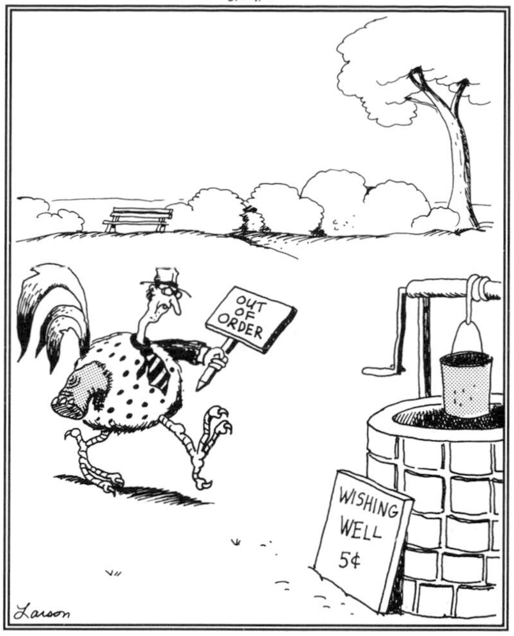
OUT OF ORDER
WISHING WELL 5¢
Larson

5/26/80

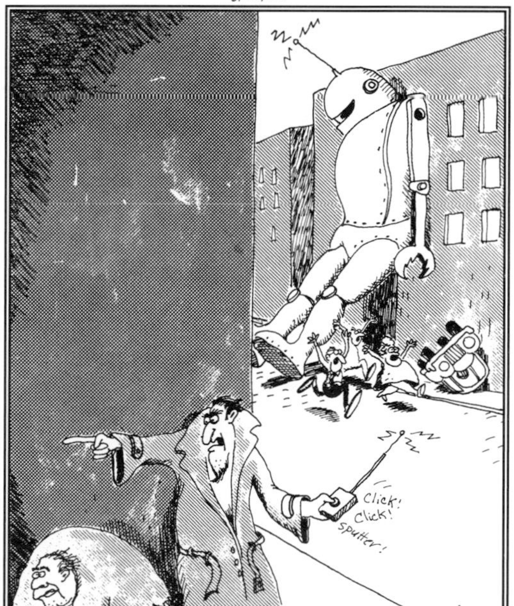
Click! Click! Sputter!
Larson

"Curses! ... Quick, Igor! Run down to the store and get two size D flashlight batteries!"

5/27/80

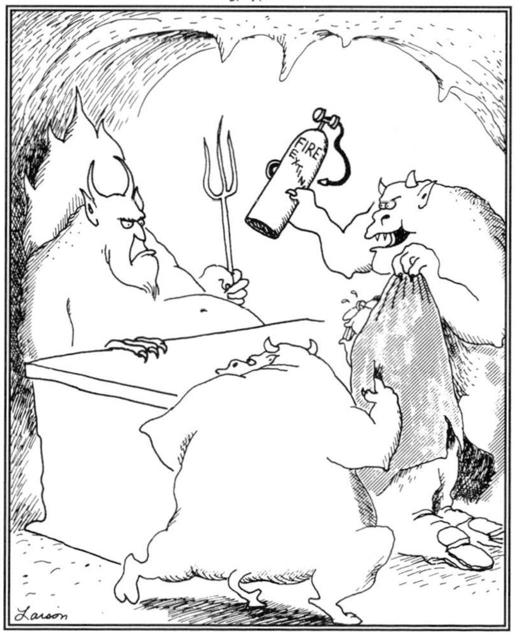
FIRE EXT.
Larson

"Yes, sir ... we caught him trying to smuggle this in under his coat."

May 1980

5/28/80

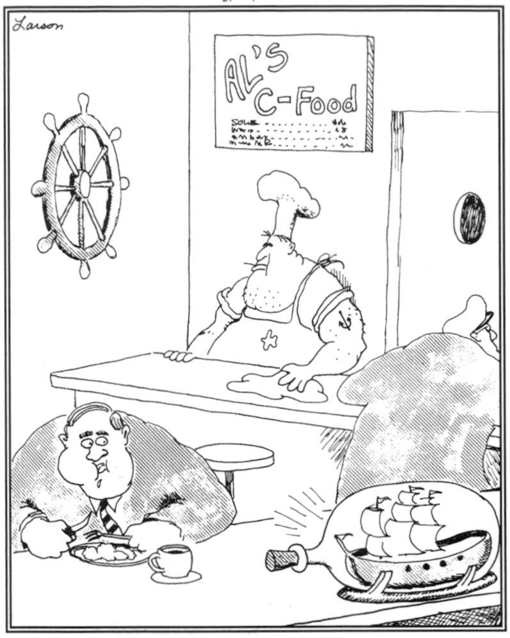
Larson
AL'S
C-Food

"Okay, it's settled—tonight at midnight, when the place is closed, we sail!"

5/29/80

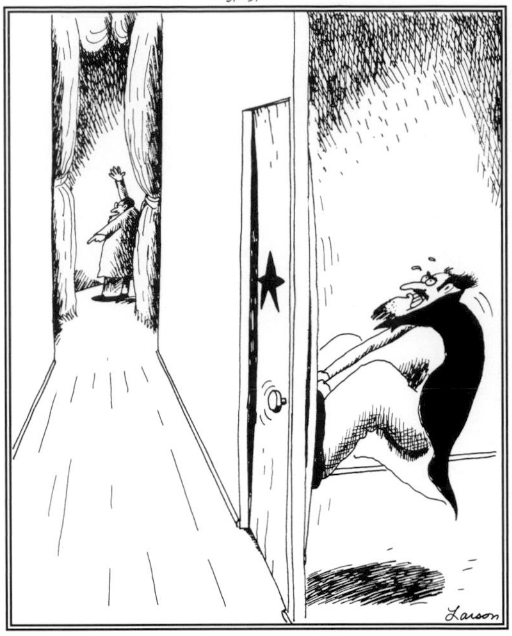
Larson

"And now, ladies and gentlemen, I give you the world's greatest escape artist ... THE GREAT WALDO!"

5/30/80

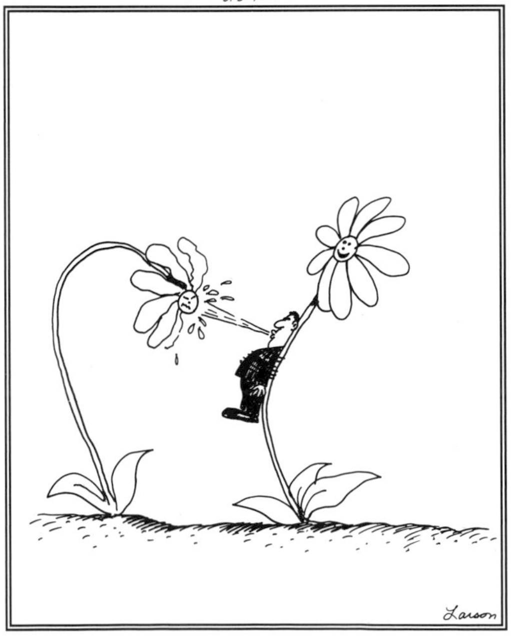
Larson

5/31/80

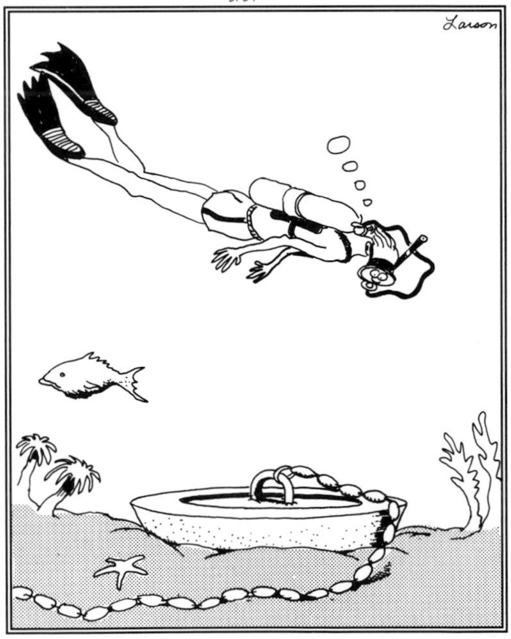
Larson

6/2/80

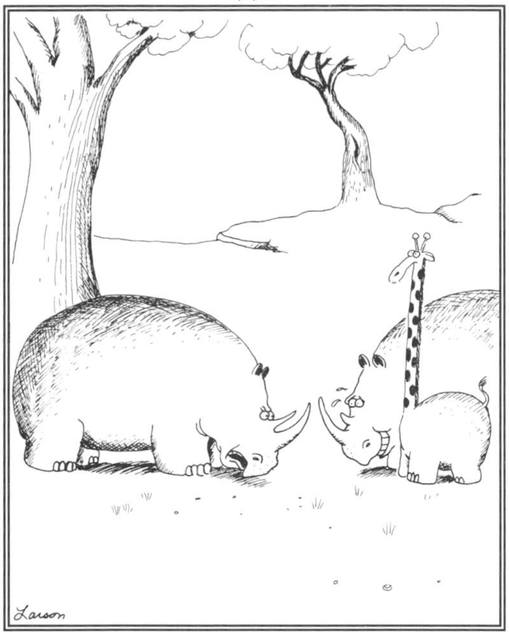
Larson

"There's something different about that kid."

6/4/80

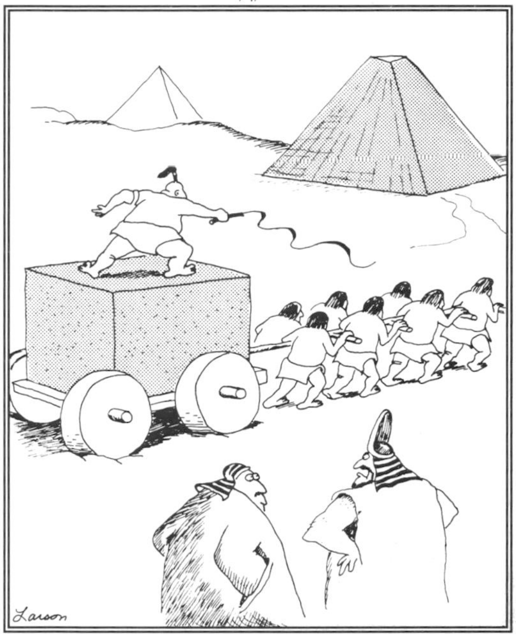
Larson

"Well, if it'll keep my razor blades sharp, that's all I ask."

6/3/80

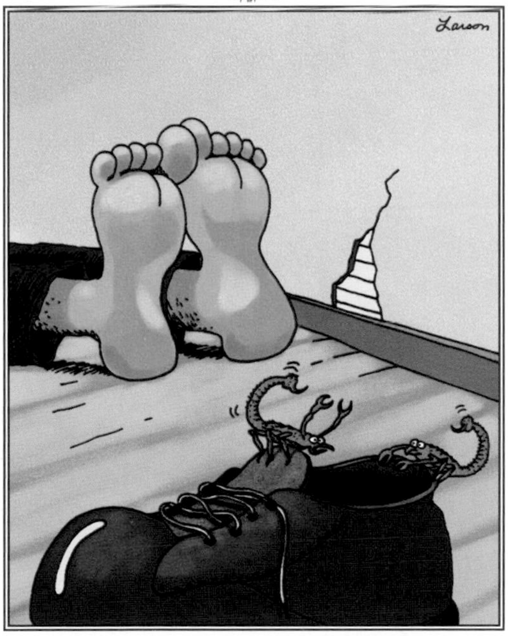
Larson

"There I was—asleep in this little cave here, when suddenly I was attacked by this hideous thing with five heads!"

6/5/80

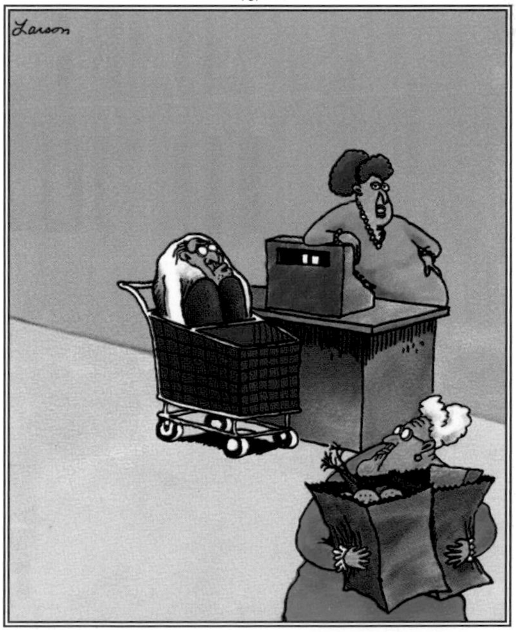
Larson

"Oh, Mrs. Oswald ... you've forgotten something again."

6/9/80

Larson

"'That's fine,' I said. 'Good nose,' I said. But no, you had to go and hit the chisel one more time."

6/6/80

Larson

6/7/80

7636
BAKERY DEPT.
Ernie,
Here's the file you wanted.
Good luck.
Love, Rosey
Larson

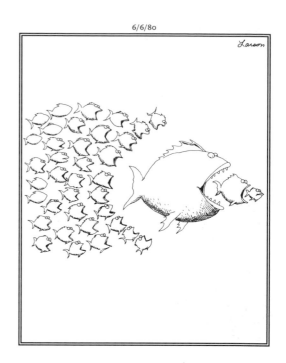

6/11/80

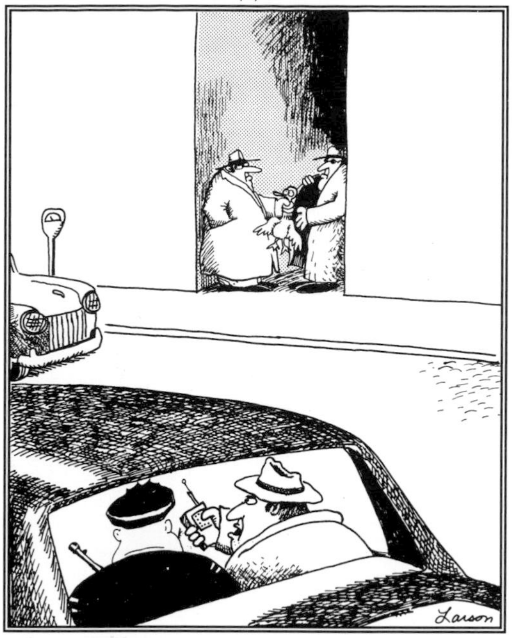

"All units prepare to move in! ... He's givin' him the duck now!"

6/12/80

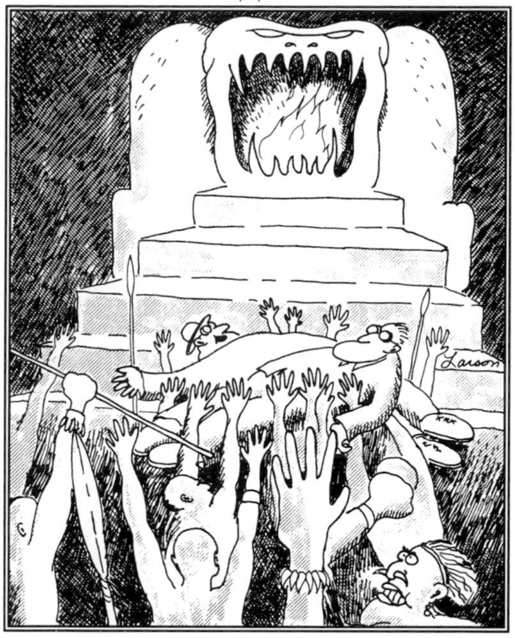

"By Jove, Andrew! ... It's just like being the heroes of some football game!"

6/13/80

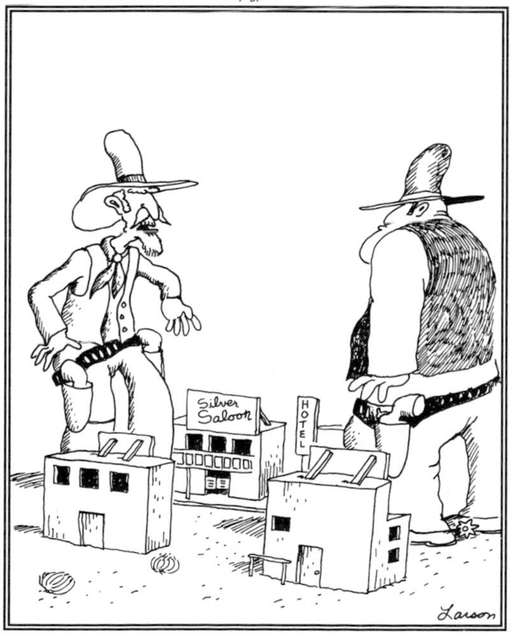
Silver Saloon
HOTEL

"This town ain't big enough for both of us, Redeye."

6/14/80

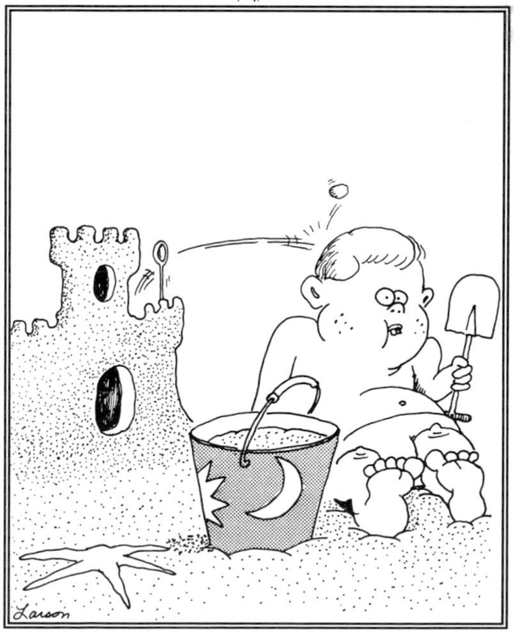

6/10/80

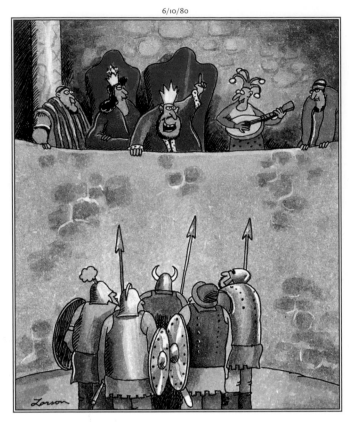

"And the last gladiator left alive will win the contest.
But first ... the egg-toss!"

6/16/80

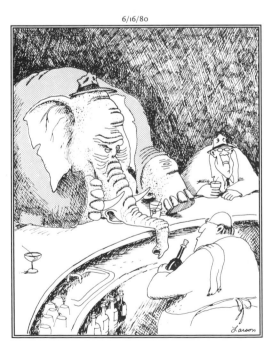

"It's no use. I drink and I drink, and I
still can't forget."

6/17/80

"Get ready! He's put the rubber ducky down
and now he's reaching for the bar of soap!"

6/19/80

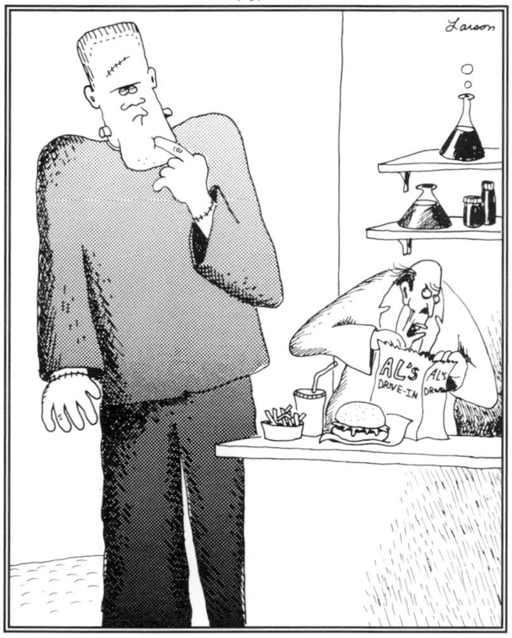
Larson
AL'S DRIVE-IN

"What? No tartar sauce? ... You'd forget your own head if it wasn't bolted on!"

6/20/80

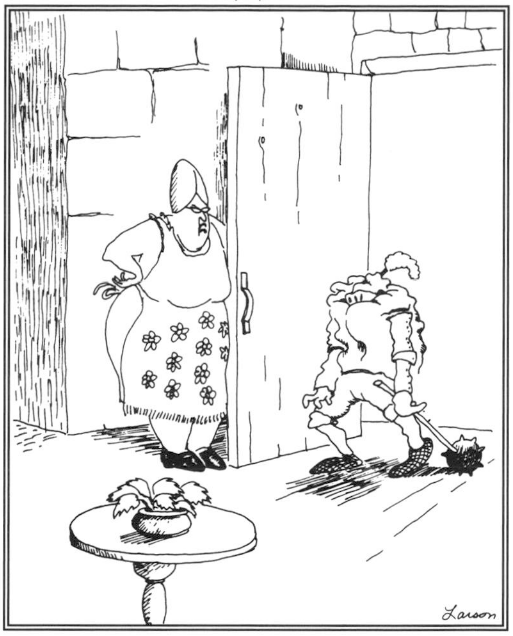
Larson

"So! You've been fighting again! ... And in your new suit, too!"

6/18/80

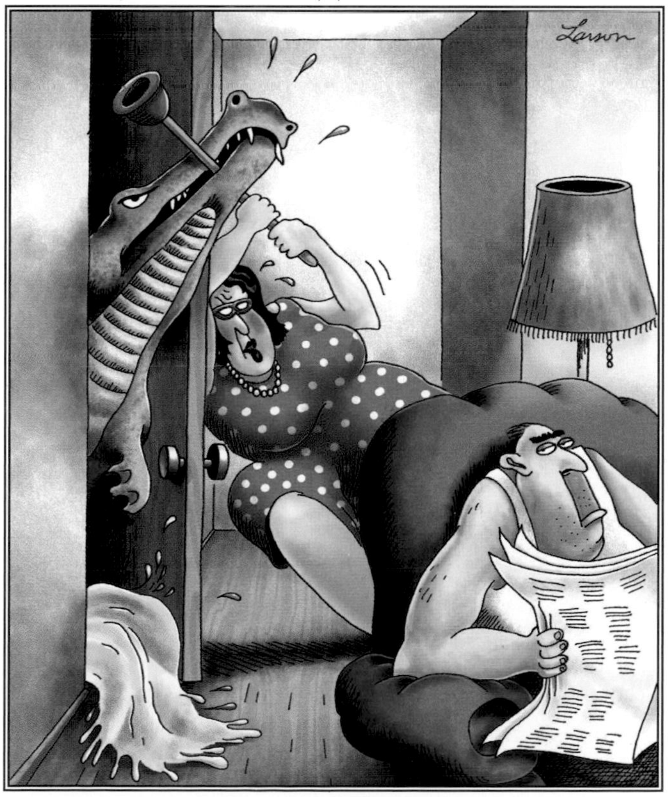
Larson

"Curse this New York City sewer system! ... It's backing up again."

6/21/80

Larson

"Nice guy ... except for that zebra-breath."

6/23/80

Larson

"Thank God! ... It was only a cat!"

6/25/80

Larson

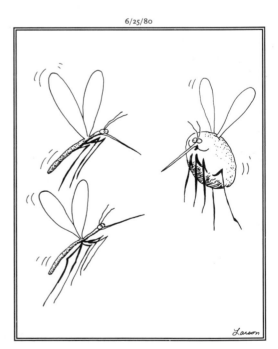

"Head five miles west until you come to a river, then fly upstream about a mile until you come to the sign 'Sunshine Nudist Camp.'"

6/27/80

Larson

"Oh Thorg! The new bird feeder is *wonderful!*"

6/24/80

"You'll never get away with this!"

6/26/80

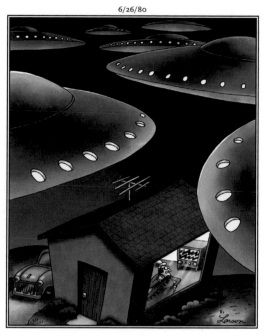

"Yeah, Sylvia—my set too. ... And in the middle of *Laverne and Shirley*."

6/30/80

"REMEMBER THE ... uh ... REMEMBER THE ... REMEMBER THAT PLACE IN TEXAS!"

6/28/80

"The curse of every albatross—that ship's been following us for days!"

July 1980

7/1/80

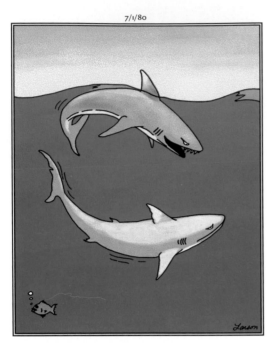

"Say, honey ... didn't I meet you last night at the feeding frenzy?"

7/2/80

YUTH'S
Fountain & Snack bar

"When we get back, I'm gonna wring de León's neck!"

7/3/80

"What the? ... Margaret! Margaret! Wake up! ... The bed's covered with coconuts!"

7/4/80

AL'S
CHART

"Set the hook! Set the hook!"

7/8/80

"And that goes for Lancelot, Galahad, and the rest of you guys—no more stickin' your gum under the table."

7/5/80

"Aha!"

7/7/80

"Gad, that's eerie. ... No matter where you stand the nose seems to follow."

7/9/80

"Just look at those stars tonight. ... Makes you feel sort of small and insignificant."

7/10/80

"And while you're out there, bring in a
couple of them frozen dinners."

7/11/80

"It's the attendant ... he's been trampled."

7/14/80

"So then this little sailor dude whips out this
can of spinach, this crazy music starts playin',
and ... well, just *look* at this place."

7/15/80

"Now here's one of the mysteries of the
universe. ... Which came first?"

7/17/80

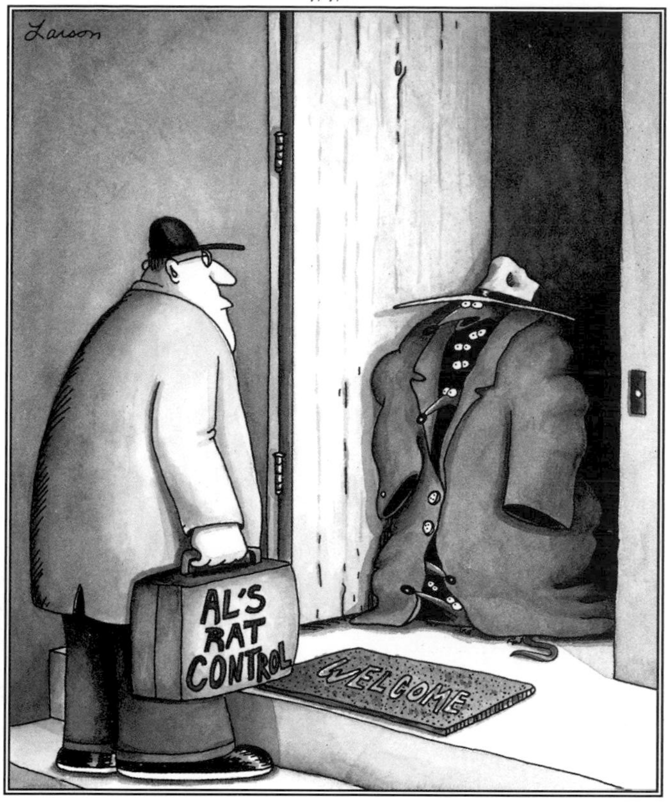
Larson
AL'S RAT CONTROL
WELCOME

"I'm sorry, we did call an exterminator ... but we've changed our minds."

7/19/80

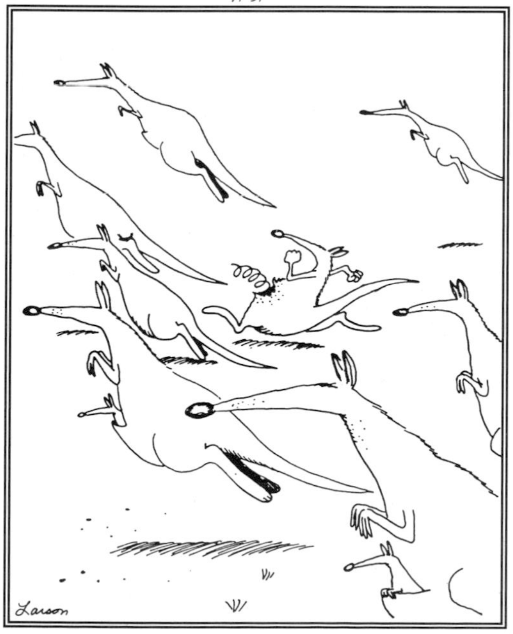
Larson

7/16/80

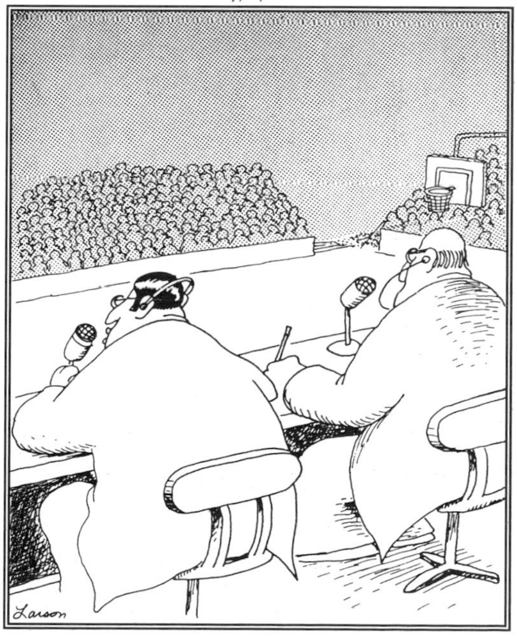
Larson

"Well, I guess that does it, folks. ... Number 26 is taking his ball and going home."

7/12/80

"Look! Down there! ... It's a worm!"

7/18/80

7/21/80

"Two, four, six, eight, who do we appreciate ..."

7/22/80

HELLOOOOOoo
HELLOOOOOOOOOOO
OW! HEY!
OH! OW!
HEY! OW!

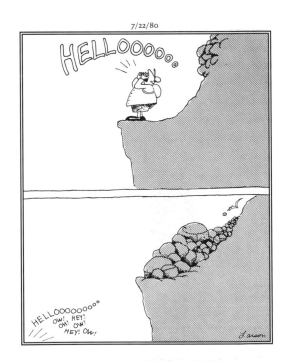

7/23/80

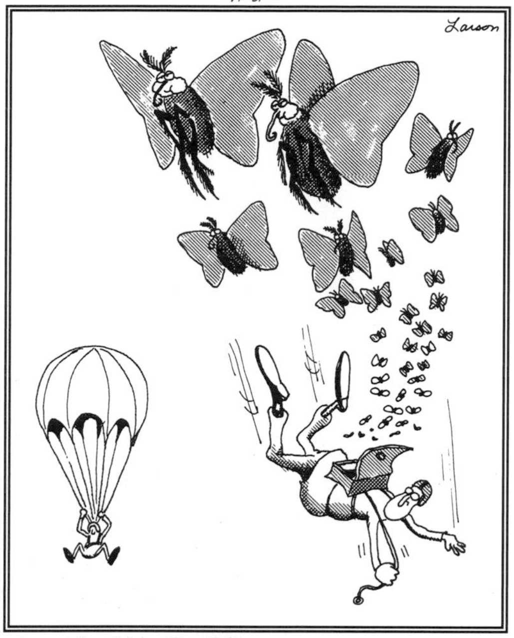
Larson

7/24/80

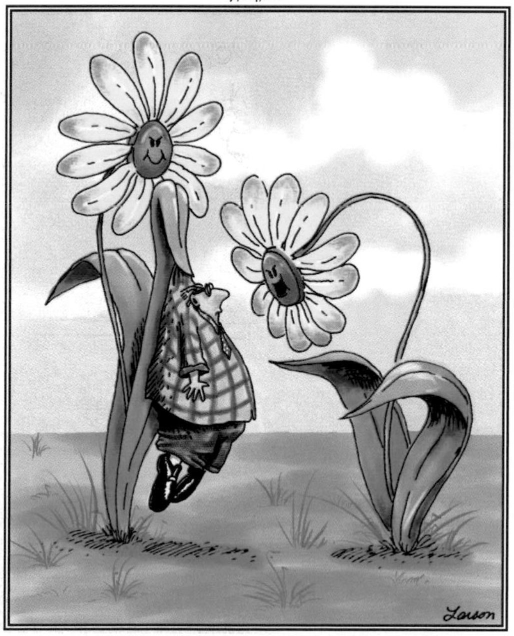
Larson

"And now *we're* going to play she-loves-me, she-loves-me-not!"

7/26/80

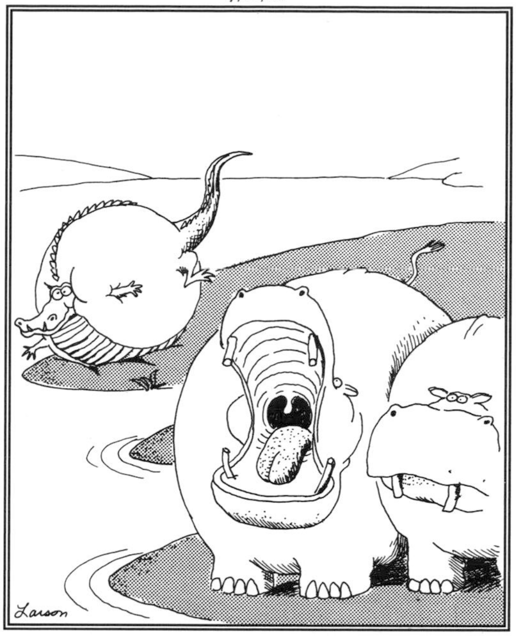
Larson

"AAAAAAAAAAlbert!"

7/25/80

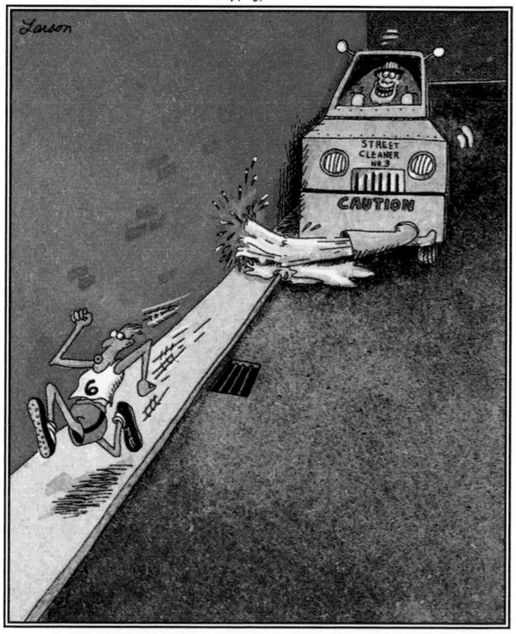
Larson
STREET
CLEANER
CAUTION
6

7/28/80

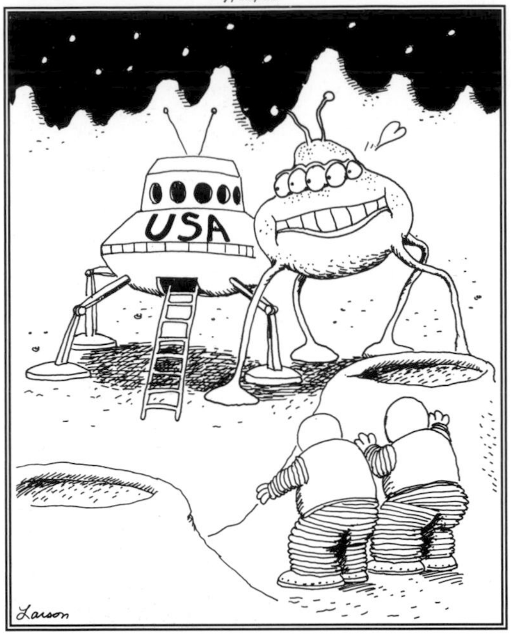
USA
Larson

7/29/80

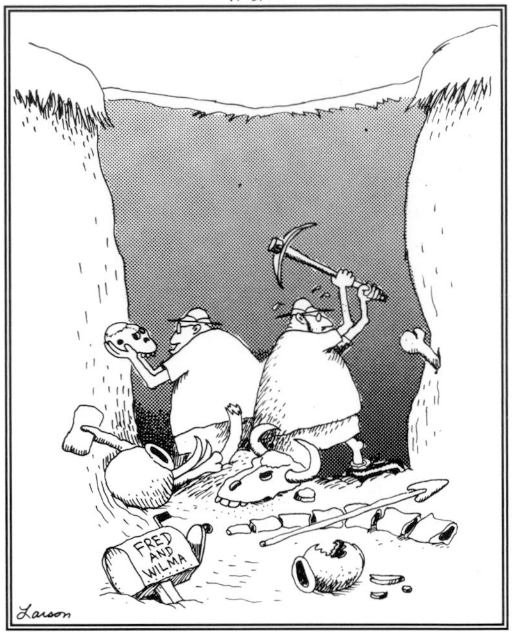
FRED AND WILMA
Larson

7/30/80

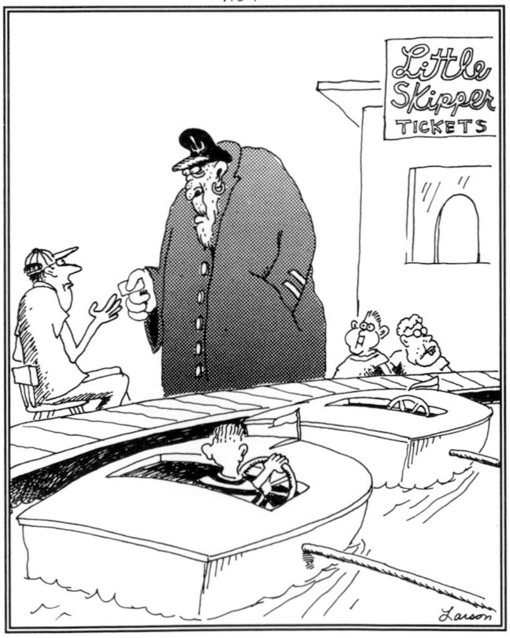
Little Skipper TICKETS
Larson

7/31/80

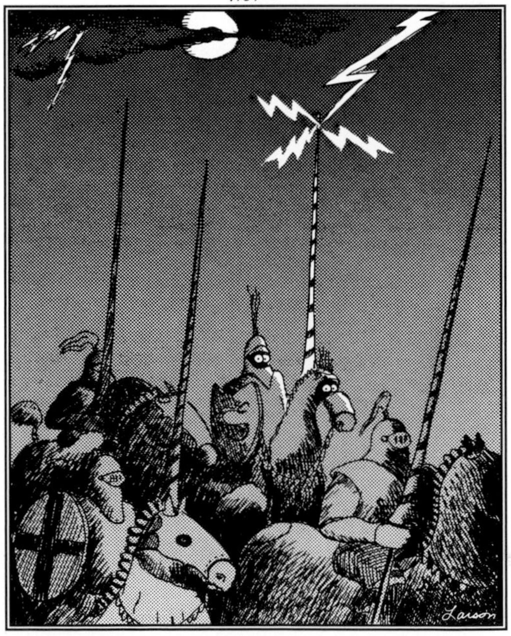
Larson

8/1/80

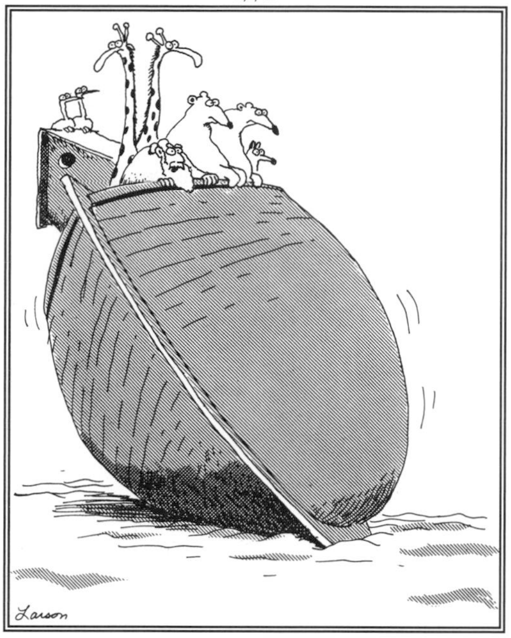
Larson

"Blast! ... The elephants are sick again!"

8/2/80

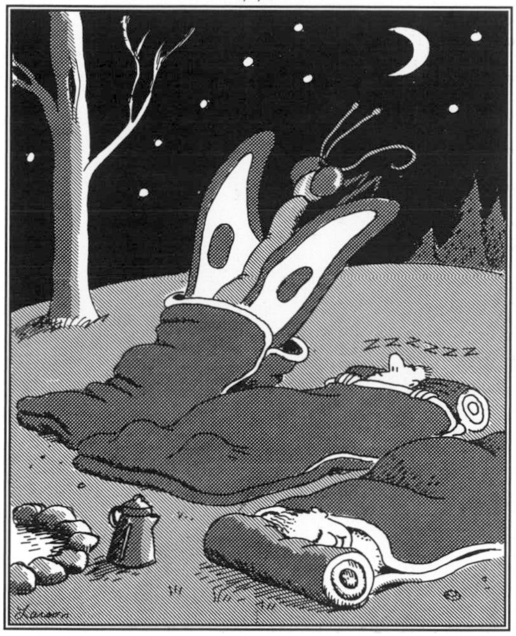
ZZZZZZ
Larson

8/5/80

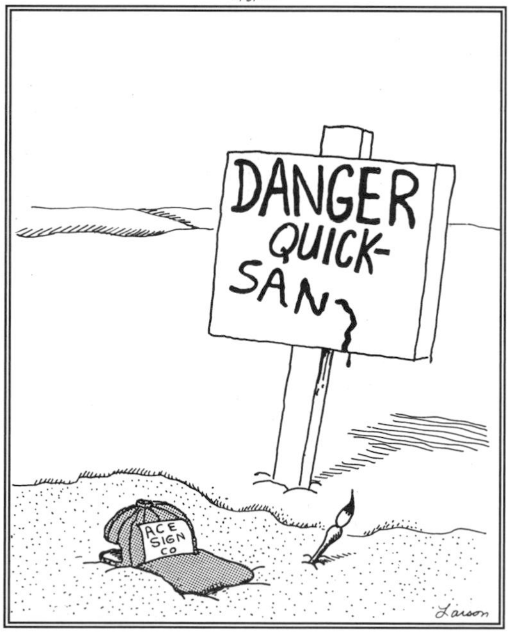
DANGER
QUICK-
SAN
ACE
SIGN
CO
Larson

8/7/80

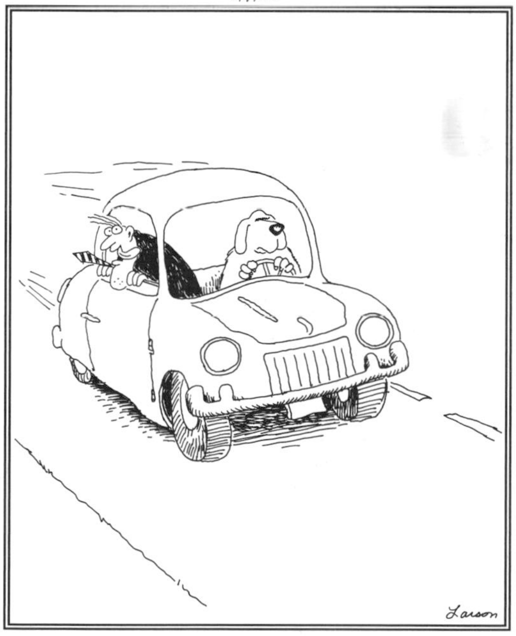
Larson

8/4/80

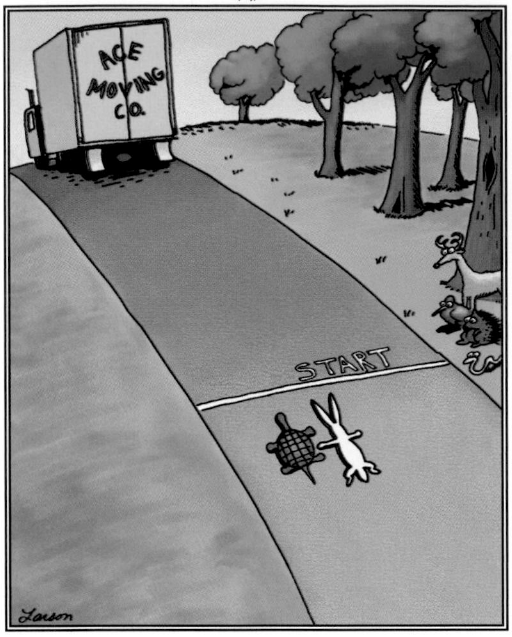
ACE
MOVING
CO.
START

8/6/80

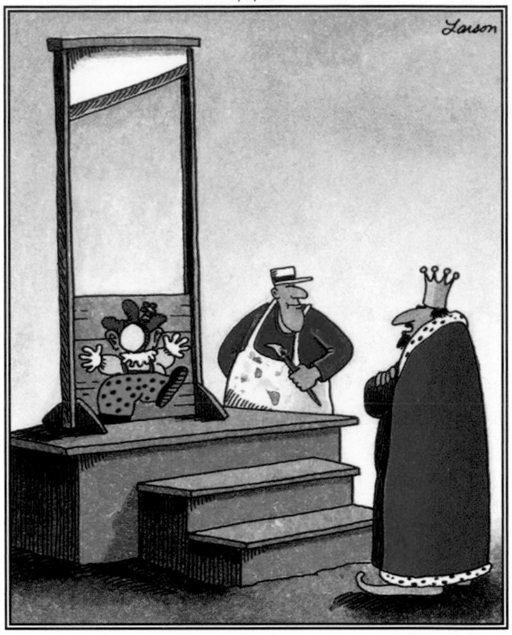

"I like it ... I like it."

8/8/80

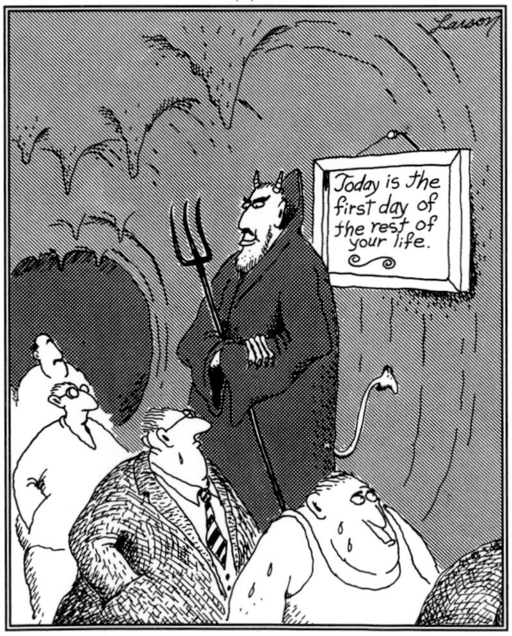
Today is the first day of the rest of your life.

8/9/80

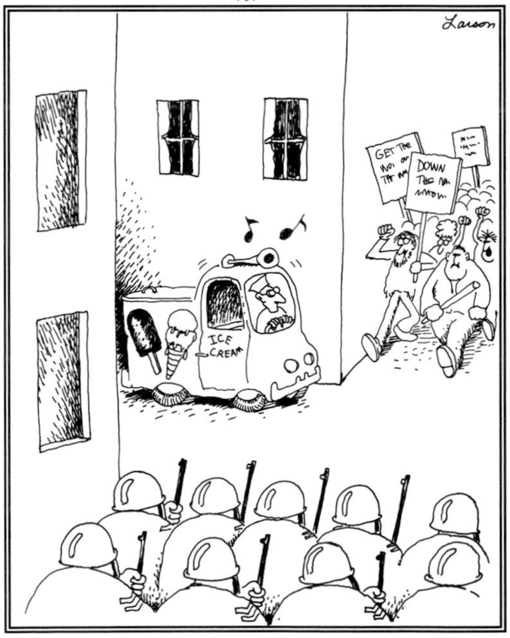
GET THE
DOWN THE
ICE CREAM

Dear Stan:

I wonder if we might gather some of the reactions I have had to Gary Larson--editors' comments--and weave them into a story of some kind for E&P (or even a note for general circulation--or both). The initial response to this cartoon has been quite funny and un-editor-like, if you think as I often do of newspaper editors as cautious and diplomatic people--judicious in their praise, given rarely to hyperbole or boundless laughter at the slightest occasion--above all, as having an immunity to outrage (a languor in the face of eccentricity) that borders on world-weariness!...And then, all of a sudden, with Gary Larson on their desk, what human sparks emerge! What has made this interesting to me is not knowing as I travel from one place to the next what <u>kind</u> of response to expect--the reactions are so diverse, unpredictable--even from editors I know fairly well. I don't know if I am going to be offered another cup of Sanka or shown the door. There is a lot of outright laughter incidentally a lot of silence too with intermittent nervous laughter--and then there is some deep groaning, a miserable sound to hear. Anyway, here are some of the comments:

"I hate it, it's sick."

"Oh dear, OH DEAR!"

"The best thing since Doonesbury as far as I am concerned. And
                they're <u>all</u> good!"

Editor's note: This is a memo from Stuart Dodds to his boss, Stan Arnold, general manager of Chronicle Features Syndicate. Dodds, the sales manager for the syndicate, had the unenviable job of being the first person to try and sell The Far Side *to newspaper editors (who tend to be a rather cynical lot). It was written late at night in a small motel room in the desert outside of Tucson on his portable typewriter.*

2--Larson

"What a mind this man has. He's brilliant!"

"He's insane."

"Jesus...Jesus Christ."

"It might go over in San Francisco..."

"This is <u>not</u> a Buffalo product" (Buffalo Evening News)

"I don't know what this is but it's not for us."

"This is an excellent feature you have."

"This is the strangest thing I have seen in my life."

"Funny as hell."

"We'd get too much flack. I'd like to watch it for a while."

"Who is this guy?"

(There could follow a humorous biography of Larson.)

Editors by their nature are drawn towards controversy. If we can cast it about that this <u>is</u> a controversial feature, that it has brought on the highest praise from some quarters and made others hair stand on end, we'd build up curiosity--the inquiries would flow in and a percentage of them would buy it. Maybe we could send parts of this memo to E&P as "Notes From the Field" or some such thing, with one or two of the more horrifying cartoons... Those are my fevered thoughts in the desert tonight...

8/2/80--Tucson

8/11/80

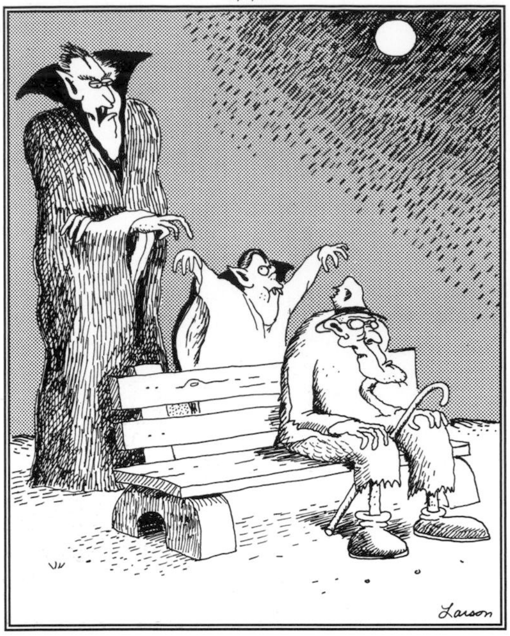
Larson

"No, no, Wendell ... you can't get blood out of a turnip."

8/12/80

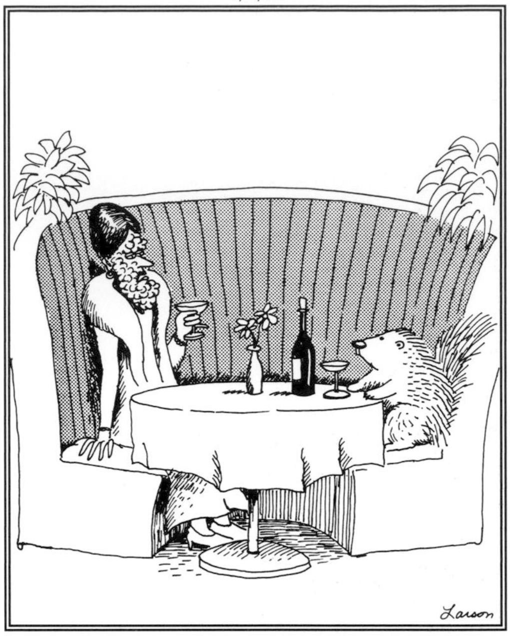
Larson

"Look. I just don't feel the relationship is working out."

8/13/80

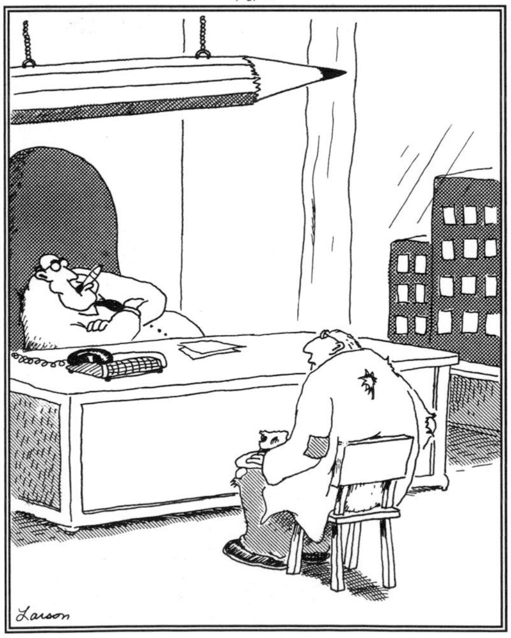
Larson

"So ... you wanna sell our pencils, do you?"

8/14/80

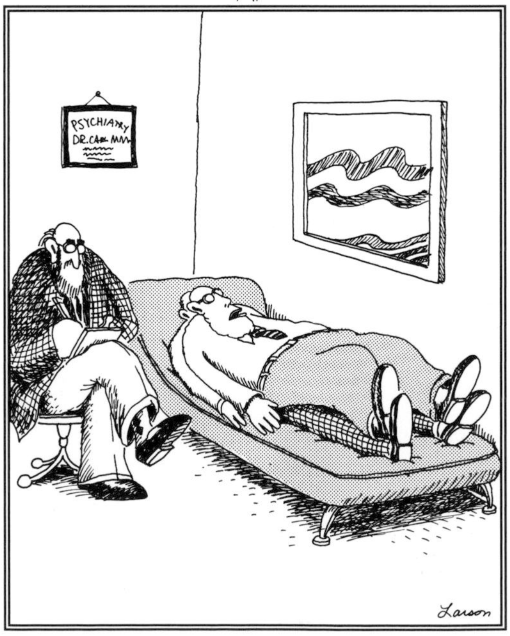
PSYCHIATRY
Larson

"It's quite strange ... almost like I'm being followed."

8/15/80

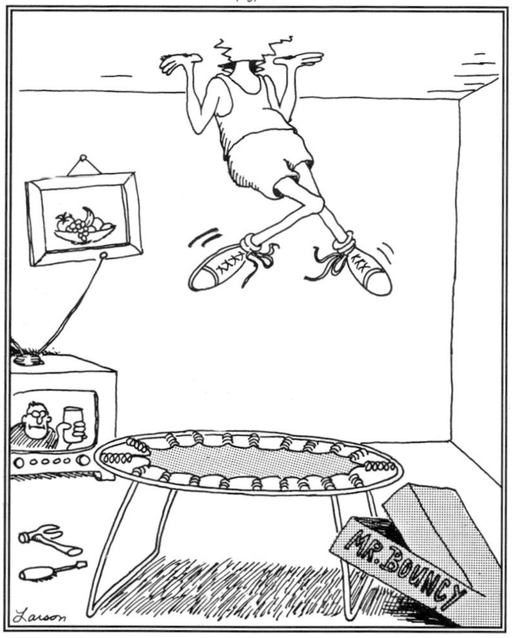
MR. BOUNCY
Larson

8/16/80

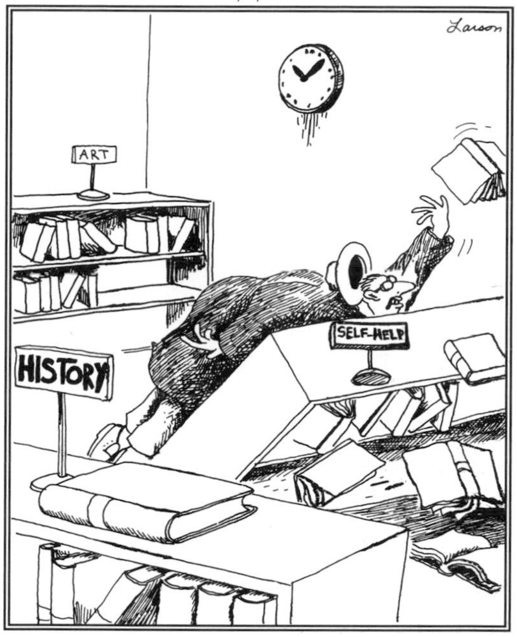
Larson
ART
SELF-HELP
HISTORY

8/18/80

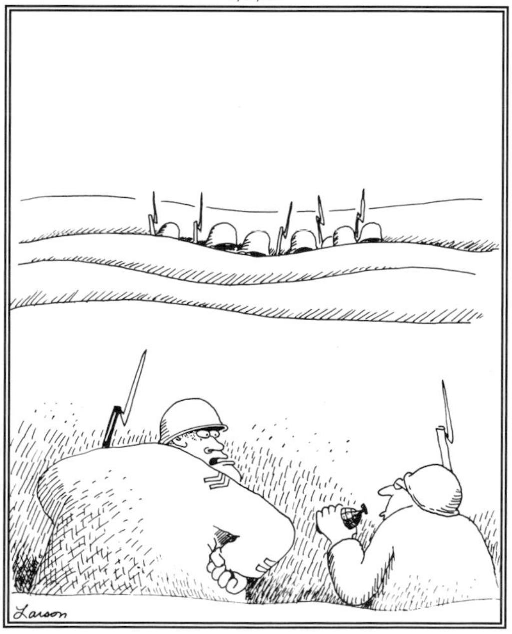
Larson

"This time, Johnson, just pull the pin, throw the grenade, and refrain from yelling 'Heads!'"

8/20/80

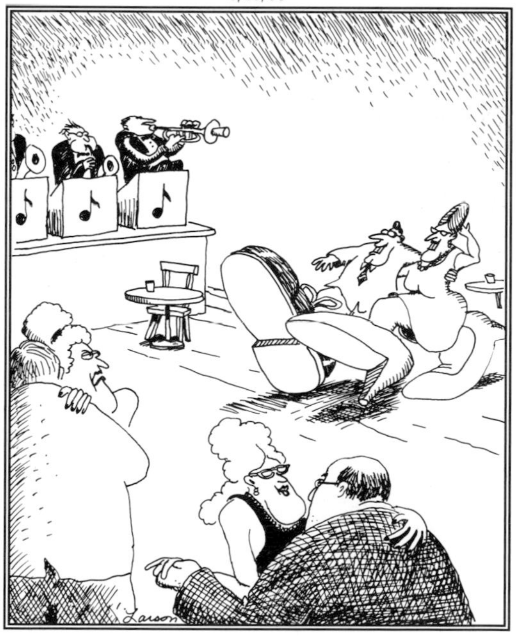
Larson

"Gad! Clear the dance floor—here come the Nelsons again."

8/19/80

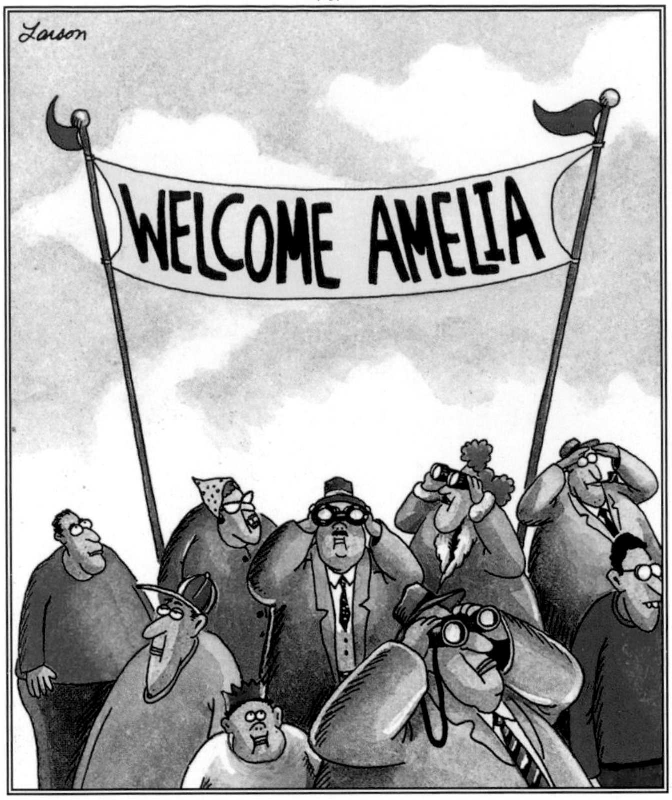
Larson
WELCOME AMELIA

"Well, I'm just starting to worry about that roast in the oven, that's all."

8/21/80

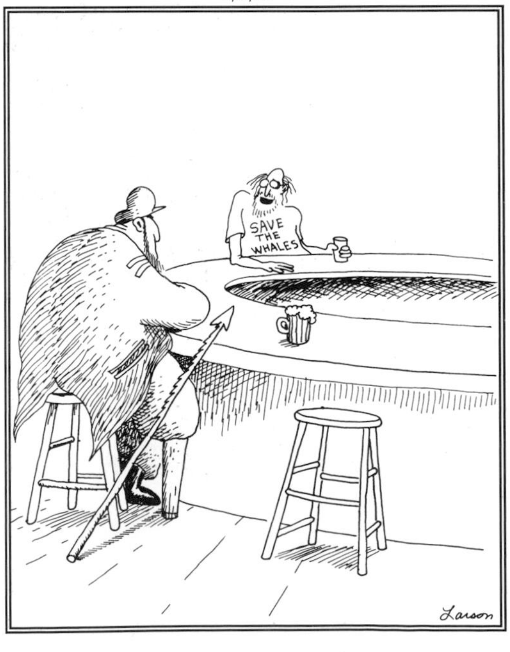
SAVE THE WHALES
Larson

"Oh, sure—*white* whales. ... We've got plenty of *them*."

8/23/80

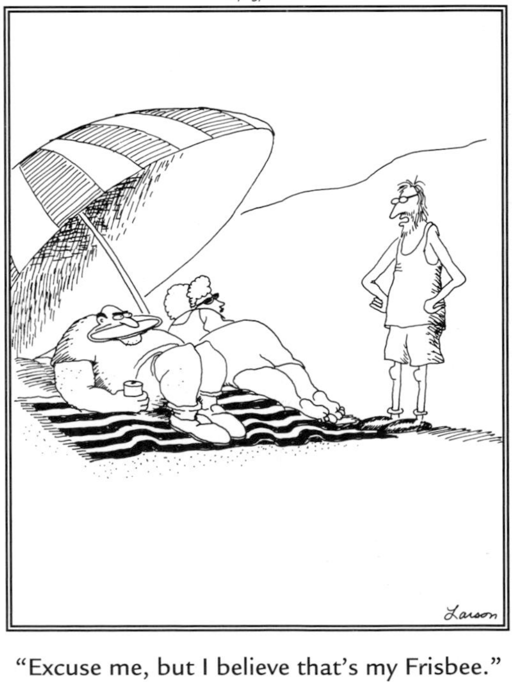
Larson

"Excuse me, but I believe that's my Frisbee."

8/22/80

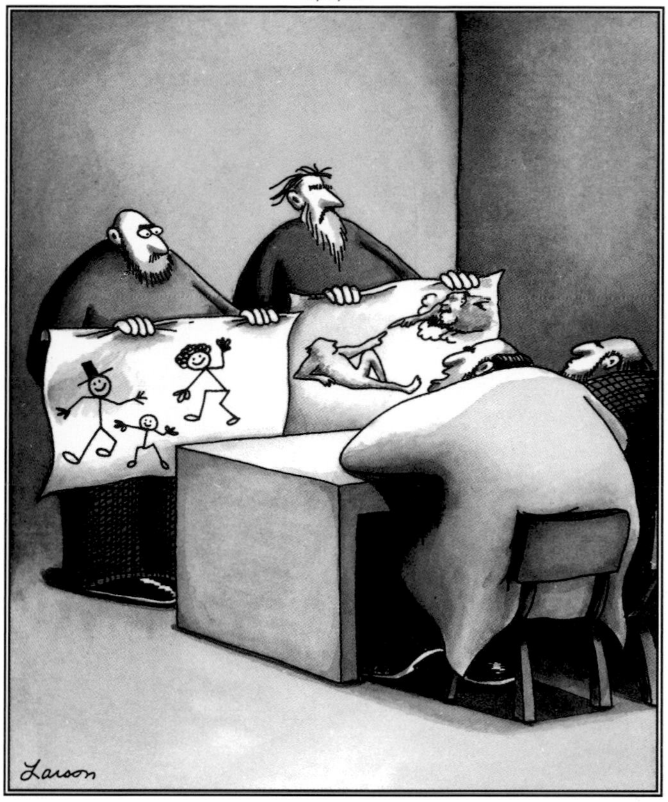

"I'm sorry, Mr. Funucci, but we've decided to award the ceiling project to Michelangelo."

8/25/80

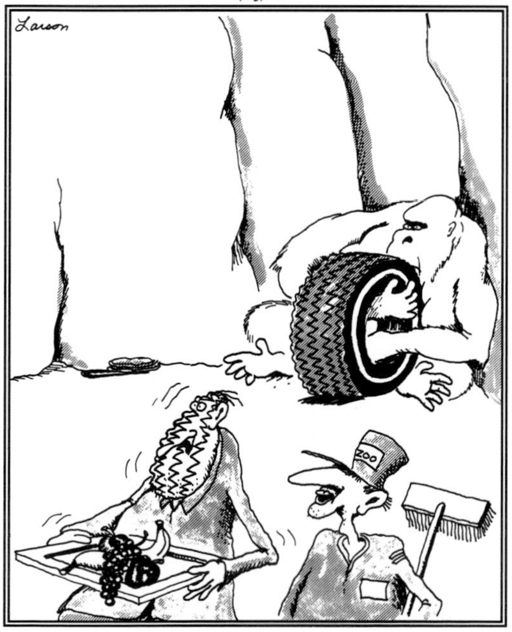
ZOO

"Quick, powerful, and totally unpredictable— that's our Bobo."

8/26/80

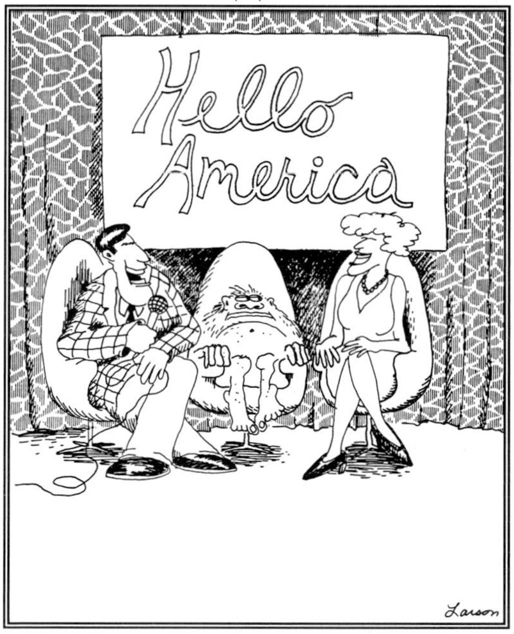
Hello
America

"And so, after being frozen in ice for almost 50,000 years, we'll ask our friend here what dramatic changes he's noticed."

8/27/80

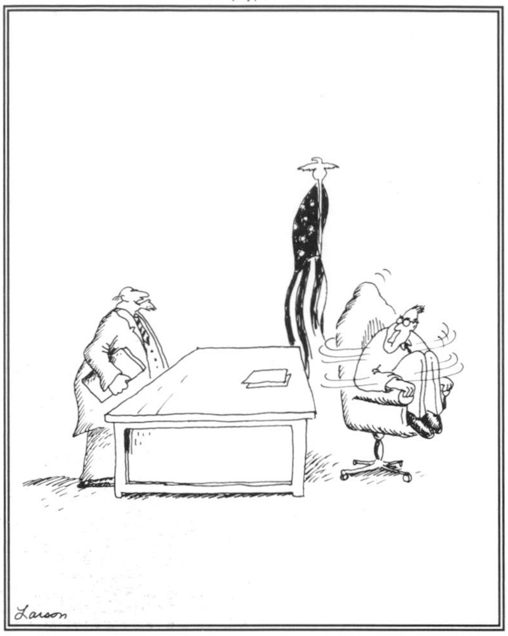

"I'm afraid you'll have to do better than that, sir. ... The former president could spin twenty-six times before stopping."

8/28/80

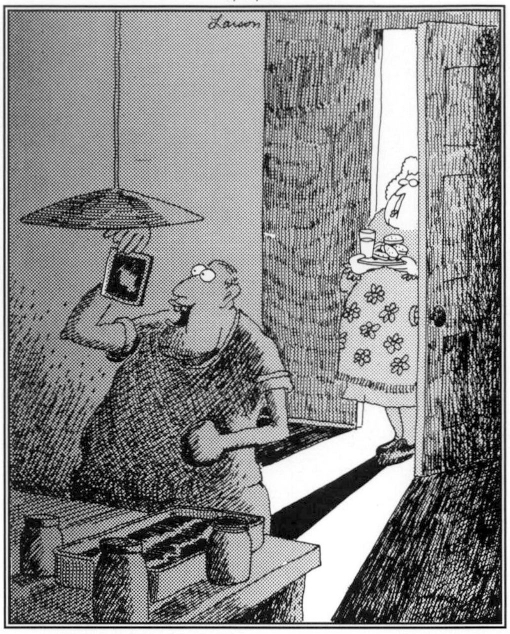

"I've done it! The first real evidence of a UFO! ... And with my own camera, in my own darkroom, and in my own ..."

8/29/80

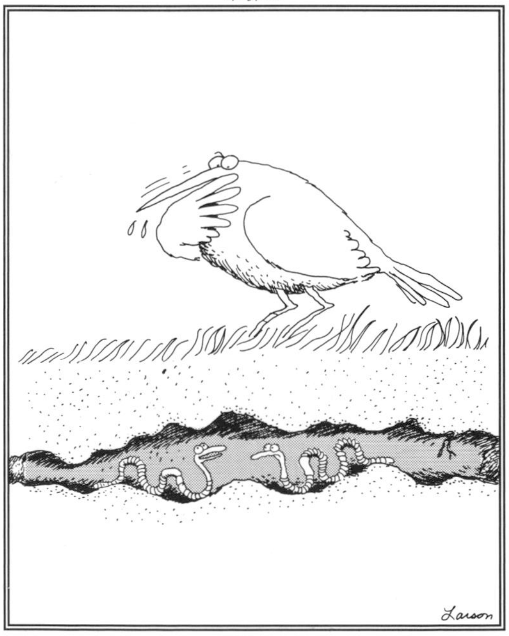

"Gesundheit!"

8/30/80

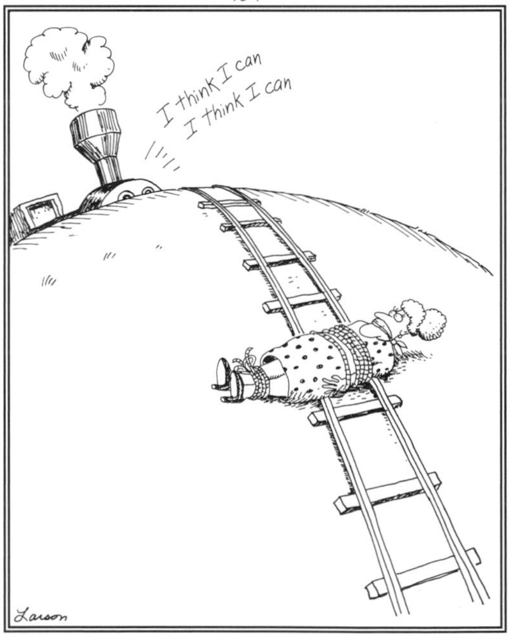
I think I can
I think I can

9/1/80

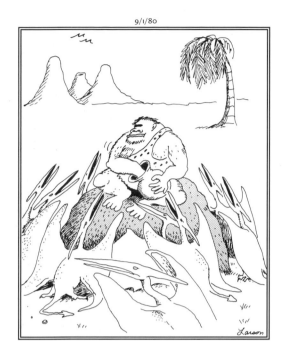

Larson

9/2/80

Larson

"Hmmm ... not bad, Kemosabe ... but this one little better maybe."

9/3/80

Larson

"Okay, okay, settle down! ... Now who wants dark meat and who wants white?"

9/4/80

Larson

"Gad ... I gotta get this thing in for a tune-up."

9/5/80

Larson

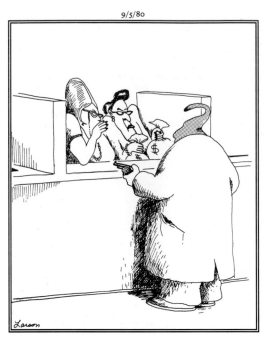

"God, Harriet ... check out the run in his nylon."

9/6/80

Larson

9/8/80

Larson

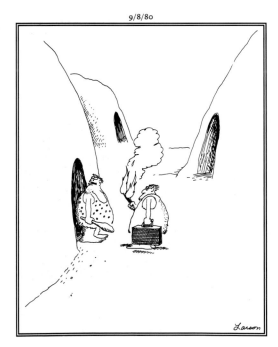

"Hey, Oona! Did you order some of this stuff?"

9/9/80

Larson

"Andrew, go out and get your grandfather. ... The squirrels have got him again."

9/10/80

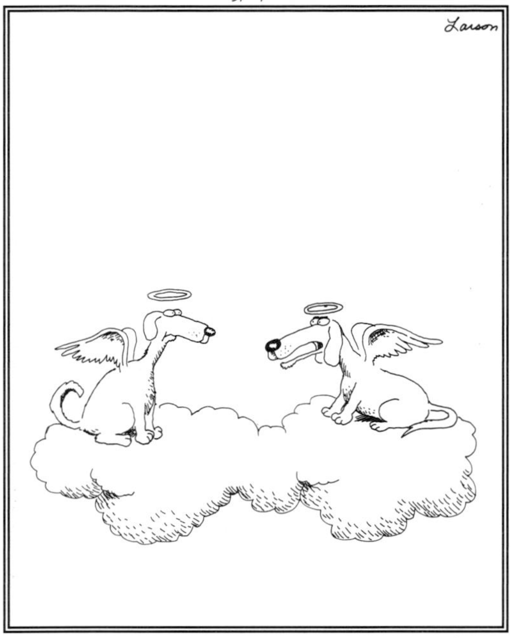
Larson

"For twelve perfect years I was a car-chaser. Pontiacs, Fords, Chryslers—I took 'em all on ... and yesterday my stupid owner backs over me in the driveway."

9/11/80

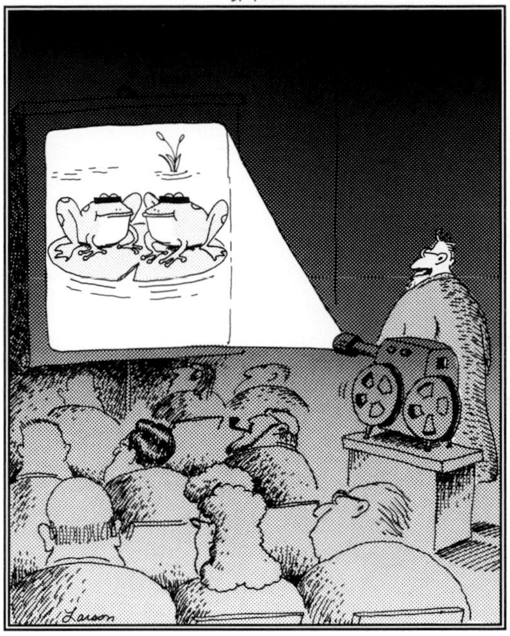
Larson

"And now, as you will observe, the male *Bufo boreas* begins his courtship display as the female responds to the vocal stimulus."

9/12/80

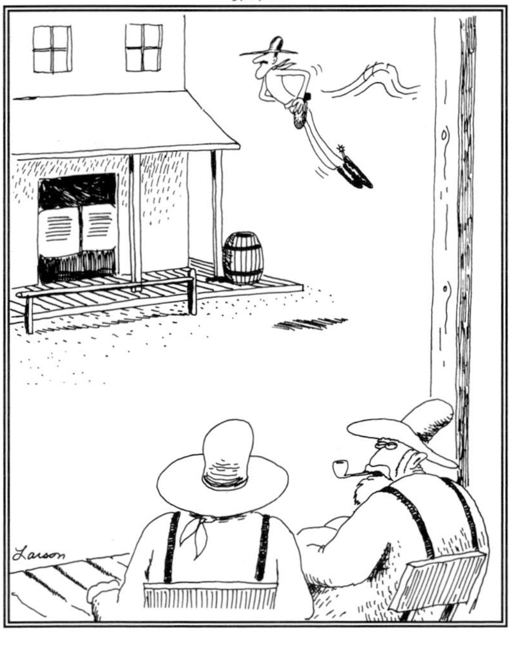
Larson

"Looks like some drifter comin' into town."

9/13/80

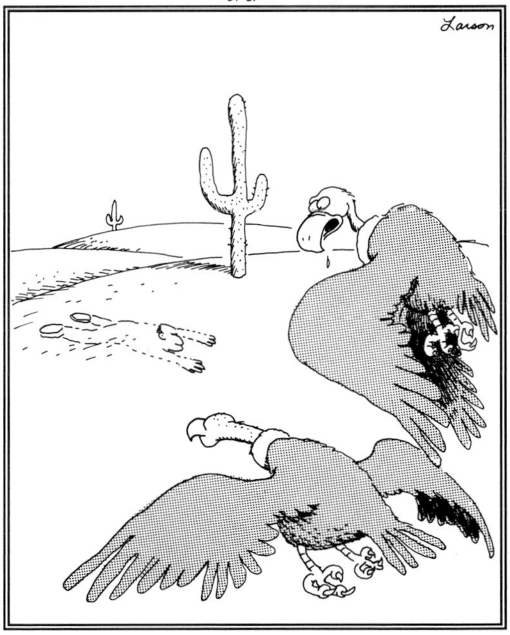
Larson

"You moron! ... I told you it was only a mirage!"

9/16/80

"Pie trap! ... We're in Zubutu country,
all right."

9/17/80

RETURN OF THE KILLER WINDSHIELD

9/15/80

"Nice try."

9/20/80

"Well, there goes the neighborhood."

9/18/80

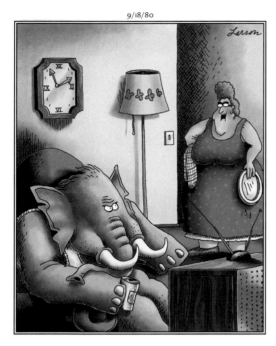

"Mother was right! ... I never should have married outside my own species!"

9/19/80

"Yoo-hoo! Oh, yoo-hoo! ... I think I'm getting a blister."

9/23/80

"I can't take this curse any longer! ... Every sunrise I change into this hairless, frail little man who couldn't hurt a fly."

9/24/80

"Zag and Thena! ... Come on in and act uncivilized!"

9/22/80

"I guess he made it. ... It's been more than a week
since he went over the wall."

9/25/80

"Hey, Zoran! What's happenin'? ...
Give me six!"

9/26/80

"We're in luck. I don't think he sees it."

9/27/80

Larson

9/30/80

Larson
CLASSIFIEDS

"Hey! Here's one! ... 'Mad scientist needs assistant.'"

9/29/80

Larson

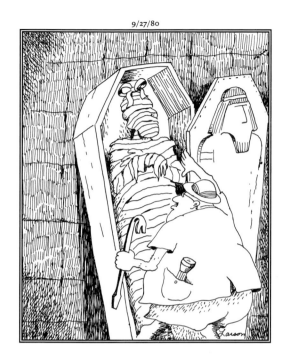

"Oh hey! I just love these things! ... Crunchy on the outside and a chewy center!"

10/1/80

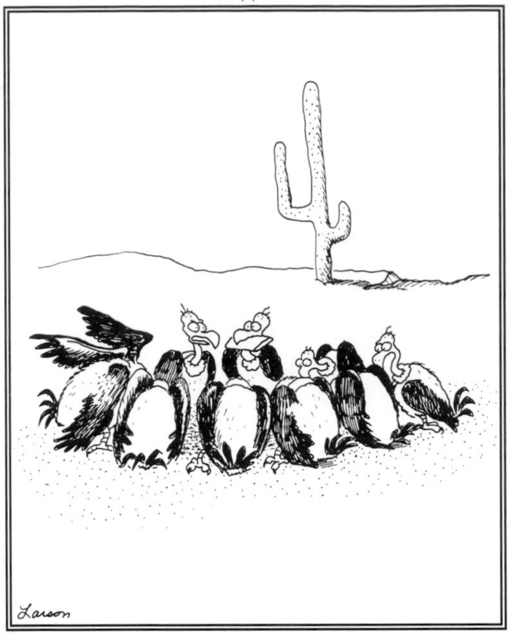

"You fool! You can't eat that ... it's a wallet!"

10/2/80

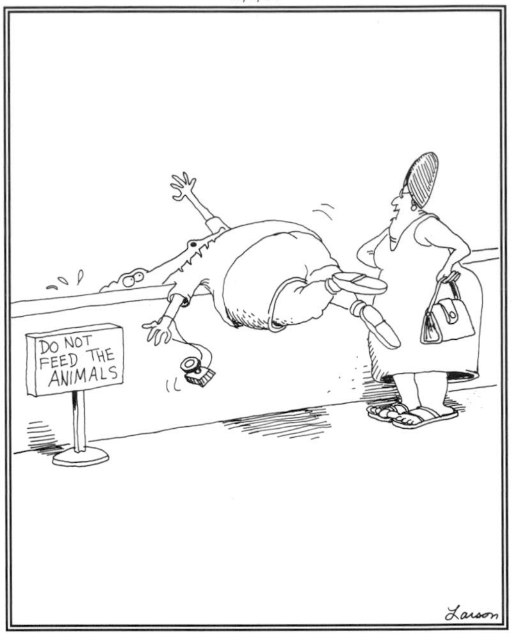
DO NOT
FEED THE
ANIMALS

"You're embarrassing me, Warren."

10/3/80

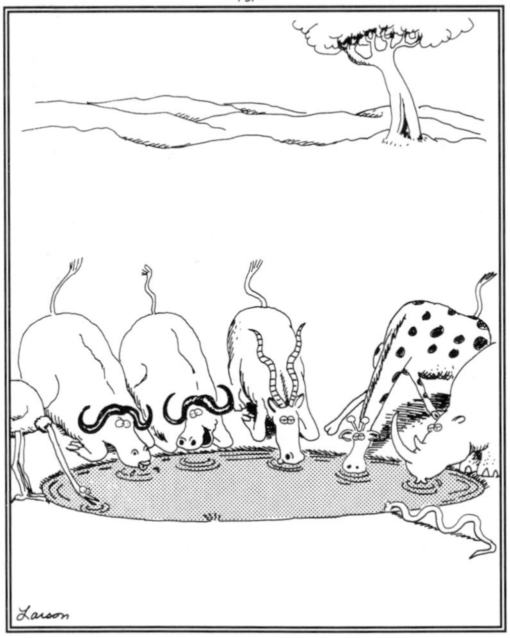

"So ... come here often?"

10/4/80

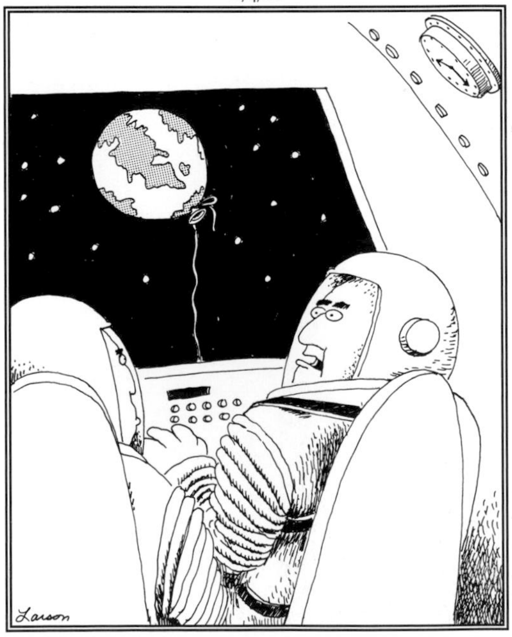

"Listen. I think we better keep this quiet."

10/9/80

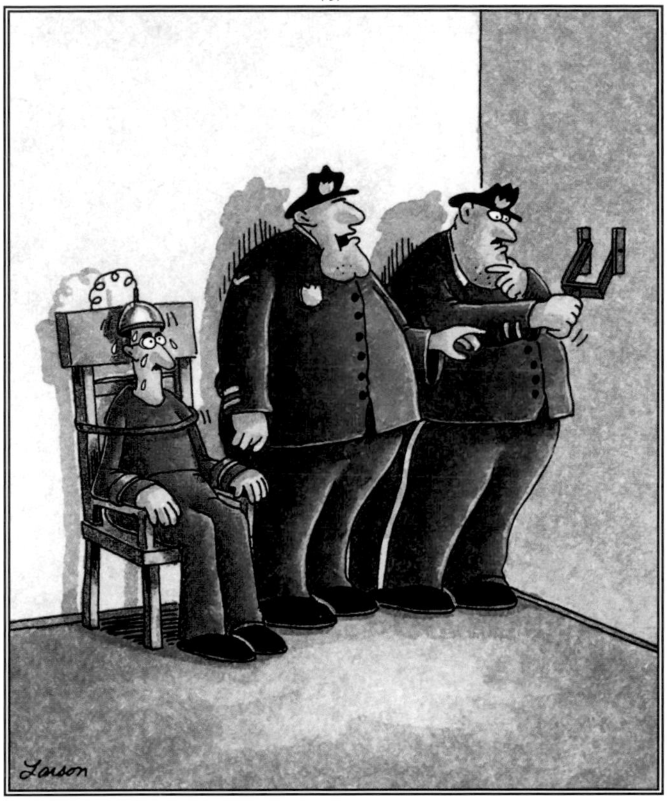
Larson

"The contact points must be dirty. ... Just click it up and down a few times."

10/6/80

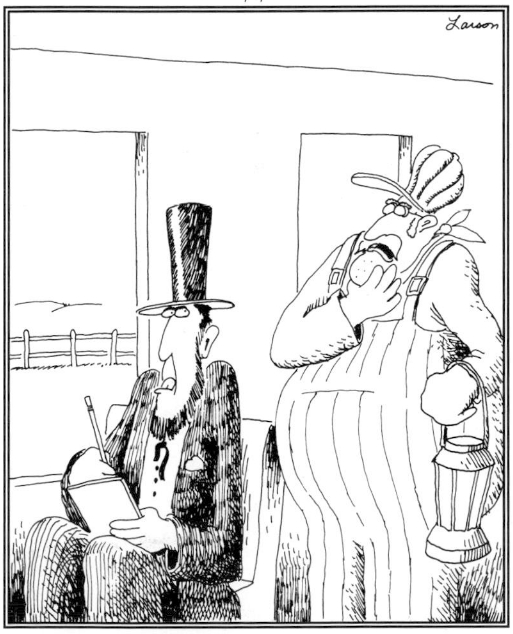
Larson

"Well, Mr. President, let's see—carry the one, take away three, carry the two ... that would be four score and seven years ago."

10/7/80

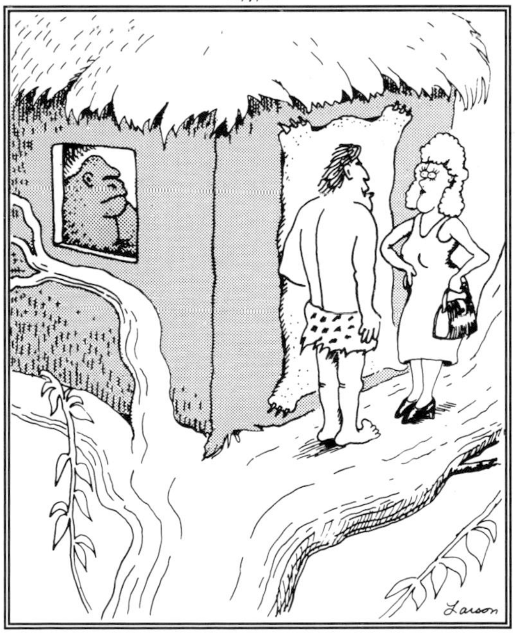
Larson

"My folks are a little different ... just ignore them if they start looking through your hair for fleas and things."

October 1980

10/8/80

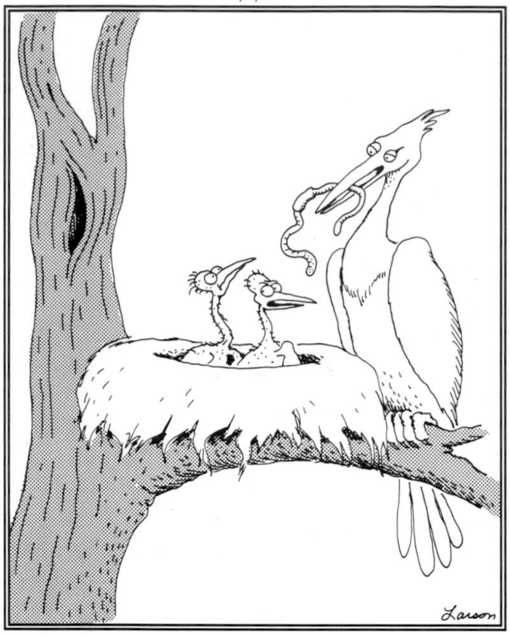

"We better eat it ... or we'll get that old lecture again about the birds starving in Asia."

10/11/80

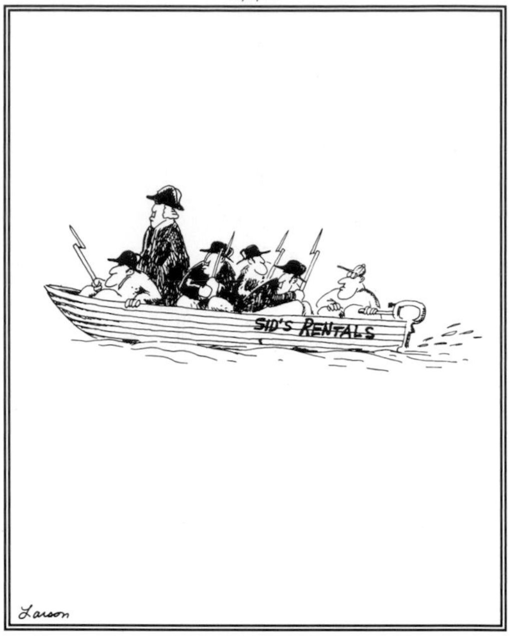
SID'S RENTALS

10/13/80

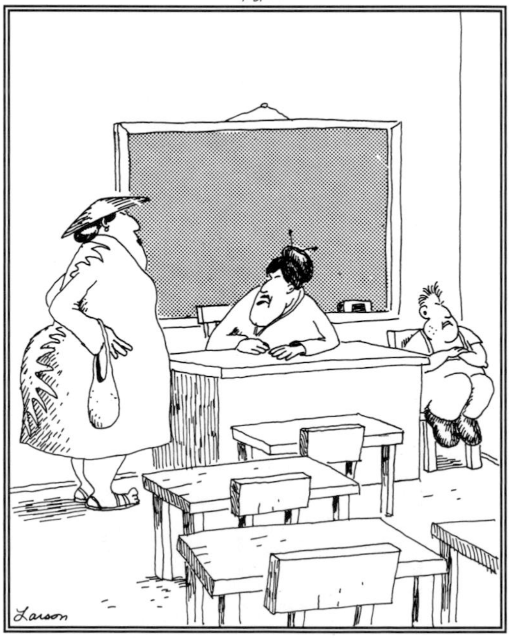

"And in addition, Mrs. Khan, little Genghis disrupts the class, fights with other children, and completely lacks any leadership ability."

10/15/80

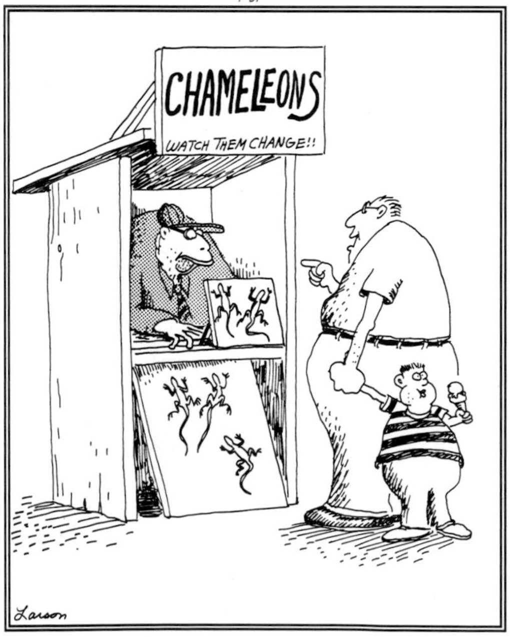
CHAMELEONS
WATCH THEM CHANGE!!

"Well, my gosh, Mr. Turner ... I remember you selling these things thirty years ago!"

10/17/80

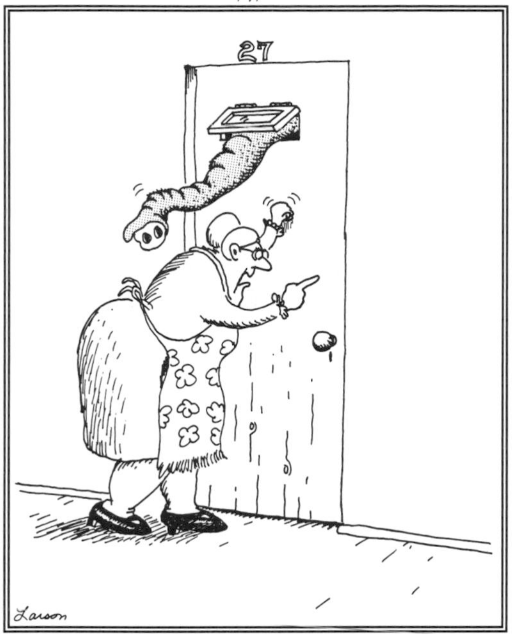
27
Larson

"Young man, if you've got a pet in there ..."

10/16/80

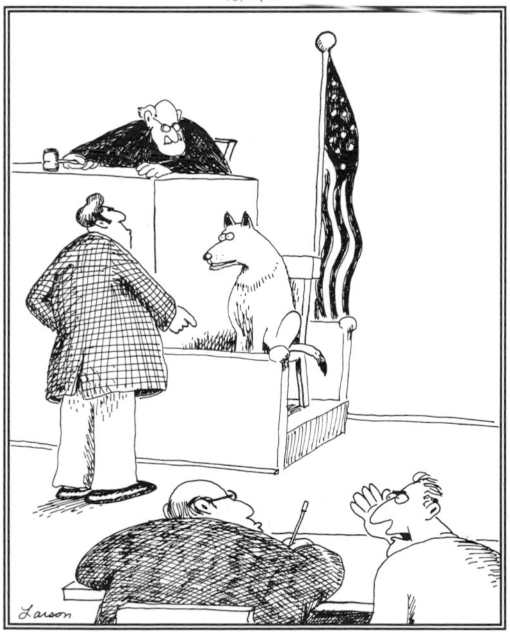
Larson

"I could have guessed. ... My friends all warned me that this breed will sometimes turn on you."

10/14/80

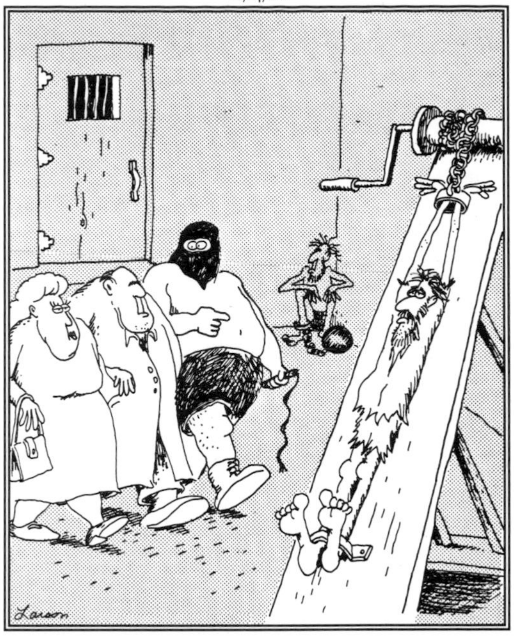
Larson

"Now over here, Mom and Dad, is what we call 'The Rack,' and I'll show you how it works."

10/18/80

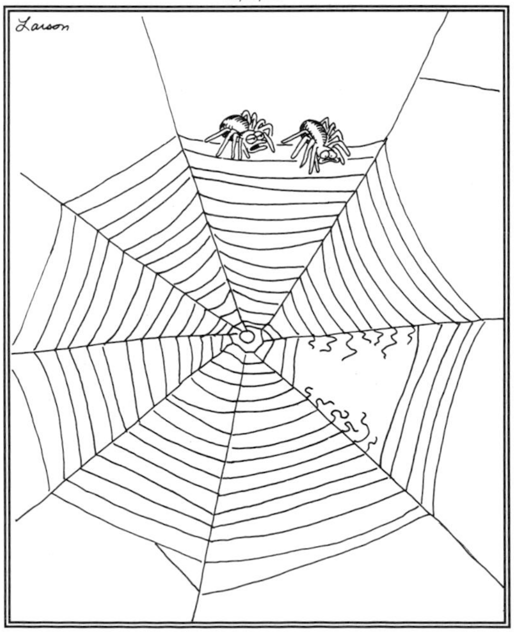
Larson

"Don't take it so hard. ... Everyone's got a story about the one that got away."

October 1980

10/10/80

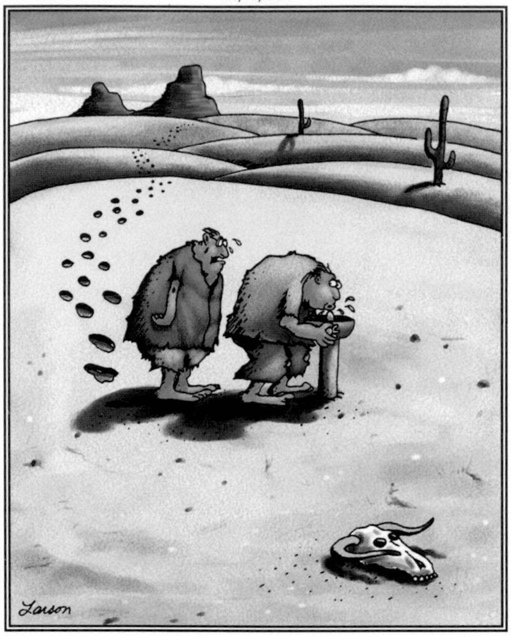
Larson

"Hey c'mon! Don't put your mouth on it!"

10/20/80

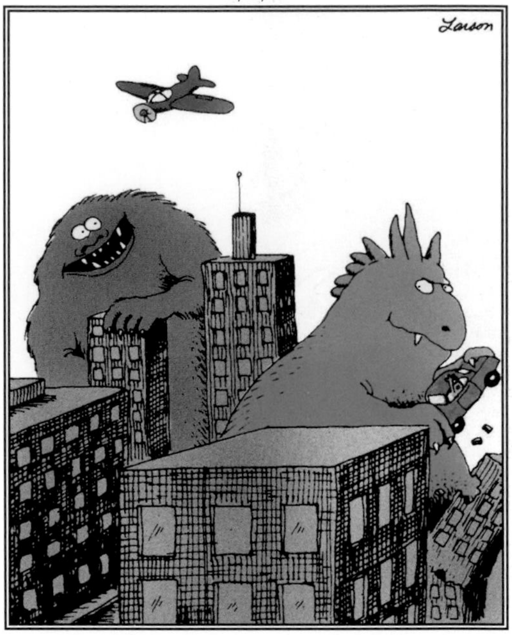
Larson

"Hey! Is that you, Dave? ... Small world!"

10/21/80

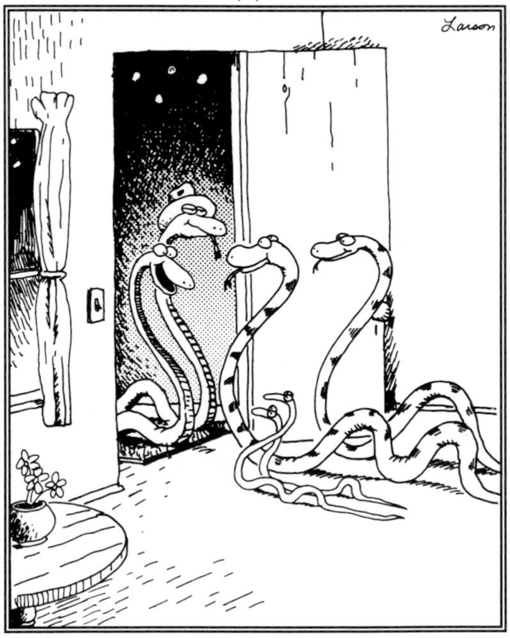
Larson

"And oh my goodness! ... Aren't the children getting *long!*"

10/23/80

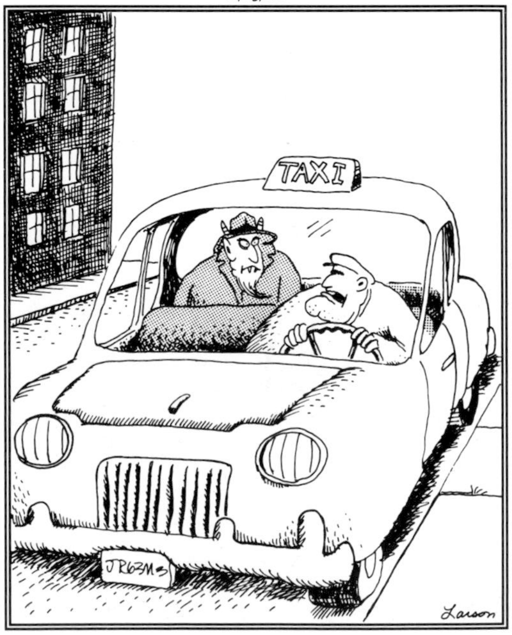
TAXI
Larson

"Hey, Buddy! Nobody tells me to go *there* and gets away with it!"

10/27/80

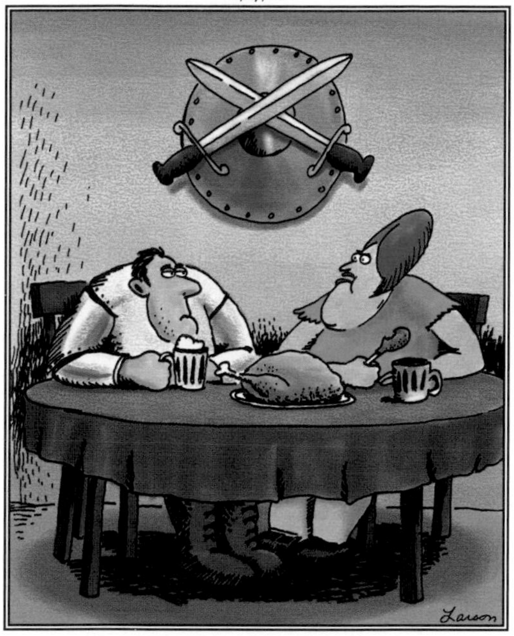
Larson

"And another thing! ... I want you to be more assertive! I'm tired of everyone calling you Alexander the Pretty-Good!"

10/22/80

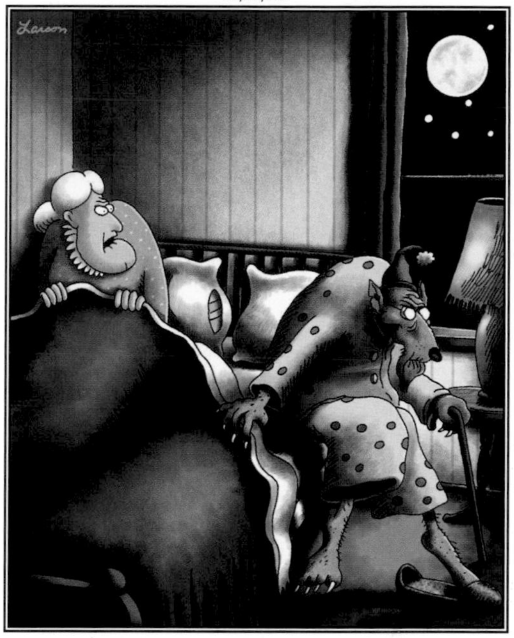
Larson

"Well I just think I've been putting up with this silly curse of yours long enough!"

10/25/80

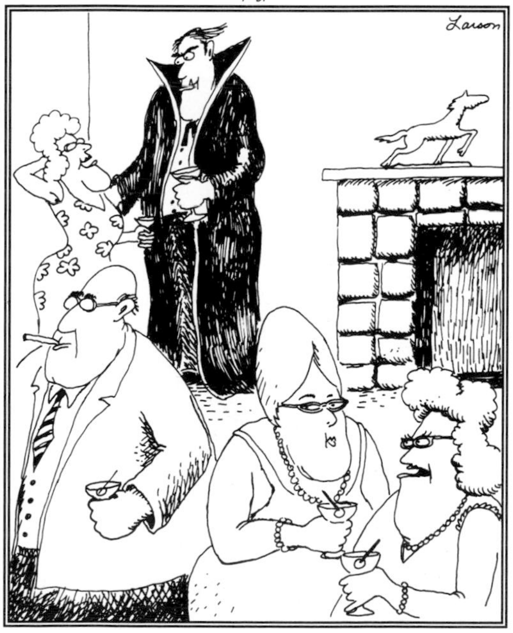
Larson

"Well, it looks like Sylvia has latched on to another fly-by-night boyfriend."

10/29/80

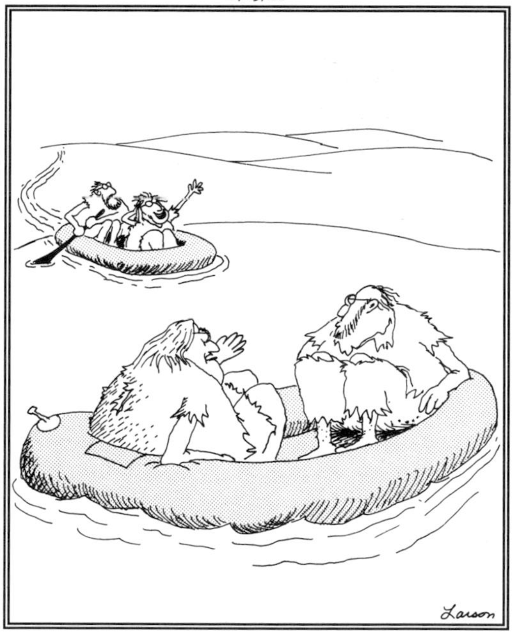
Larson

"Gad! Here come those pesky Andersons again ... probably want to borrow a cup of water."

10/30/80

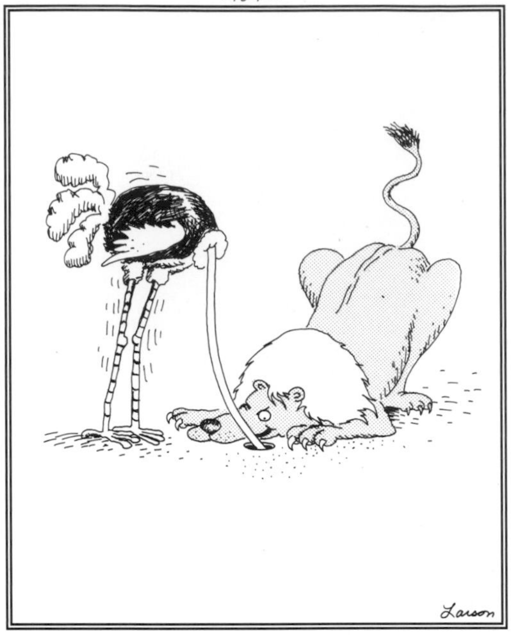
Larson

"I seeeeeee you!"

10/31/80

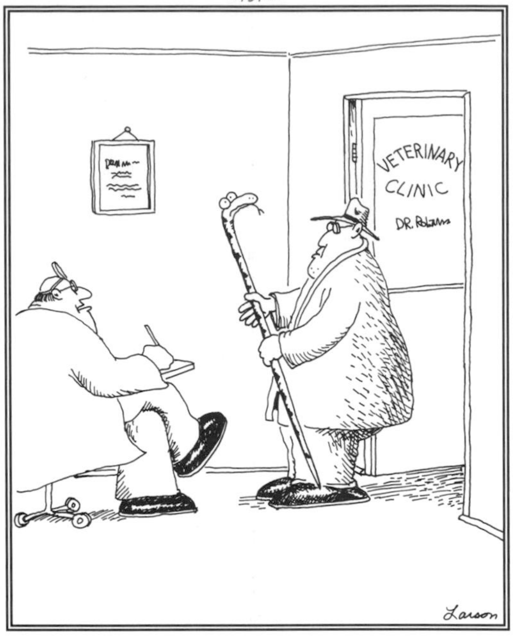
VETERINARY
CLINIC
Larson

"Just keep him calm for a couple of days. ...
He's got lockbody."

10/24/80

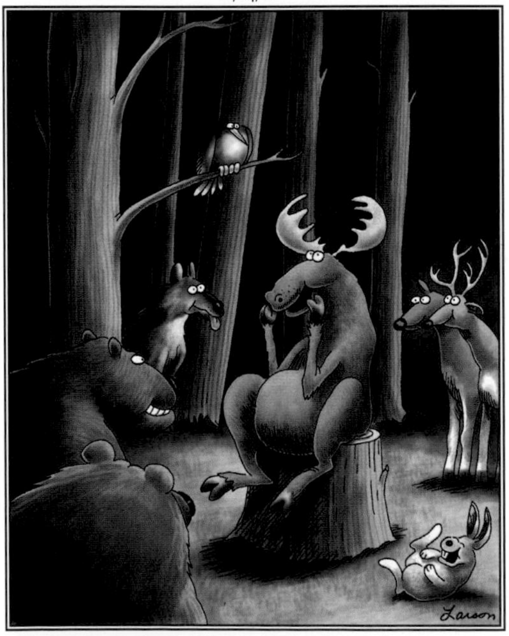
Larson

"Wait! Wait! Here's another one—the screams of a man lost in the woods."

10/28/80

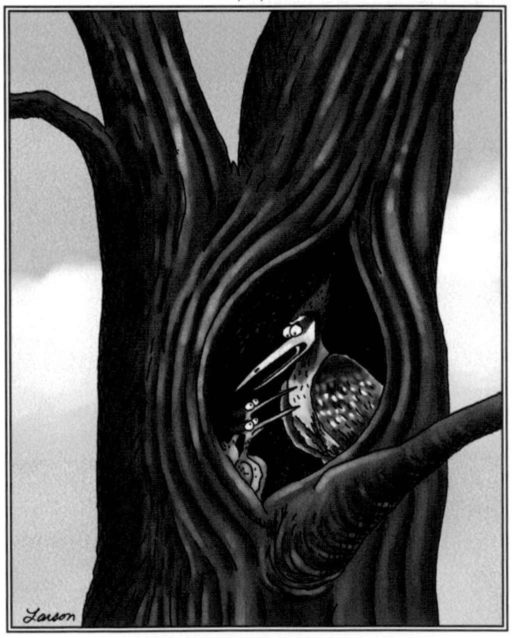
Larson

"I don't know where your father is tonight. ...
No doubt out bangin' his head against some tree."

11/1/80

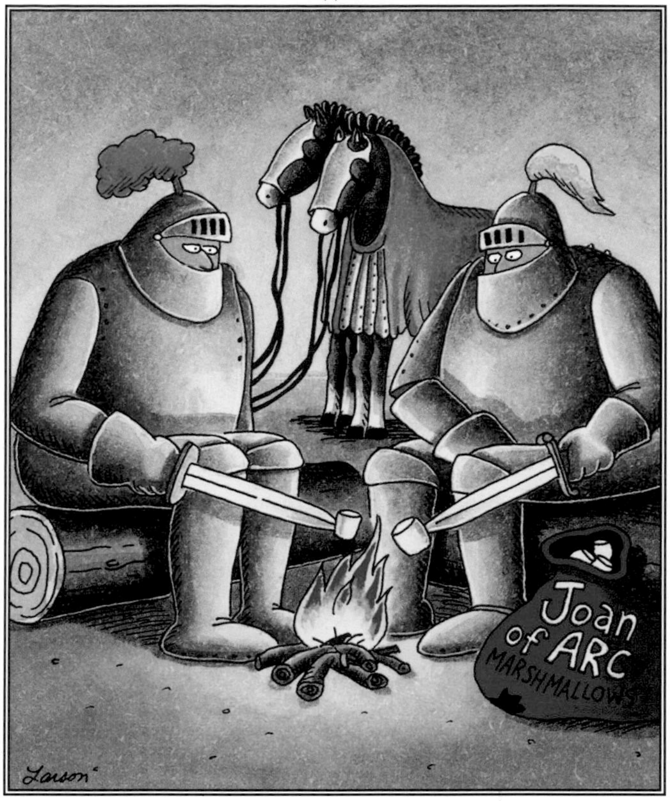
Joan
of ARC
MARSHMALLOWS
Larson

11/4/80

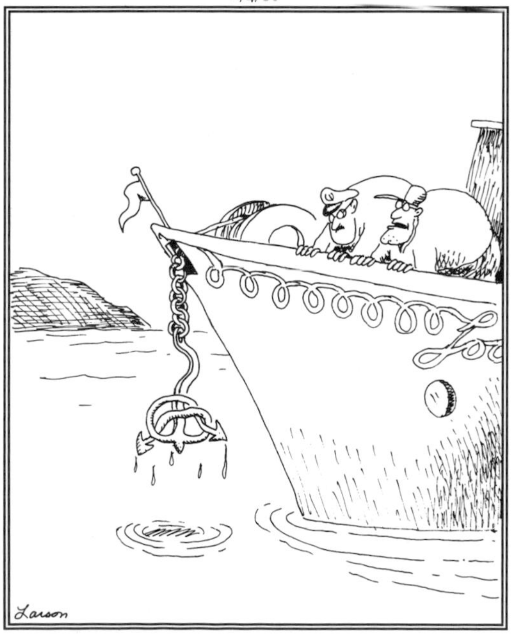
Larson

"Listen, Wadsworth ... as far as I'm concerned we can just go anchor somewhere else."

11/3/80

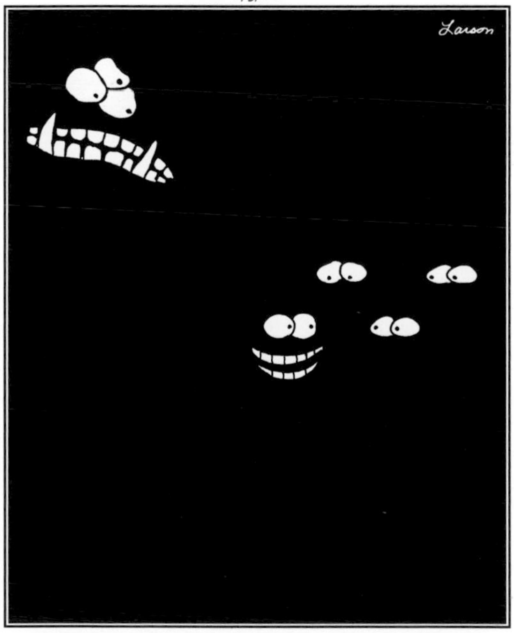
Larson

"Well ... since the elevator's power is dead, why don't we all just introduce ourselves?"

11/8/80

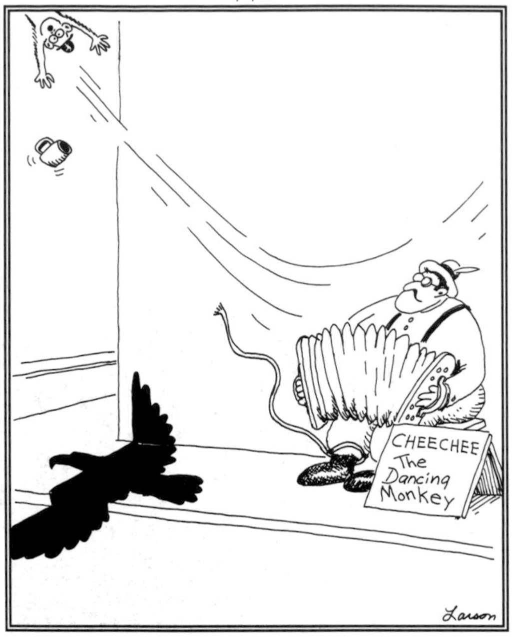
CHEECHEE
The Dancing Monkey
Larson

11/10/80

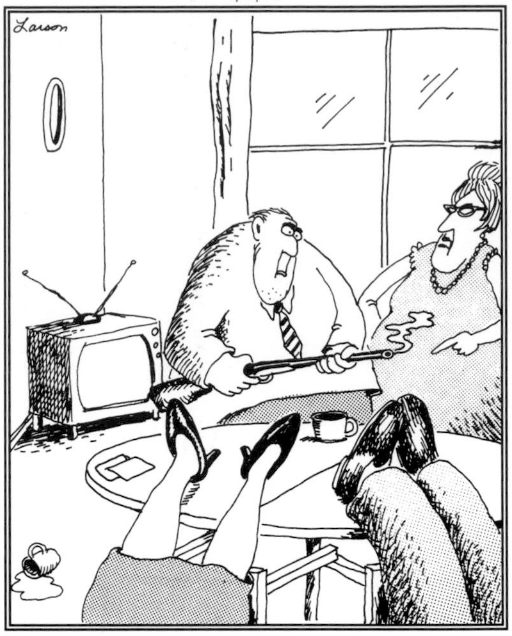
Larson

"That settles it, Carl! ... From now on, you're getting only decaffeinated coffee!"

11/7/80

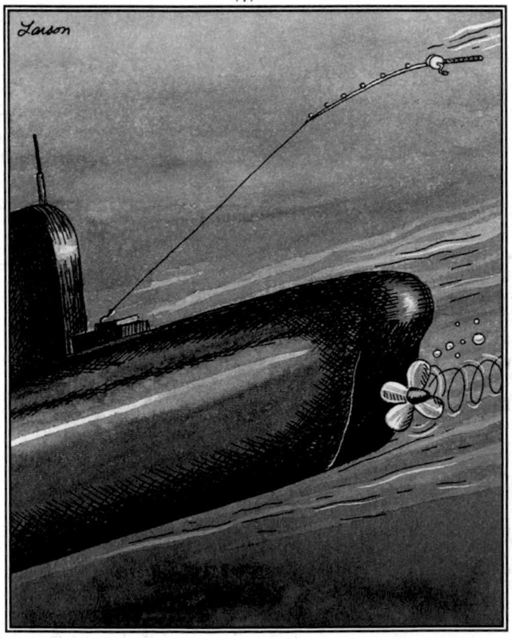
Larson

11/6/80

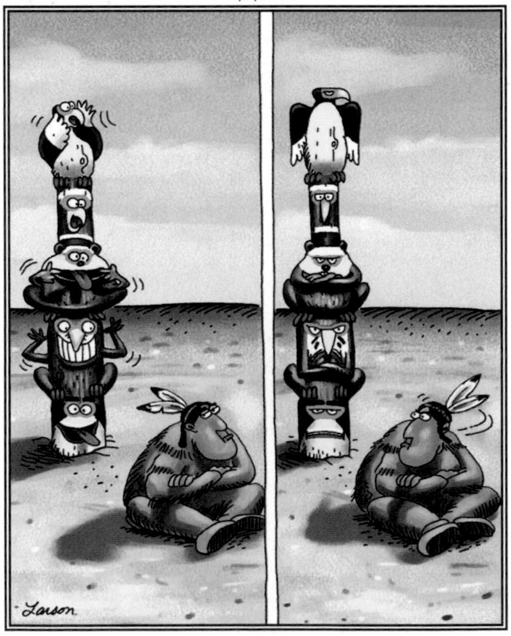
Larson

11/13/80

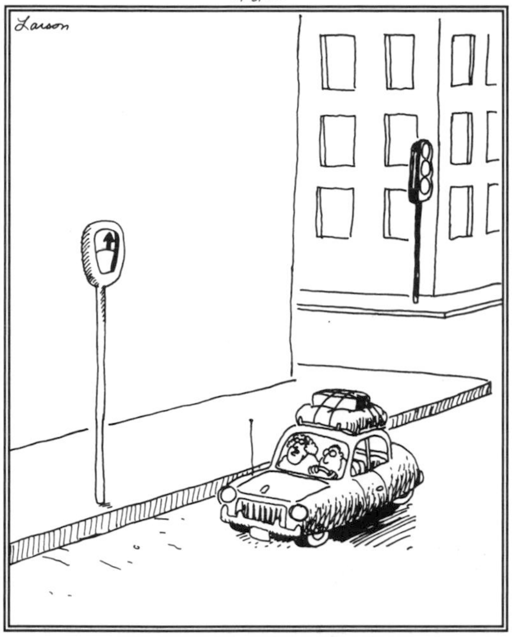
Larson

"Well, we both knew there'd be some adjustments moving from a small town to a big city."

11/12/80

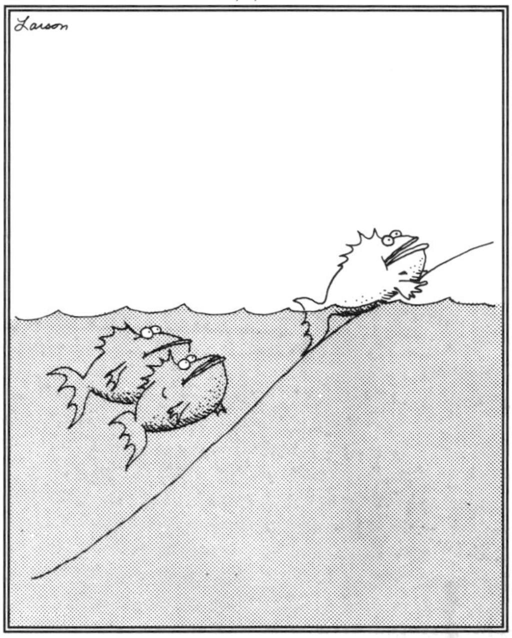
Larson

"One small step for a fish, one giant leap for fishkind."

11/14/80

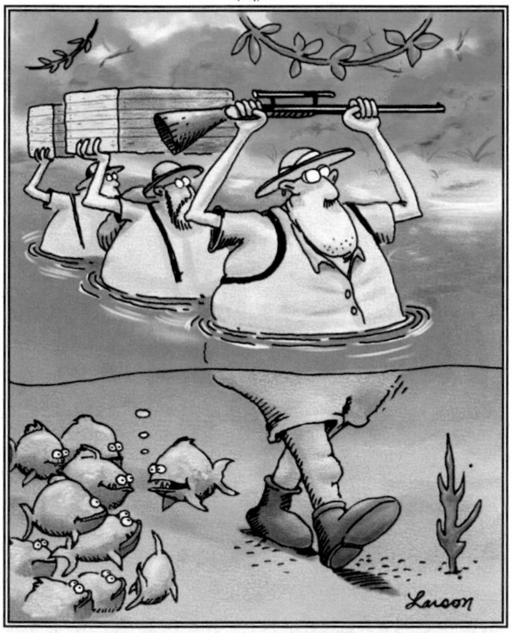
Larson

"Just nibble at first. ... But when you hear them yell 'Piranha!'—go for it."

11/11/80

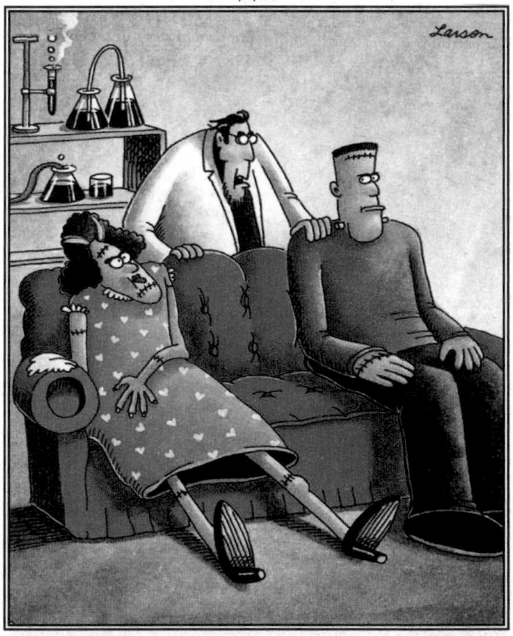
Larson

"Hey, c'mon now! ... You two were *made* for each other!"

11/5/80

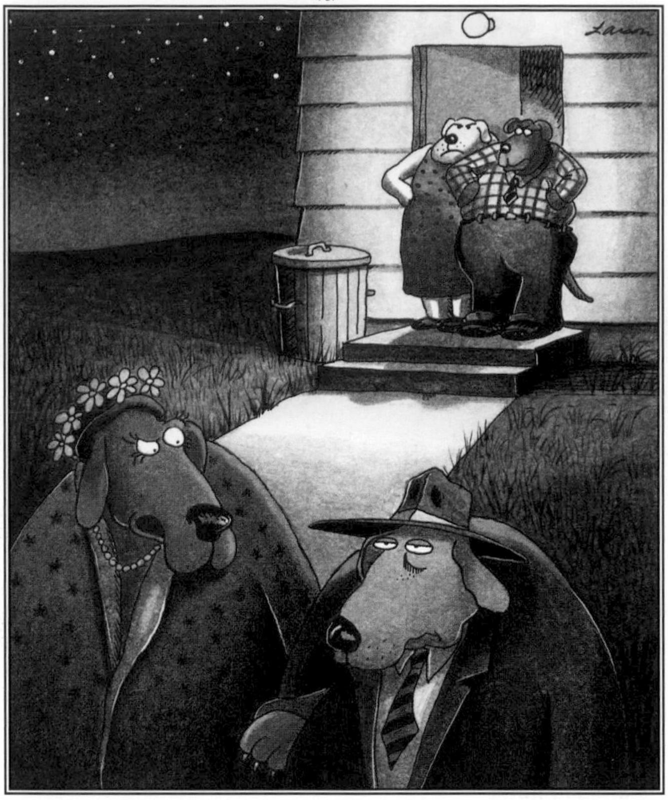
Larson

"One of the nicest evenings I've ever spent at the Wilsons' ... and then you had to go and do that on the rug!"

11/15/80

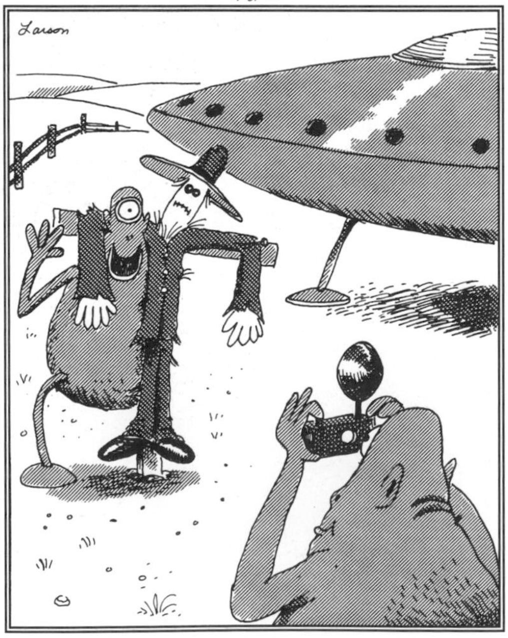
Larson

11/17/80

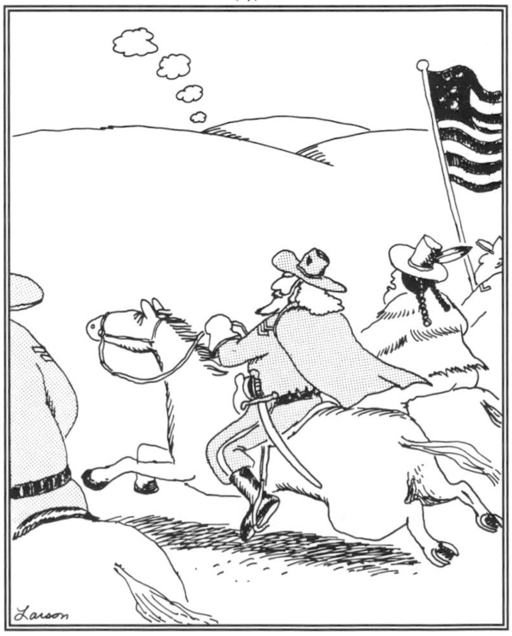
Larson

"Excuse me, General Custer, sir ... but smoke signals say, 'Ready ... or ... not ... here ... we ... come.'"

11/18/80

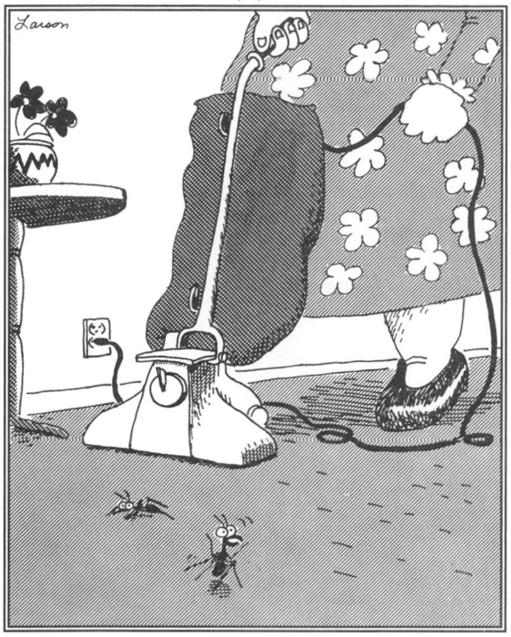

"Look out! ... It's a black hole!"

11/19/80

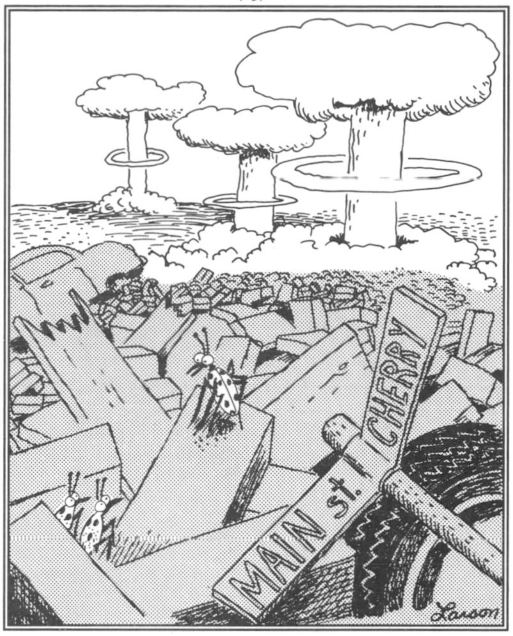
MAIN st.
CHERRY

"Come on out. ... I think they're through."

11/20/80

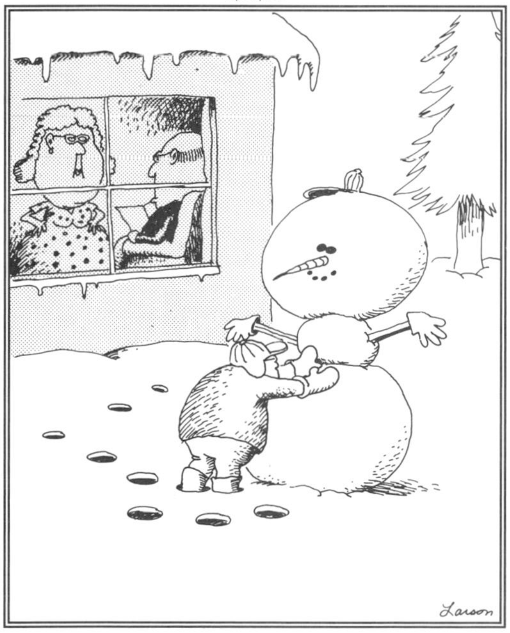

11/21/80

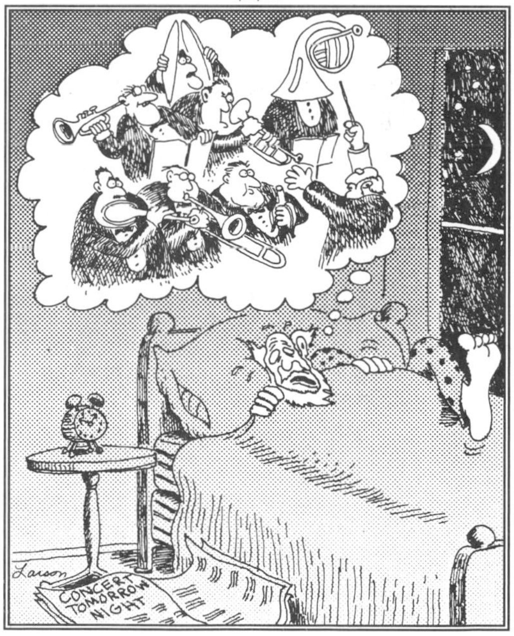
CONCERT TOMORROW NIGHT

11/22/80

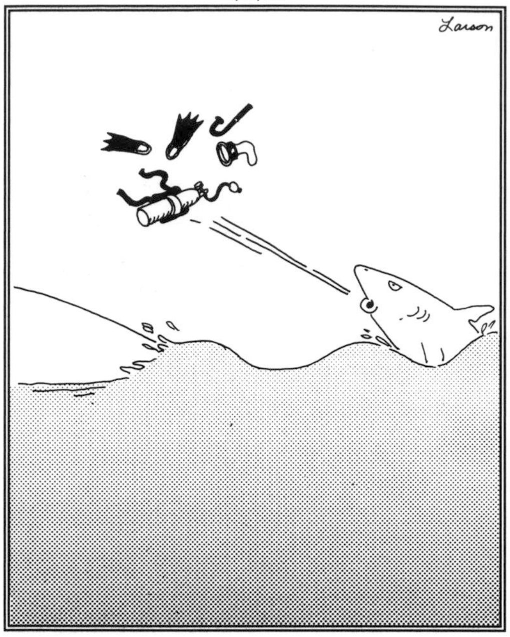
Larson

11/24/80

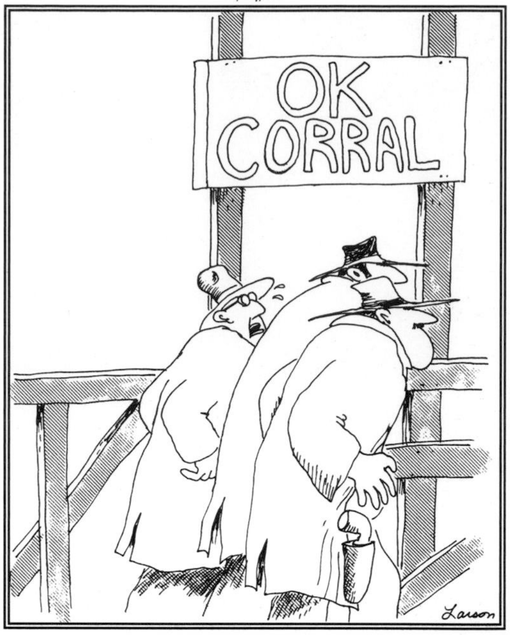
OK
CORRAL
Larson

"Hey look, guys ... maybe we got the wrong address."

11/25/80

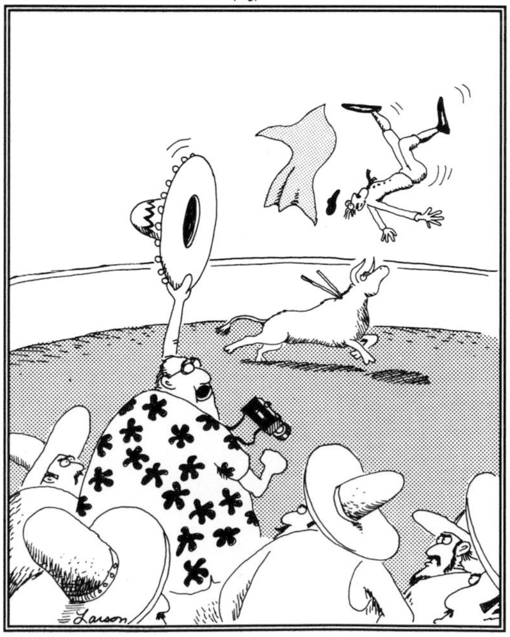
Larson

"Olé!"

11/26/80

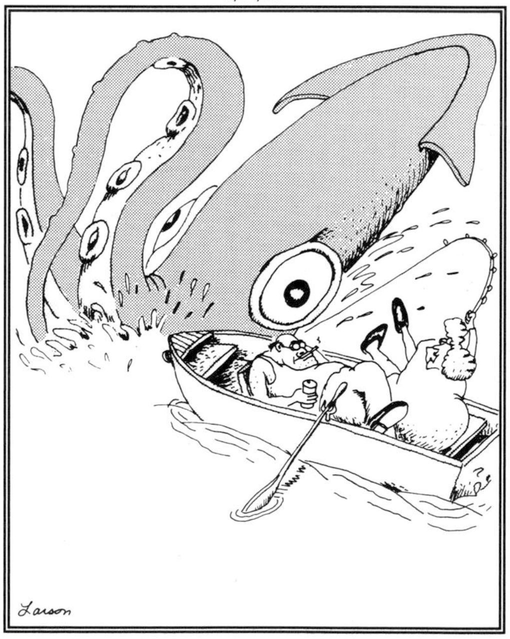
Larson

"Oh, Sidney! Look! I *wasn't* snagged on the bottom!"

11/27/80

11/28/80

11/29/80

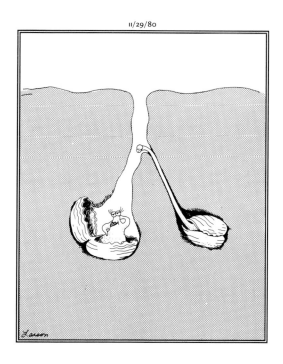

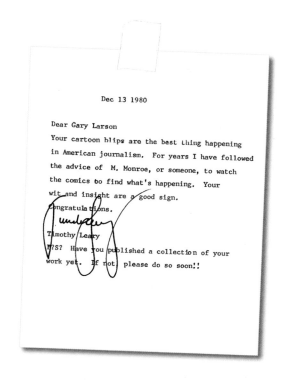

Dec 13 1980

Dear Gary Larson

Your cartoon blips are the best thing happening in American journalism. For years I have followed the advice of M. Monroe, or someone, to watch the comics to find what's happening. Your wit and insight are a good sign. Congratulations.

Timothy Leary

P?S? Have you published a collection of your work yet. If not, please do so soon!!

12/1/80

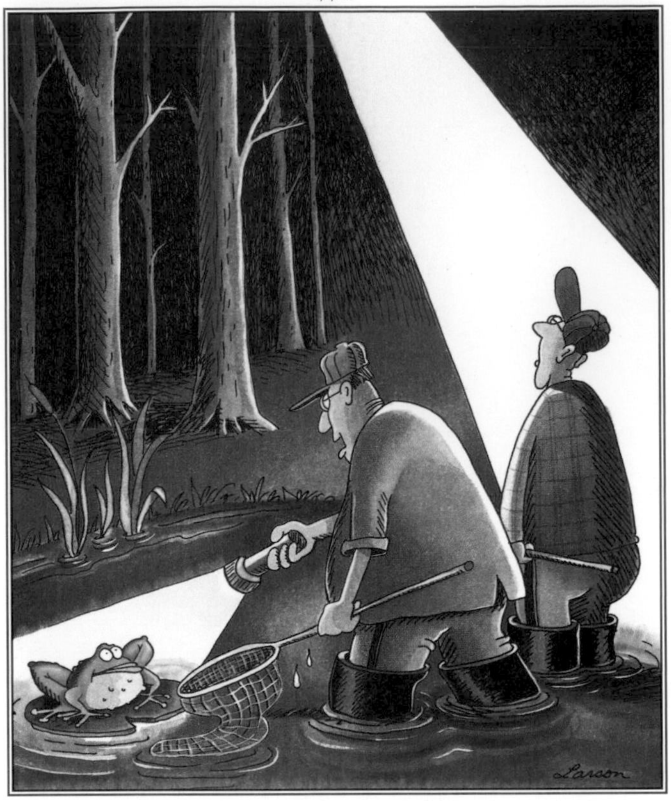

"See, Frank? Keep the light in their eyes and you can bag them without any trouble at all."

12/2/80

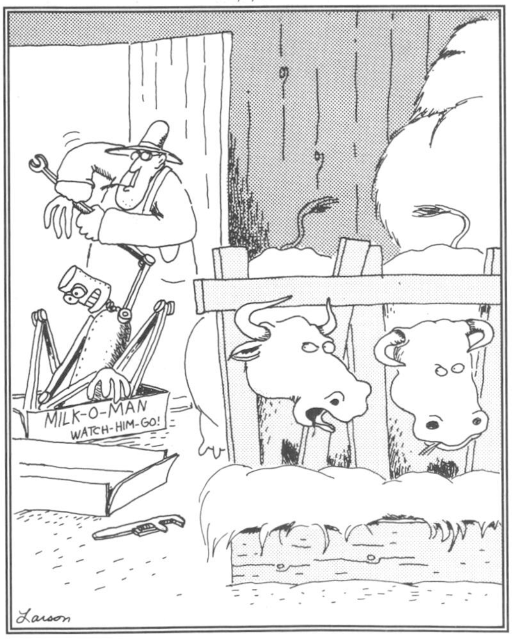
MILK-O-MAN
WATCH-HIM-GO!

"I don't like the looks of this."

12/4/80

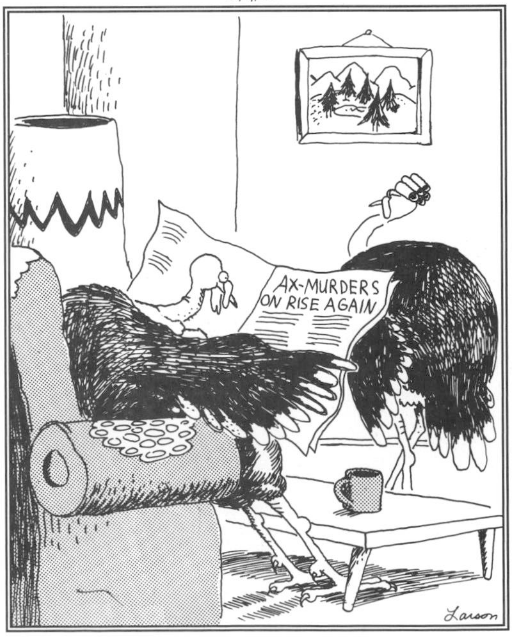
AX-MURDERS
ON RISE AGAIN

12/5/80

NUTS
Larson

12/6/80

Larson

12/8/80

Larson

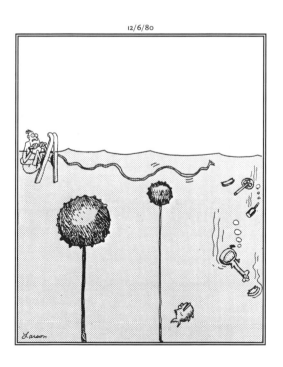

"Go for it, Sidney! You've got it! You've got it! Good hands! Don't choke!"

12/3/80

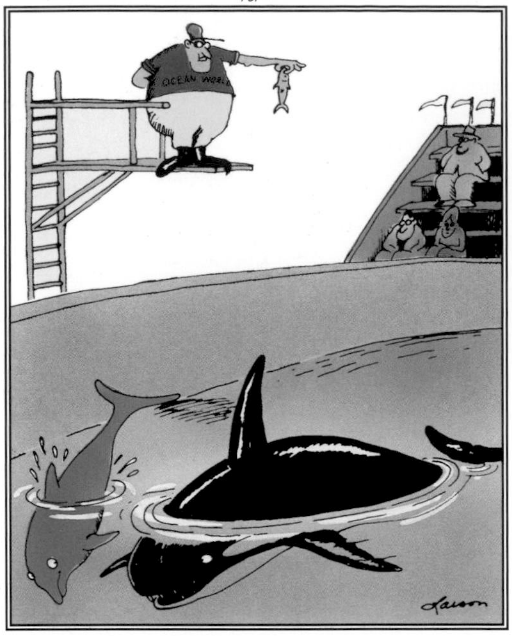
OCEAN WORLD

"The herring's nothin'. ... I'm going for the whole shmeer!"

12/12/80

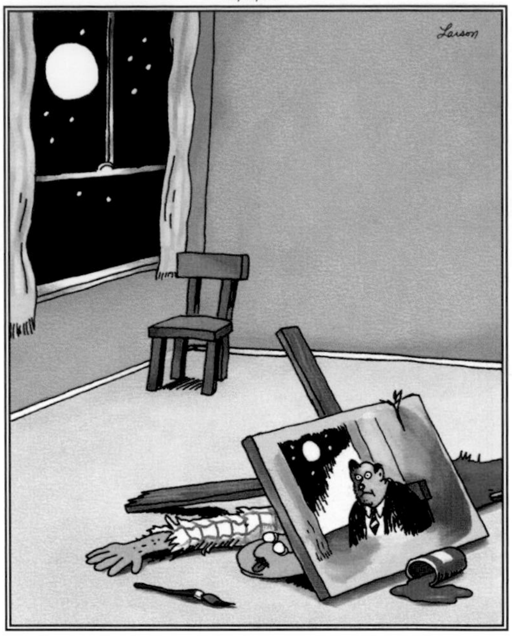

12/9/80

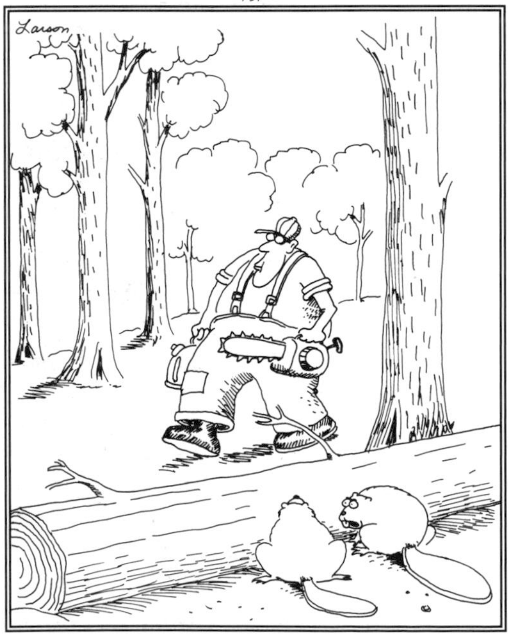

"Here he comes again ... and he's carrying the thundertooth."

12/10/80

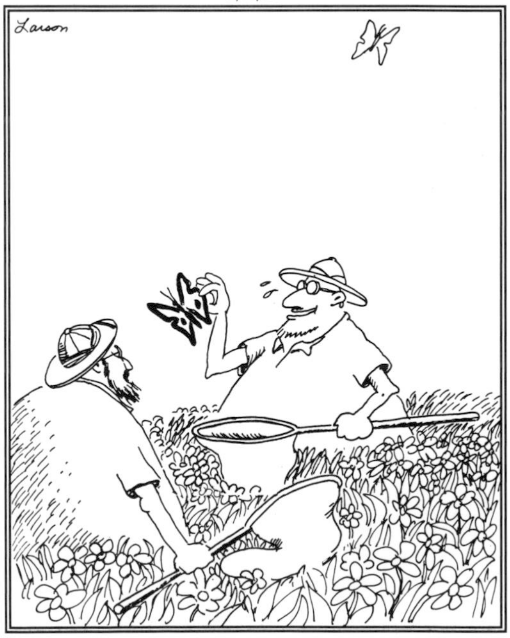

"An excellent specimen ... the symbol of beauty, innocence, and fragile life. ... Hand me the jar of ether."

12/15/80

12/17/80

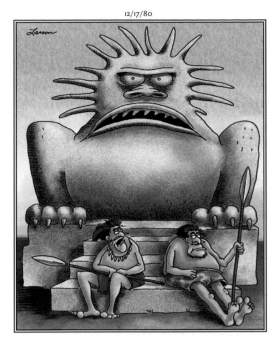

"Twelve sacrifices already this week. ...
Thank Goran it's Friday!"

12/11/80

"Uh-oh—looks like the zipper has stuck on
that thing again."

12/13/80

12/16/80

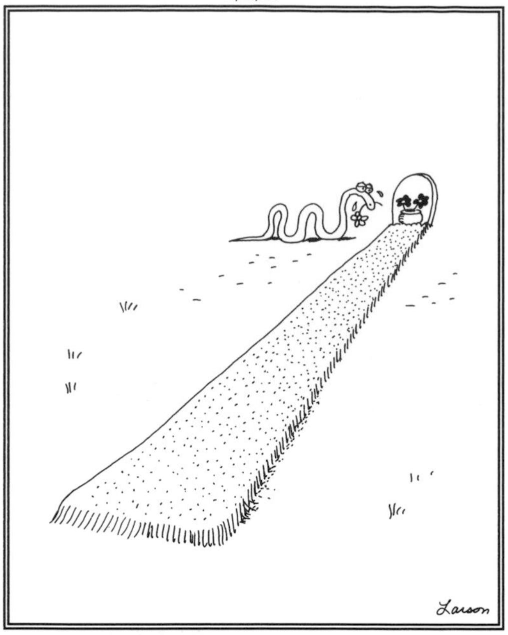
Larson

12/18/80

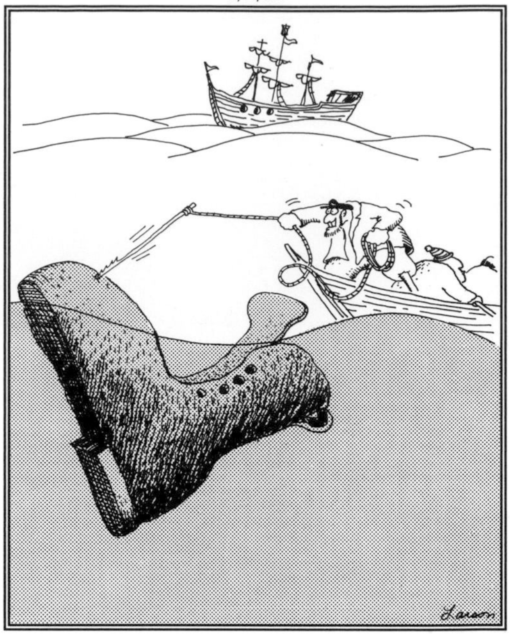
Larson

12/19/80

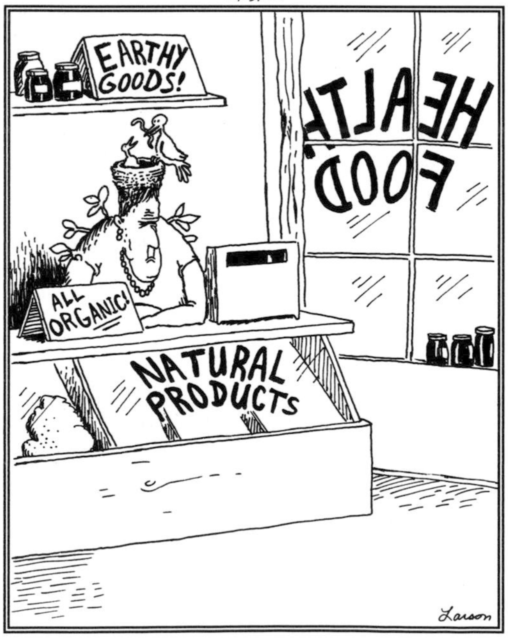
EARTHY GOODS!
HEALTH FOOD
ALL ORGANIC!
NATURAL PRODUCTS
Larson

12/20/80

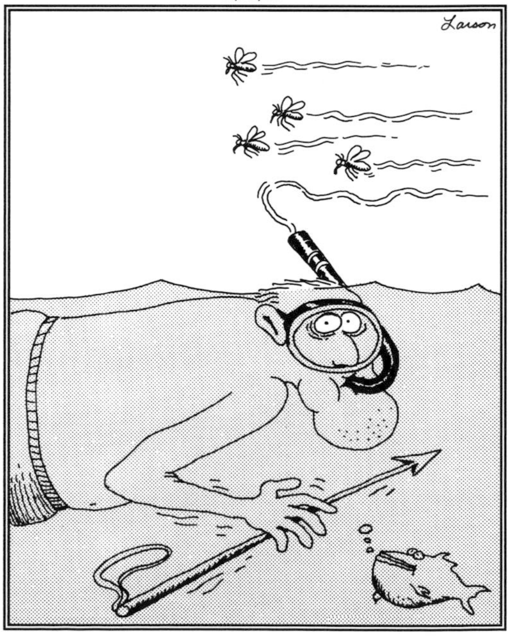
Larson

12/23/80

Larson

"Quick! Back the other way!
Back the other way!"

12/24/80

Larson

12/25/80

MR. Tomato
Larson

12/26/80

Larson

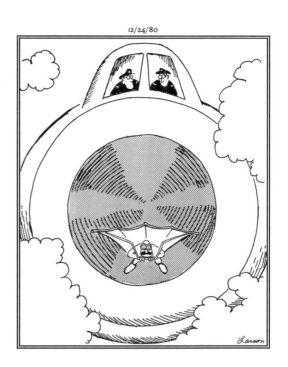

12/22/80

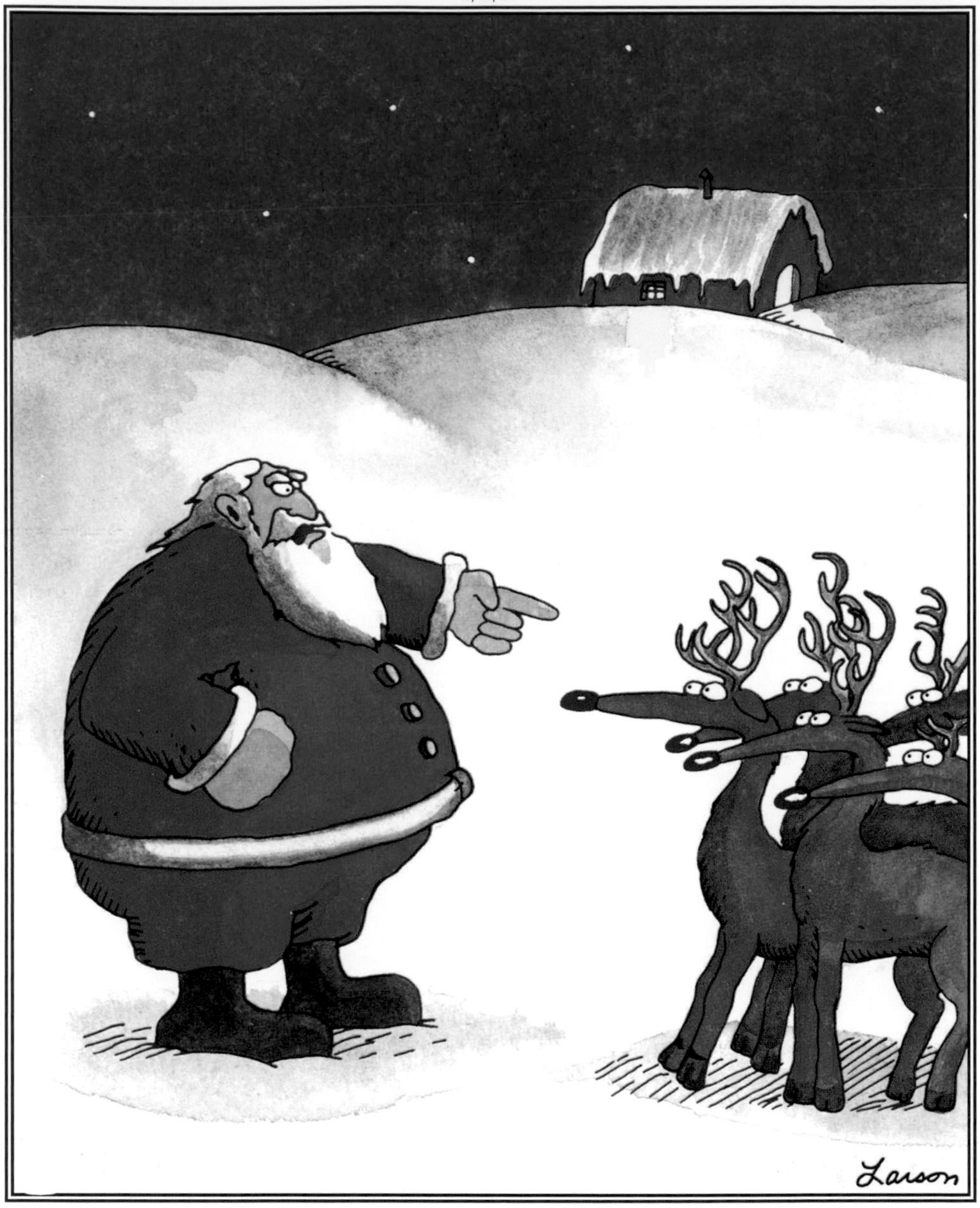
Larson

"And I've only one thing to say about all these complaints I've been hearing about ... *Venison!*"

12/27/80

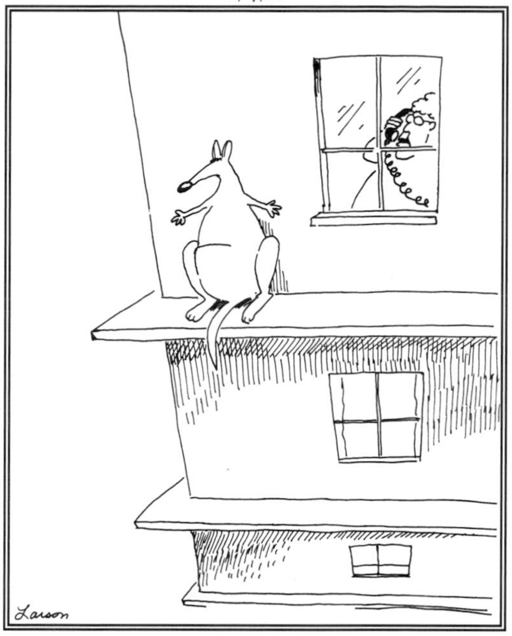
Larson

"Well, you better get someone over here right away. ... He really looks like he's going to jump."

12/29/80

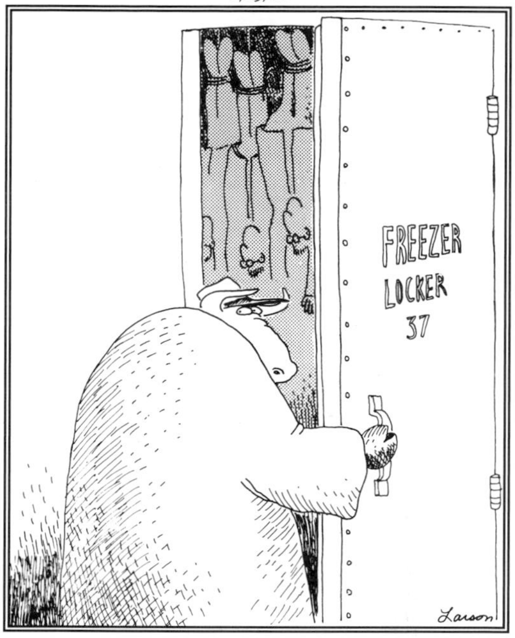
FREEZER
LOCKER
37
Larson

12/30/80

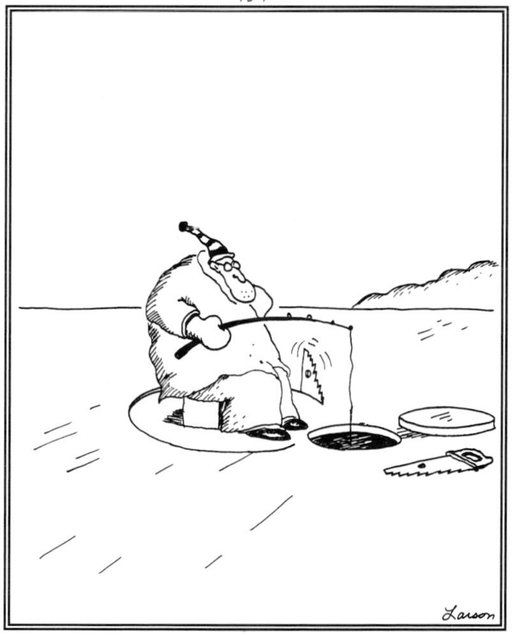
Larson

12/31/80

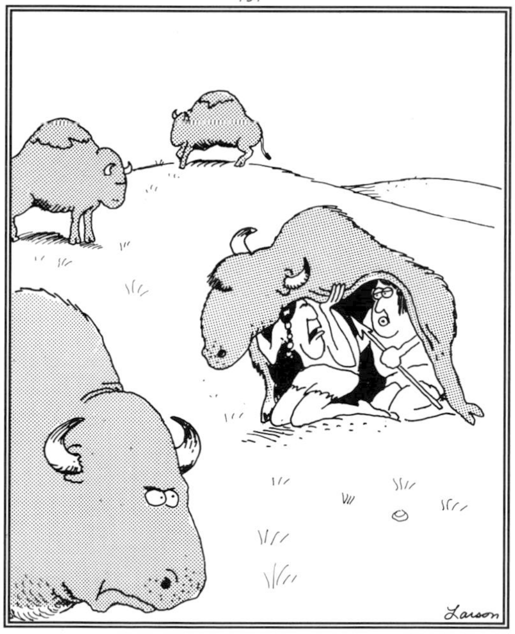
Larson

"I said act nonchalant—that doesn't mean whistling!"

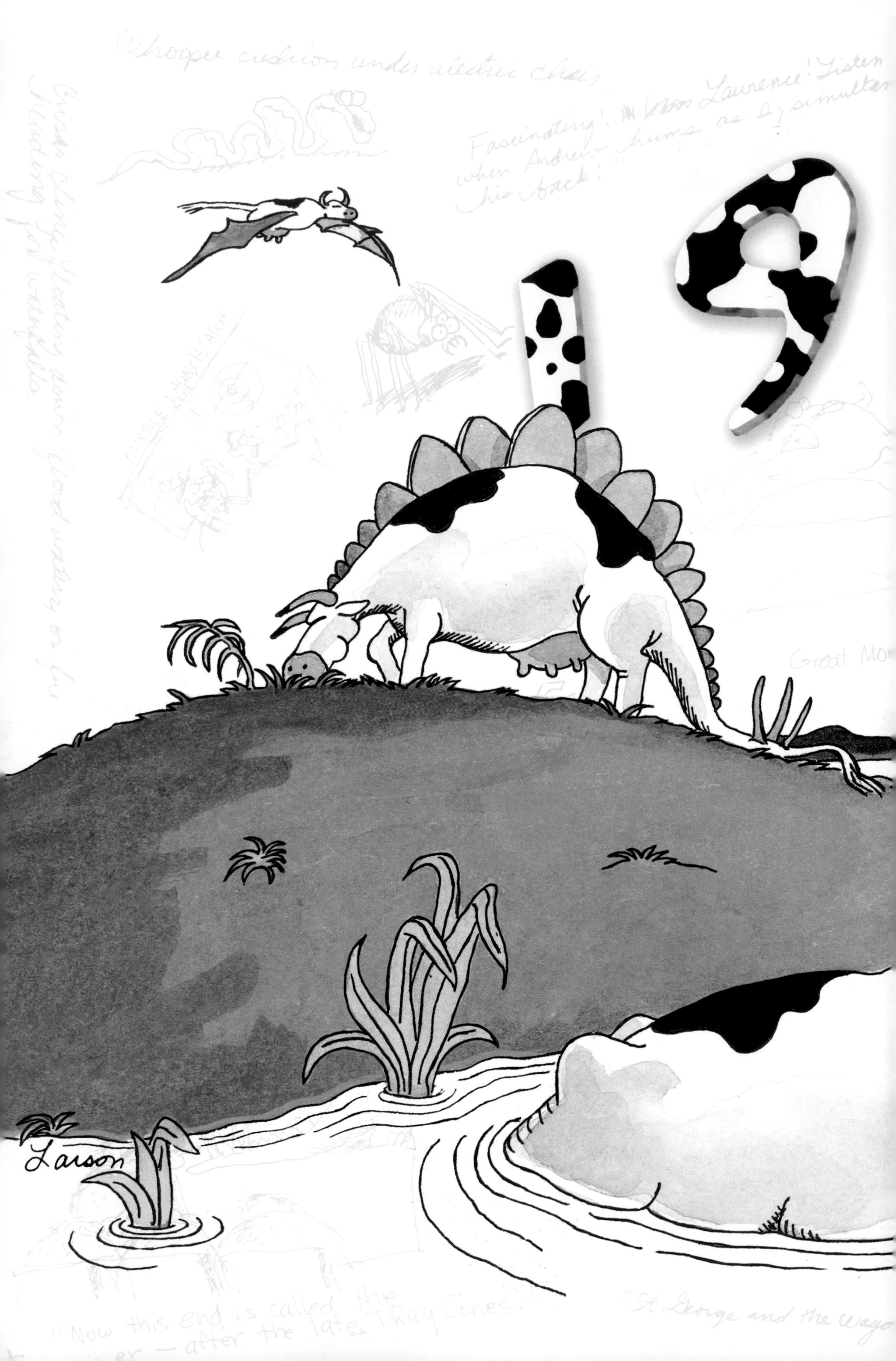

19
Larson

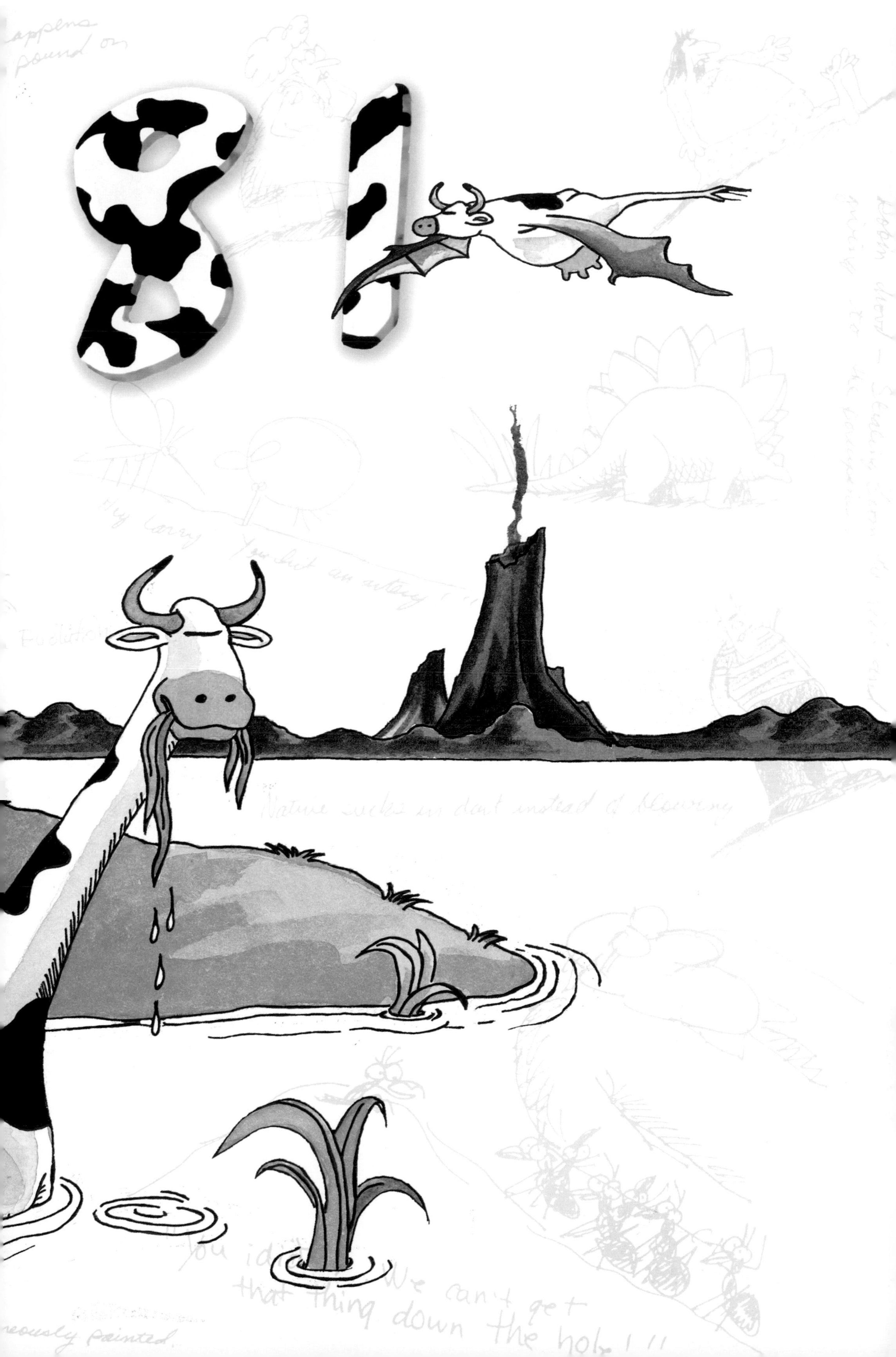
81
We can't get
that thing down the hole!!

With a Friend Like This ...

Many years ago, I traveled with my friend Ernie to a remote, mountainous area in northern Mexico. Ernie was the curator of reptiles at our local zoo, and he had invited me to accompany him on a mission to capture and bring back a little-known species of Mexican king snake. (Okay—it's not everyone's dream vacation, I grant you; but getting a tan on a beach somewhere always gave me the willies.) Oh, one other thing: Ernie was insane. Not clinically insane, of course—just your garden variety, watch-your-ass-when-you're-around-this-person kind of insane.

One afternoon we had been exploring a potential king snake habitat when I turned over a rock and discovered a couple of huge whip scorpions. (Some people call them vinegarroons, but for the three entomologists who have always dogged my trail on these details, I'll formally identify them as *Mastigoproctus giganteus*.)

I wanted to photograph these interesting critters, but I had left my camera back at camp. I did, however, have a large collection jar in my backpack. Gingerly, I herded the slow-moving scorpions into the container, figuring I would simply schlep the happy couple back to camp, photograph them, and release them later. But we didn't get back to camp until dusk, so the photo-op would have to wait a day. I set the jar aside, next to some gear.

The next morning, warm and cozy inside my sleeping bag, I awoke to hear Ernie moving about, making a fire and getting breakfast together. I was reluctant to get up myself, since it was always so cold in the mornings before the sun got a good grip on the day. So I just lay there in my bag with only my face exposed. I still remember the tranquility of it all—surrounded by saguaro cacti, listening to the crackling fire, staring up at the Mexican sky.

That's when Ernie walked over. He paused and stood over me, then lifted a corner of my bag with one arm and plunged his other arm deep inside. He quickly withdrew it and leaped backward. A few seconds later, he was doubled up with laughter.

I still wasn't fully awake, and I remember just looking at him, wondering, what was the deal? And then I saw something in his hand. It was a jar. *The* jar. Whip Scorpion Inn. And the Inn was now vacant.

The basic scenario came groggily into focus. Ernie plus jar, minus whip scorpions, plus strange behavior (common with Ernie), plus laughter equals WHIP SCORPIONS (or, technically, *Mastigoproctus giganteus*) IN MY SLEEPING BAG!

There are people who claim your entire life flashes before you when disaster is imminent. I assure you that if the disaster involves something that looks like this (close to life-size, I might add) …

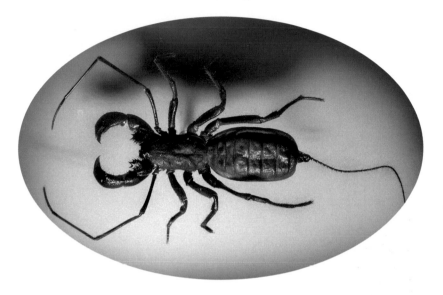

your life will definitely not flash. This is all you're going to see.

I was now awake. Whip scorpions are not dangerous (no stingers), but look at this animal again. I ask you: Does it matter it can't sting?

It's interesting to note how quickly the nervous system can switch gears. Without a hitch, my brain shifted from dreamily contemplating the Natural World to the more basic there's-a-scorpion-in-my-bed mode. As a cartoonist, I enjoyed plumbing this aspect of human nature, the phobias and common fears many of us have to one degree or another—I just don't like to be personally involved in the research. (Especially, I might add, when it involves an arachnid whose Latin name ends with *giganteus*.)

I didn't bother with the zipper; I just shot out of that bag as if it was on fire—screaming, I'm afraid, like a girl cartoonist. When I finally stopped jumping around, one of the whip scorpions was clinging to my shirt collar. Another round of jumping, please. Between fits of laughter, Ernie kept saying, "God, if only I had a camera!"

Ah, friends. To any scorpion fanciers out there, rest assured that the little creatures were unharmed. And likewise rest assured, I did get my revenge on Ernie—but that's a story he can share in his own book.

1/1/81

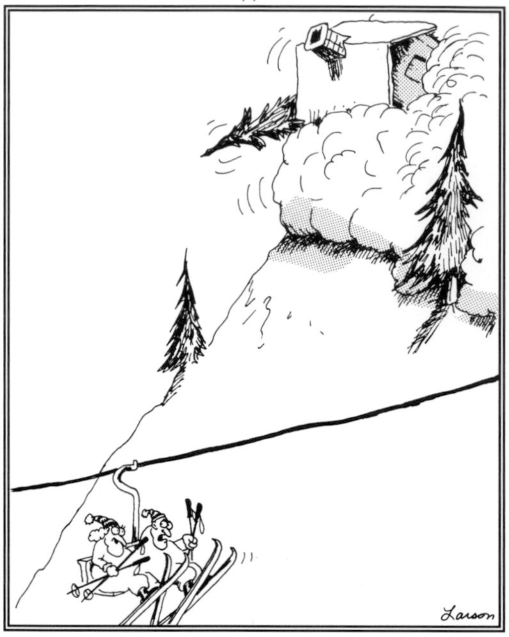

"My stomach? ... *Your* stomach's rumbling!"

1/2/81

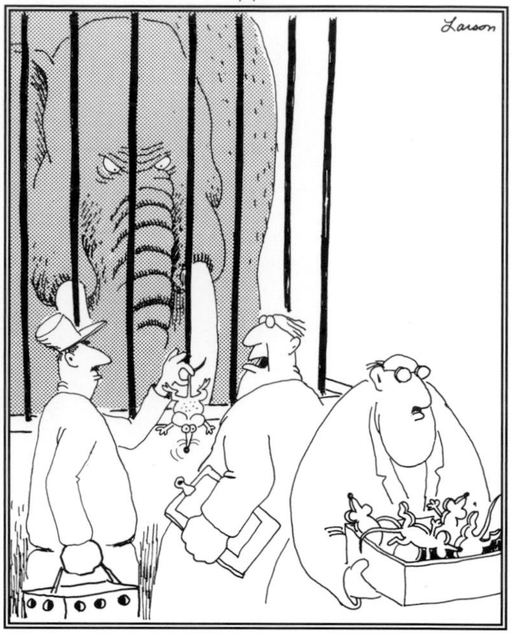

"That won't be necessary, Carl. ... I think we can safely conclude that they're definitely not afraid of mice."

1/3/81

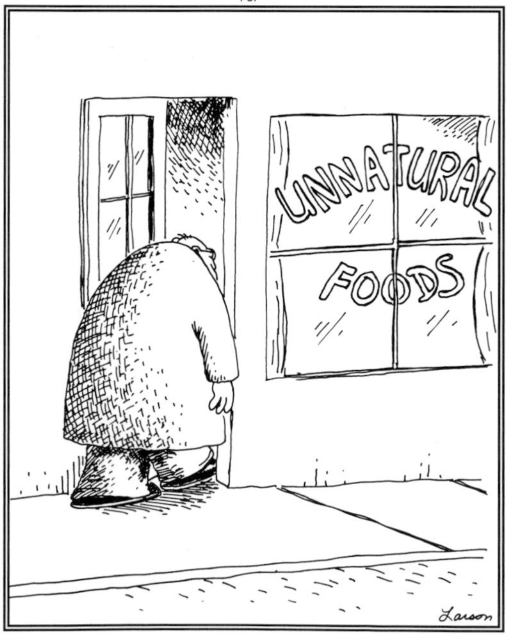
UNNATURAL
FOODS

1/5/81

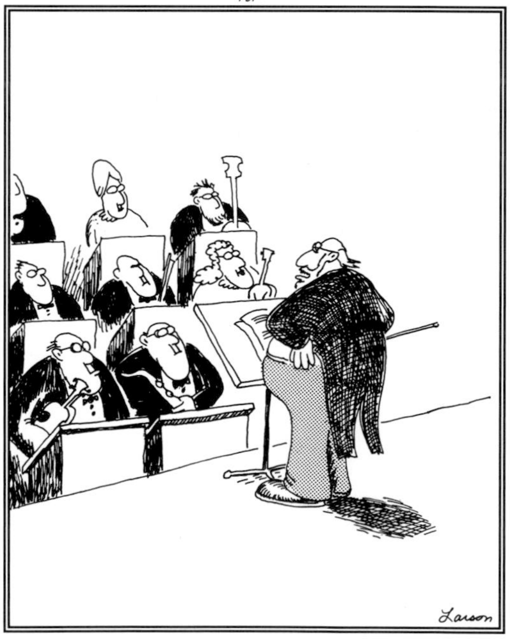

"I don't know which one of you is doing it, but at the end of the sonata we shall refrain from playing 'Shave and a Haircut.'"

1/7/81

"I told you guys to slow down and take it easy or
something like this would happen."

1/6/81

"You idiot! ... Twenty bucks for a smoke
alarm and we don't even know what
the stuff is!"

1/9/81

1/8/81

Larson

"Disgusting! ... It's just a sort of heavy huffing and puffing."

1/12/81

Larson

"Well that's how it happened, Sylvia. ... I kissed this frog, he turns into a prince, we get married, and WHAM! ... I'm stuck at home with a bunch of pollywogs."

1/13/81

Larson

"Come out of that cave and meet your doom, you miserable dragon! You can't hide in there forever, you overgrown chameleon!"

1/10/81

Larson

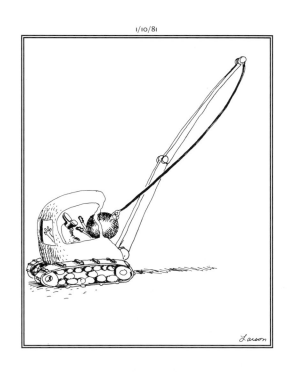

1/20/81

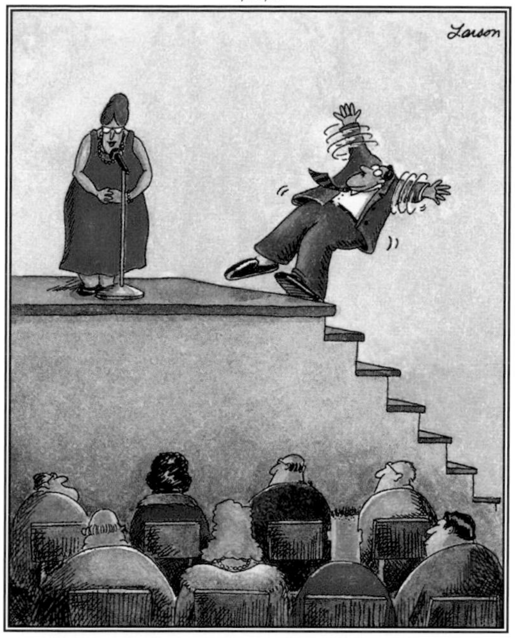
Larson

"And now, standing at my side, I give you the man who conquered Everest, the Matterhorn, Kilimanjaro ..."

1/22/81

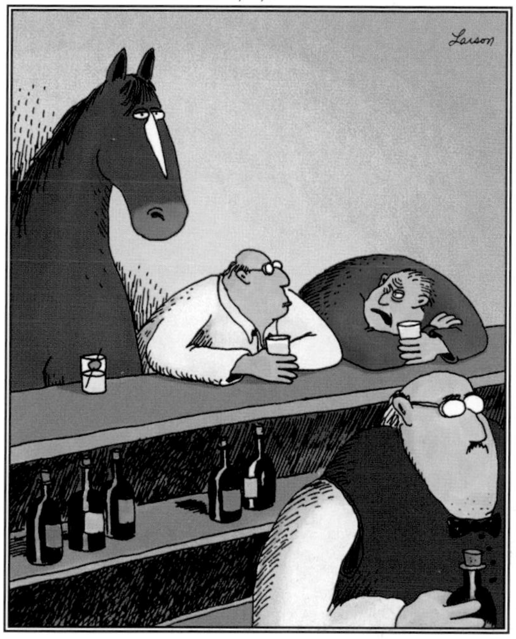
Larson

"Sure—but can you make him drink?"

1/14/81

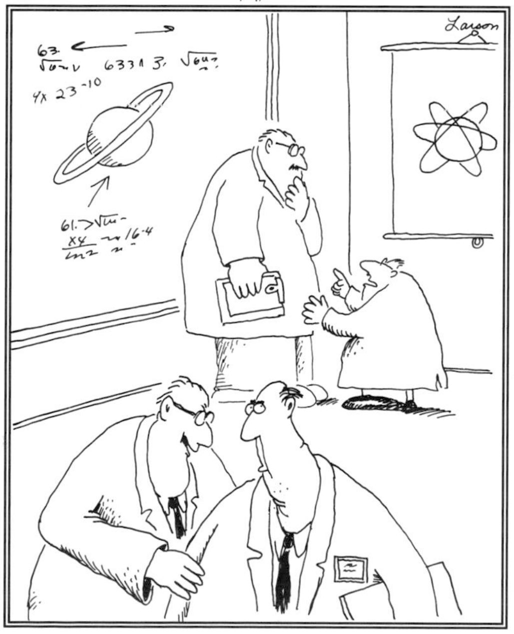
Larson

"There goes Williams again ... trying to win support for his Little Bang theory."

1/15/81

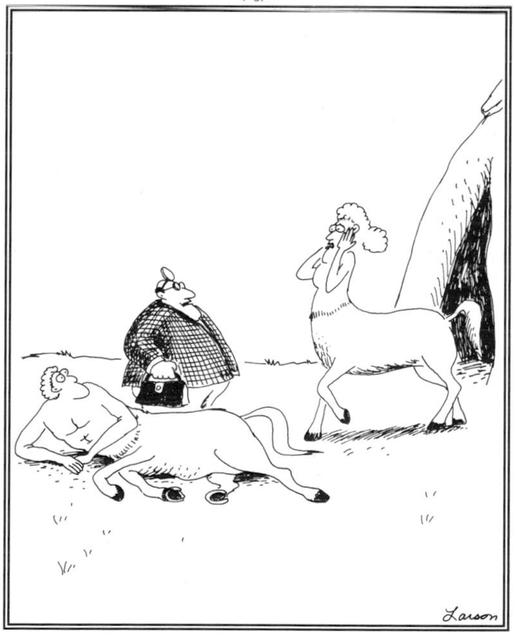
Larson

"I'm afraid his leg is broken, Ma'am. ... He'll have to be shot."

1/16/81

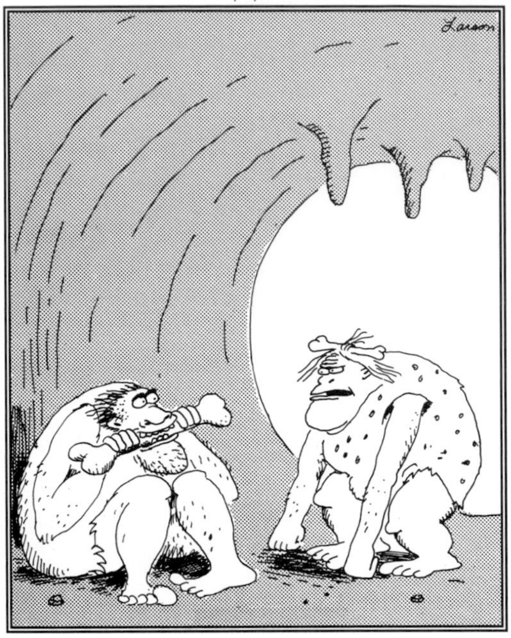

"I'm leaving you for another, Zog. ... His cranium is larger, his thumbs are more opposable, and he's really going somewhere."

1/17/81

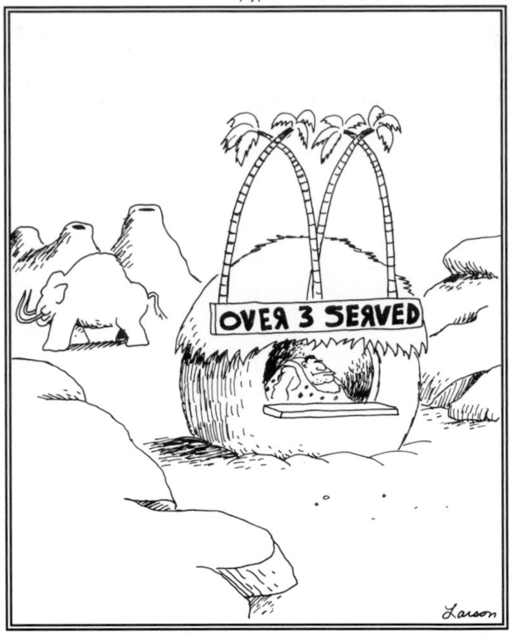
OVER 3 SERVED

1/19/81

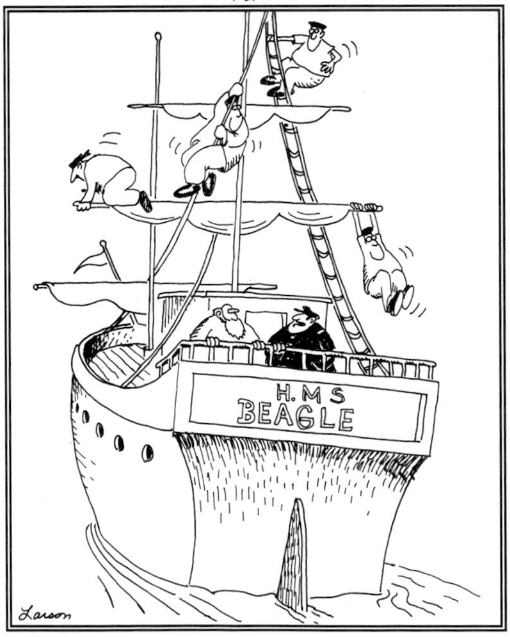
H.M.S
BEAGLE

"Well, Mr. Darwin ... have you reached any conclusions so far?"

1/23/81

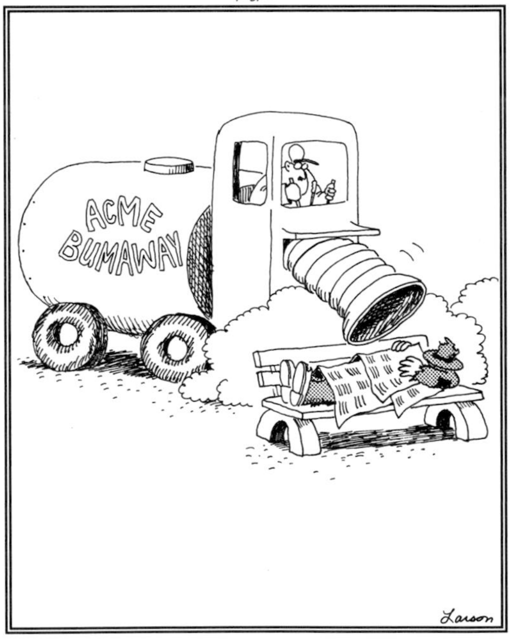
ACME
BUMAWAY

1/24/81

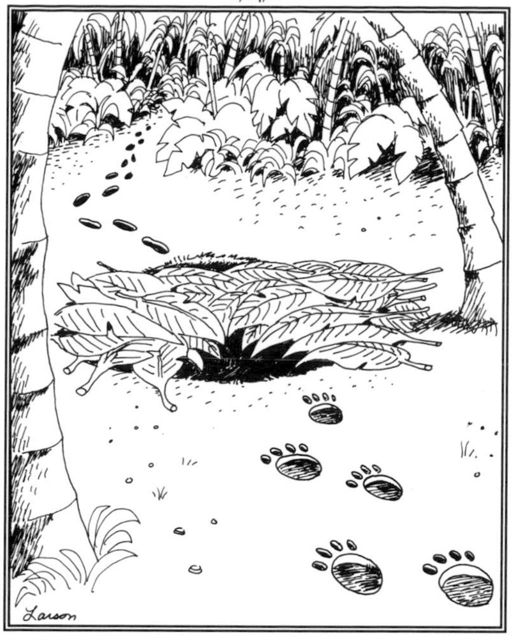
Larson

1/26/81

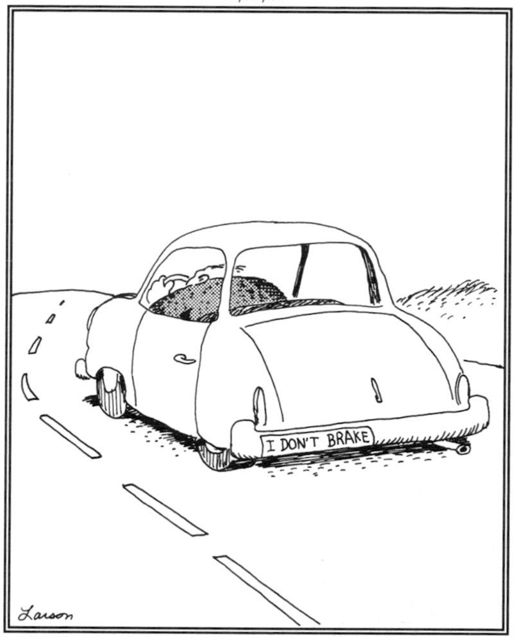
I DON'T BRAKE
Larson

1/27/81

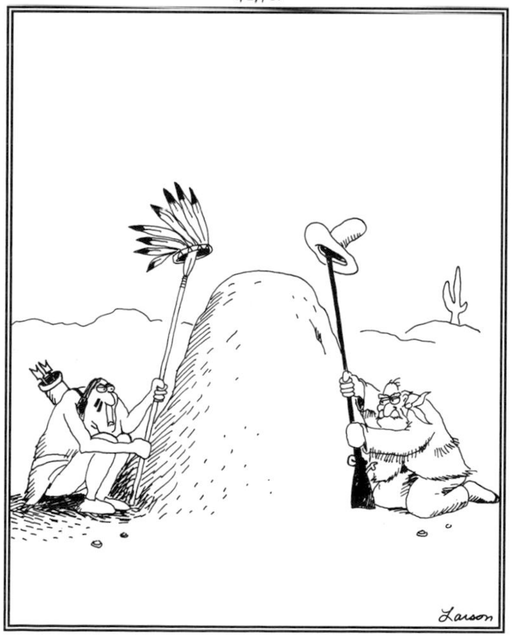
Larson

1/28/81

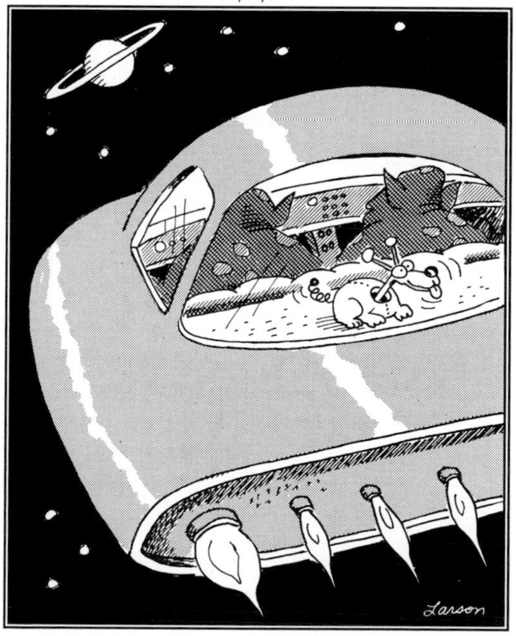
Larson

1/21/81

Larson

"Hold still, Carl! ... Don't ... move ... an ... *inch!*"

1/29/81

Larson

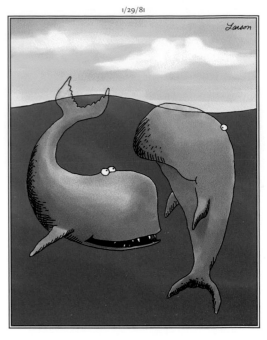

"Gee, I don't know, Eddie ... how many college students do you think you could eat at one time?"

1/30/81

ANYWHERE
Larson

"C'mon, Sylvia ... where's your spirit of adventure?"

1/31/81

Larson

"Bird calls! Bird calls, you fool! ... Not mountain lions!"

2/2/81

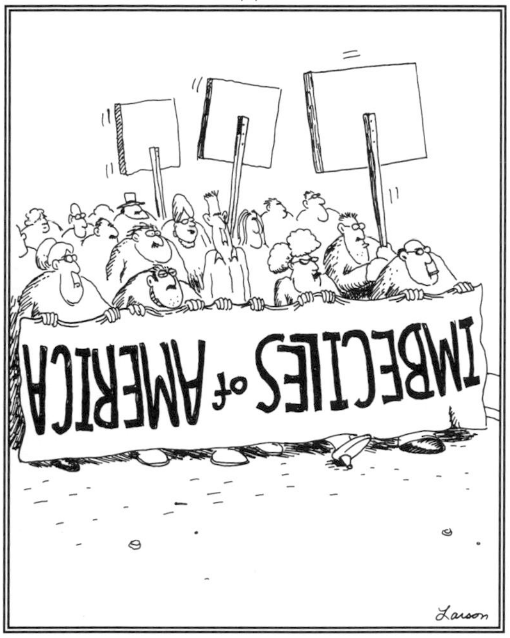
IMBECILES of AMERICA
Larson

2/3/81

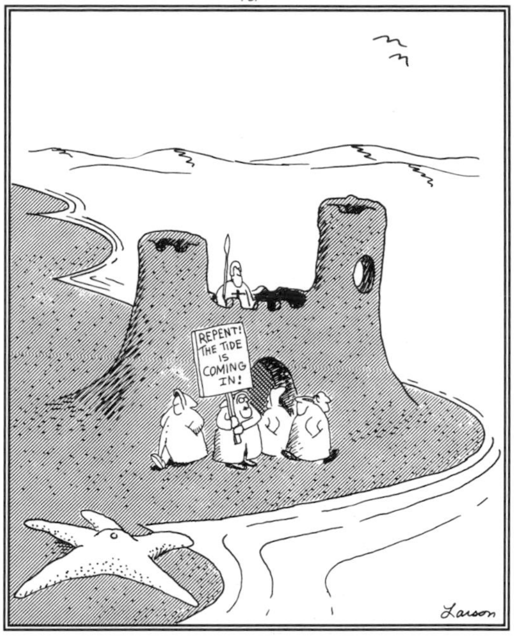
REPENT! THE TIDE IS COMING IN!
Larson

2/5/81

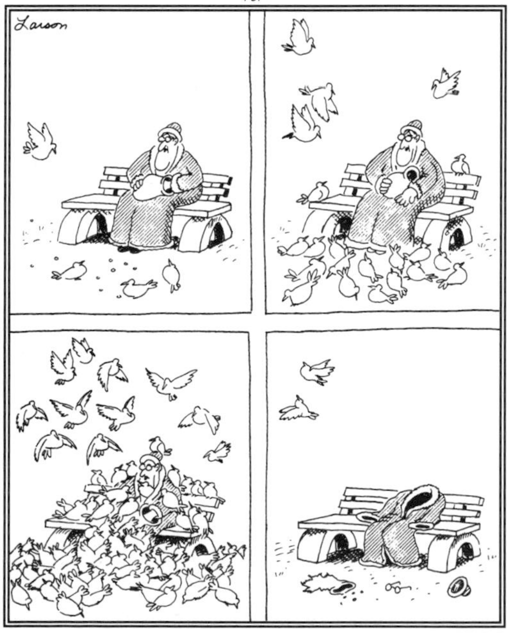
Larson

2/6/81

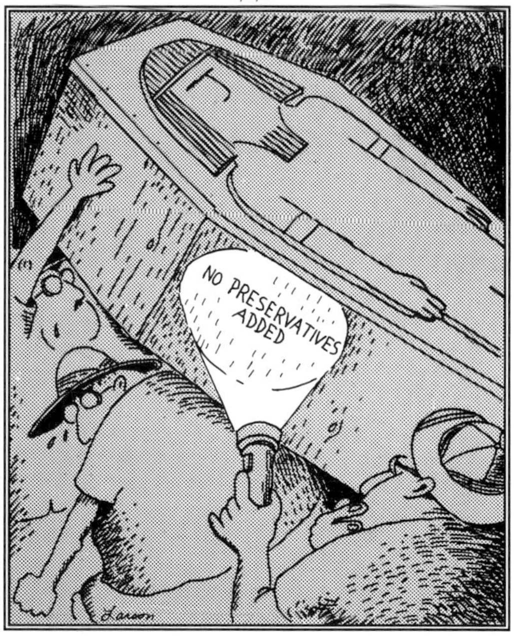
NO PRESERVATIVES ADDED
Larson

2/10/81

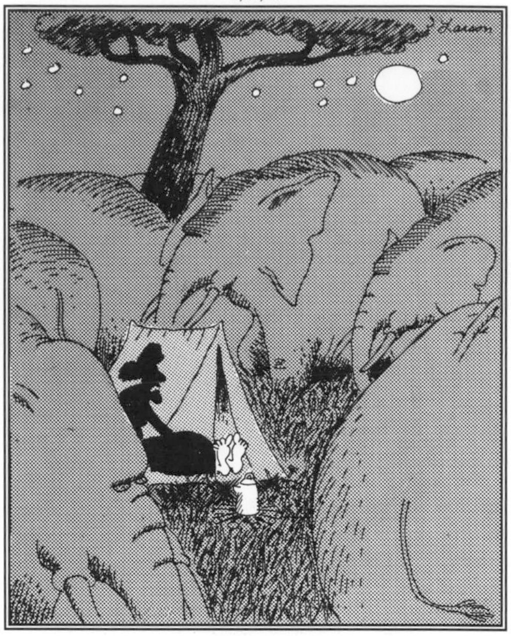

"Lester! Wake up! Lester! ... I think I heard footsteps."

2/7/81

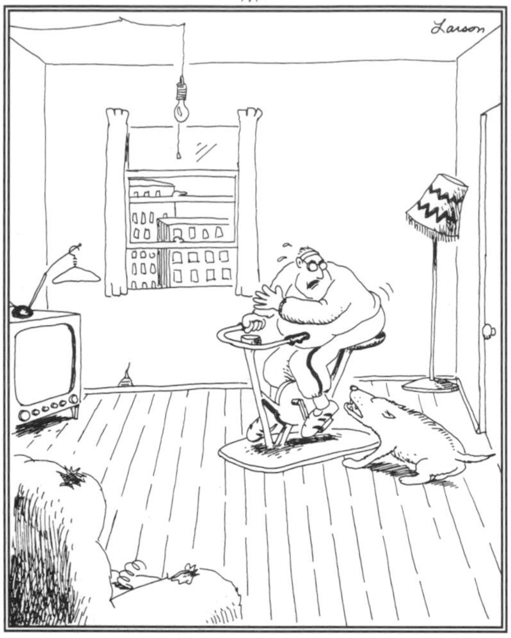

2/4/81

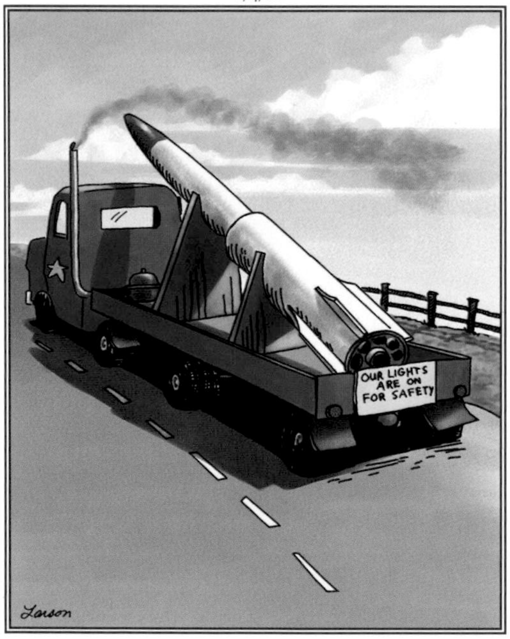
OUR LIGHTS ARE ON FOR SAFETY

2/9/81

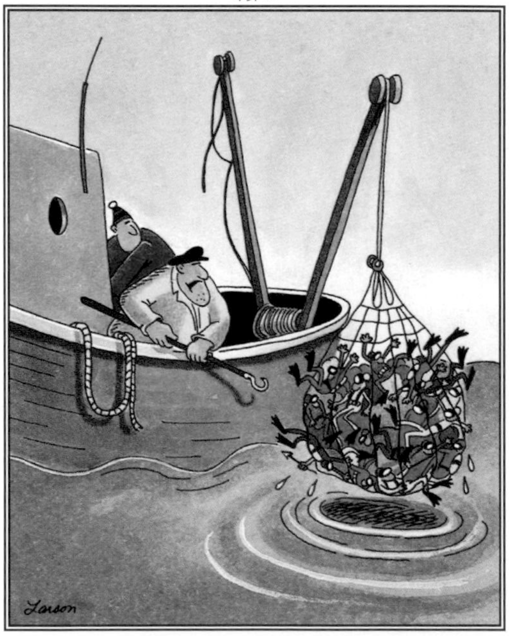

"I'm not sure, Al, but we sure got into a mess of 'em."

2/12/81

Larson

"This is General Sherman! The march to the sea is over! Turn back, I say! HALT! HAAAAAALT!"

2/11/81

Larson

"Thag, this is Noona. Noona, this is Thag. ... Thag is a Hunter and Gatherer."

2/16/81

HOT DOGS
HAMBURGE
Larson

2/13/81

Larson

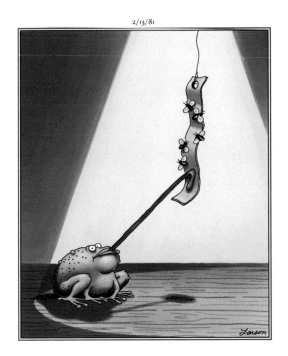

February 1981

2/14/81

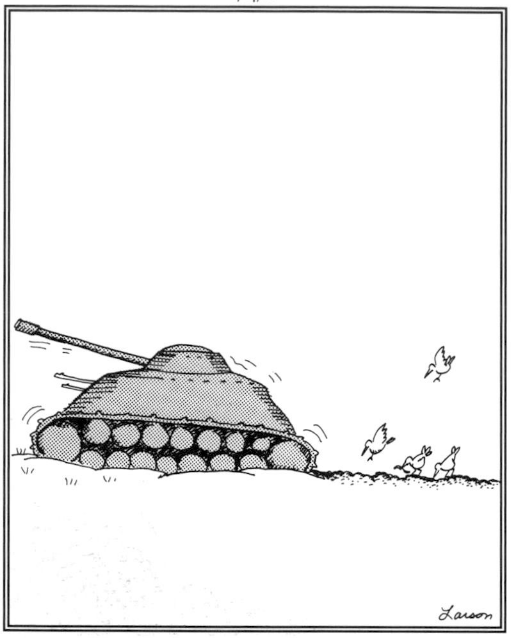
Larson

2/17/81

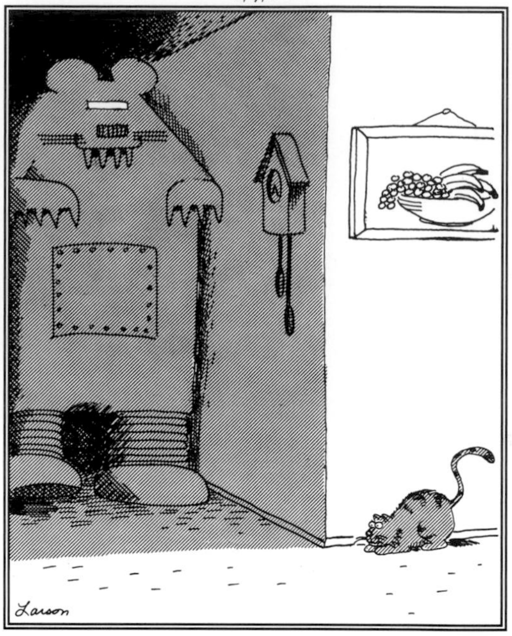
Larson

2/18/81

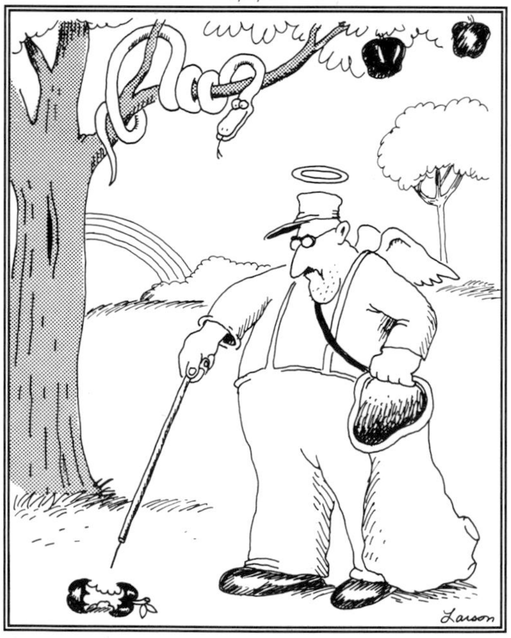
Larson

2/19/81

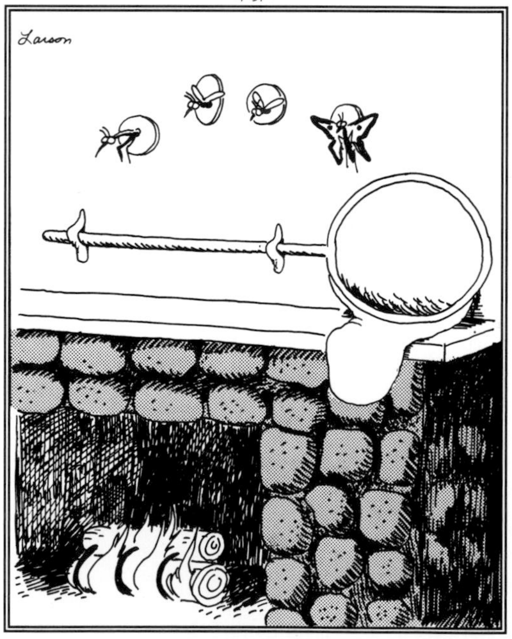
Larson

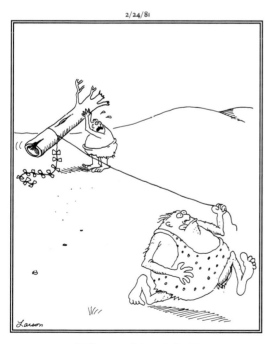

2/20/81

Larson
BEWARE
OF
BEAVER

2/21/81

Larson

2/24/81

Larson

"Okay, Bob! Go! Go!"

2/25/81

Larson
CAFE

"Oh! Here he comes. ... Now, whatever you do, don't say anything about his ears."

2/26/81

"Get 'em up there!"

2/28/81

"THAAAAAAR SHE BLOOOOOOWS!"

2/23/81

"And I'm not going to tell you again—
clean up your room!"

2/27/81

"We're here, Eric! Antarctica! ...
Bottom of the world!"

3/2/81

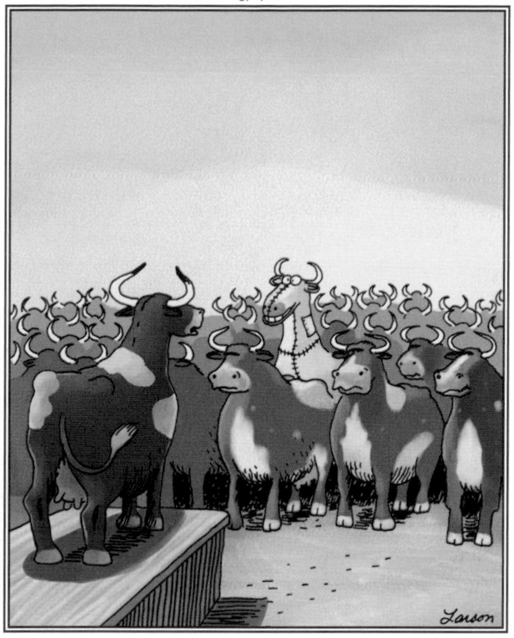

“The revolution has been postponed. ... We’ve discovered a leak.”

3/3/81

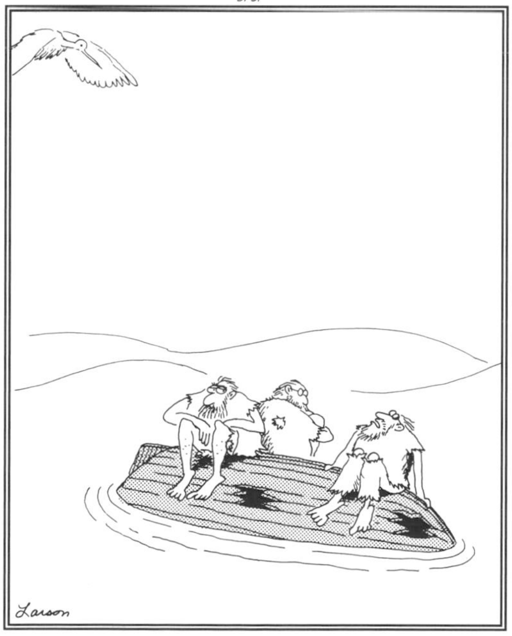

“Oh no! An albatross! ... Well, there goes our luck.”

3/4/81

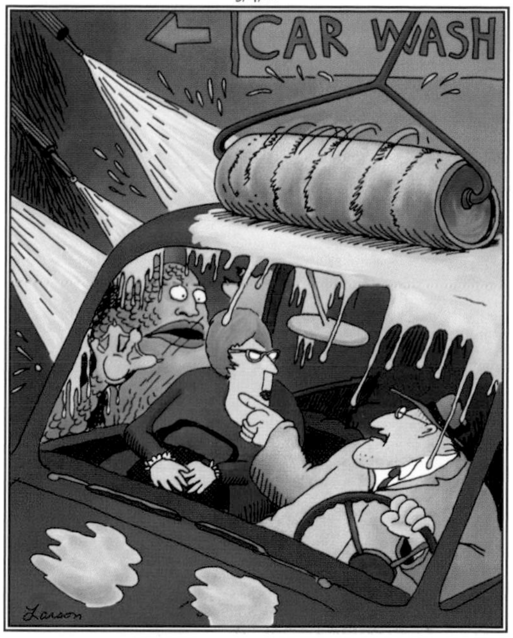
CAR WASH

“Quick, Agnes! Look! ... There it is again!”

3/5/81

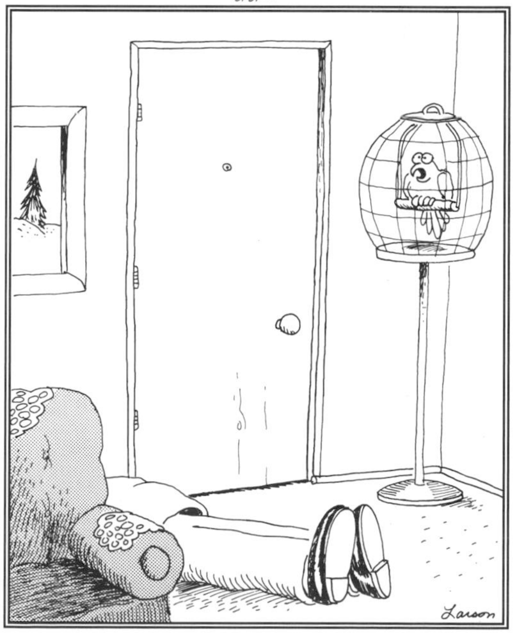

“Knock, knock, knock ... ding-dong, ding-dong ... anybody home? ... knock, knock, knock ... ”

"Give up, Sir James. ... You've lost."

"*Now* we'll see if that dog can get in here!"

3/10/81

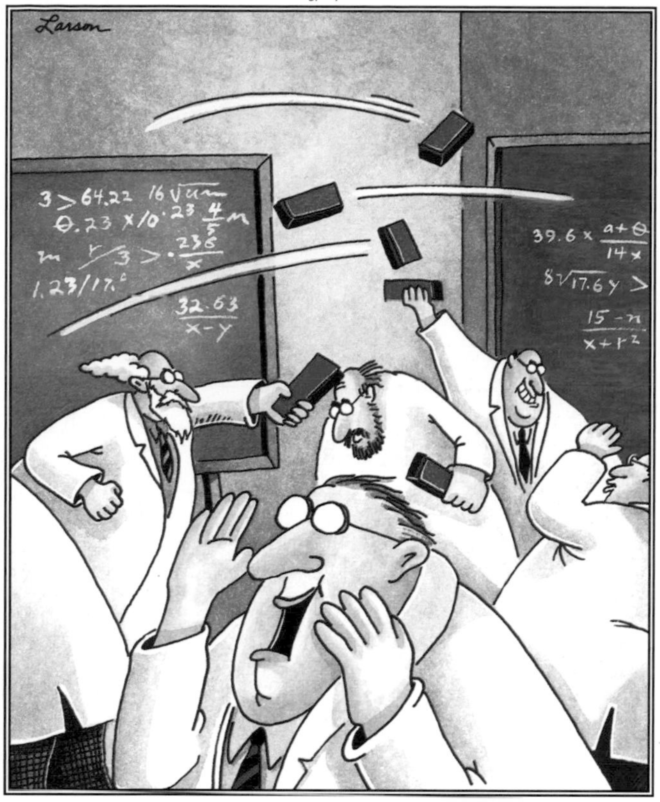
Larson

"Eraser fight!!"

3/11/81

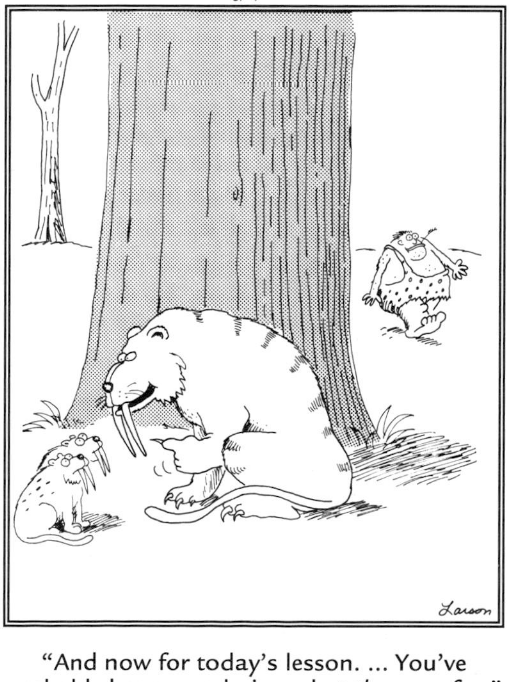
Larson

"And now for today's lesson. ... You've probably been wondering what *these* are for."

3/12/81

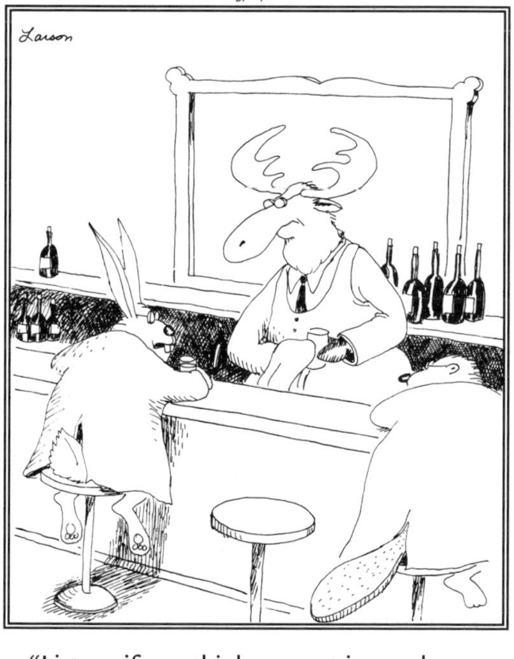
Larson

"Listen—if you think you got it rough, you should try *my* child-support payments."

3/13/81

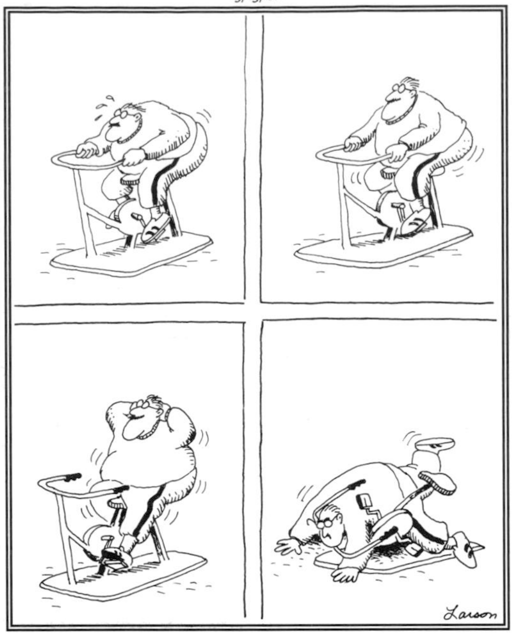
Larson

3/14/81

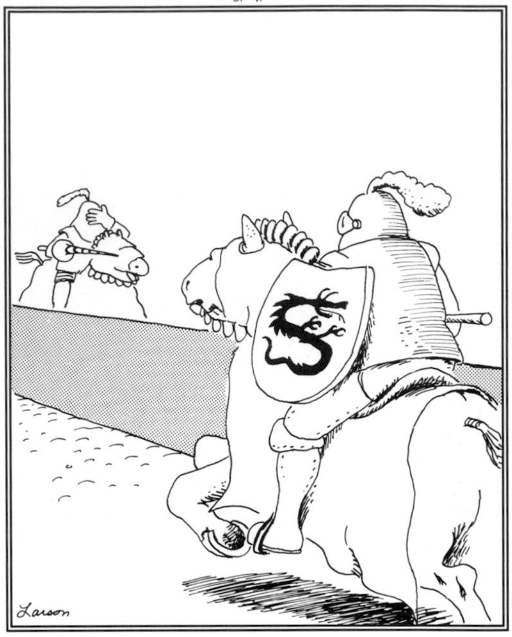
Larson

3/16/81

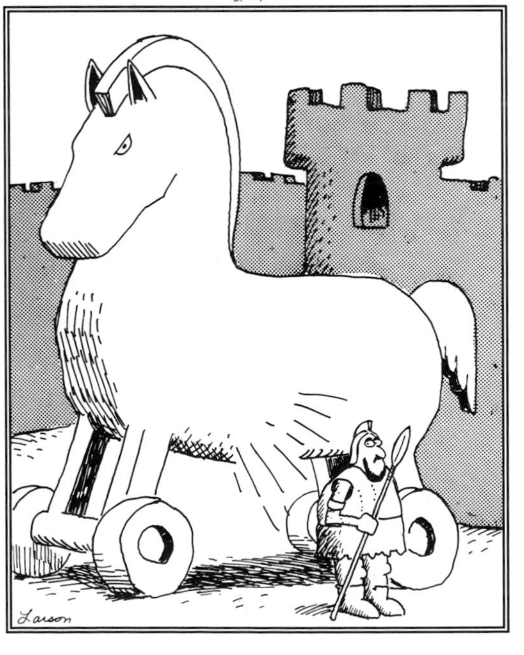
Larson

"You should have thought of that earlier, Cornelius. ... You're just going to have to hold it until nightfall."

3/17/81

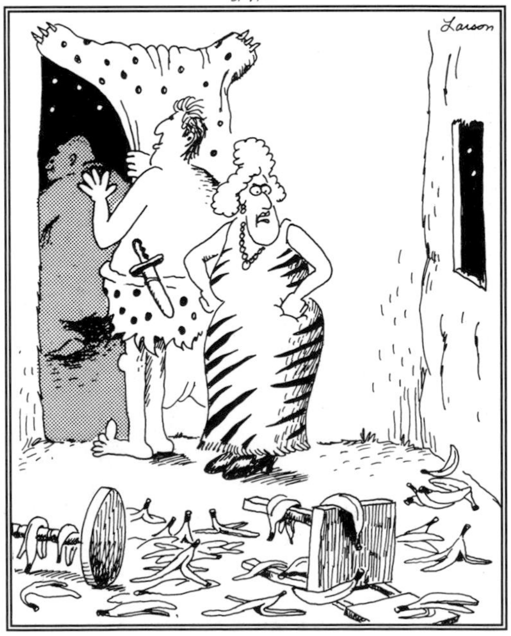
Larson

"Well, that's the last of 'em ... but just look at this place!"

3/18/81

"This may be hard, son, but your mother and I
agreed it was time you were told the truth. ...
You were adopted."

3/19/81

"Andrew! Listen! ... You can hear the ocean!"

3/20/81

"Hang on, Bernard! You've got him! ...
Give him slack!"

3/21/81

"Hey, Bob! So how's death been treating you?"

"FOOD!"

"So then Carl says to me, 'Look—let's invite
over the new neighbors and check 'em out.'"

"Okay, Billy. ... Tide's coming in now. ...
Dig me out, Billy. ... Billy, I don't want
to get angry. ..."

3/28/81

3/30/81

"And now we'll see if it attacks its
own reflection."

3/25/81

"You heard me, Simmons! You get that
cursed bugle fixed!"

3/31/81

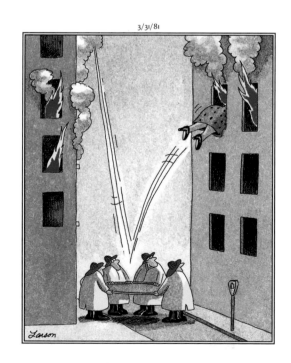

"Curse you, Zog! I've told you a hundred
times to get them screens up!"

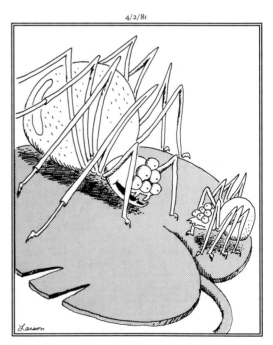

"Of course, that was back in the days when
you were just a twinkle in your father's eyes."

4/3/81

4/7/81

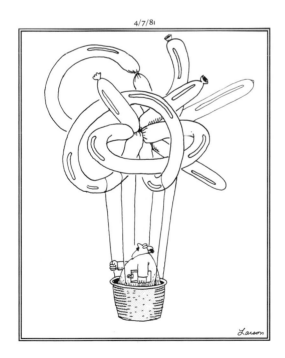

4/8/81

"Watch it, Randy! ... She's on your case!"

4/9/81

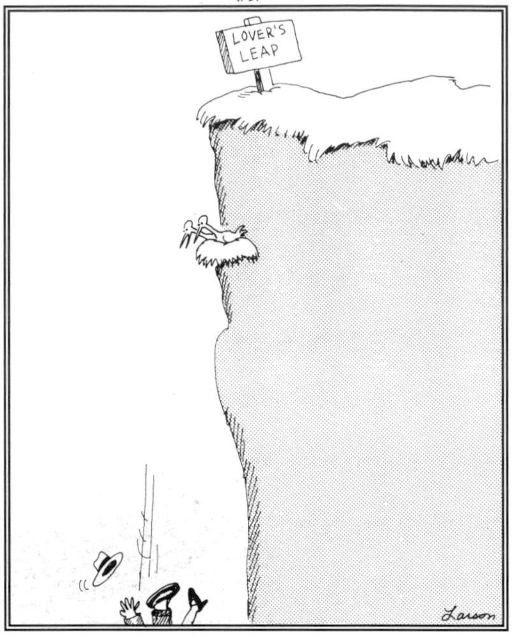
LOVER'S
LEAP

"There they go again ... leaving the nest too early."

4/20/81

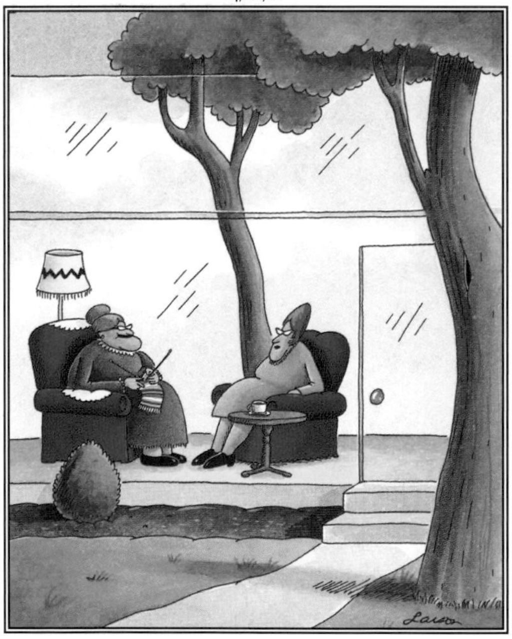

"Of course, living in an all-glass house has its disadvantages ... but you should see the birds smack it."

4/11/81

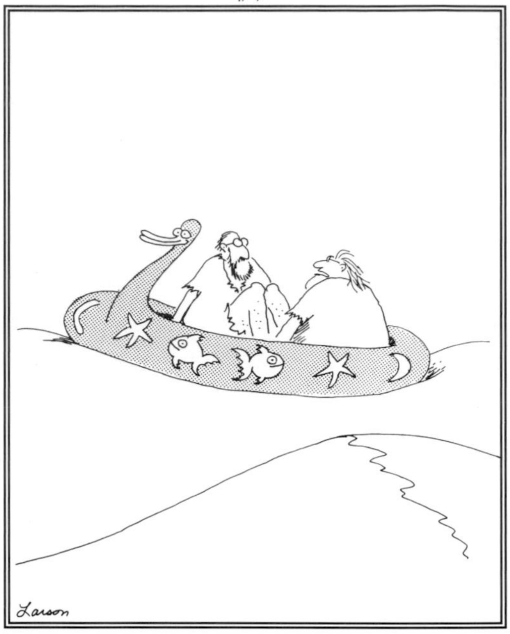

"Seven days at sea ... but thank God no one's seen us yet."

4/10/81

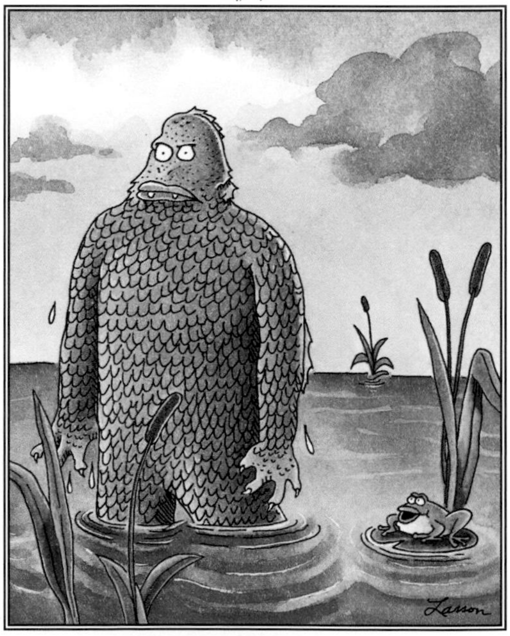

"Go get 'em, brother."

4/13/81

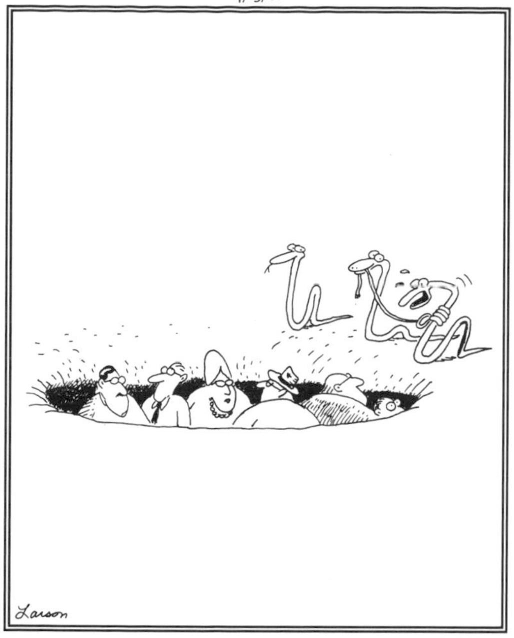

"No! No! Not that! Not *the pit!*"

4/14/81

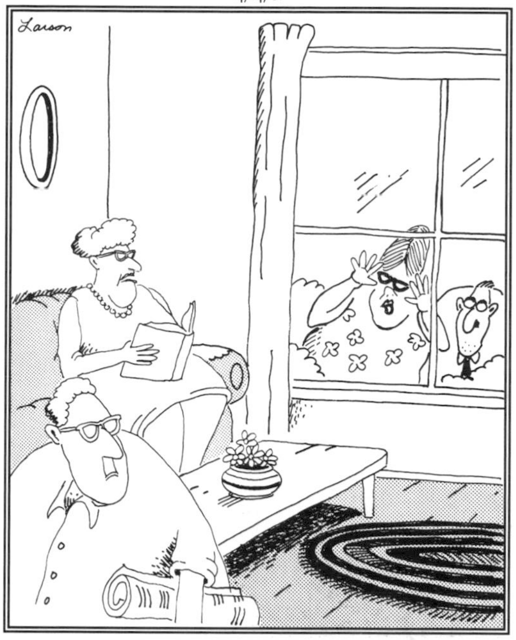

"Uh-oh, Warren. ... The Williamses are checking us out again."

4/21/81

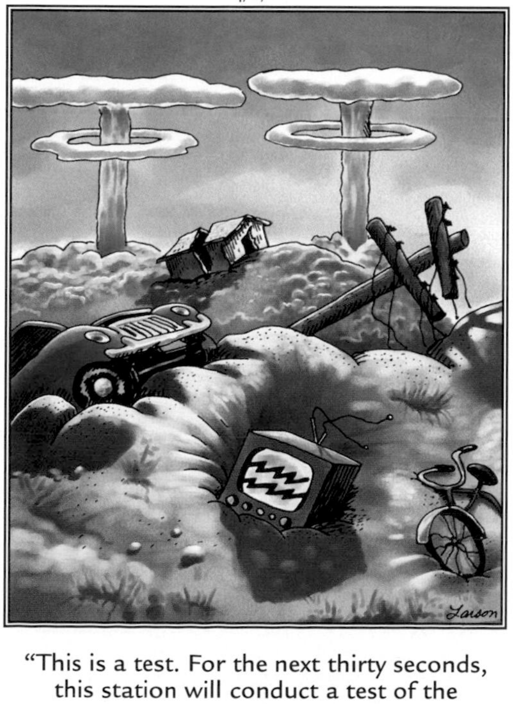

"This is a test. For the next thirty seconds, this station will conduct a test of the emergency broadcast system ..."

4/25/81

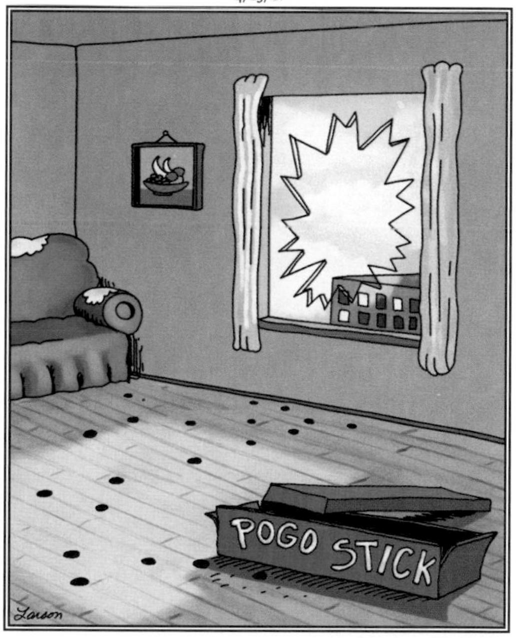
POGO STICK

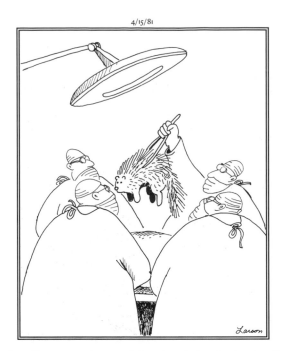

"Well, I guess that explains the abdominal pains."

"Now, close your eyes and go back to sleep, honey. ... There's nothing in your closet."

"Remember, Thag, approach her carefully. If she doesn't recognize your courtship behavior, she might eat you."

"So there he was—this big gorilla just lying there. And Jim here says, 'Do you suppose it's dead or just asleep?'"

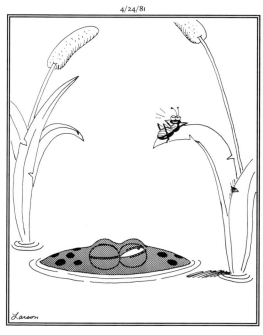

"Ahhhh ... life!"

119

April 1981

4/28/81

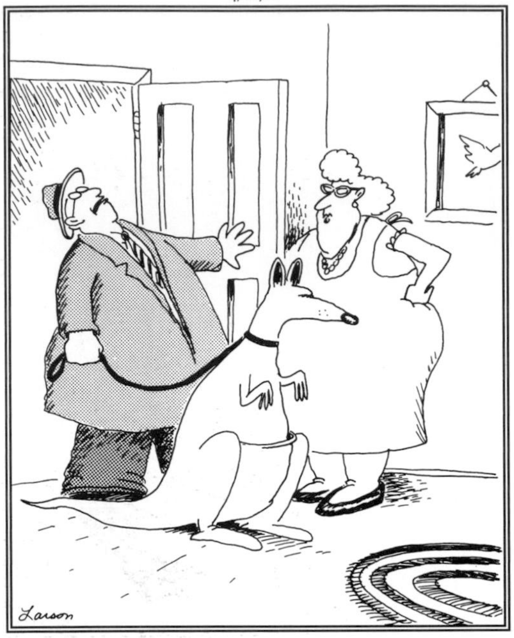

"Florence! It's my neck again! ...
I can't move it!"

4/29/81

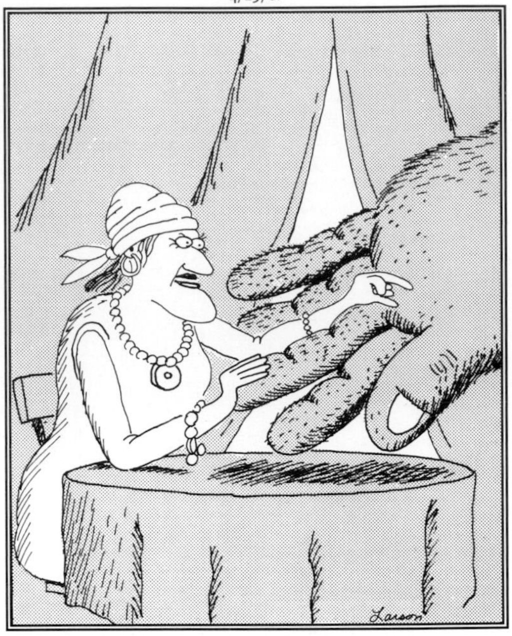

"And you should definitely stay away from short blondes and tall buildings."

4/30/81

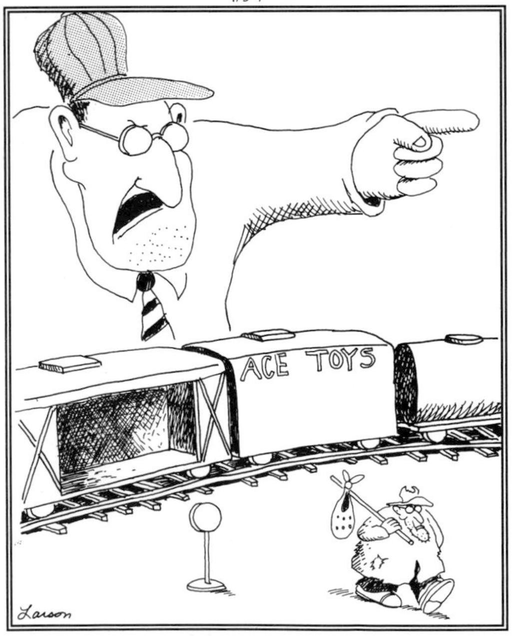
ACE TOYS

"And *stay* off!"

4-30-81

Editor
Los Angeles Times
Times Mirror Square
Los Angeles, CA

Sirs:

I must register strong exception to your cartoon "The Far Side" by Gary Larson in today's paper.

Being an old railroader and model railroad fan for longer than I care to admit I must inform you and Gary Larson that no model railroader in his right mind would force a perfectly sculptured "bum" from his railroad "layout".

A model railroader seeks perfection in his miniture world. A miniture creature would be welcomed as heartily as the perfect switch or a track that never gets greasy.

His only complaint would be if the "bum" was "out of scale."

HOn3 forever,
Howard Decker

5/4/81

5/6/81

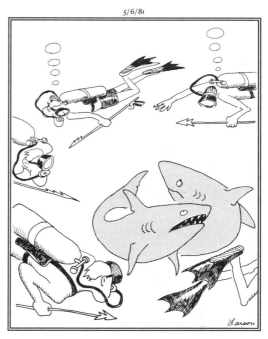

"Just stay calm and don't make any
erratic movements."

5/8/81

The Dawn of Man

5/9/81

"Now follow me. Step, step, slither, step ...
step, step, slither, step ..."

5/1/81

Larson

5/2/81

Larson

5/11/81

Larson

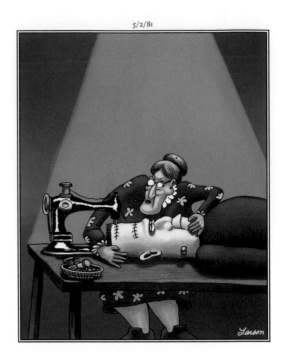

"We better do as he says, Thag. ...
He's got the drop on us."

5/13/81

Larson

"Oh, yeah? ... And I suppose you got those
suction marks at the meeting, too!"

5/5/81

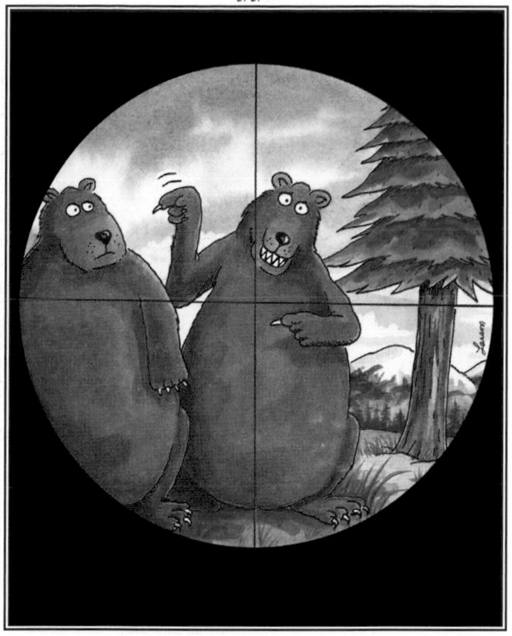

5/7/81

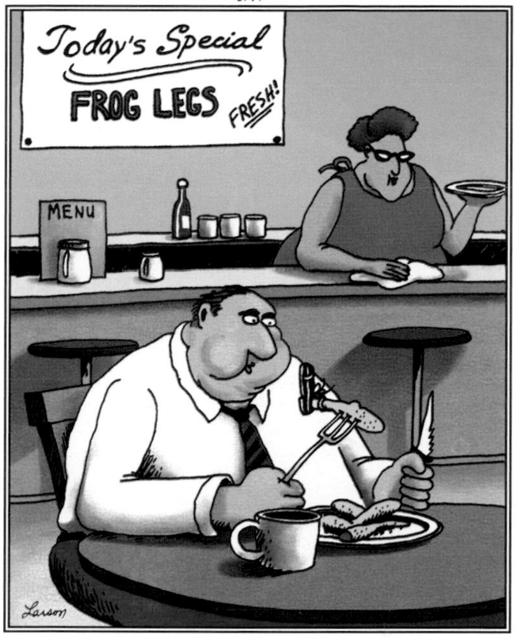
Today's Special
FROG LEGS
FRESH!
MENU

5/12/81

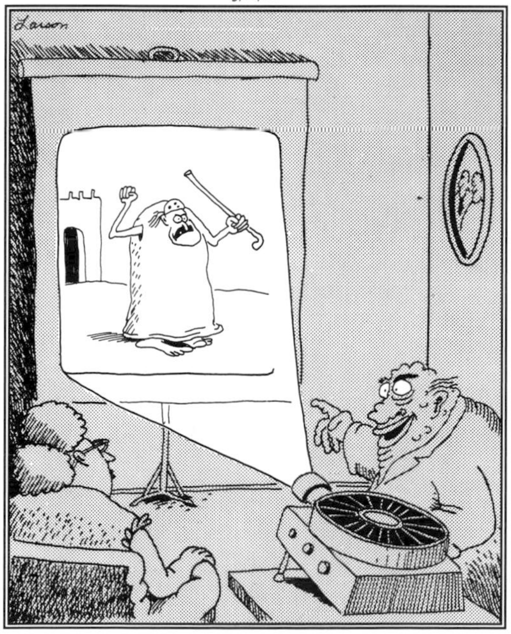

"Now I remember, Helen! ... That's the old peasant woman who said she'd put a curse on me if I snapped her!"

5/19/81

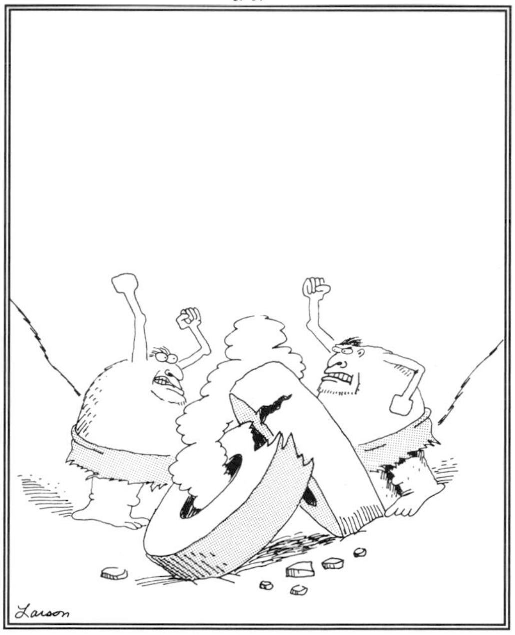

May 1981

5/15/81

Larson

"Okay, okay, okay. ... Everyone just calm down and we'll try this thing one more time."

5/14/81

Larson

"This ain't gonna look good on our report, Leroy."

5/16/81

Larson

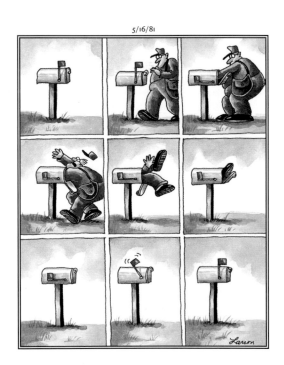

5/20/81

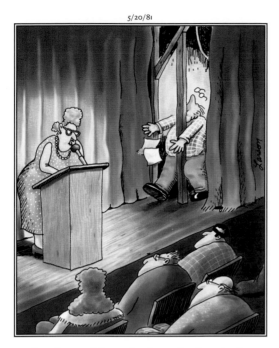

"And so, without further ado, here's the author of *Mind over Matter* ..."

5/23/81

BREKFUST
SURVDED ANYTiM

5/27/81

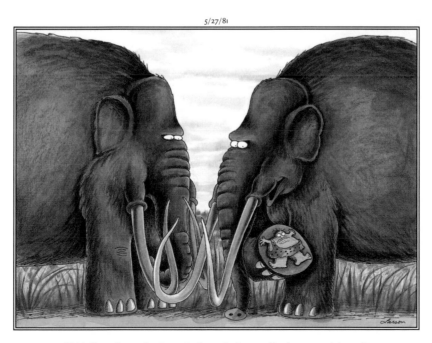

"Well, what the? ... I *thought* I smelled something."

5/18/81

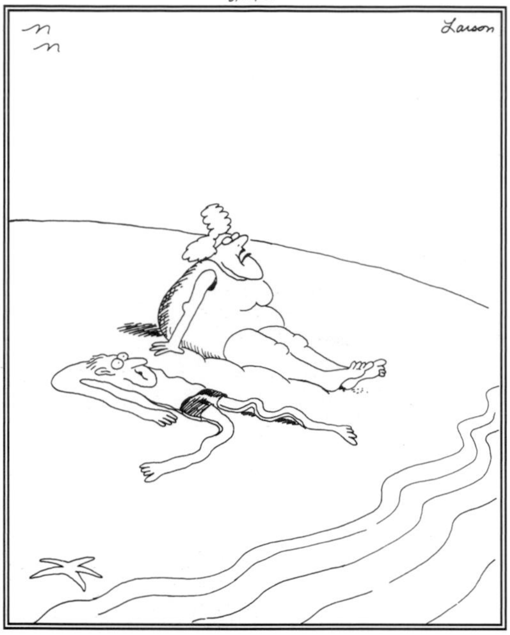
Larson

"My goodness, Harold! ... Now there goes one big mosquito!"

5/21/81

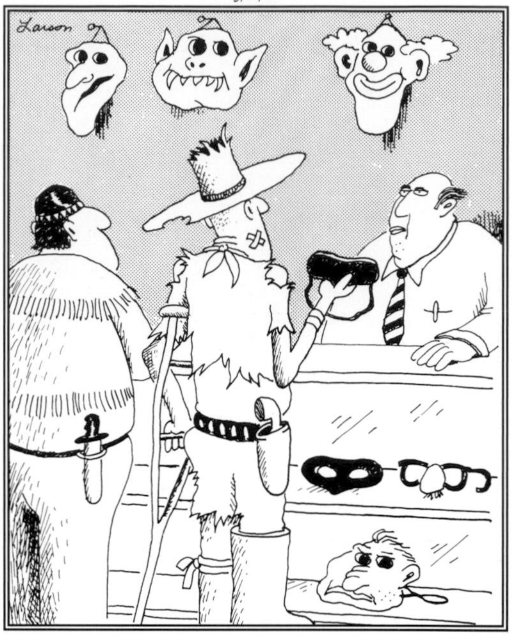
Larson

"Say ... wasn't there supposed to be a couple of holes punched in this thing?"

5/22/81

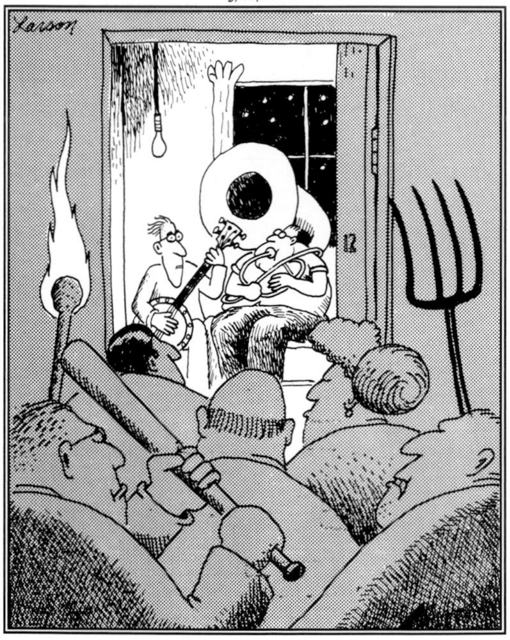
Larson
12

5/25/81

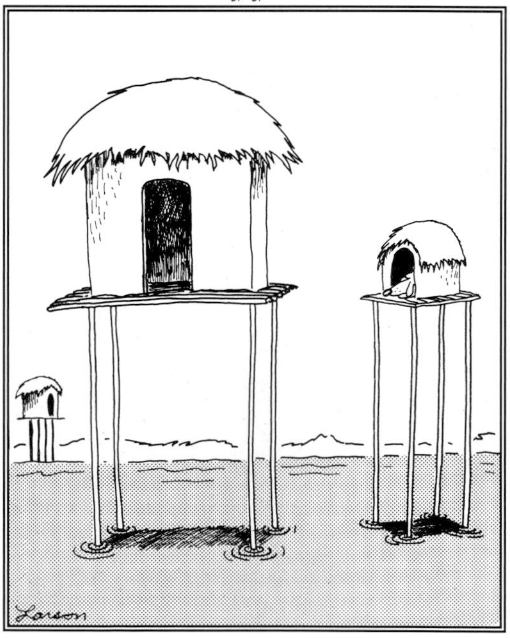
Larson

5/26/81

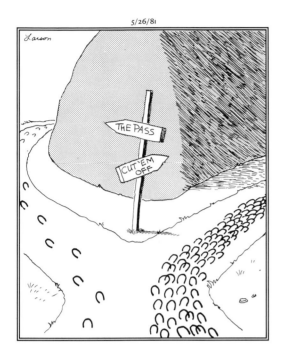

Larson
THE PASS
CUT 'EM OFF

5/28/81

Larson

"Well, the Answer Man says, 'If the wheels start to spin, try rocking the car back and forth'..."

5/29/81

Larson

5/30/81

Larson

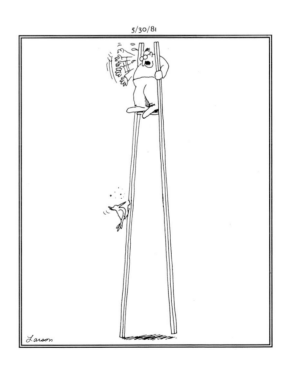

June 1981

6/1/81

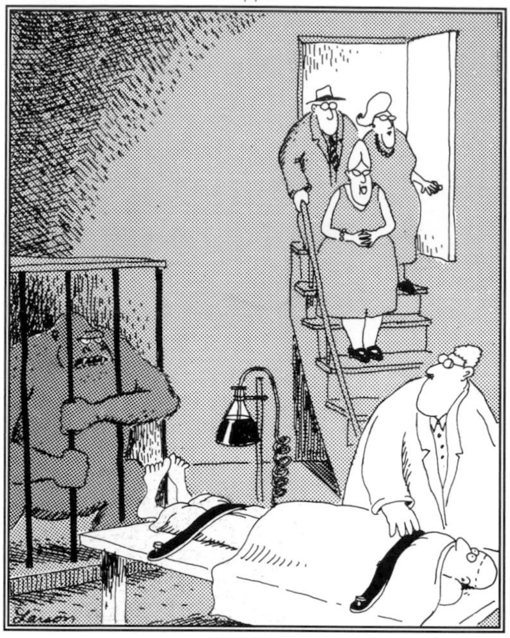

"Honey, the Merrimonts are here. ... They'd like to come down and see your ape-man project."

6/2/81

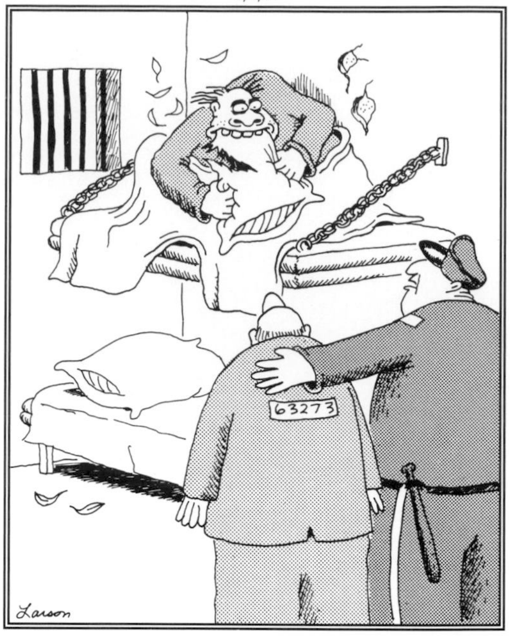
63273

"Hey, Durk! ... New cellmate, Durk! ... New cellmate! ... Friend, Durk! ... Friend!"

6/3/81

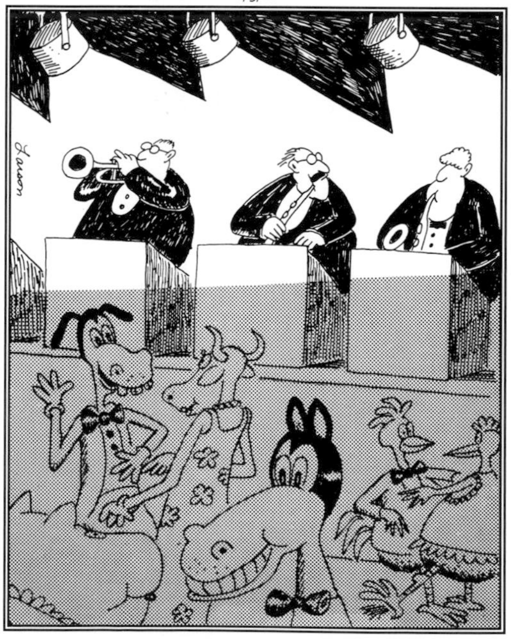

"That does it, Carl. ... You're through doing the bookings."

6/6/81

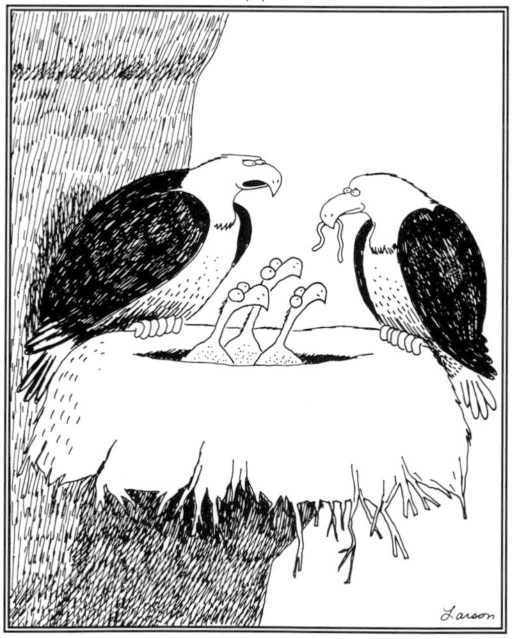

"Well, well. ... The great hunter returneth."

6/5/81

"And then, whenever I come to the word 'chicken,' the couple here in front will jump up and make clucking sounds!"

6/8/81

"Faster! He's still there!"

6/10/81

"Well, I learned one thing. ... This works good on clothes, but don't try it on your dog."

6/11/81

BEGINNING DANCE

6/4/81

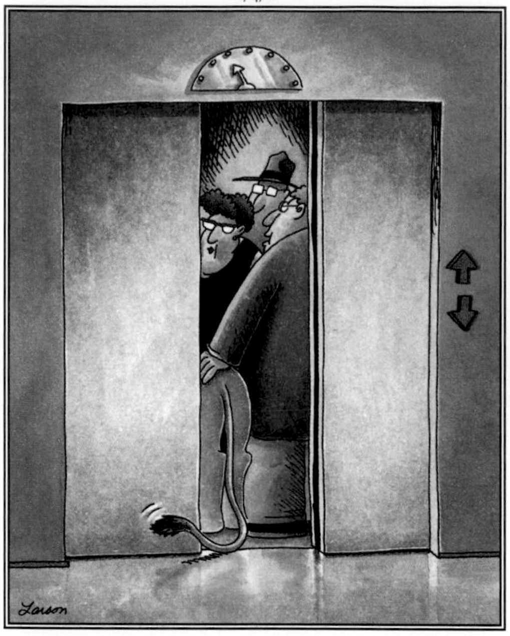
Larson

"Don't be alarmed, folks—he's completely harmless unless something startles him."

6/9/81

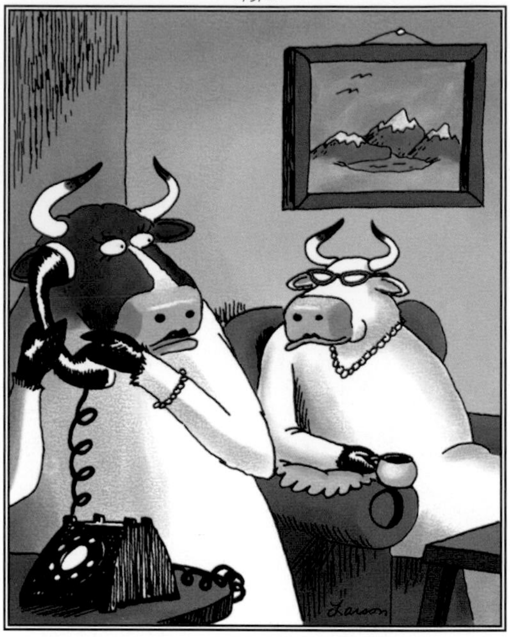
Larson

"Agnes! It's that heavy, chewing sound again!"

6/12/81

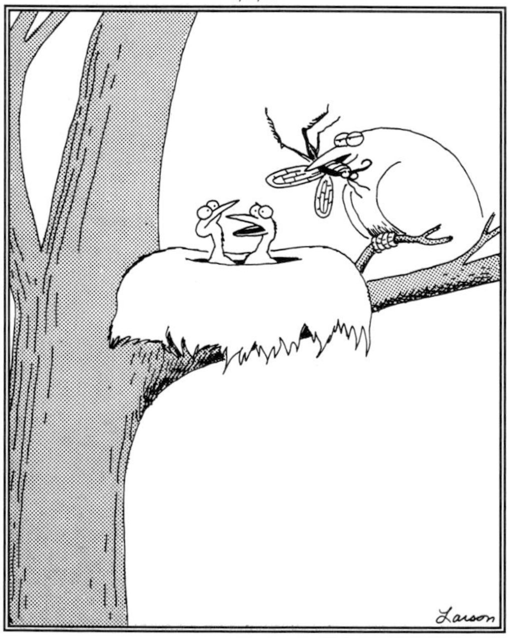
Larson

"No way! ... This time *I* get the legs and thighs; *you* get the wings and back!"

6/13/81

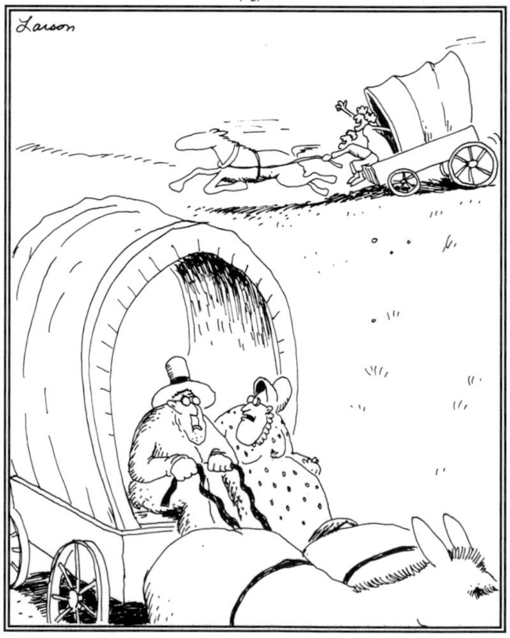
Larson

"I wish they'd keep those danged teenagers off the trails."

6/15/81

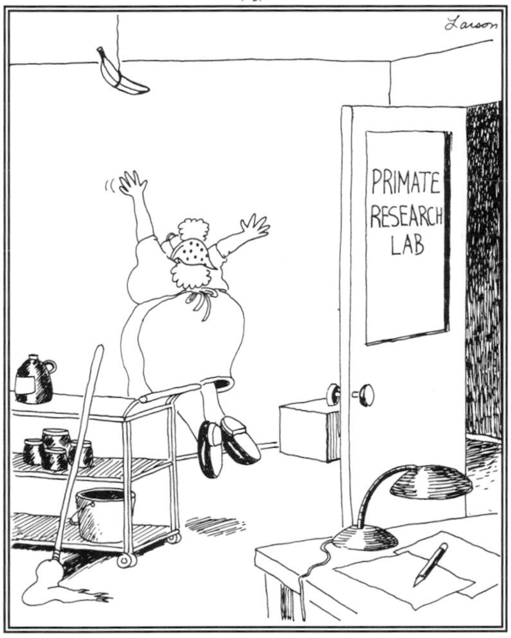
Larson
PRIMATE
RESEARCH
LAB

6/16/81

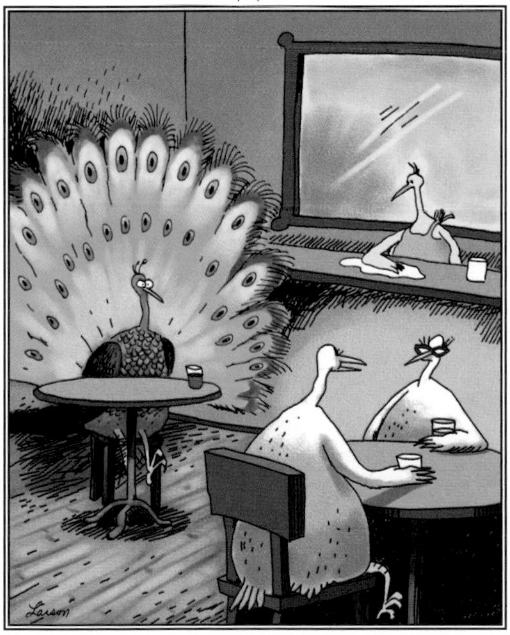
Larson

"Don't encourage him, Sylvia."

6/20/81

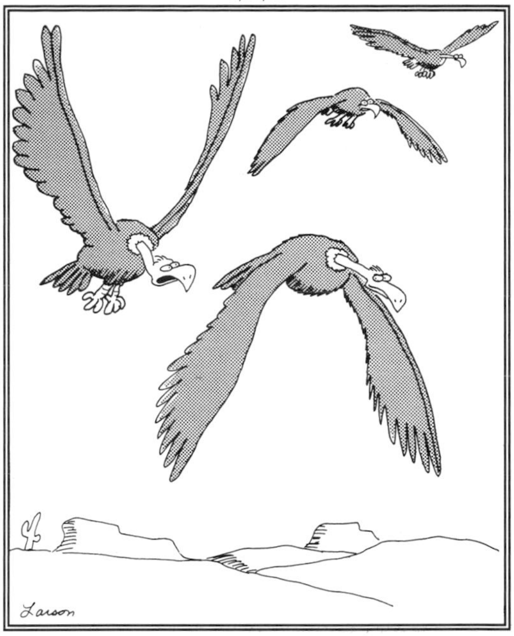
Larson

"Well, this better not be just a wild goose chase. ... Little Big Horn, huh?"

6/18/81

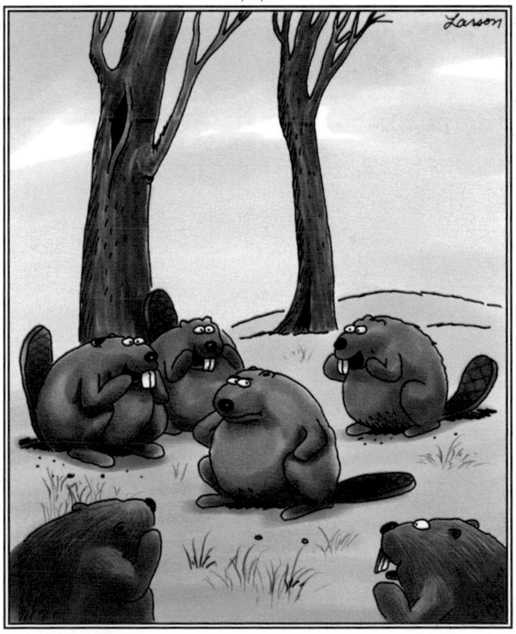
Larson

"Doesn't have buck teeth, doesn't have buck teeth, doesn't have ..."

6/17/81

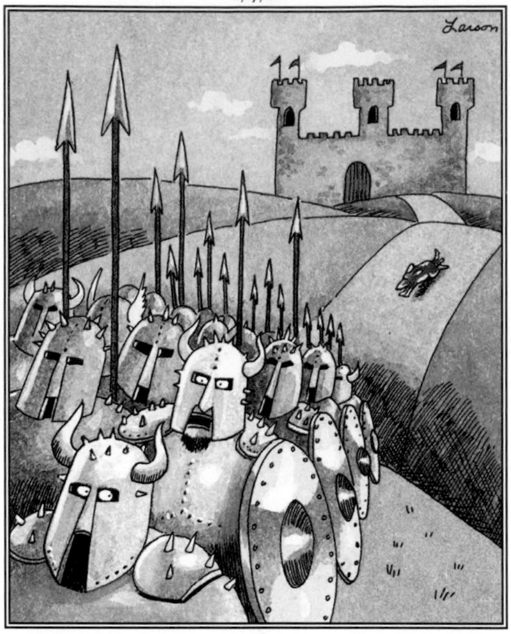
Larson

"Hey, Richard! Your stupid dog's following us again!"

6/19/81

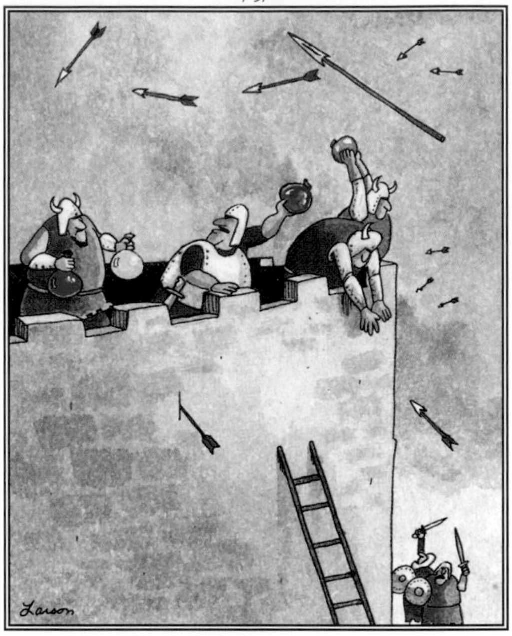
Larson

"Hot oil! We need hot oil! ... Forget the water balloons!"

6/26/81

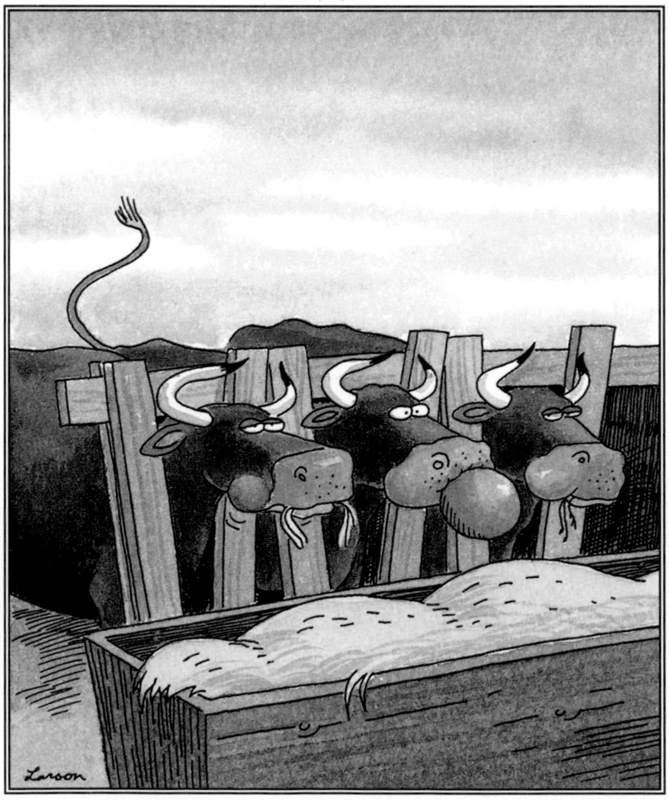
Larson

6/24/81

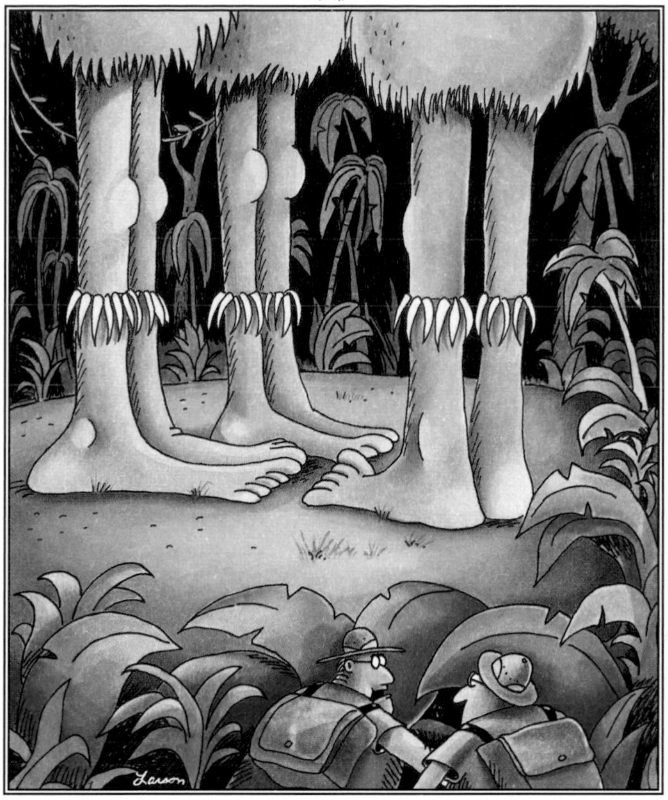

"With a little luck, they may revere us as gods."

6/23/81

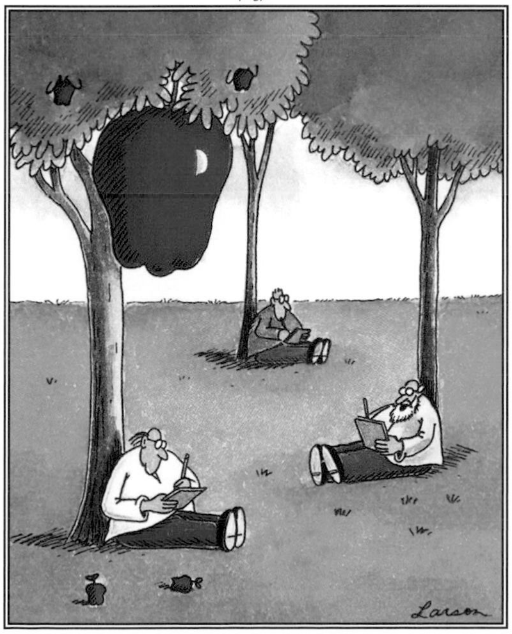

"Nothing yet. ... How about you, Newton?"

6/27/81

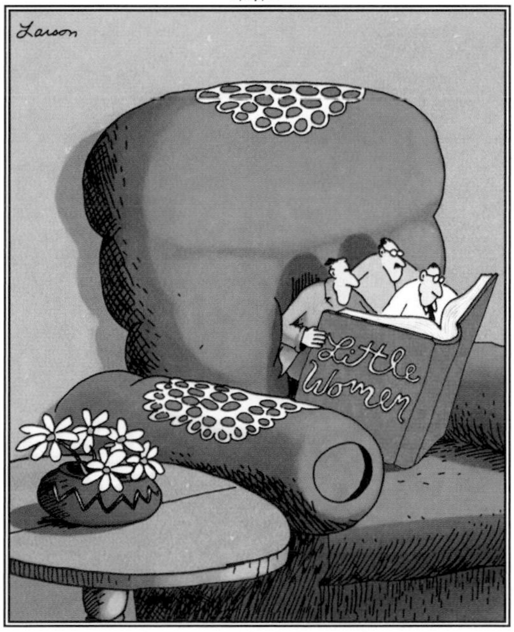
Little Women

6/22/81

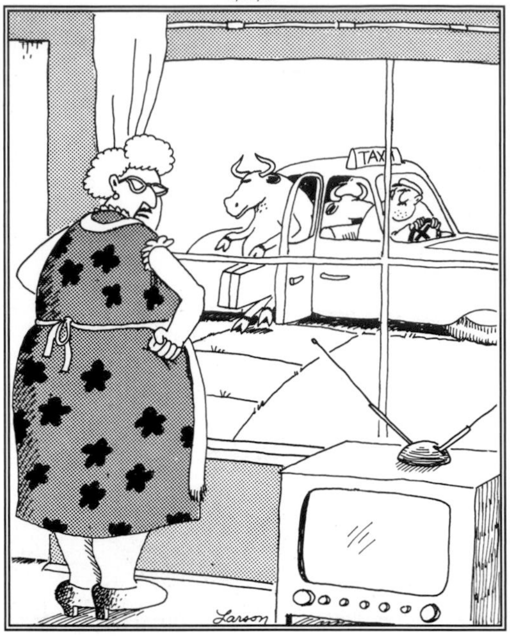

"Andrew ... the cows have come home."

6/25/81

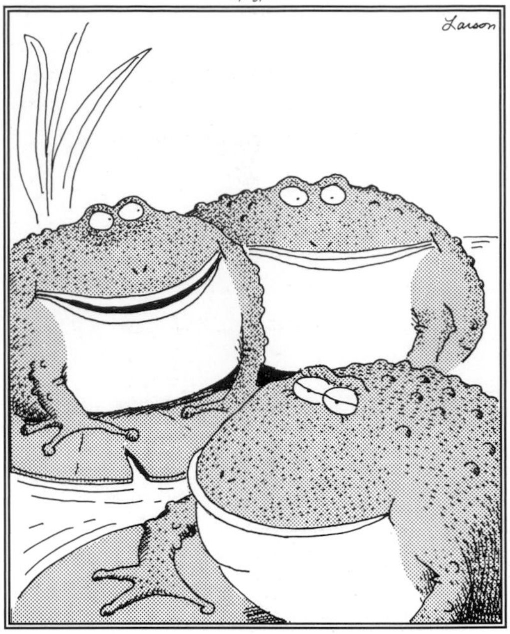

"Vive la difference."

6/29/81

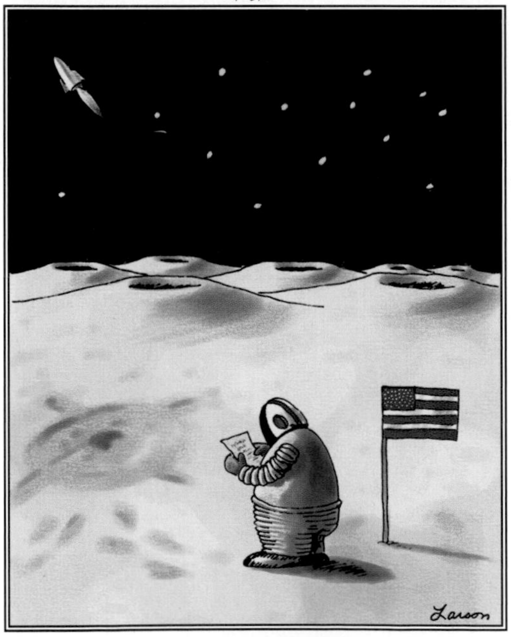

"Dear Henry: Where were you? We waited and waited but finally decided that ..."

6/30/81

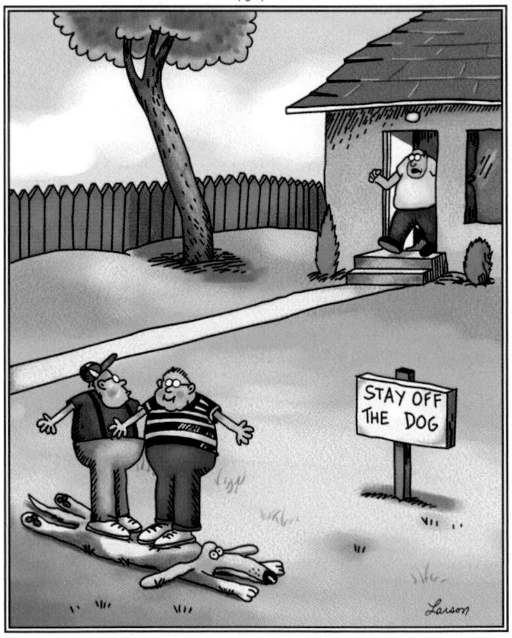
STAY OFF THE DOG

"Hey! You kids! ... Can't you read?"

7/1/81

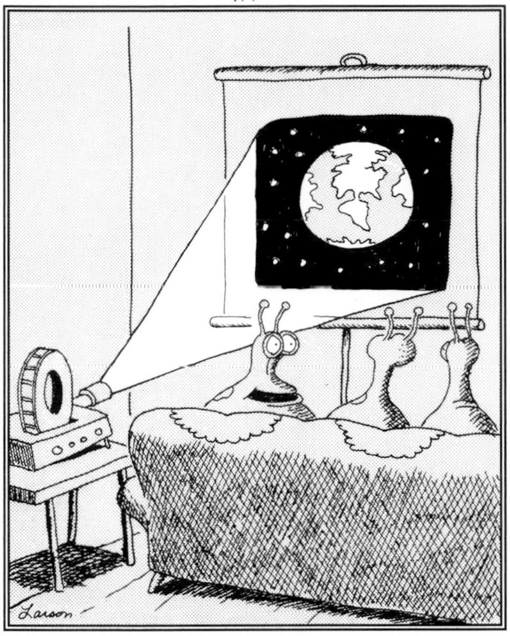
Larson

"Oh, yeah. ... Now that place was *really* a greasy spoon!"

7/2/81

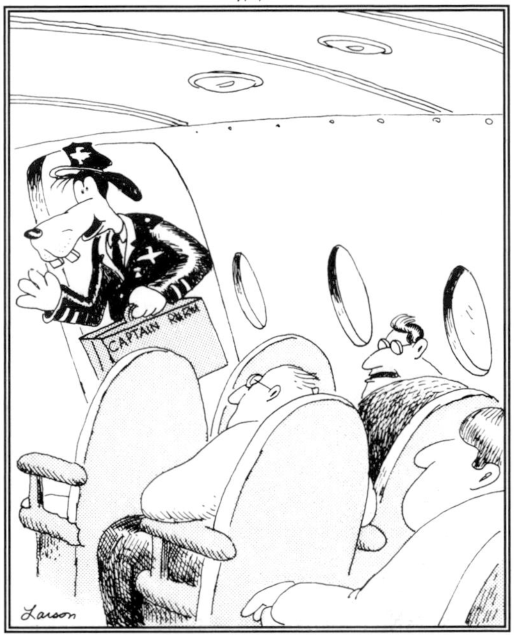
CAPTAIN
Larson

"God help us all."

7/3/81

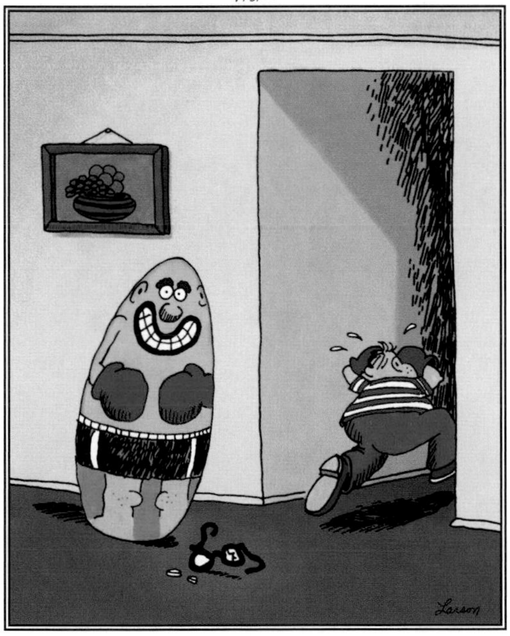
Larson

7/6/81

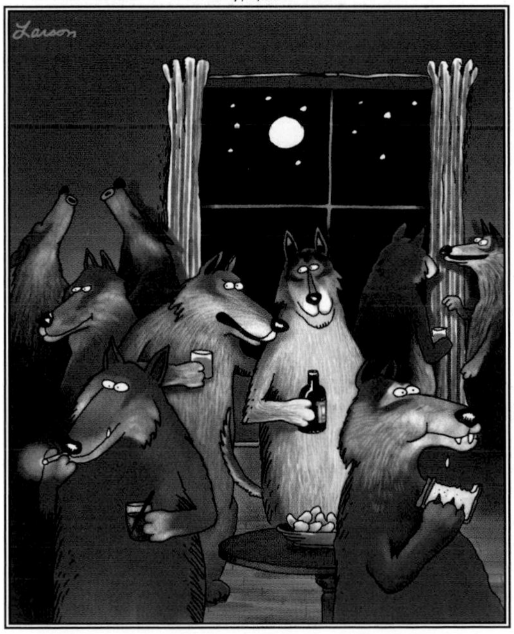
Larson

"Listen ... this party's a drag. But later on, Floyd, Warren, and myself are going over to Farmer Brown's and slaughter some chickens."

7/8/81

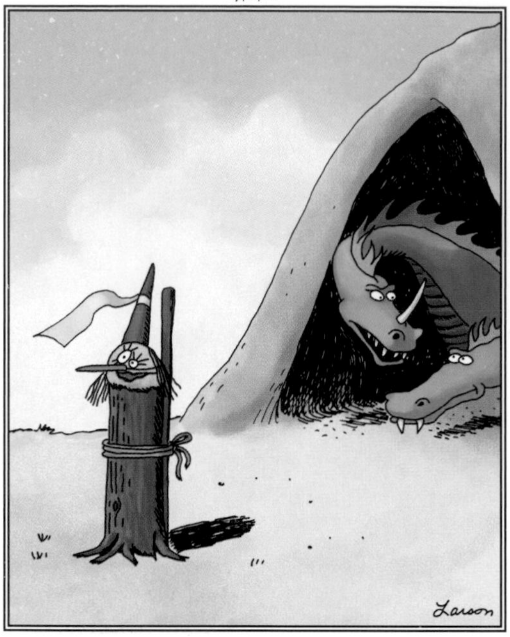
Larson

"It's no use. ... We've just got to get ourselves a real damsel."

7/9/81

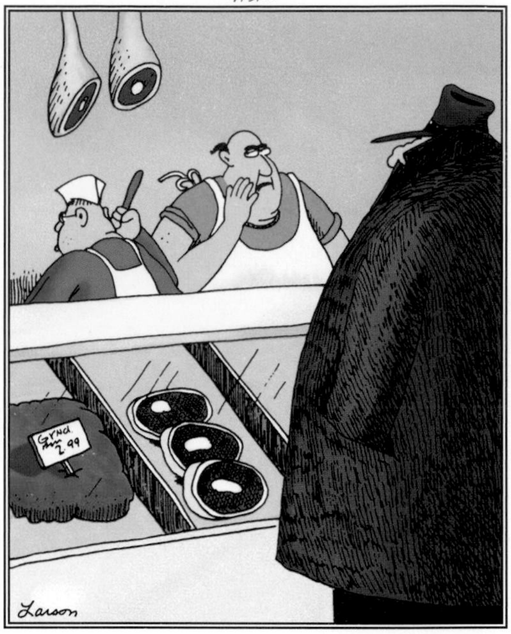
Larson

"Well, I never thought about it before ... but I suppose I'd let the kid go for about $1.99 a pound."

7/4/81

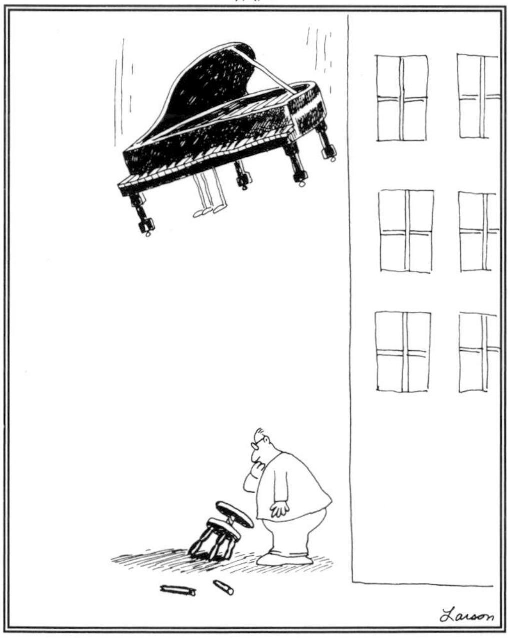
Larson

7/7/81

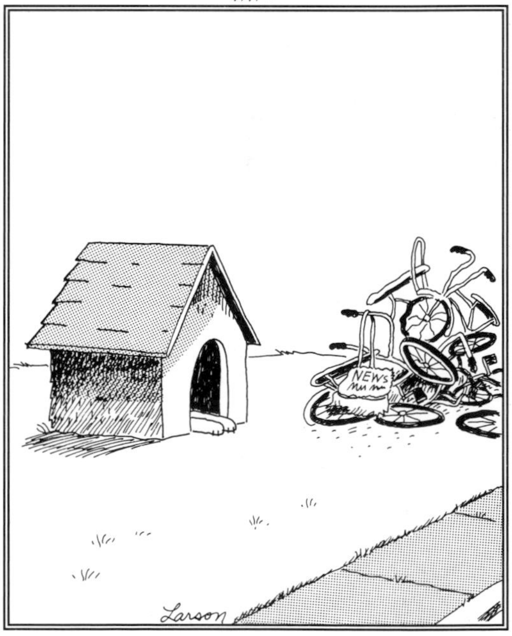
NEWS
Larson

7/13/81

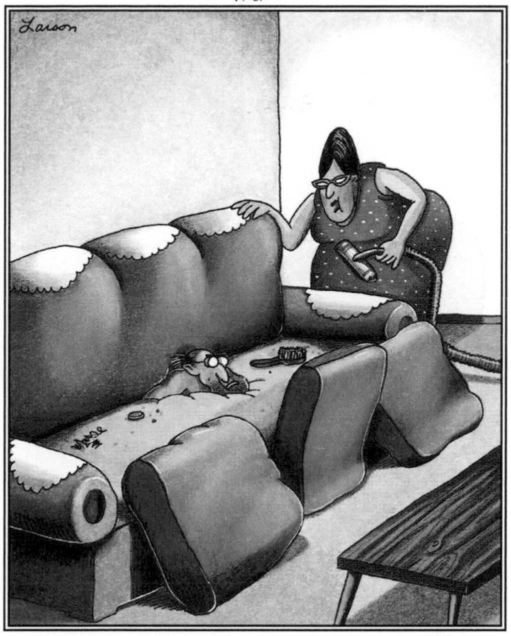

"Andrew! So that's where you've been! And good heavens! ... There's my old hairbrush, too!"

7/10/81

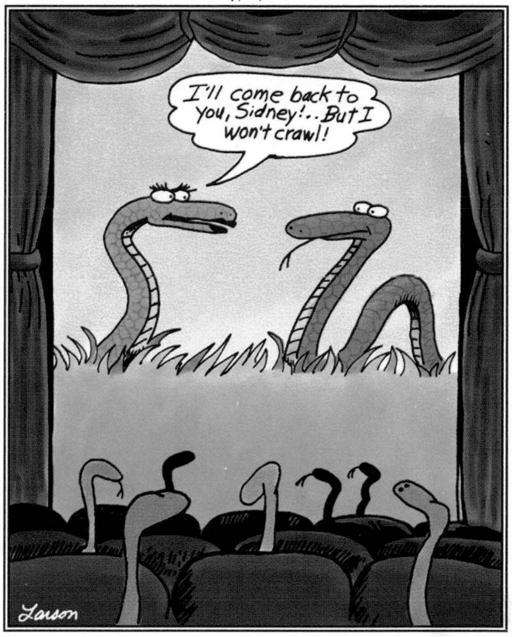
I'll come back to you, Sidney!.. But I won't crawl!

7/14/81

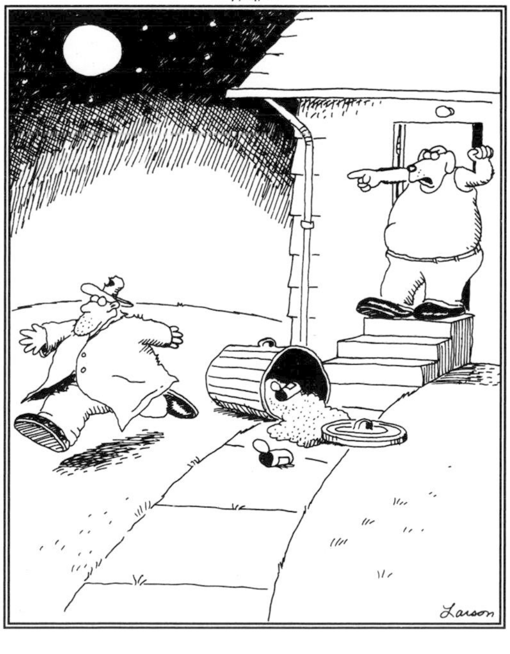

7/15/81

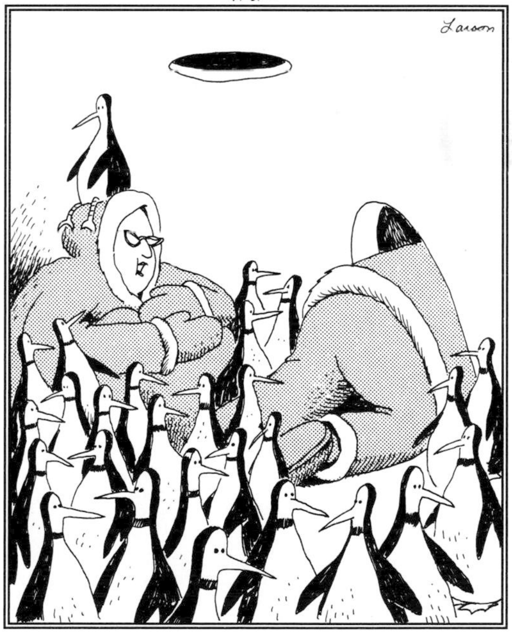

"Remember, milk, eggs, loaf of bread ... and pick up one of those No-Penguin-Strips."

7/17/81

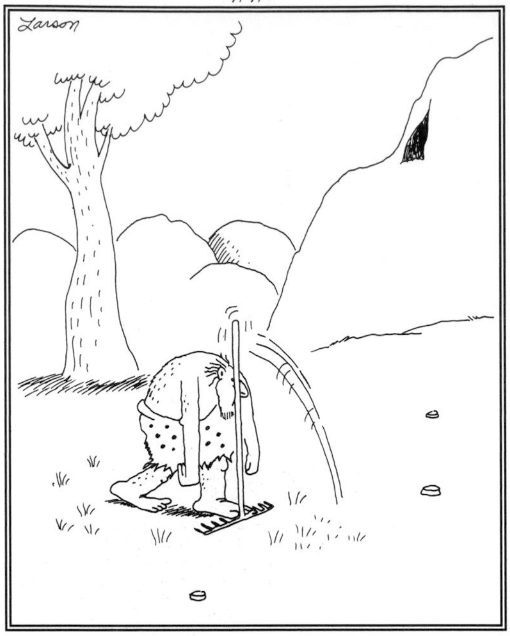

The discovery of tools

7/18/81

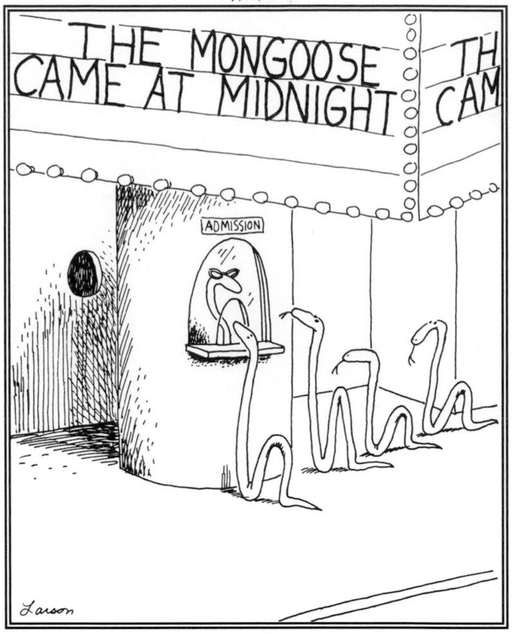
THE MONGOOSE
CAME AT MIDNIGHT
TH
CAM
ADMISSION

7/11/81

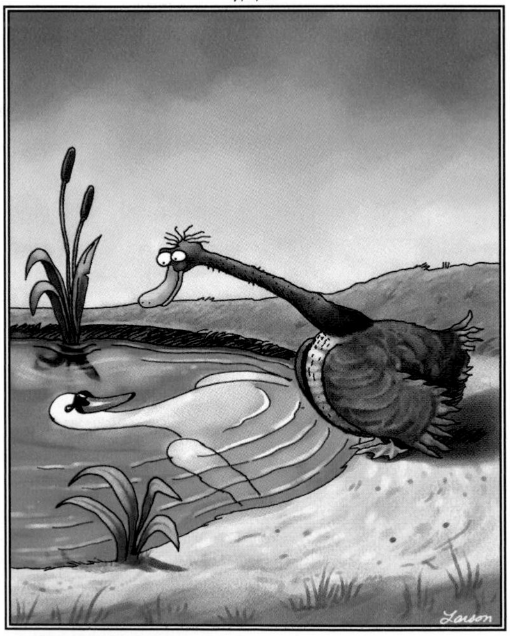

7/16/81

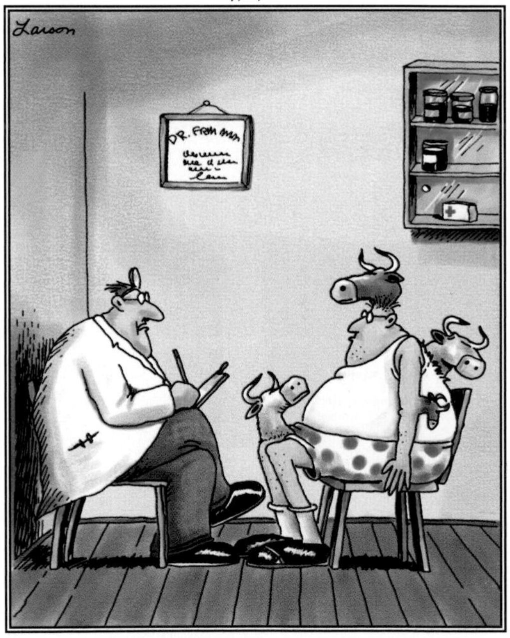

"I'm afraid you've got cows, Mr. Farnsworth."

7/20/81

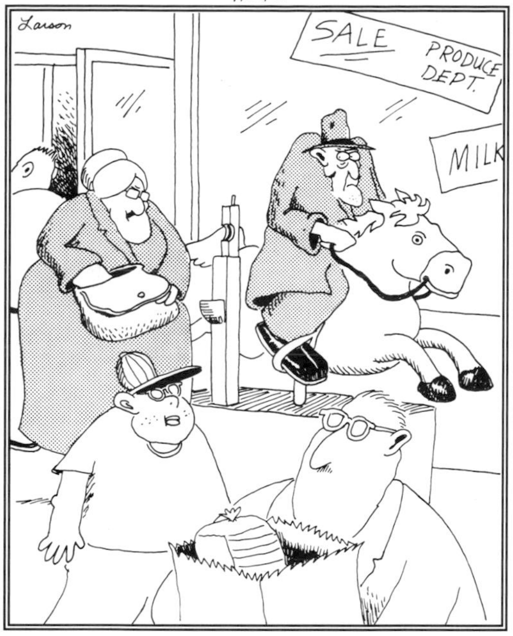
Larson
SALE
PRODUCE DEPT.
MILK

"Oh, all right, Barnaby! ... One more quarter and *then* we're going home!"

7/23/81

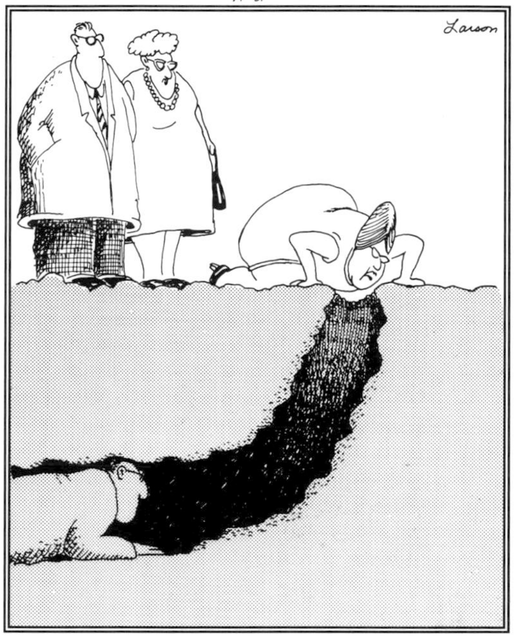
Larson

"Reuben! The Johnsons are here! You come up this instant ... or I'll get the hose!"

7/29/81

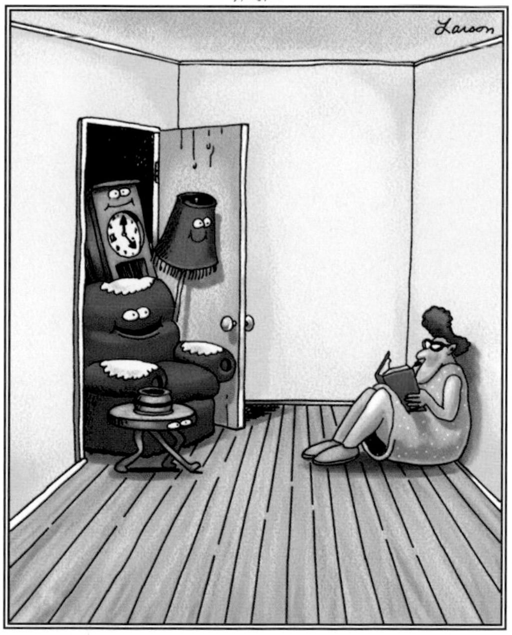
Larson

"Well, we're back!"

7/21/81

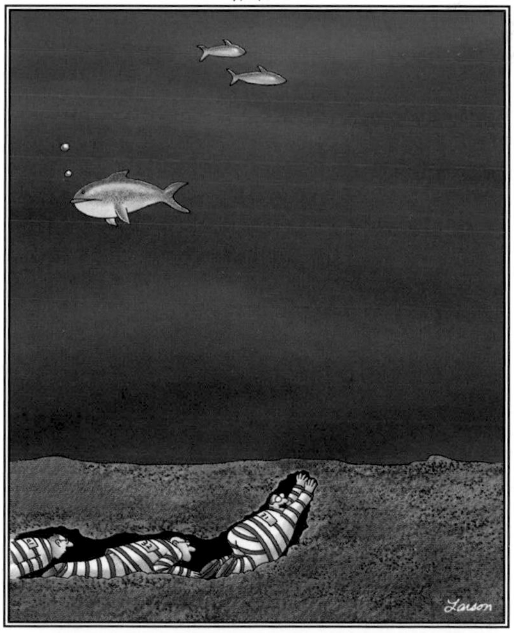
Larson

"We're almost free, everyone! I just felt the first drop of rain!"

7/22/81

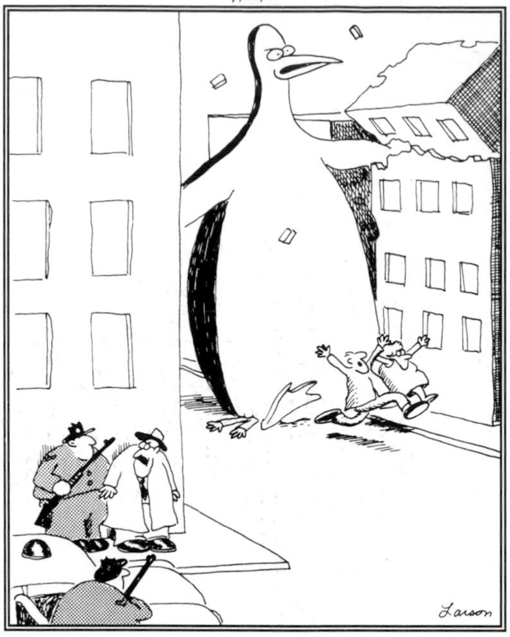
Larson

"Other cities get giant gorillas or dinosaurs. ... But what do *we* get?"

7/24/81

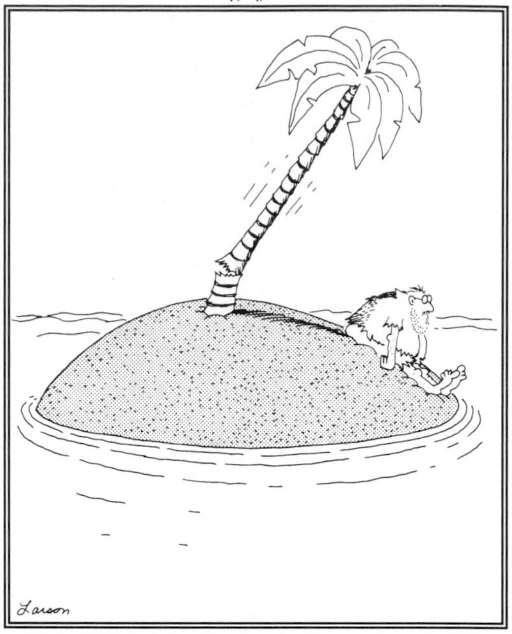
Larson

7/25/81

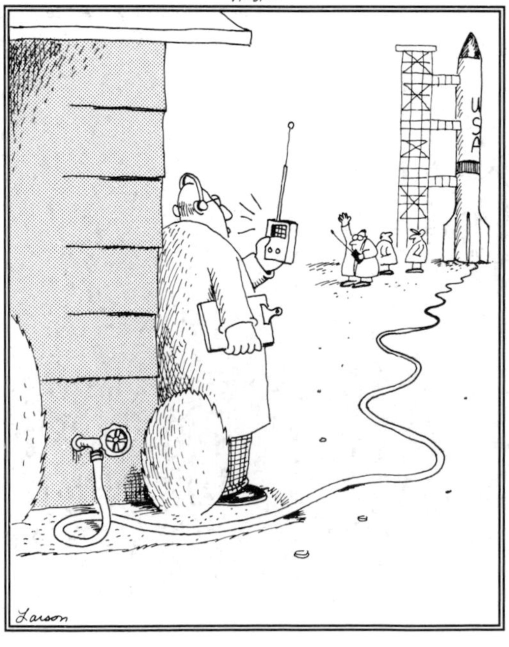
Larson

"Okay, Pete! Start the pressure nice and easy."

7/28/81

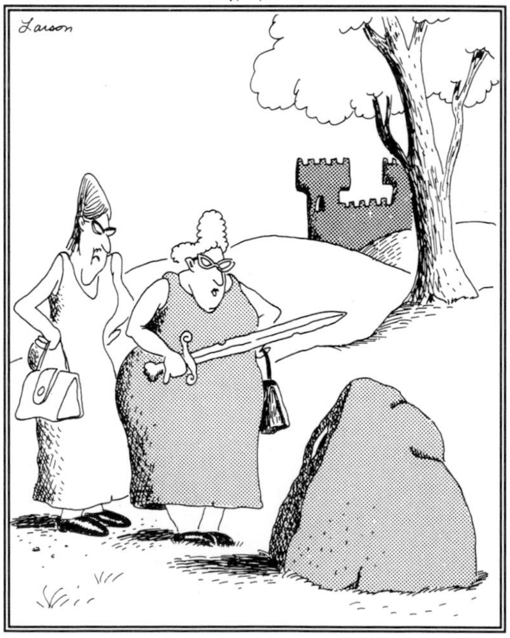
Larson

"Put it back in the rock, Barbara—you couldn't even slice a tomato with that old thing."

7/27/81

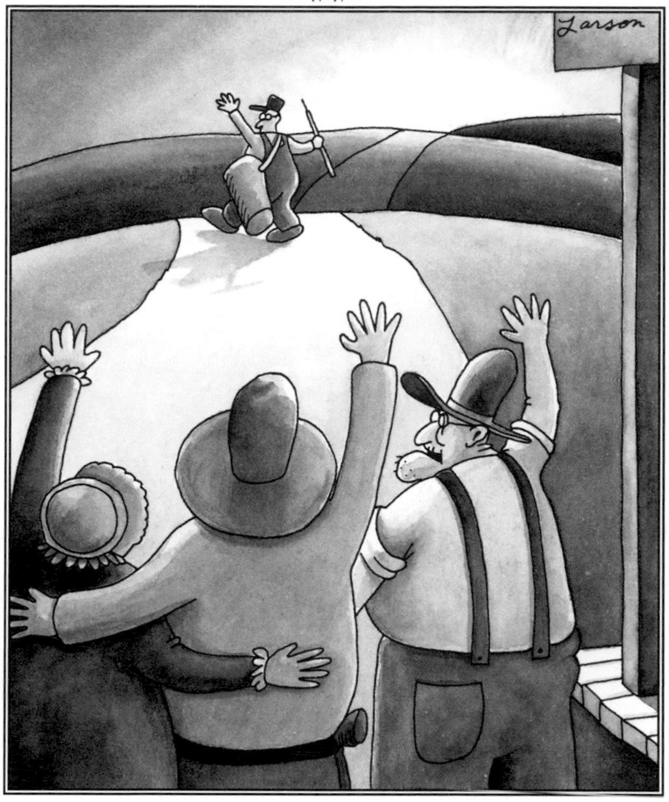
Larson

"I never got his name, but he sure cleaned up this town."

7/30/81

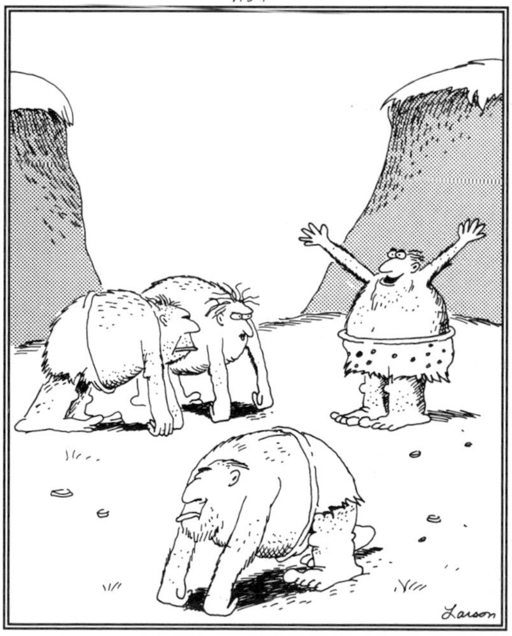
Larson

"Hey! Look! ... No hands!"

7/31/81

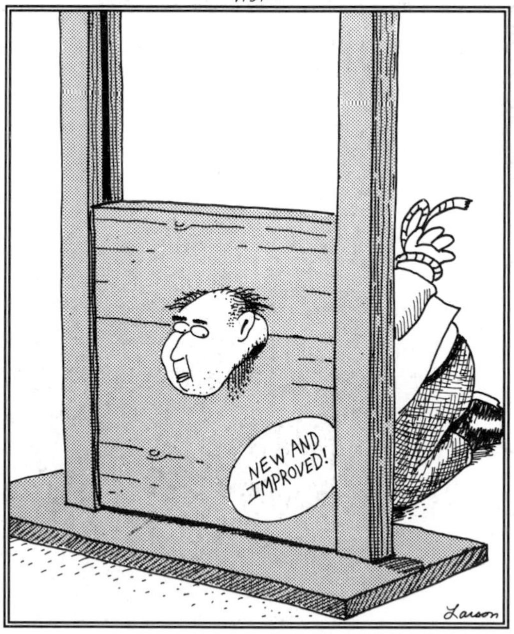
NEW AND IMPROVED!
Larson

August 1981

8/3/81

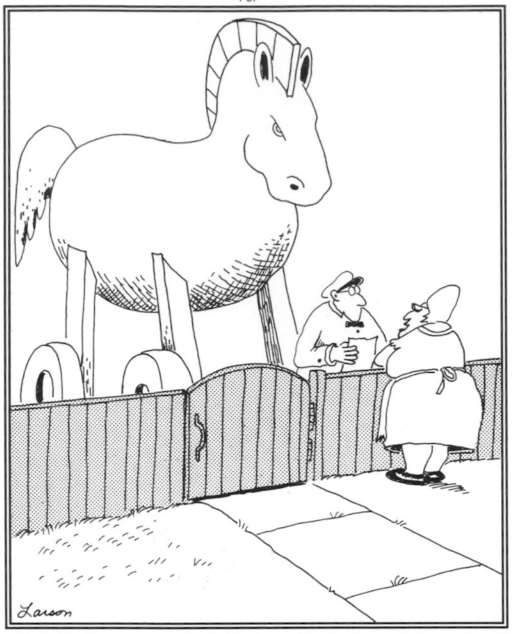
Larson

"No ... this is 221 Chestnut Drive. ... You want the big place around the corner."

8/1/81

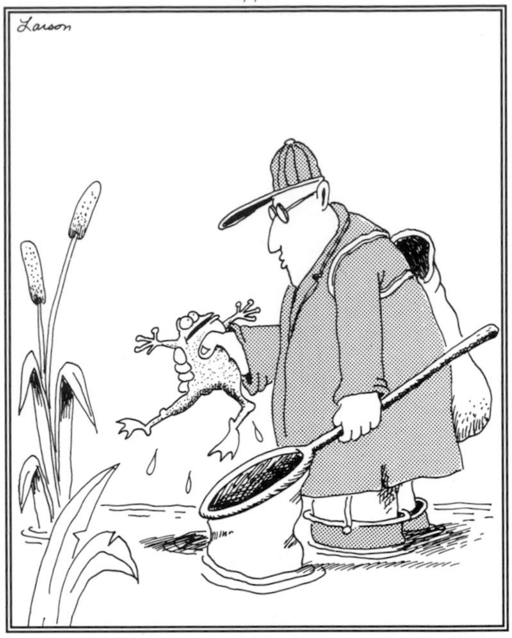
Larson

"Skinny legs! ... I got skinny legs!"

8/4/81

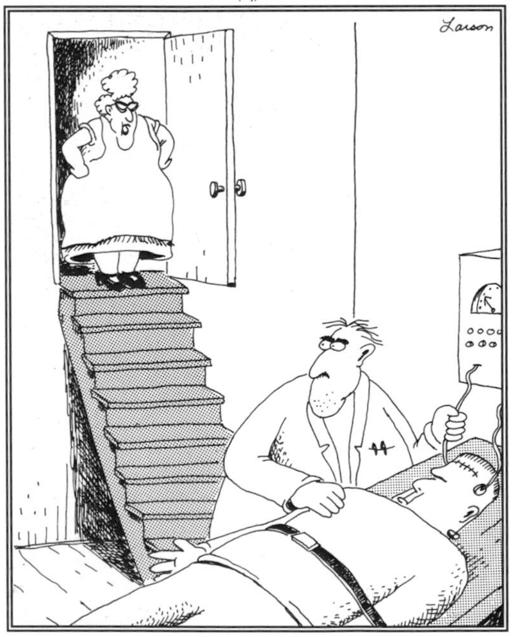
Larson

"Dear ... have you seen the beef brains I bought for supper tonight?"

8/5/81

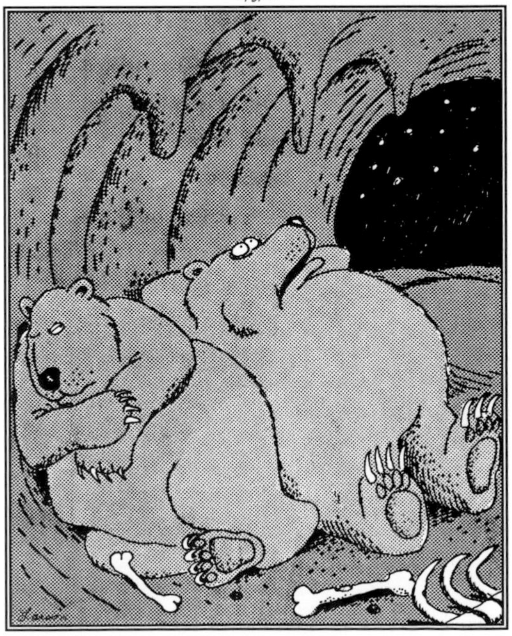
Larson

"Damn! ... I can't hibernate."

8/6/81

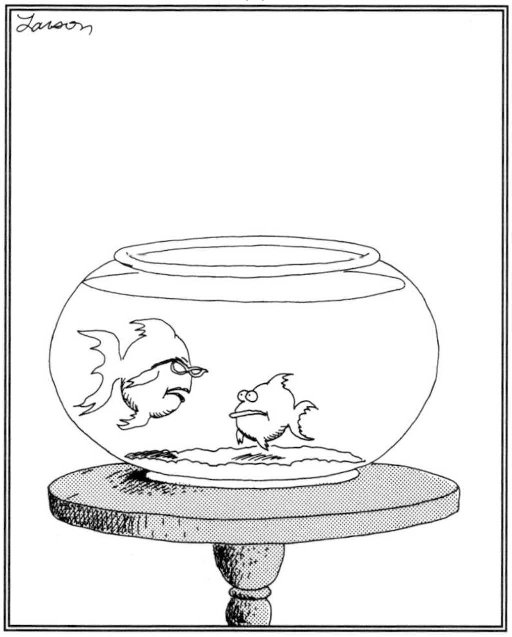
Larson

"That's not funny, Malcolm! There will be no more floating belly-up on the surface!"

8/11/81

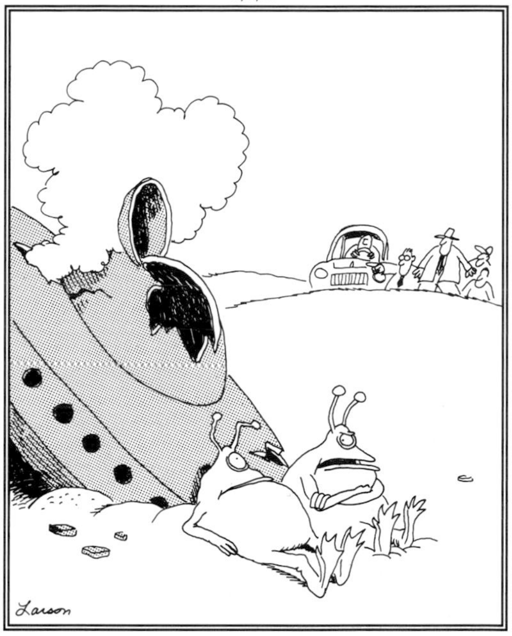
Larson

"I can't believe it! One lousy little bee gets inside and you just freak out!"

8/12/81

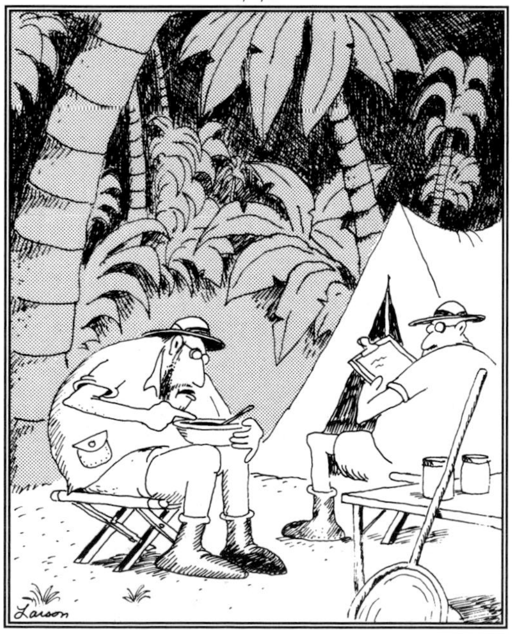
Larson

"Hey! What's this *Drosophila melanogaster* doing in my soup?"

8/14/81

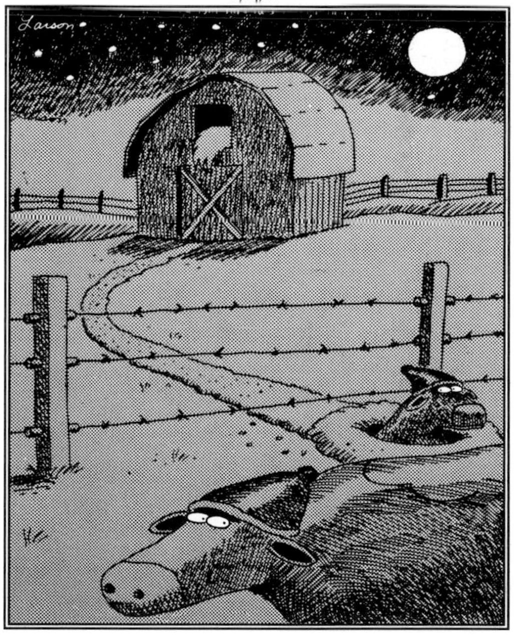
Larson

8/7/81

8/8/81

8/18/81

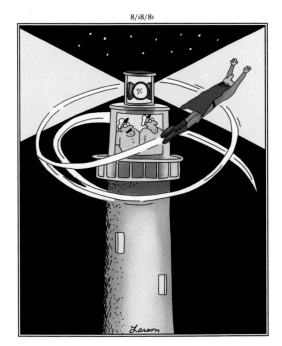

"For God's sake, kill the lights, Murray—
he's back again!"

8/10/81

8/19/81

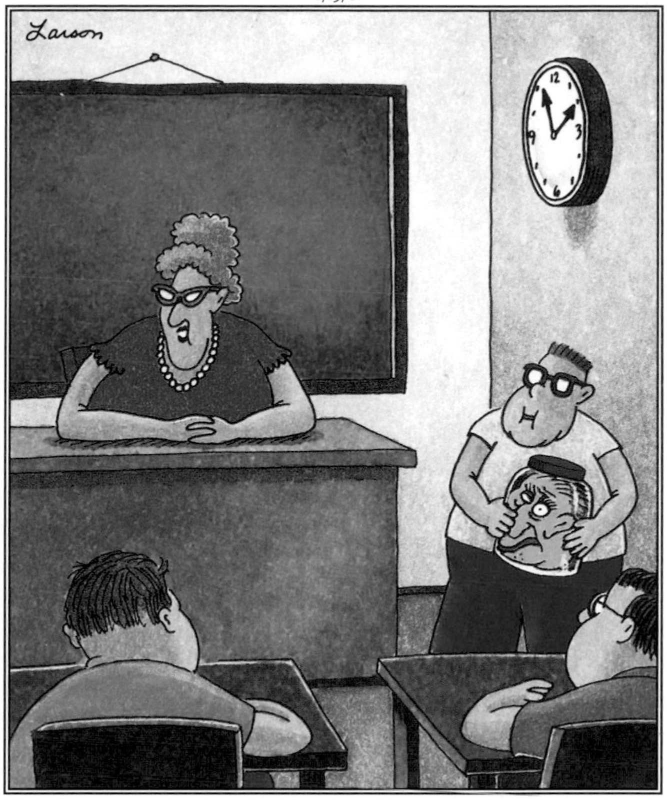
Larson

"And next, for show-and-tell, Bobby Henderson says he has something he found on the beach last summer. ..."

8/13/81

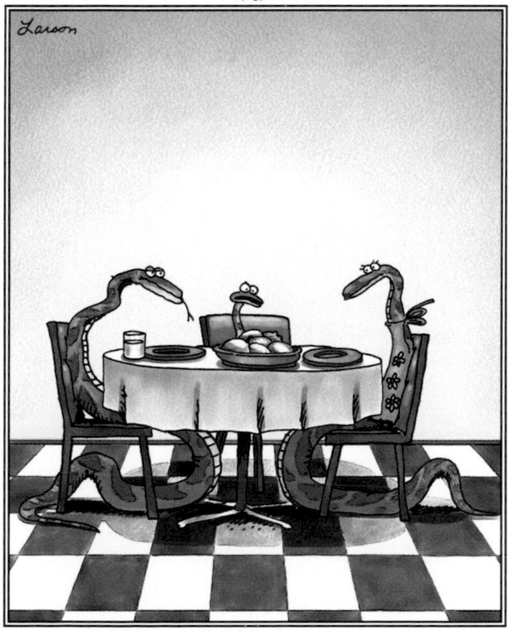
Larson

"Oh, brother! ... Not hamsters again!"

8/20/81

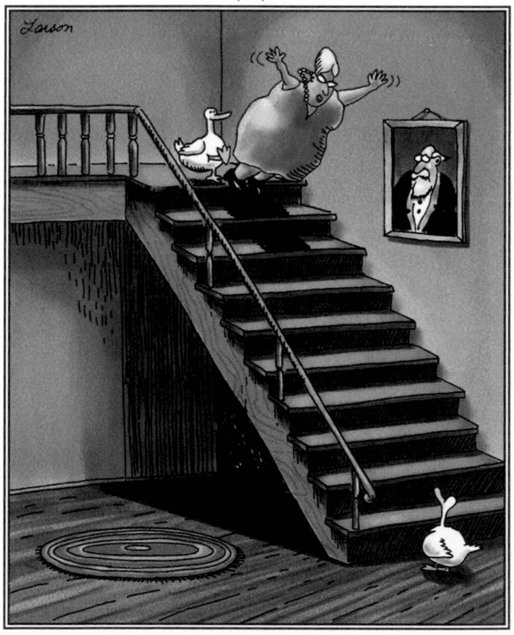
Larson

As the first duck kept Margaret's attention, the second one made its move.

8/15/81

8/17/81

"Blast it, Agnes! If you're going to put your cold feet on me, you could at least dry them first."

8/21/81

"Sure, I like her ... but she doesn't even know I exist."

8/22/81

"ALERT! ALERT! ... IT'S THE SUCKING DEATH!"

August 1981

8/24/81

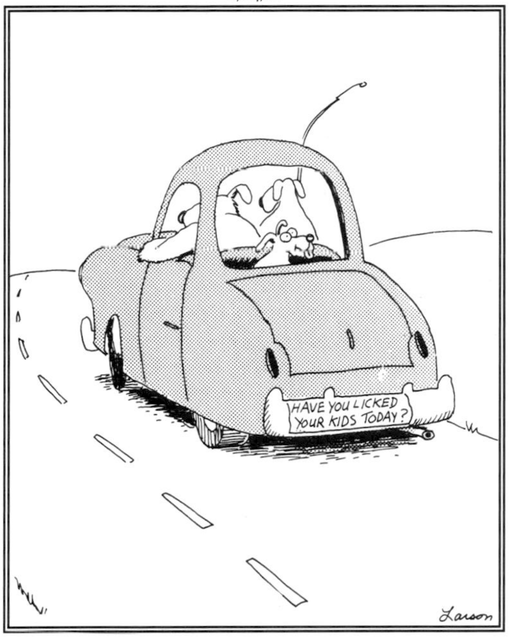
HAVE YOU LICKED YOUR KIDS TODAY?

8/26/81

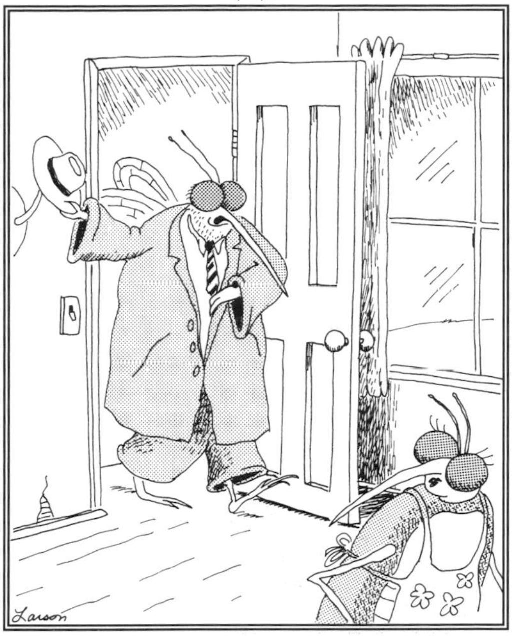

"What a day! I must have spread malaria across half the country."

8/29/81

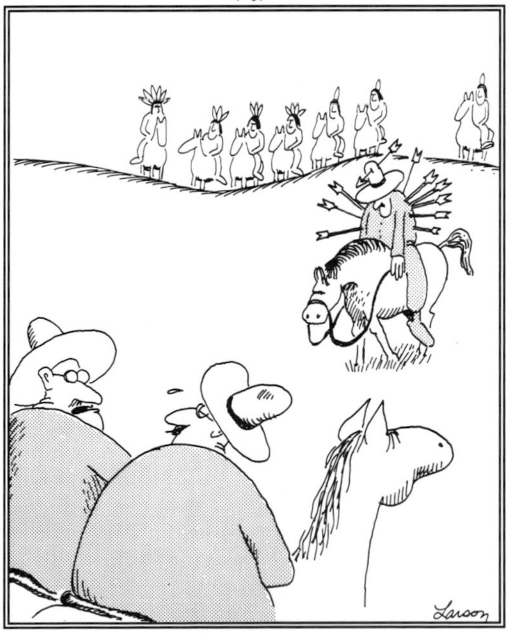

"Now stay calm. ... Let's hear what they said to Bill."

8/27/81

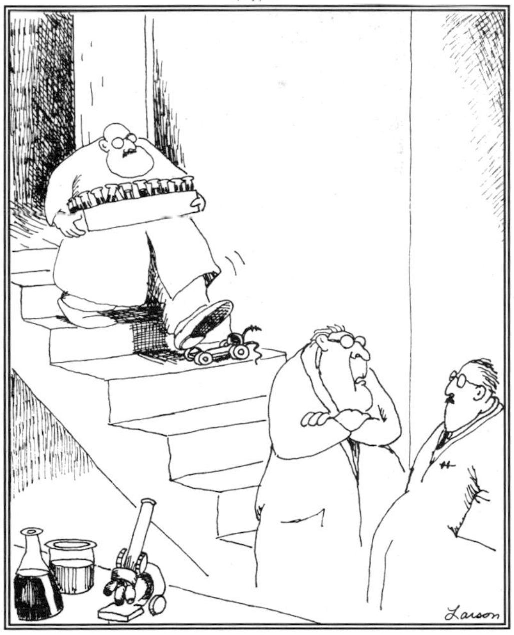

"And, as you shall soon observe, we are quite proud of our test tube baby progress."

8/25/81

"On the other hand, what if we aren't alone
in the universe?"

8/31/81

"So! ... You *still* won't talk, eh?"

8/28/81

9/5/81

9/2/81

"I can't believe this! Can't *anyone* here get
the lid off the mayonnaise?"

9/8/81

"You're kidding! I was struck twice by lightning too!"

149

9/1/81

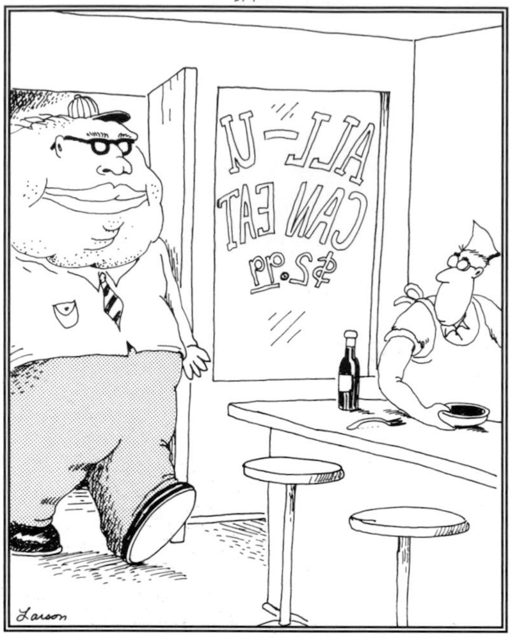
ALL-U
CAN EAT
$2.99
Larson

9/3/81

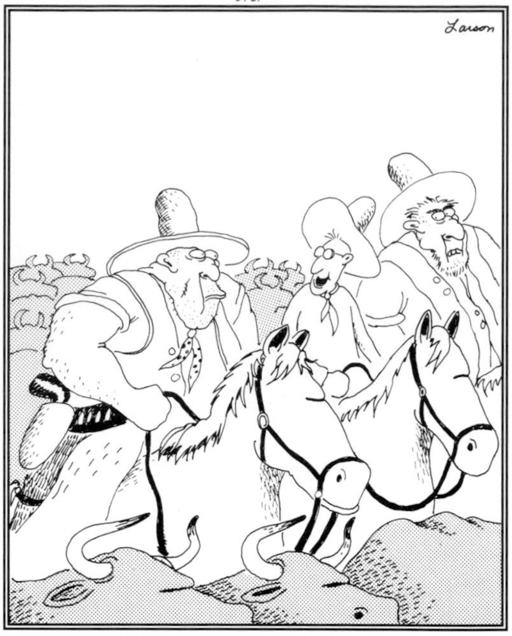
Larson

"Anyone for a chorus of 'Happy Trails'?"

9/4/81

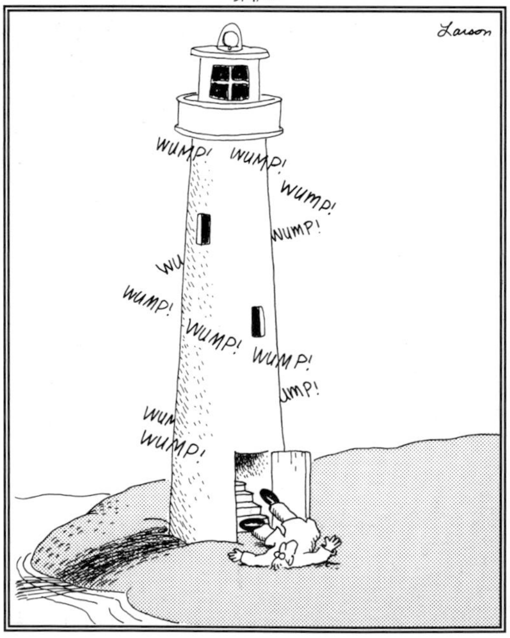
Larson
WUMP!
WUMP!
WUMP!
WUMP!
WUMP!
WUMP!
WUMP!
WUMP!

9/7/81

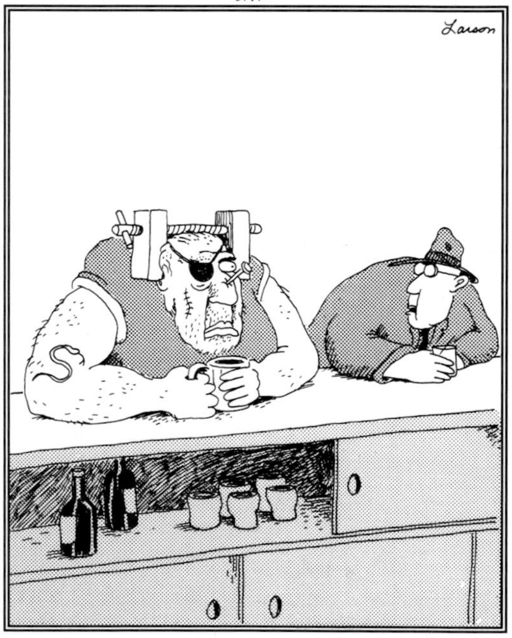
Larson

"Tough-guy, huh?"

9/9/81

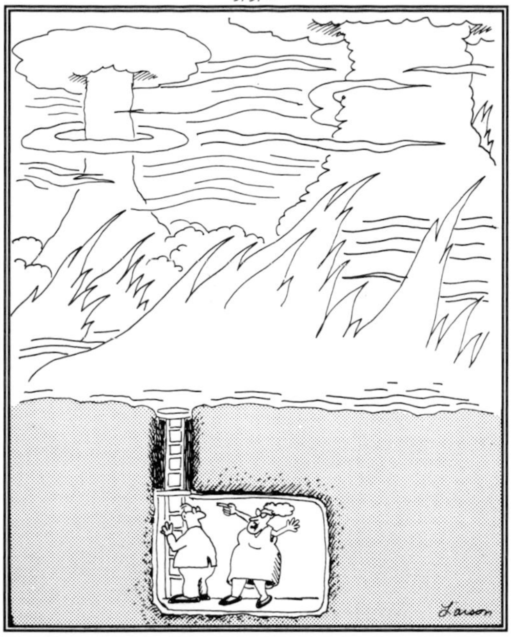
Larson

"Arnold! The bird! The bird! ... You get back up there and get the bird!"

9/10/81

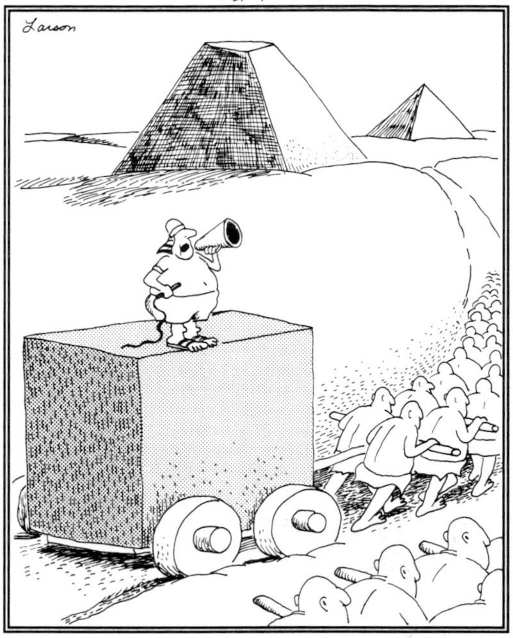
Larson

"C'mon, let's go! Remember Pharaoh's favorite mottoes: 'Many hands make light work, a job worth doing is worth doing well, and death to the laggard!'"

9/11/81

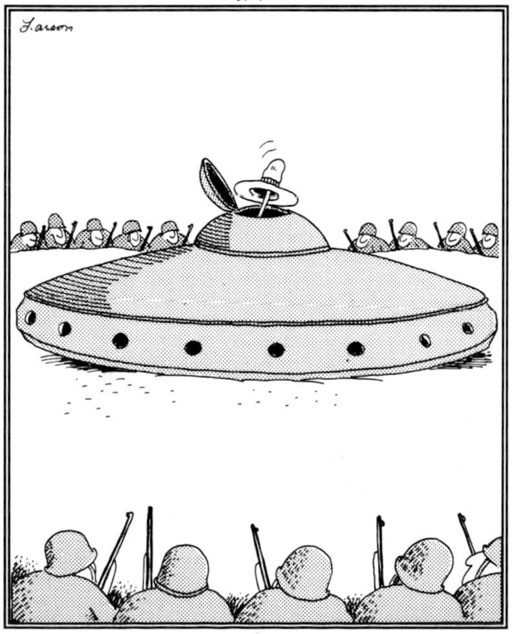
Larson

9/12/81

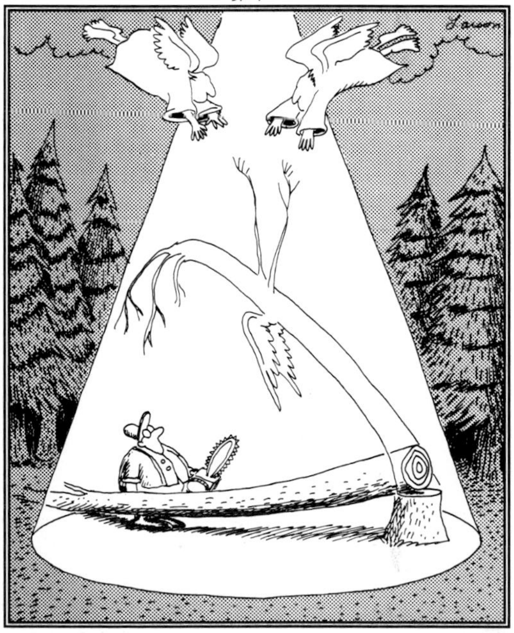
Larson

9/14/81

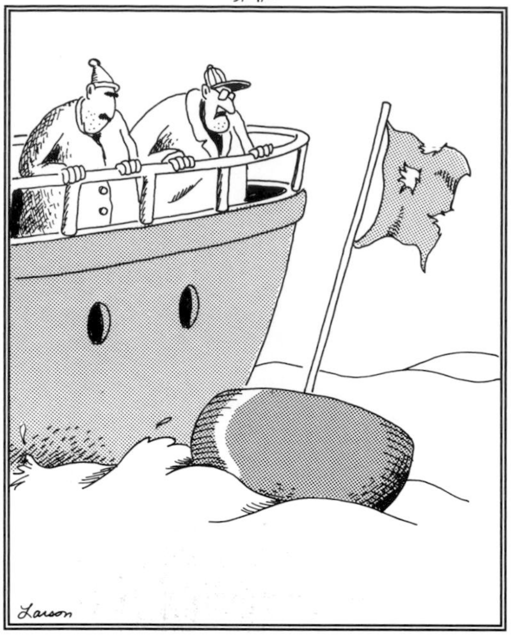
Larson

"What do you make of it, Earl? ... A small, pea-green boat, drifting way out here—empty, except for those two little skeletons."

9/15/81

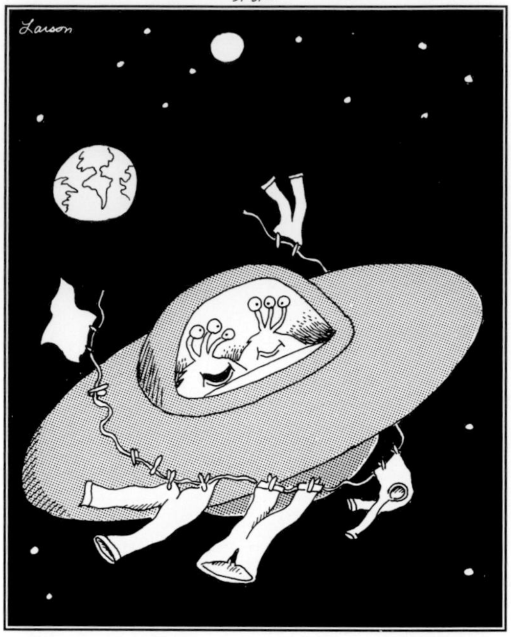
Larson

"I daresay there's a woman in Mayfield, Nebraska, who believes in UFOs."

9/16/81

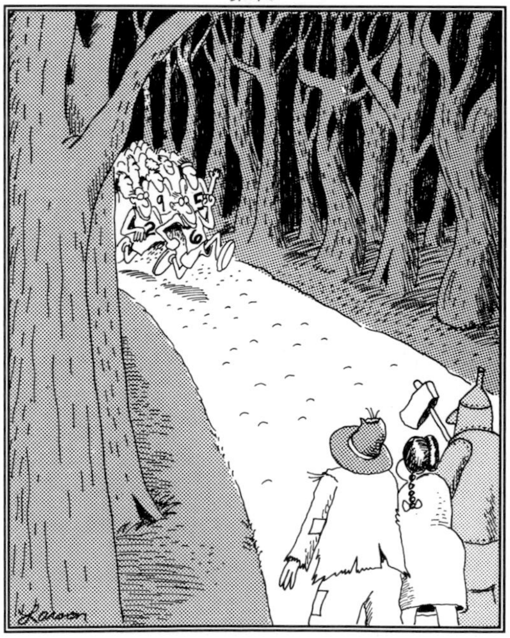
Larson

9/17/81

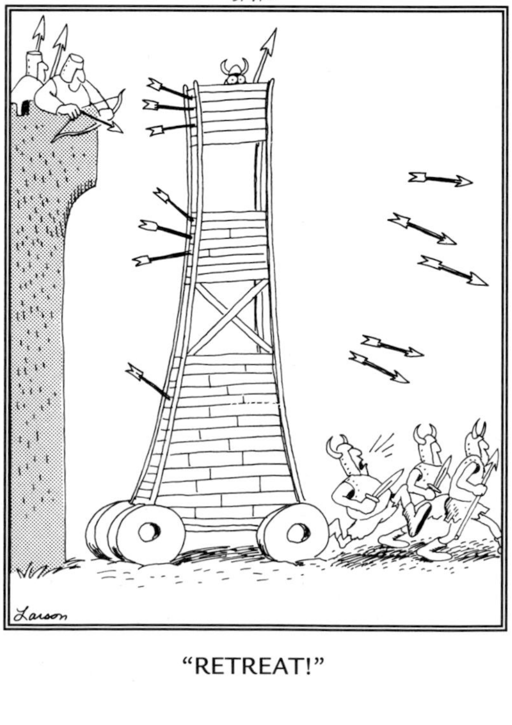
Larson

"RETREAT!"

9/18/81

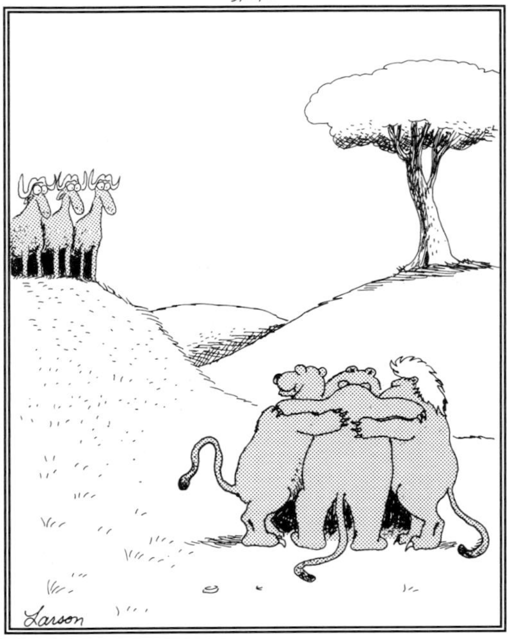

9/19/81

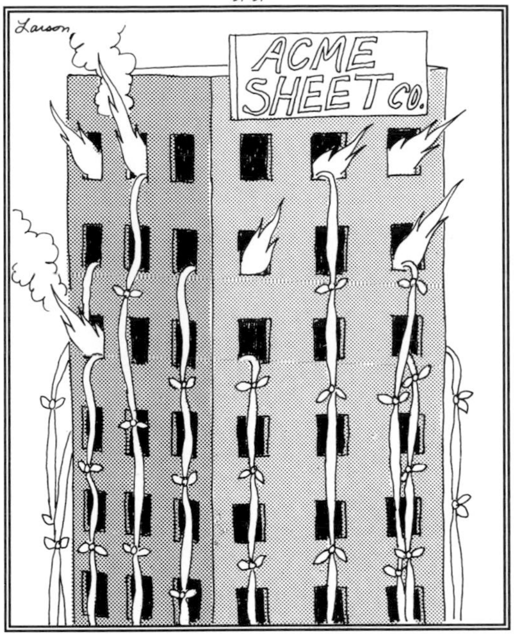
ACME SHEET Co.

9/21/81

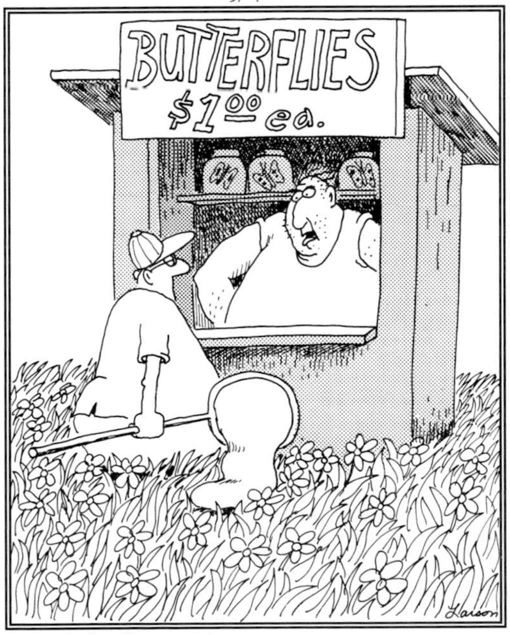
BUTTERFLIES
$1.00 ea.

"Well, they ain't free anymore, buddy."

9/23/81

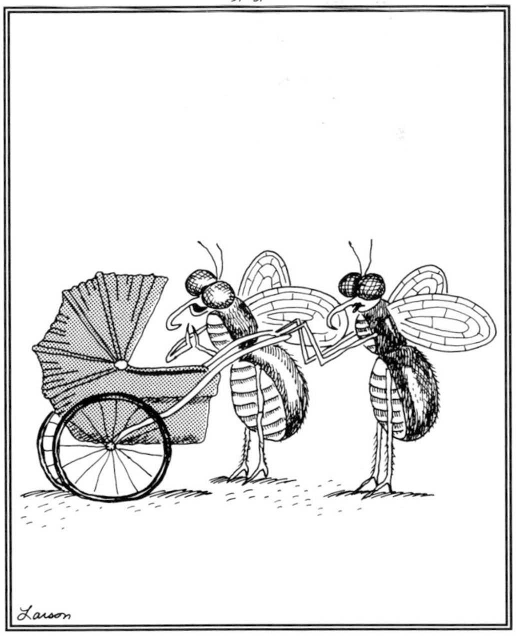

"Oh, my! ... What a *cute* little maggot!"

9/22/81

Larson

"Egad, Alex! I'm losing some wrinkles!"

9/24/81

Larson

"So! ... Out bob bob bobbing along again!"

9/25/81

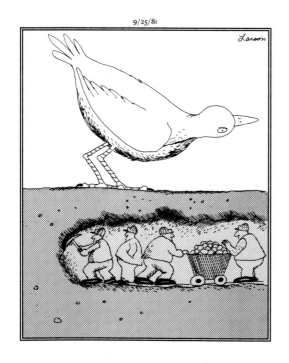

Larson

9/28/81

WORMS
50¢
doz.
Larson

"Well, I dunno. This one's a little beak-worn. ...
How much do you want for it?"

9/26/81

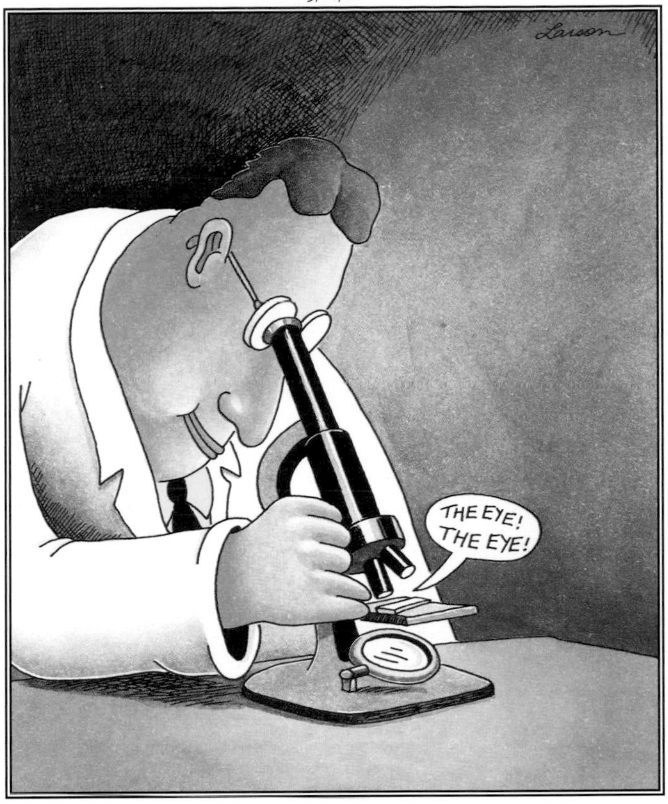
Larson
THE EYE! THE EYE!

9/29/81

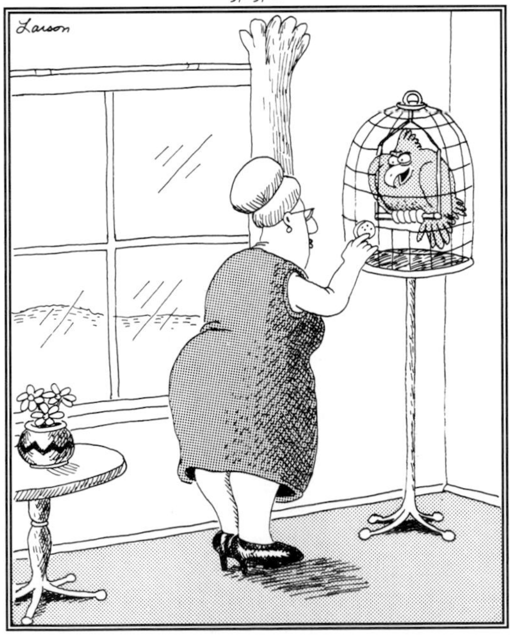
Larson

"Polly wanna finger."

9/30/81

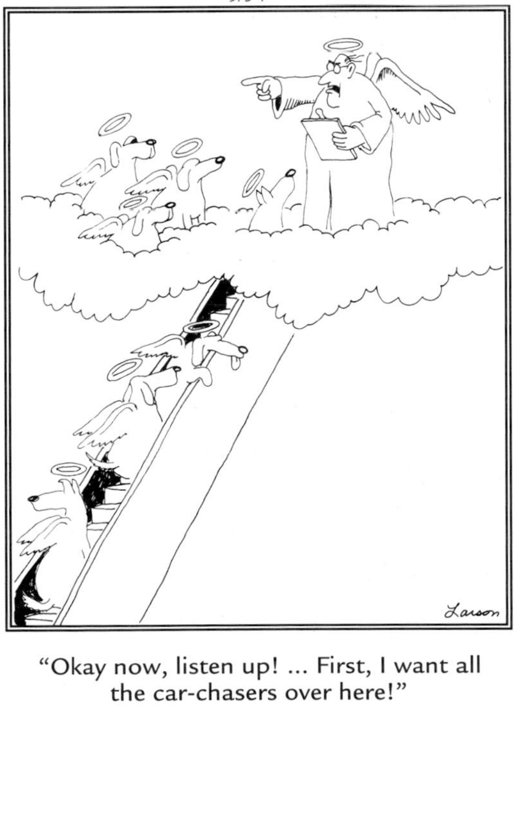
Larson

"Okay now, listen up! ... First, I want all the car-chasers over here!"

10/2/81

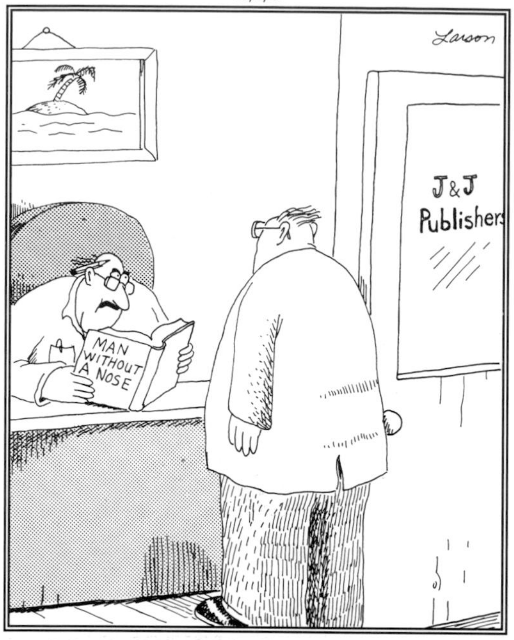
Larson
J&J
Publishers
MAN
WITHOUT
A NOSE

"Autobiography I presume?"

10/3/81

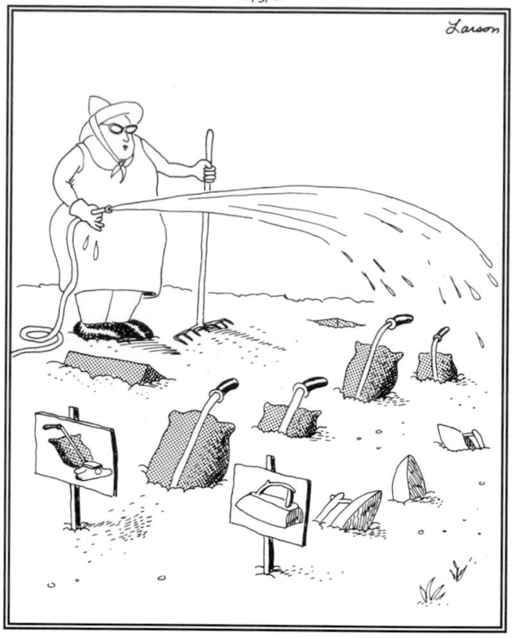
Larson

10/1/81

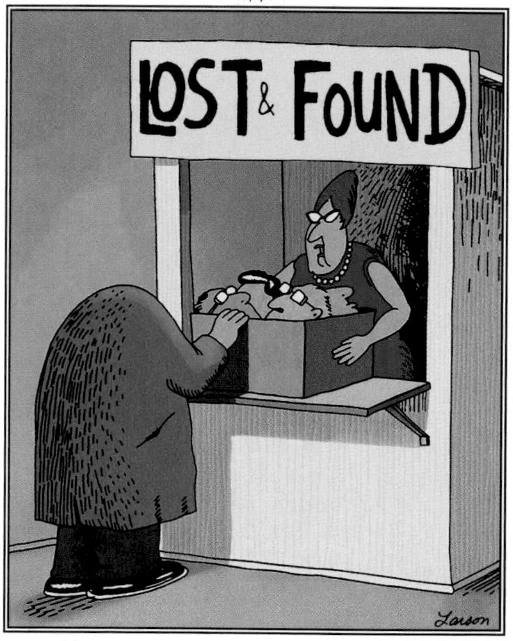
LOST & FOUND
Larson

"C'mon, c'mon! Either it's here or it isn't!"

10/6/81

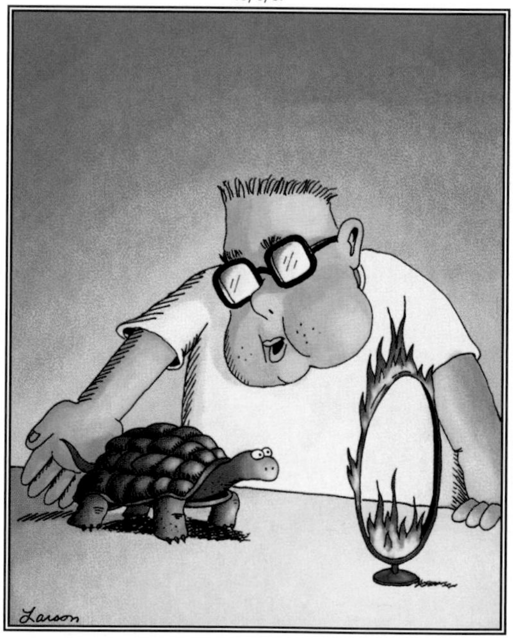
Larson

"Through the hoop, Bob! Through the hoop!"

October 1981

10/7/81

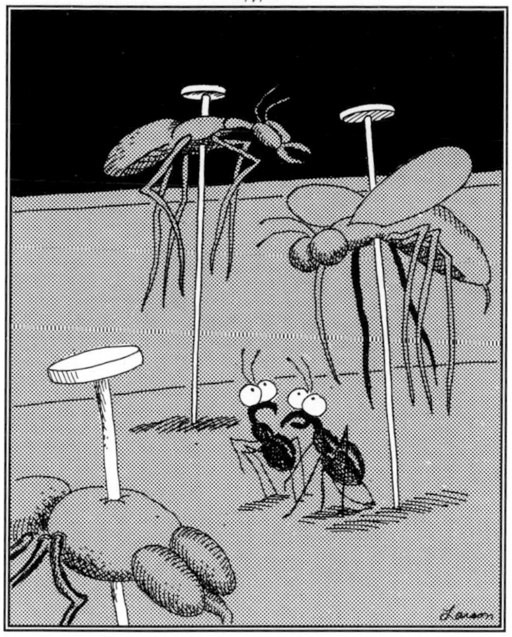
Larson

"Gad, I hate walking through this place at night."

10/5/81

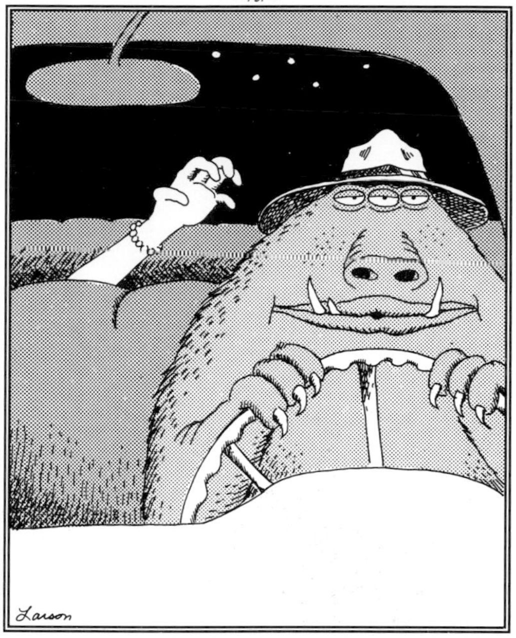
Larson

10/9/81

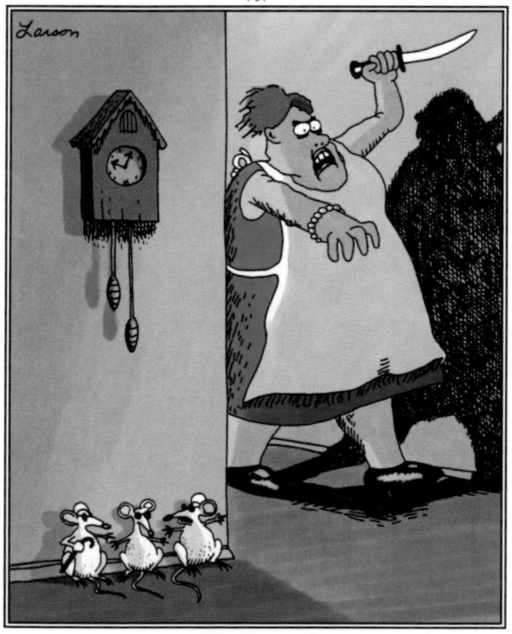
Larson

"Egad! ... Sounds like the farmer's wife has really flipped out this time!"

10/10/81

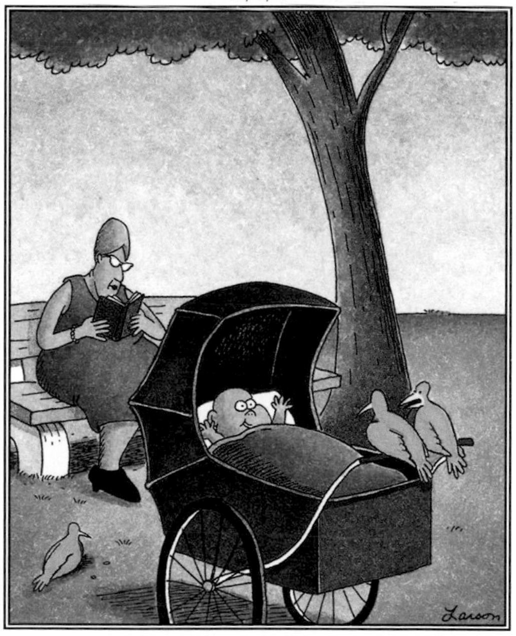
Larson

"It's still hungry ... and I've been stuffing worms into it all day."

10/8/81

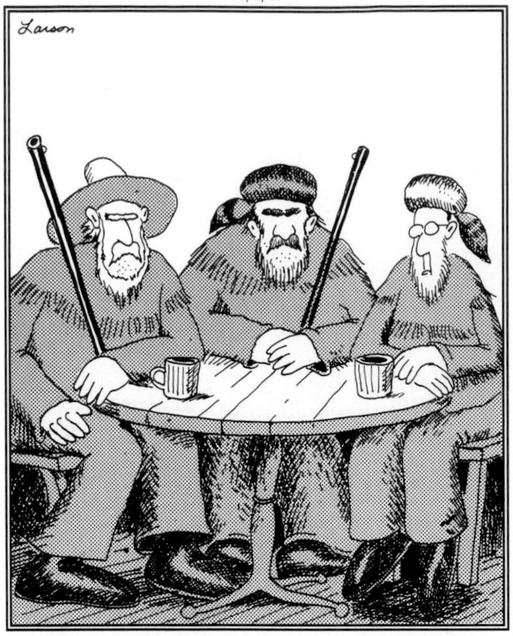
Larson

Buffalo Bill, Grizzly Adams, and Pigeon Jones

10/12/81

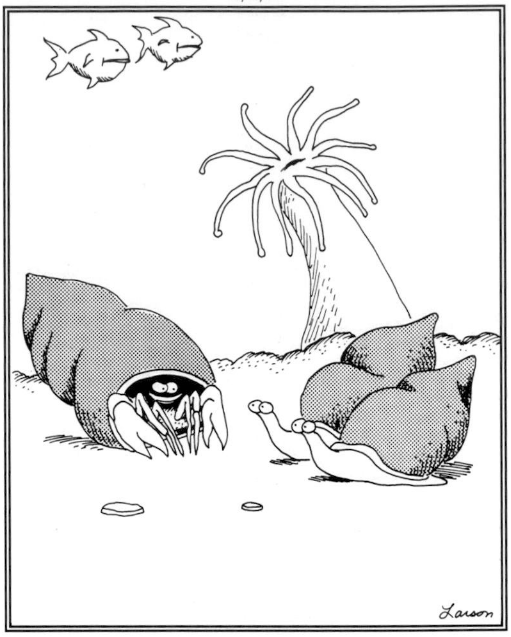
Larson

"Sorry—Carl doesn't live here anymore."

10/13/81

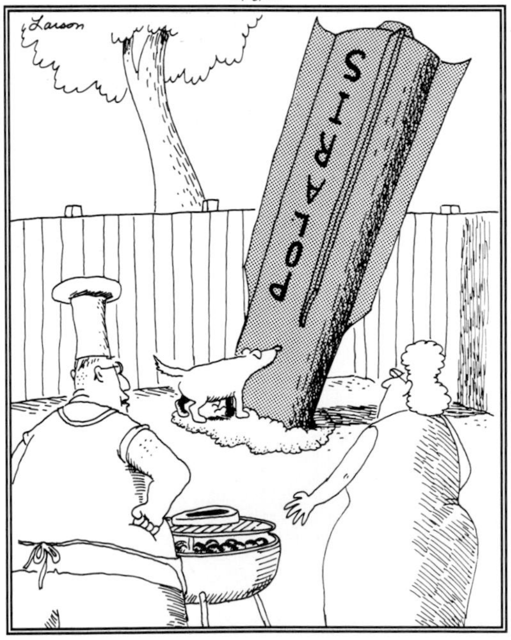
Larson

"Let's not overreact, Agnes. ... For one thing, it was only a dud."

10/14/81

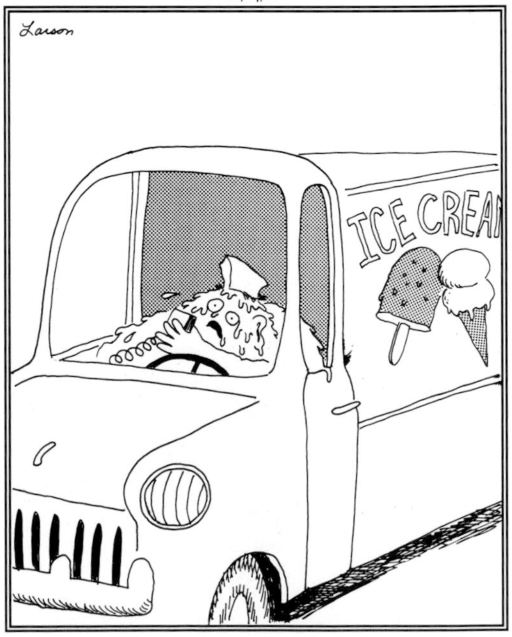
Larson
ICE CREA

"This is Harold Schwartz! ... Something horrible is happening out here!"

10/15/81

Larson

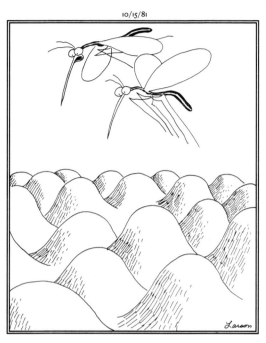

"Looks like this place has been pretty much sucked over."

10/21/81

Larson

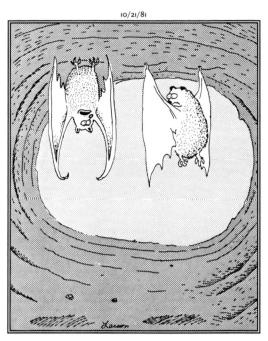

"Sure, go ahead—if you want the blood to rush to your feet."

10/22/81

Larson

"Sidney, just take one—don't handle every fly."

10/23/81

Goodbye
World
Larson

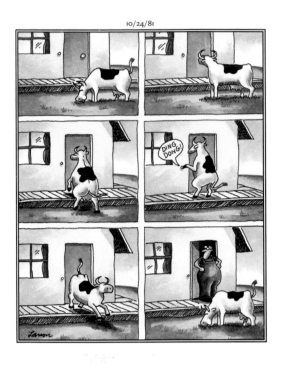

"C'mon! Look at these fangs! Look at these claws! You think we're supposed to eat just honey and berries?"

"Hey, wait a minute! This is grass! We've been eating grass!"

10/20/81

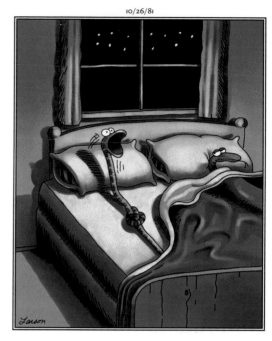

10/26/81

"CHARLEY HORSE!"

10/27/81

10/28/81

"Well, I'll be! Eggbeater must have missed that one."

10/30/81

10/31/81

10/29/81

"Counterclockwise, Red Eagle!
Always counterclockwise!"

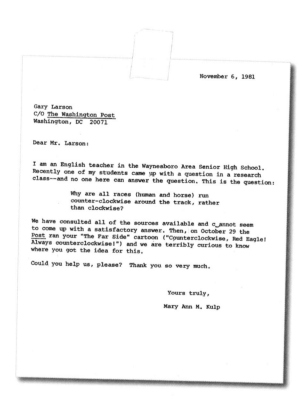

November 6, 1981

Gary Larson
C/O The Washington Post
Washington, DC 20071

Dear Mr. Larson:

I am an English teacher in the Waynesboro Area Senior High School.
Recently one of my students came up with a question in a research
class—and no one here can answer the question. This is the question:

Why are all races (human and horse) run
counter-clockwise around the track, rather
than clockwise?

We have consulted all of the sources available and c_annot seem
to come up with a satisfactory answer. Then, on October 29 the
Post ran your "The Far Side" cartoon ("Counterclockwise, Red Eagle!
Always counterclockwise!") and we are terribly curious to know
where you got the idea for this.

Could you help us, please? Thank you so very much.

Yours truly,

Mary Ann M. Kulp

11/2/81

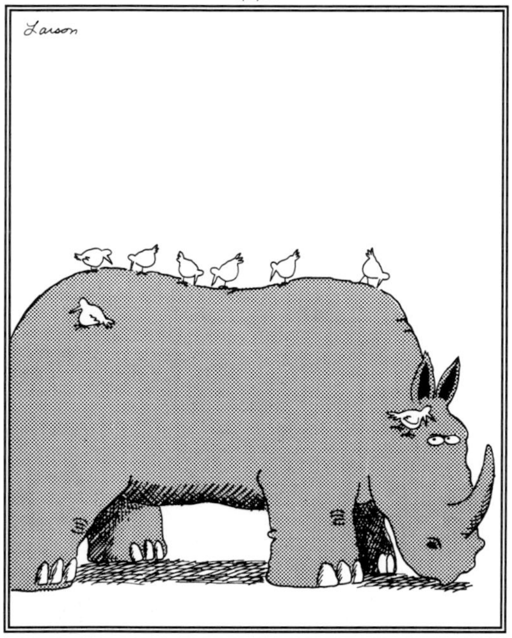
Larson

"Mind if we check the ears?"

11/3/81

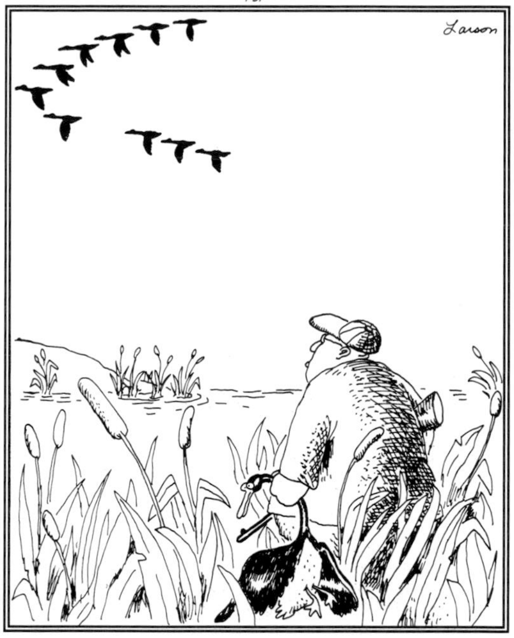
Larson

11/4/81

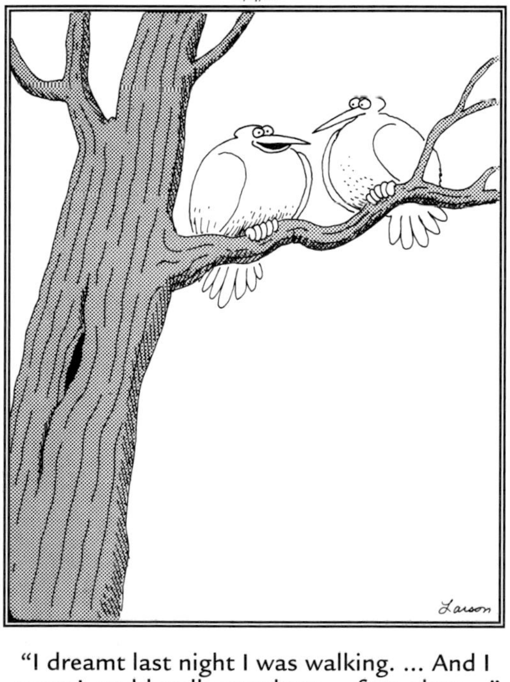
Larson

"I dreamt last night I was walking. ... And I mean I could walk anywhere ... fast, slow ..."

11/7/81

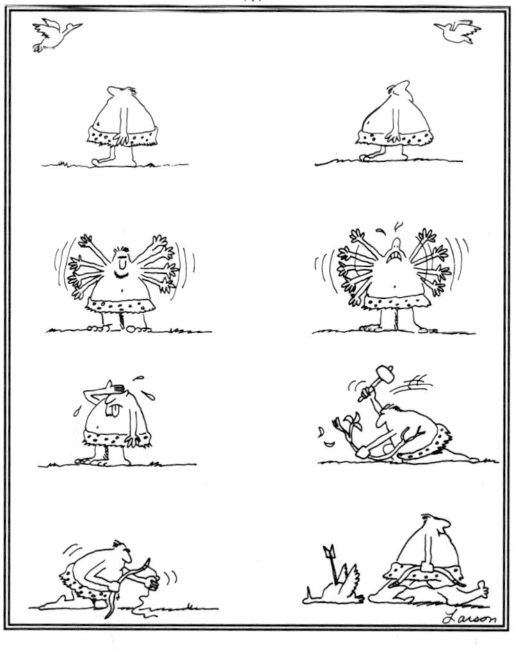
Larson

11/5/81

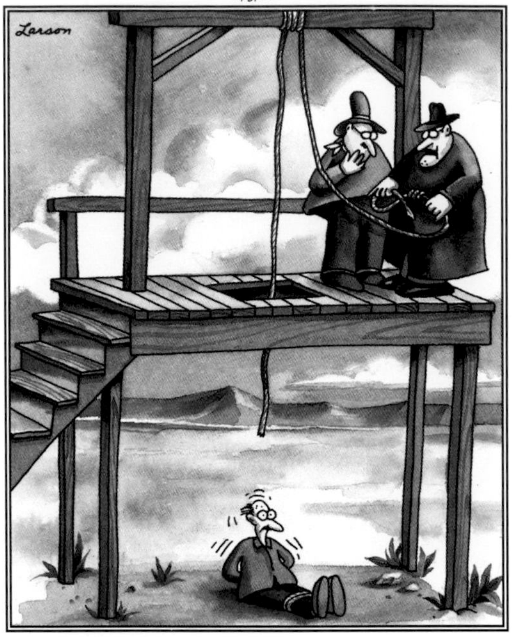
Larson

"You meathead! Now watch! ... The rabbit goes through the hole, around the tree five or six times ..."

11/6/81

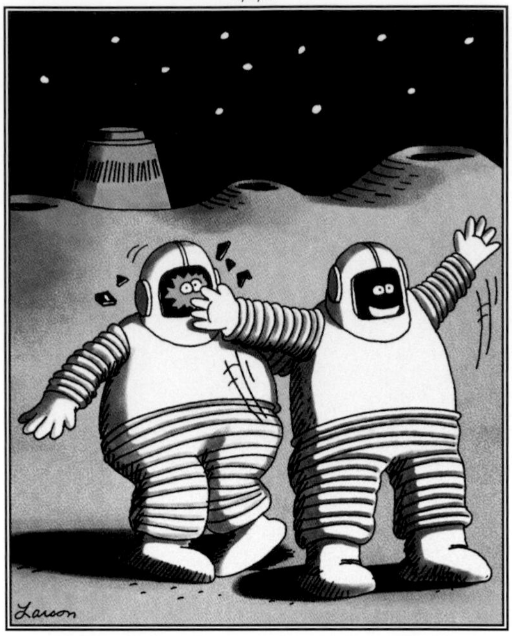
Larson

"We've made it, Warren! ... The moon!"

11/9/81

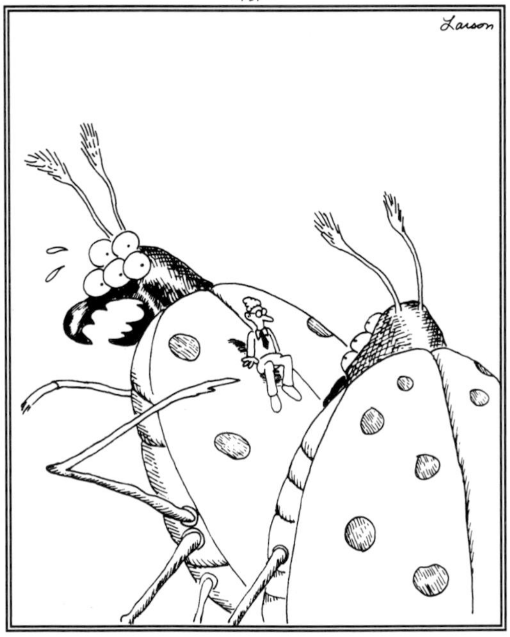
Larson

"Get it off me! Get it off me!"

11/10/81

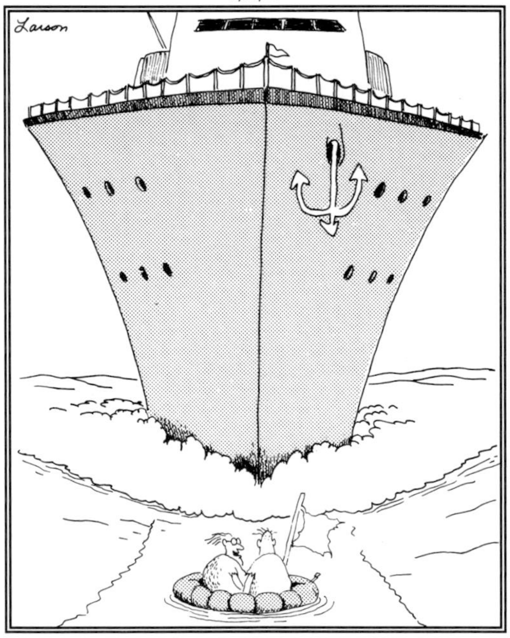
Larson

"Thank goodness, Malcolm! We've finally been spotted!"

11/11/81

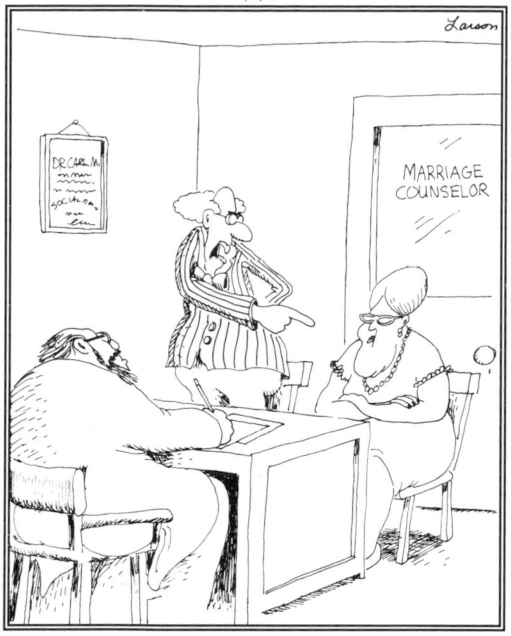
Larson
MARRIAGE COUNSELOR

"Bozo? Did you hear that?
She called me a bozo!"

11/12/81

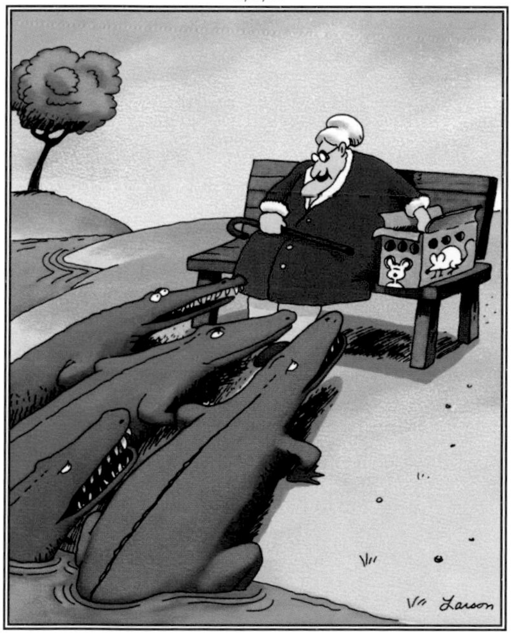
Larson

"Yes, yes ... now don't fuss. ... I have
something for you all."

11/13/81

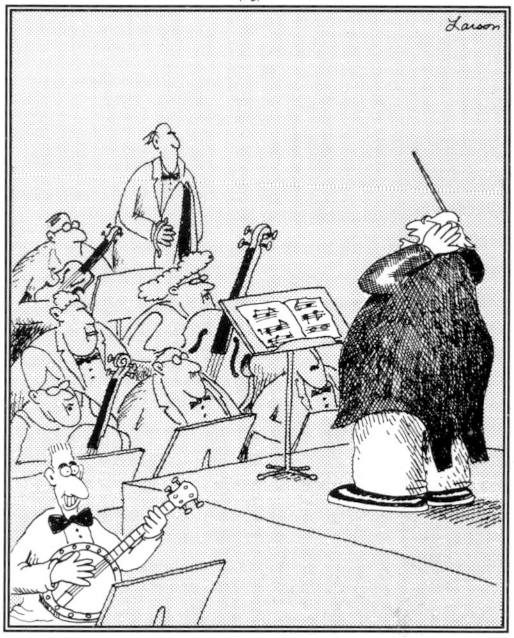
Larson

"Stop! Stop! What's that sound?
What's that sound?"

11/14/81

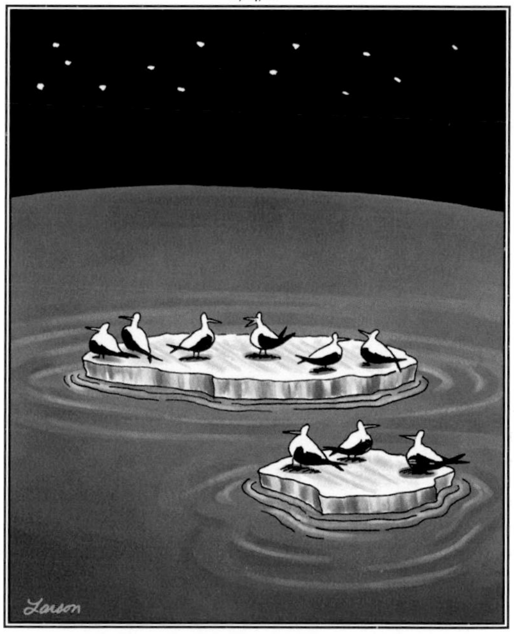
Larson

"You imbecile! We flew 12,000
miles for THIS?"

"First the good news, sir! ... I count only one Indian!"

"Uh-oh! It says here: 'A good mimic, this bird should not be exposed to foul or abusive sounds.'"

11/19/81

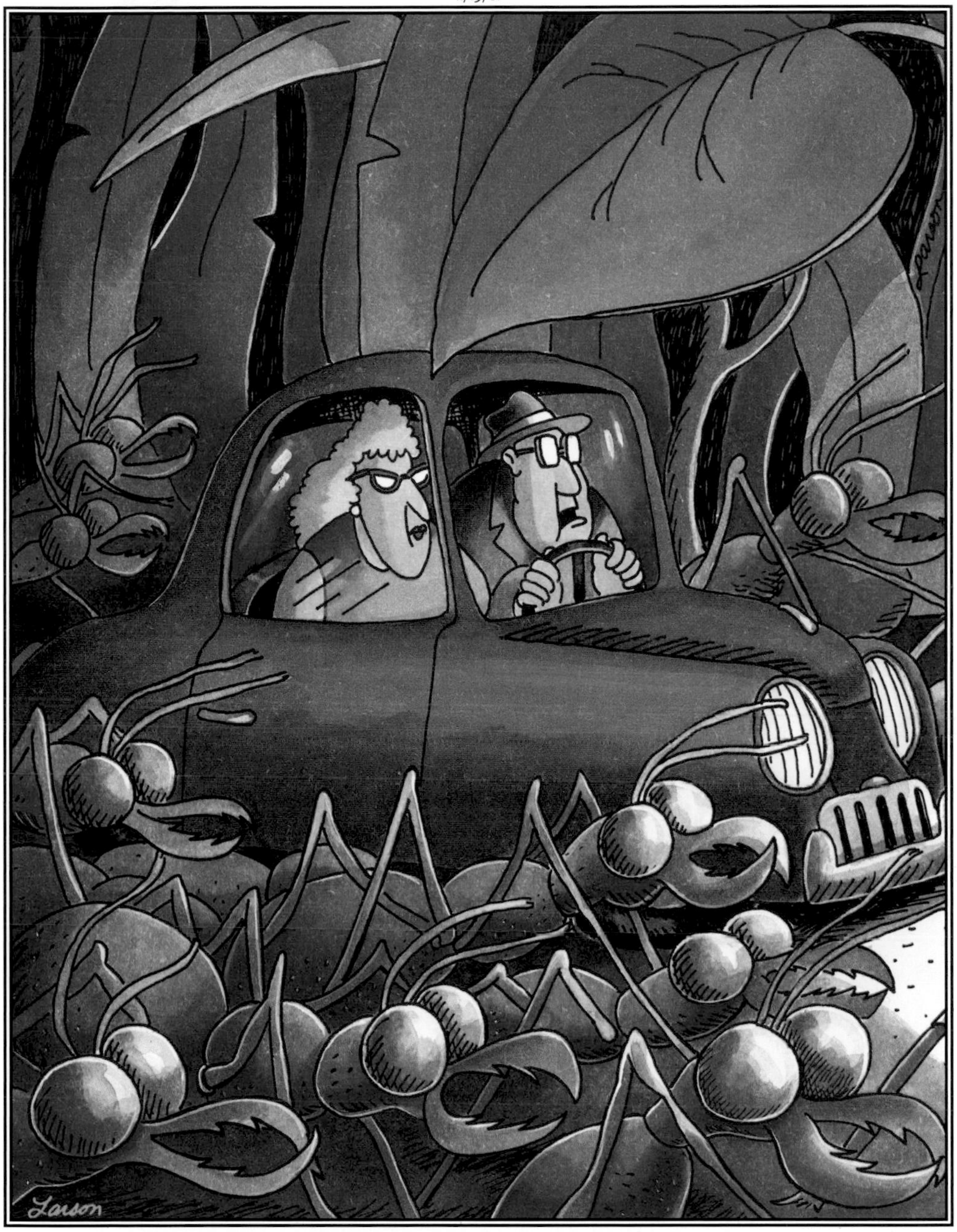
Larson

"Something's wrong here, Harriet. This is starting to look less and less like Interstate 95."

11/21/81

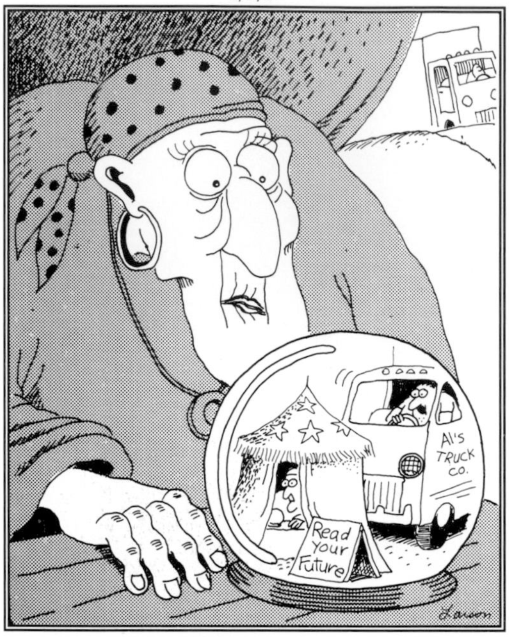
Al's
TRUCK
CO.
Read
Your
Future
Larson

11/23/81

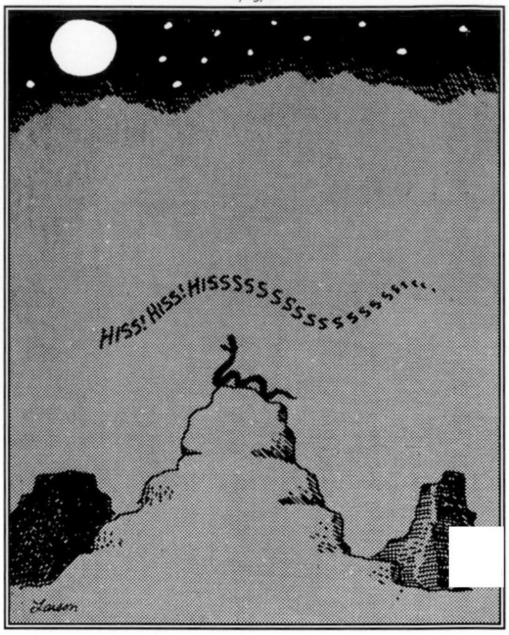
HISS! HISS! HISSSSSSSSSSSSSSSSSSS...
Larson

11/24/81

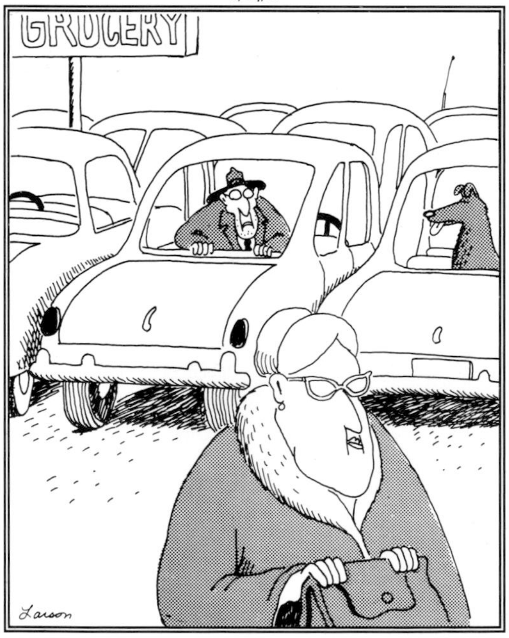
GROCERY
Larson

11/25/81

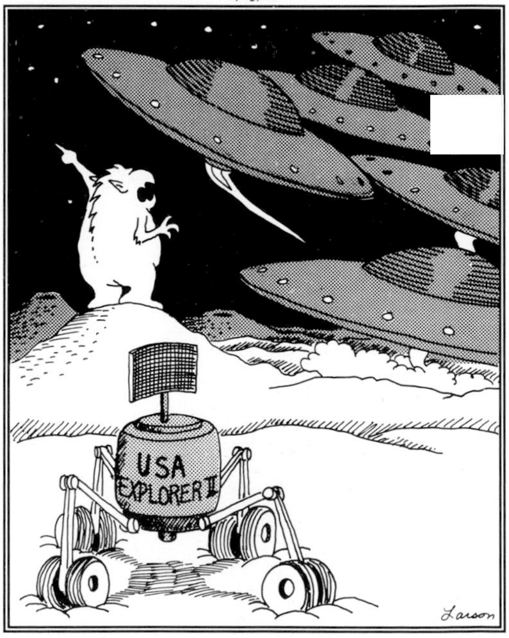
USA
EXPLORER II
Larson

"FIND THEM!"

11/26/81

11/27/81

11/28/81

11/30/81

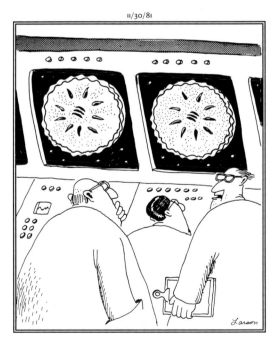

"We estimate it to be 7,000 kilometers in diameter, 130,000 kilometers away—and we're on a collision course!"

12/2/81

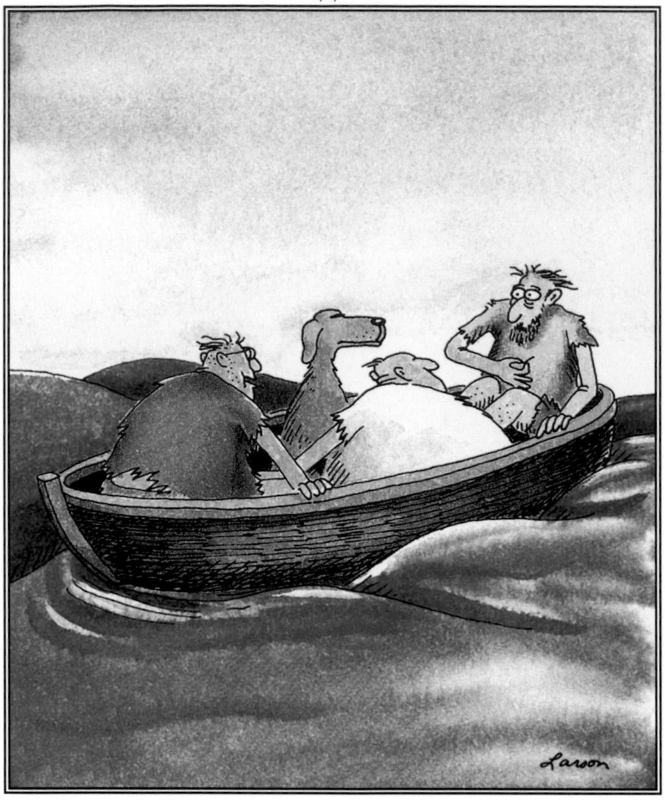
Larson

"Fair is fair, Larry. ... We're out of food, we drew straws—you lost."

12/1/81

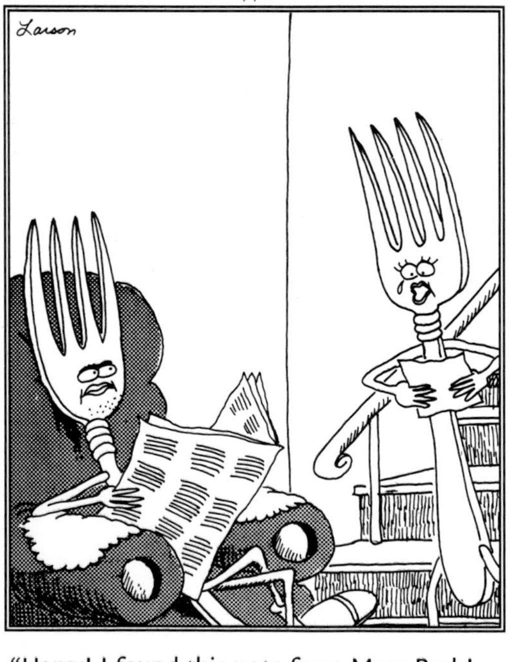
Larson

"Harry! I found this note from Mary Beth! ... She's run off with a spoon!"

12/3/81

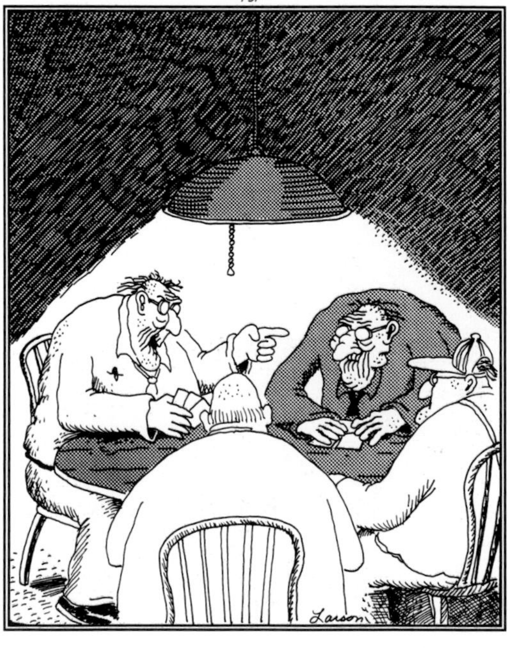
Larson

"Ha! I knew you were bluffing, Amos! You never did have much of a poker face!"

December 1981

12/5/81

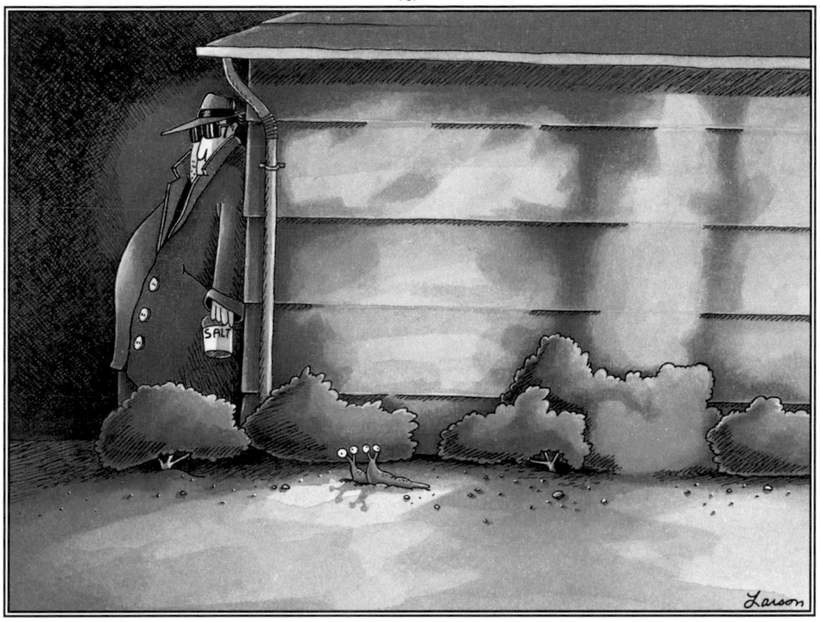
SALT
Larson

12/4/81

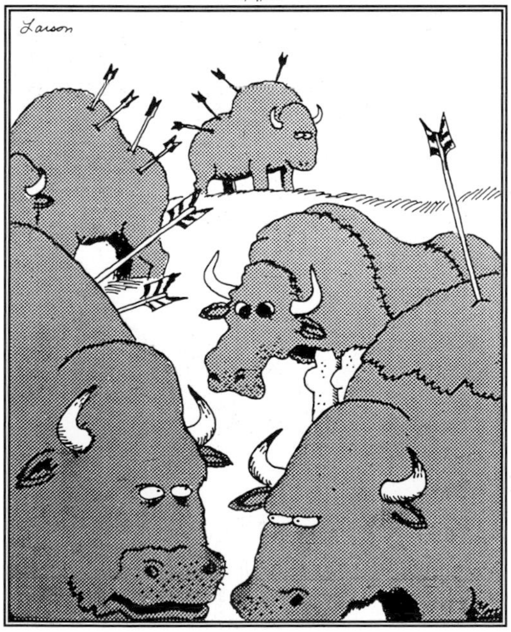
Larson

"Say ... maybe it's not just a bad swarm of horseflies."

Comics Editor
Minneapolis Tribune
Minneapolis, Minnesota

I am quite liberal when it comes to various types of comics and even go so far as to enjoy the cartoons and jokes in magazines like Playboy and High Society.

But I must strongly protest the cartoon; The Far Side, by Gary Larson. A sample is attached.

Larson has some kind of sickness in that he has to portray animals in some kind of suffering situation. I think we have enough people in the world who inflict pain on helpless animals and we don't have to encourage this craziness on the comic pages.

I am able to accept comics that deal with people-to-people violence simply because people have some control over how they may or may not feel toward each other. I cannot stomach the violence of people against animals who have no way of knowing when danger is imminent.

The Minneapolis Tribune should drop The Far Side until Gary Larson completes psychotherapy to overcome his problem. The Far Side does not represent humor. It represents illness.

Please send Gary Larson a copy of this letter. He needs to know that a whole lot of people don't think he's funny.

Thanks very much.

R. E. Enger
Minneapolis

P.S. I should add that the Minneapolis Tribune comic page is excellent (expect for an occasional Far Side) and urge you not to eliminate any of its other fine comics.

"So ... you must be the one they call Mr. Long."

"Thank God, Sylvia! We're alive!"

"Okay, buddy. Then how 'bout the right arm?"

December 1981

12/10/81

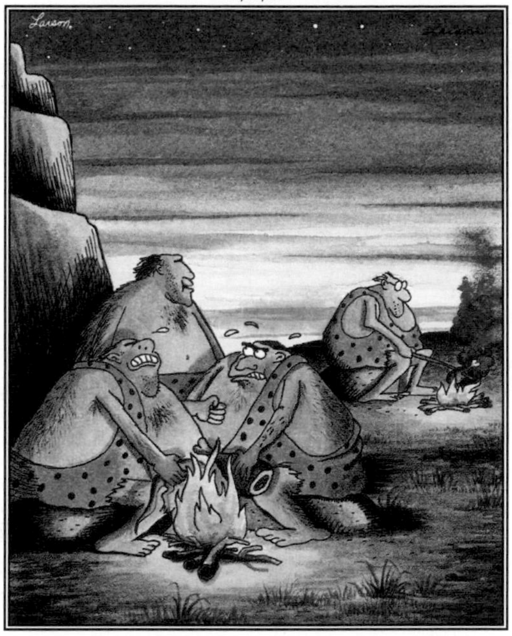

"Hey! Look what Zog do!"

12/14/81

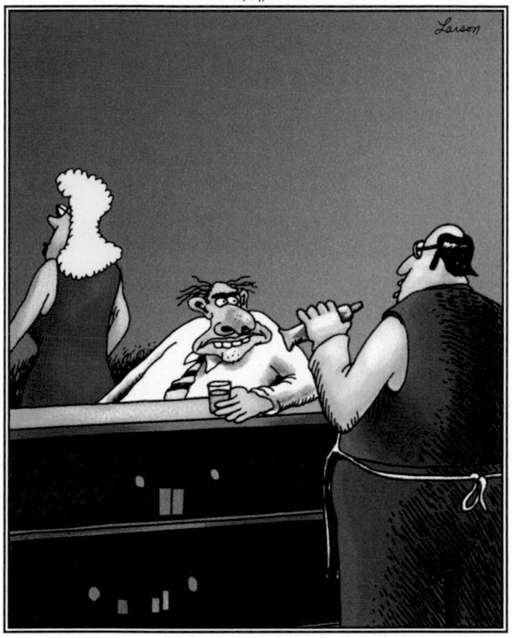

"Rejected again, huh Murray? Have you heard about this new breath-freshening toothpaste?"

12/12/81

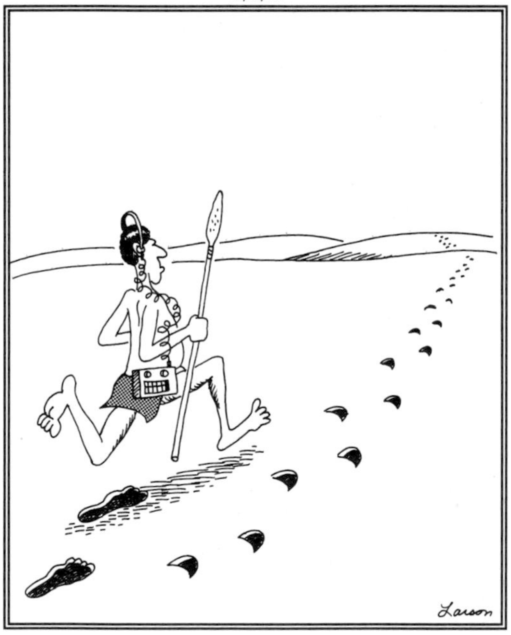

12/15/81

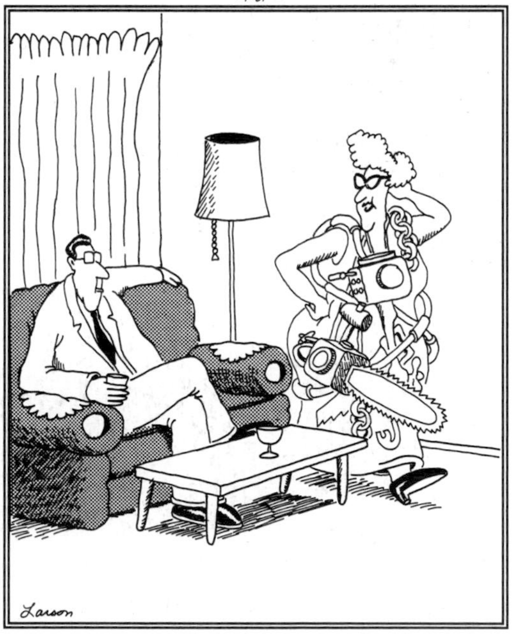

"Excuse me, Harold, while I go slip into something more comfortable."

December 1981

12/16/81

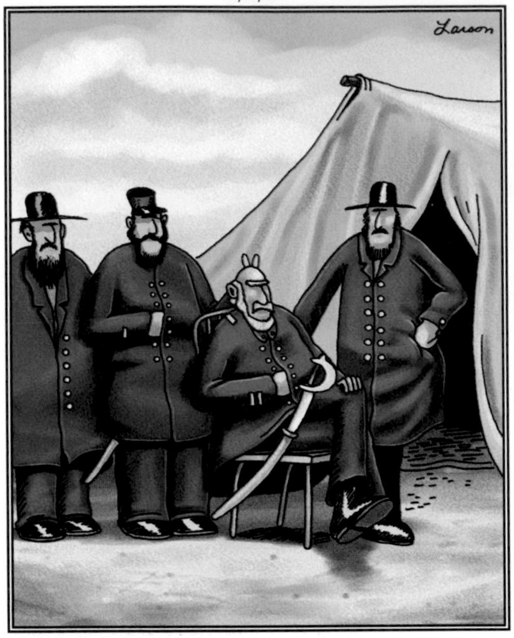
Larson

Near Gettysburg, 1863: A reflective moment

12/17/81

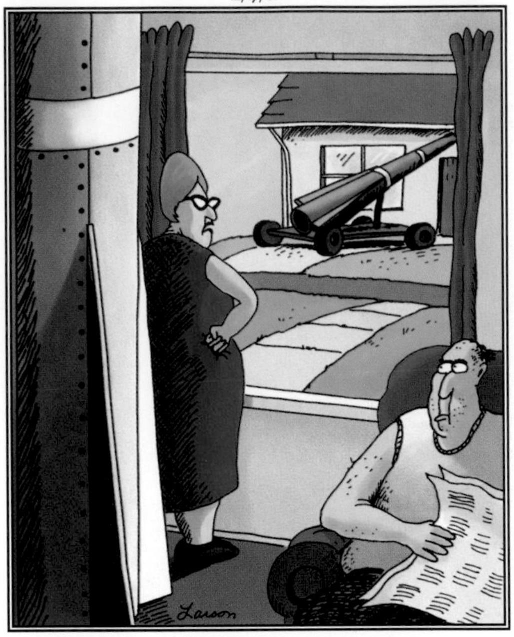
Larson

"Wouldn't you know it! Now the Hendersons have the bomb."

12/18/81

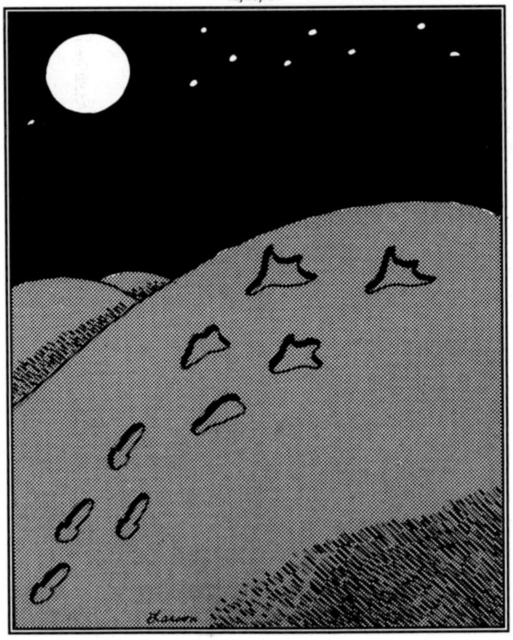
Larson

The wereduck cometh.

12/19/81

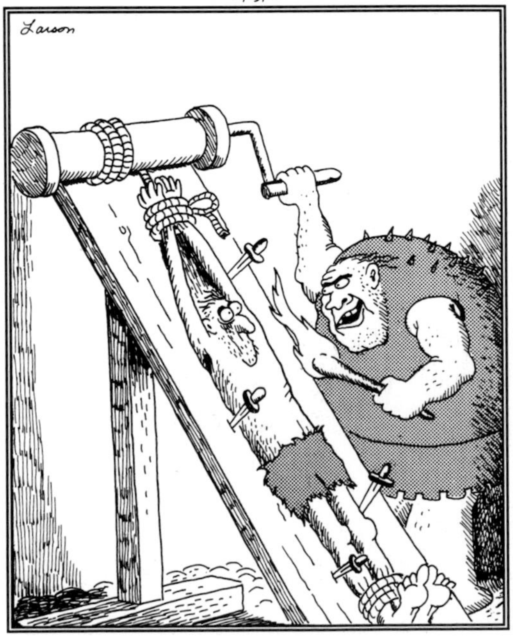
Larson

"Still won't talk, huh? ... Okay, no more Mr. Nice Guy."

12/22/81

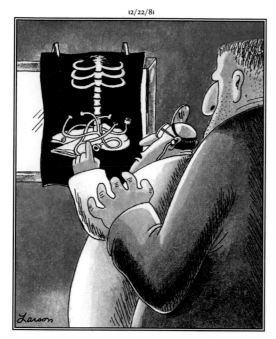

"My goodness, Mr. Osgood! Your X-ray reveals
several stethoscopes, a smock, and ..."

12/21/81

"Uh-oh, Stan. I guess it *wasn't* a big,
blue mule deer."

12/25/81

12/30/81

"Well, that does it! ... Tomorrow he dies."

12/23/81

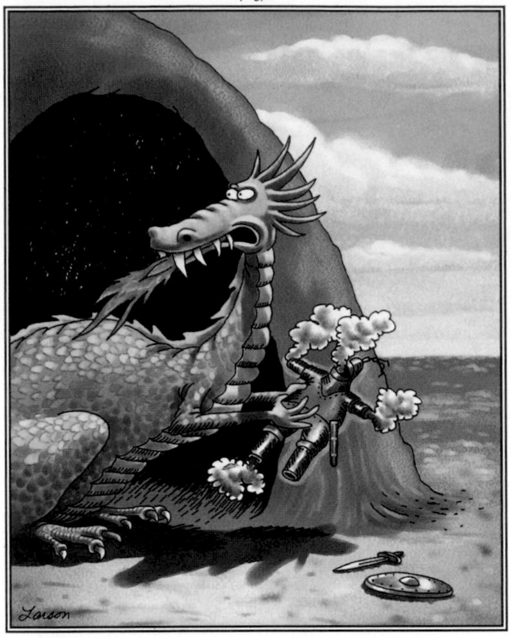
Larson

"Ooo! Ow! Blast it, Phyllis! ... Hurry up with them hot pads!"

12/26/81

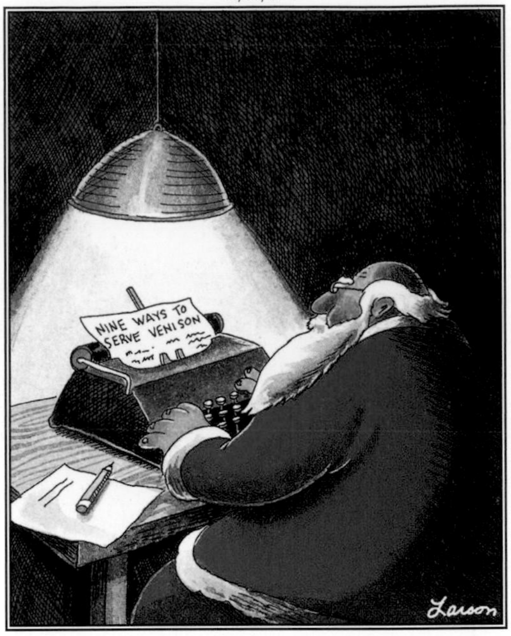
NINE WAYS TO
SERVE VENISON
Larson

12/24/81

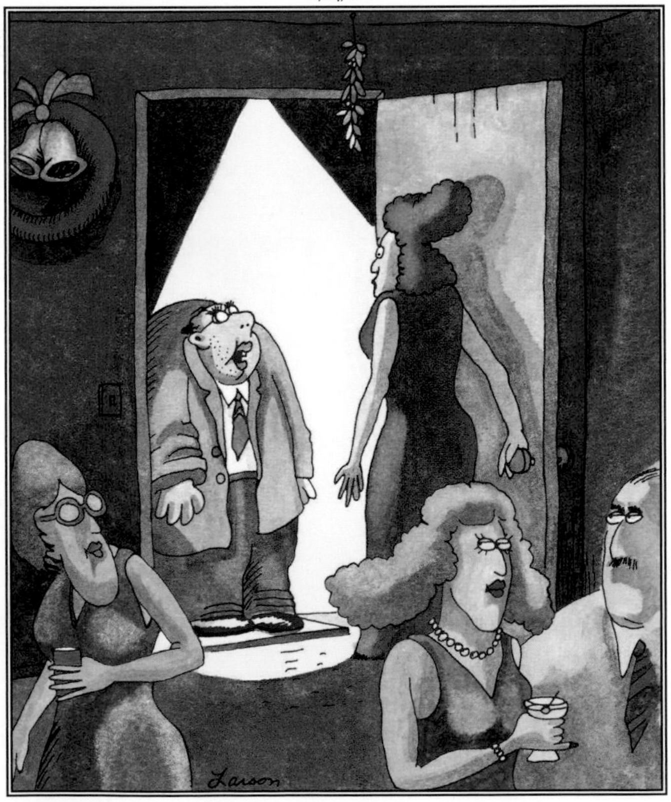
Larson

"Hello, I'm Clarence Jones from Bill's office and ... Oh! Hey! Mistletoe!"

12/28/81

Larson
OK
NO
good

12/29/81

Larson

12/31/81

Larson

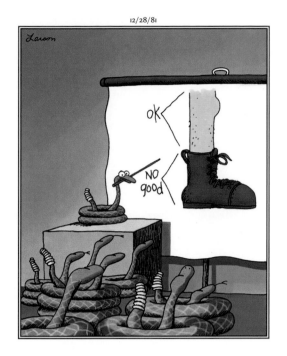

"Well, so much for the unicorns. ... But, from now on, all carnivores will be confined to 'C' deck."

19

Little boy approaching front of class w
a head inside a jar, Teacher: "Okay, Nov
will see what Bobby Henderson has
brought for Show & Tell."
Dracula getting sunlamp
Cows getting out of Taxi with luggage etc., woma
in window, "Arnold... The cows have come home.

82

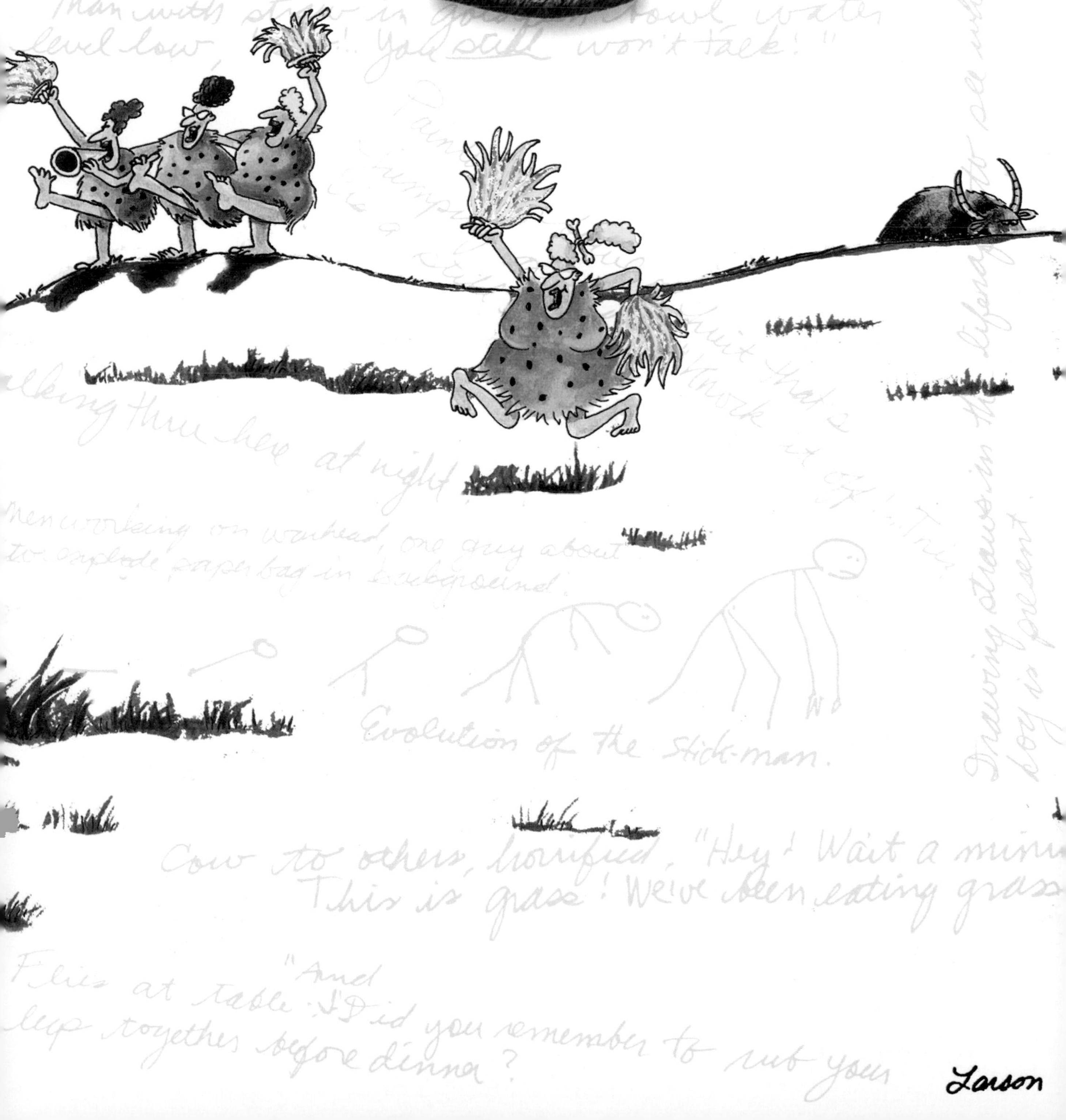

The Syndrome

The last time it struck me was a few years ago, while my wife and I were on vacation in Indonesia. Frankly, my syndrome hadn't surfaced for years, and up until this rather embarrassing "Bali episode," I had foolishly thought I was completely free of its grip.

I had just left the Hotel Bali Oberoi's outdoor bar and was heading back to our "hut," bearing a couple of those tropical drinks that look like someone had stuffed a clown into a blender. Just then, across the beautifully landscaped grounds, maybe a hundred feet from where I stood, strolled an enormous black lizard, perhaps three feet in length.

Outwardly, I was calm. Inwardly, I was completely undone. I put the drinks down on the lawn and immediately started moving toward this mysterious reptile. (Some kind of monitor lizard, I later determined.) And as it kept a watchful eye on me, maintaining a constant distance, I started moving a little faster. As did the lizard. As did I. Within a few minutes I was running full out, dodging palm trees and startled tourists. I was focused on that lizard, that big, beautiful, scaly creature of my dreams.

Hello to my little problem. Or, as my brother (who was also doomed to suffer under its spell) and I "scientifically" designated it, the *ohpleaseohplease syndrome*. For both of us, it first showed up in childhood.

On any given day or night, under optimum conditions (no school, essentially), Dan and I would gather up our boots, nets, and collecting jars and head for the local swamps or tidelands. We were on a quest for living treasure: the wetland fauna of western Washington.

Our passion for frequenting wetlands was not the syndrome per se: It was merely setting the stage. The syndrome itself, however, was always waiting in the wings, ready to pounce. Allow me to put you in my boots, and I will attempt to walk you through a typical "episode" of *ohpleaseohplease*.

It's night. You are at the edge of a big swamp, wading through the muddy shallows, staying close to the reeds. Your trusty net is in one hand, your less trusty flashlight in the other. The only sounds you hear are frogs and occasionally creatures of unknown origin. Your flashlight sweeps back and forth in a slow, smooth arc, its beam searching for denizens of the not-so-deep. And then … your heart nearly stops. You can barely breathe. There, not far from where you stand frozen, illuminated in your light beam, is the most beautiful, the most incredible _____ (fill in the creature of your own dreams) that you have ever laid eyes on! Now the syndrome kicks in.

For a while, you dare not move. But soon you find yourself moving (or is it being "pulled"?) in slow motion toward this beautiful, amazing ______ . And as you raise your net into capture position with the practiced skill of an Amazonian Indian (wearing glasses), knowing that at any moment the ______ might realize your intent and instantly vanish, you hear, over and over again, a single voice pounding in your head: *ohpleaseohplease!* It's an all-out begging of the gods to deliver yonder animal unto thy net. And while that voice implores away inside your brain, you experience a total eclipse of everything else in the known universe. All you see is that amazing, beautiful, incredible ______ that's staring back at you.

Like a full moon shining down on some werewolf, that huge lizard in Bali had triggered my own curse. I *wanted* that lizard. I *had* to have that lizard. I *lusted* after that lizard!

In the end, that big reptile just ran into some bushes. Gone like a lizard. And so there I stood, drenched in sweat—the only tell-tale sign that I had just experienced another attack of *ohpleaseohplease.*

Years ago, my brother and I concluded we were probably not alone with our affliction. Biologists, naturalists, all people who find themselves inexplicably drawn to look under rocks, down holes, up trees, under water, or wherever else you might discover some beautiful beastie, must also suffer from bouts of *ohpleaseohplease.* Very simply, it's the obsession to capture and to hold, if only for a few moments, some living, natural wonder, to observe it, examine it, have it touch your skin, feel its heartbeat against your hand—to "drink it in" before it once again slips back over that invisible wall that separates Us from Them.

Whether directly or indirectly, the memory of *ohpleaseohplease* was the genesis for a number of my cartoons. I guess in the end, you are what you draw. A scary thought.

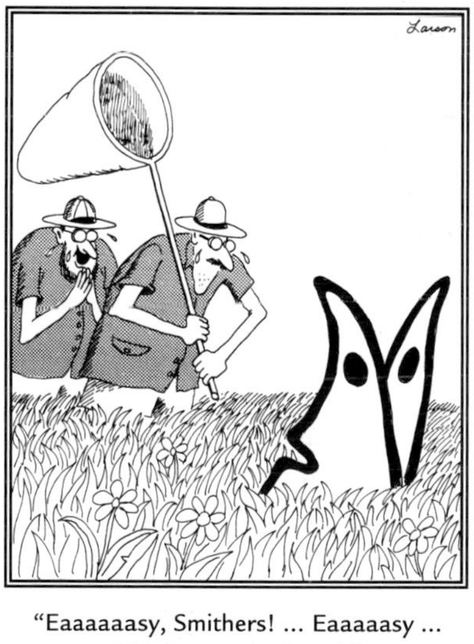
Larson

"Eaaaaaasy, Smithers! ... Eaaaaasy ... Oh please, oh please!"

1/2/82

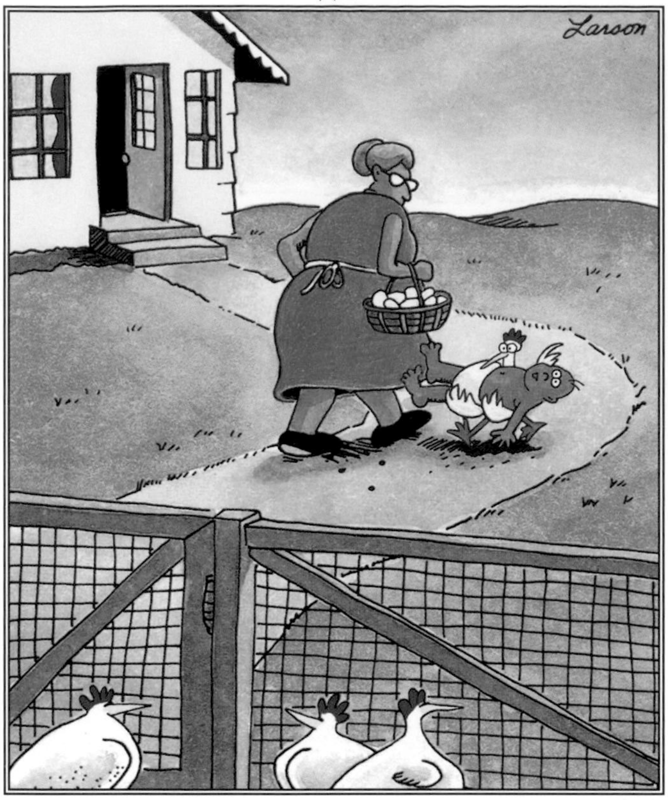
Larson

1/1/82

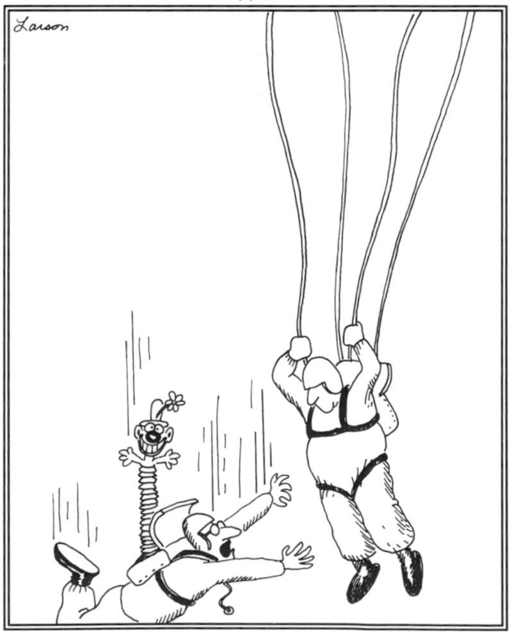
Larson

1/4/82

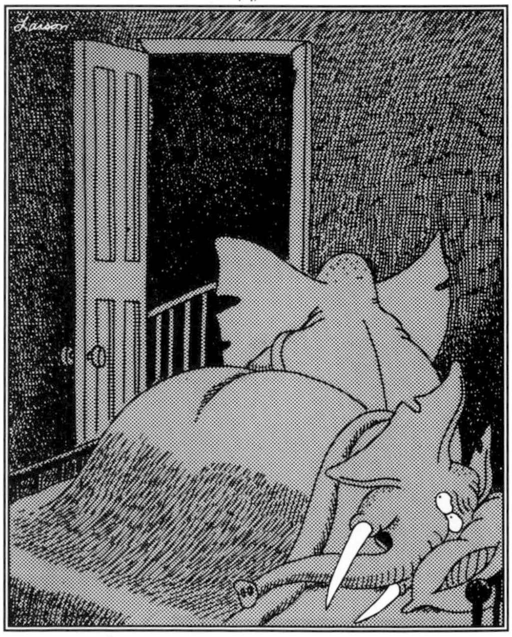
Larson

"For crying out loud! ... You're *always* hearing something moving around downstairs!"

1/6/82

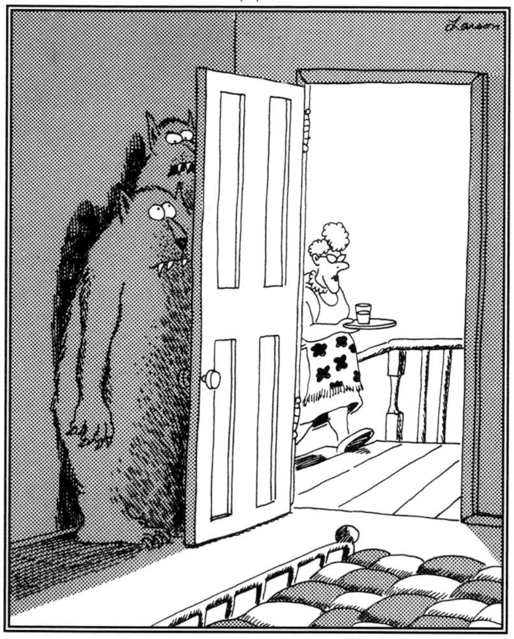

"Shove off, buddy ... I've been working this neighborhood for years."

1/9/82

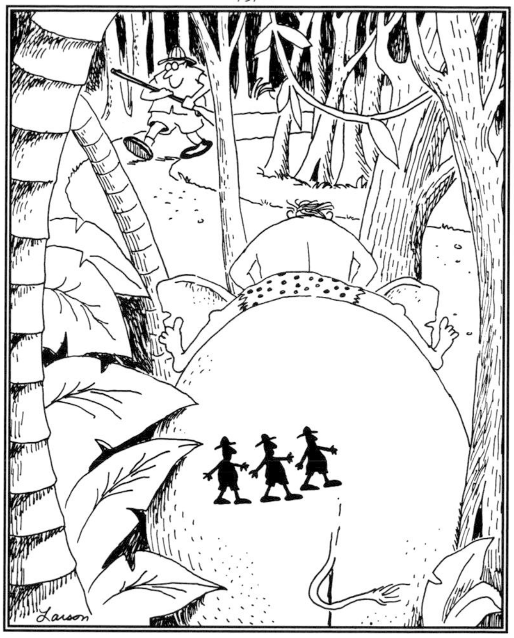

1/7/82

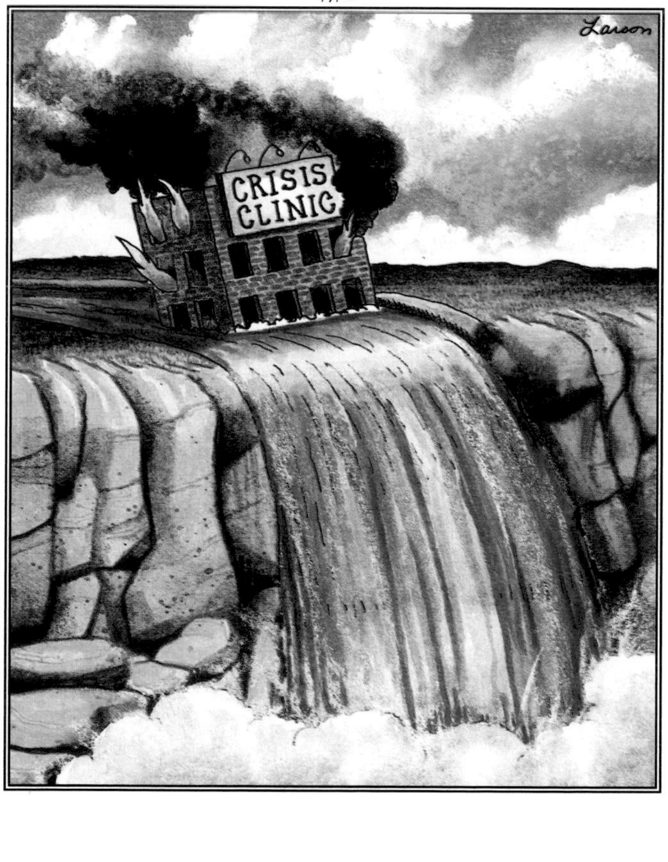
CRISIS CLINIC

1/5/82

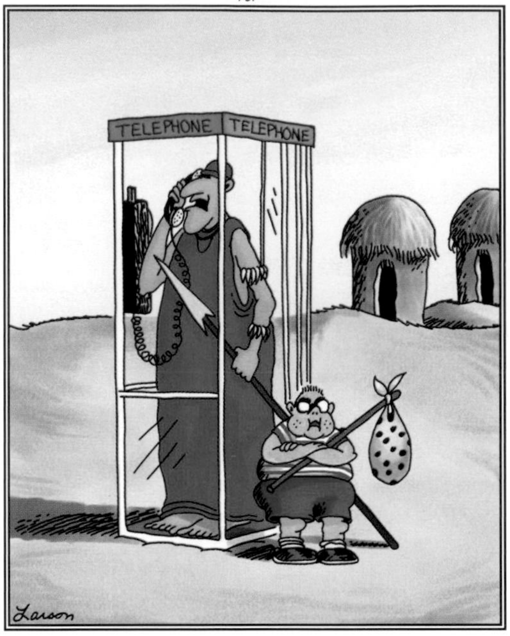
TELEPHONE
TELEPHONE

"Mrs. Harriet Schwartz? This is Zathu Nananga of the Masai. ... Are you missing a little boy, Mrs. Schwartz?"

1/8/82

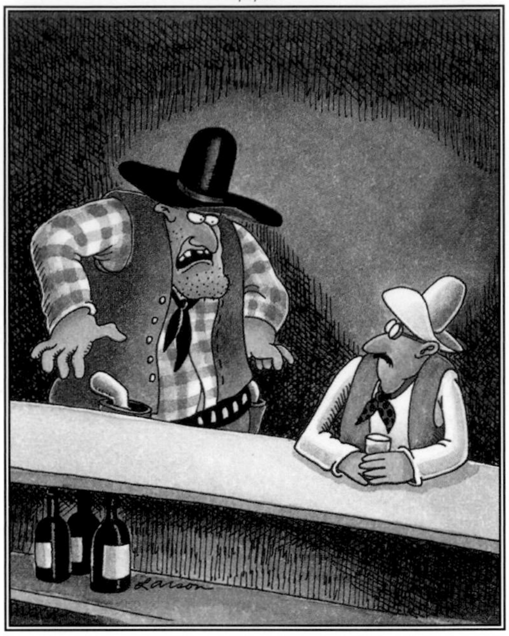

"I *asked* you a question, buddy. ... What's the square root of 5,248?"

1/12/82

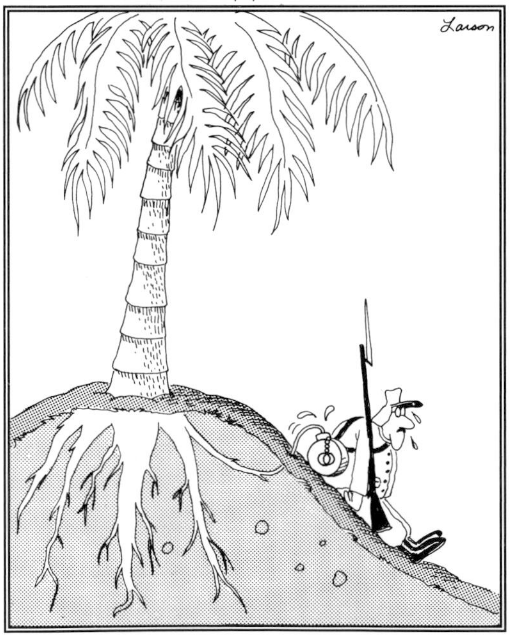

1/13/82

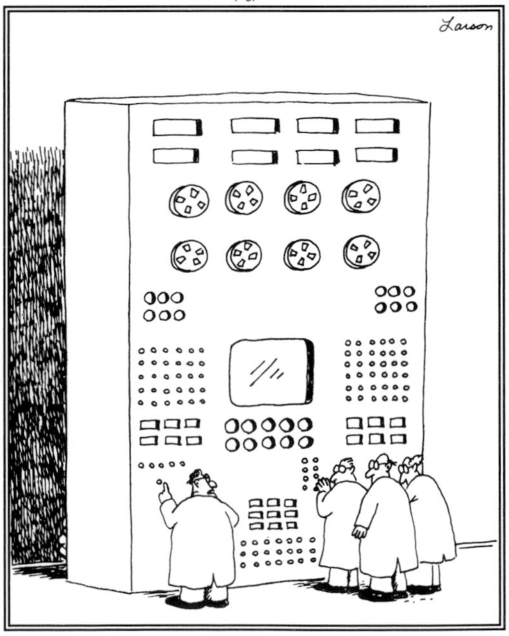

"Wait a minute, gentlemen. ... Here's the 'on' switch over here."

1/14/82

Larson

"Why, yes ... we do have two children who won't eat their vegetables."

1/11/82

BONK!
BONK!
BONK!
BONK!
Larson

1/15/82

Larson
SAFARI
SEE WILD ANIMALS UP CLOSE!

1/16/82

Larson

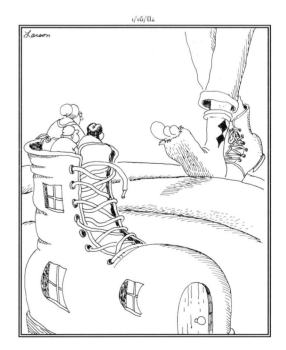

1/18/82

"This is just not effective. ... We need to get some chains."

1/19/82

"Hathunters!"

1/20/82

"I can't stand it. ... They're so *cute* when they sit like that."

1/21/82

Africa's deadliest game

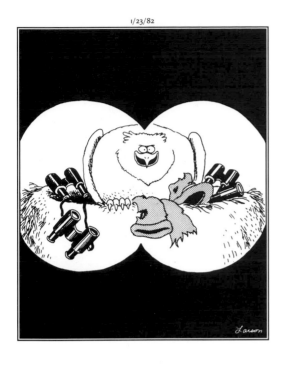

"Hey, buddy ... you wanna buy a hoofed mammal?"

"Okay, Williams, we'll just vote. ... How many here say the heart has four chambers?"

"Okay, so you're Grizzly Adams. ... Let's see some proof!"

1/22/82

1/26/82

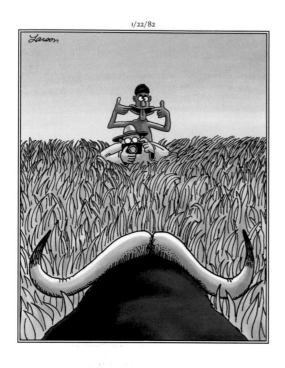

"These little ones are mice. ... These over here are hamsters. ... Ooh! This must be a gerbil!"

1/29/82

"Hey! Is that you, Arnie? ... Small petri dish!"

1/30/82

PEARLY GATES
WE'VE MOVED TO 4223 Maple Ave.

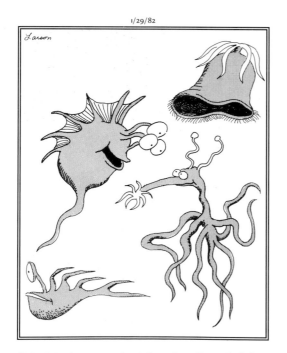

2/1/82

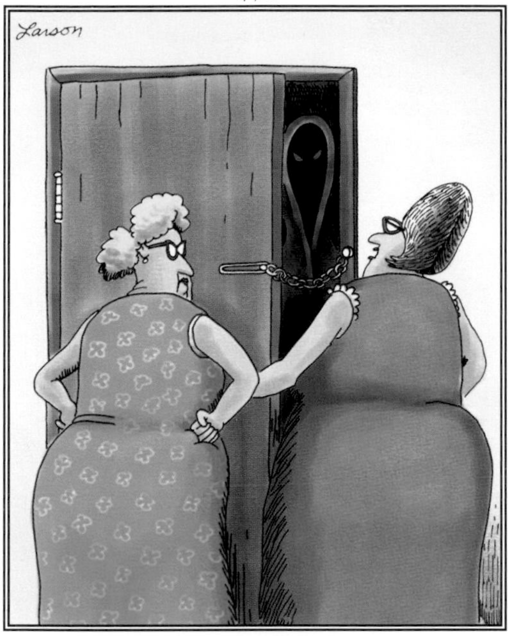
Larson

"Now wait just a minute here. ... How are we supposed to know you're the *real* Angel of Death?"

2/2/82

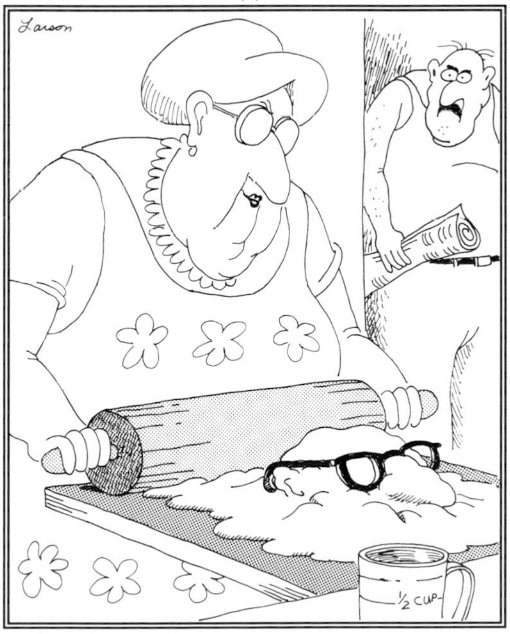
Larson
½ CUP

"Blast it, woman! ... Have you seen my reading glasses?"

2/3/82

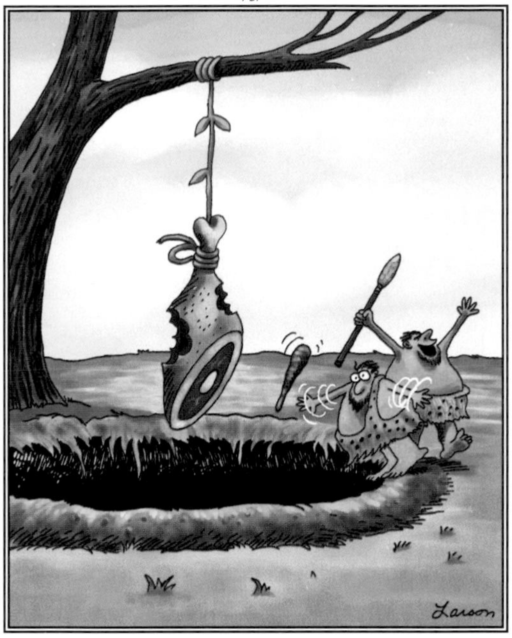
Larson

"Big one, Thag! ... We caught biiiiiig one!"

2/4/82

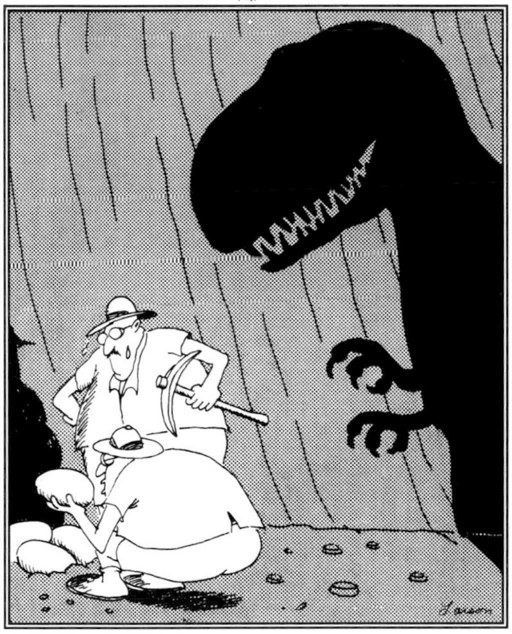
Larson

"Millions of years old and they look as if they were laid yesterday!"

2/6/82

"MOBY DICK"
CHAPTER 1
Call me
CHAPTER 1
Call me Bill
CHAPTER1
Call me Al.
CHAPTER 1
Call me Larry
Call me Roge
CHAPTER1
Call me Warren.

2/8/82

"Your room is right in here, Maestro."

2/5/82

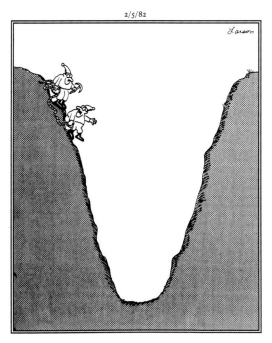

"Because it's not there."

2/9/82

"Yes. Will you accept a collect call from a Mr. Aaaaaaaaa?"

2/11/82

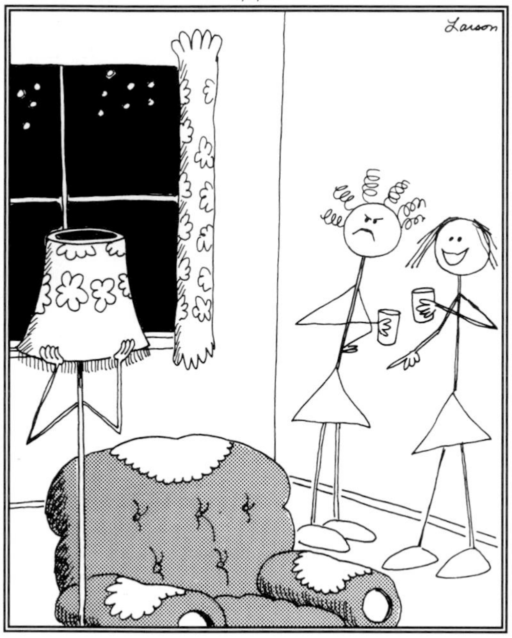

"Uh-oh, Gladys. ... Looks like your Sidney has had too much to drink again."

2/12/82

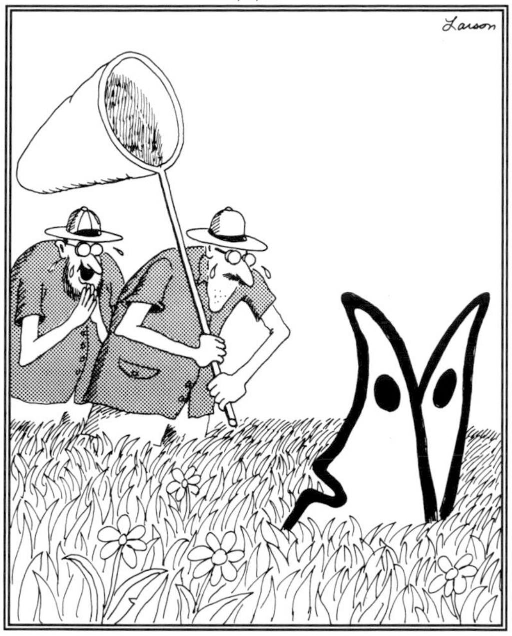

"Eaaaaaasy, Smithers! ... Eaaaaasy ... Oh please, oh please!"

2/10/82

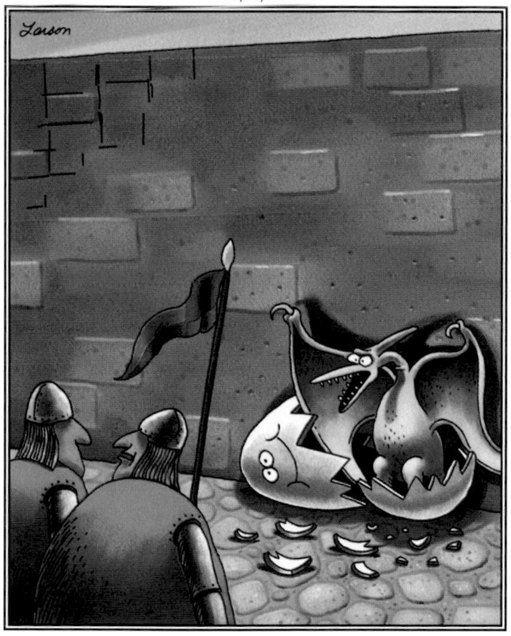

"Look. ... *You* wanna try putting him back together again?"

2/13/82

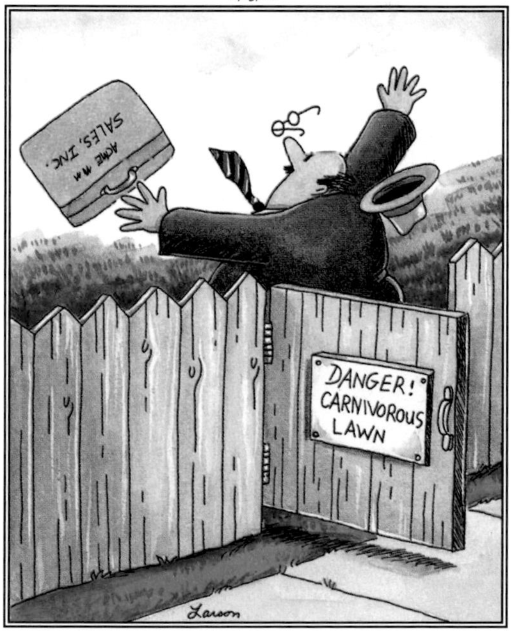
DANGER!
CARNIVOROUS
LAWN

2/15/82

"You idiots! ... We'll never get that thing down the hole!"

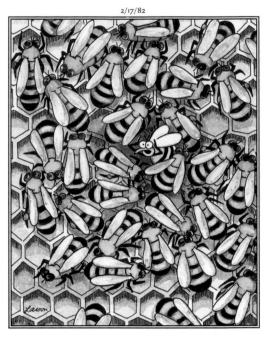

2/17/82

"No more! No more! I can't take it! ...
That incessant buzzing sound!"

2/16/82

Great moments in evolution

2/18/82

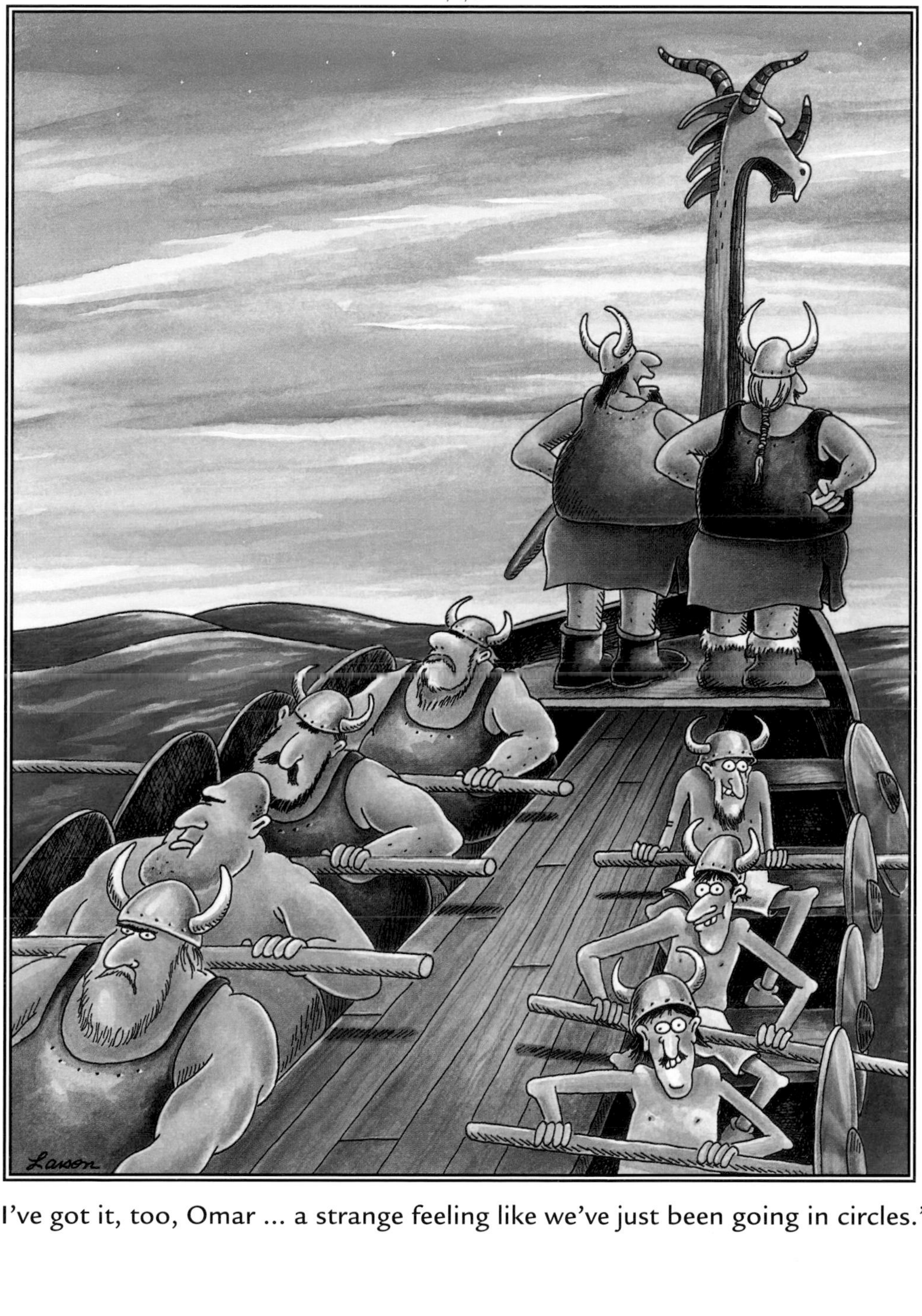
Larson

"I've got it, too, Omar ... a strange feeling like we've just been going in circles."

2/23/82

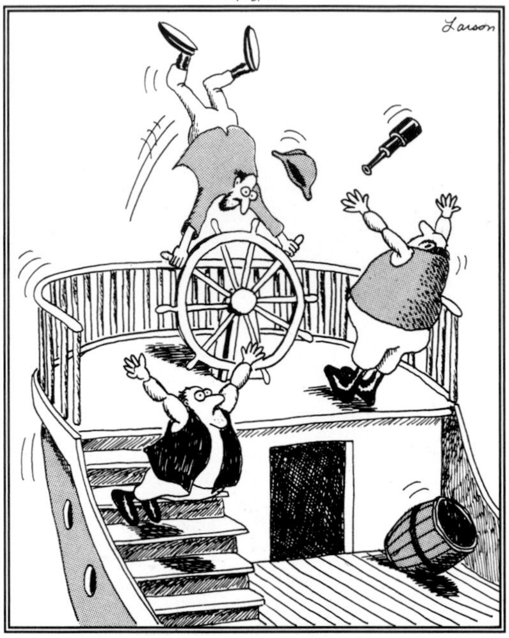

Columbus discovers America.

2/24/82

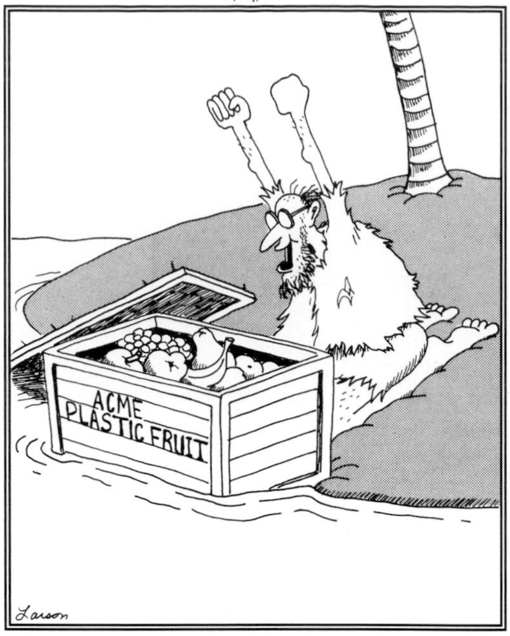
ACME
PLASTIC FRUIT

2/19/82

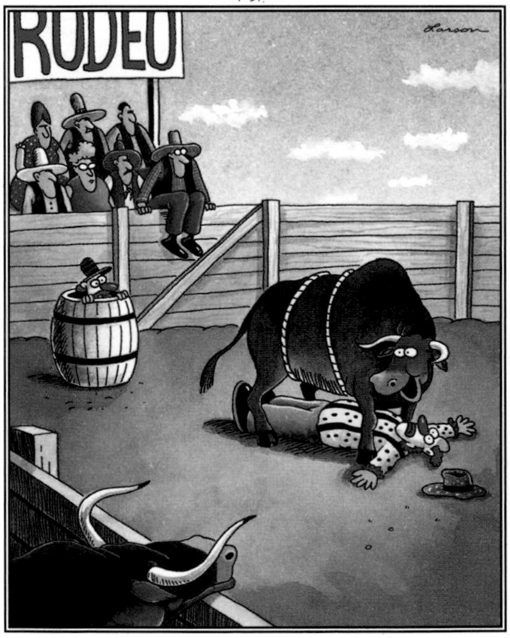
RODEO

"Hey! I got one! I got one!"

2/20/82

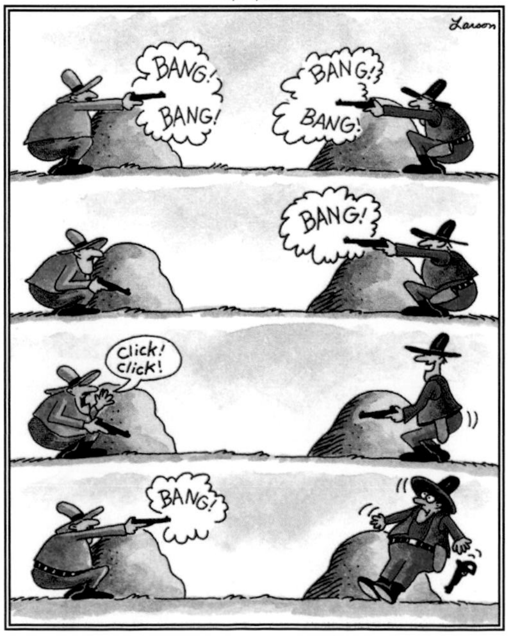
BANG!
BANG!
BANG!
BANG!
BANG!
Click! click!
BANG!

2/26/82

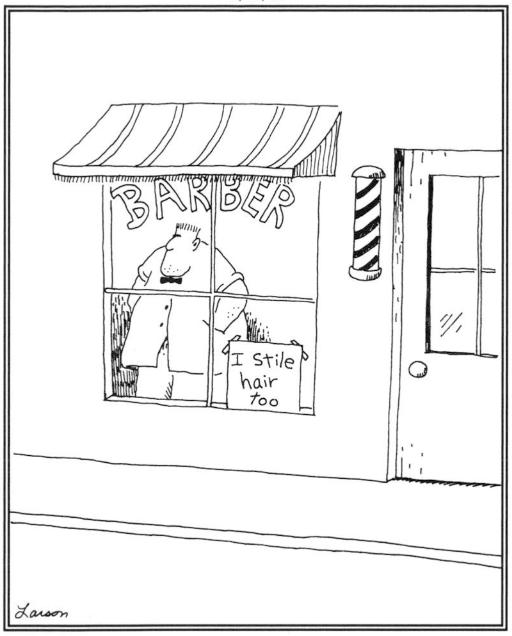
BARBER
I stile
hair
too
Larson

2/27/82

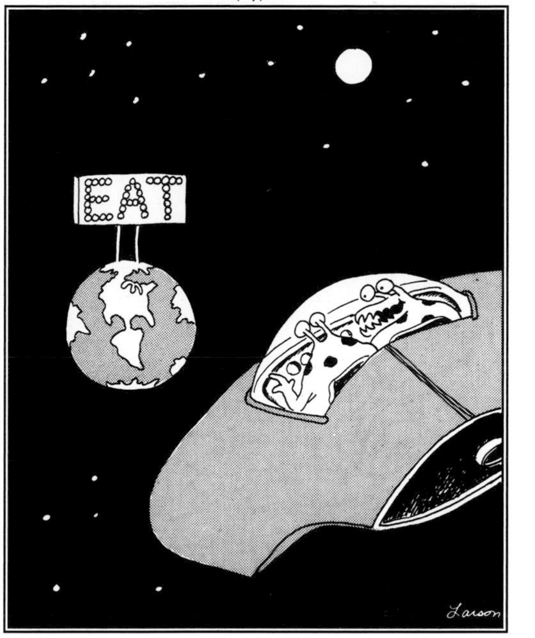
EAT
Larson

"Say ... I could go for something."

2/22/82

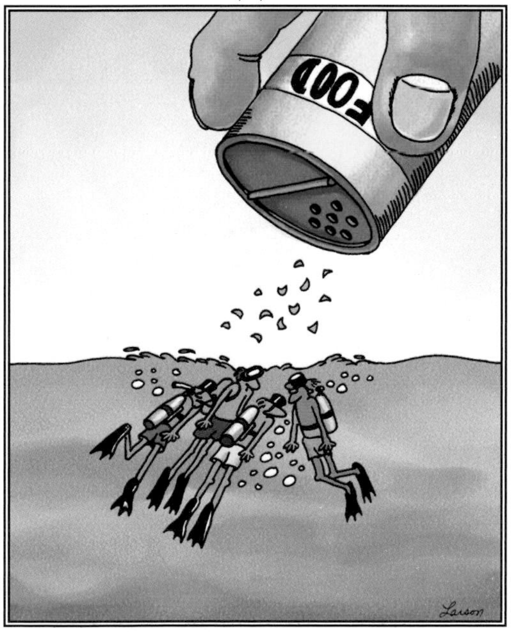
FOOD
Larson

2/25/82

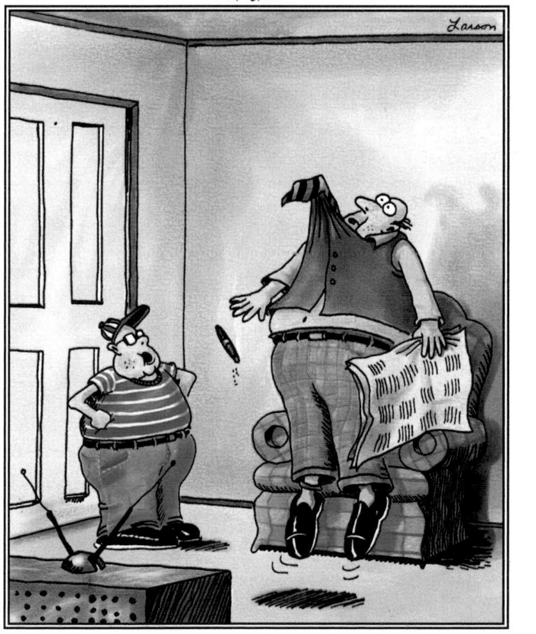
Larson

"Big Bob says he's getting tired of you saying he doesn't really exist."

3/1/82

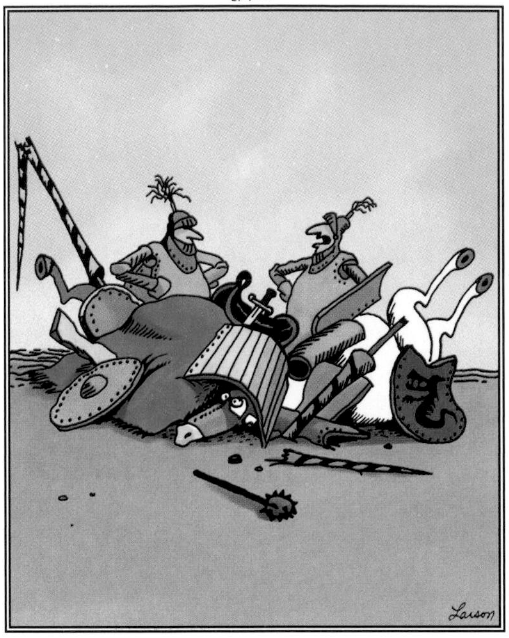

"Me? I *was* charging on the right, when you suddenly went left, so I went left, and then you went right again, you idiot!"

3/2/82

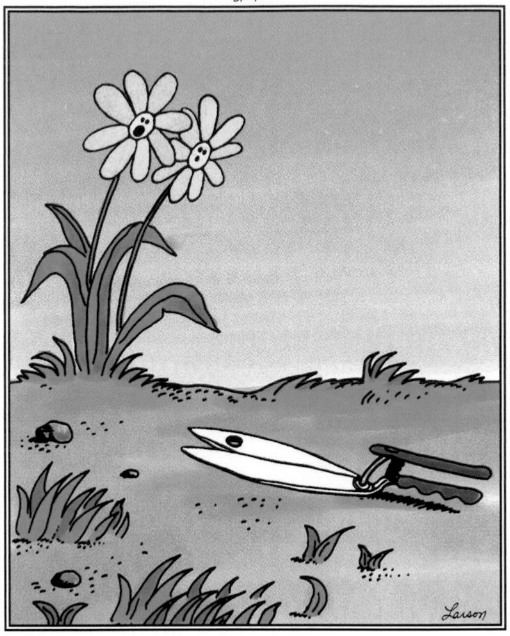

"There! There! See it, Larry? ... It moved a little closer!"

3/4/82

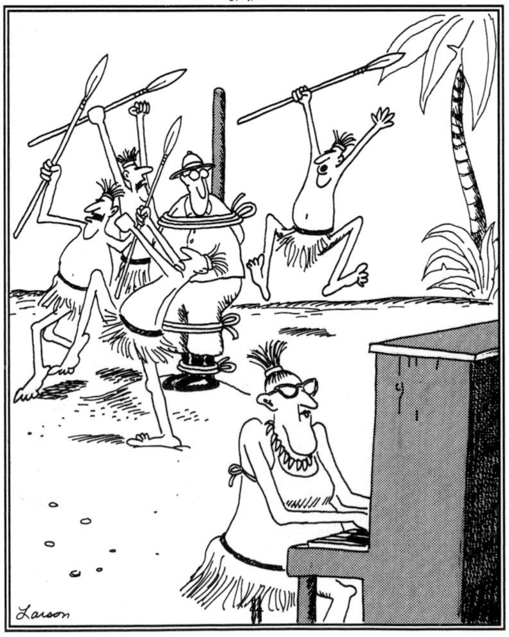

3/5/82

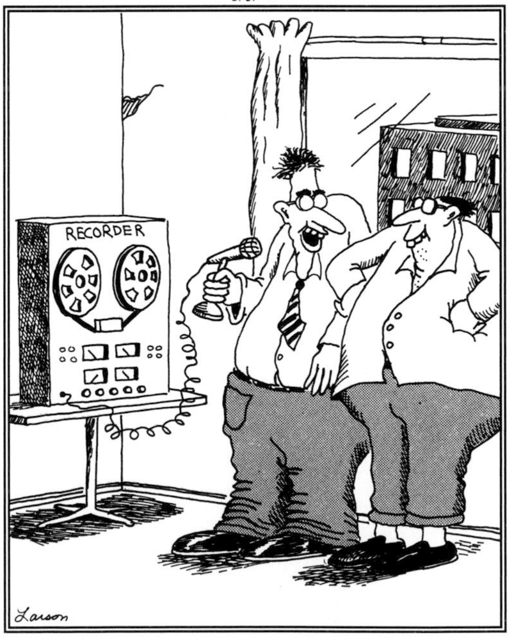
RECORDER

"Oh, wow! I can't believe this thing! ... Does my voice really sound that funny?"

3/3/82

Larson

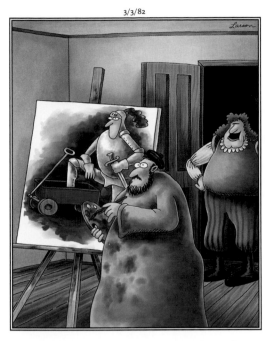

"So, Andre! ... The king wants to know how you're coming with *St. George and the Dragon.*"

3/12/82

Larson

"*Look* at that! ... Give me the good ol' days when a man carried a club, walked semi-erect, and had a brain the size of a walnut."

3/6/82

Larson

3/8/82

Larson

"FEEDING FRENZY!"

3/9/82

"My word, Walter! ... Sounded like a
good-size bird just hit the window."

3/10/82

"And this little piggy went weee, weee, weee,
weee ... but soon stopped struggling
and was eaten."

3/11/82

"Ha! Check this out, Andrews. ... Seems
there's some kind of ancient curse on
those who defile this crypt."

3/13/82

"Dang it! Doris! Hit the light! ... I think
there's a mosquito after me!"

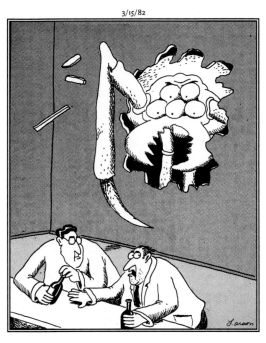

3/15/82

"Wait! Wait! ... Don't open
that brand of beer!"

3/16/82

"Hey! Look in here! ... There's all kinds of
cool movie cameras and junk!"

3/17/82

"Aphids! Aphids, Henry! ... Aphids are loose
in the garden!"

3/19/82

"I don't mean to be callous, Earl, but can
I have your stereo?"

3/23/82

3/20/82

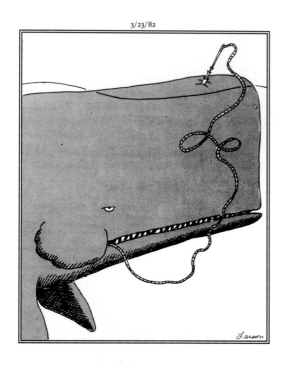

"I'd hate to be in a box canyon with those coming at me!"

3/24/82

"Now let me get this straight. ... We hired you to babysit the kids, and instead you cooked and ate them *both?*"

3/25/82

Grrrrr haruff! Arfa rawrg
bah huff grargh woof woof?

3/26/82

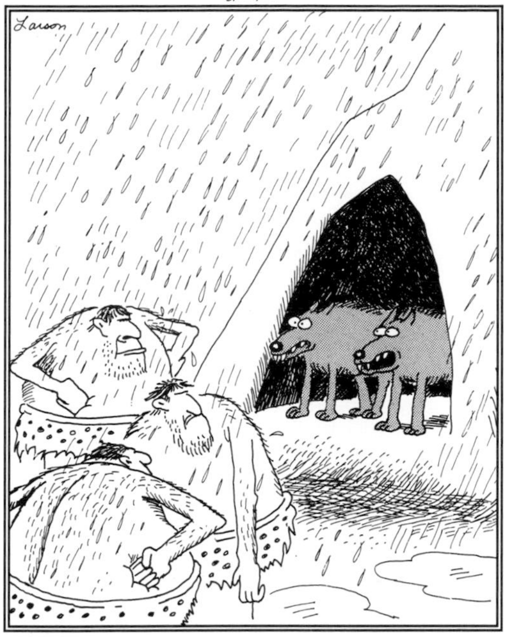
Larson

"Be firm, Arnold. ... Let them in once and they'll expect it every time."

3/27/82

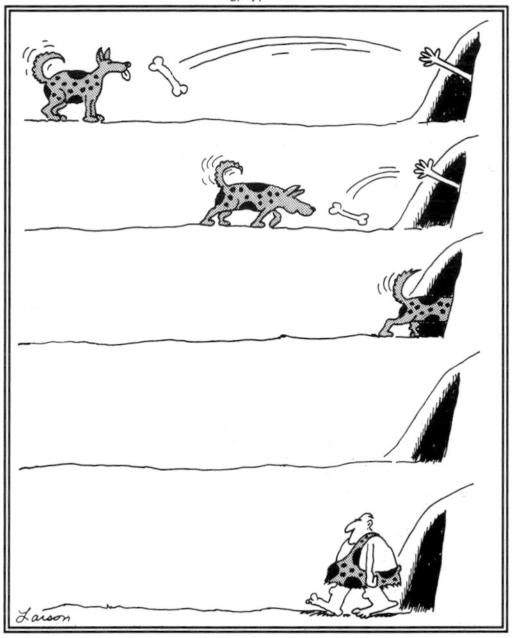
Larson

First encounters

3/30/82

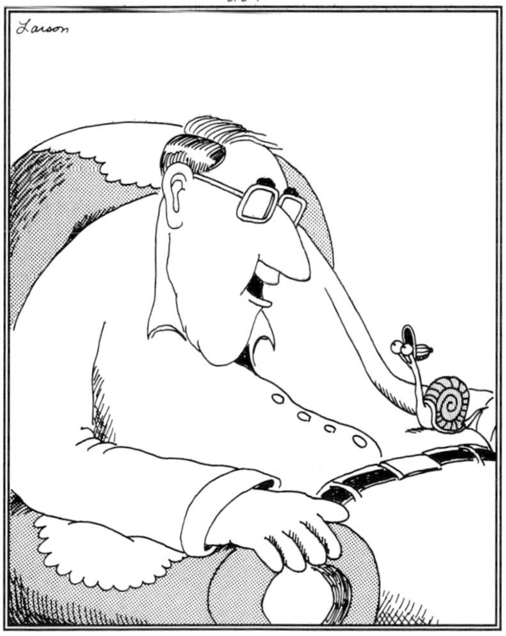
Larson

"That's right, Jimmy. ... One day your mother and I found you underneath a cabbage leaf."

3/31/82

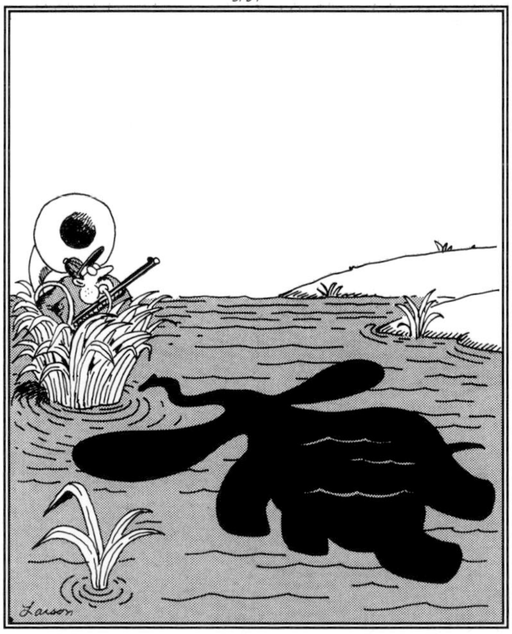
Larson

3/18/82

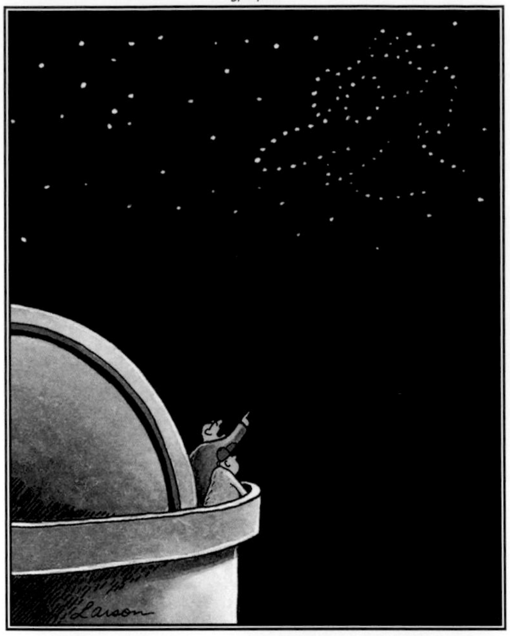

"Now that constellation, Jimmy, is simply called 'The Big Dip.'"

3/22/82

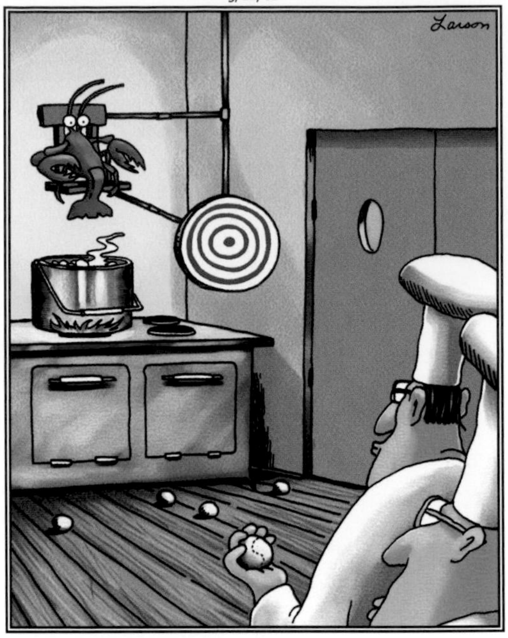

3/29/82

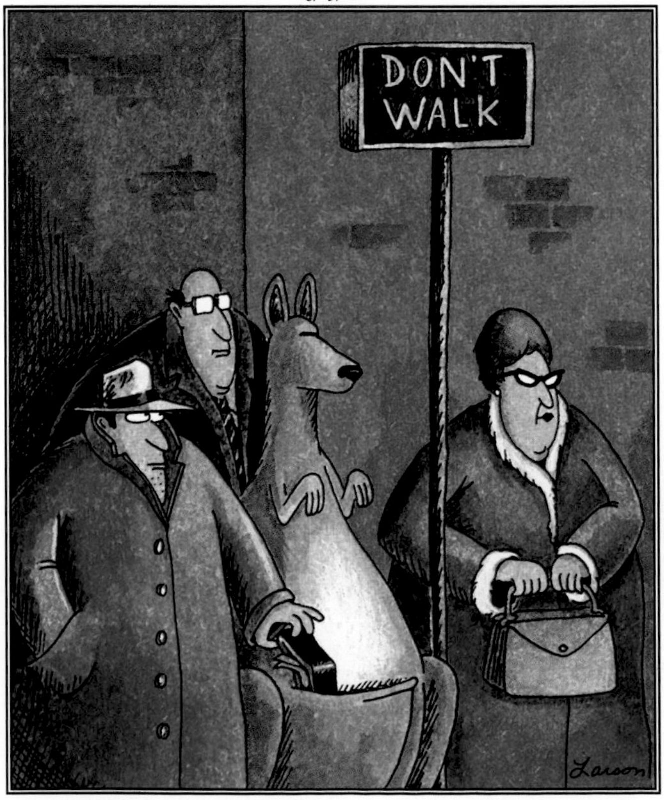
DON'T
WALK

4/2/82

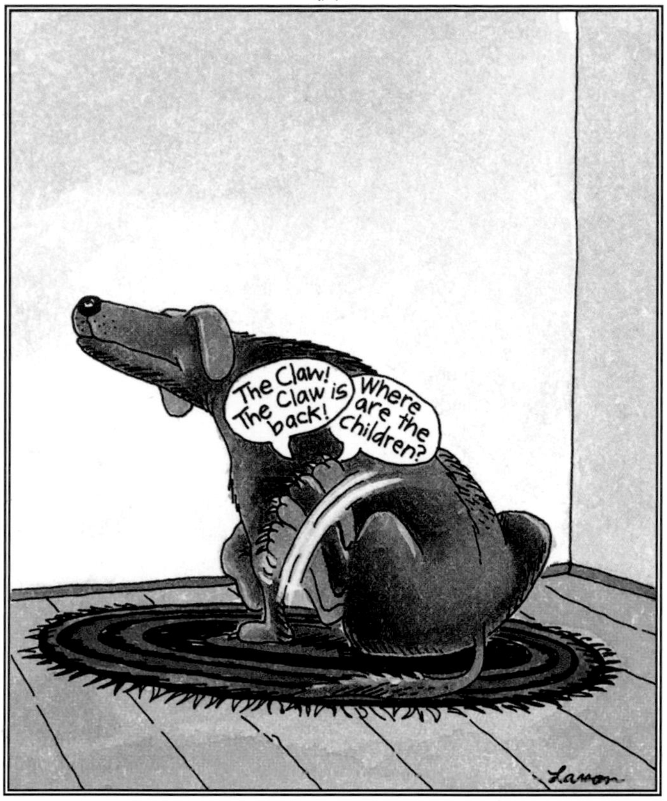
The Claw! The Claw is back!
Where are the children?
Larson

4/5/82

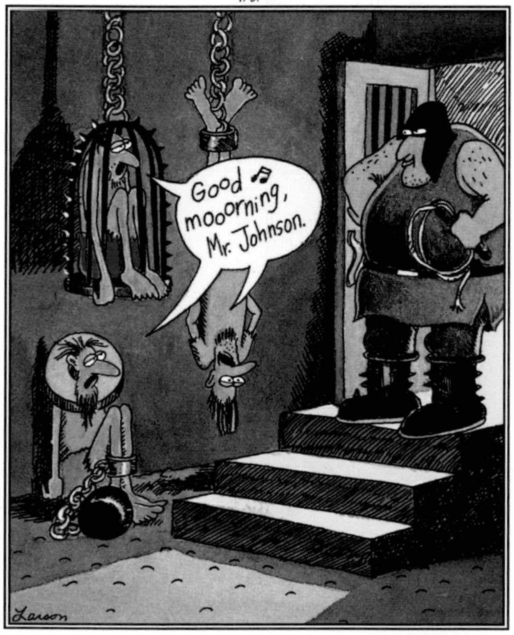
Good moooorning, Mr. Johnson.
Larson

Los Angeles Times
Comics

I cannot understand the cleverness of this Gary Larson. Do these come from the inmates of prisons & are sold to him which he in turn sells (them) to you?

What lies behind these warped cartoons? I wish some one would clear their meaning (of them) to me.

To me they are a waste of space and are an insult to a L.A. Times reader who can find no reason for them in your newspaper.

R. E. Lewis

4/3/82

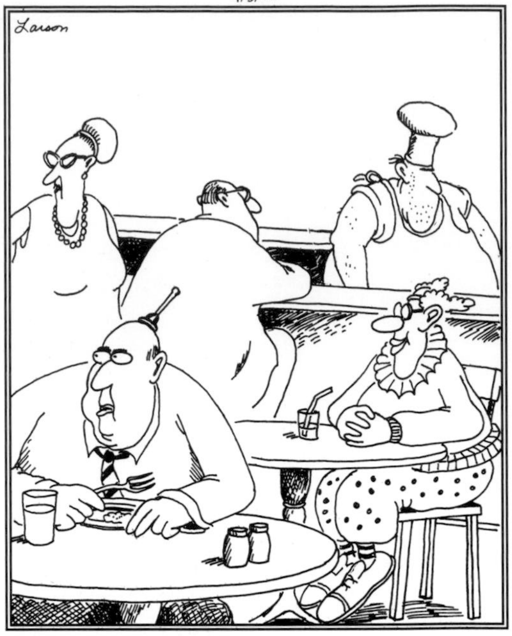
Larson

4/1/82

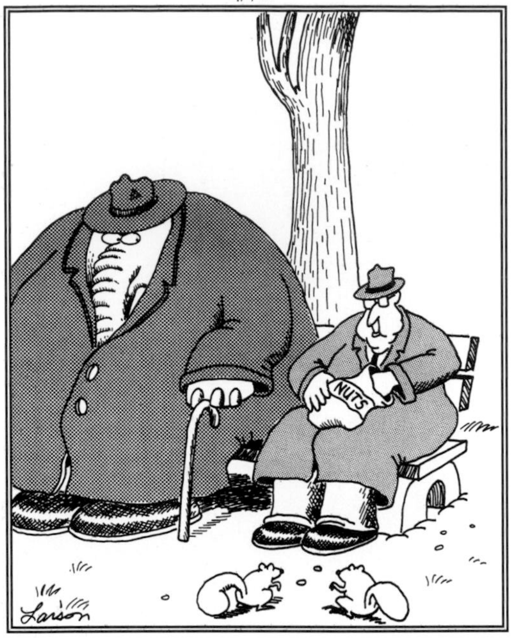
NUTS
Larson

4/8/82

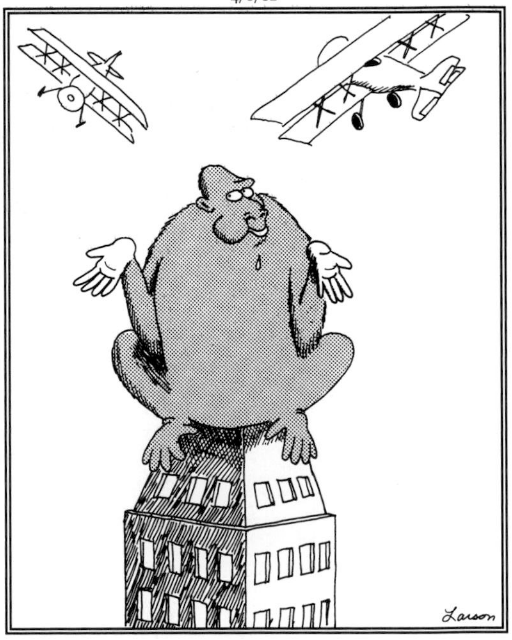
Larson

4/6/82

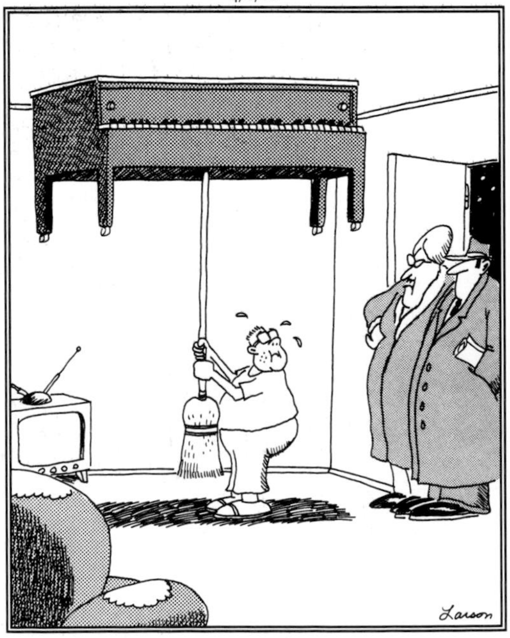
Larson

"So, Billy! Seems your father and I can never leave without you getting yourself into some kind of trouble!"

4/7/82

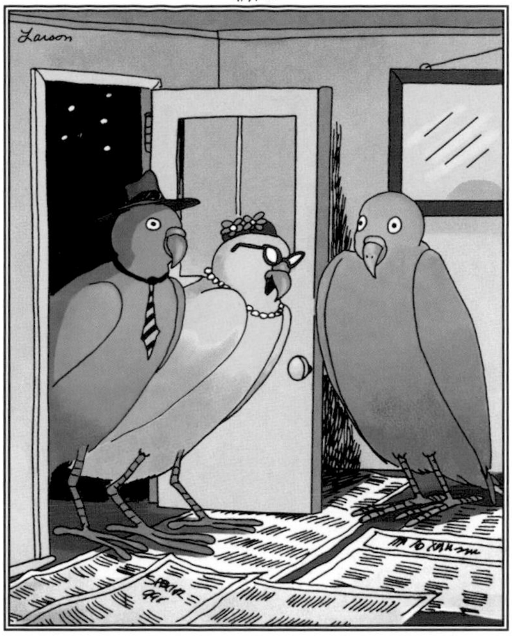
Larson

"What a lovely home, Edna! ... And look at the fresh newspaper, Stanley!"

4/12/82

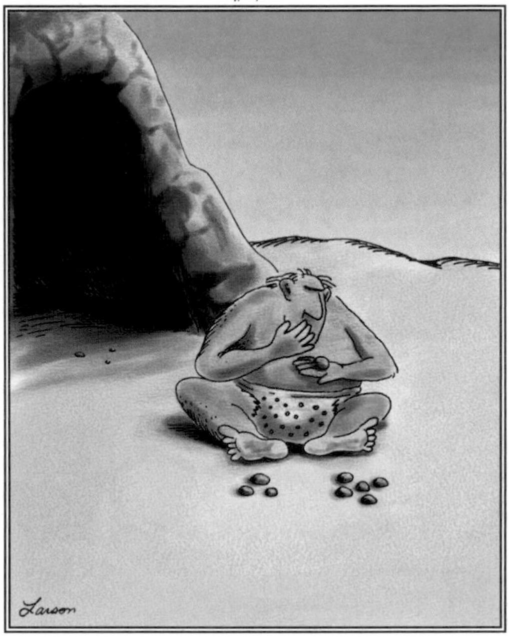
Larson

Early stages of math anxiety

4/13/82

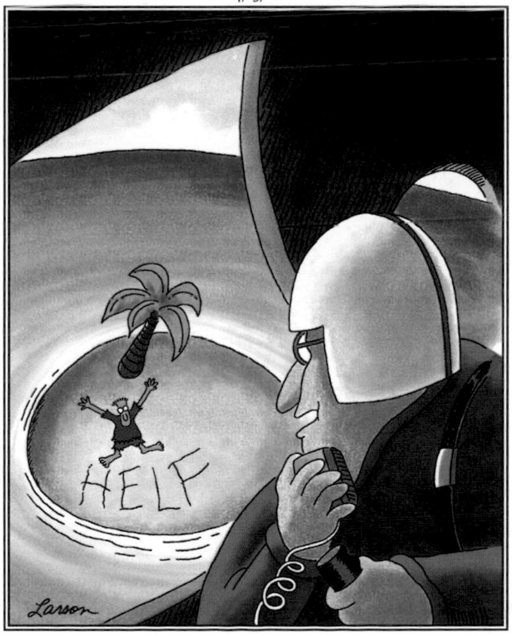
Larson

"Wait! Wait! Cancel that. ... I guess it says 'helf.'"

4/17/82

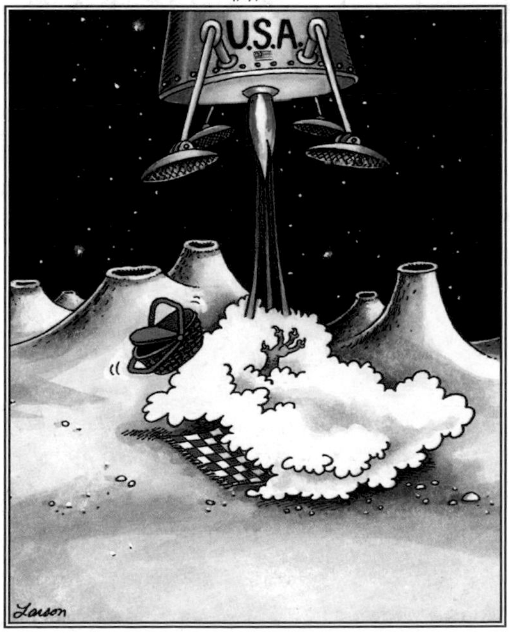
U.S.A.
Larson

4/9/82

"For crying out loud! ... We were supposed to turn south after that last mountain range!"

4/10/82

"I found him in the park. ... I pulled a thorn from his foot and he just sort of followed me home."

4/14/82

CONSTRUCTION AREA

4/15/82

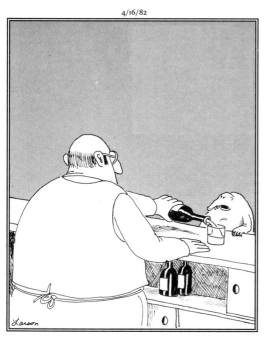

4/16/82

Larson

"Sho I shez to her, 'Hey, look! I'm tired of livin' in this hole, diggin' dirt, and eatin' worms!'"

4/19/82

Larson

"I'm not telling you kids again! ... Stand on one leg, turn your head straight back, and go to sleep!"

4/20/82

Larson

"Wouldn't you know it! ... A quiet day at the beach, and a real person shows up!"

4/23/82

Larson

"Quick! ... Run up and tell Him we found them!"

4/22/82

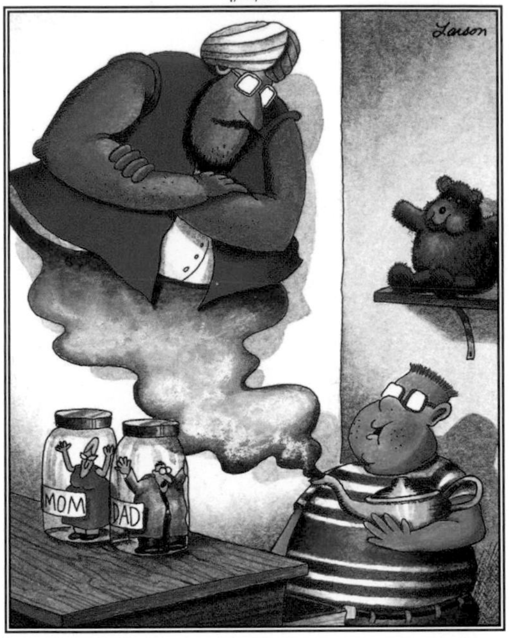
Larson
MOM
DAD

"Gee, whiz ... you mean I get a *third* wish, too?"

4/21/82

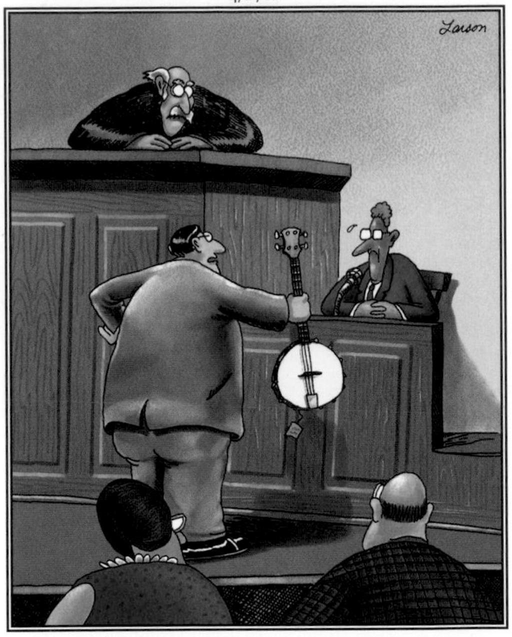
Larson

"So! You admit that this is, indeed, your banjo the police found at the scene, but you expect this jury to believe you were never in the kitchen with Dinah?"

4/24/82

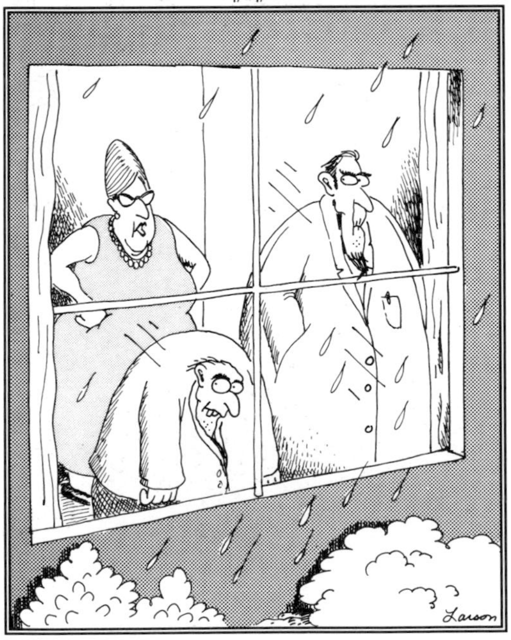
Larson

"Oh, c'mon now. ... *I* know! Why don't you two go downstairs today and build a monster?"

4/26/82

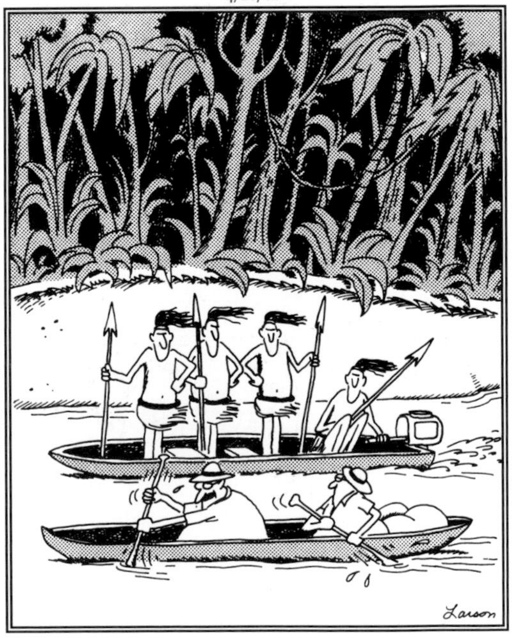
Larson

"Are they gaining, Huxley?"

4/27/82

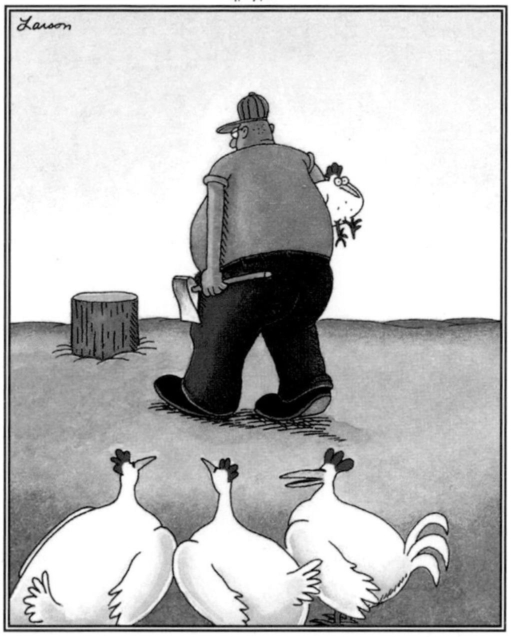
Larson

"Well, when it's my turn, I just hope I go quietly. ... You know—without a lot of running around."

4/30/82

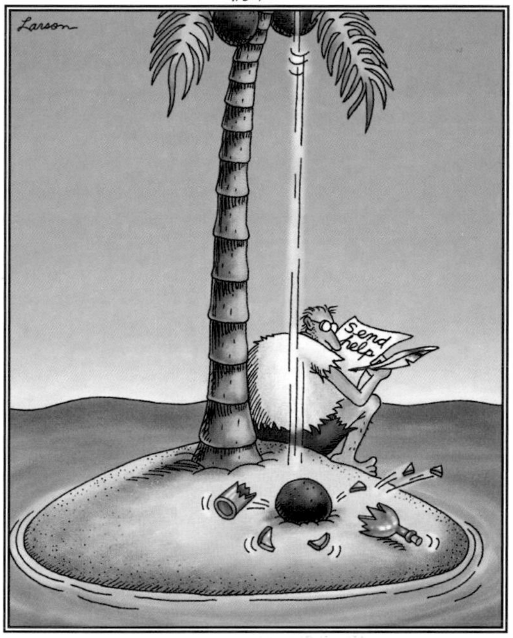
Larson
Send help

4/28/82

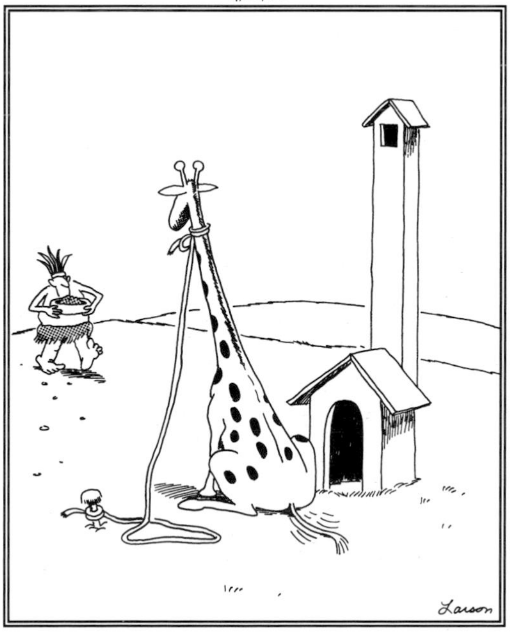
Larson

4/29/82

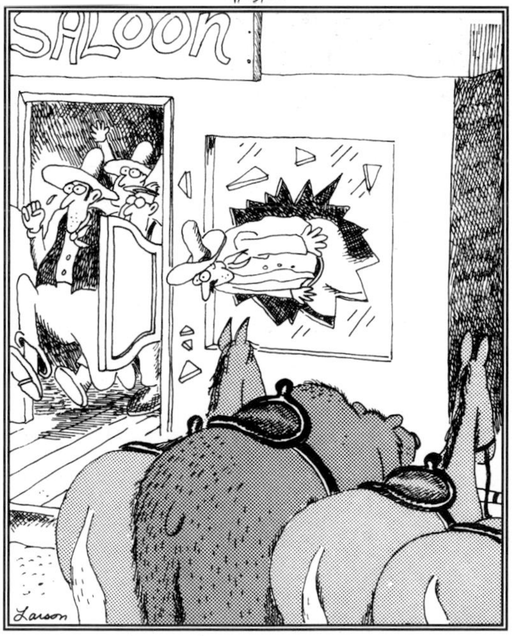
SALOON
Larson

5/1/82

MARINE
BIOLOGY
Larson

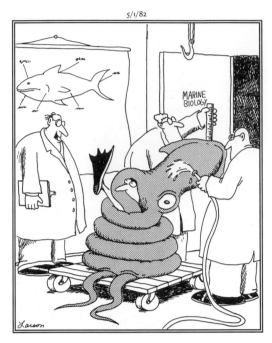

"Excuse our excitement, Mr. Farnsworth, but your cries for help have afforded science a rare opportunity."

5/4/82

Larson

The volcano god of the Nerdesians

5/3/82

Larson

"What? ... You mean *no one* brought the buns?"

5/6/82

"ARMY ANTS!"

5/7/82

"See, Agnes? ... It's just Kevin."

5/5/82

"Sorry to bother you, Sylvia, but your Henry's over
here and he's got my cat treed again."

5/8/82

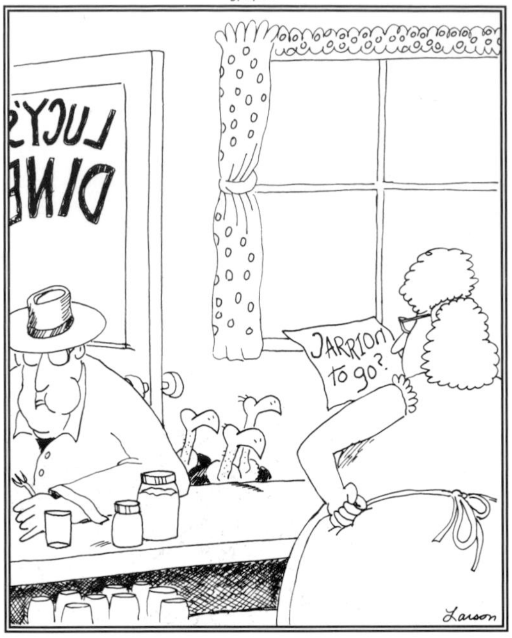
LUCY'S
DINE
CARRION
to go?
Larson

5/10/82

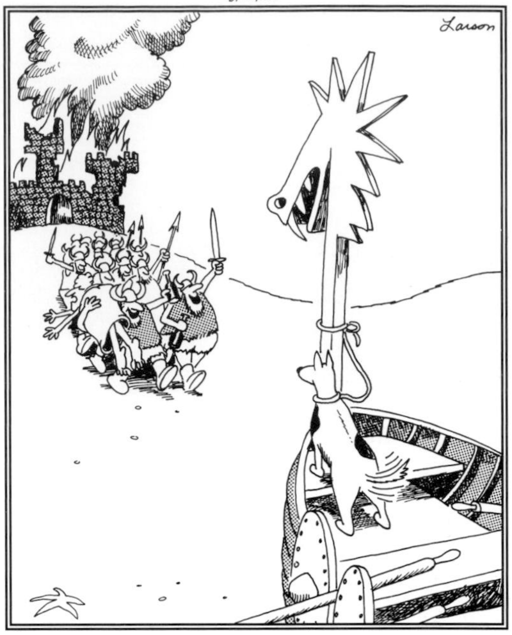
Larson

5/11/82

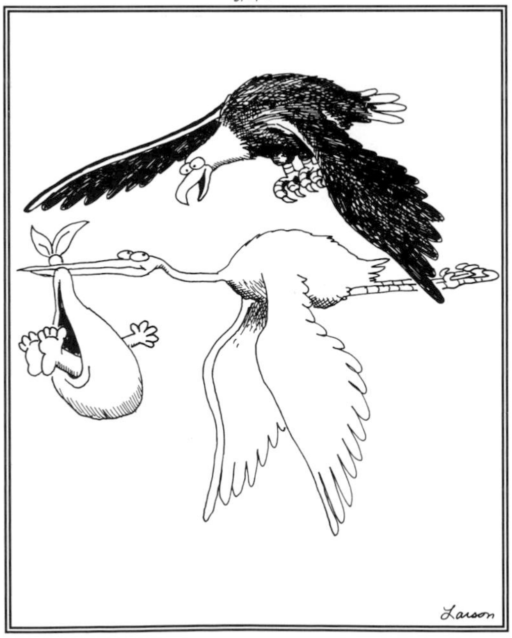
Larson

"Say ... would you like to contribute to an endangered species?"

5/12/82

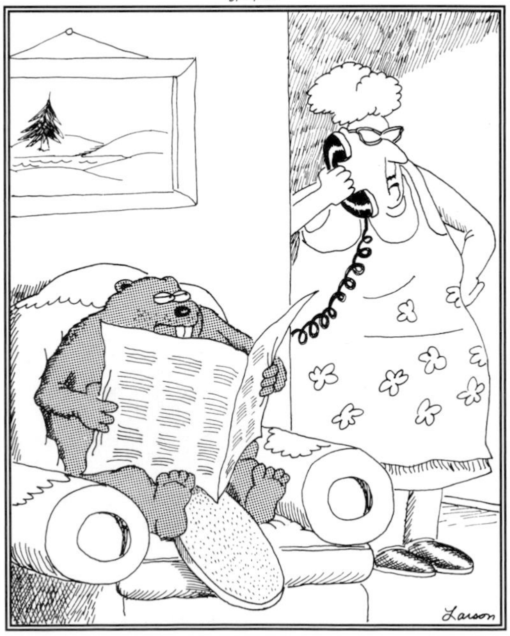
Larson

"No, he's not busy. ... In fact, that whole thing is just a myth."

May 1982

5/13/82

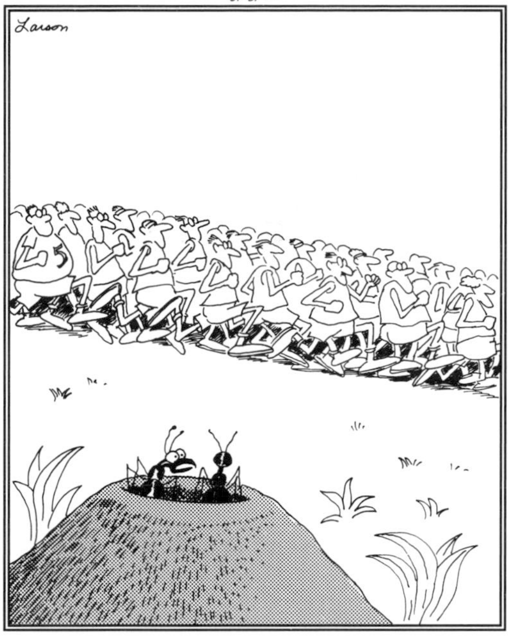
Larson
5

"Uh-oh ... I think Bobby Joe went foraging in that direction."

5/14/82

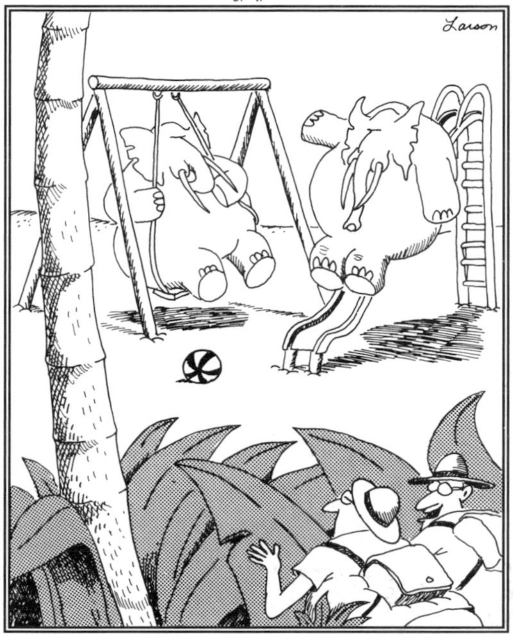
Larson

"By Jove! We've found it, Simmons! ... The Secret Elephant Playground!"

5/15/82

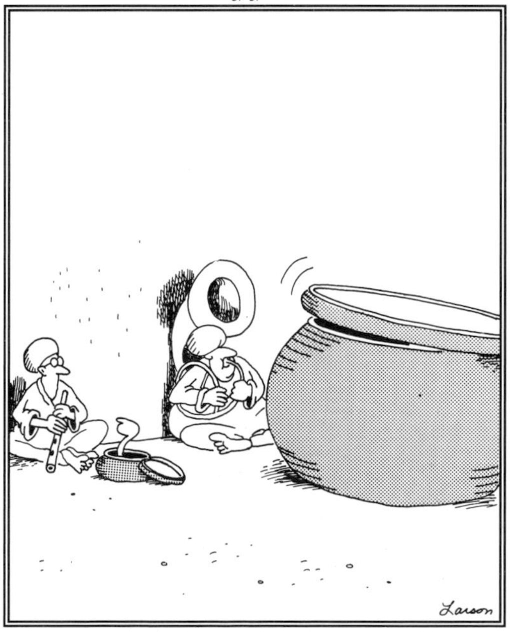
Larson

5/17/82

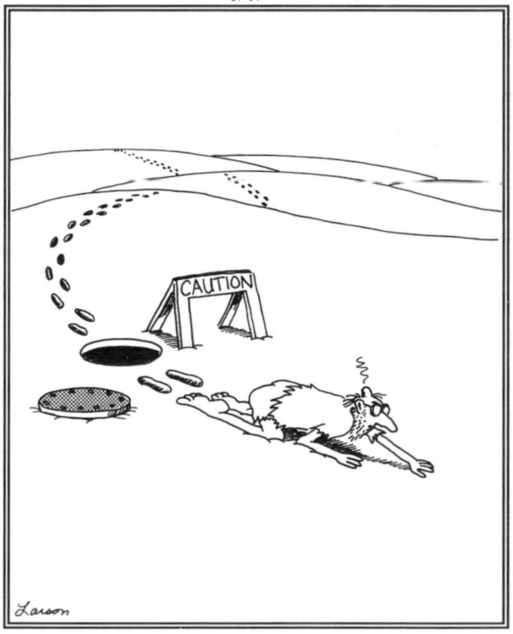
CAUTION
Larson

5/18/82

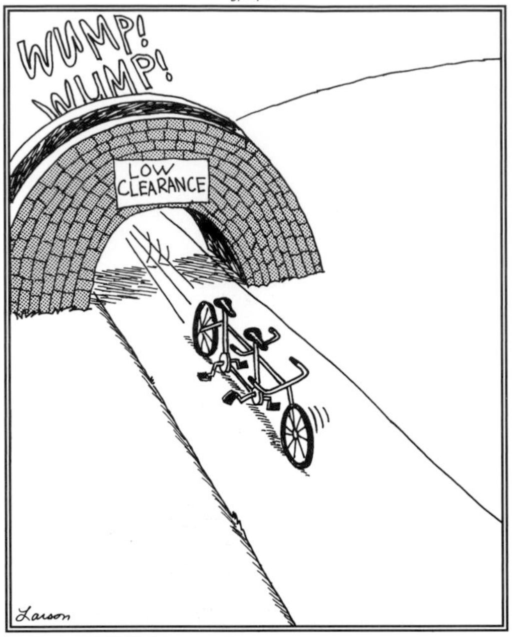
WUMP!
WUMP!
LOW CLEARANCE

5/20/82

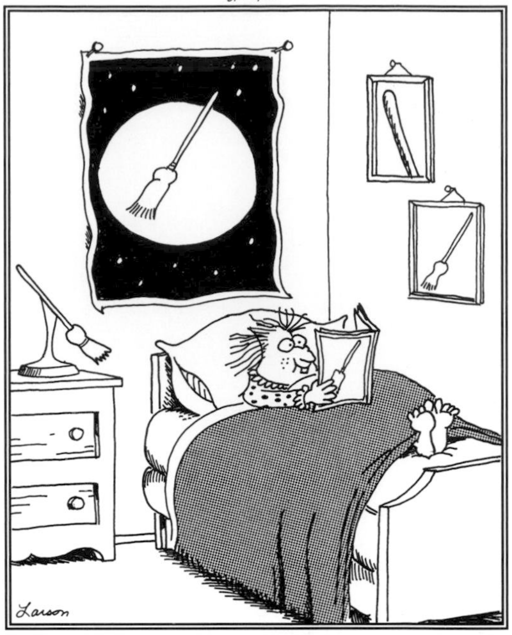

5/22/82

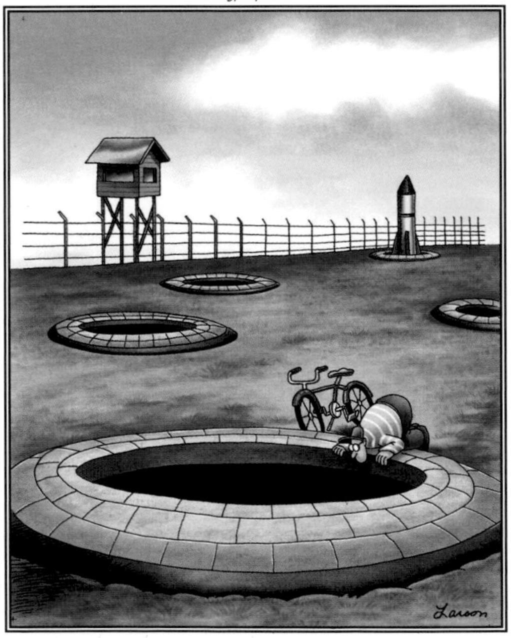

Never, never do this.

5/19/82

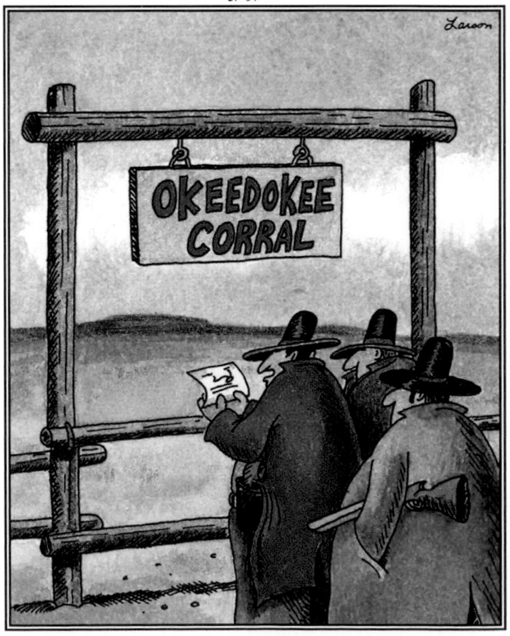
OKEEDOKEE CORRAL

"Well, no wonder! ... This ain't the place."

5/21/82

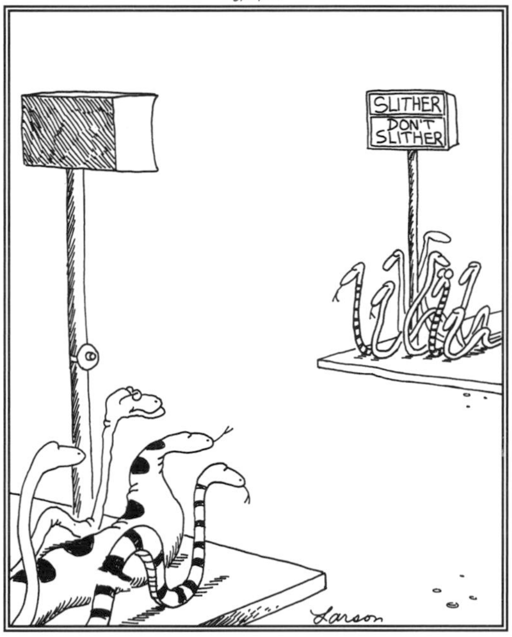
SLITHER
DON'T
SLITHER
Larson

5/25/82

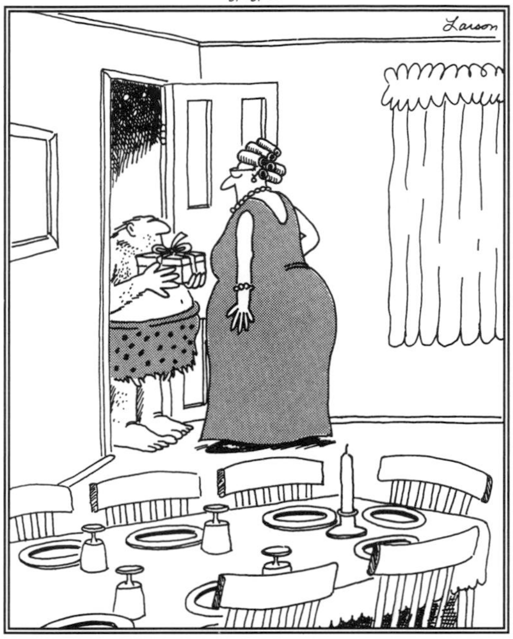
Larson

Early Man

5/27/82

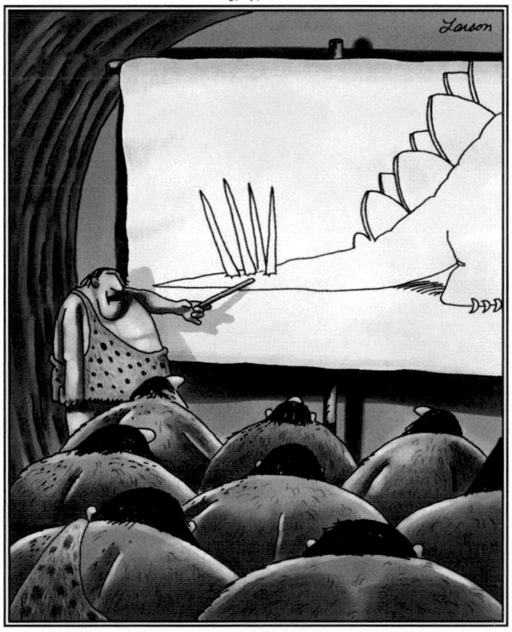
Larson

"Now, this end is called the thagomizer ...
after the late Thag Simmons."

5/29/82

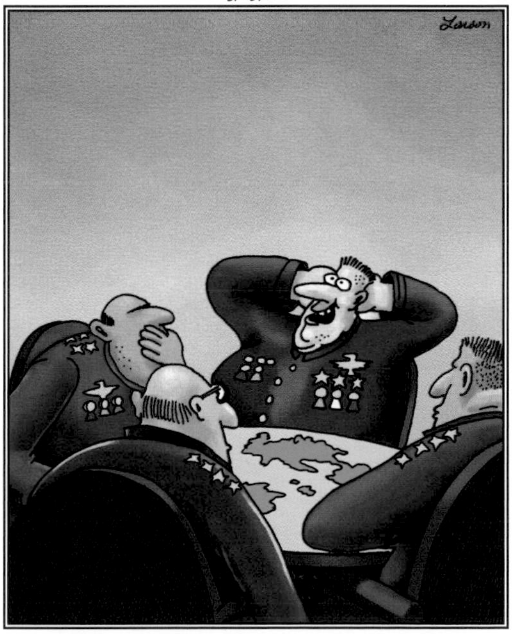
Larson

"On the other hand, gentlemen, what if we
gave a war and *everybody* came?"

5/24/82

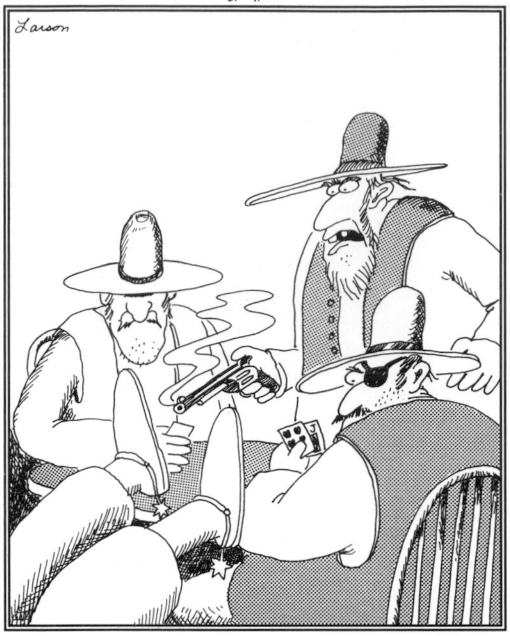
Larson

"Dirty, low-down skunk! ... I saw him slip that last card from his sleeve just before he yelled 'Fish!'"

5/26/82

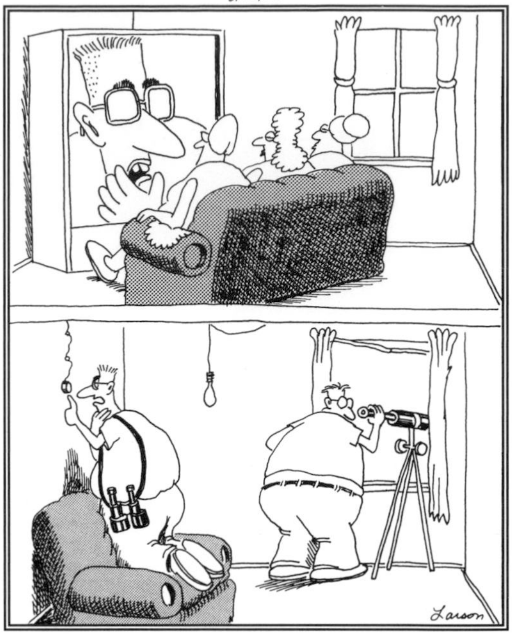
Larson

"Say, Carl ... forget the Hendersons for a second and come look at this thing."

5/28/82

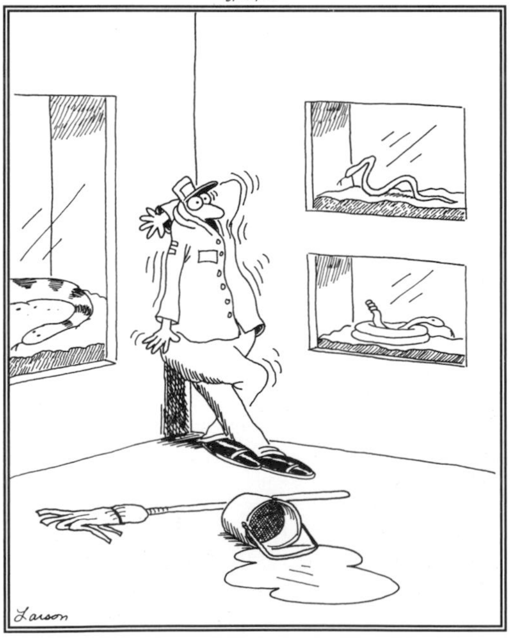
Larson

After 23 uneventful years at the zoo's snakehouse, curator Ernie Schwartz has a cumulative attack of the willies.

5/31/82

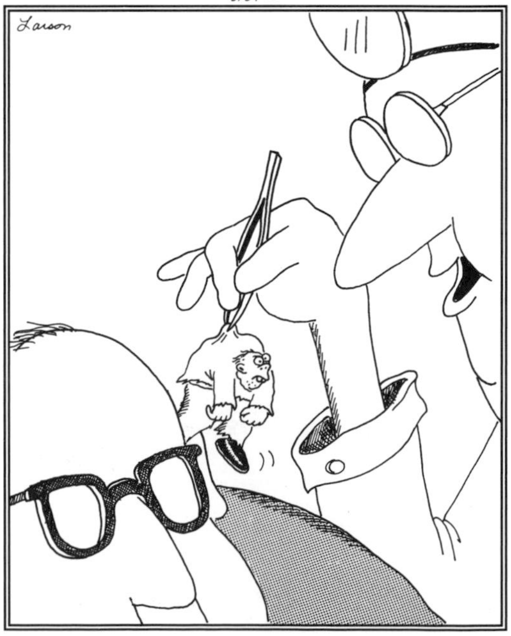
Larson

"Well, well ... seems we've found what's been causing that ringing sensation in your ear, Mr. Foley."

6/1/82

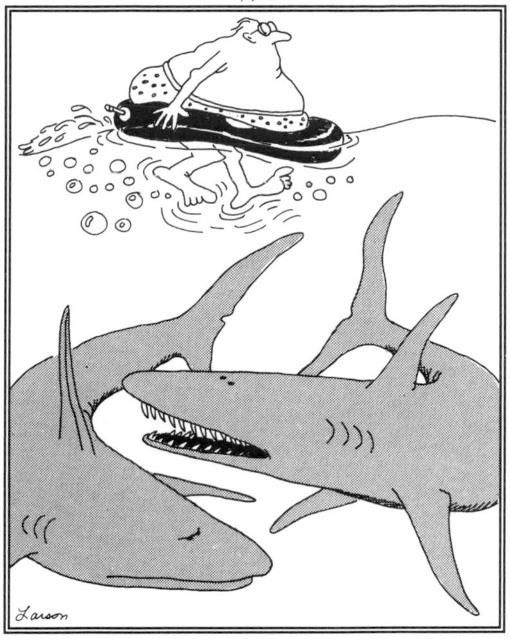
Larson

"I'm tempted, but it looks really high in cholesterol."

6/2/82

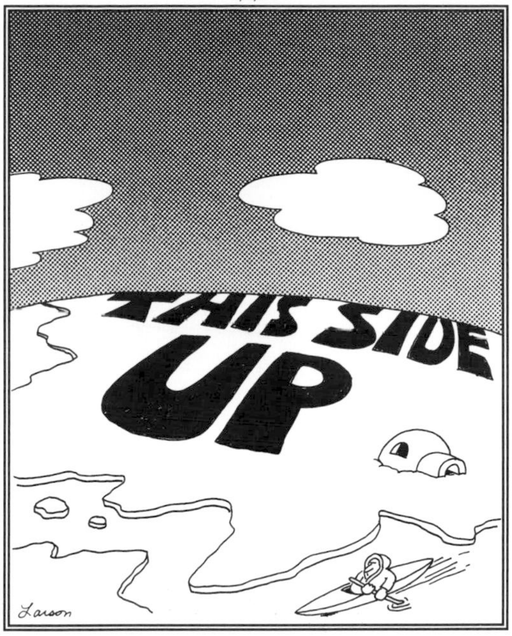
THIS SIDE UP
Larson

6/3/82

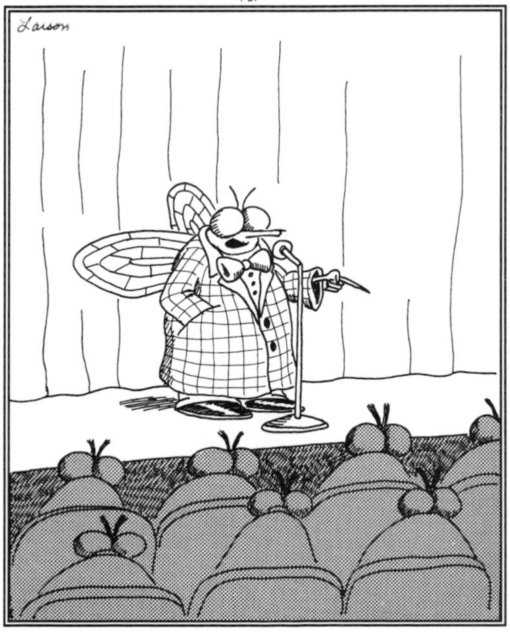
Larson

"Larry? Betty? ... Stand up, will ya? ... These are some friends of mine, folks, who flew all the way in from the dump."

6/4/82

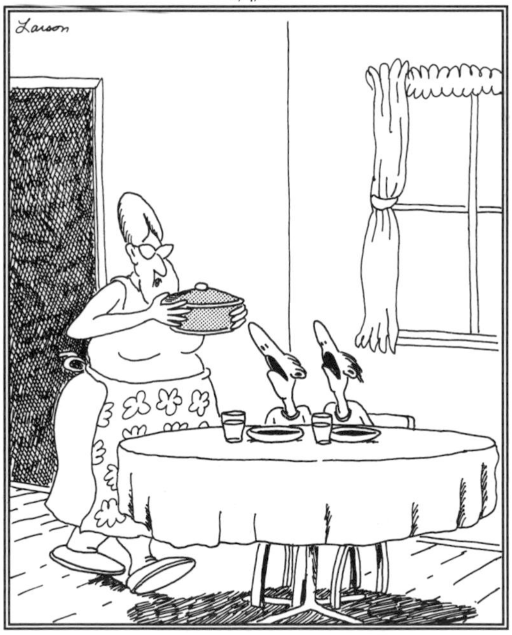
Larson

Dinnertime for the young Wright brothers

"Well, that should do it. ... When Mr. Warner comes around, make sure he gets all the ice cream he wants."

"This is it, Carl! ... We head straight at each other and the first one to veer off is 'chicken.'"

"I say it every time, 'Watch your head, Frank! Watch your head!'... But do you listen?"

6/12/82

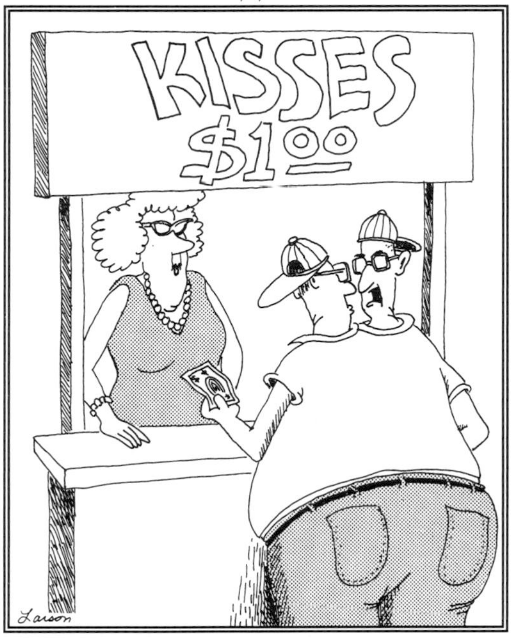
KISSES
$1 00
Larson

"It's *my* turn, Randy! Or I warn you ... I'll start making weird sucking sounds again!"

6/15/82

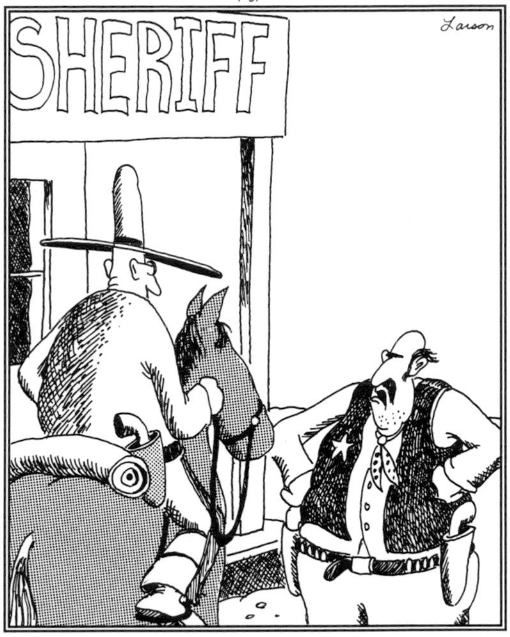
SHERIFF
Larson

"Hold it right there, stranger. We got us a hat-check law in this town ... so just take it off niiiiice and slow."

6/17/82

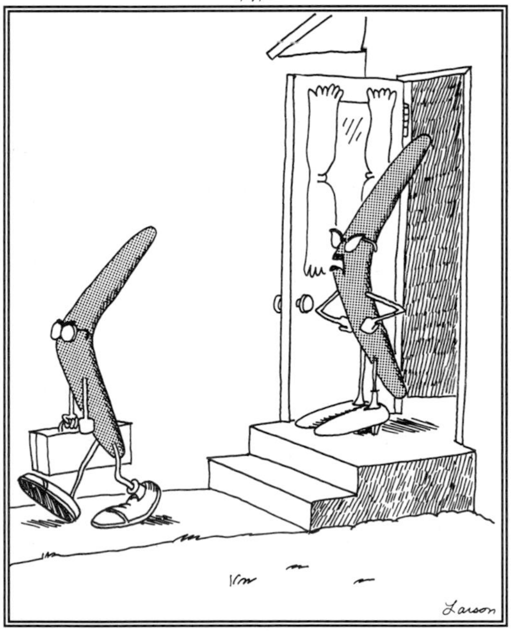
Larson

"Ha! Just like every time, you'll get about a hundred yards out, make a big arc, and start heading back."

6/18/82

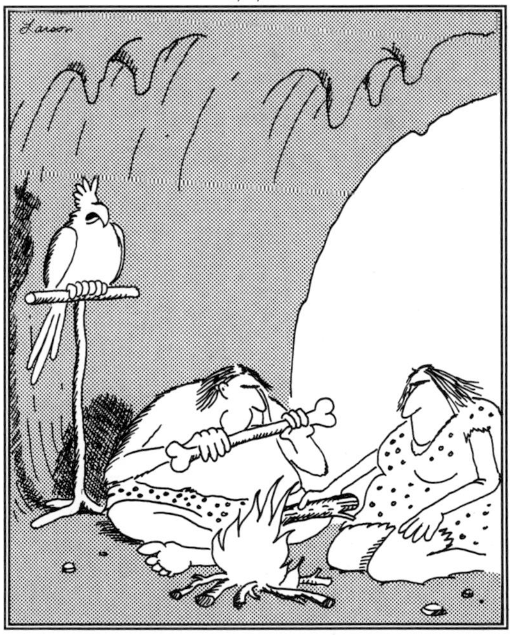
Larson

"Grunt, snort ... grunt grunt, snort ..."

6/11/82

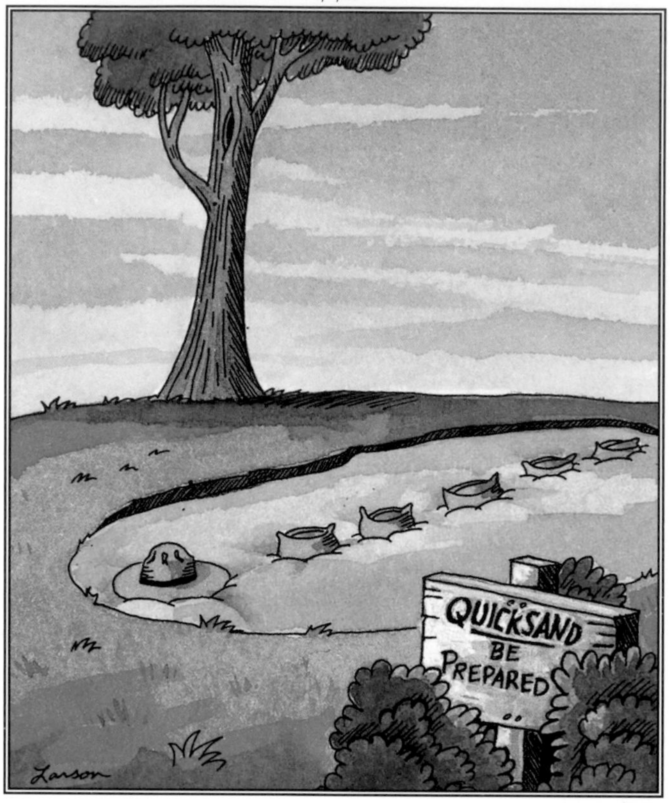
QUICKSAND
BE
PREPARED

6/9/82

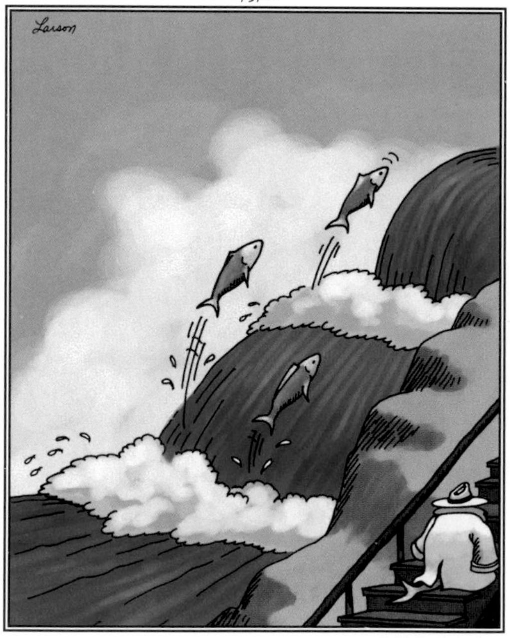

6/14/82

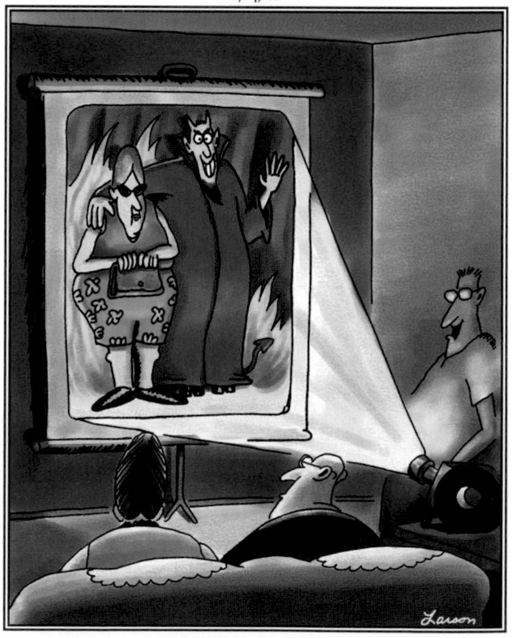

"Oh. Now this is from last summer, when Helen and I went to hell and back."

6/19/82

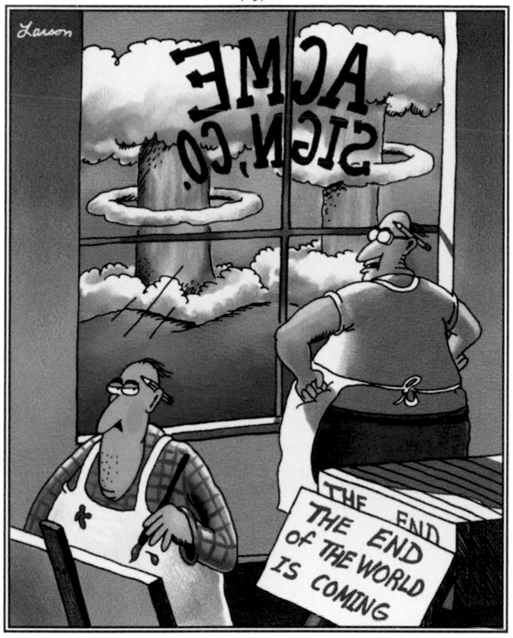
Larson
ACME SIGN CO.
THE END
THE END OF THE WORLD IS COMING

"Well, wouldn't you know it! ... There goes our market for these things!"

6/23/82

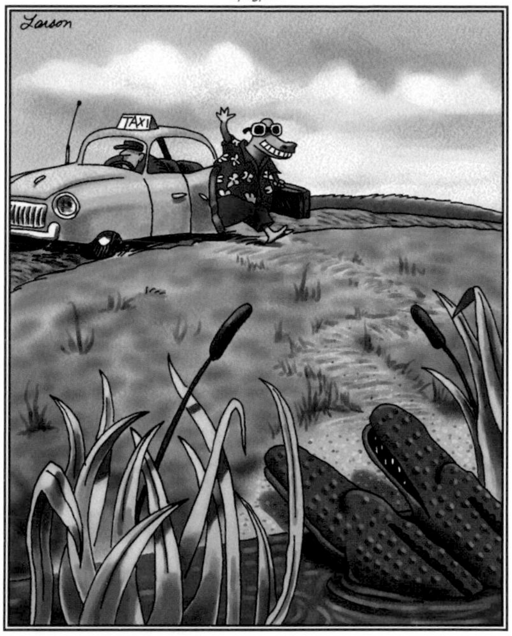
Larson
TAXI

"Well, for crying out loud! ... It's Uncle Irwin from the city sewer!"

6/16/82

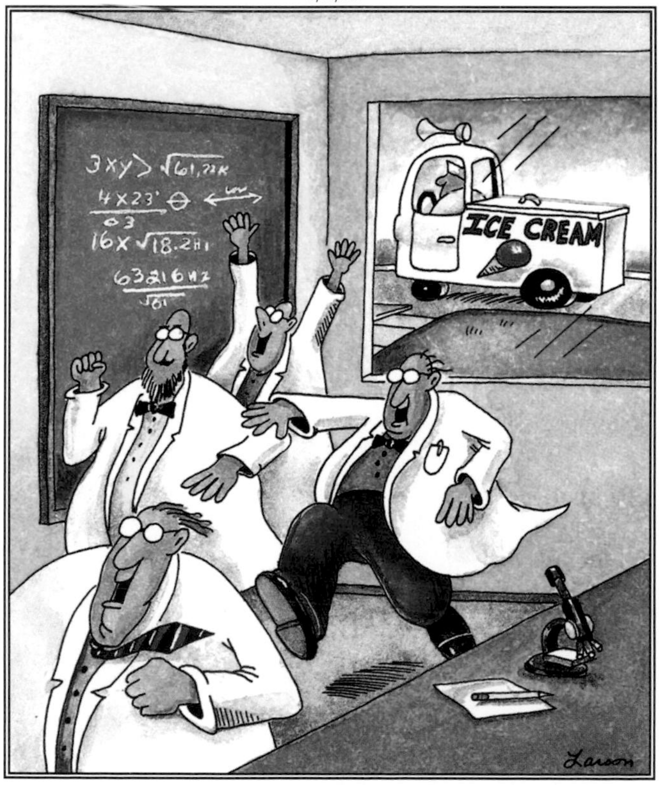
ICE CREAM
Larson

6/25/82

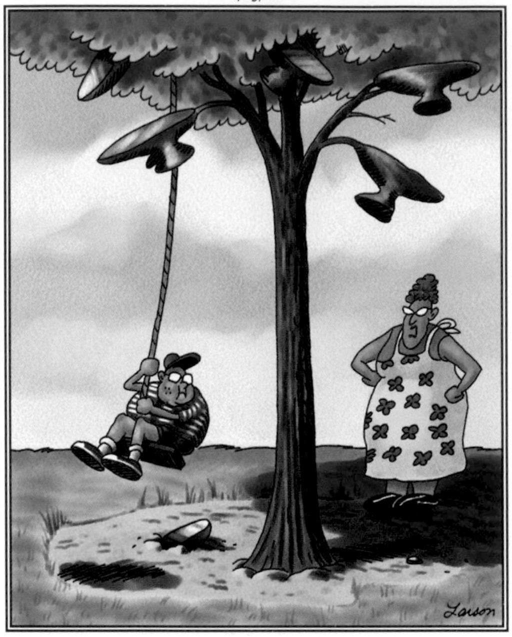
Larson

"All right, Billy, you just go right ahead! ...
I've warned you enough times about
playing under the anvil tree!"

6/26/82

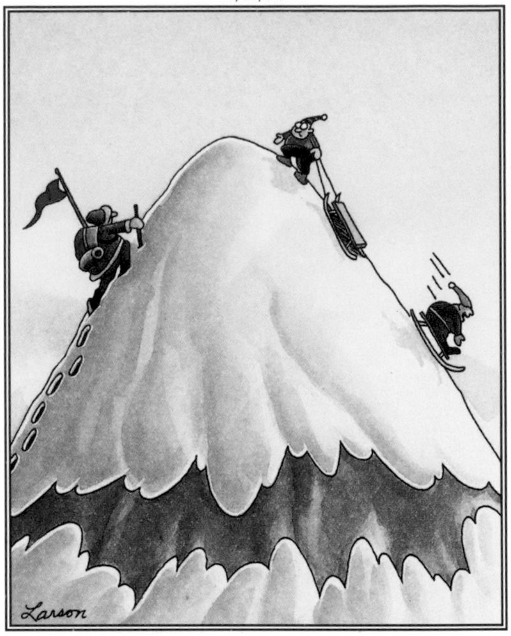
Larson

6/21/82

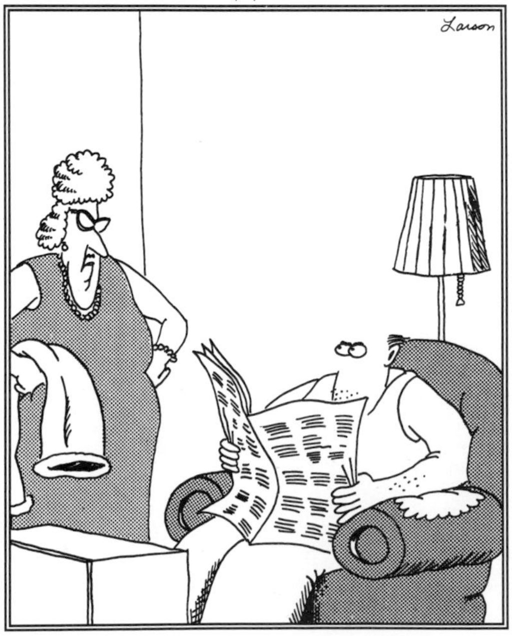
Larson

"For heaven's sake, Murray! ... We're
supposed to leave in five minutes
and you're not even drawn yet!"

6/22/82

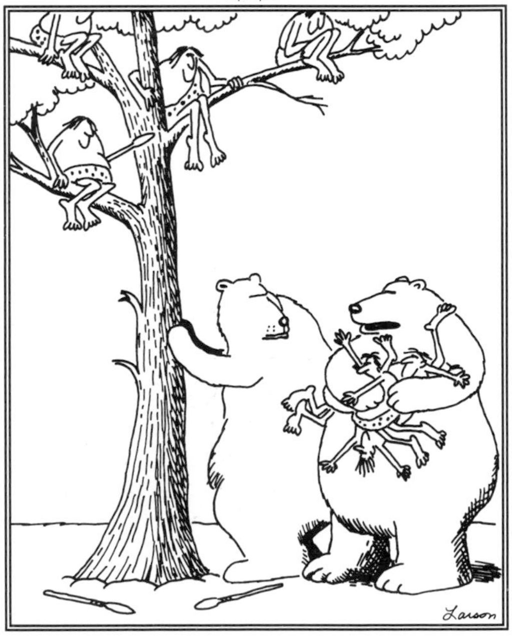
Larson

"Let's see ... I guess your brother's coming
over, too—better give it one more shake."

"Well, well, King ... looks like the new neighbors have brought a friend for you, too."

"I'm sorry, Irwin. ... It's your breath. It's ... it's fresh and minty."

Left to right: Old Man Winter, River, and Higgins

"I assume you're being facetious, Andrews. ... I distinctly yelled 'second!' before you did."

7/1/82

Yes!.. we're OPEN!

7/2/82

ACE LADDER Co.

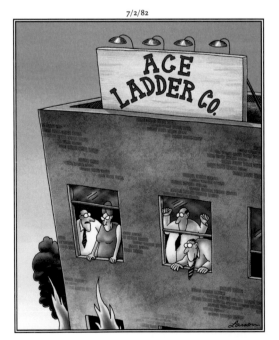

"Wait a minute! Say that again, Doris! ... You know, the part about 'If only we had some means of climbing down.'"

7/3/82

DOUBLE YOUR IQ OR NO MONEY BACK!

"Well, I dunno. ... Okay, sounds good to me."

7/6/82

CHIN-UP BAR

7/7/82

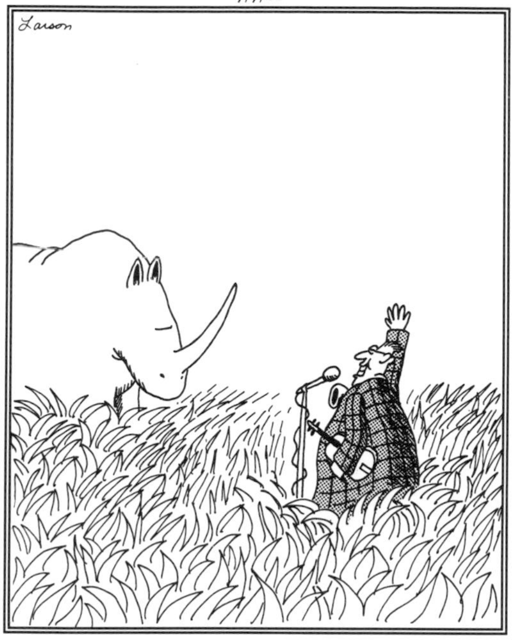
Larson

The African rhino: an animal with little or no sense of humor.

7/9/82

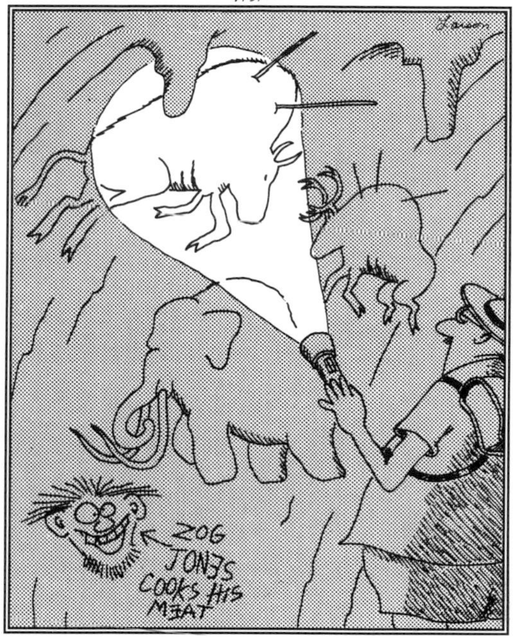
Larson
ZOG
JONES
COOKS HIS
MEAT

7/13/82

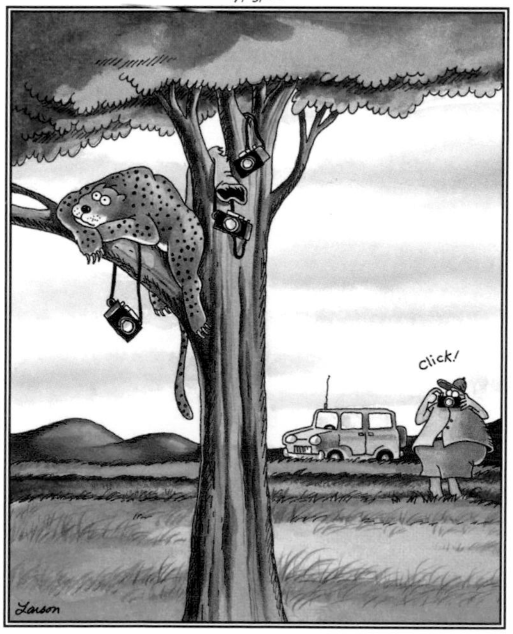
click!
Larson

7/5/82

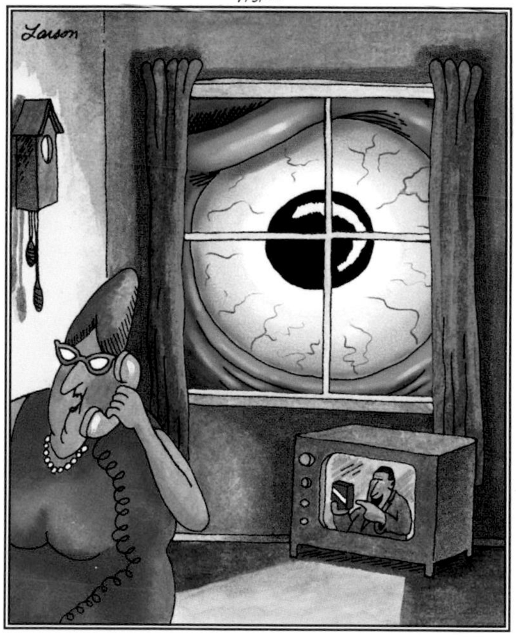
Larson

"Hello, Emily. This is Gladys Murphy up the street. Fine, thanks. ... Say, Emily, could you go to your window and describe what's in my front yard?"

7/8/82

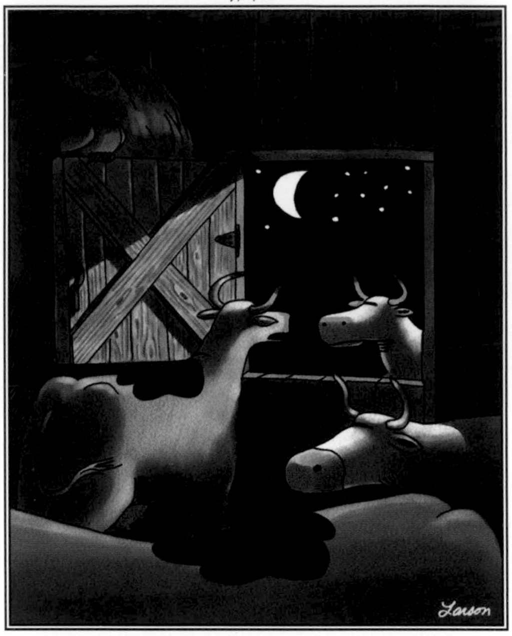
Larson

"I'm sorry, but we haven't any room. ... You'll have to sleep in the house."

7/15/82

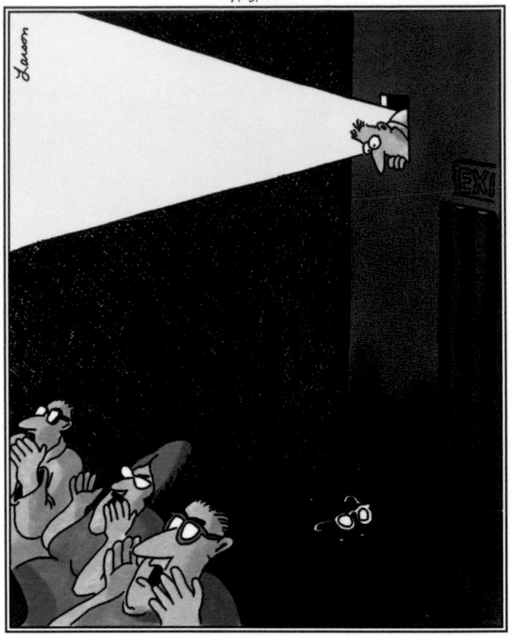
Larson

"FOCUS! ... FOCUS!"

7/10/82

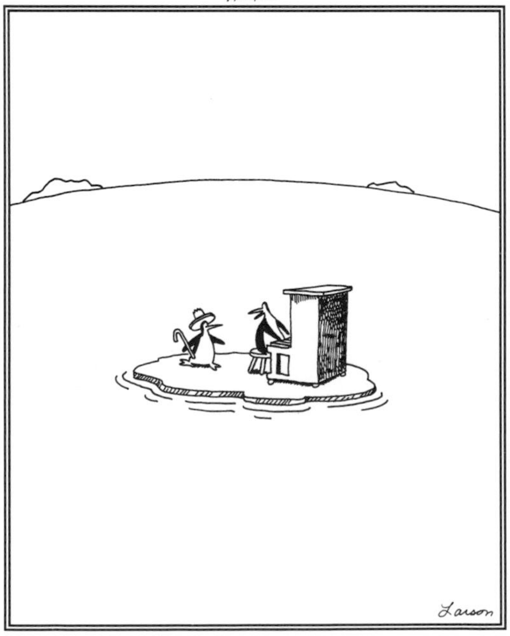
Larson

"No, no, no! Now, try it again! ... Remember, this is our one and only ticket out of here!"

7/12/82

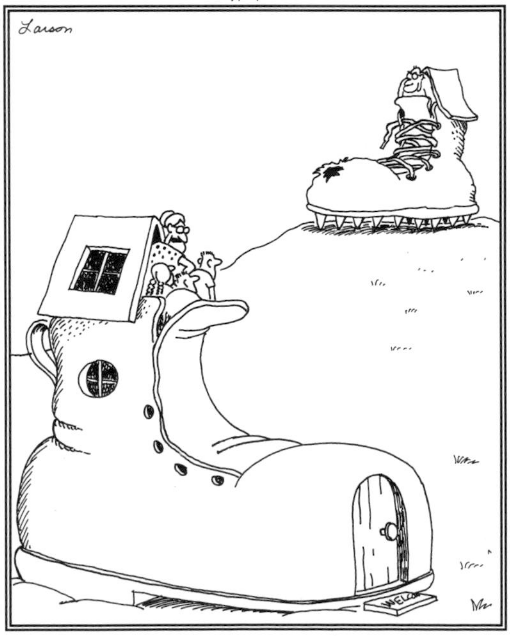
Larson

"Now don't you kids forget—stay away from old Mr. Weatherby's place."

7/17/82

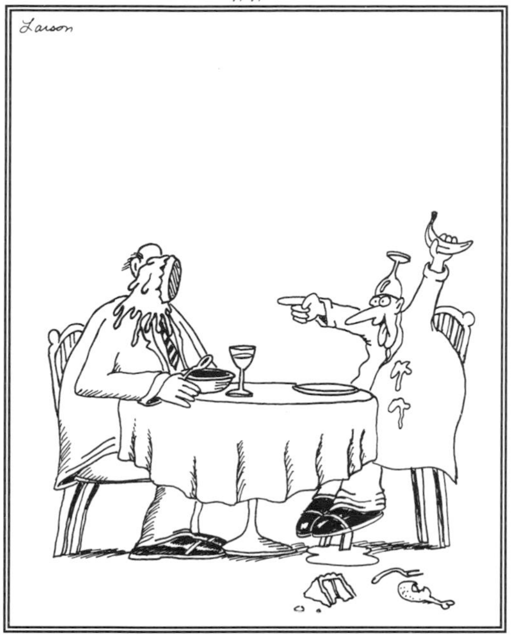

My dinner with Andy

7/14/82

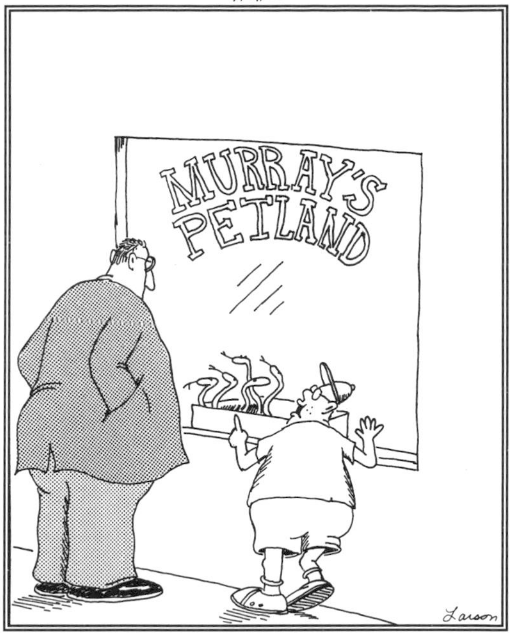
MURRAY'S PETLAND

"Oh, please, oh, please, Dad! ...
The little brown one!"

7/20/82

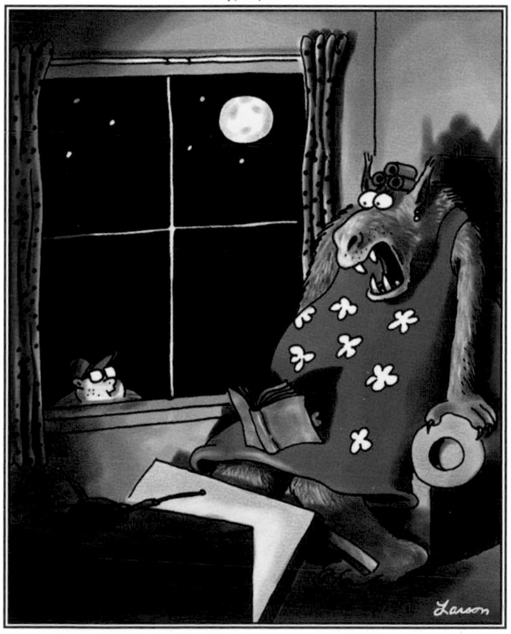

7/23/82

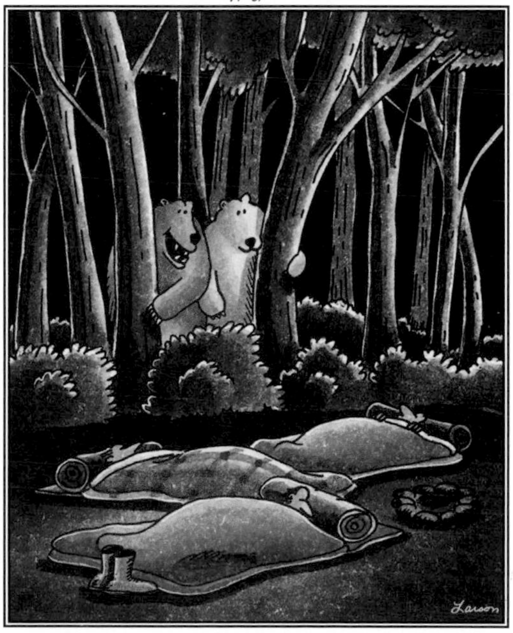

"Sandwiches!"

7/19/82

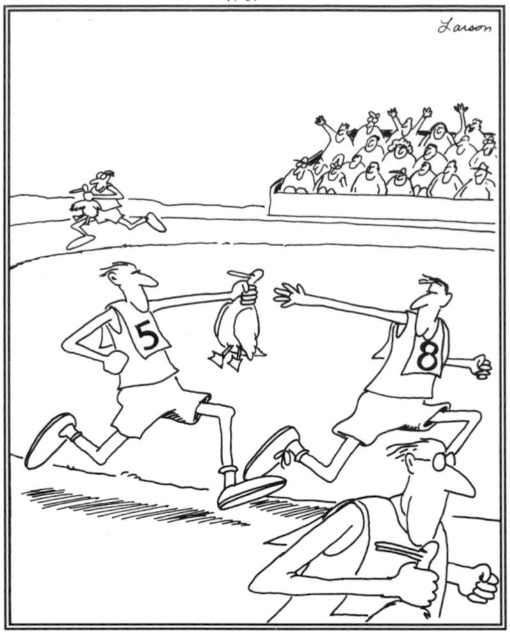
Larson
5
8

The duck relays

7/24/82

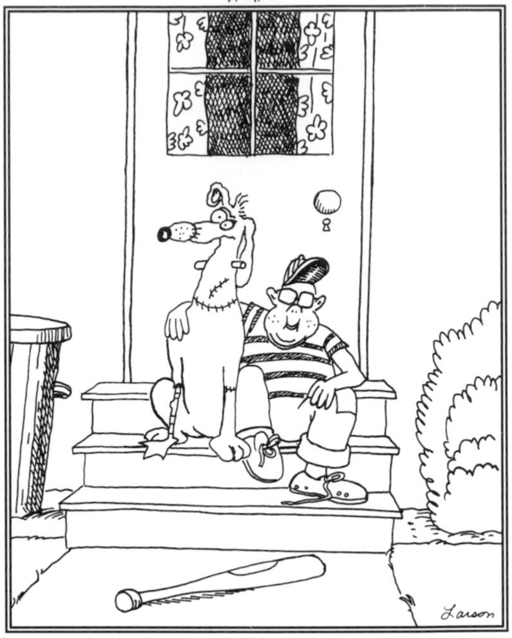
Larson

Young Jimmy Frankenstein

7/21/82

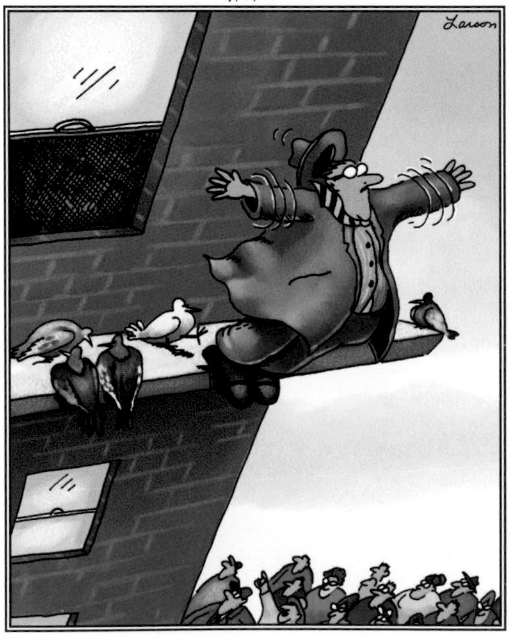
Larson

7/22/82

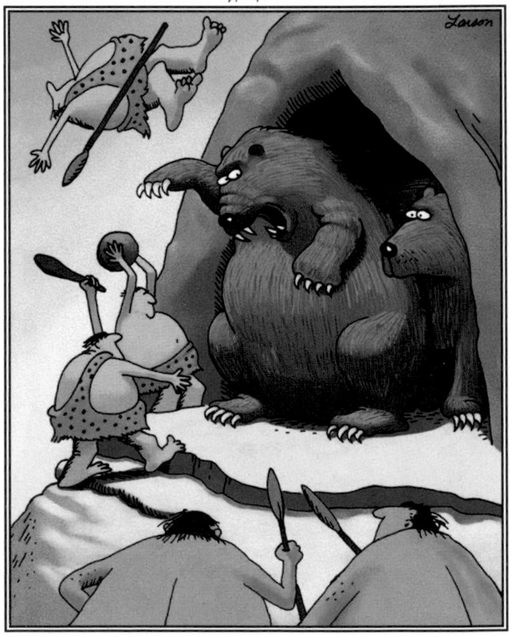
Larson

"Crimony! ... It seems like every summer there's more and more of these things around!"

7/16/82

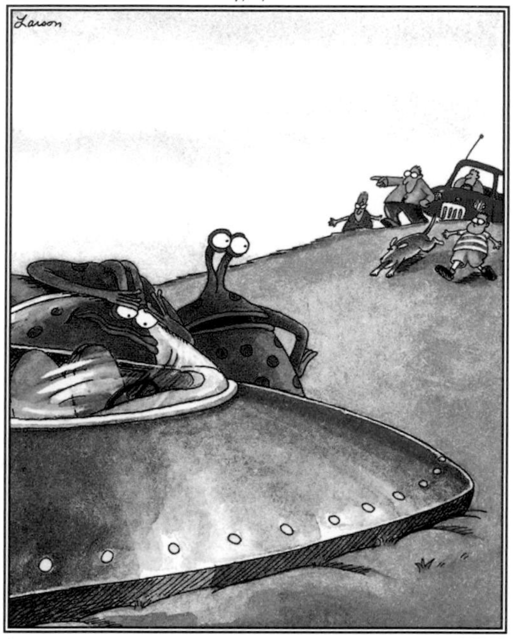
Larson

"Well, here they come. ... You locked the keys inside, you do the talkin'."

7/26/82

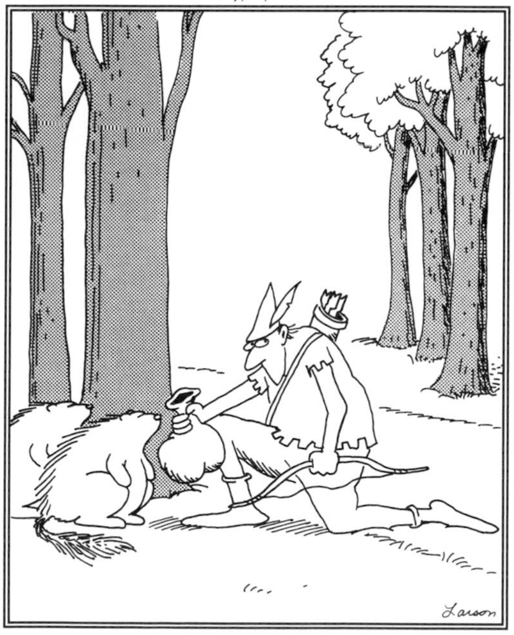
Larson

Historic note: Until his life's destiny was further clarified, Robin Hood spent several years robbing from the rich and giving to the porcupines.

7/27/82

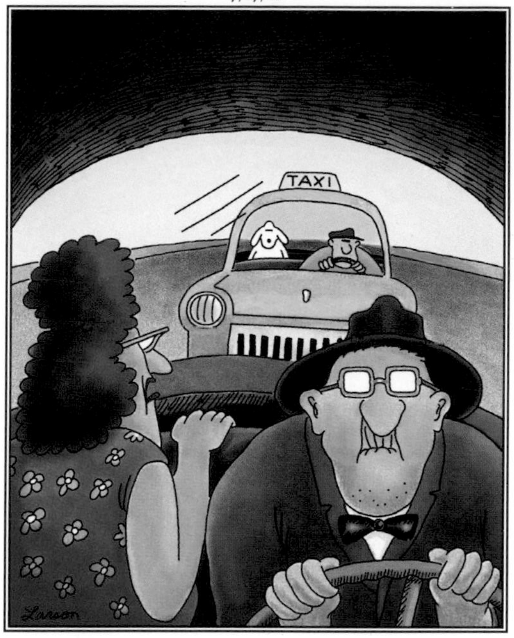
TAXI
Larson

"Blast it, Henry! ... I think the dog is following us."

7/30/82

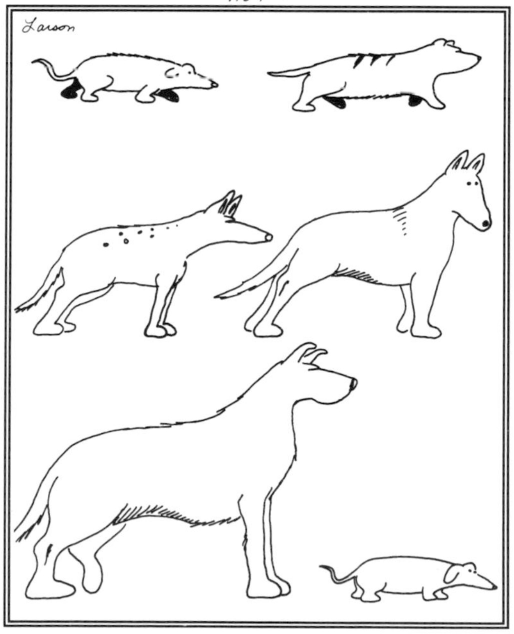
Larson

Evolution of the dog

7/29/82

"DOWN IN FRONT! ... SIT DOWN! ...
SIT DOWN!"

7/28/82

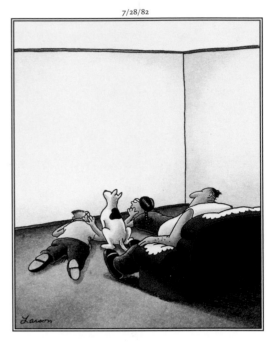

In the days before television

7/31/82

Late at night, and without permission, Reuben
would often enter the nursery and conduct
experiments in static electricity.

8/2/82

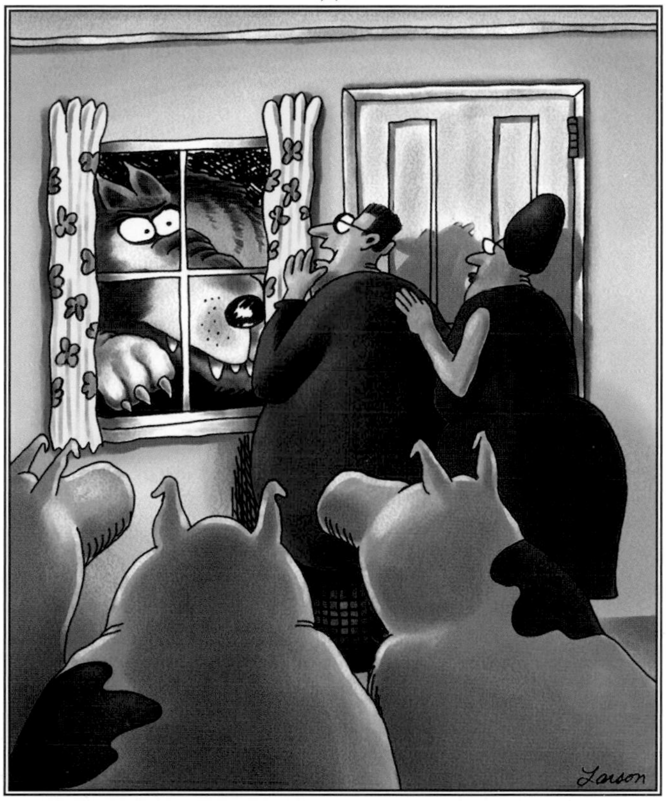

"Listen out there! We're George and Harriet Miller! We just dropped in on the pigs for coffee! We're coming out! ... We don't want trouble!"

8/5/82

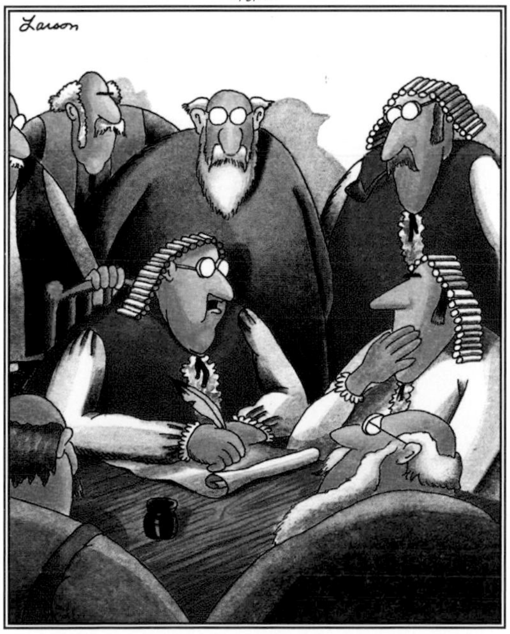

"So, then ... would that be 'us the people' or 'we the people'?"

8/6/82

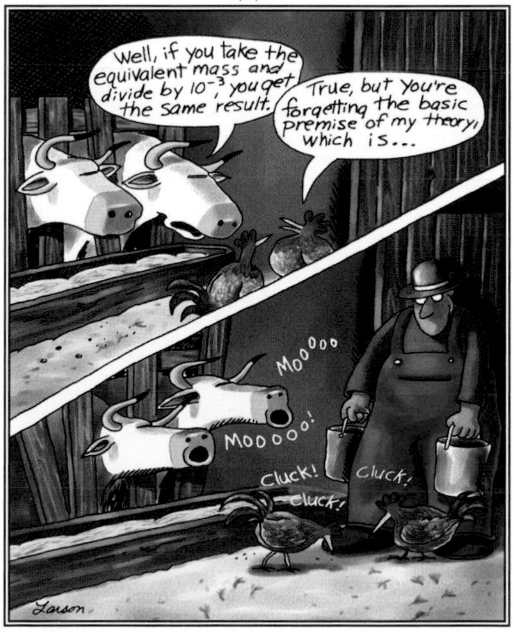
Well, if you take the equivalent mass and divide by 10^{-3}, you get the same result.
True, but you're forgetting the basic premise of my theory, which is...
Moooo
Moooo!
Cluck!
cluck!
Cluck!

8/3/82

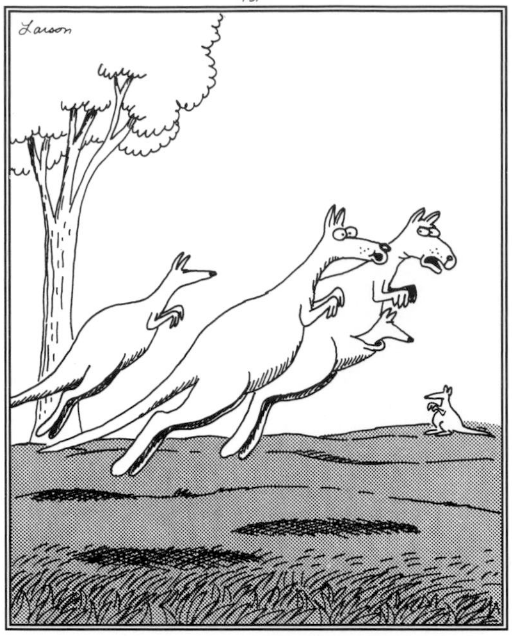
Larson

"Just jump, fool! ... You don't have to go, 'Boing, boing, boing!'"

8/9/82

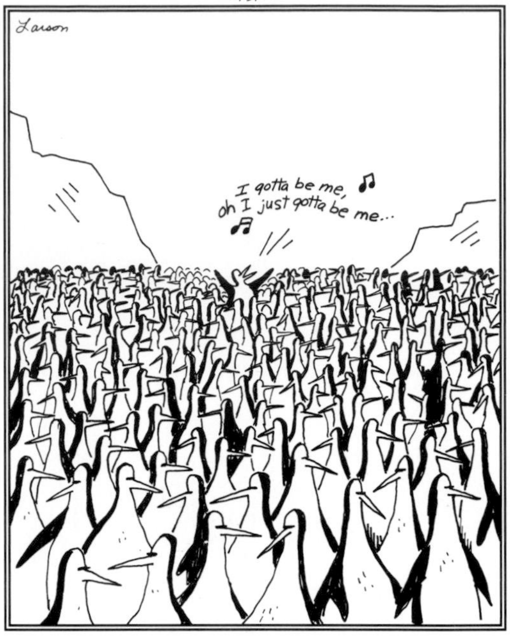
Larson
I gotta be me,
oh I just gotta be me...

8/7/82

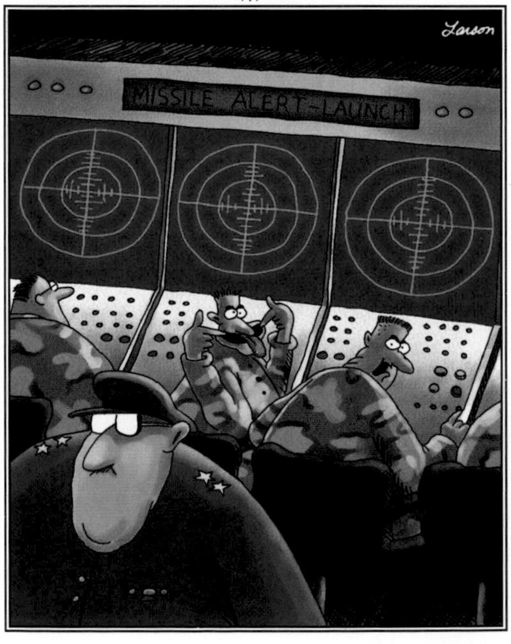
Larson
MISSILE ALERT-LAUNCH

"General! Quick! Look! ... Henderson is doing it again!"

8/11/82

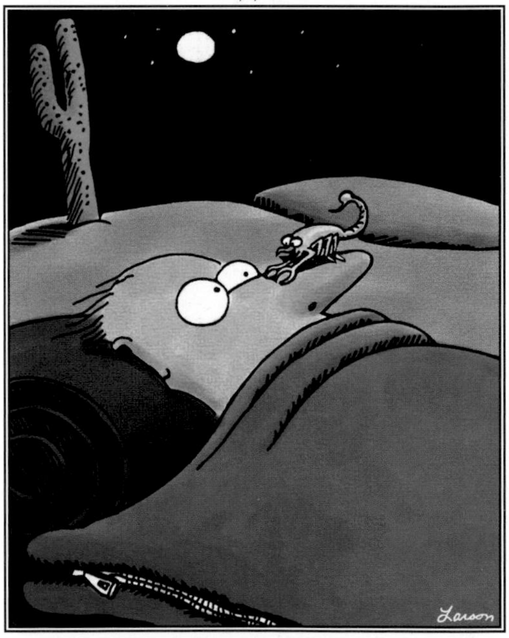
Larson

"Excuse me, but the others sent me up here to ask you to please not roll around so much."

8/18/82

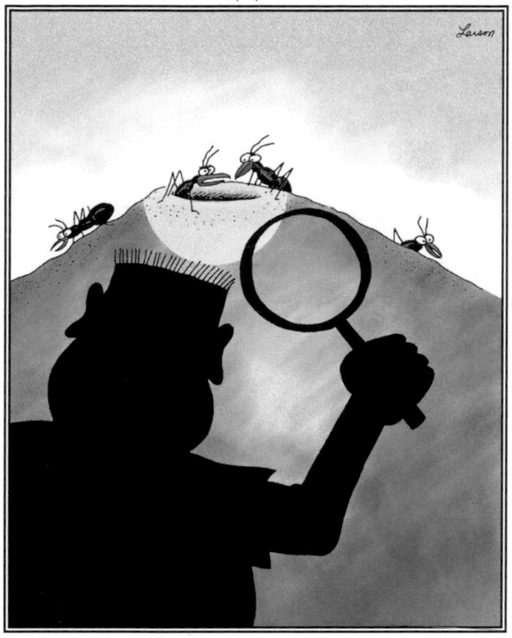

"Say ... now *I'm* starting to feel kinda warm!"

8/16/82

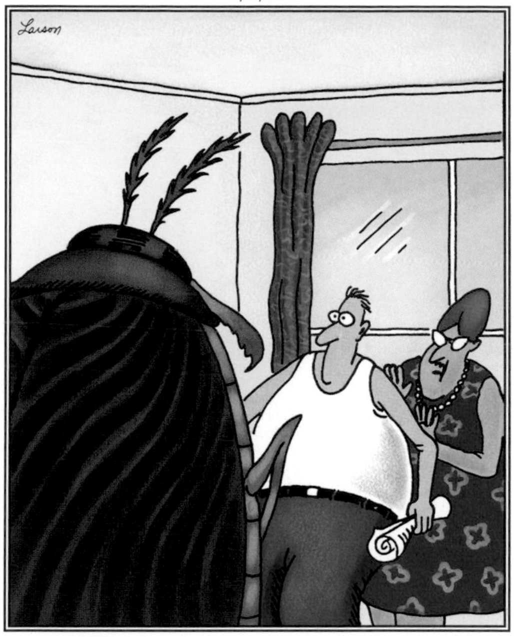

"Step on it, Arnold! STEP ON IT!"

8/4/82

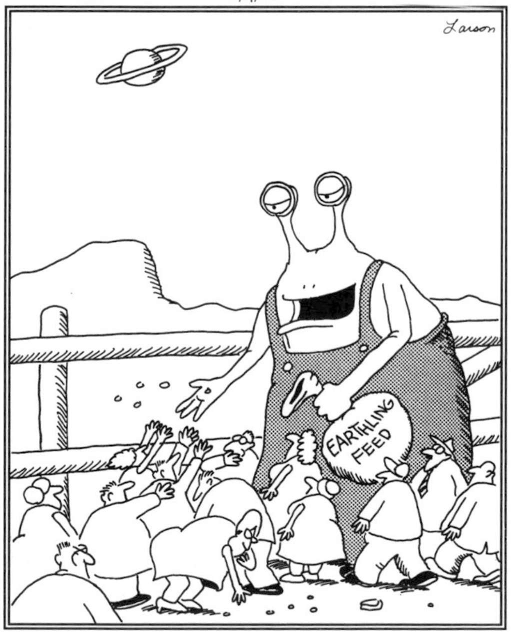
EARTHLING
FEED

"Heeeeeere, yakity yak yak yak! ...
Come, come, yakity yak yak yak!"

8/10/82

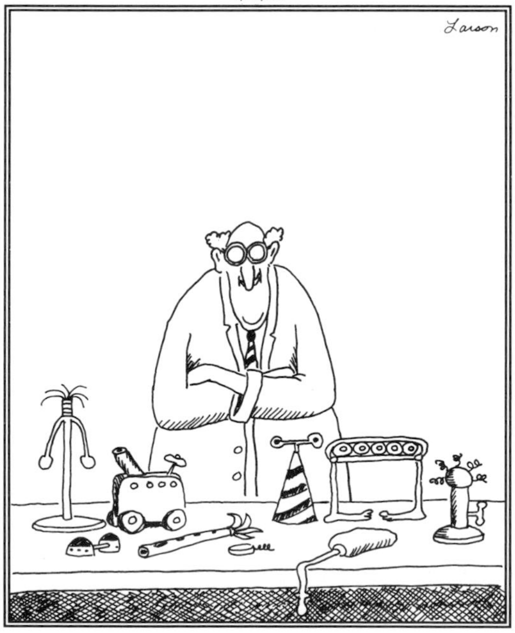

Professor E. F. Gizmo and some of
his many inventions

8/13/82

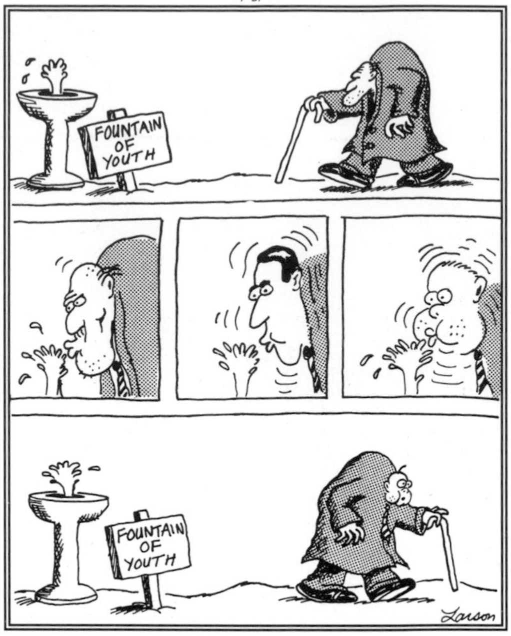
FOUNTAIN OF YOUTH
FOUNTAIN OF YOUTH

8/12/82

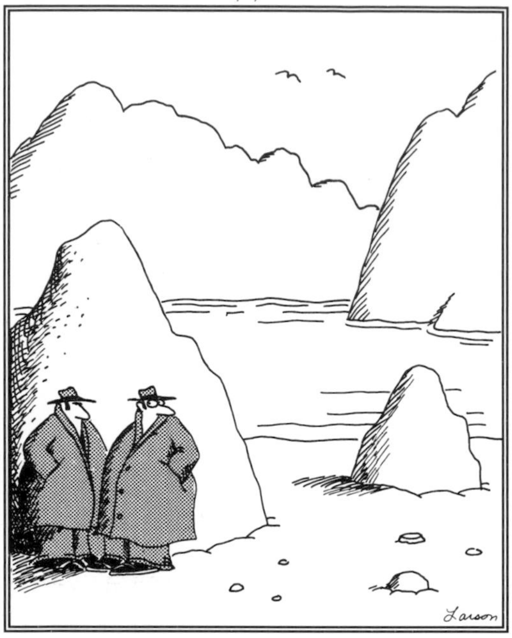

Loch Ness mobsters

8/20/82

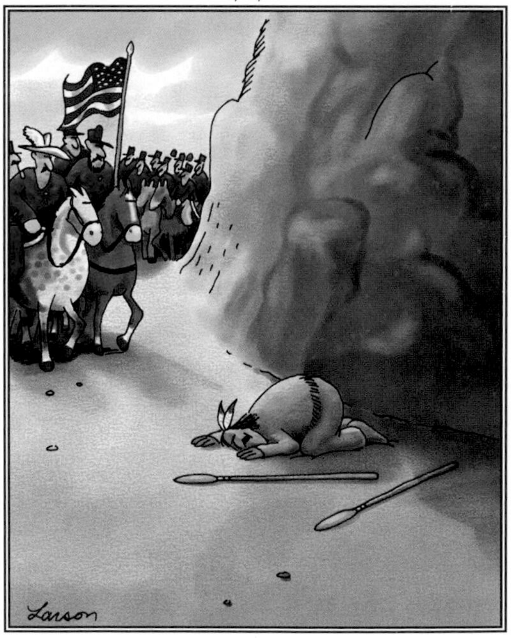

"I say fifty, maybe a hundred horses. ...
What you say, Red Eagle?"

8/19/82

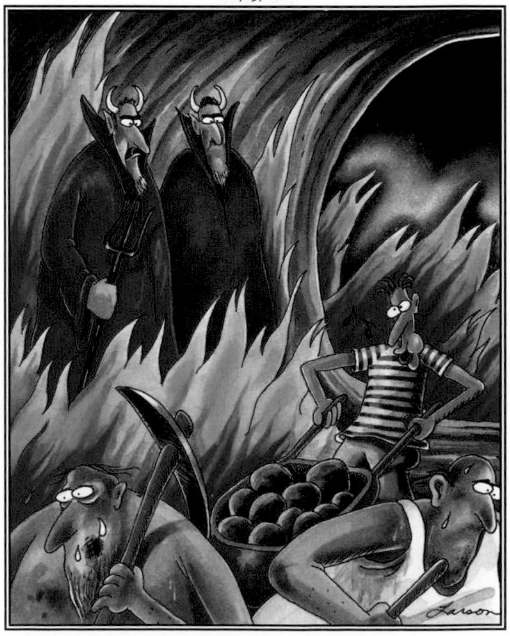

"You know, we're just not reaching that guy."

8/14/82

"Somethin's in the air, Carl. ... The doc's gettin' that old twinkle in his eye again."

8/17/82

8/21/82

"THE GOLDEN ARCHES! ... THE GOLDEN ARCHES GOT ME!"

8/24/82

Inevitably, their affair ended: Howard worried excessively about what the pack would think, and Agnes simply ate the flowers.

8/23/82

"Look! Look, gentlemen! Purple mountains! Spacious skies! Fruited plains! ... Is someone writing this down?"

8/28/82

"And notice, gentlemen, the faster I go, the more Simmons sounds like a motorboat."

8/25/82

"And now there go the Wilsons! ... Seems like everyone's evolving except us!"

8/26/82

"One!"

Things that go bump in the night

"Listen ... you go tell Billy's mother, and I'll start looking for another old tire."

"Mom! Dad! ... The nose fairy left me a whole quarter!"

"Uh-oh, Lorraine ... someone seems to be checking you out."

"Do you know me? I have to deal with lions, wolves, and saber-toothed tigers. ... That's why I carry one of *these*."

"Hey! Hey, you idiots! The train has stopped! ... Come on down from there!"

9/6/82

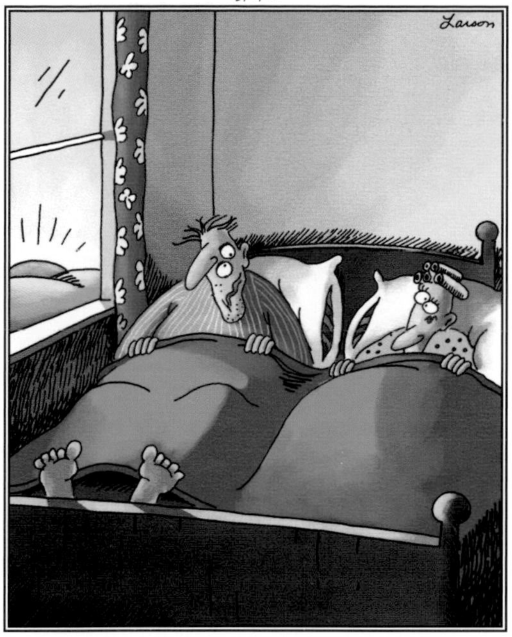
Larson

The embarrassment of "morning face"

9/8/82

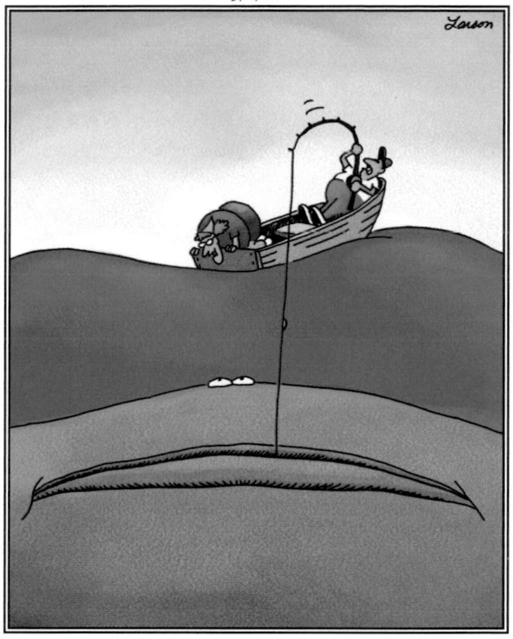
Larson

"Good heavens, Stuart! ... We're definitely going to need the net!"

9/10/82

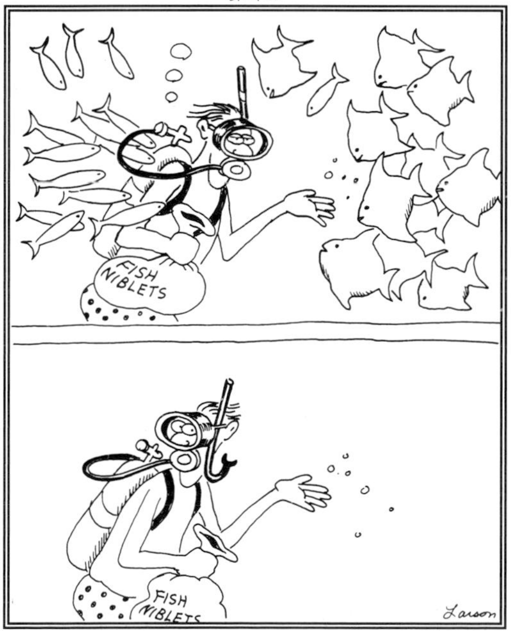
FISH NIBLETS
FISH NIBLETS
Larson

Nature's subtle signs of danger

9/21/82

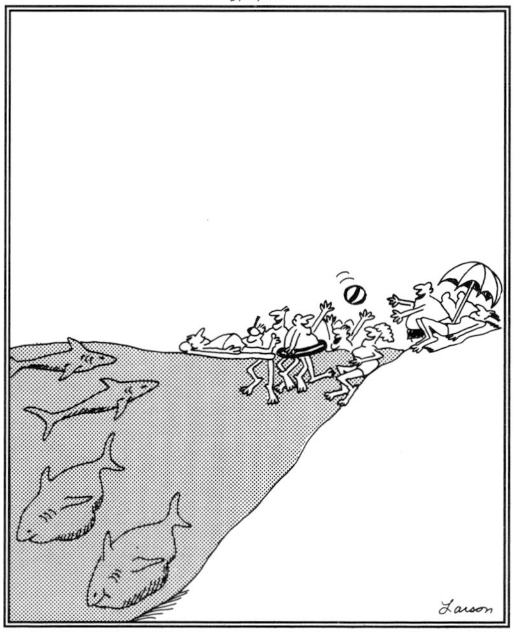
Larson

9/9/82

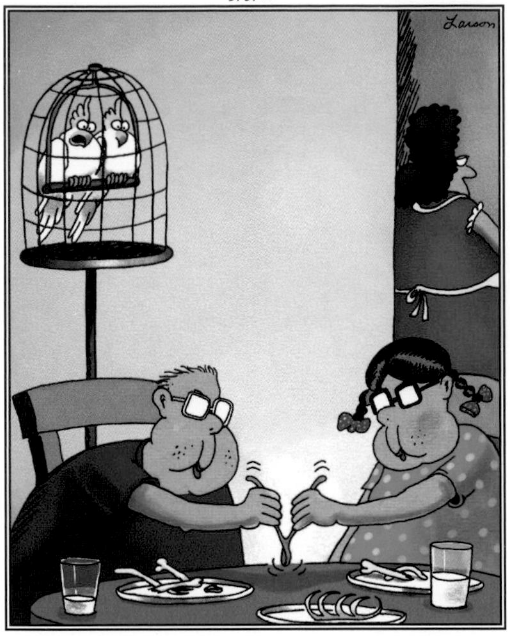
Larson

"Now here comes the barbaric finale."

9/11/82

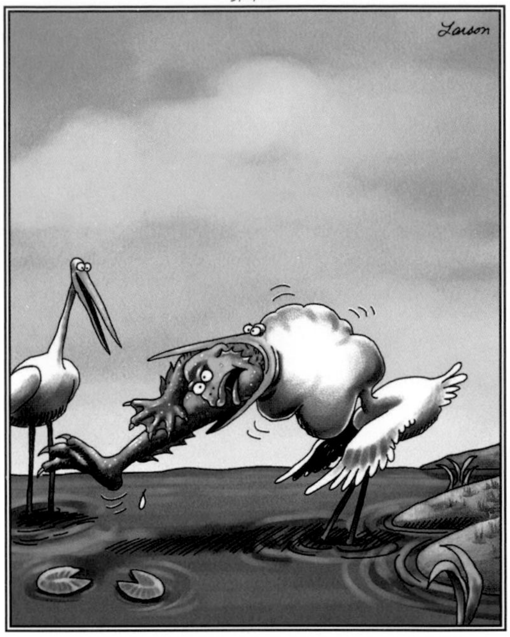
Larson

"*Now* you've got him, Vinnie!"

9/7/82

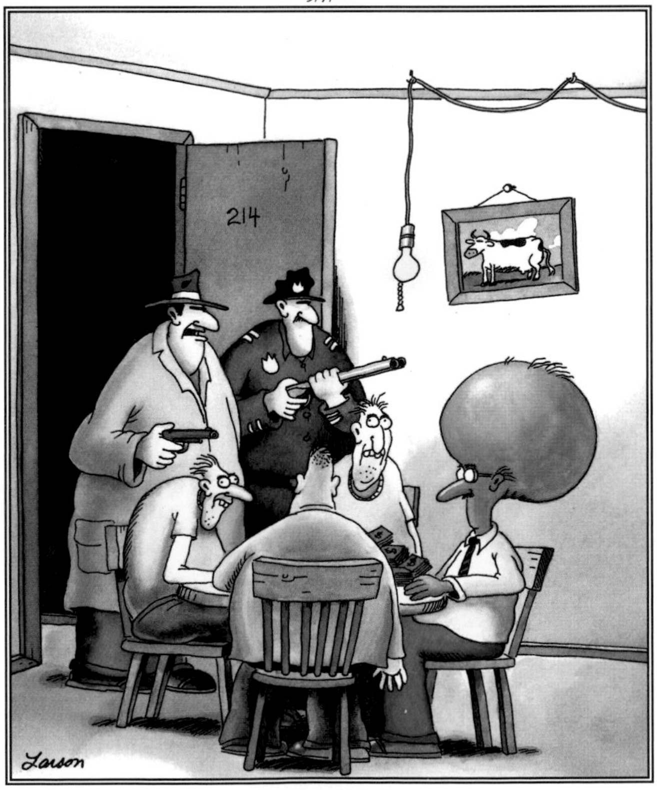
214
Larson

"FREEZE! ... Okay, now ... who's the brains of this outfit?"

September 1982

9/16/82

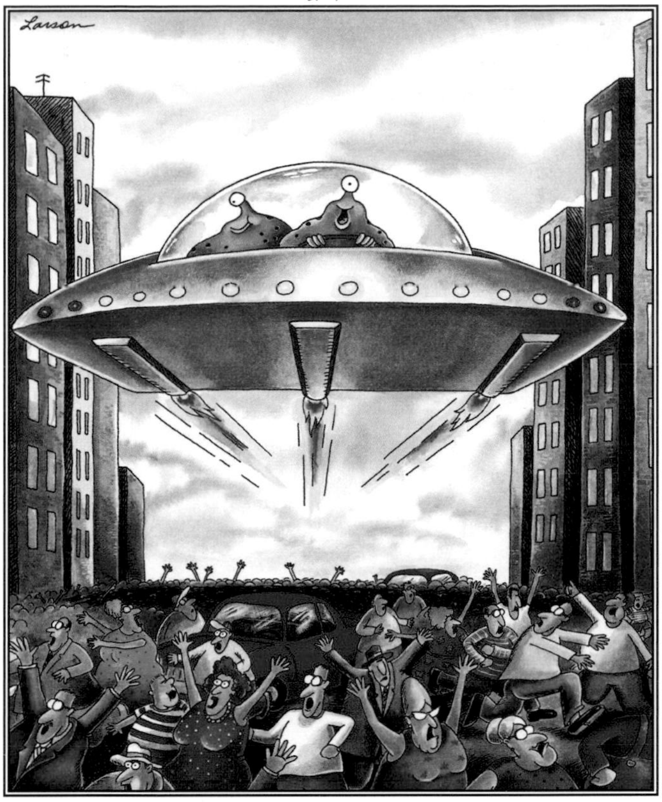
Larson

"YEEEEEHAAAAAAAAA!"

9/13/82

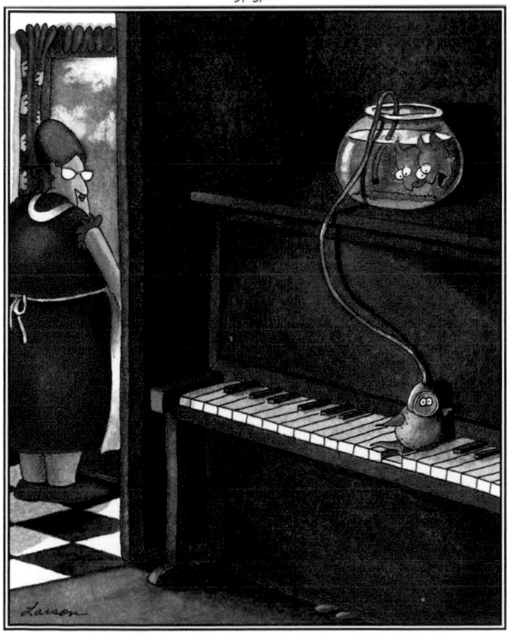
Larson

"The fool! ... He's on the keyboard!"

9/17/82

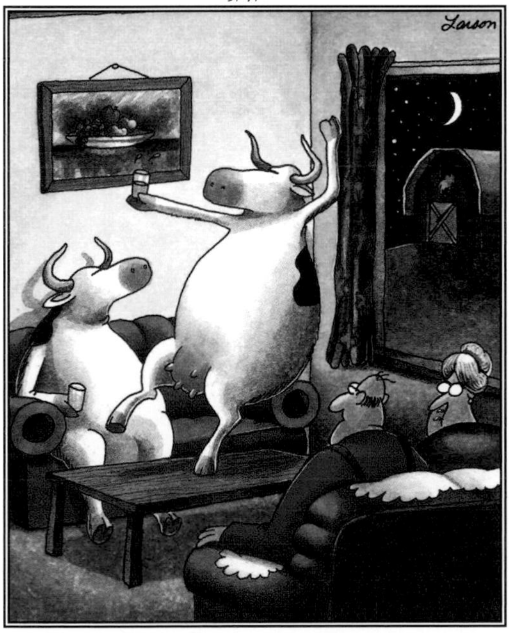
Larson

"Satisfied? ... I warned you not to invite the cows in for a few drinks."

9/14/82

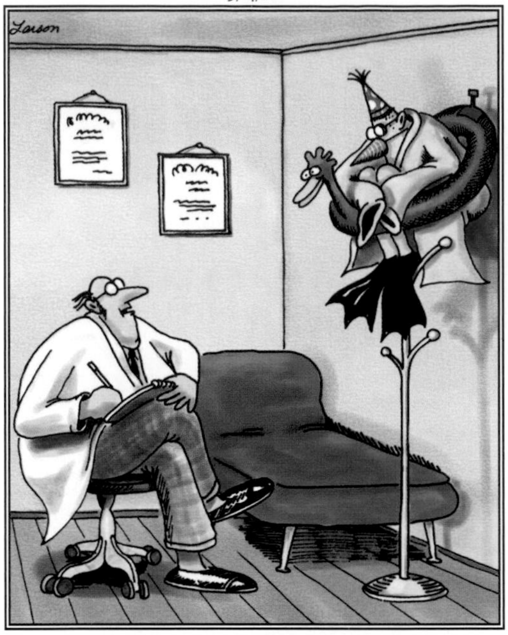
Larson

"So, Mr. Fenton ... let's begin
with your mother."

9/15/82

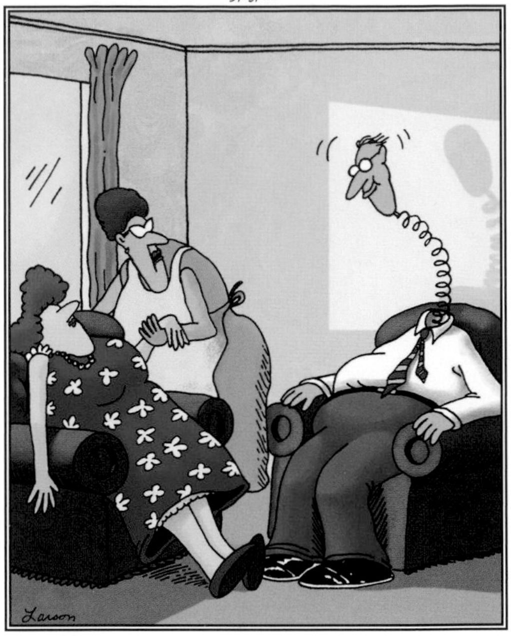
Larson

"Well, Emily is out like a light. ... Just can't
resist pulling that little stunt of yours,
can you, Earl?"

9/25/82

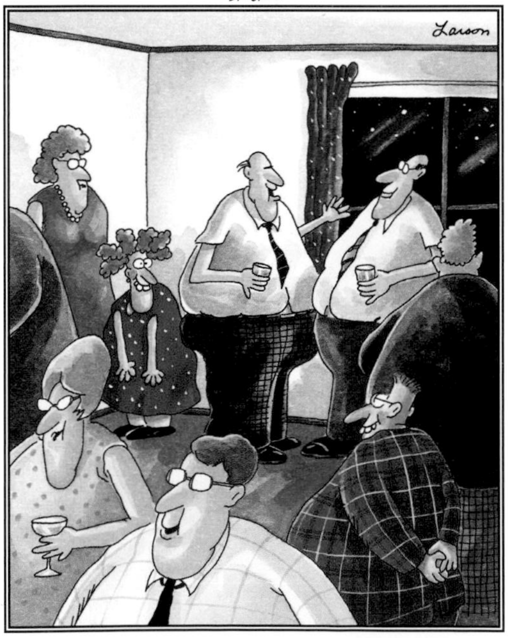
Larson

And then, from across the room,
their eyes met.

9/24/82

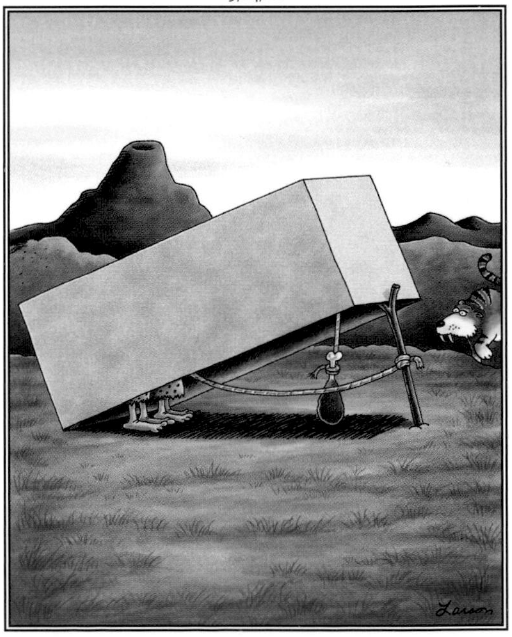
Larson

"Shhhh, Zog! ... Here come one now!"

9/18/82

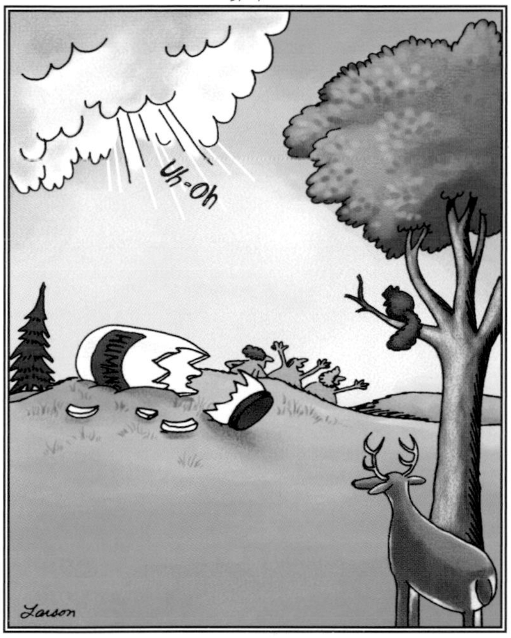
Uh-Oh
Larson

9/23/82

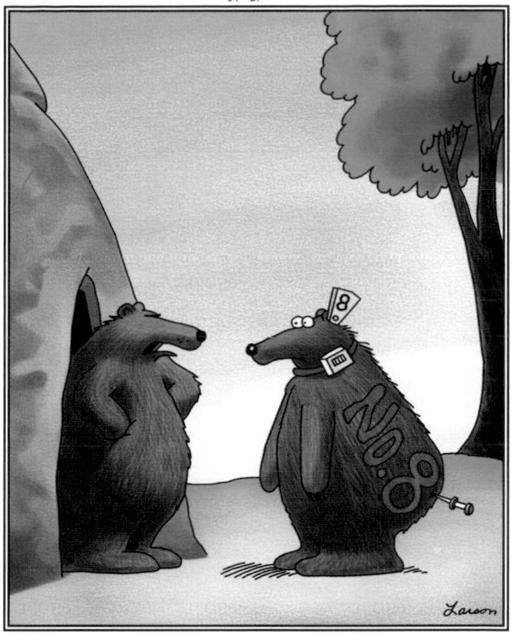
No. 8
Larson

"Late again! ... This better be good!"

9/28/82

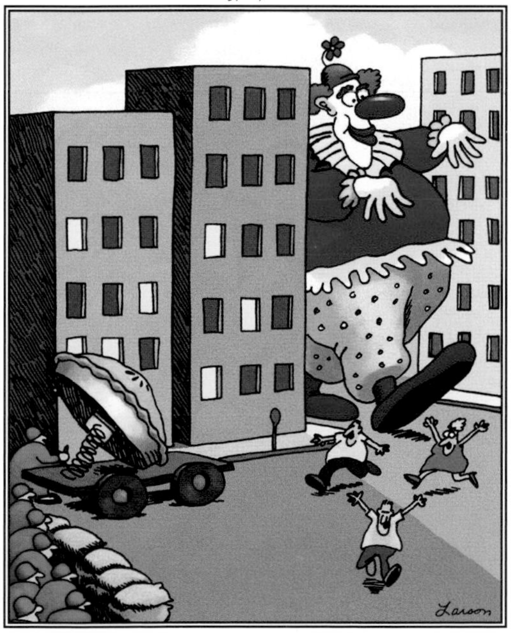
Larson

9/29/82

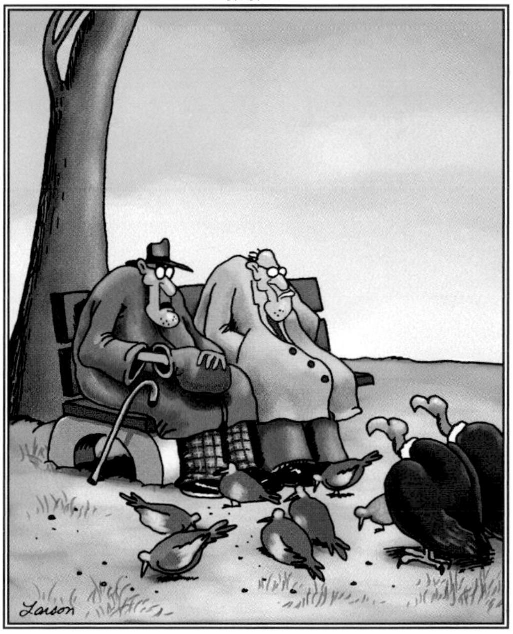
Larson

"Now take them big birds, Barnaby. ...
Never eat a thing ... just sit and stare."

September 1982

9/20/82

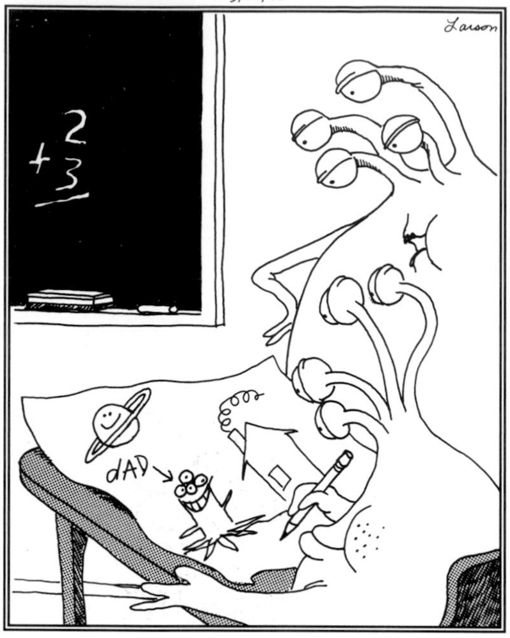
2
+3
dAD

"Verrrrrrry good, Ernie!"

9/22/82

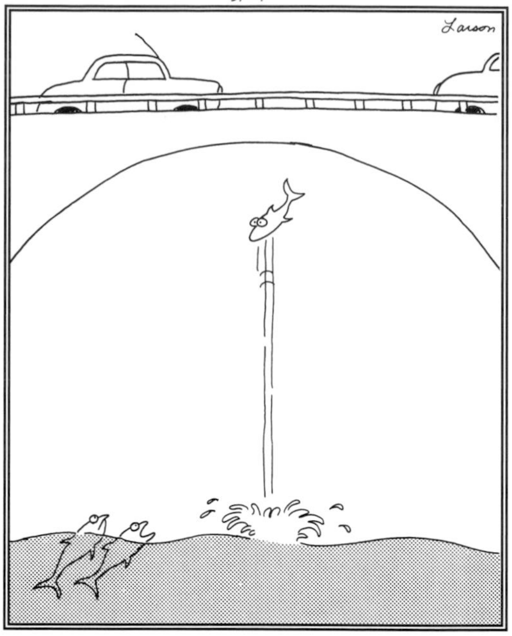

"We're too late! ... He jumped!"

9/27/82

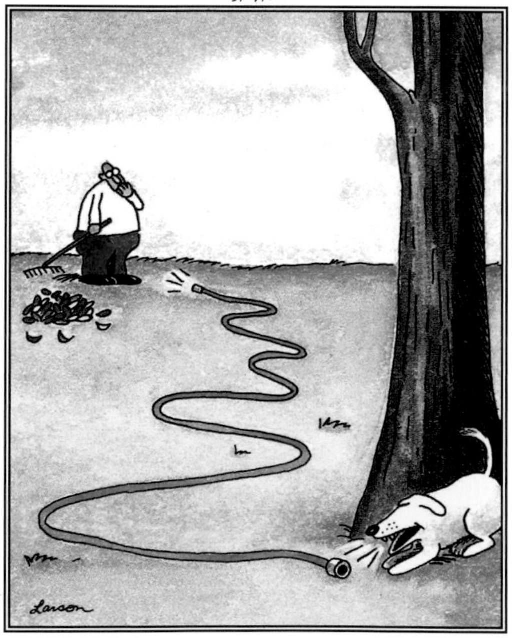

9/30/82

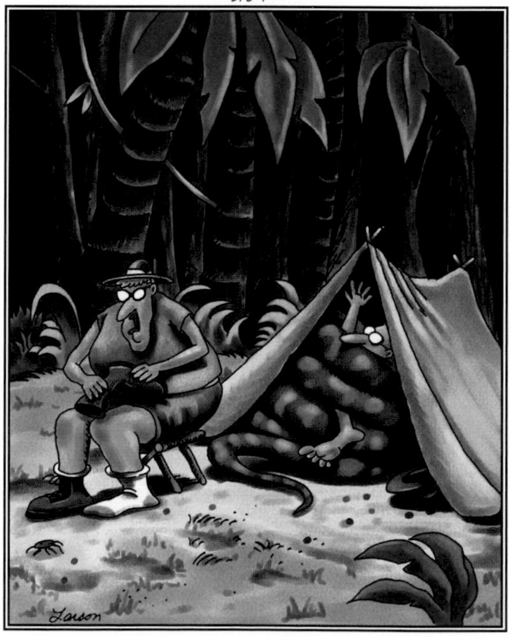

"AAAAAAAAA! MURRAY! ... A spider was in my shoe!"

10/2/82

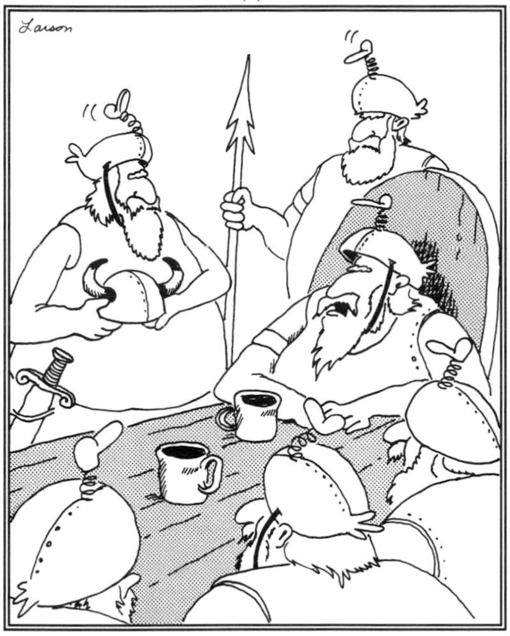
Larson

"Now, on to other business ...
Bjorn Jorgensen here has a new
helmet design to show us!"

10/1/82

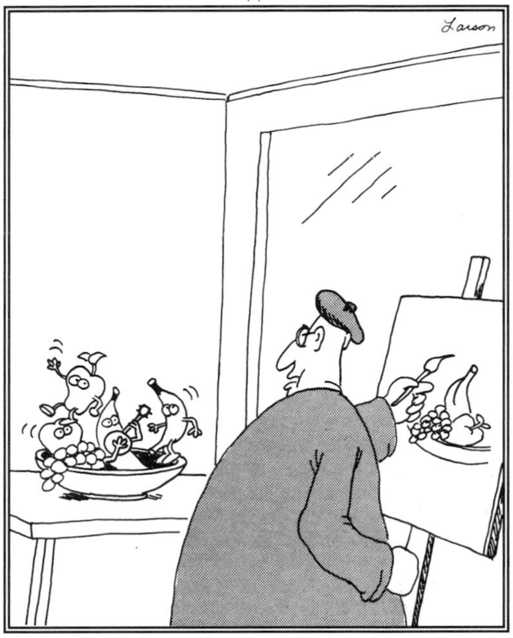
Larson

"Knock it off, I said! ... This is a still life!"

10/5/82

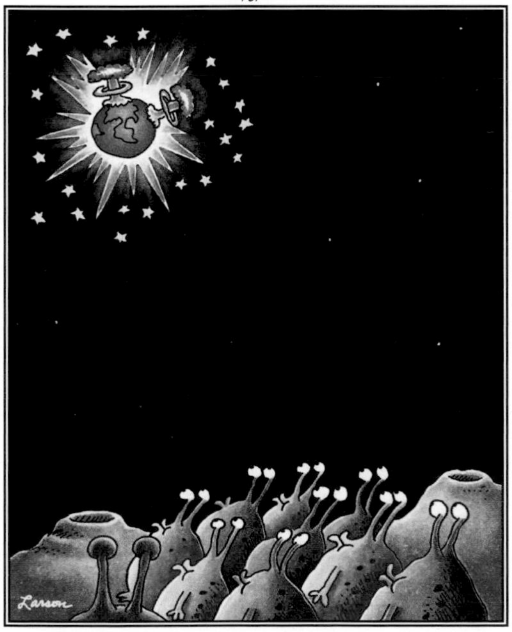
Larson

"Oooooooooooooo!"

10/7/82

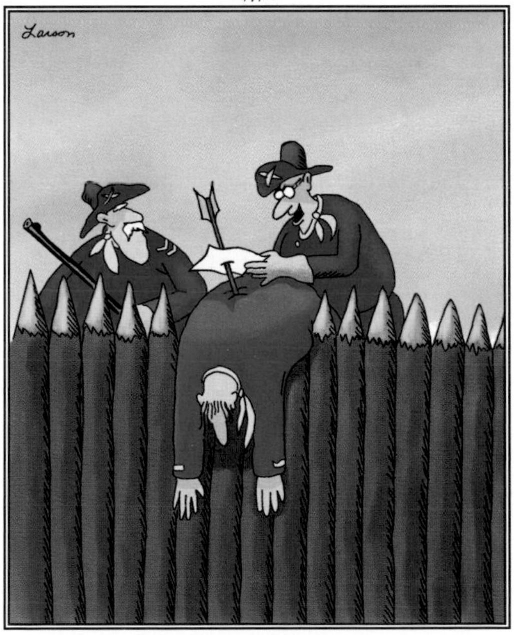
Larson

"Ha! The idiots spelled 'surrender'
with only one 'r'!"

10/4/82

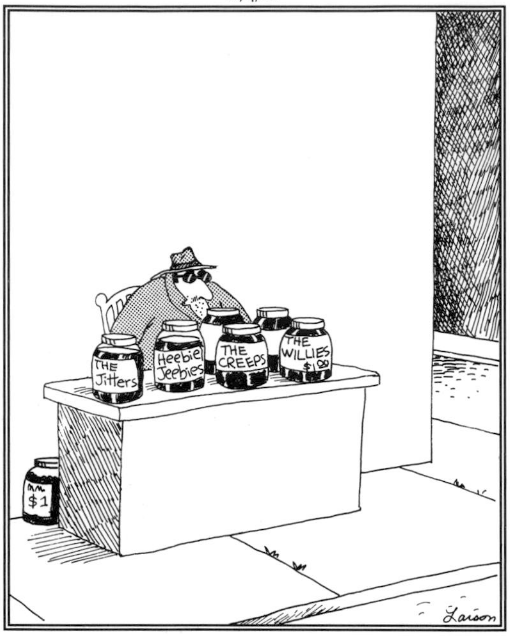
THE Jitters
Heebie Jeebies
THE CREEPS
THE WILLIES $1.00
$1
Larson

10/6/82

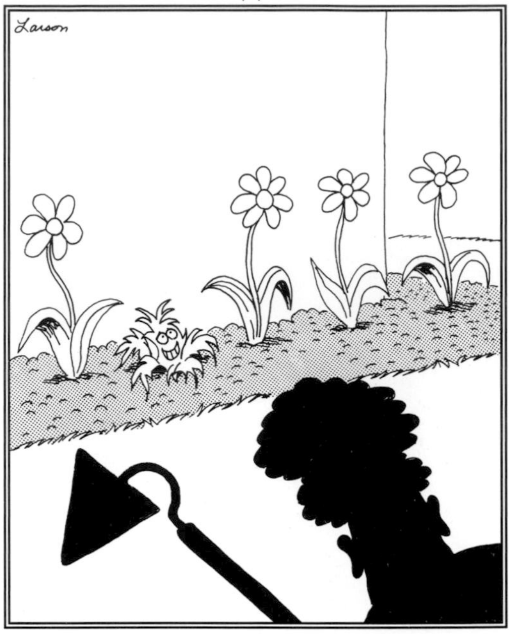
Larson

10/11/82

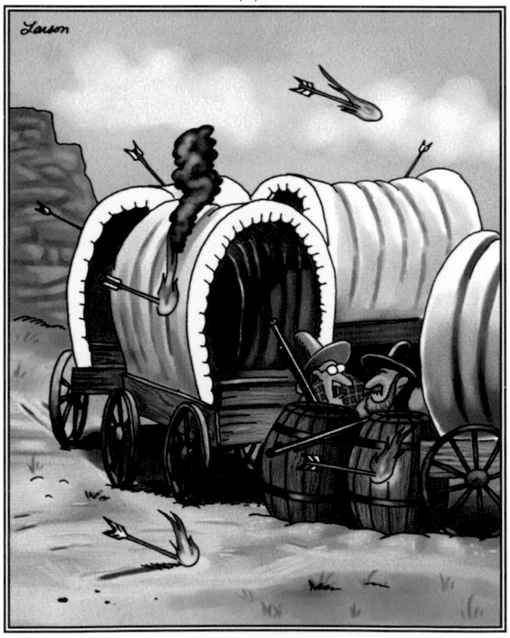
Larson

"Hey! They're lighting their arrows! ...
Can they *do* that?"

10/12/82

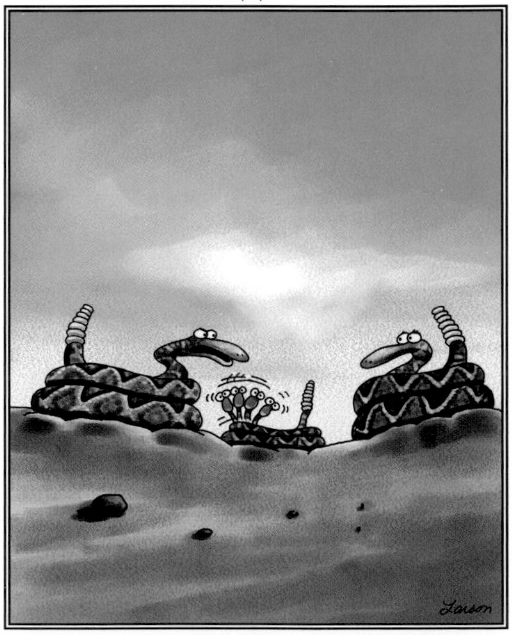
Larson

"This is your side of the family, you realize."

10/8/82

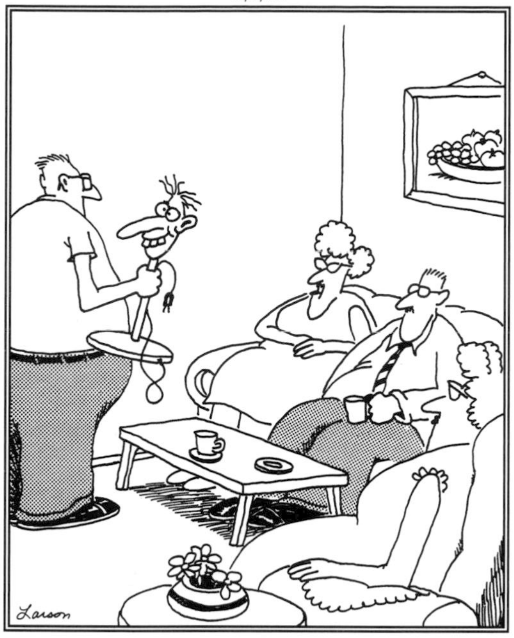

"For heaven's sake, Andrew! ... You're not going to plug that horrible thing in, are you?"

10/9/82

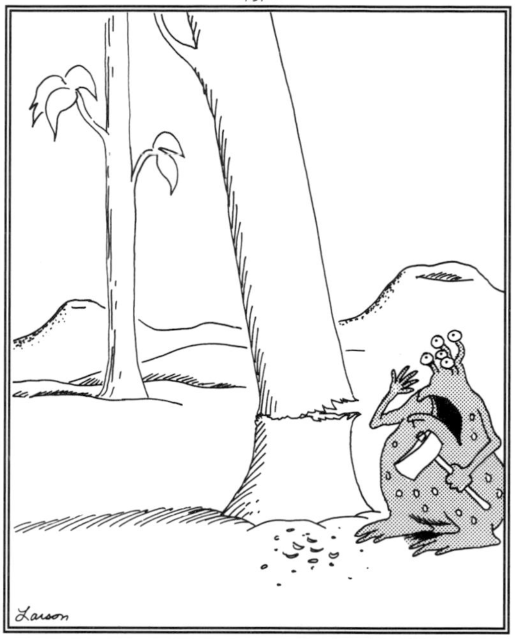

"Raaaaaaaaaaxphoooooooooorg!"

10/13/82

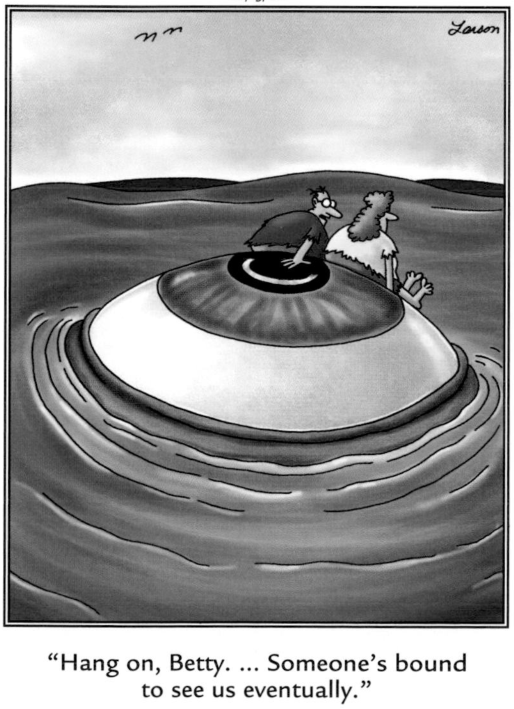

"Hang on, Betty. ... Someone's bound to see us eventually."

10/14/82

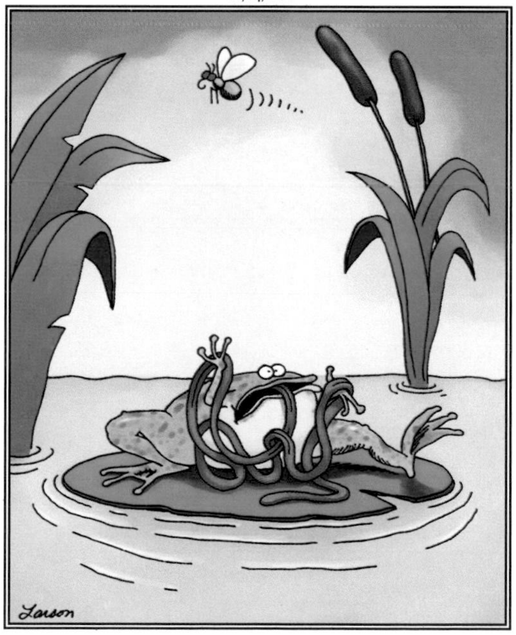

"Blasted recoil unit!"

10/15/82

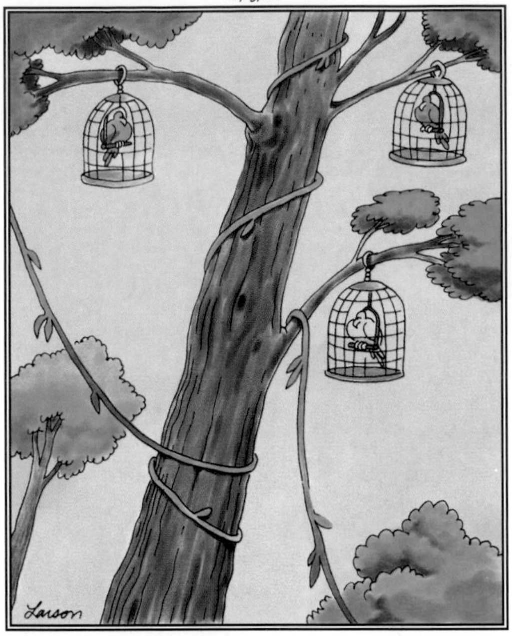
Larson

Where parakeets come from

10/16/82

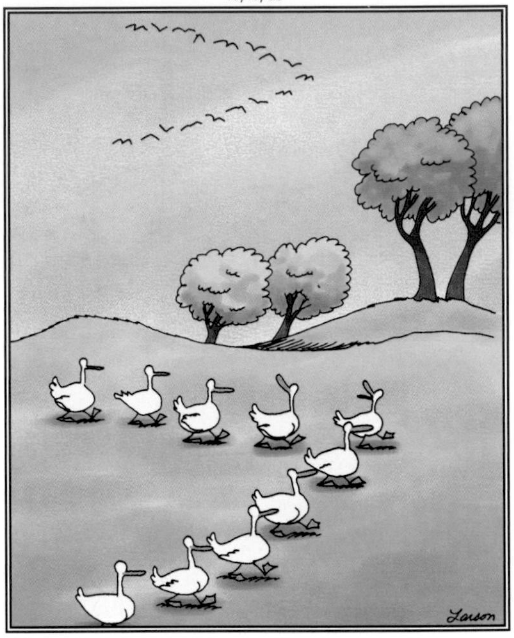
Larson

"Say ... look what *they're* doing."

10/18/82

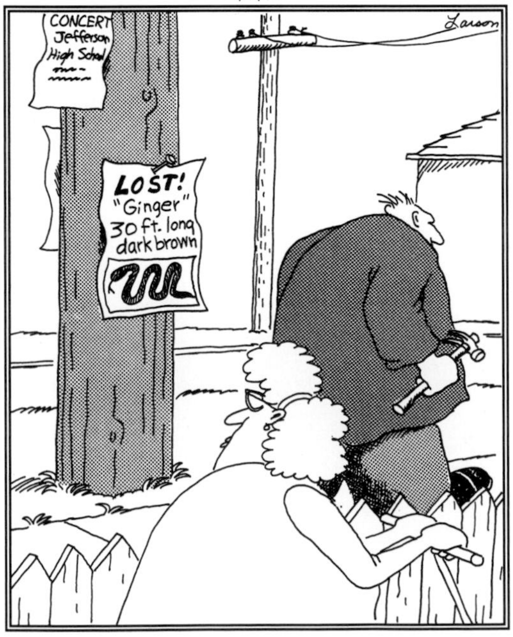
CONCERT
Jefferson
High School
LOST!
"Ginger"
30 ft. long
dark brown
Larson

10/20/82

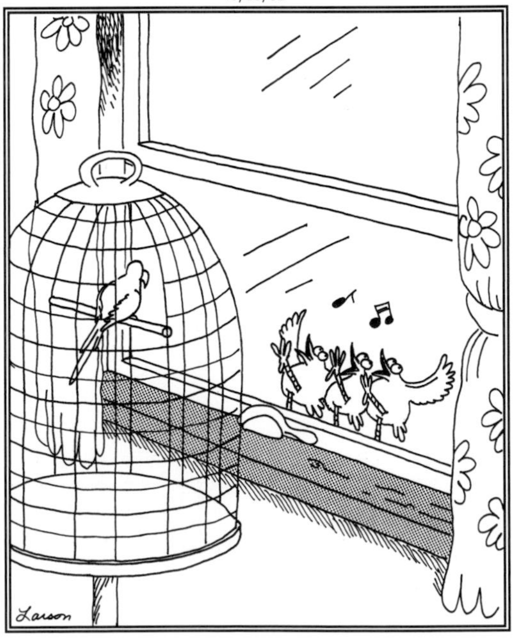
Larson

10/19/82

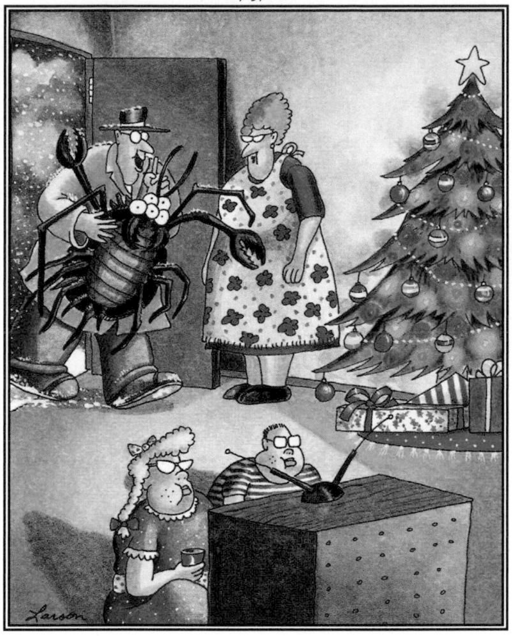

"Shhhhhh ... I wanna surprise the kids."

10/21/82

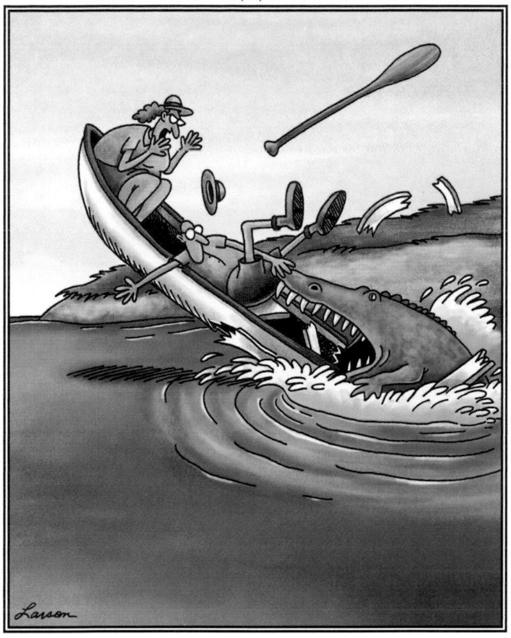

"RUB HIS BELLY, ERNIE! RUB HIS BELLY!"

10/22/82

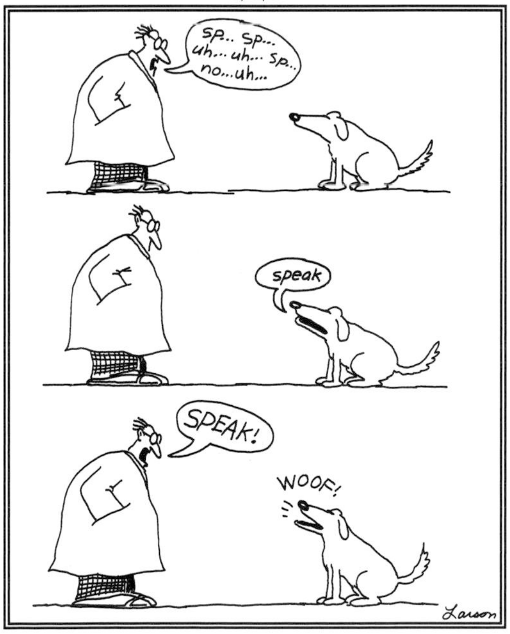
sp.. sp... uh... uh... sp.. no...uh...
speak
SPEAK!
WOOF!

10/25/82

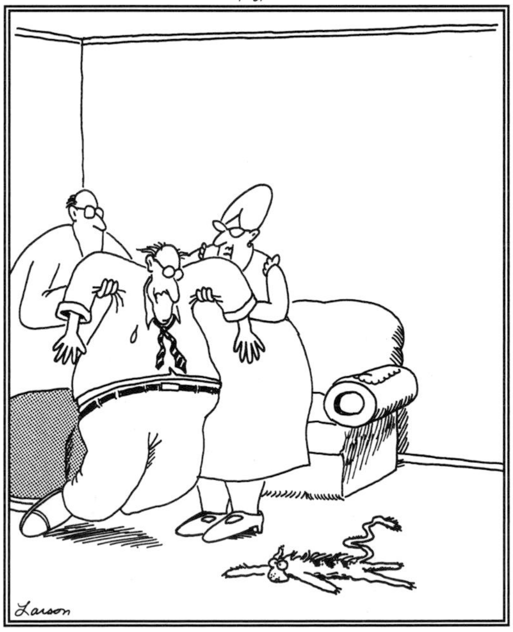

"Well, I guess both Warren and the cat are okay. ... But thank goodness for the Heimlich maneuver!"

10/23/82

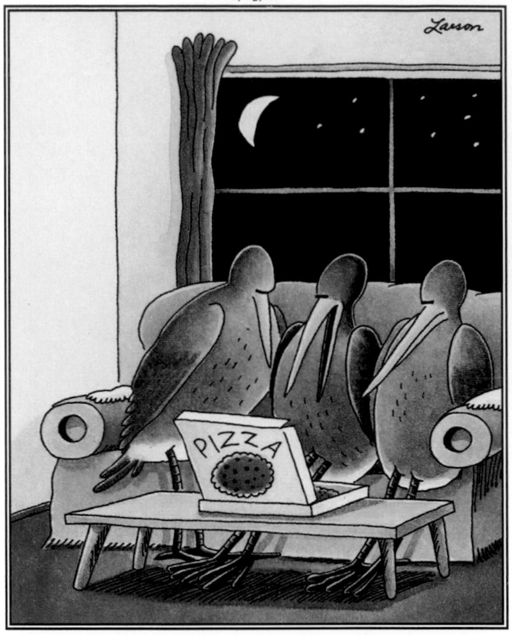
Larson
PIZZA

"Let's see—mosquitoes, gnats, flies, ants ... what the? ... Those jerks! We didn't order stinkbugs on this thing!"

10/30/82

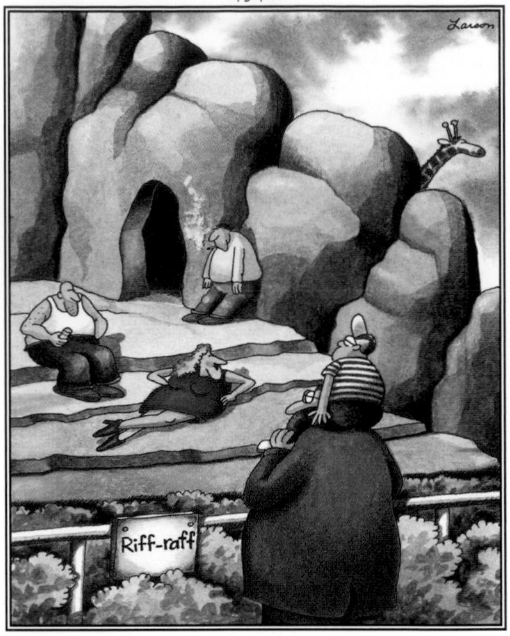
Larson
Riff-raff

10/26/82

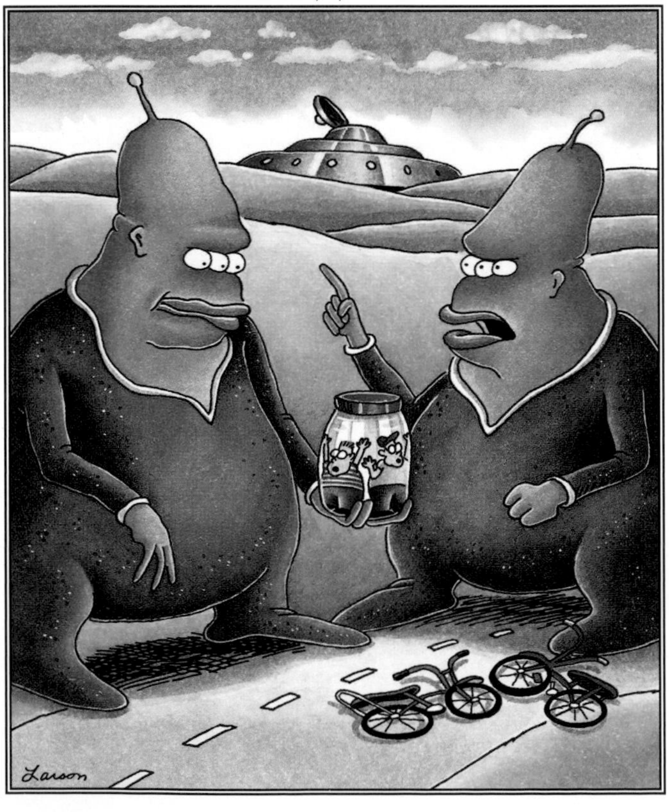
Larson

"Now, don't forget, Gorok! ... *This* time punch some holes in the lid!"

The Lexington Leader, Lexington, Ky., Monday, November 8, 1982

Comic too far out for 'Far Side' fans

By JODY JAFFE
Knight-Ridder Newspapers

Cow tools? It didn't make much sense to a lot of people.

Chronicle Features, the syndicate that handles Gary Larson and his *Far Side* cartoons was deluged with calls after his cartoon captioned "Cow Tools," ran in newspapers across the country. Editors and readers were begging for an explanation.

(That cartoon did not appear in *The Leader*, one of 71 papers in the U.S. and Canada which carry the *Far Side*. *Leader* editor Steve Wilson said another *Far Side* cartoon was used in its place "because we didn't understand the gag.")

"The phone never stopped ringing for two days," said Chronicle Features general manager Stuart Dodds, between chuckles about the whole mess. Dodds said he got the joke right off.

"It didn't seem like the greatest joke that Gary had made," Dodds said. "Those who didn't get it were searching for far-fetched explanations. Further than Gary's wildest thoughts."

But that's not the worst of it. Larson's own mother, Doris, didn't get the joke.

"She said, 'Dear, I don't think I quite understood this one,' " Larson said in a telephone interview from his home in Seattle. (Doris Larson, according to her son, understands most of his off-beat jokes, "except for these occasional slip ups.")

After countless explanations to countless *Far Side* fans, Dodds decided to go public with the punchline. For the first time in Chronicle Features history, it sent out letters of explanation by the cartoonist to all 71 newspapers that carry Larson's daily cartoon.

"This cartoon was meant as an exercise in silliness," Larson wrote.

"I've never met a cow who could make tools, but if I had, I feel sure that its efforts would lack something in sophistication and would resemble the crude specimens shown in the cartoon."

That's it, folks, the punchline: If cows could build tools, those are the kind they'd build.

For those who want further explanation, read on. Larson came up with the joke after remembering a definition of mankind: one of the things that separates human beings from animals is that humans can build tools.

"I started thinking of well ... cows," said Larson, who at one time, worked at a humane society. "I like cows. I just think there's almost something intrinsically humorous about them. I even just like the name 'cow.'

"I thought obviously cows don't make tools, but if they did, they would look like this. At the time I thought it was hysterical ... Wrong."

10/28/82

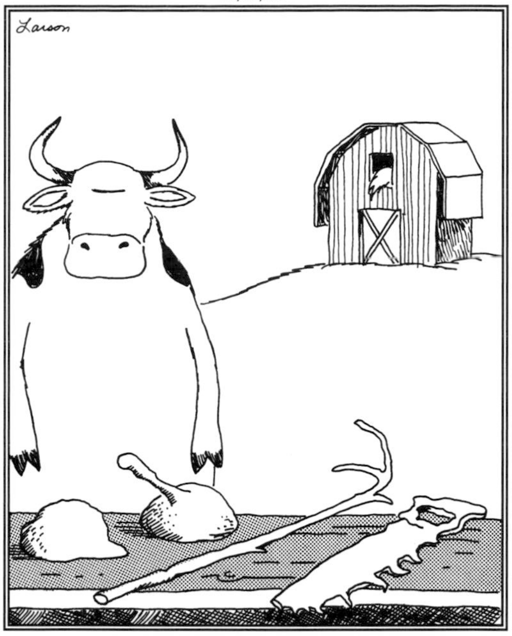

Cow tools

10/27/82

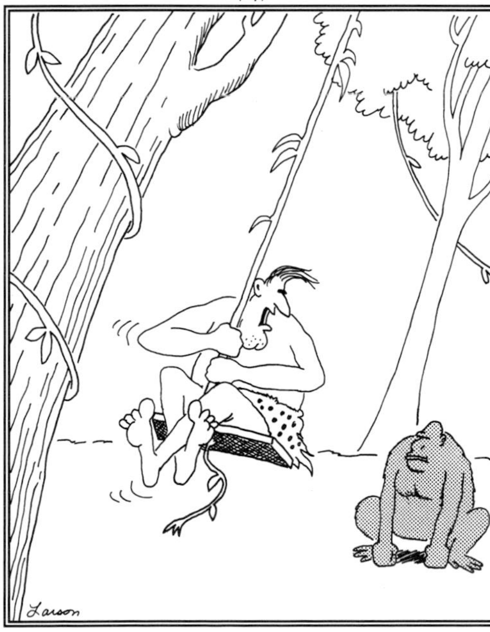

"Stop the swing! I'm getting sick! Stop the swing! Oongowa! Oongowa!"

10/29/82

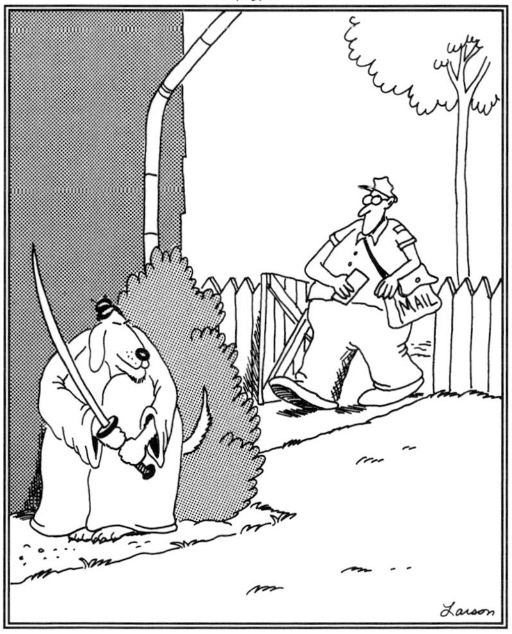
MAIL

11/1/82

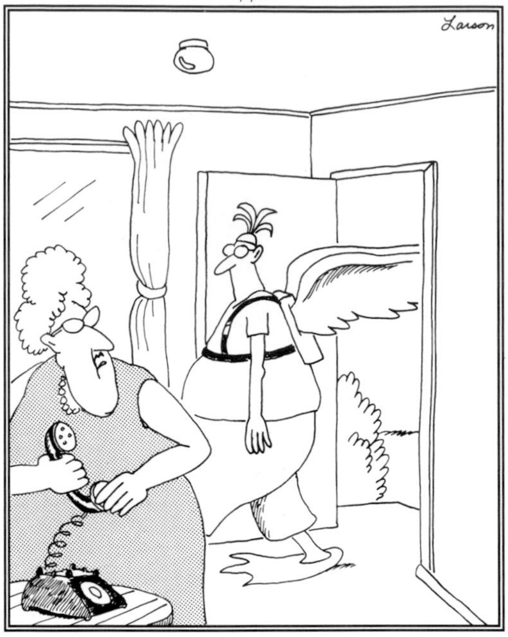

"Arnold, it's Mr. Wimberly on the phone. ... He says the next time you buzz his house, he'll have his 12-gauge ready."

11/2/82

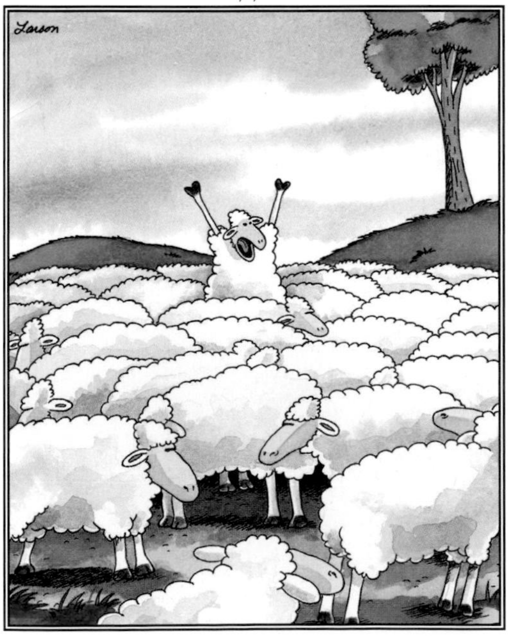

"Wait! Wait! Listen to me! ... We don't *have* to be just sheep!"

11/3/82

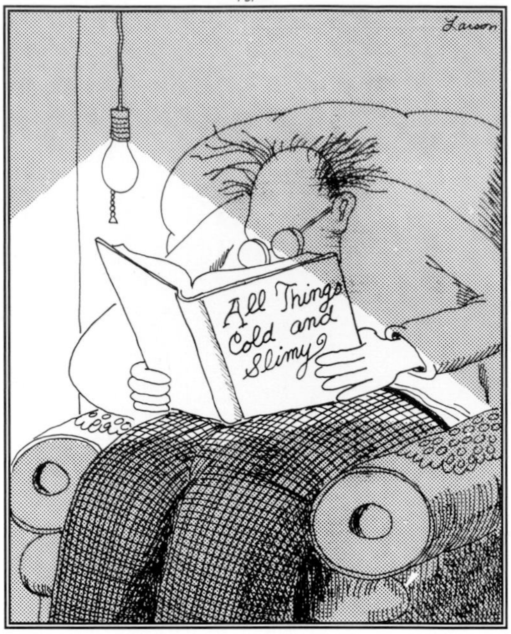
All Things Cold and Slimy

11/4/82

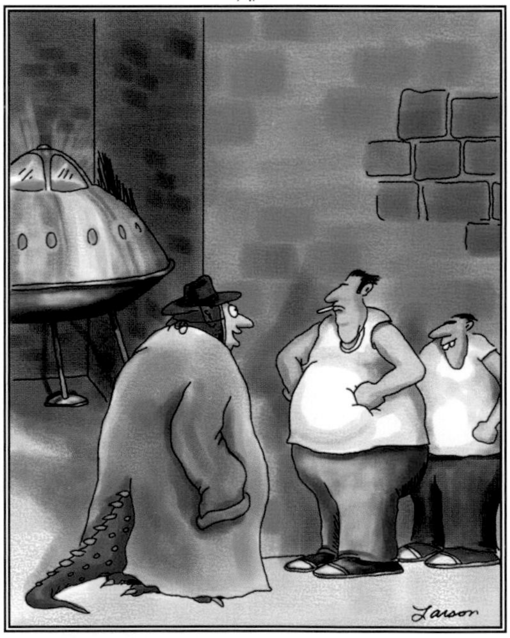

"Why ... yes ... thank ... you ... I ... would ... like ... a ... knuckle ... sandwich."

11/9/82

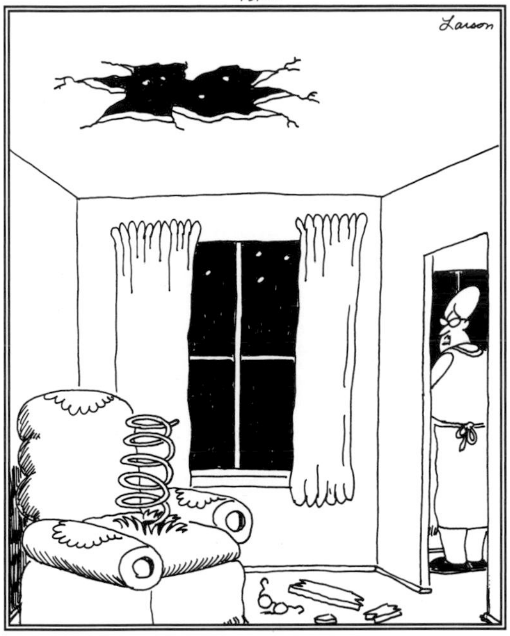

"Good heavens, Ronald! ... I think something just landed on the roof!"

11/10/82

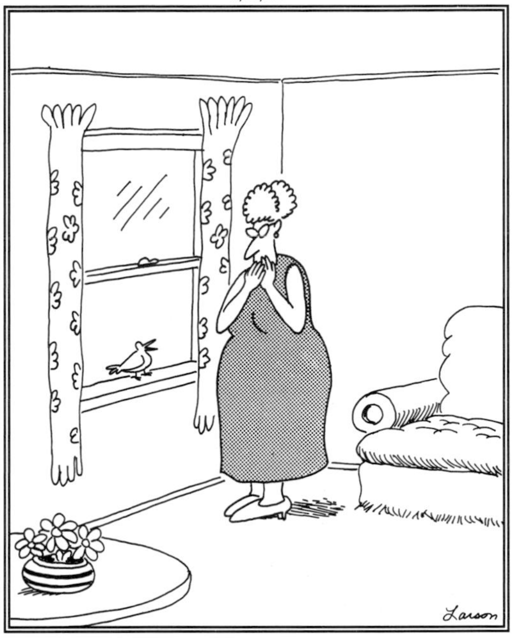

"I'm sorry, Margaret, but it's time I spread my wings and said goodbye."

11/5/82

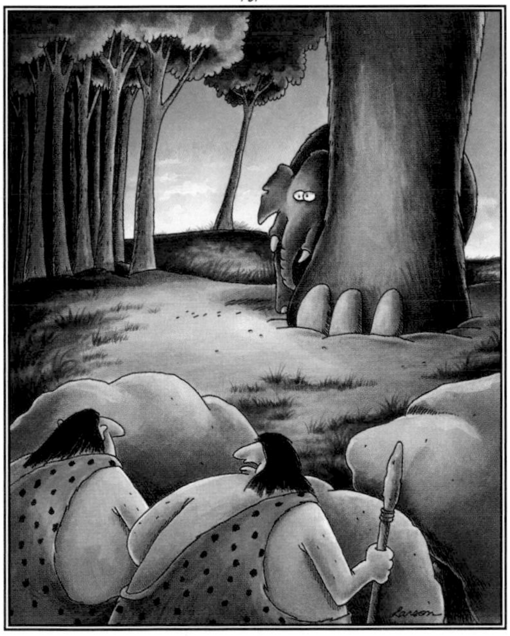

"Ha! We got him now!"

11/6/82

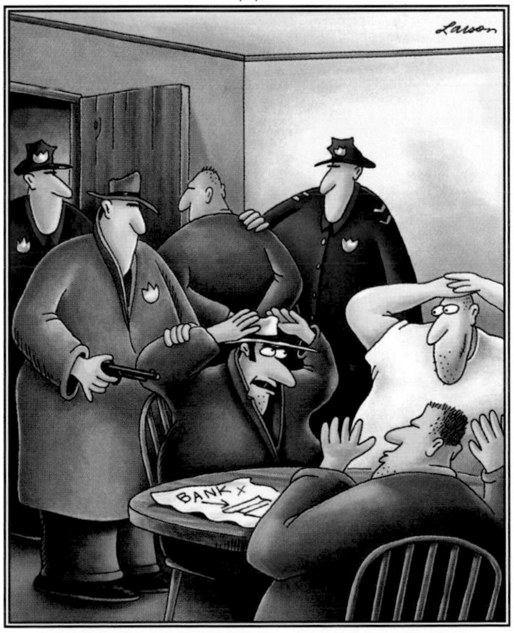
BANK

"I knew it! I just knew it. ... 'Shave and a Haircut' was a lousy secret knock."

11/8/82

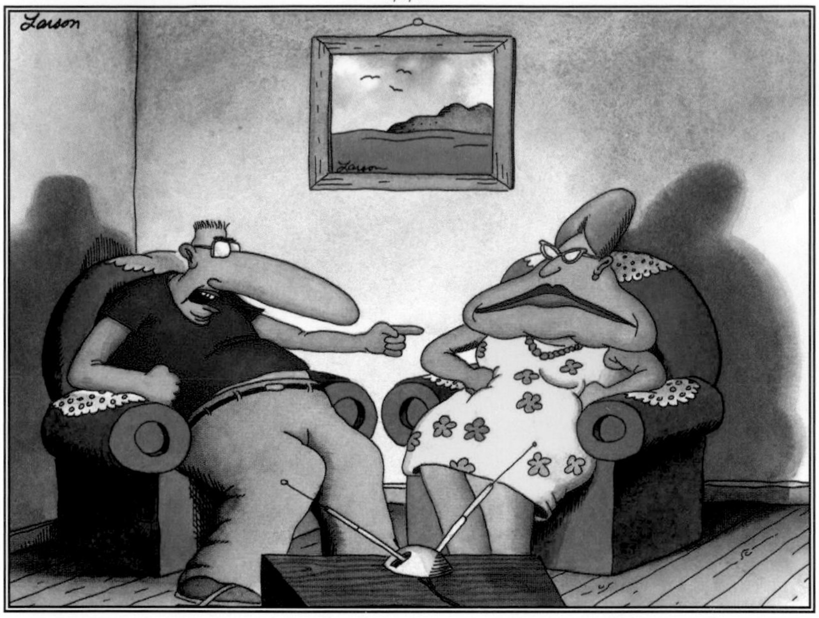

"Oh! Is that so? ... Well, *you've* got a big *mouth!*"

11/12/82

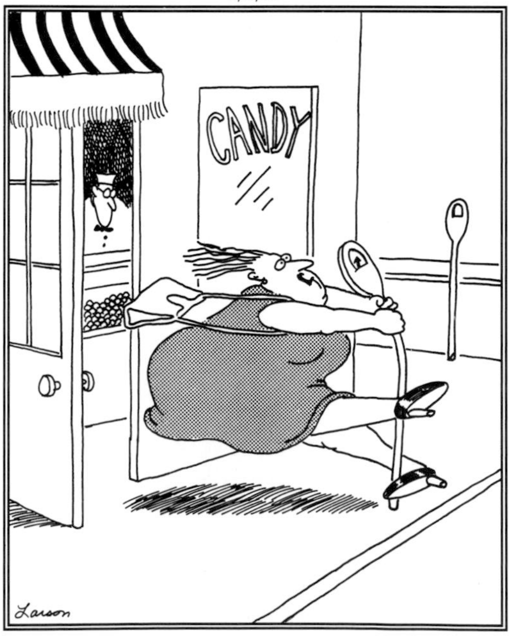
CANDY

11/13/82

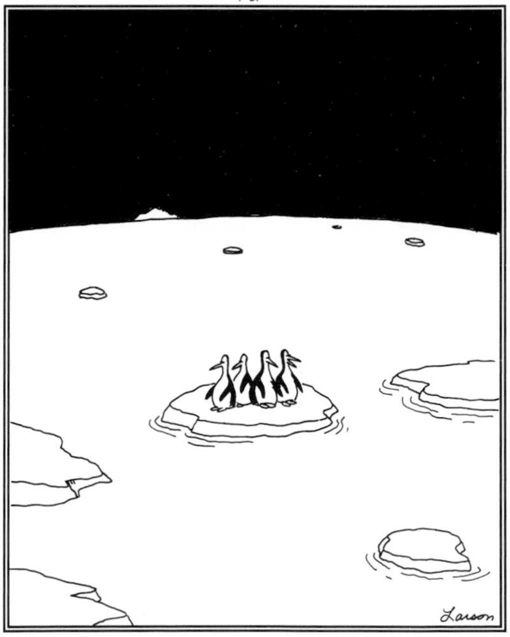

"Well, once again, here we are."

11/15/82

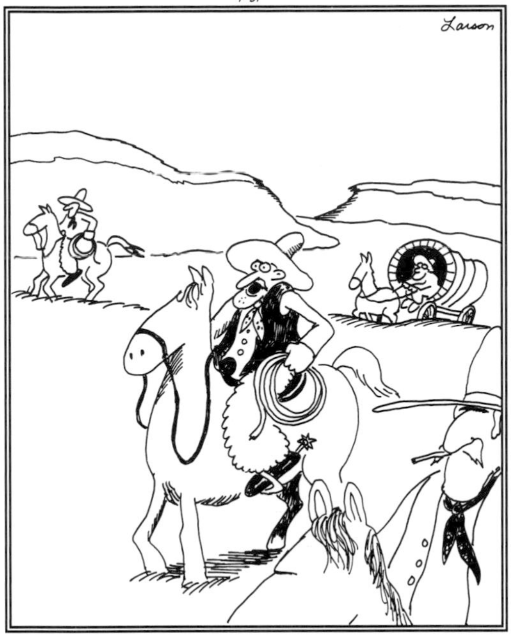
Larson

"Say ... wait just a dang minute, here. ... We forgot the cattle!"

11/22/82

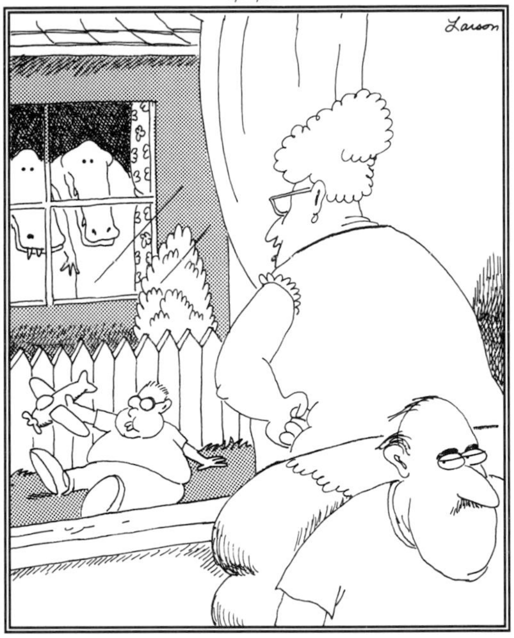
Larson

"I just don't like it, Al. ... Whenever Billy goes outside, the new neighbors seem compelled to watch every little thing he does."

11/11/82

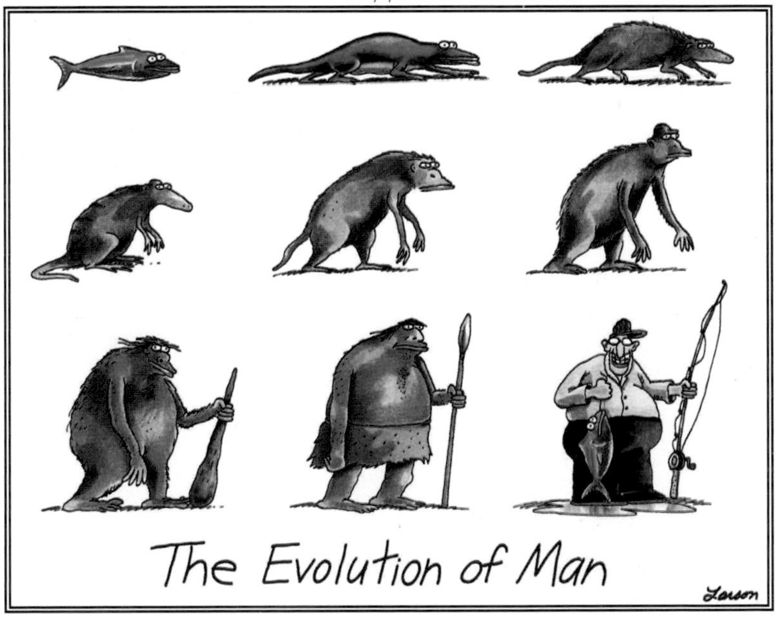
The Evolution of Man
Larson

11/16/82

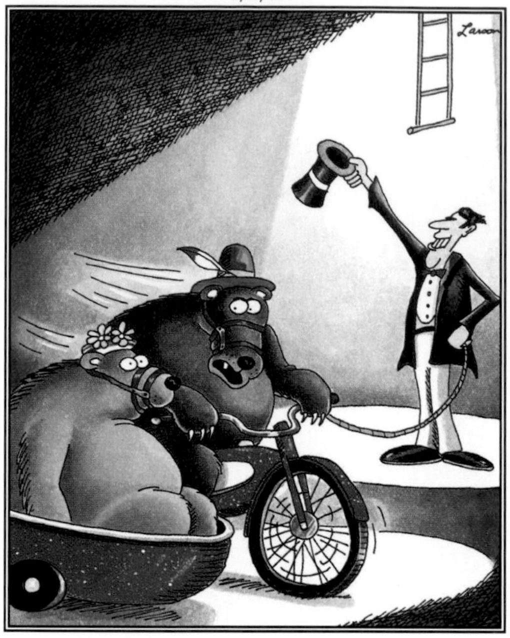
Larson

"'Looks like a trap,' I said. 'Nonsense,' you said. 'No one would set a trap way out here in the woods,' you said."

11/17/82

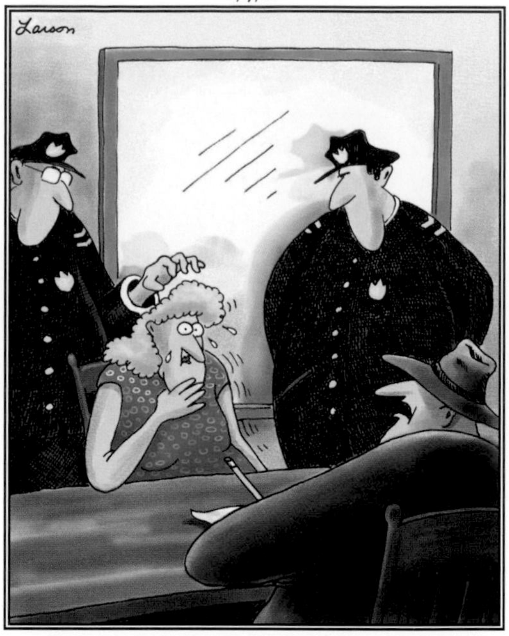
Larson

"Try to relax, ma'am. ... You say it was dark and you were alone in the house, when suddenly you felt a hand reaching from behind and ... JOHNSON! KNOCK IT OFF!"

11/18/82

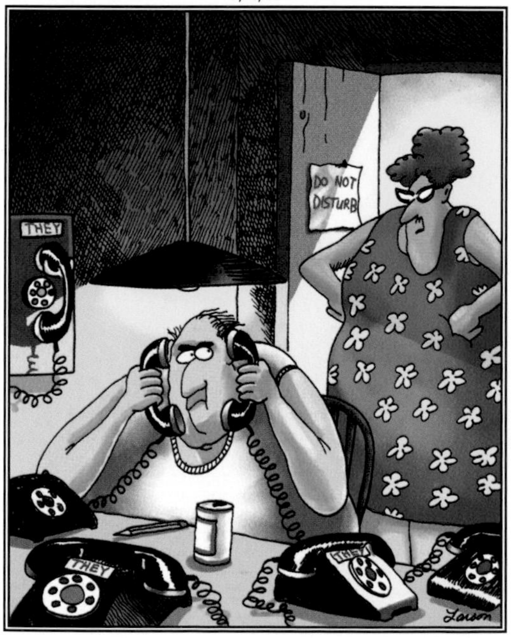
THEY
DO NOT DISTURB
THEY
THEY
Larson

"*You,* Bernie Horowitz? ... So *you're* the 'they' in 'that's what they say'?"

11/19/82

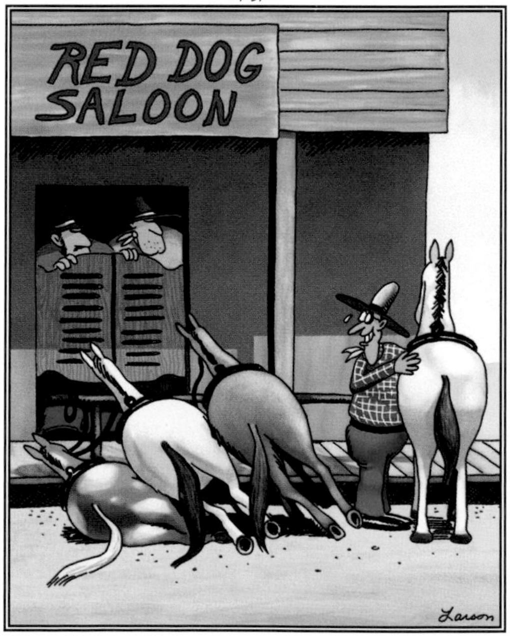
RED DOG SALOON
Larson

11/23/82

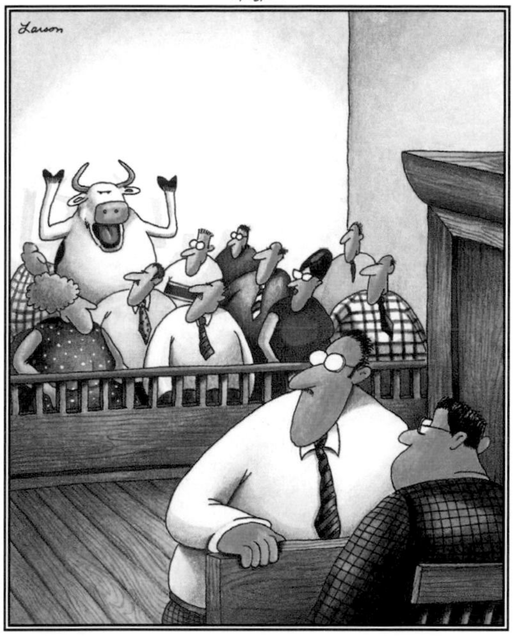
Larson

"All right! All right! I confess! I did it! Yes! That's right! The cow! Ha ha ha! And I feel great!"

11/24/82

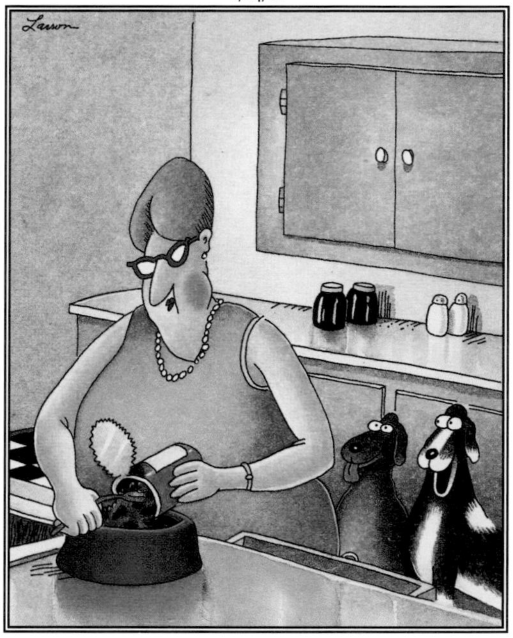
Larson

"Oh boy! ... It's dog food *again!*"

11/20/82

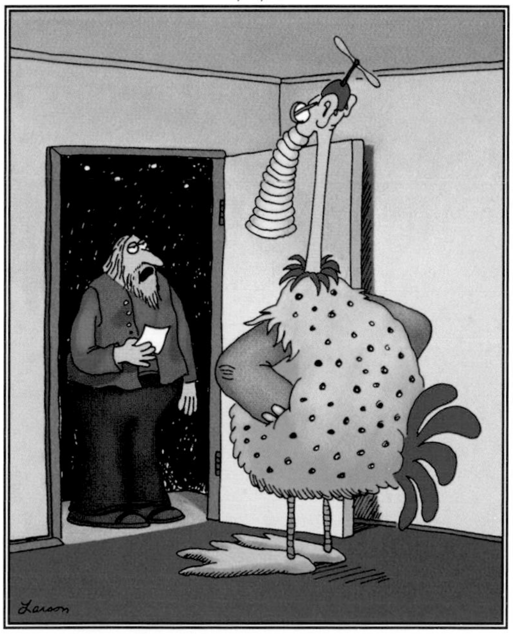
Larson

"I wonder if you could help me. ... I'm looking for 523 West Cherry and ... Oh! Wow! Déjà vu!"

11/27/82

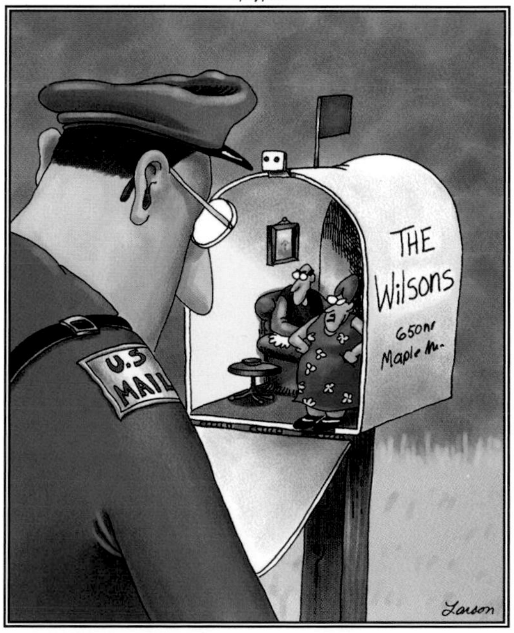
THE
Wilsons
U.S
MAIL
Larson

"We're the Wilsons, bozo! ... What's it say on the box?"

11/26/82

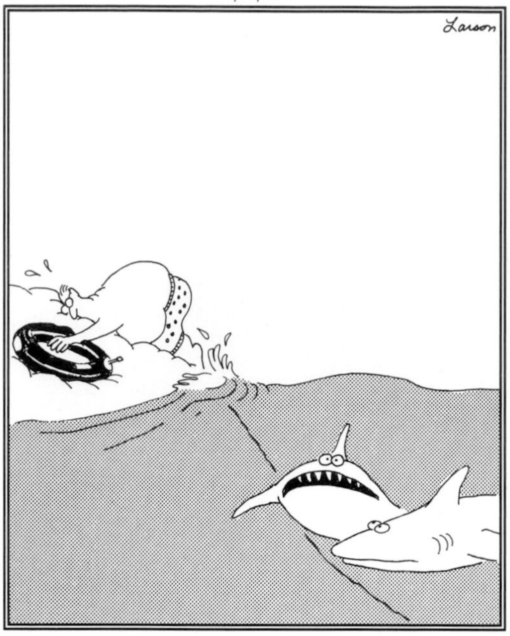

"He was magnificent! Just magnificent! And I almost had him! ... I can't talk about it right now."

11/25/82

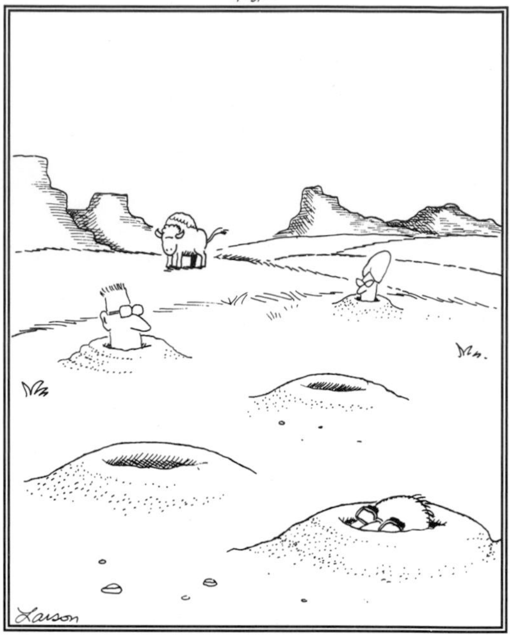

The rare and timid prairie people

11/29/82

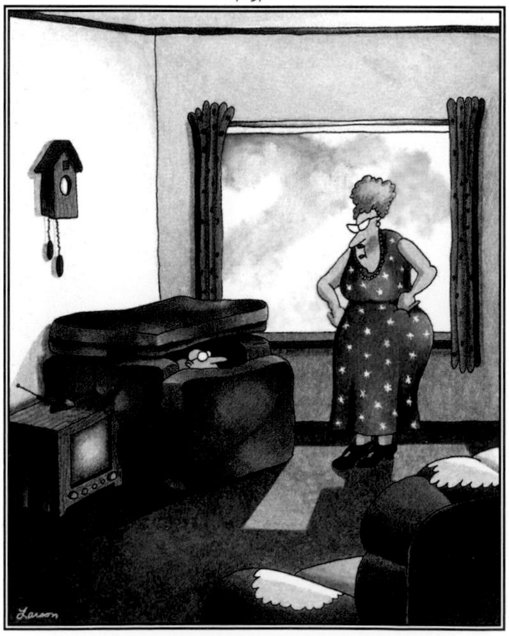

"Well, you can just rebuild the fort later, Harold. ... Phyllis and Shirley are coming over and I'll need the cushions."

11/30/82

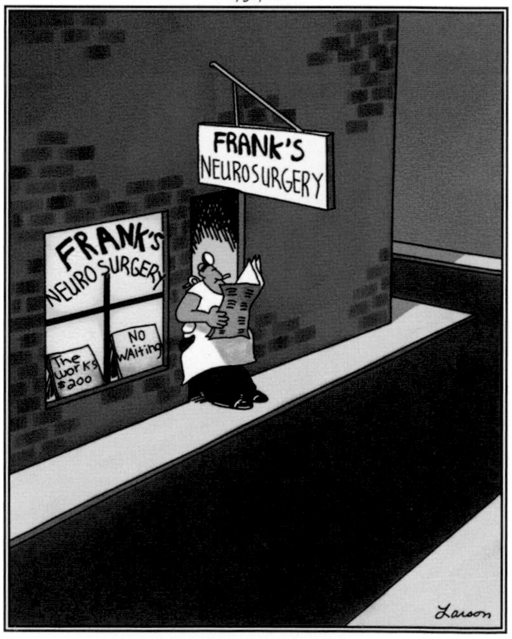
FRANK'S
NEUROSURGERY
FRANK'S
NEUROSURGERY
The works $200
NO waiting

"THE CAPE, LARRY! GO FOR THE CAPE!"

"You boys got a bottle opener?"

"Shhh! Knock off that crunching noise! ...
Pass it on!"

Jungle-wise characters

12/4/82

"See, Barbara? There's no one in here, no one outside. ...
I'll even open the drapes and have a look."

12/6/82

"Now wait a minute. ... He said two jerks
means 'more slack' and three meant
'come up'... but he never said nothin'
about one long, steady pull."

12/3/82

History and the snake

12/9/82

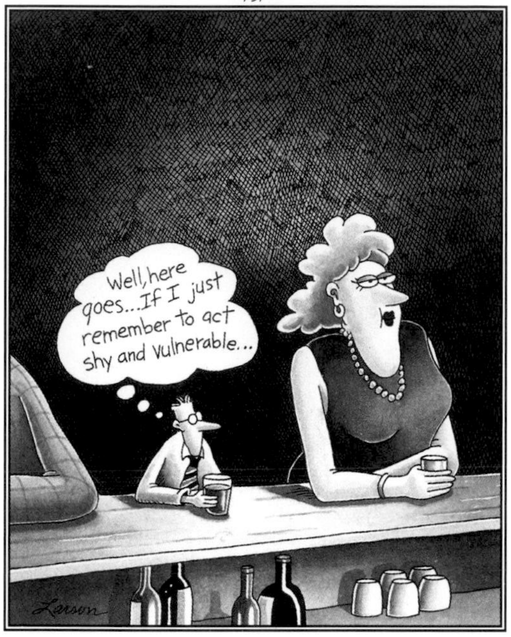
Well, here goes... If I just remember to act shy and vulnerable...

12/8/82

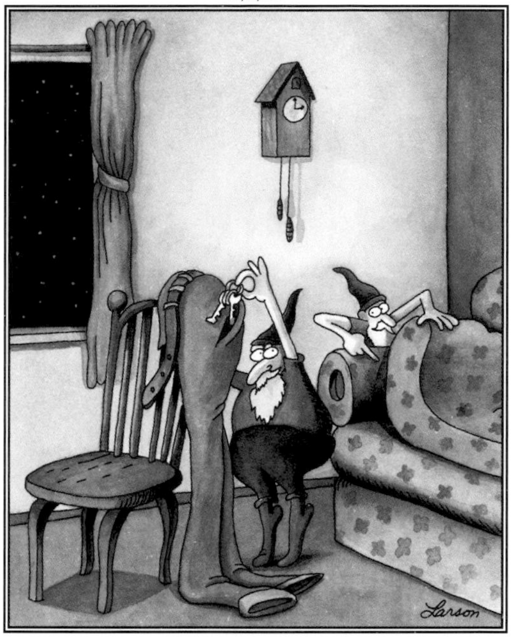

Car key gnomes

12/10/82

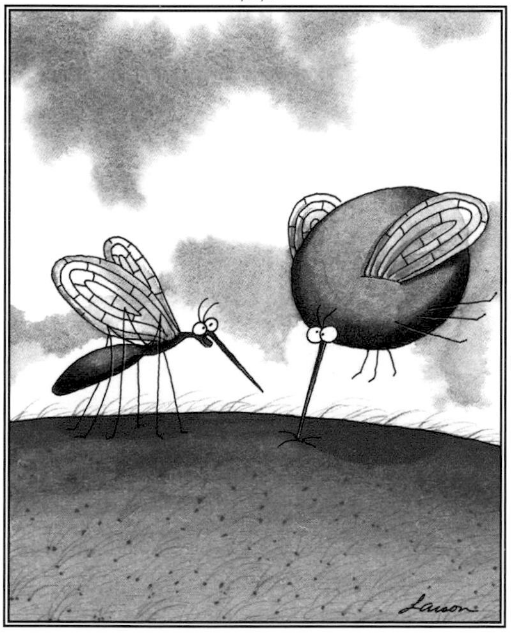

"Pull out, Betty! Pull out! ... You've hit an artery!"

12/13/82

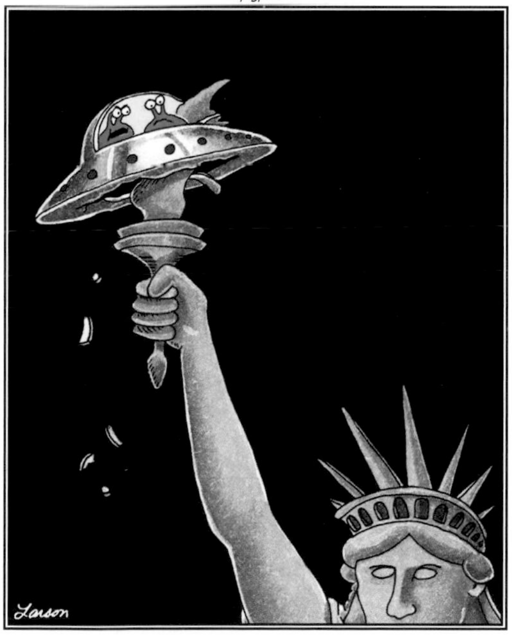

"Well, Zoron ... is *this* a close enough look for you?"

12/14/82

Larson

"Ha! Webster's blown his cerebral cortex."

12/16/82

Larson

12/17/82

Larson

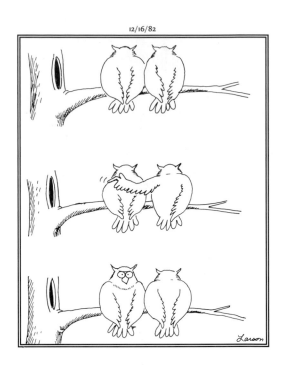

"I'm not warning you again, Sparky! ... You chew with your mouth *open!*"

12/18/82

Larson

"Egad! ... It's got most of Uncle Jake!"

12/20/82

Larson

Edwin lived reclusively in his midtown apartment with his dog, Lola, whom he secretly loathed.

12/22/82

Larson

Metamorphosis

12/23/82

Larson

It was a beautiful day, the sun was shining, and Zog had just finished washing his new invention.

12/24/82

Larson

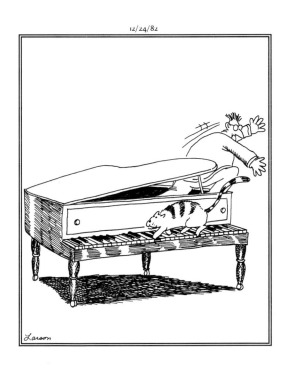

12/15/82

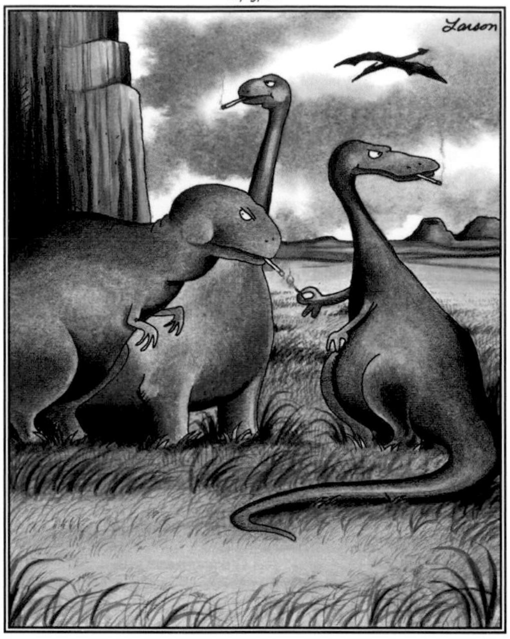
Larson

The real reason dinosaurs became extinct

12/21/82

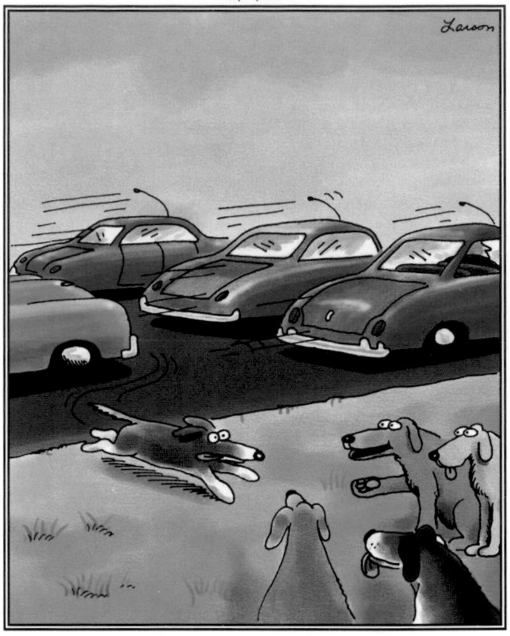
Larson

"All right! Rusty's in the club!"

12/25/82

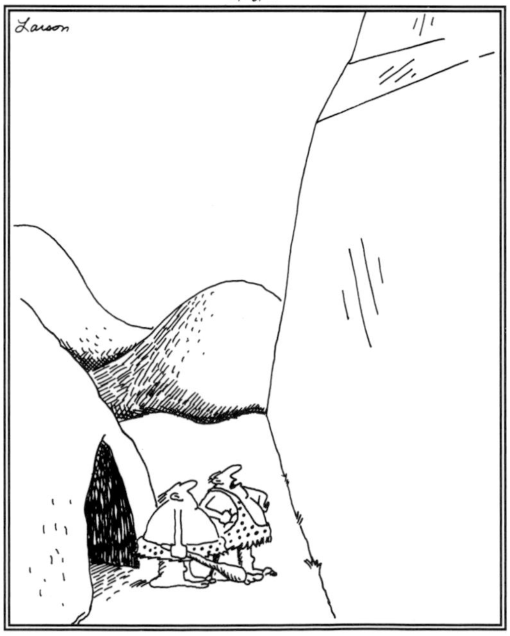
Larson

"Say, Thag ... wall of ice closer today?"

12/27/82

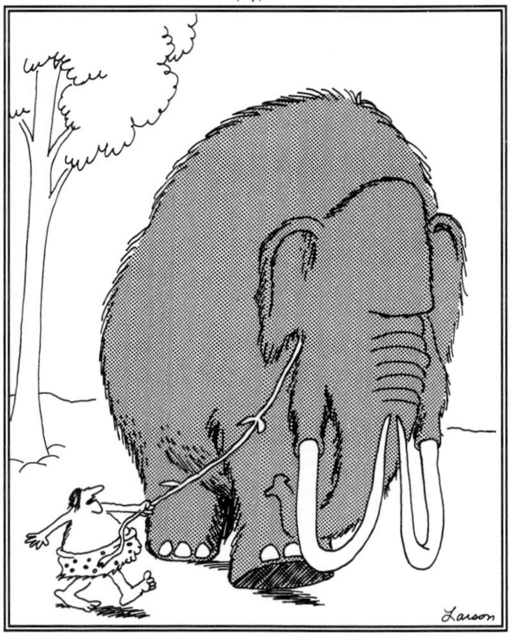
Larson

"Walkies! Walkies!"

12/28/82

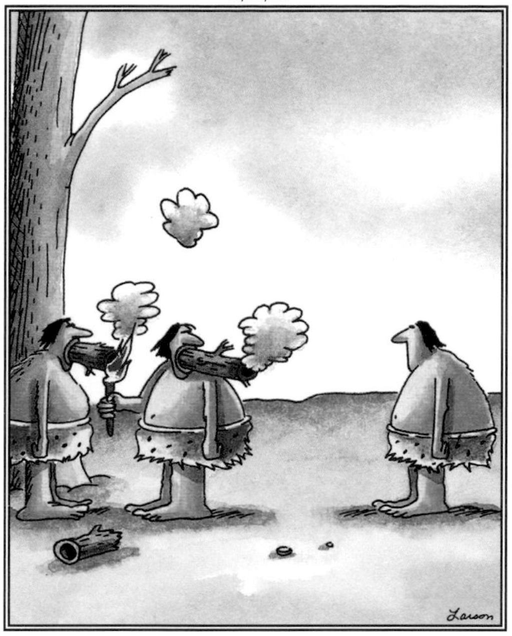

Primitive peer pressure

12/30/82

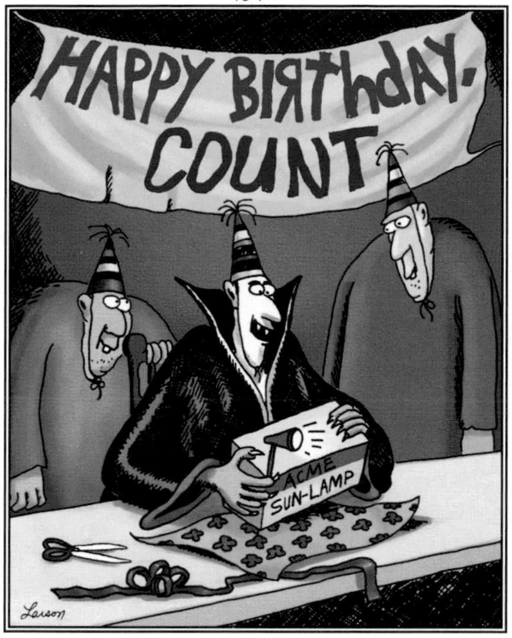
HAPPY BIRThdAY, COUNT
ACME SUN-LAMP

"Well, for goodness sakes! ...
What *is* this thing?"

12/29/82

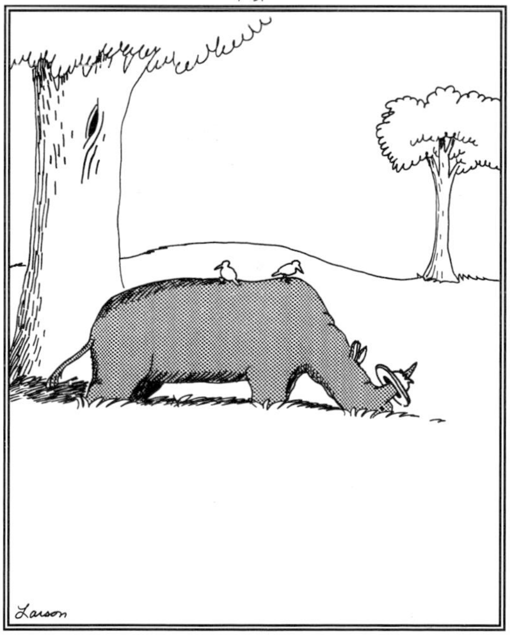

12/31/82

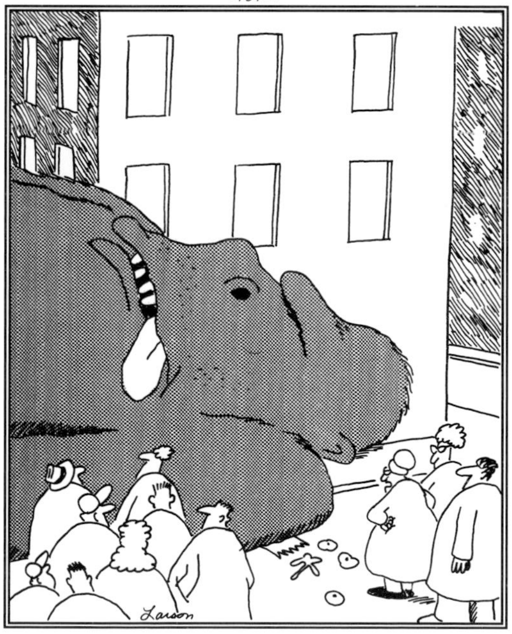

"Well, that does it for my tomatoes."

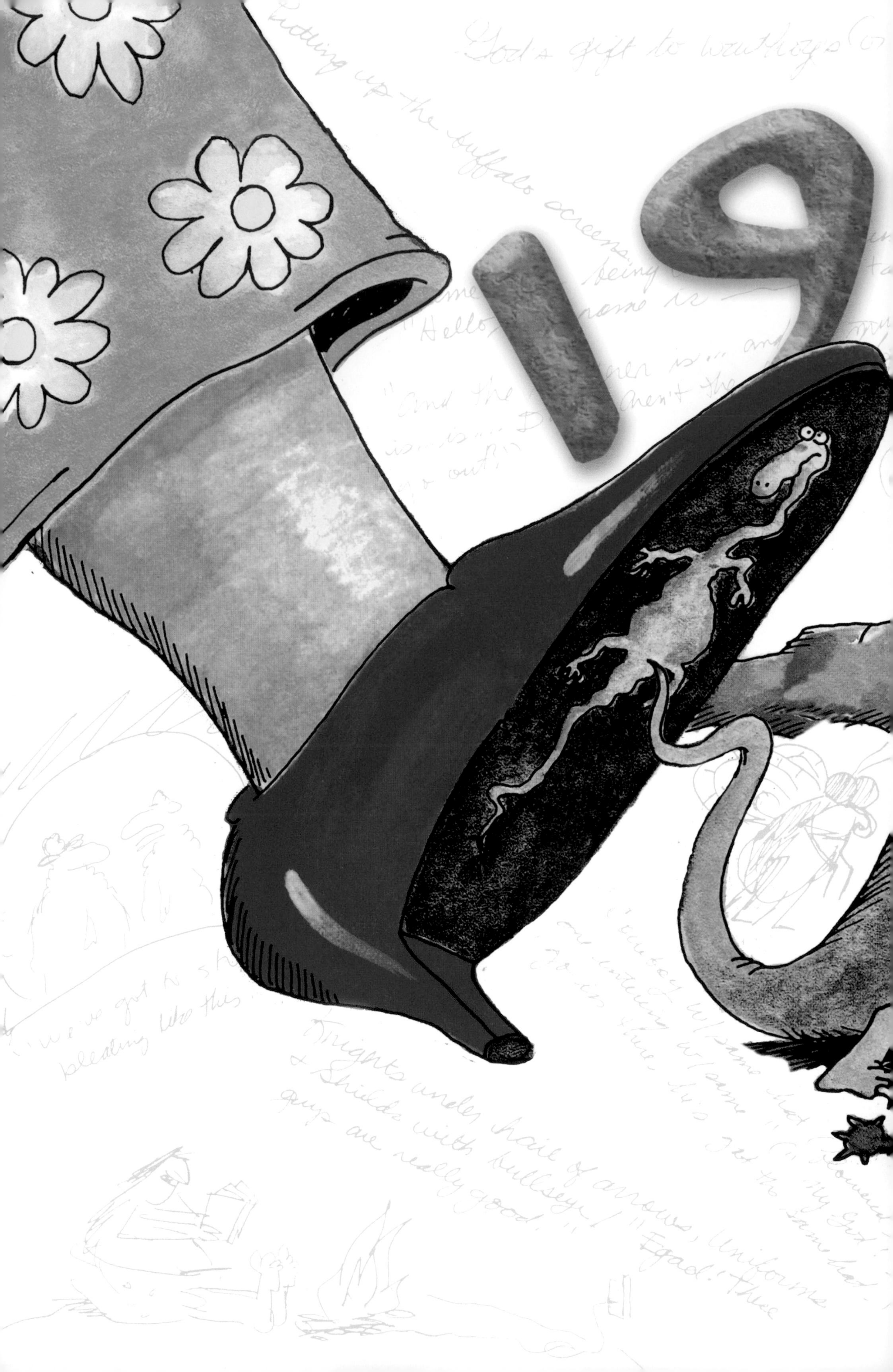
19

83

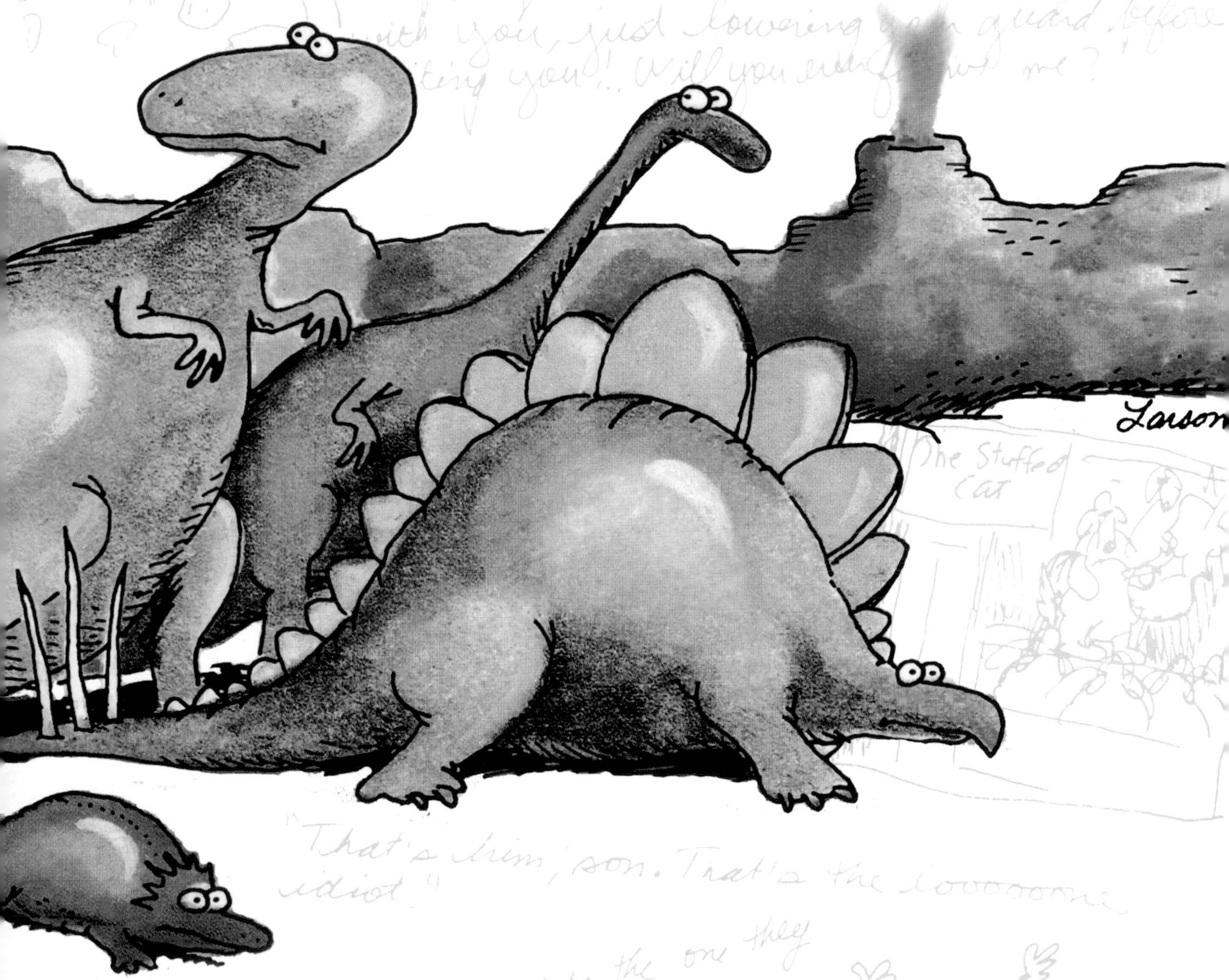
Larson

On Monsters

My childhood fear of monsters is a theme I've often explored. (Hell, you're looking at 1,278 pages of therapy, folks.) Under the bed, in the closet, up in the attic, the laundry room, that storage room at the end of the hall—monsters were everywhere in our house, lying in wait. Lying in wait for *me*.

But where they all came from, where these monsters all lived, was obviously one place: The Basement. I mean, all basements provide perfect conditions for any unnatural beast: dark, cold, drafty, lots of shadowy places to lurk—a complete monster ecosystem. All they needed was a little kid chow thrown to them now and then.

Now, in our house, the door to the basement was in the kitchen, and for some ungodly reason the light switch for the basement was controlled on the kitchen side. For a monster-fearing kid, especially one with an older brother who had obviously entered into some kind of evil pact with these same monsters in order to save his own skin, this was not a good thing.

One evening that I would like to forget, I was about halfway up the stairs, returning with some firewood. (Wouldn't it be nice if you could hear the sound track to your own life? At least you'd have a clue that danger was imminent.) And that's when it happened. With an audible click, the light switch went off and I was plunged into darkness. Welcome to nightfall in the Monster Serengeti.

I dropped the wood (the cacophony of which wrung out the last few drops that still remained in my adrenal gland) and scrambled blindly to the top of the stairs. There, my desperate hand finally found the doorknob. Locked, of course. (Did I mention the lock, also controlled from the kitchen side? Such a fun house to grow up in.) And then, in an eerie, lilting tone, my brother's voice could be heard from the other side: "It's coming for you, Gary! Do you hear it? It's cooominnnnng for youuuu!"

Just like the mother wildebeest, my own mother could always recognize the sound of one of her calves in distress. Soon she arrived, hooves flying, driving off the hyena (the laughing variety, as usual) and saving me from certain death at the hands of God-knows-what that was slowly ascending the stairs behind me.

Over the years, I can't help but think about how often people have asked me, "How do you come up with ideas?"

God, it is so easy.

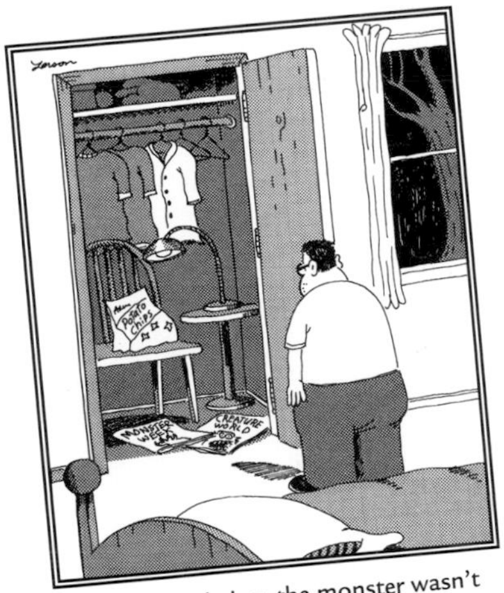

For the time being, the monster wasn't in Ricky's closet. For the time being.

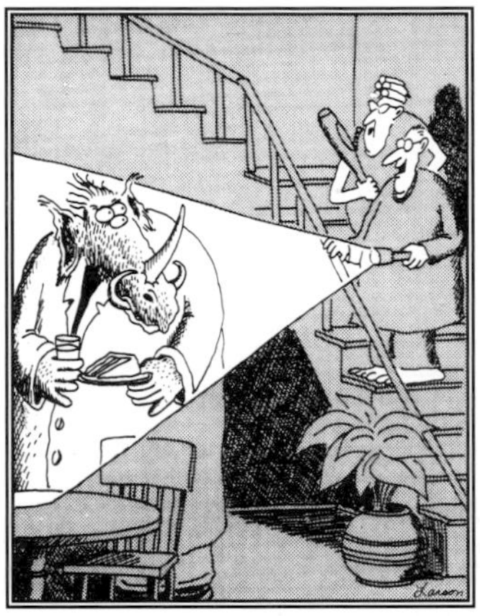

"See, Agnes? ... It's just Kevin."

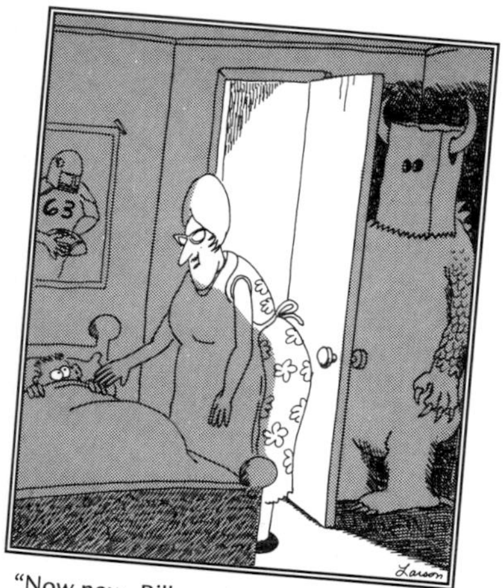

"Now now, Billy. ... How could you have seen a monster if you can't even describe him?"

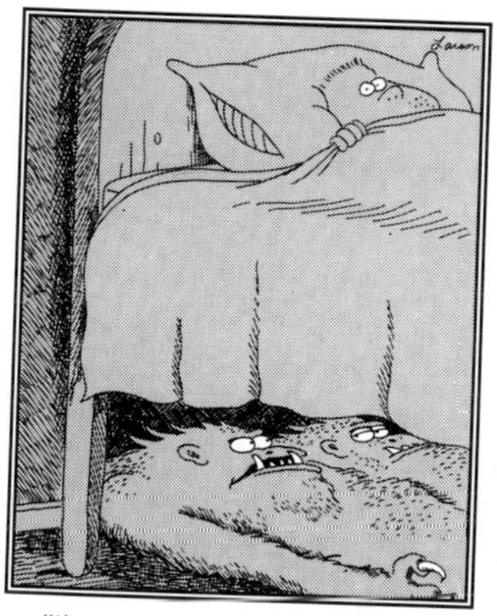

"I've got it again, Larry ... an eerie feeling like there's something on top of the bed."

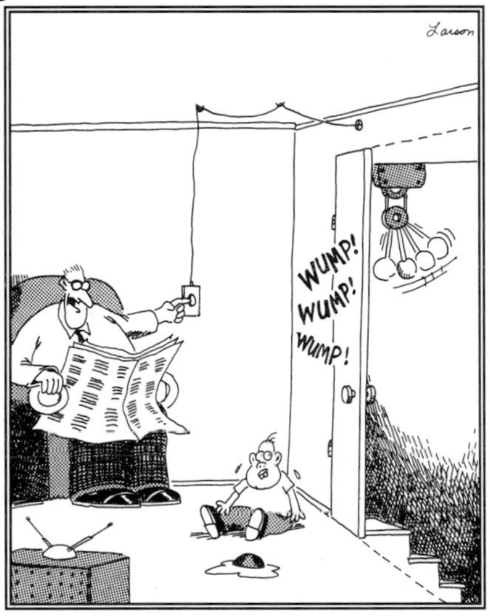
WUMP!
WUMP!
WUMP!

"Uh-oh, Donny. Sounds like the monster in the basement has heard you crying again. ... Let's be reeeeal quiet and hope he goes away."

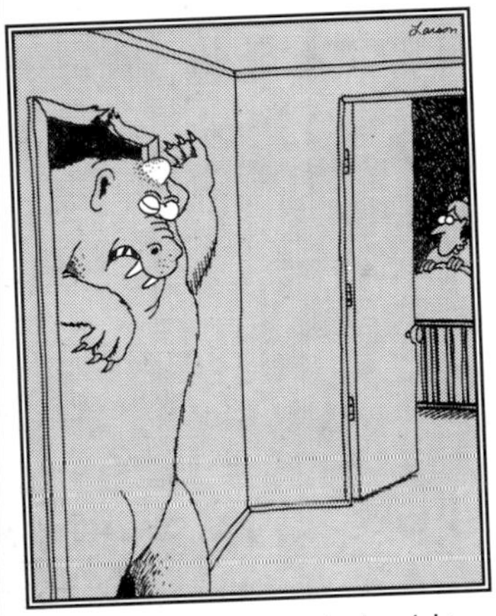

Things that go bump in the night

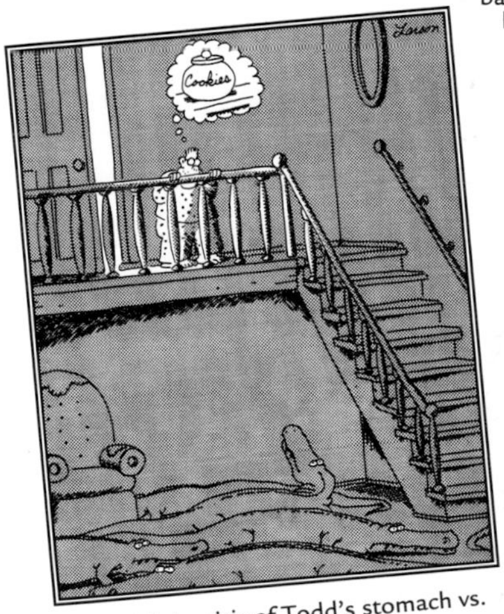
Cookies

The nightly crisis of Todd's stomach vs. Todd's imagination

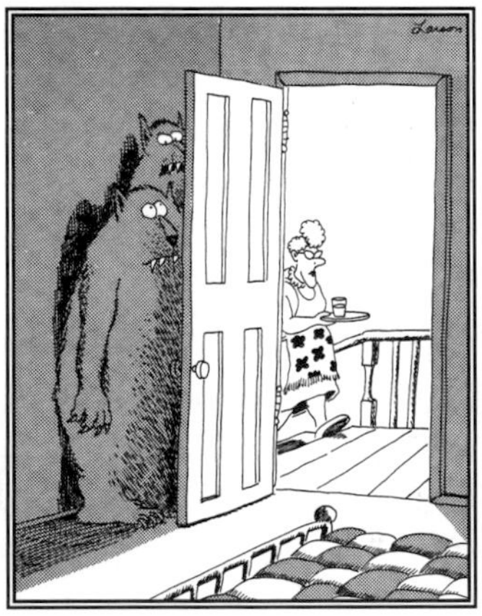

"Shove off, buddy ... I've been working this neighborhood for years."

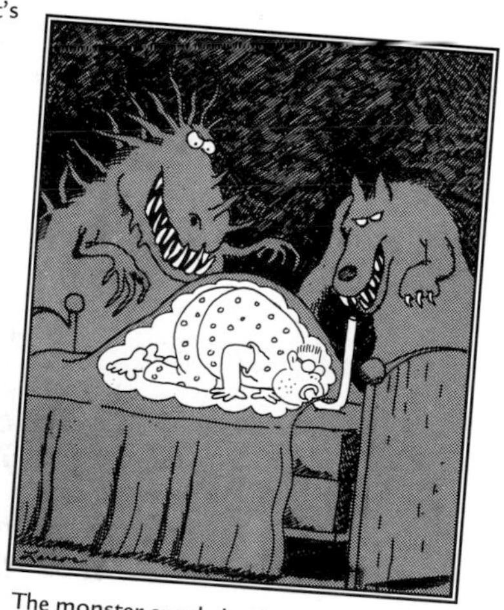

The monster snorkel: allows your child to breathe comfortably without exposing vulnerable parts to an attack.

1/1/83

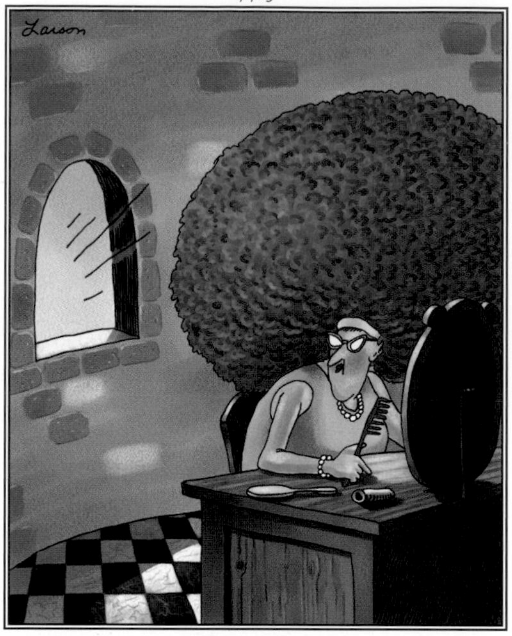
Larson

"RAPUNZEL, RAPUNZEL! ... LET DOWN YOUR HAIR!"

1/5/83

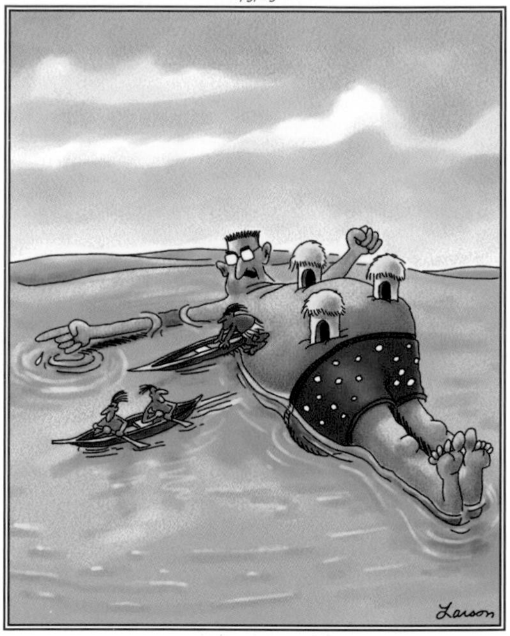
Larson

No man is an island.

1/3/83

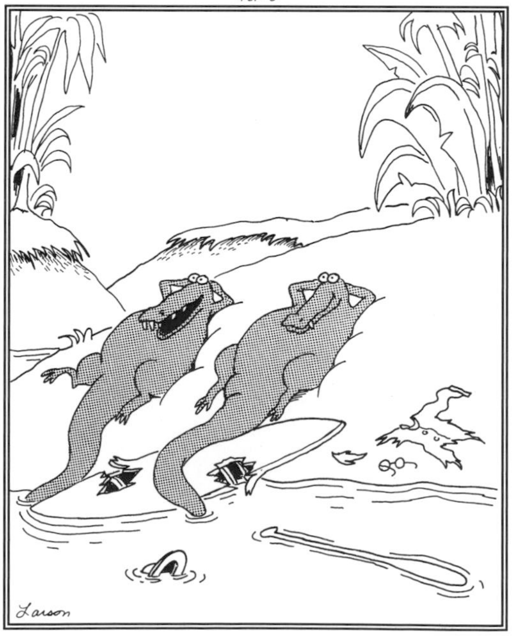
Larson

"That was incredible. No fur, claws, horns, antlers, or nothin' ... just soft and pink."

1/4/83

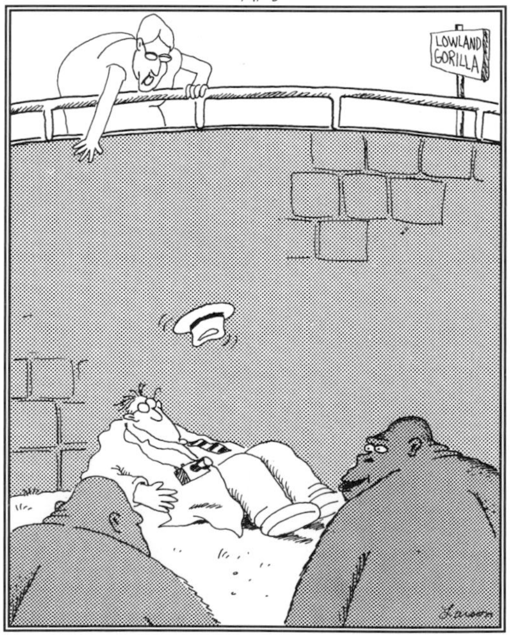
LOWLAND GORILLA
Larson

"Well, well ... looks like it's time for the old luggage test."

"Well, don't bring the filthy things in here, you imbecile! ... Take 'em down to the lake!"

"And see this ring right here, Jimmy? ... That's another time when the old fellow miraculously survived some big forest fire."

1/10/83

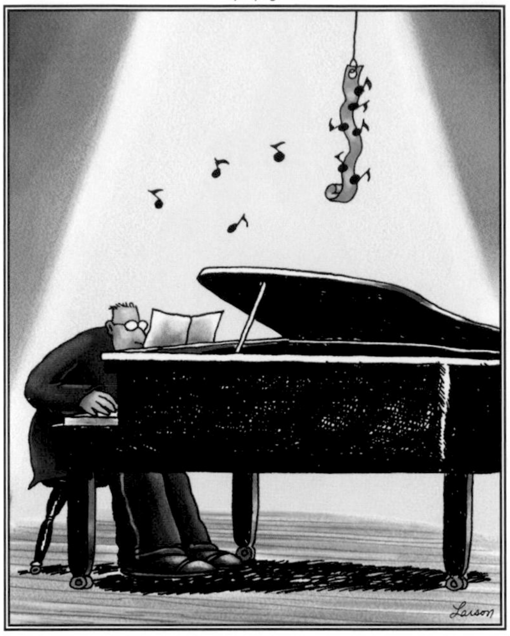

1/12/83

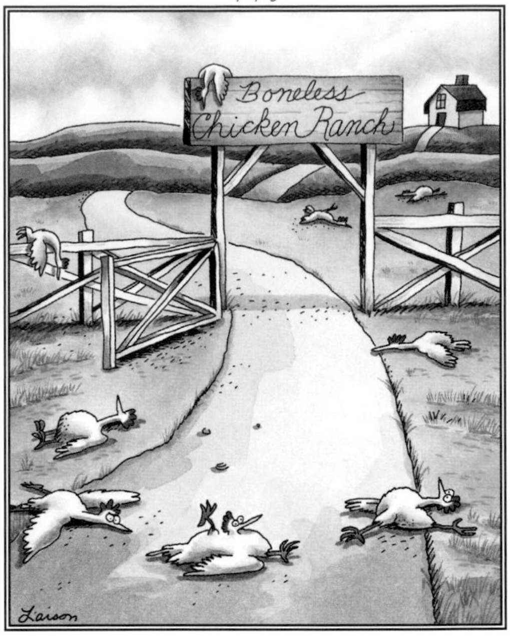
Boneless
Chicken Ranch

1/13/83

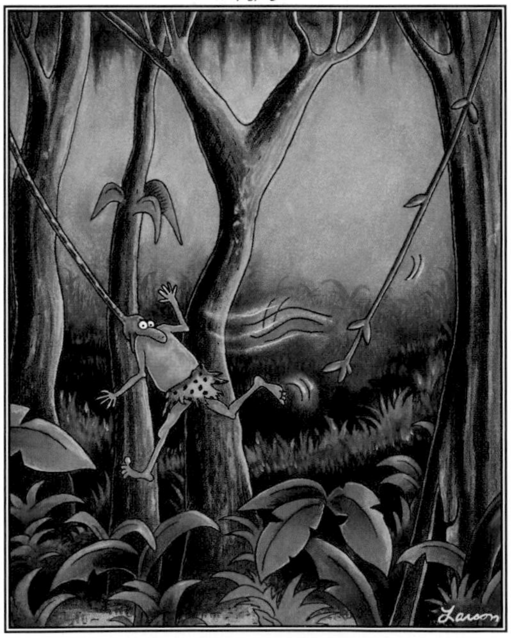

1/11/83

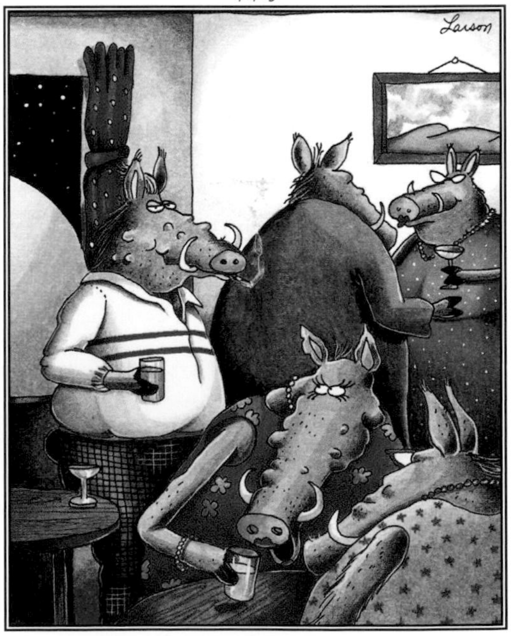

"Well, look who's here. ... God's gift to warthogs."

1/15/83

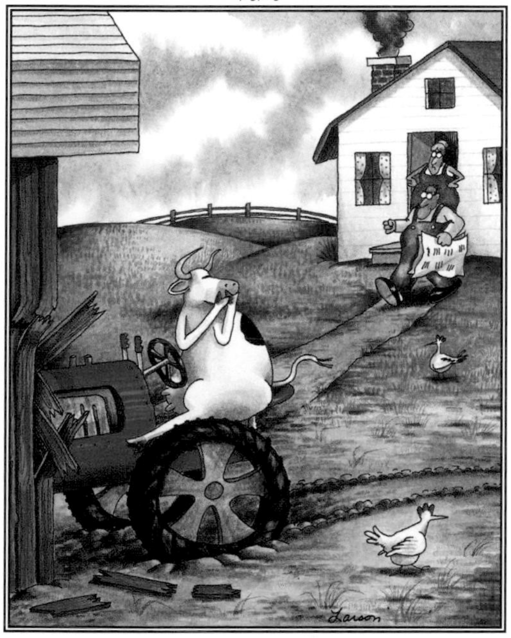
Larson

With a reverberating crash, Lulu's adventure on the tractor had come to an abrupt end.

1/18/83

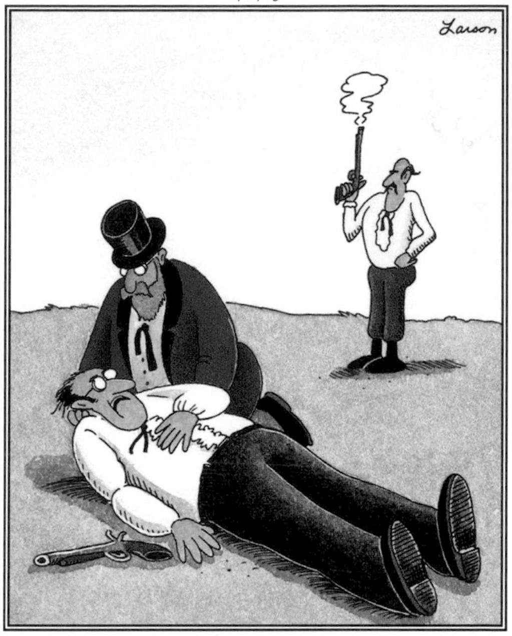
Larson

"I ... could ... have ... sworn ... you ... said ... eleven ... steps."

1/21/83

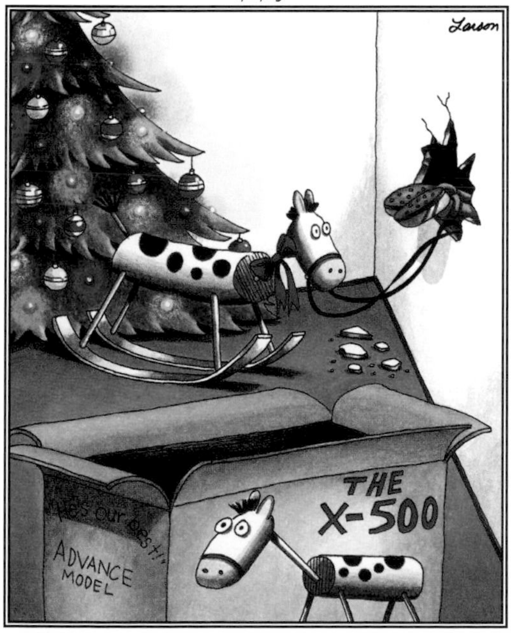
Larson
THE
X-500
ADVANCE
MODEL

1/17/83

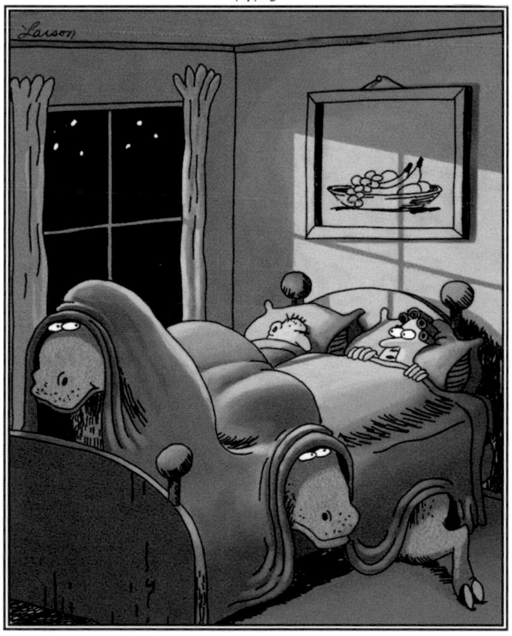
Larson

"For heaven's sake! Harold! Wake up! We've got bed buffaloes!"

"Fool! This is an eleven-sixteenths. ... I asked for a five-eighths!"

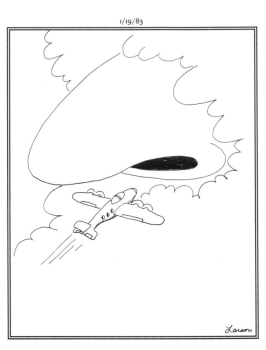

Mistakenly flying into the nose of a hurricane

"Yes ... I believe there's a question there in the back."

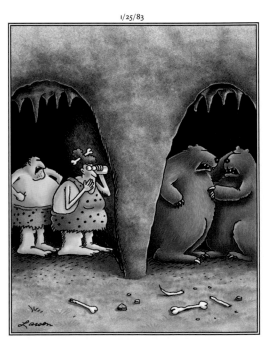

"There you go again! ... Every time the bears fight, you're right there!"

1/20/83

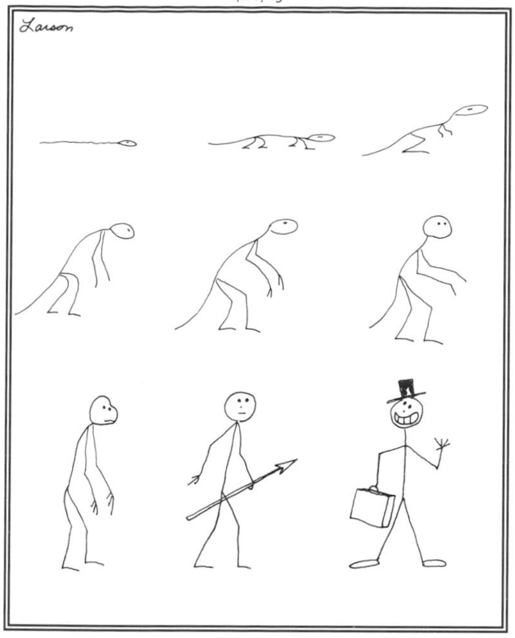
Larson

Evolution of the Stickman

1/24/83

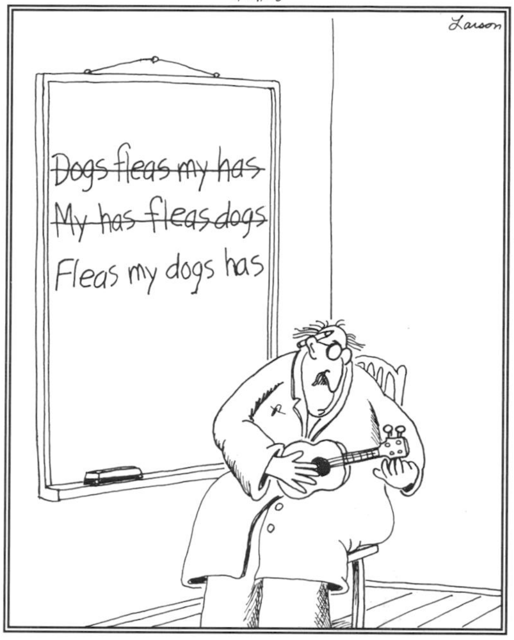
Larson
Dogs fleas my has
My has fleas dogs
Fleas my dogs has

1/26/83

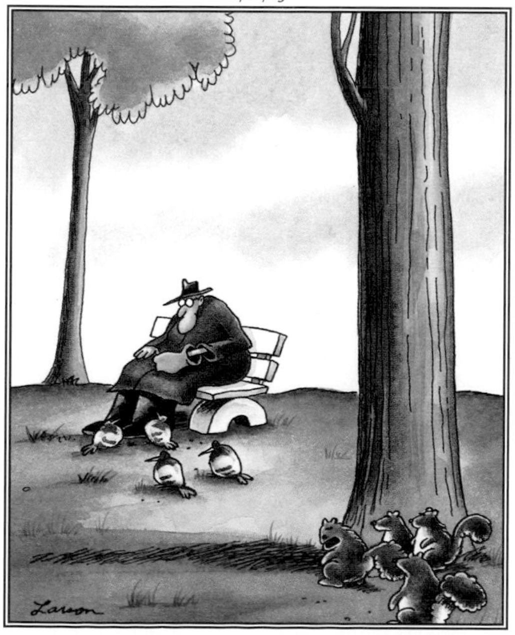
Larson

"Okay, here we go! Remember, wiggle those noses, stuff those cheeks, and act cute—and no smoking, Carl."

1/27/83

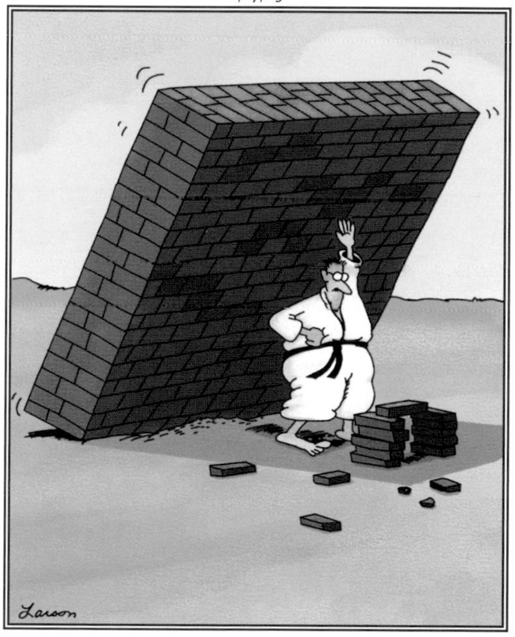
Larson

1/28/83

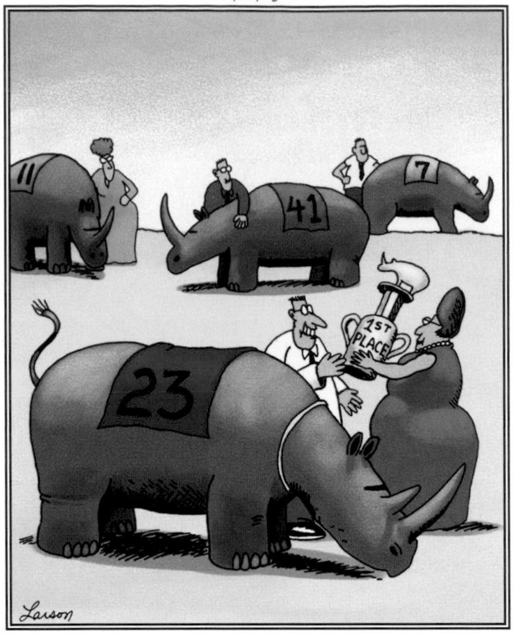
11
41
7
1ST
PLACE
23
Larson

1/29/83

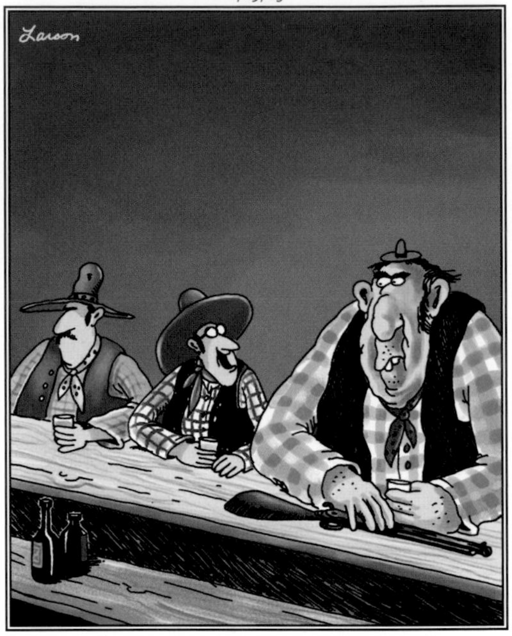
Larson

"Say ... now *there's* a little hat!"

1/31/83

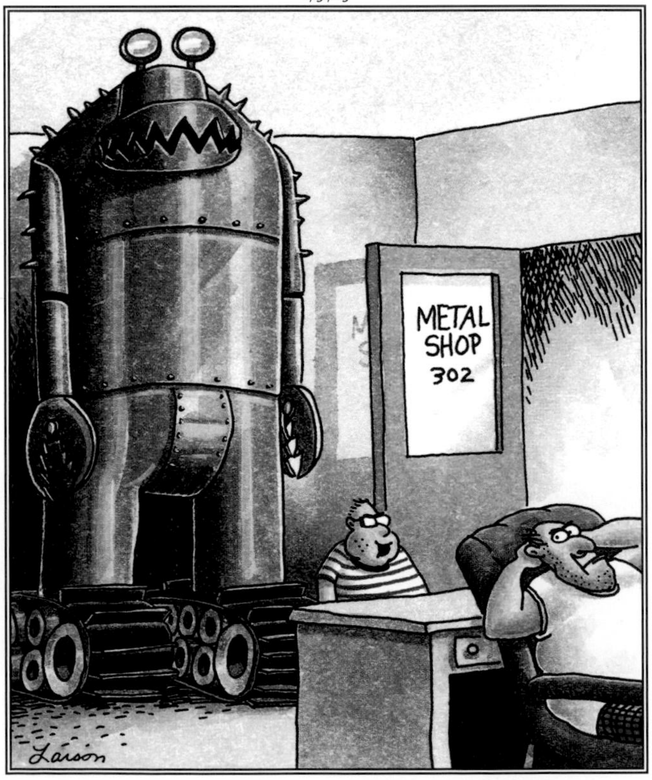
METAL
SHOP
302
Larson

"My project's ready for grading, Mr. Big Nose. ...
Hey! I'm talkin' to YOU, squidbrain!"

2/2/83

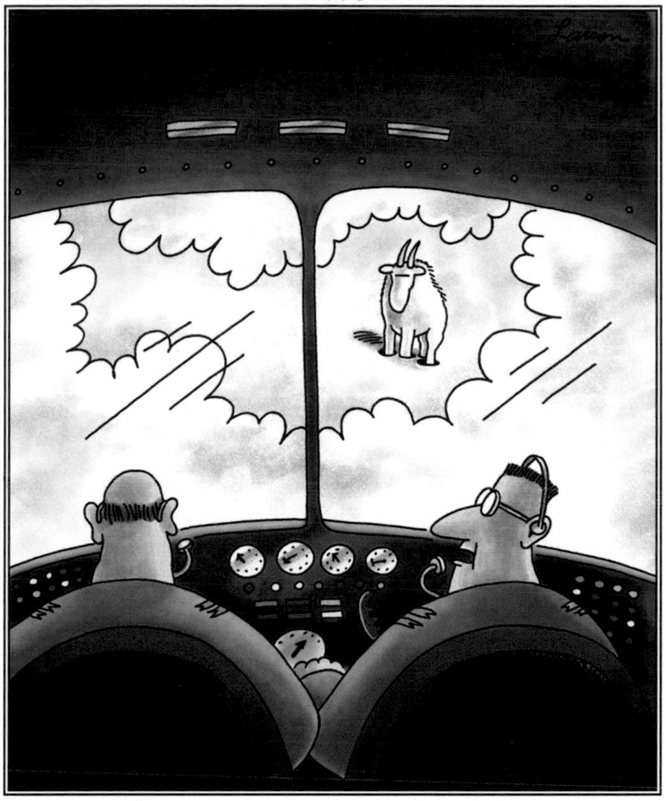

"Say ... what's a mountain goat doing way up here in a cloud bank?"

2/4/83

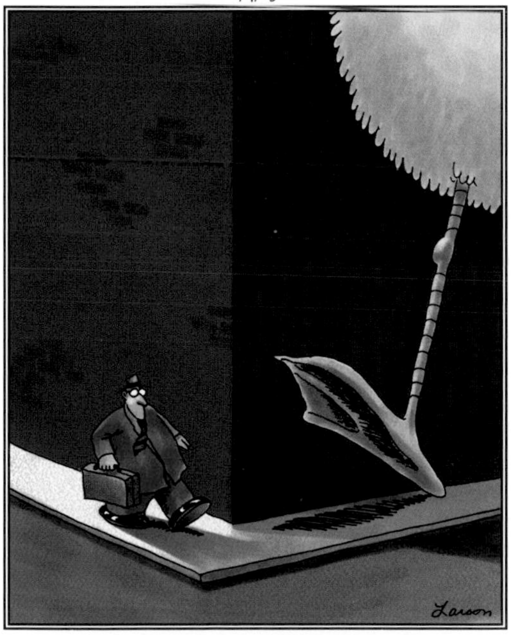

Harold would have been on his guard, but he thought the old gypsy woman was speaking figuratively.

2/9/83

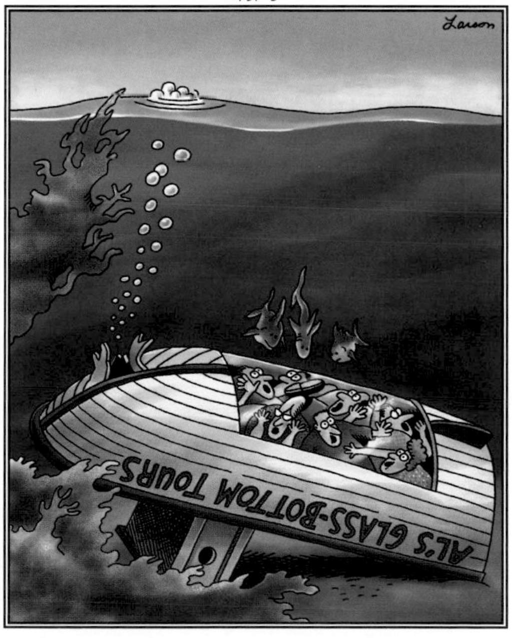
AL'S GLASS-BOTTOM TOURS

2/1/83

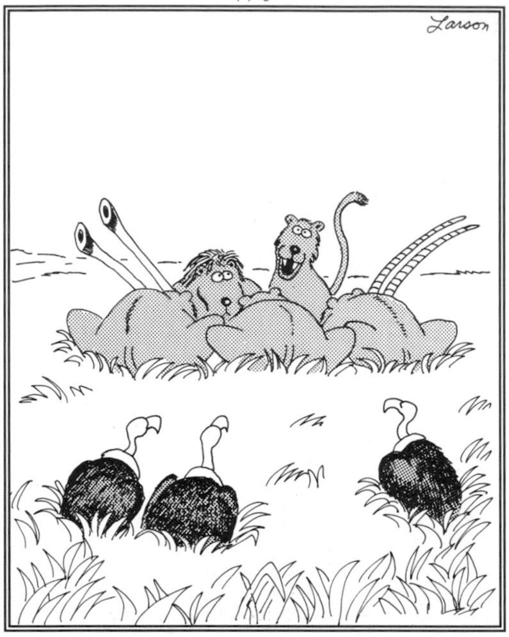
Larson

"You know? ... I think I'd like a salad."

2/3/83

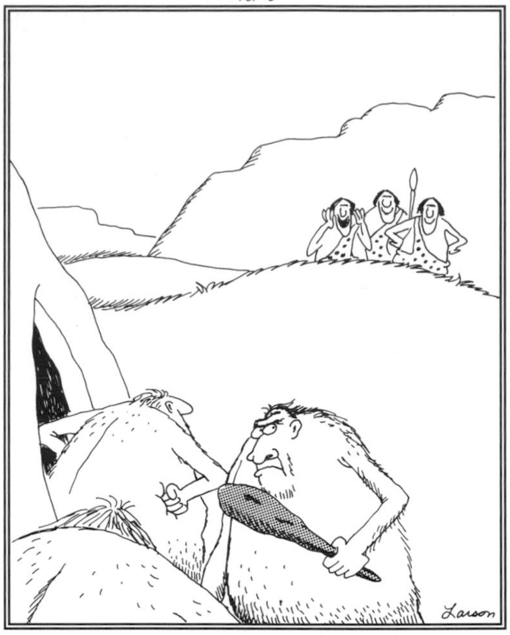
Larson

"Neanderthals, Neanderthals! Can't make fire! Can't make spear! Nyah, nyah, nyah!"

2/5/83

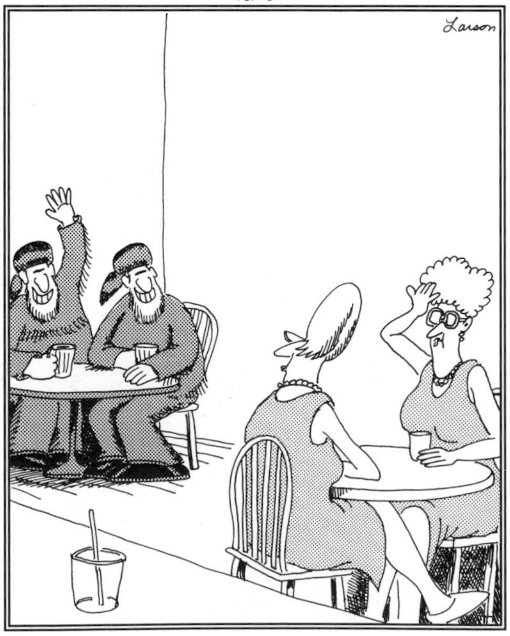
Larson

Lewis and Clark meet Sylvia and Rhonda.

2/7/83

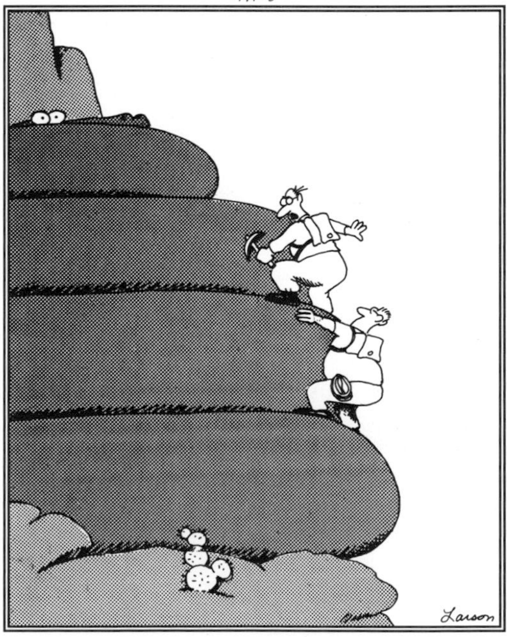
Larson

"Freeze, Earl! Freeze! ... Something rattled!"

2/8/83

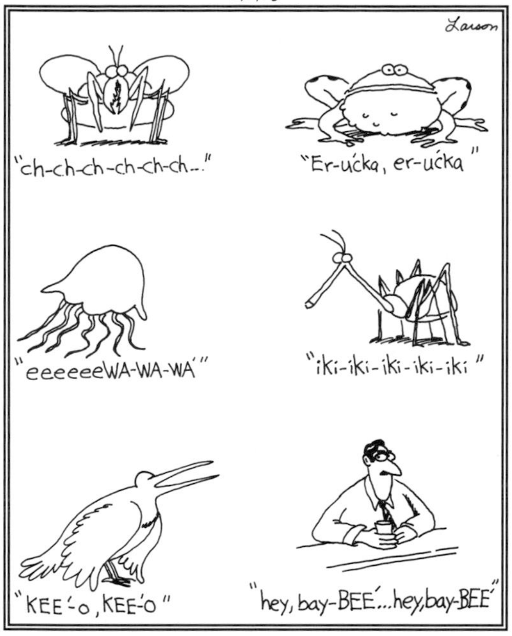
Larson
"ch-ch-ch-ch-ch-ch..."
"Er-ucka, er-ucka"
"eeeeeeWA-WA-WA"
"iki-iki-iki-iki-iki"
"KEE-o, KEE-o"
"hey, bay-BEE...hey, bay-BEE"

Animals and their mating songs

2/18/83

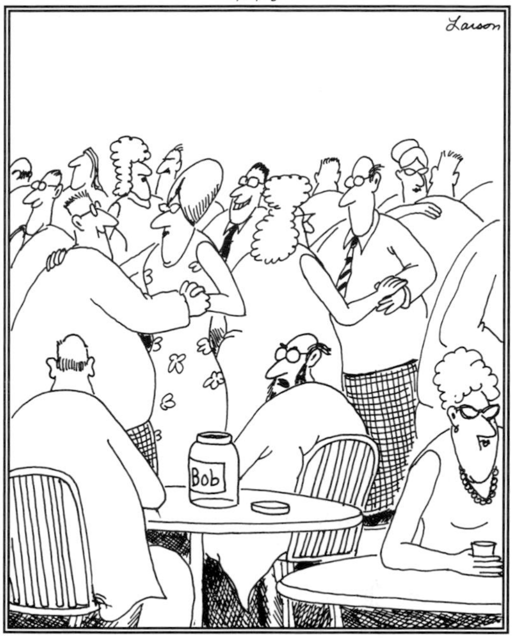
Larson
Bob

"I don't like this, Wadsworth. ... Bob never should've been allowed out on the dance floor."

2/23/83

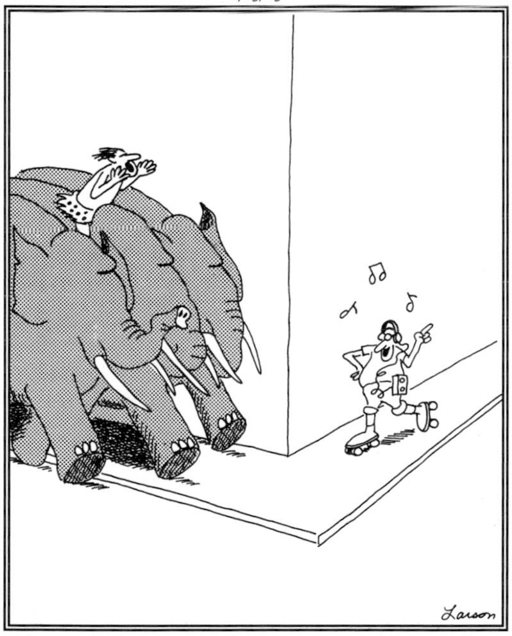
Larson

Brian has a rendezvous with destiny.

2/24/83

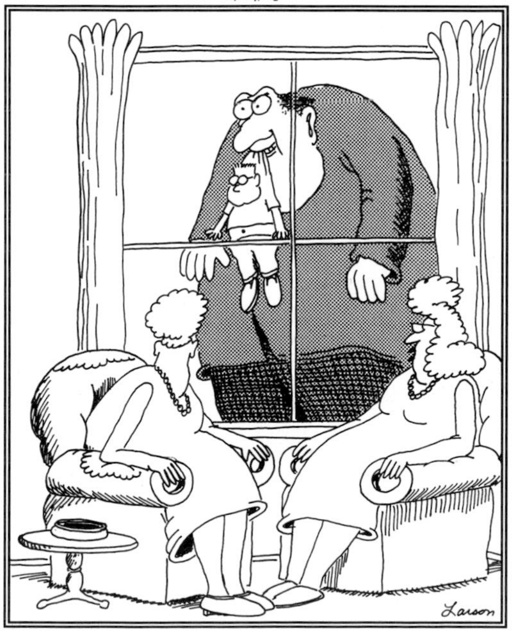
Larson

"Well, here comes Stanley now. ... Good heavens! What's he caught *this* time?"

2/10/83

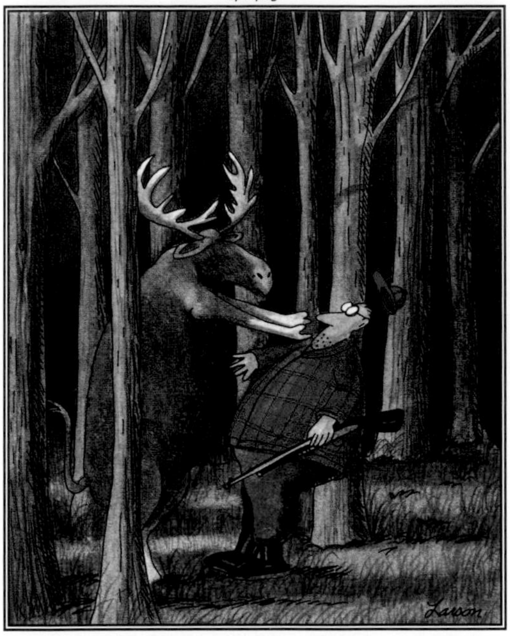
Larson

Carl shoves Roger, Roger shoves Carl, and tempers rise.

2/11/83

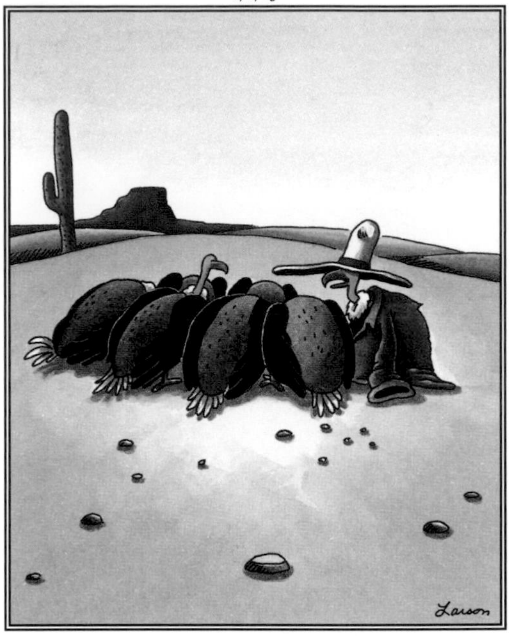
Larson

"Hey! Look at me, everybody! I'm a cowboy! ... Howdy, howdy, howdy!"

2/14/83

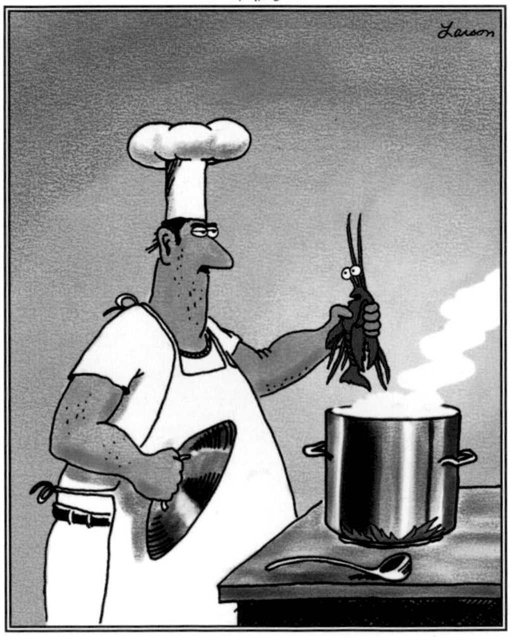
Larson

"Three wishes? Did I say three wishes? ... Shoot! I'll grant you *four* wishes."

2/15/83

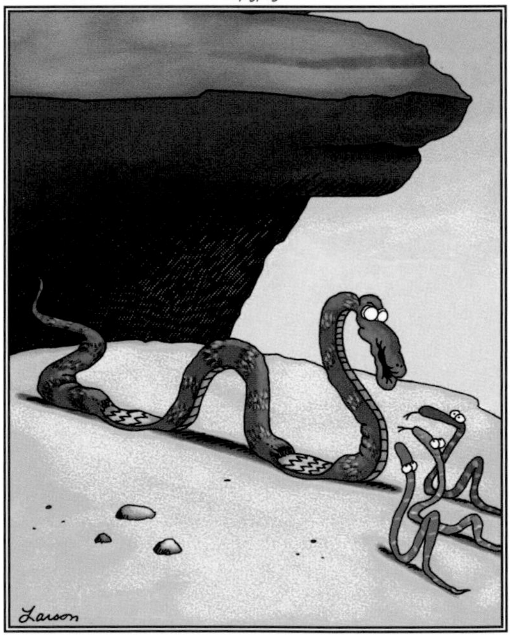
Larson

"Again? Oh, all right. ... One warm, summer evening many years ago, I was basking on a stretch of Interstate 95 not far from here ..."

2/12/83

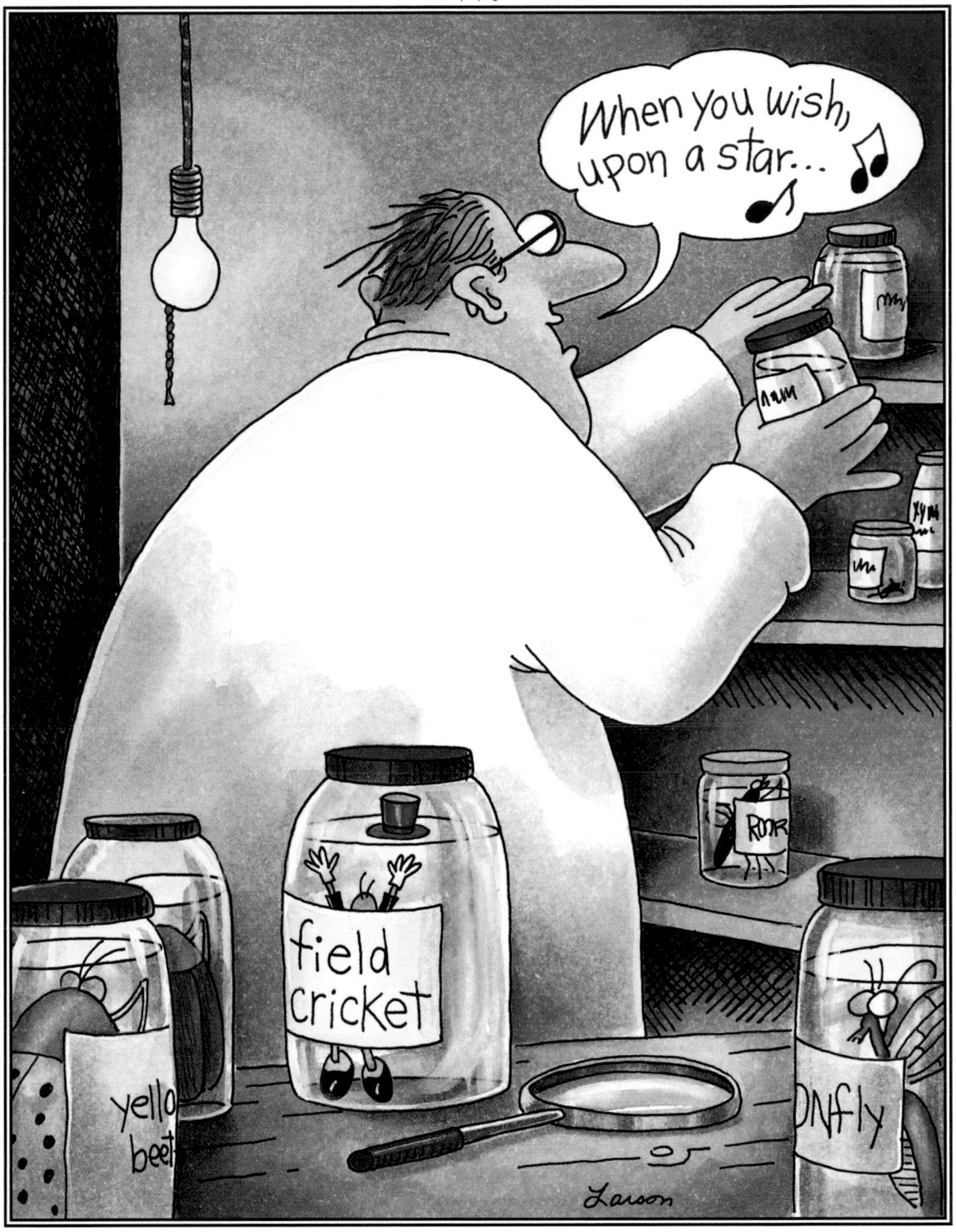
When you wish upon a star...
field cricket
yello beet
ONfly
RDDR
Larson

February 1983

2/16/83

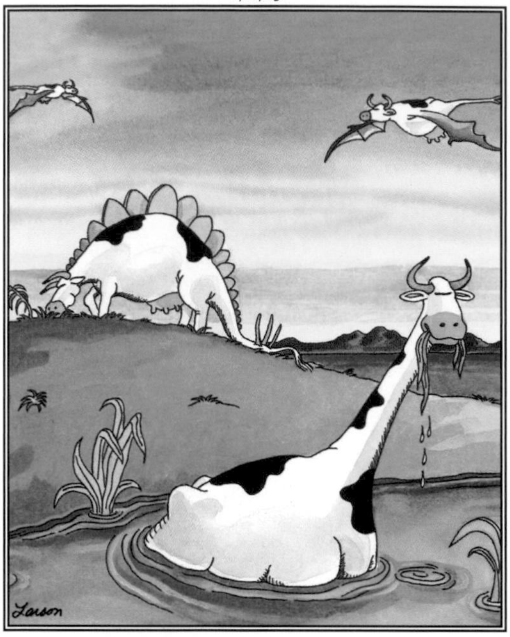

Sixty-five million years ago, when cows ruled the Earth

2/17/83

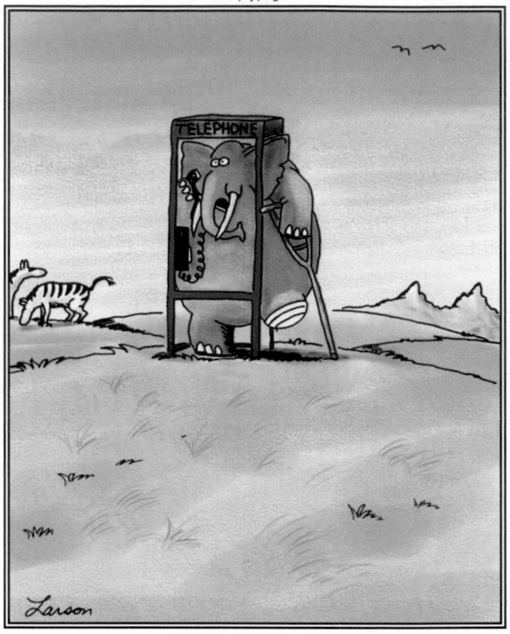
TELEPHONE

"What? ... They turned it into a WASTEBASKET?"

2/19/83

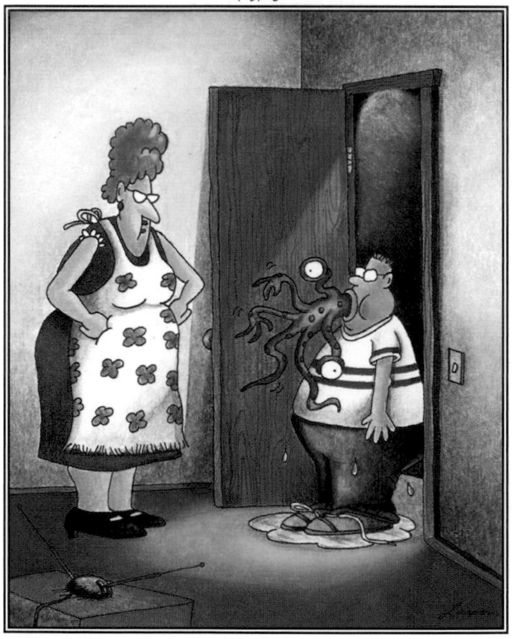

"Well, just look at you, Jimmy! ... Soaking wet, hair mussed up, shoes untied ... and take that horrible thing out of your mouth!"

2/22/83

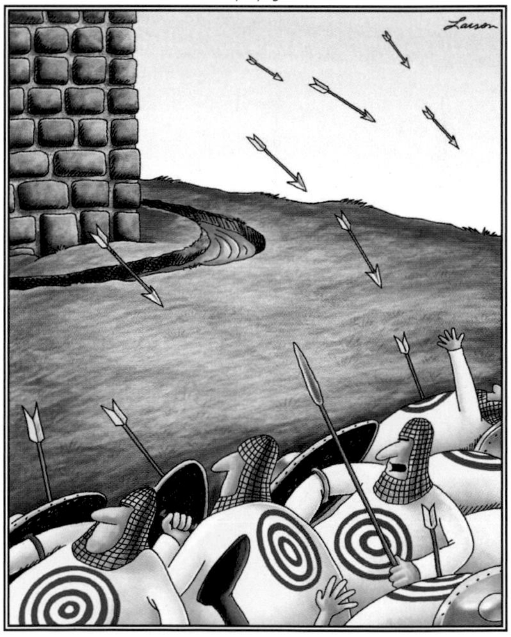

"What did I say, Boris? ... These new uniforms are a crock!"

2/21/83

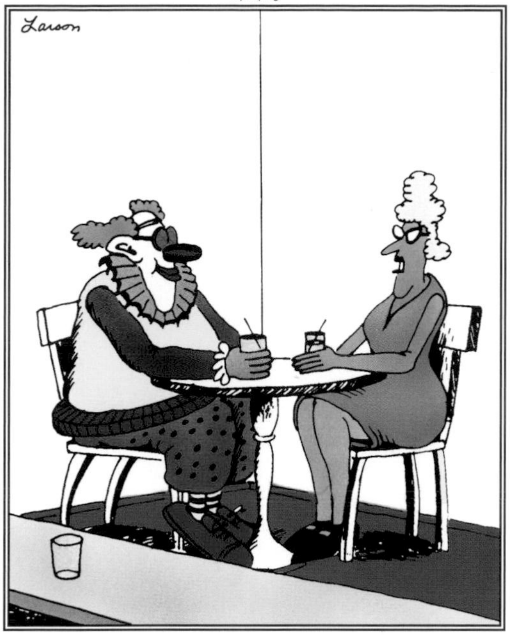
Larson

"And I like honesty in a relationship—I'm not into playing games."

2/25/83

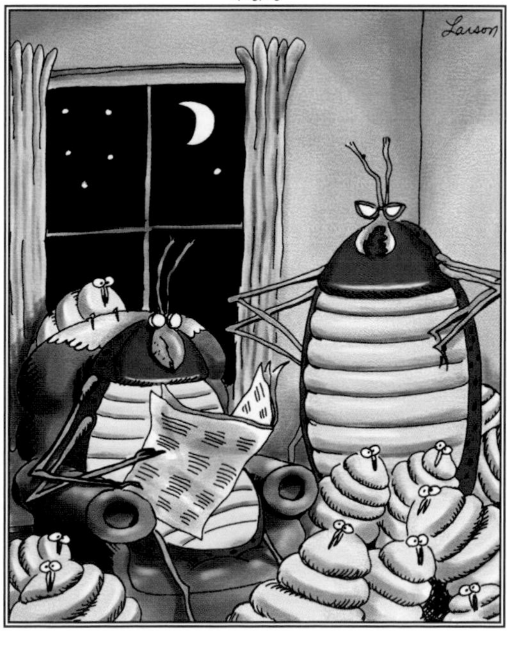
Larson

"I'm leaving you, Charles ... and I'm taking the grubs with me."

2/26/83

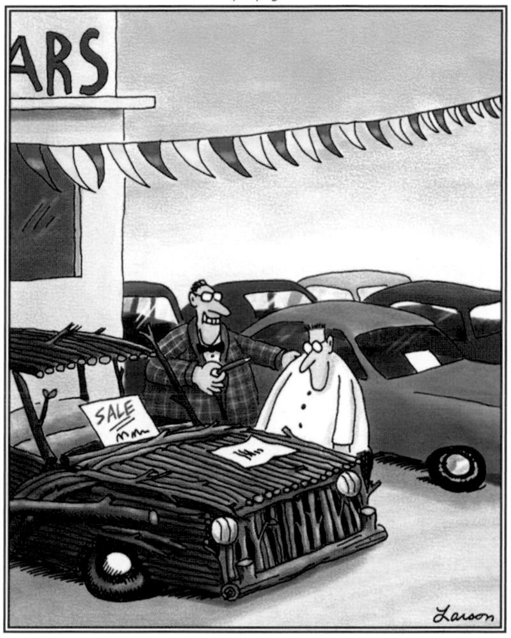
ARS
SALE
Larson

Andrew is hesitant, remembering his fiasco with the car of straw.

2/28/83

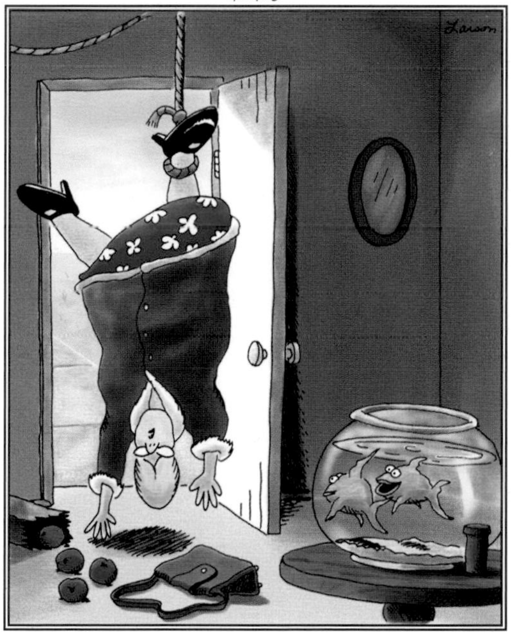
Larson

"It worked! It worked!"

3/2/83

Larson

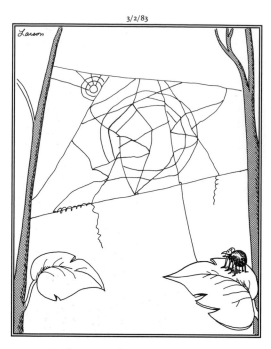

"Whoa! ... That *can't* be right!"

3/3/83

Larson

"Gesundheit."

3/1/83

Larson

"Not too close, Higgins. ... This one's got a knife."

3/4/83

Larson

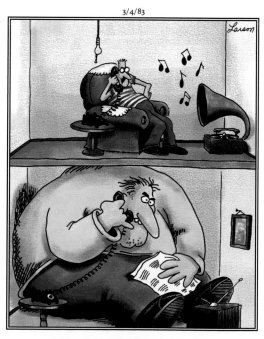

"Well, why don't you come up here and *make* me turn it down ... or do you just *talk* big, fella?"

3/7/83

"My word! I'd hate to be caught outside
on a day like this!"

3/8/83

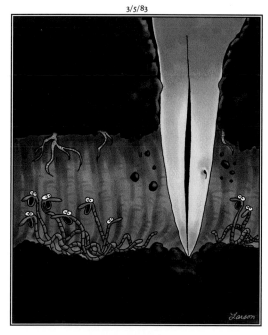

3/5/83

Night of the Robin

3/10/83

"Lunch is ready, Lawrence, and ... what?
You're *still* a fly?"

3/9/83

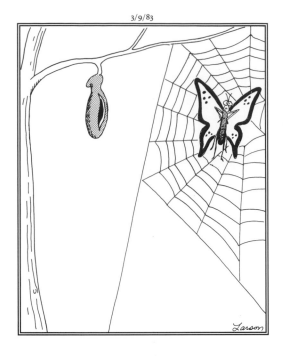

3/11/83

Al's HARDWARE
HOURS
MON-FRI
SALE!

Primitive man discovers tools.

3/14/83

"Okay! Now don't move, Andy! ... Here comes Mom!"

3/18/83

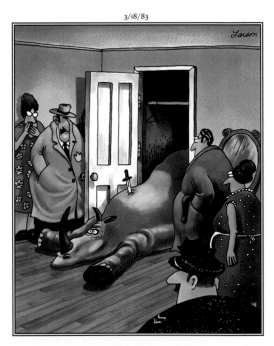

"Blast! Up to now, the rhino was one of my prime suspects."

3/16/83

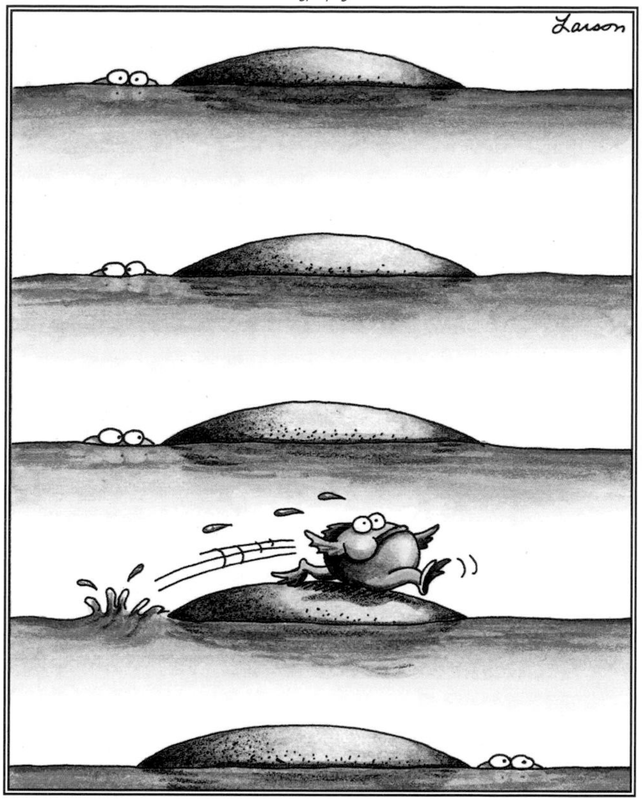
Larson

Another great moment in evolution

3/12/83

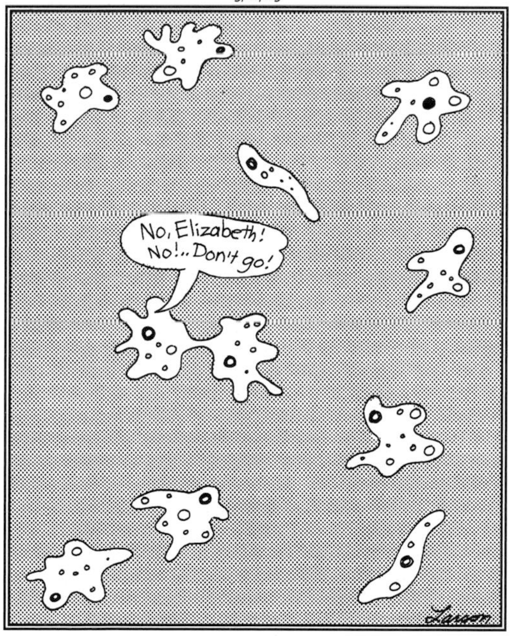
No, Elizabeth!
No!.. Don't go!
Larson

Life in the petri dish

3/15/83

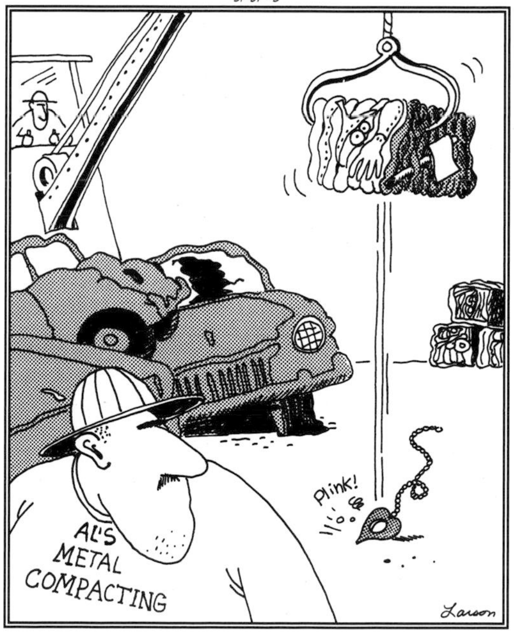
AL'S
METAL
COMPACTING
Plink!
Larson

3/19/83

The Cyclops family at breakfast

3/17/83

"How cute, Earl. ... The kids have built a little fort in the backyard."

3/22/83

"I've got it again, Larry ... an eerie feeling like there's something on top of the bed."

3/28/83

And, as you travel life's highway, don't forget to stop and eat the roses.

Cow philosophy

3/21/83

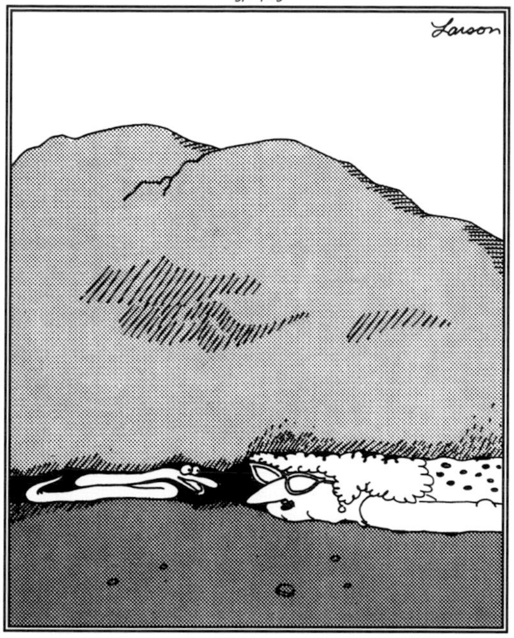

"It's true, Barbara. ... You're the first woman I've ever brought here."

3/23/83

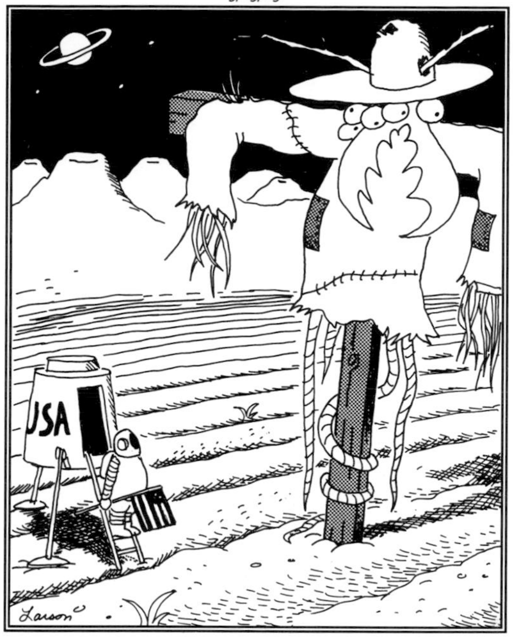
USA

3/30/83

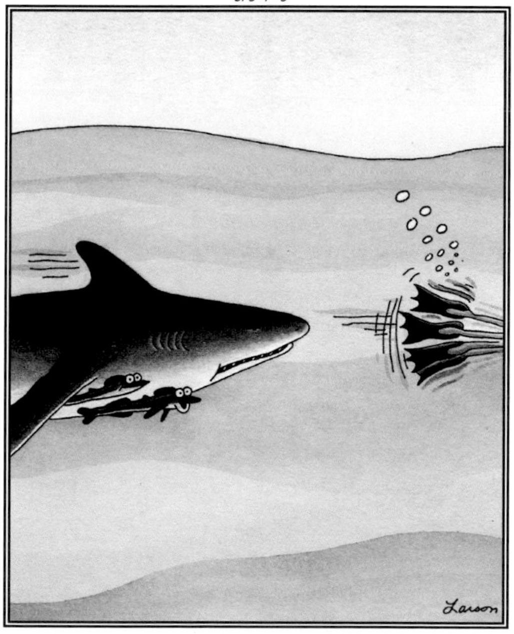

"Wheeeeeeeeeeeeeeee!"

3/31/83

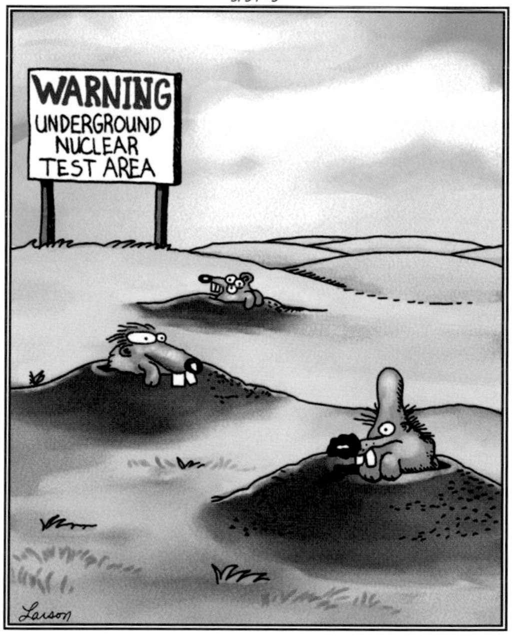
WARNING
UNDERGROUND
NUCLEAR
TEST AREA

3/24/83

"Just pull it off and apologize, Cromwell ...
or we'll go out in the hall and establish
this pecking order once and for all!"

3/25/83

"*You* again!"

3/26/83

BEWARE
OF
DOUG

ACME
SALES CO

3/29/83

"Trim the bowl, you idiots! Trim the bowl!"

4/1/83

"Now listen up! You both know the rules,
you've got equal portions, and we're going
to settle this thing once and for all. ...
On your mark ... get set ..."

4/2/83

"Dang! Wouldn't ya know it? ... The only
waterhole for a hundred miles, and
dabsmack in the middle is a giant squid."

4/4/83

"Well, look who's here ... finesse on wings!"

4/6/83

"Kids! Kids! ... The slugs are back!"

4/5/83

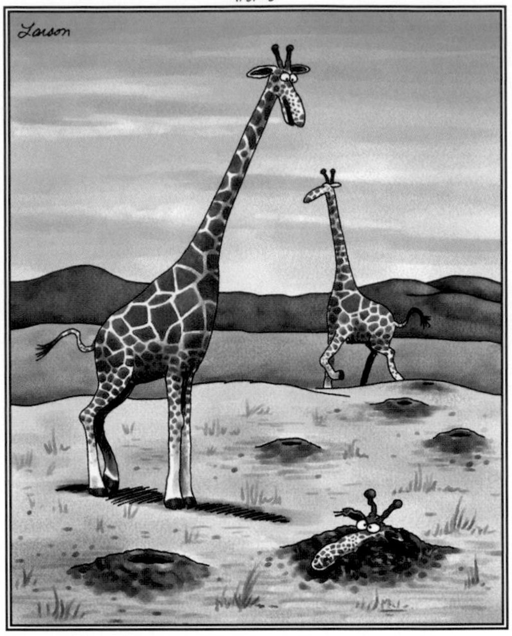

"You've got to watch out for them gopher holes, Roger."

4/7/83

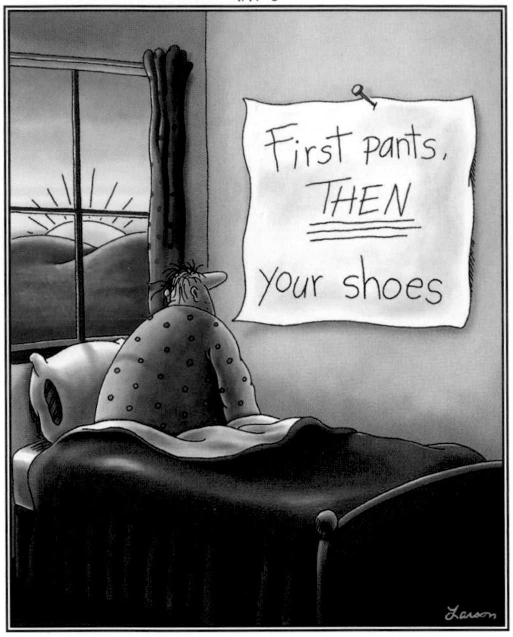
First pants,
THEN
your shoes

4/8/83

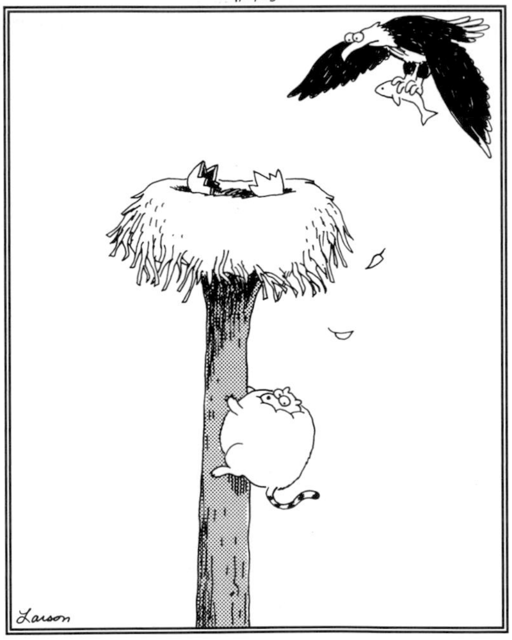

4/11/83

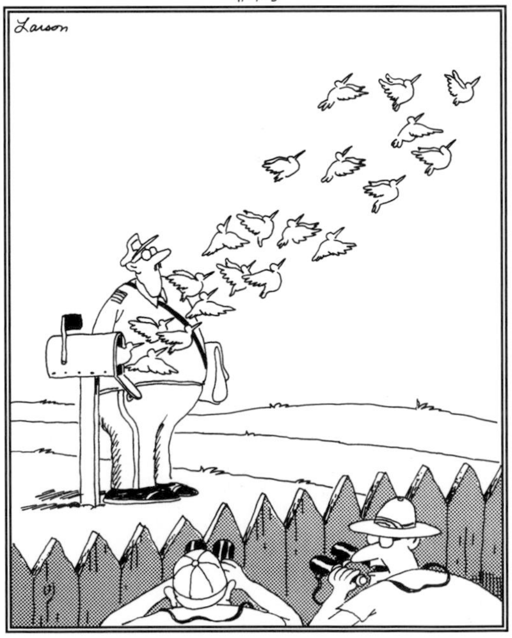

"This is it, Webster. ... We're onto the secret of migration."

4/16/83

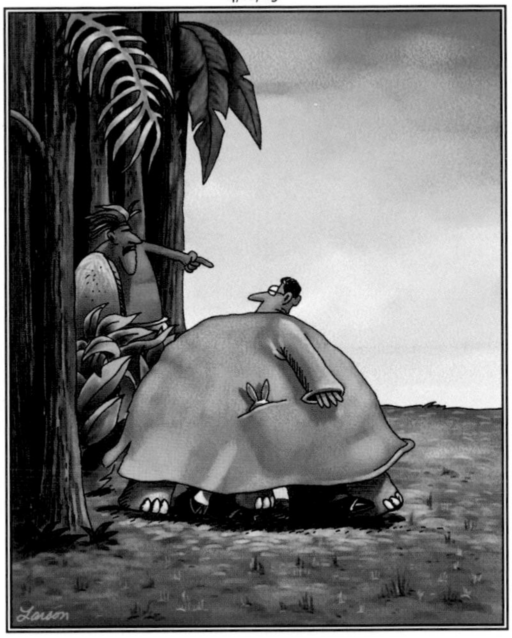
Larson

"Just a minute, young man! ... What are you taking from the jungle?"

4/20/83

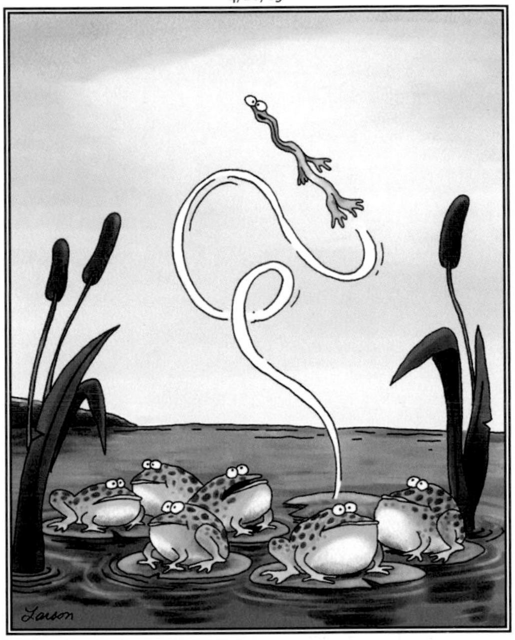
Larson

"Whoa! ... Stuart blew his air sac!"

4/12/83

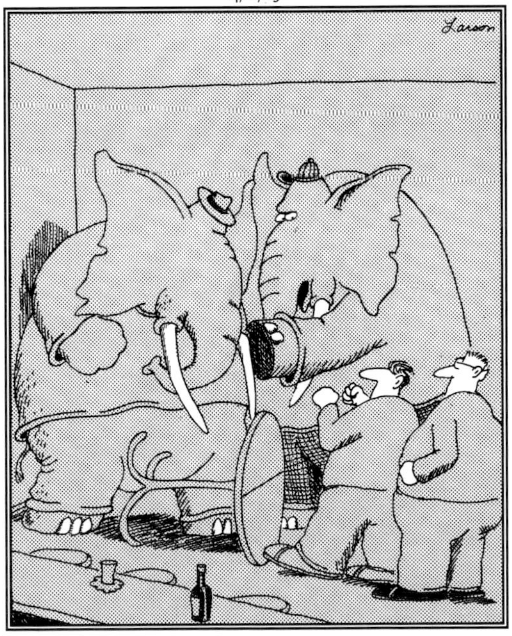
Larson

"Relax, Jerry! ... I'm sure he didn't know you were an elephant when he told that last joke!"

4/13/83

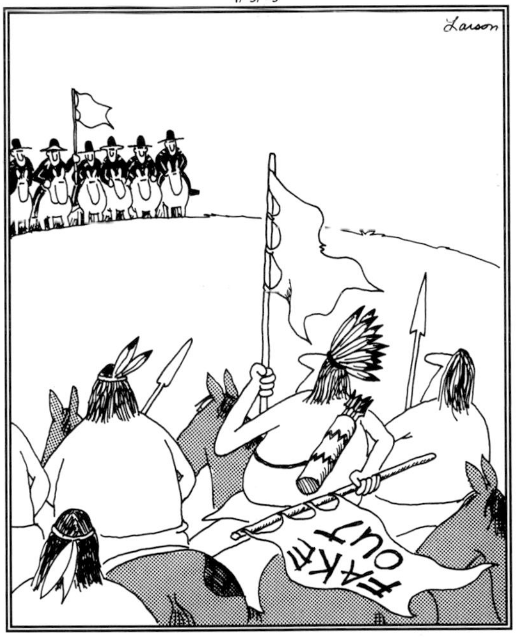
Larson
FAKE
OUT

4/9/83

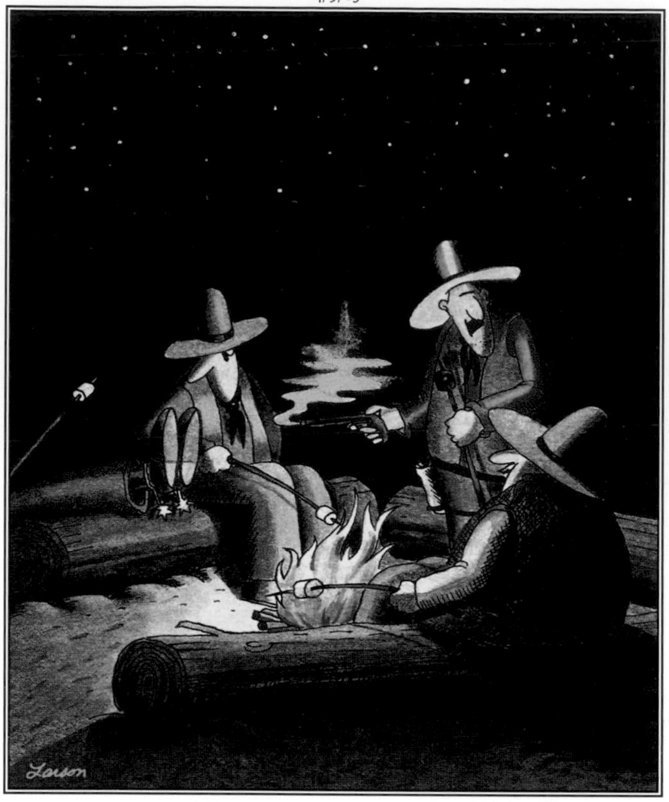
Larson

"You guys are both witnesses. ... He laughed when my marshmallow caught on fire."

4/15/83

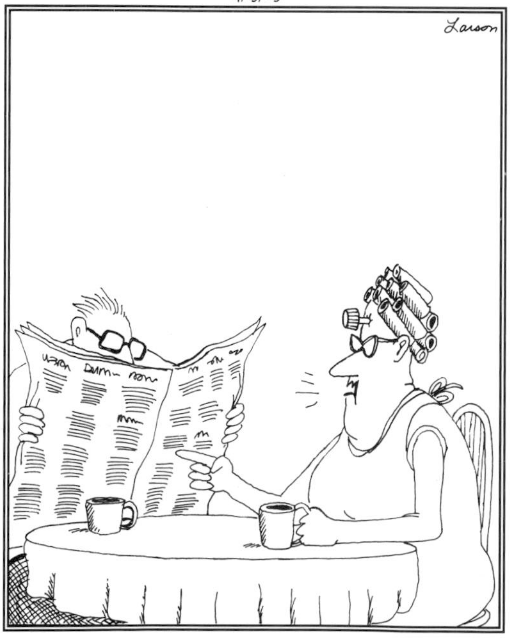
Larson

During the night, and as yet unbeknownst to Zelda, Phil had installed a volume knob.

4/18/83

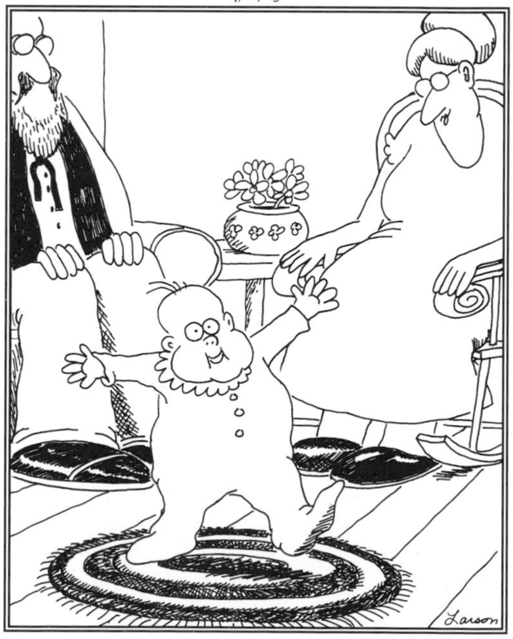
Larson

Custer's first stand

4/19/83

"Calm down, Edna. ... Yes, it's some giant, hideous insect ... but it could be some giant, hideous insect in need of help."

4/25/83

4/14/83

"I just *can't* go in there, Bart! ... Some feller in there and I are wearin' the same kind of hat!"

4/21/83

Suddenly, amidst all the confusion, Fifi seized the controls and saved the day.

4/23/83

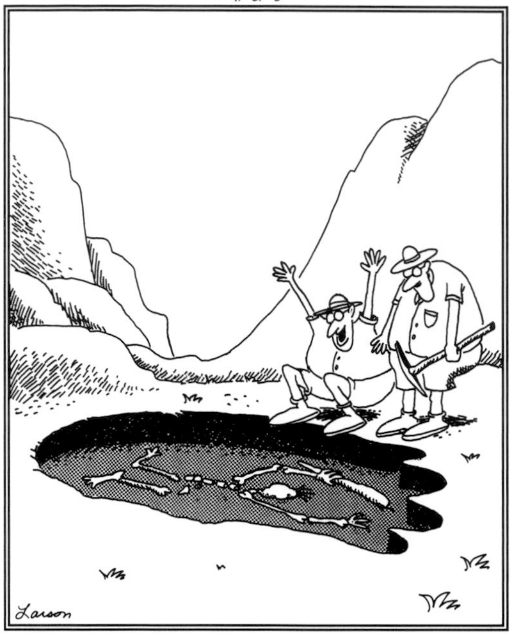

"What a find, Williams! The fossilized footprint of a Brachiosaurus! ... And a *Homo habilis* thrown in to boot!"

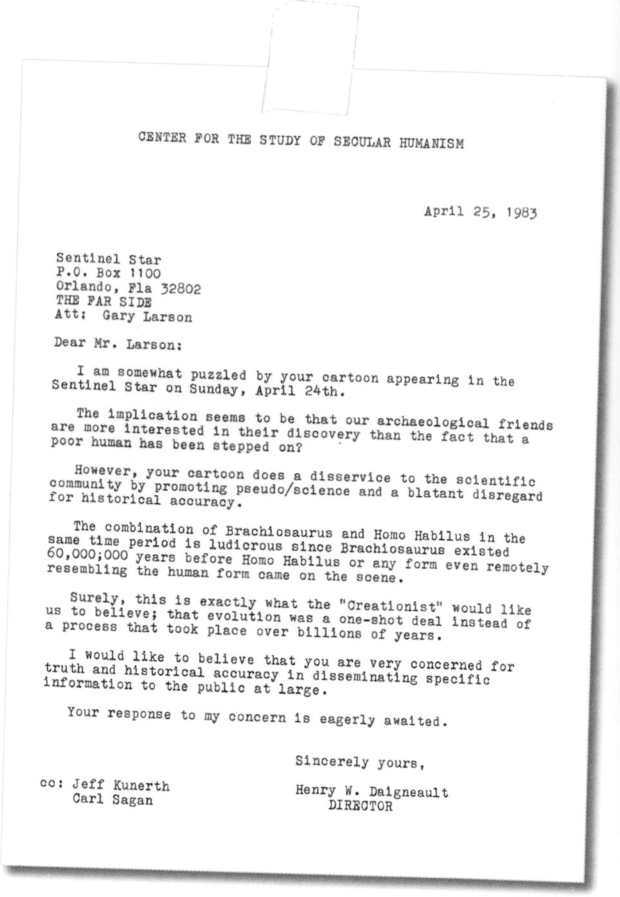

CENTER FOR THE STUDY OF SECULAR HUMANISM

April 25, 1983

Sentinel Star
P.O. Box 1100
Orlando, Fla 32802
THE FAR SIDE
Att: Gary Larson

Dear Mr. Larson:

I am somewhat puzzled by your cartoon appearing in the Sentinel Star on Sunday, April 24th.

The implication seems to be that our archaeological friends are more interested in their discovery than the fact that a poor human has been stepped on?

However, your cartoon does a disservice to the scientific community by promoting pseudo/science and a blatant disregard for historical accuracy.

The combination of Brachiosaurus and Homo Habilus in the same time period is ludicrous since Brachiosaurus existed 60,000;000 years before Homo Habilus or any form even remotely resembling the human form came on the scene.

Surely, this is exactly what the "Creationist" would like us to believe; that evolution was a one-shot deal instead of a process that took place over billions of years.

I would like to believe that you are very concerned for truth and historical accuracy in disseminating specific information to the public at large.

Your response to my concern is eagerly awaited.

Sincerely yours,

Henry W. Daigneault
DIRECTOR

cc: Jeff Kunerth
Carl Sagan

4/22/83

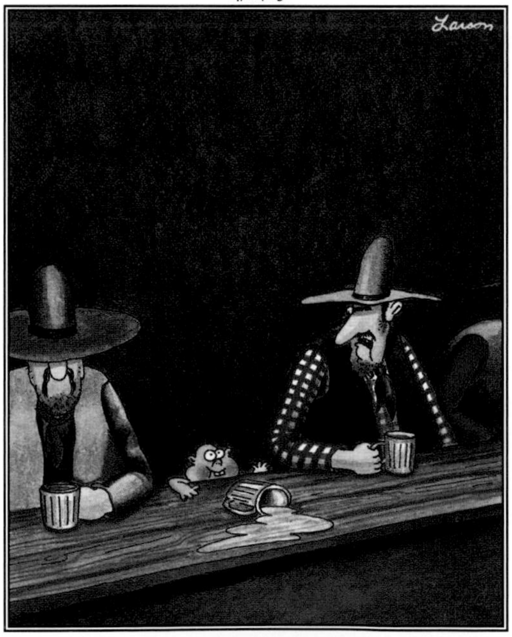

"So! ... You must be the one they call 'The Kid.'"

4/28/83

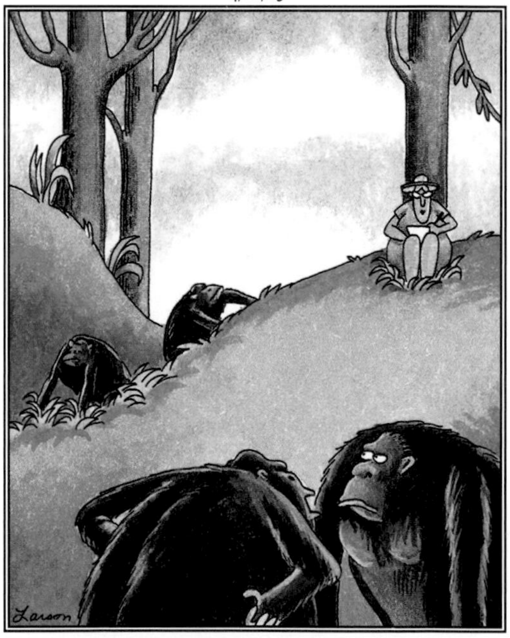

"Don't shush me—and I don't care if she *is* writing in her little notebook; just tell me where you were last night!"

4/26/83

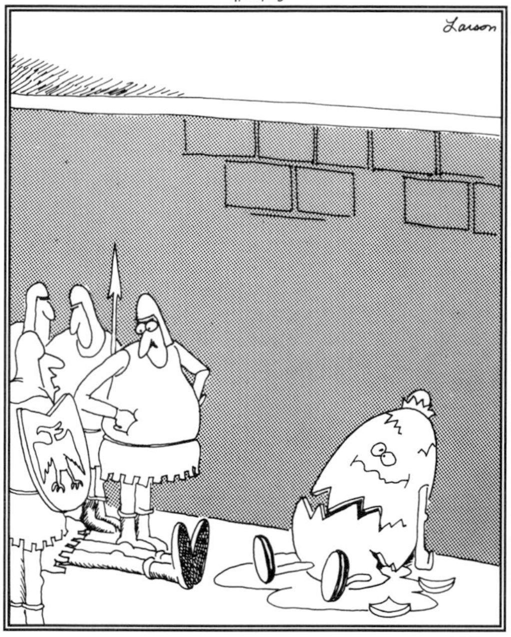
Larson

"It's Henderson again, sir. ... He always faints at the sight of yolk."

4/27/83

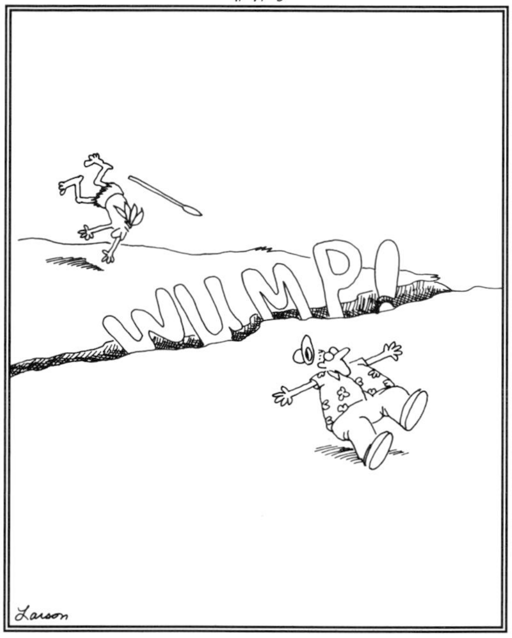
WUMP!
Larson

Continental drift whiplash

4/29/83

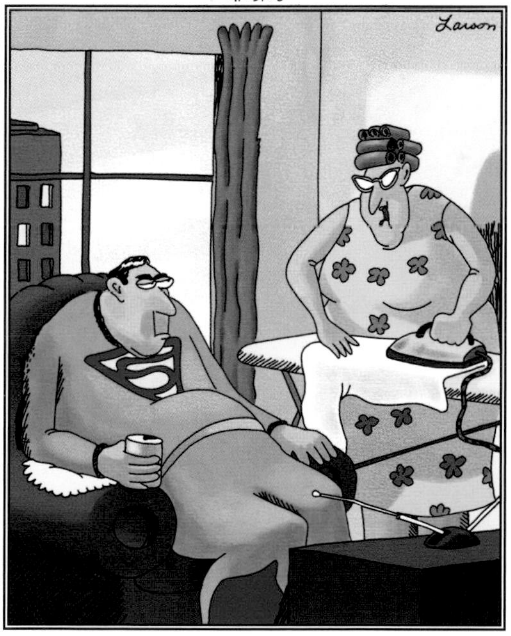
Larson

"By the way, we're playing cards with the Millers tonight, and Edna says if you promise not to use your X-ray vision, Warren promises not to bring his Kryptonite."

4/30/83

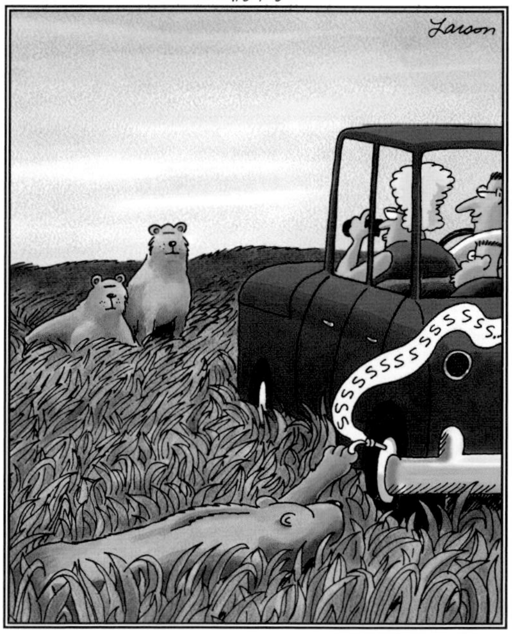
Larson

5/3/83

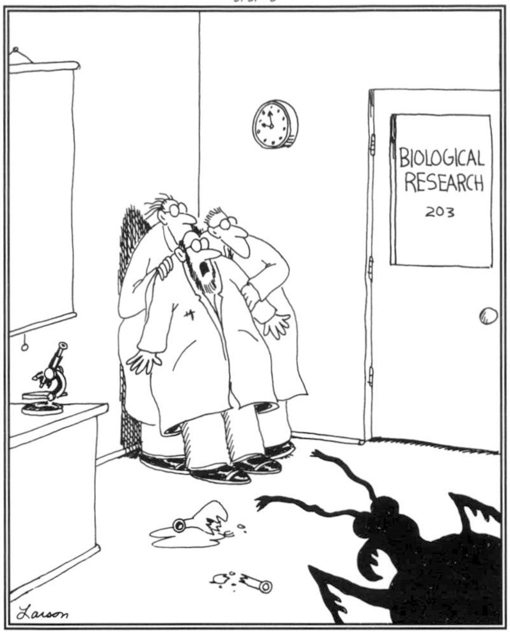
BIOLOGICAL
RESEARCH
203

"Trapped like rodentia!"

5/4/83

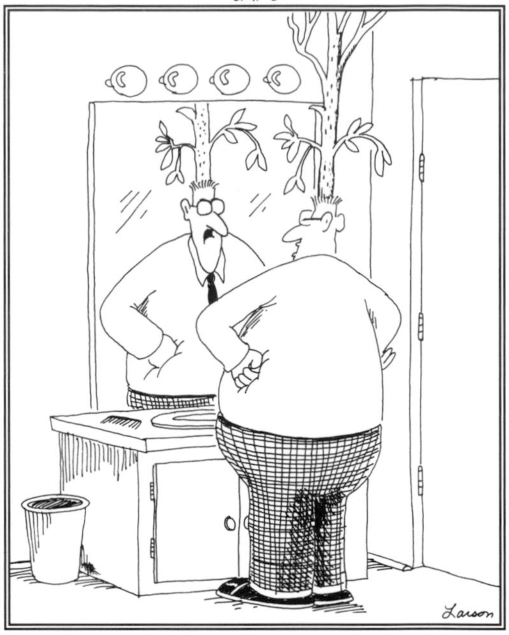

"Wouldn't you know it! ... And always just before a big date!"

5/2/83

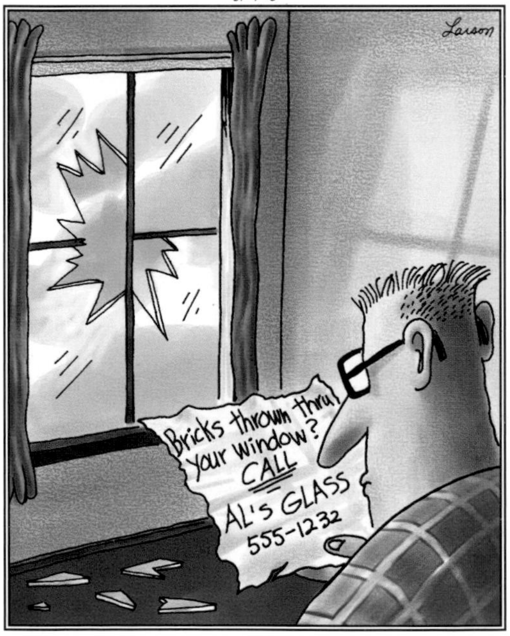
Bricks thrown thru your window?
CALL
AL's GLASS
555-1232

5/6/83

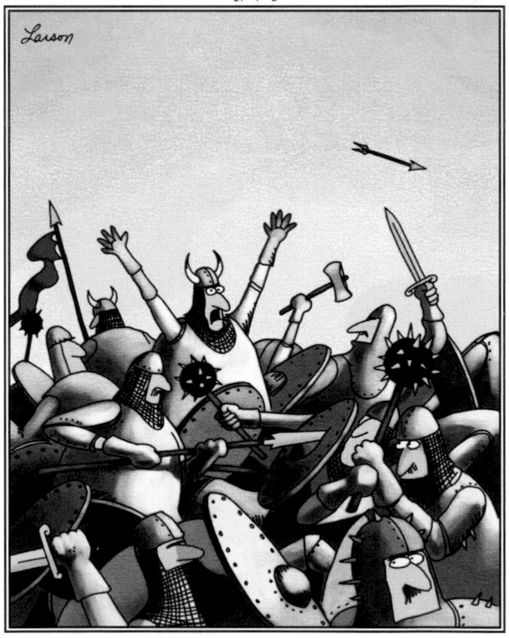

"Hey! C'mon! Hold it! Hold it! ... Or someone's gonna get hurt!"

5/5/83

TELEPHONE
Larson

5/10/83

Larson

"Chief say, 'Oh yeah? ... *Your* horse ugly.'"

5/7/83

KICK ME
Larson

5/9/83

Larson

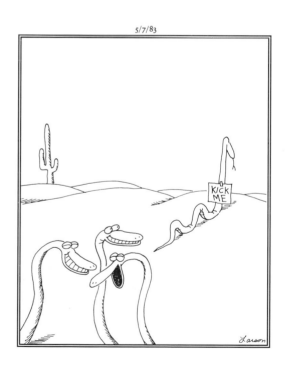

5/12/83

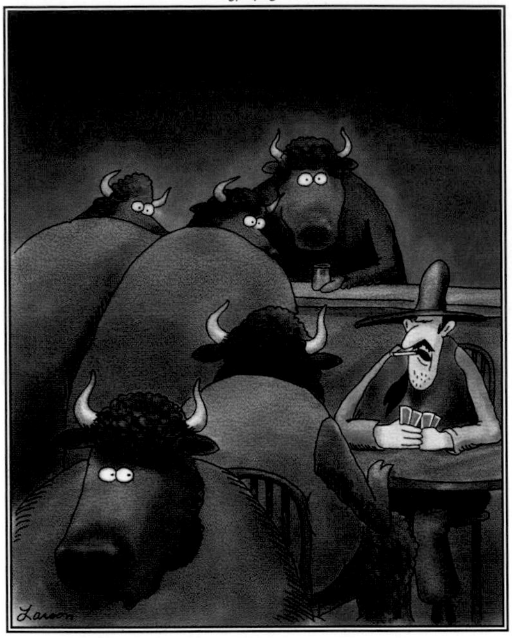
Larson

"The name is Bill ... Buffalo Bill."

5/11/83

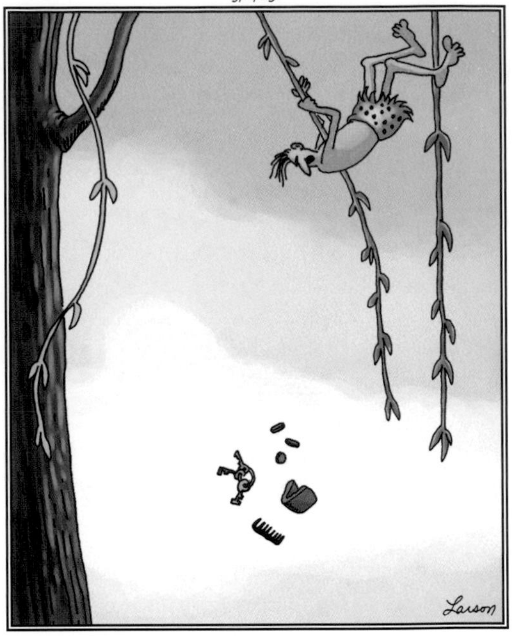
Larson

"Dang!"

5/21/83

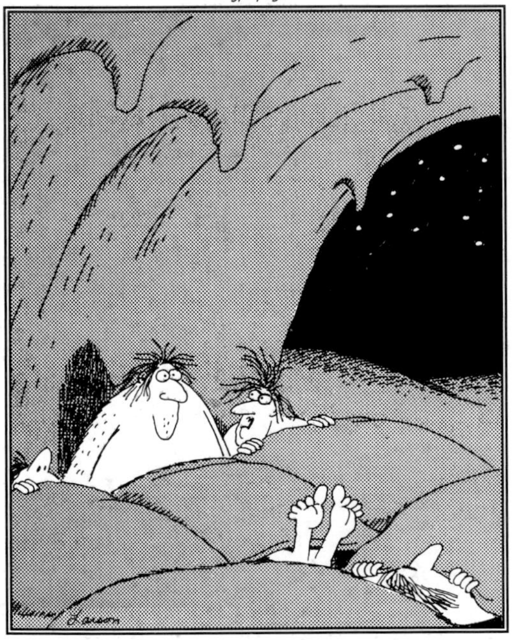

"Go back sleep, Thag. ... You only dream
we live just so long then die."

5/23/83

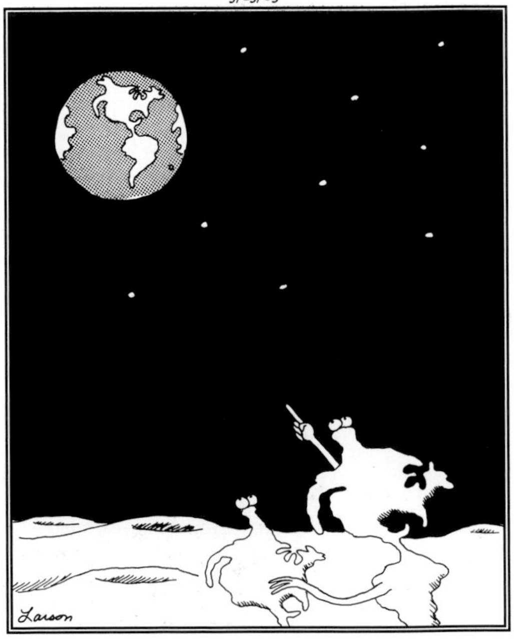
Larson

"And, if you squint your eyes just right,
you can see the zork in the Earth."

5/13/83

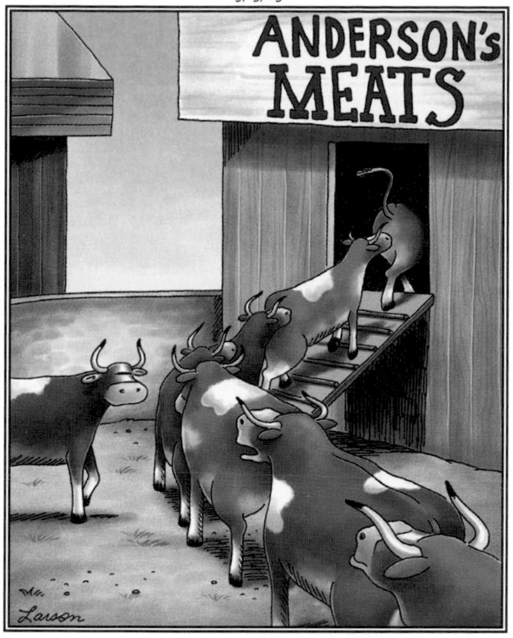
ANDERSON's
MEATS
Larson

"Hey! You! ... No cutting in!"

5/14/83

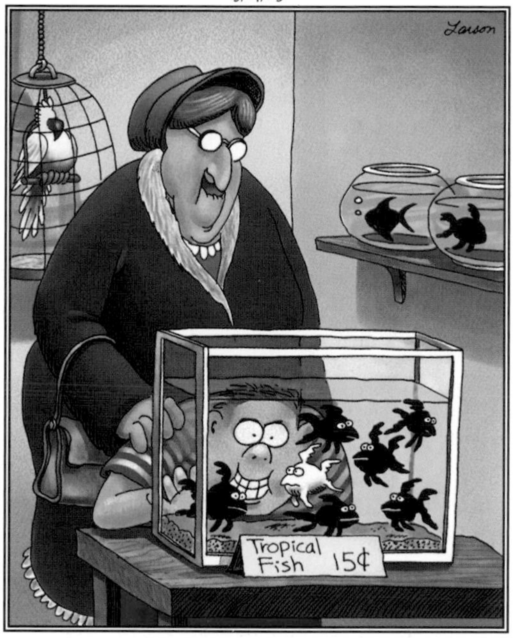
Larson
Tropical
Fish 15¢

"Okay, okay, little Ahab. ... Which one is it going to be?"

5/24/83

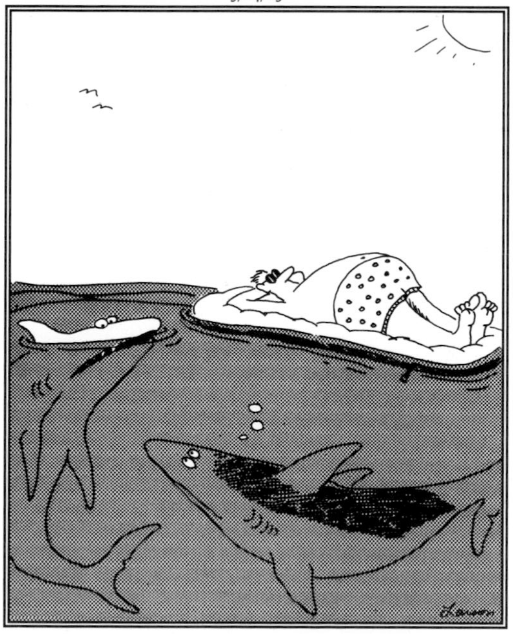
Larson

"Well, shoot ... I can never tell whether these things are done or not."

5/25/83

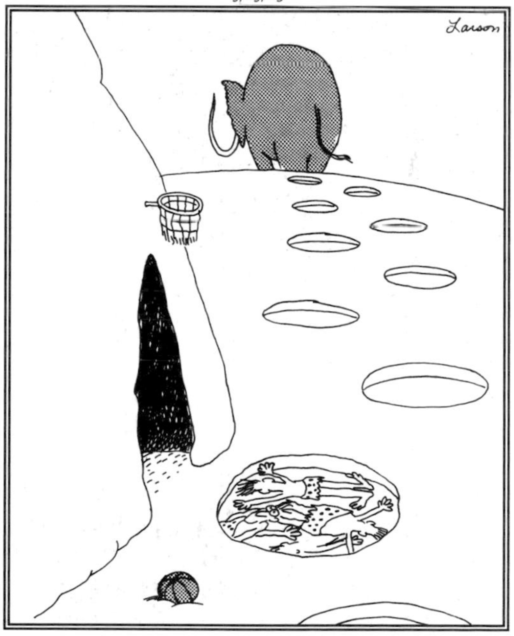
Larson

5/16/83

"And the murderer is ... THE BUTLER! Yes, the butler—
who, I'm convinced, first gored the Colonel to death
before trampling him to smithereens."

5/17/83

5/18/83

"I wouldn't do that, mister. ... Old Zeek's
liable to fire that sucker up."

5/19/83

BEAVER TRAP
BEAVER TRAP

5/20/83

"Well, good heavens! I can't believe you men. ... *I've* got some rope!"

5/26/83

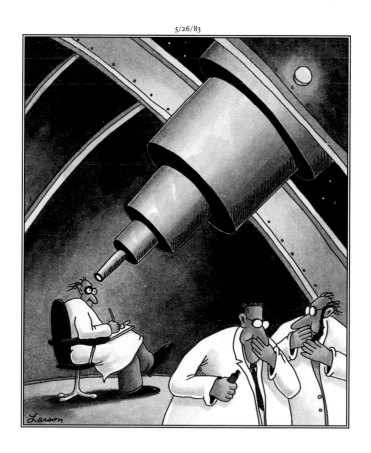

5/27/83

INVERTEBRATE
TASTE TEST
Larson

"Mmmmmm. ... Nope ... nope. ... I don't like that at all. ... Too many legs."

5/28/83

Larson
flap flap flap flap flap
Bonk!

5/30/83

USA
Larson

"First!"

5/31/83

Larson

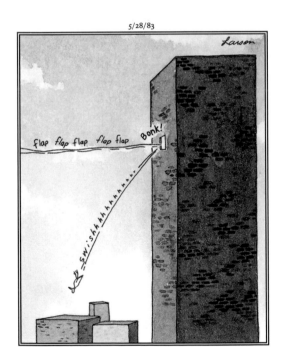

"Spiders, scorpions, and insecticides, oh my! ... Spiders, scorpions, and insecticides, oh my! ..."

6/1/83

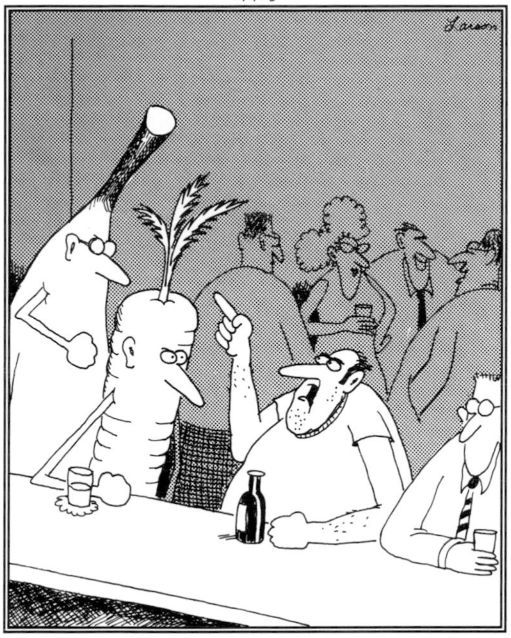
Larson

"Oh, is that so? ... Well, if there's anything I hate worse than a big, stupid carrot, it's a big, stupid banana!"

6/2/83

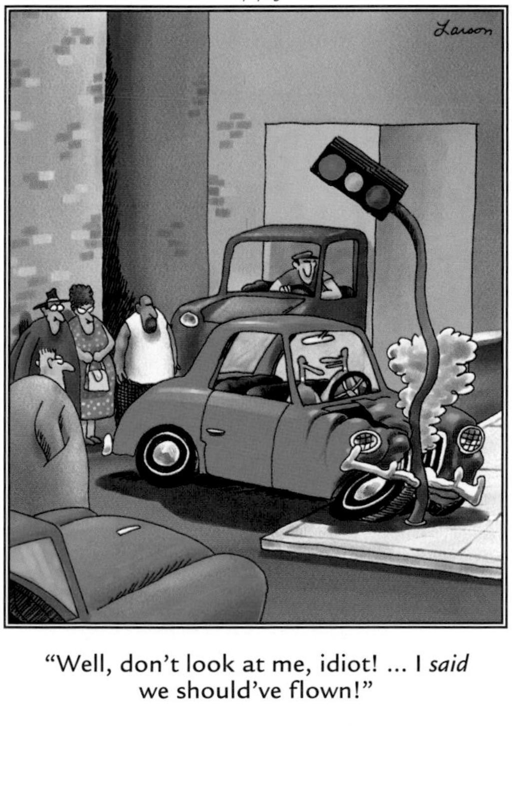
Larson

"Well, don't look at me, idiot! ... I *said* we should've flown!"

6/3/83

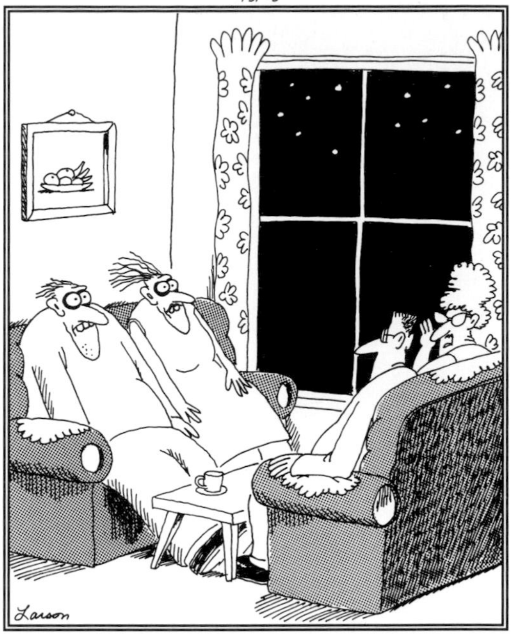
Larson

"What did I say, Alex? ... Every time we invite the Zombies over, we all end up just sitting around staring at each other."

6/9/83

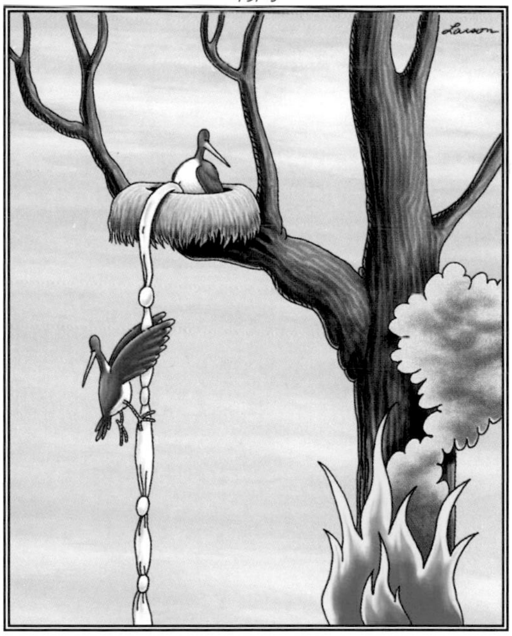
Larson

Stupid birds

6/4/83

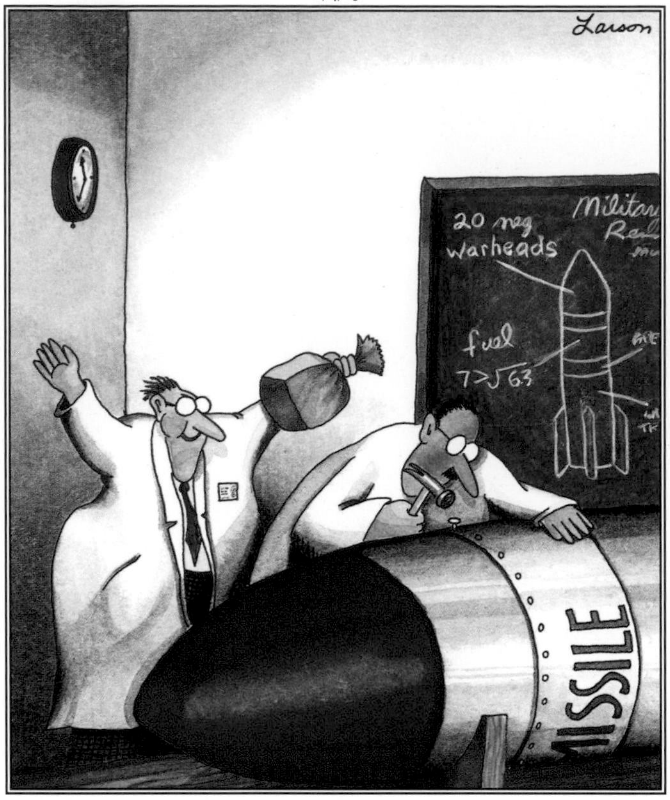
Larson
20 meg
warheads
fuel
MISSILE

6/6/83

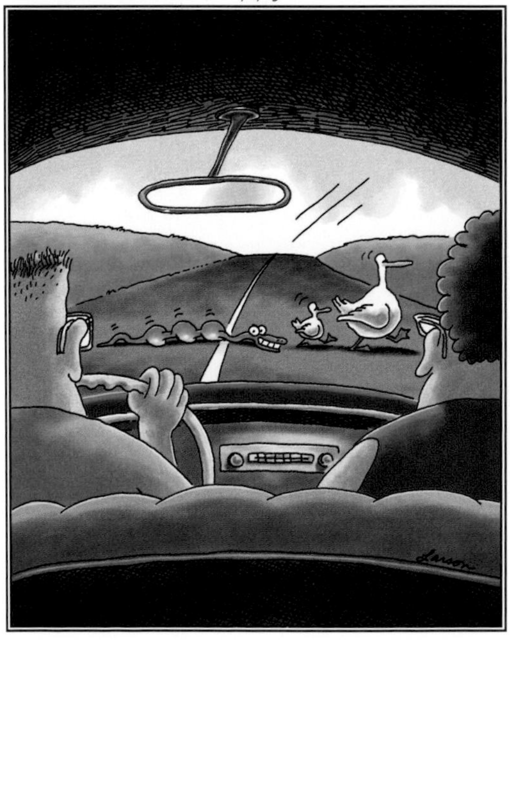
Larson

6/7/83

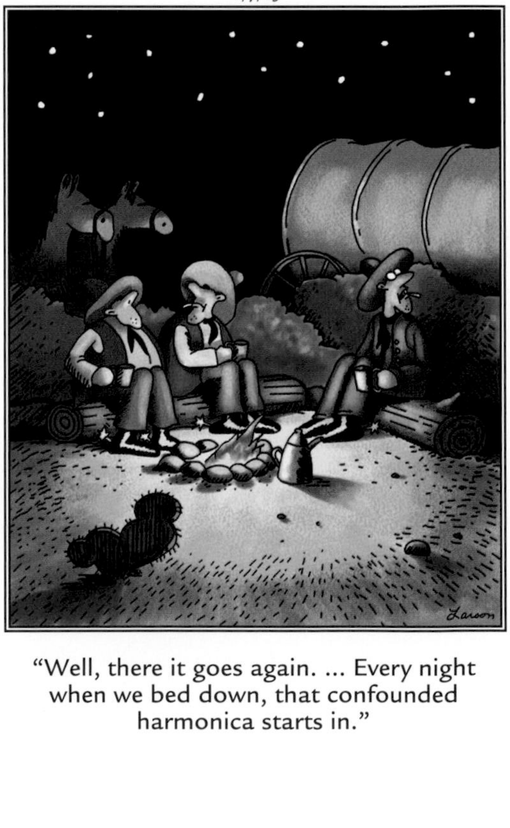
Larson

"Well, there it goes again. ... Every night when we bed down, that confounded harmonica starts in."

June 1983

6/13/83

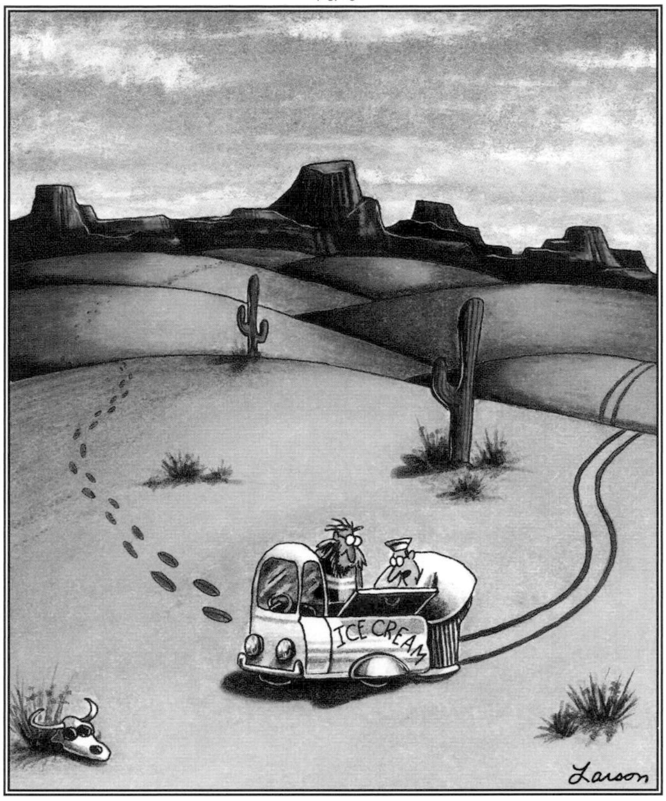
ICE CREAM
Larson

"Let's see. ... No orange ... no root beer ... no fudgesickles. ... Well, for crying out loud! ... Am I out of everything?"

6/8/83

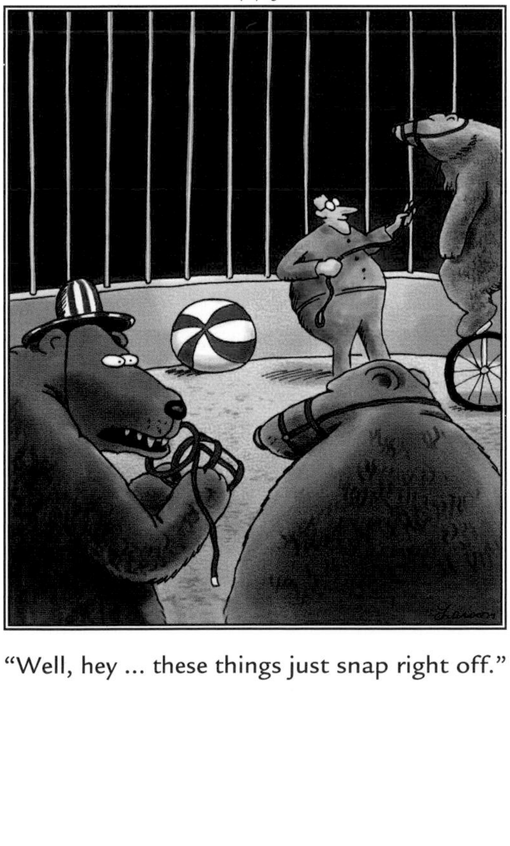

"Well, hey ... these things just snap right off."

6/11/83

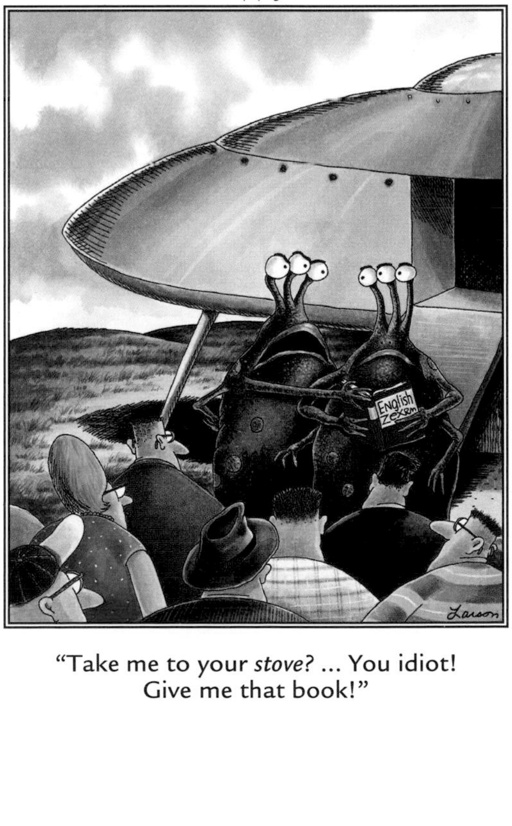
Larson

"Take me to your *stove?* ... You idiot! Give me that book!"

6/10/83

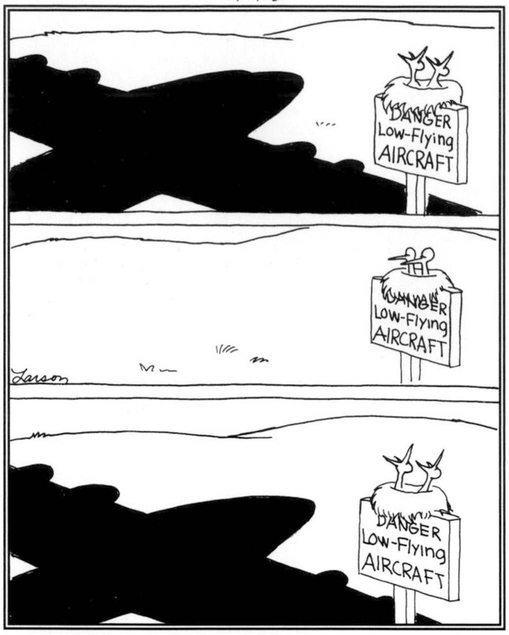
DANGER Low-Flying AIRCRAFT
DANGER Low-Flying AIRCRAFT
DANGER Low-Flying AIRCRAFT
Larson

6/14/83

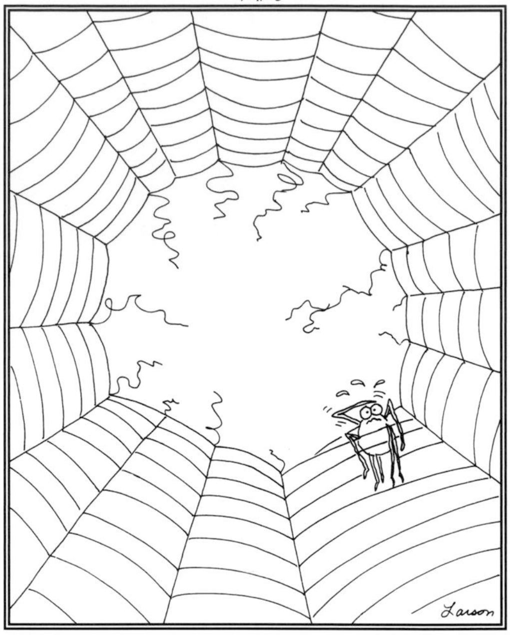
Larson

6/15/83

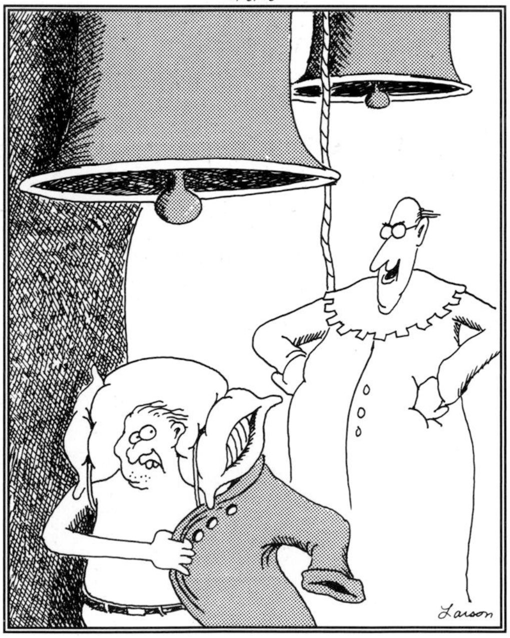
Larson

"Aha! ... My suspicions confirmed!"

6/16/83

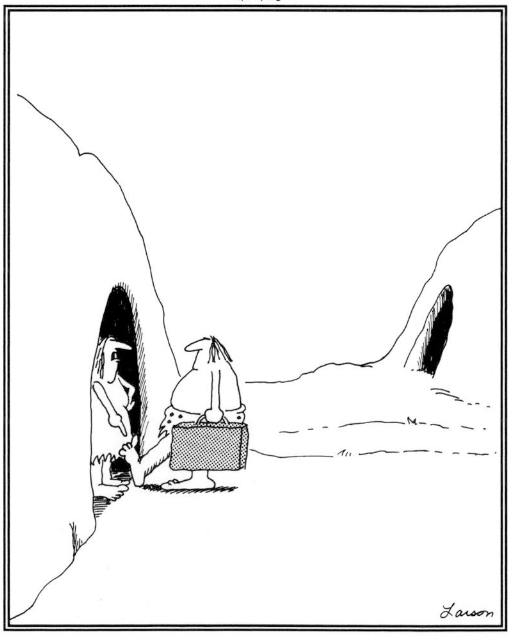
Larson

"I *said* I wasn't interested. ... Now please remove your foot from the cave."

6/17/83

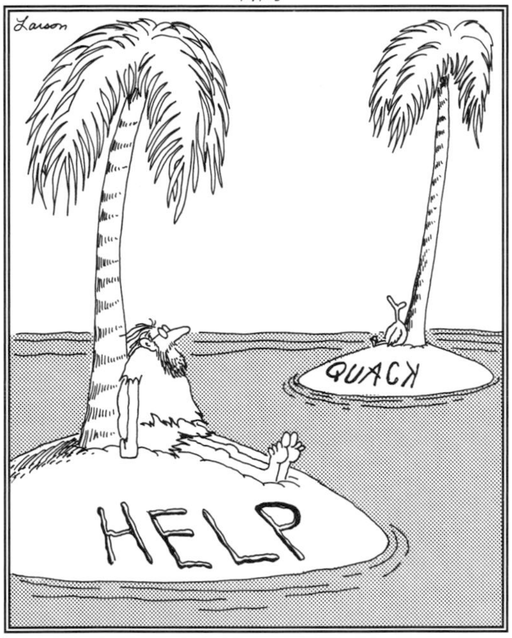
QUACK
HELP

6/23/83

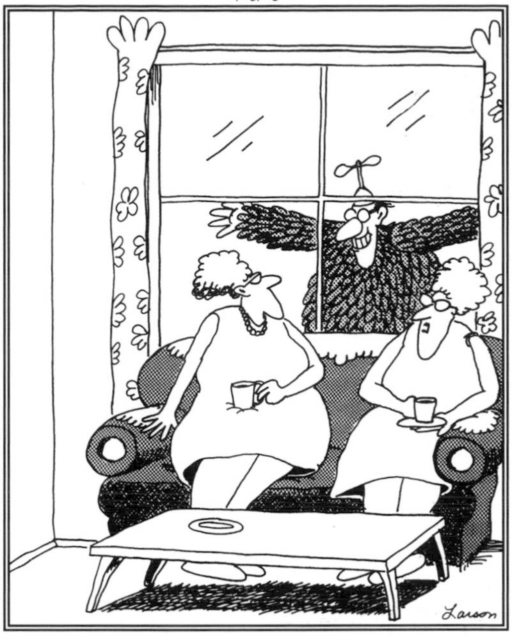

"Oh, that's Bernie Harrison from down the block. ... Bernie has lost his mind."

6/24/83

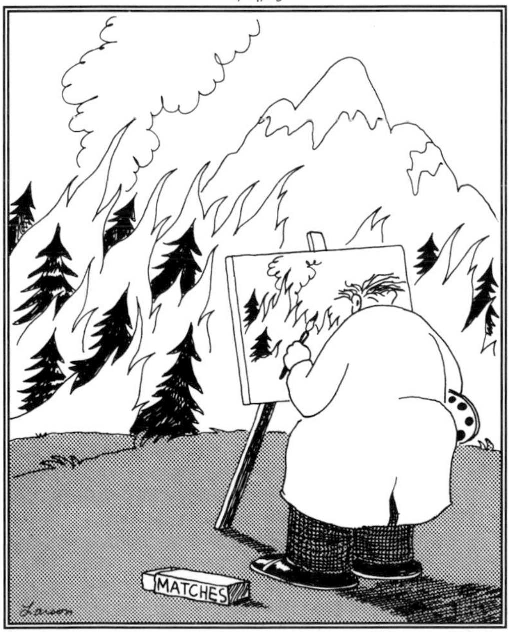
MATCHES

6/25/83

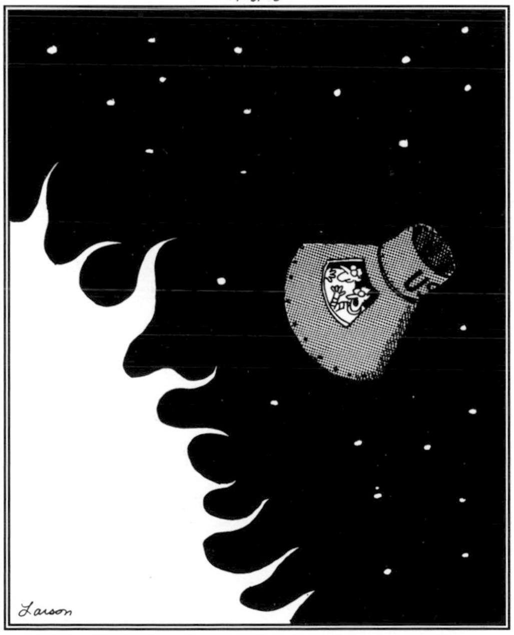

"Blast! The controls are jammed! ... We're headed straight for Mr. Sun!"

6/18/83

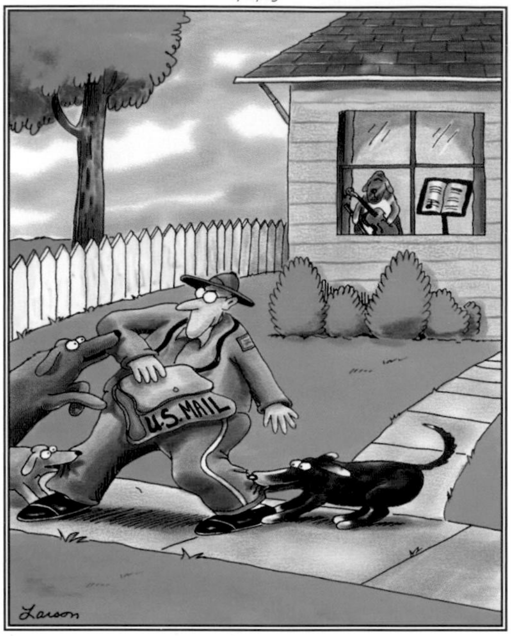
U.S. MAIL
Larson

6/20/83

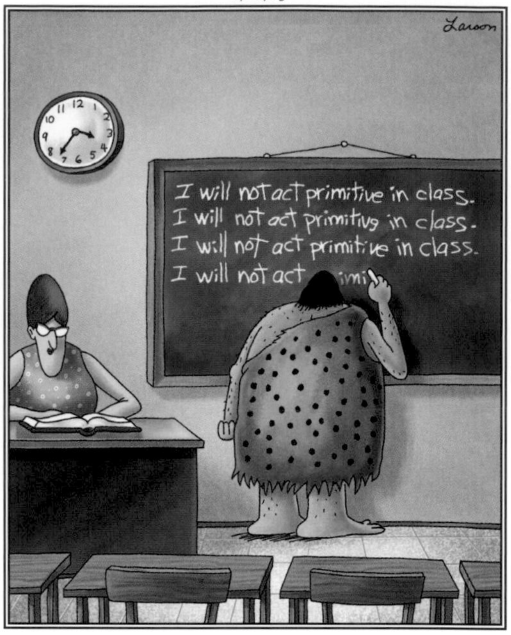
Larson
I will not act primitive in class.
I will not act primitive in class.
I will not act primitive in class.
I will not act

6/27/83

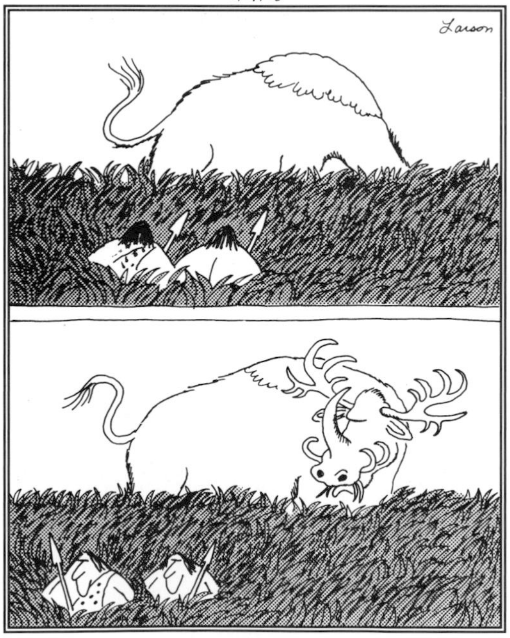
Larson

Primitive man's ability to reason

6/28/83

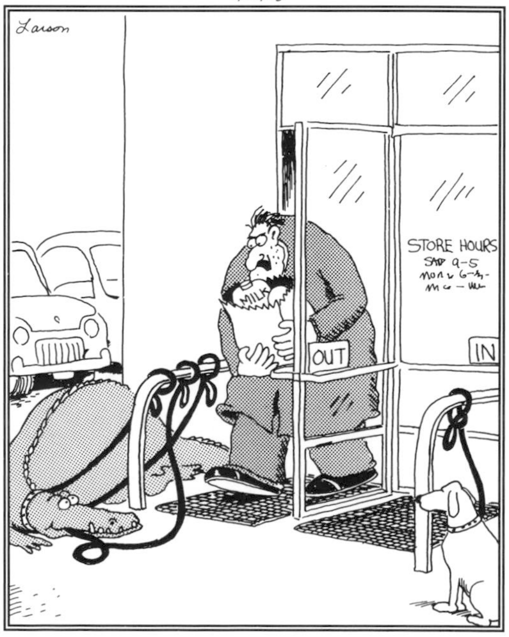
Larson
STORE HOURS
OUT
IN

"What? ... Again?"

6/22/83

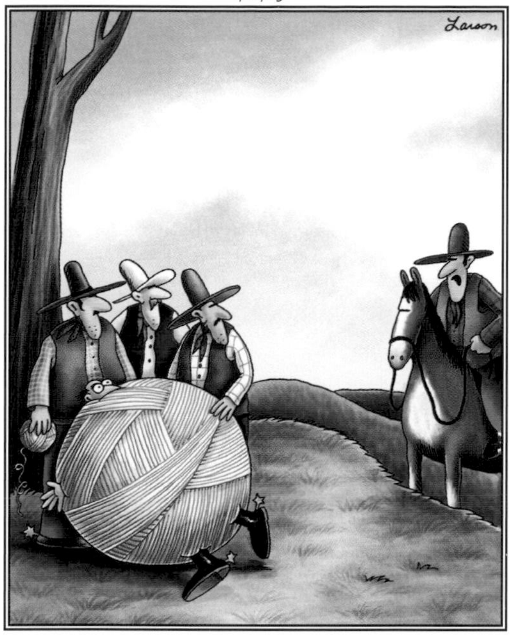

"Hang him, you idiots! Hang him! ...
'String him up' is a figure of speech!"

6/21/83

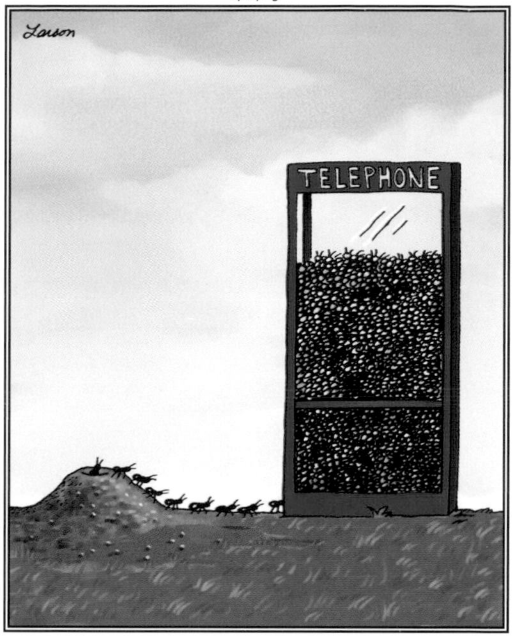
TELEPHONE

Ant games

6/29/83

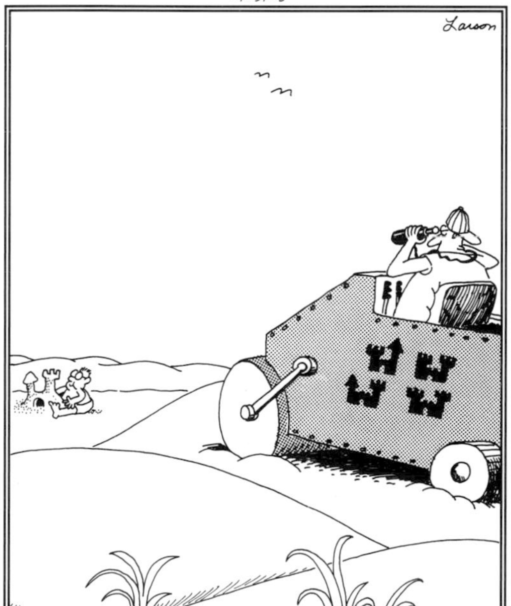

6/30/83

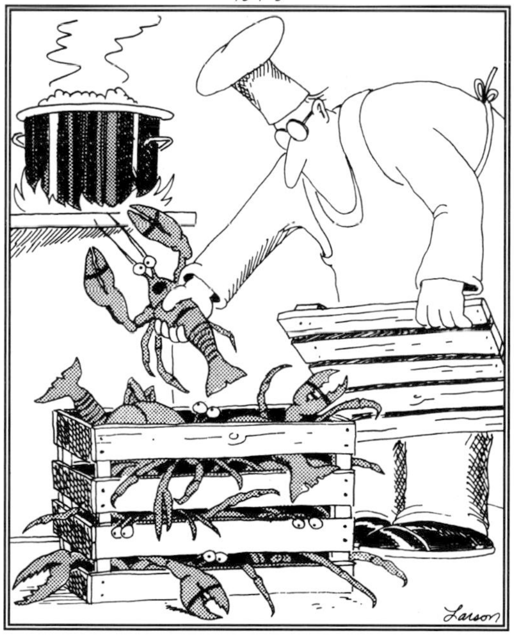

"Auntie Em, Auntie Em! ... There's no place
like home! ... There's no place like home!"

7/2/83

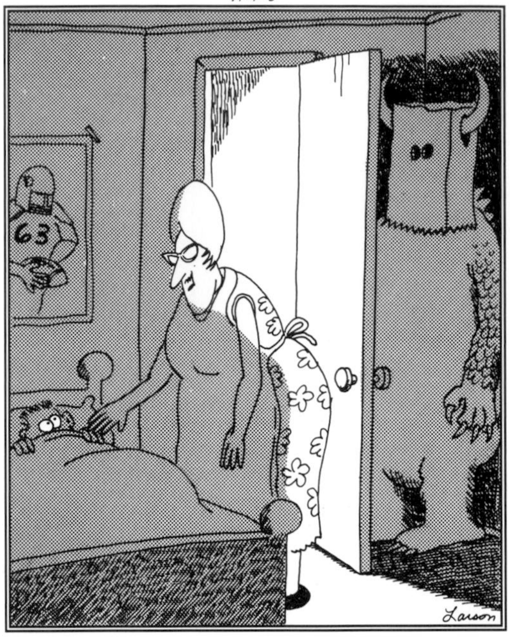
63

"Now now, Billy. ... How could you have seen a monster if you can't even describe him?"

7/8/83

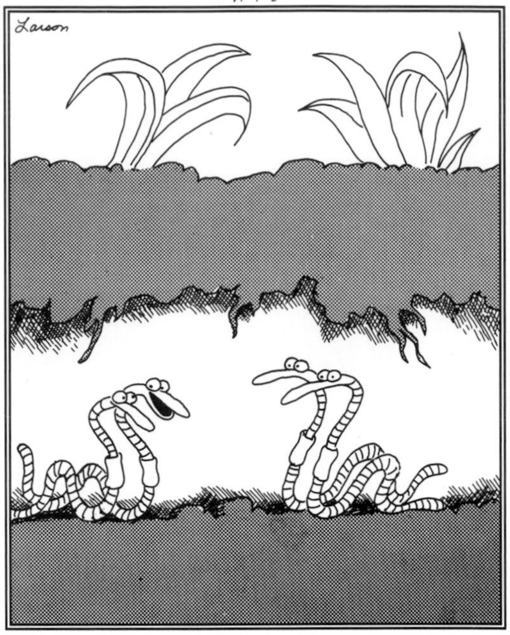

"Sally, this is Larry and his brother, Eddie. ... Larry used to be an only child until the gardener hacked him in half."

7/1/83

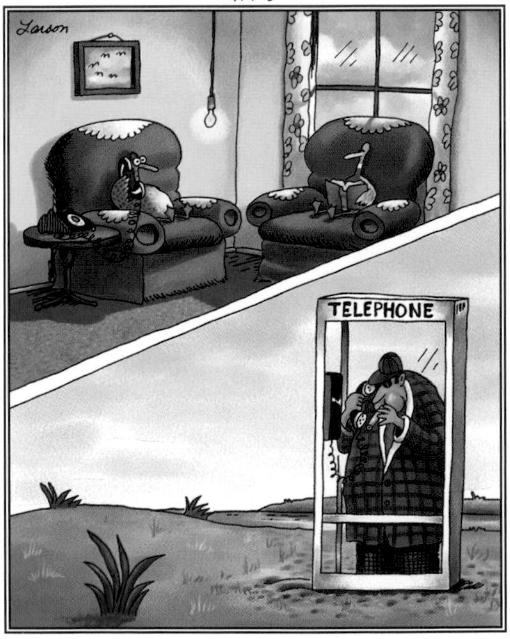
TELEPHONE

Obscene duck call

7/5/83

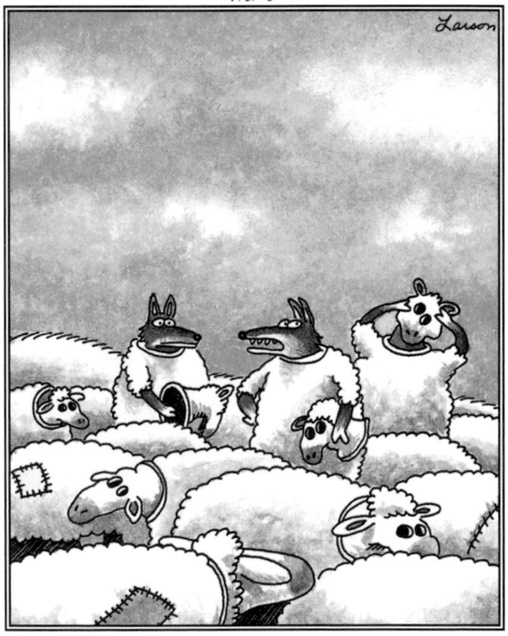

"Wait a minute! Isn't anyone here a real sheep?"

"Oo! Watch out! ... The walls are pointy!"

"Darlene is going with some new guy. ...
And *he's* got a shell."

"Okay ... which of you is the one they call
'Old-One-Eyed-Dog-Face'?"

"Wait a minute here, Mr. Crumbley. ...
Maybe it isn't kidney stones after all."

7/12/83

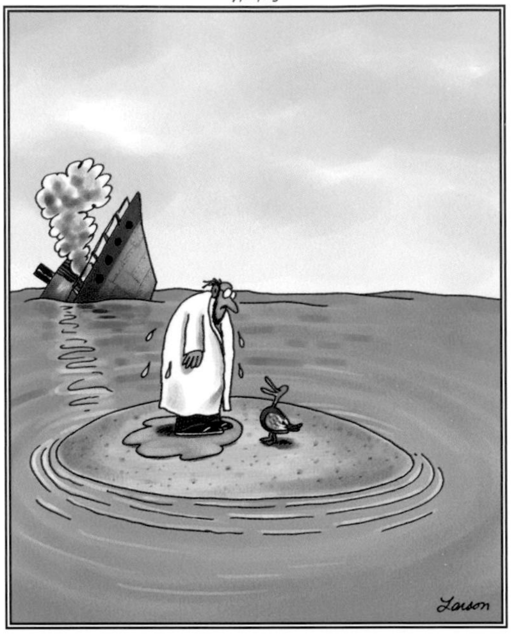
Larson

"So, Professor Jenkins! ... My old nemesis! ... We meet again, but this time the advantage is mine! Ha! Ha! Ha!"

7/13/83

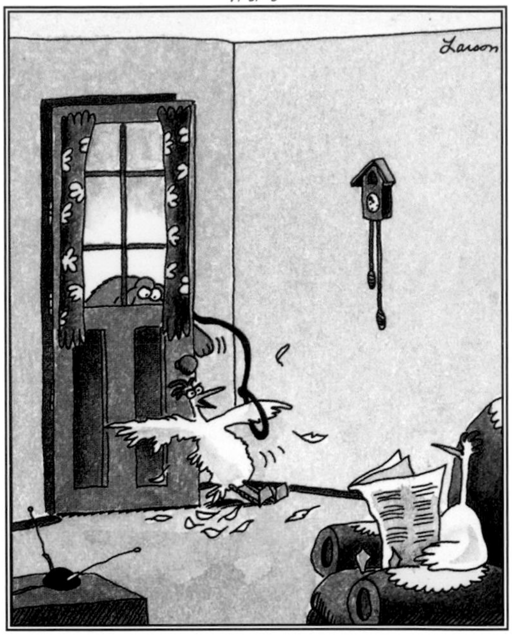
Larson

"Blast! ... You raise a dog from a pup, and suddenly one day he turns out to be a chicken killer!"

7/14/83

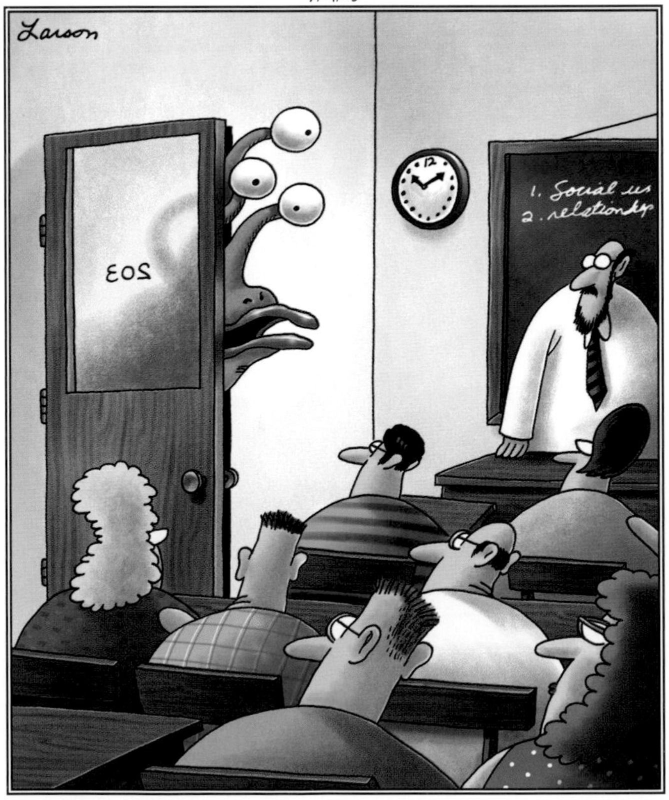
Larson

"Whoa! ... Wrong room."

7/18/83

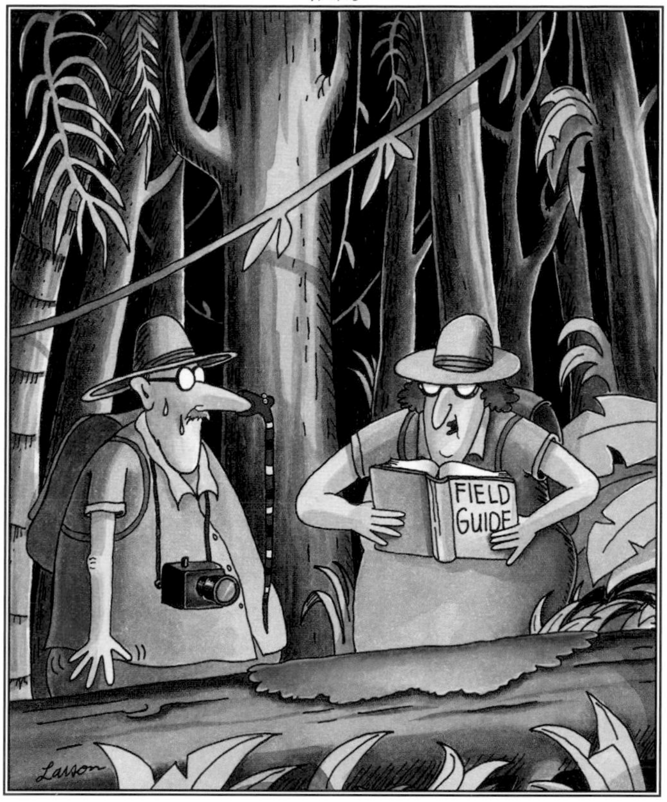
FIELD GUIDE
Larson

"'This dangerous viper, known for its peculiar habit of tenaciously hanging from one's nose, is vividly colored.'... Oo! Murray! Look! ... Here's a picture of it!"

7/15/83

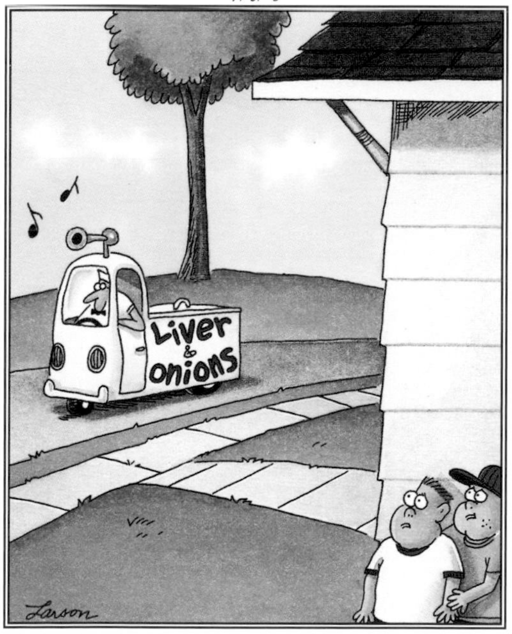
Liver & onions
Larson

7/19/83

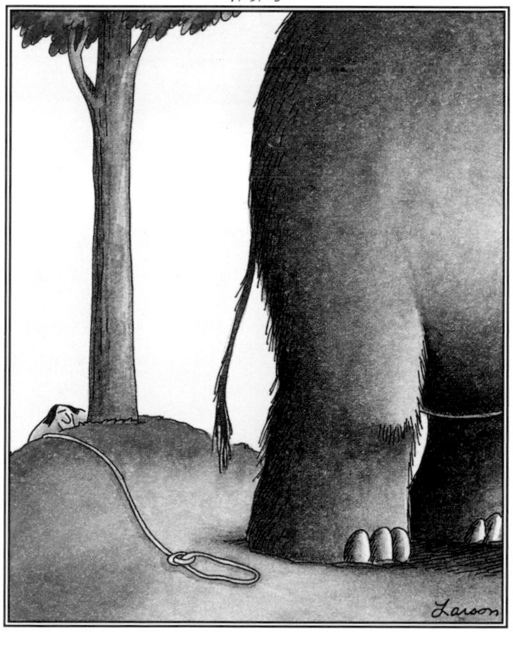
Larson

7/11/83

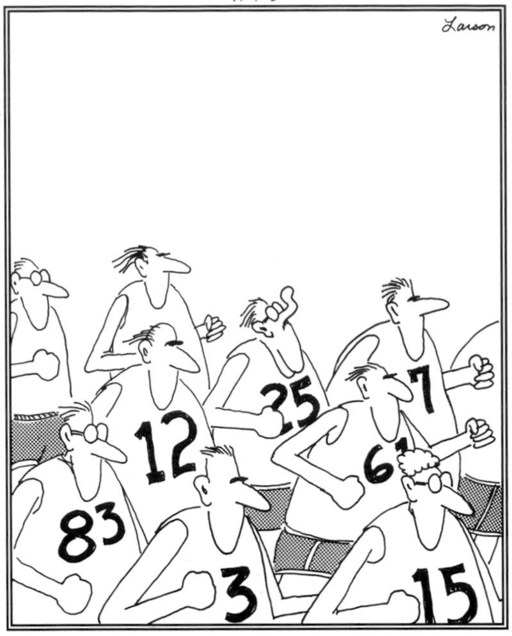
Larson
83
12
25
7
3
15

Suddenly, only a mile into the race, Ernie gets a nose cramp.

7/16/83

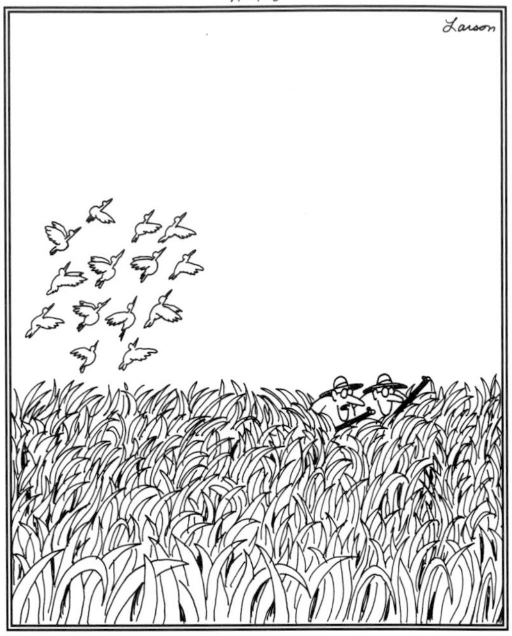
Larson

"Keep your rifle handy, Boswell. ... That wounded lion could be anywhere in this tall grass."

7/20/83

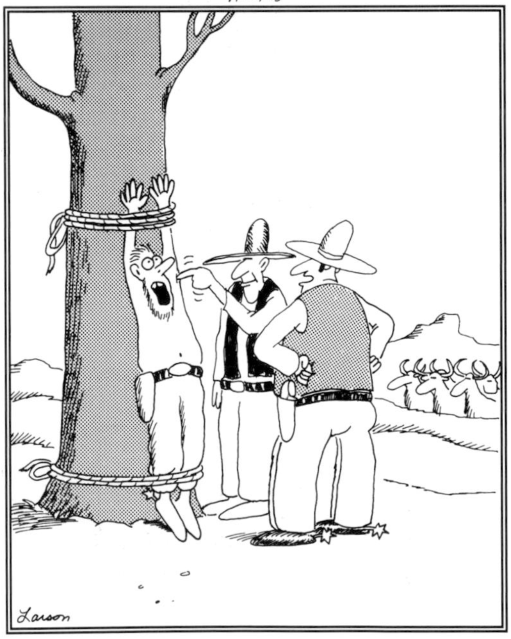
Larson

"Sorry, mister, but this is what we do to cattle rustlers in these parts."

7/21/83

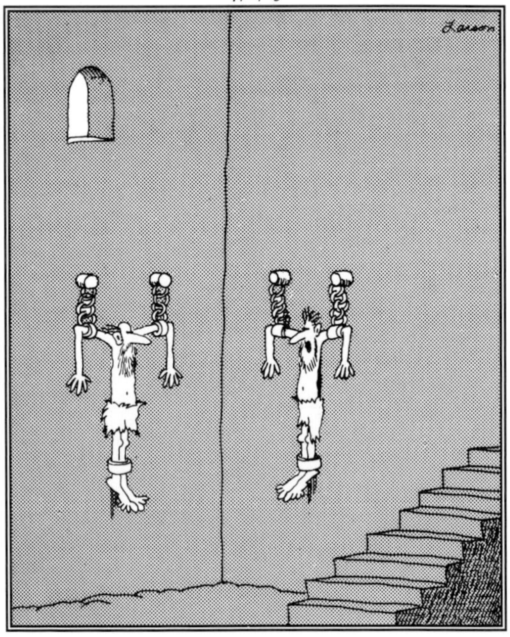
Larson

"You idiot! ... Now this time wait for me to finish the first 'row row row your boat' *before* you come in!"

7/22/83

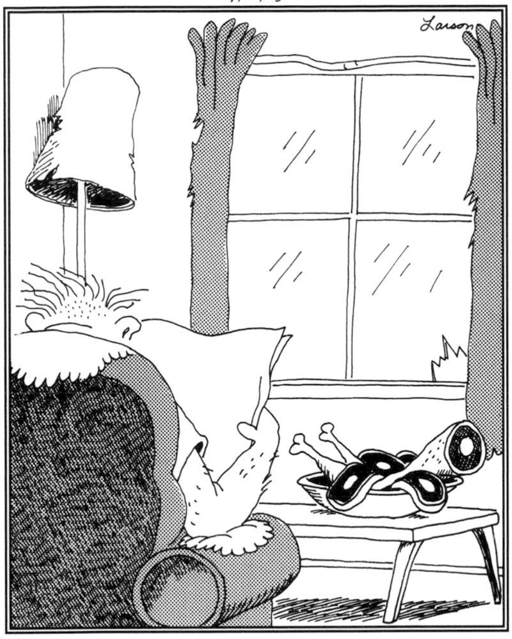
Larson

7/27/83

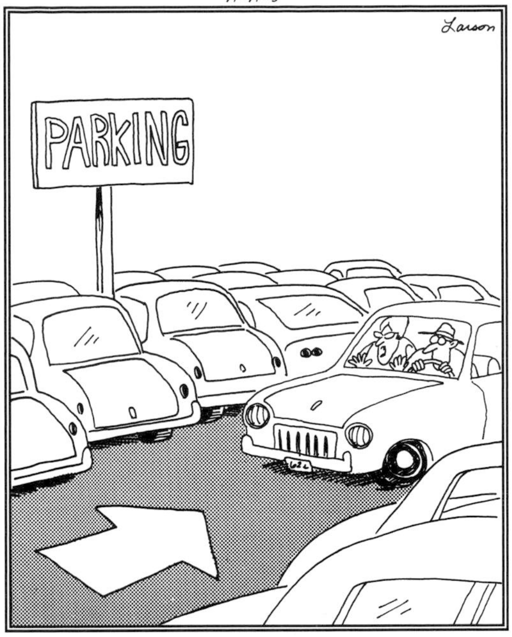
Larson
PARKING

"Harold, you fool! ... The arrow goes the other way! ... WE'RE DOOMED!"

7/28/83

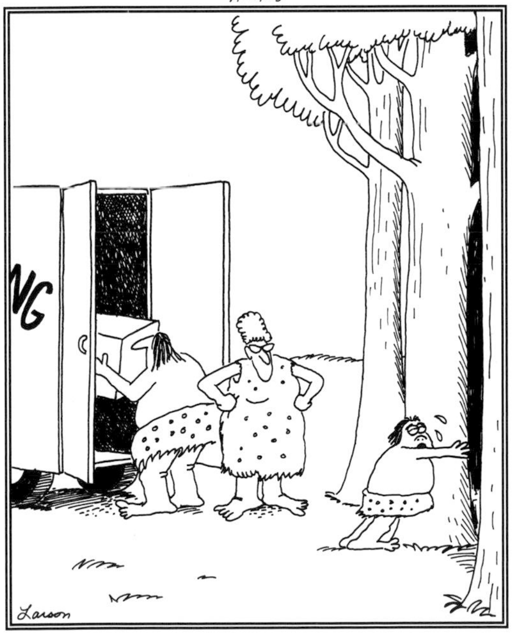
NG
Larson

Primitive Man leaves the trees.

7/30/83

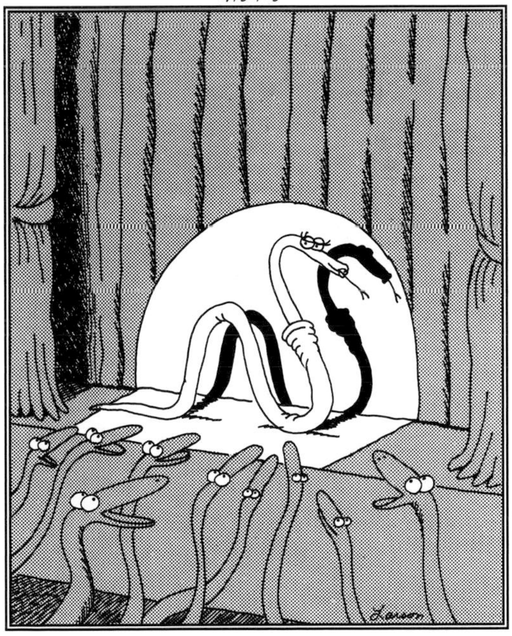
Larson

7/23/83

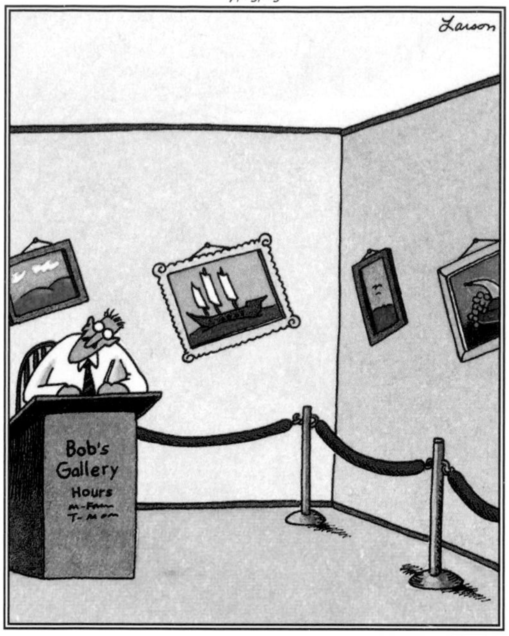
Larson
Bob's
Gallery
Hours

7/25/83

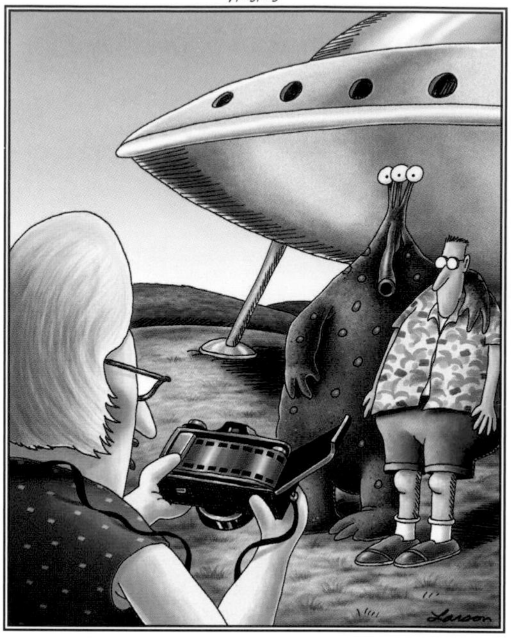
Larson

"Yes, yes, already, Warren! ... There *is* film in the camera!"

7/26/83

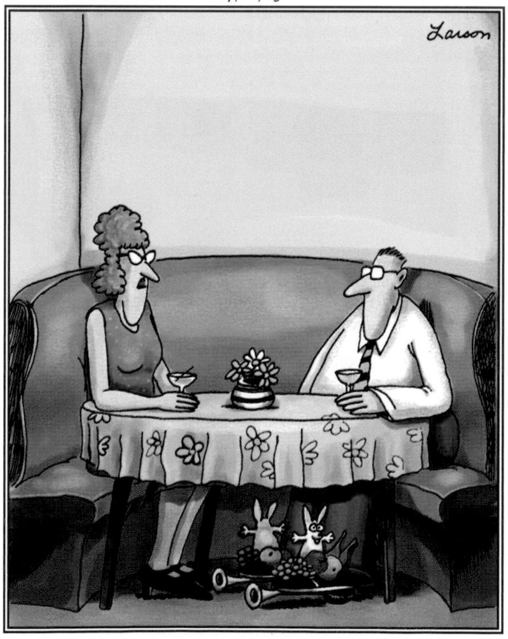
Larson

"I judge a man by the shoes he wears, Jerry."

7/29/83

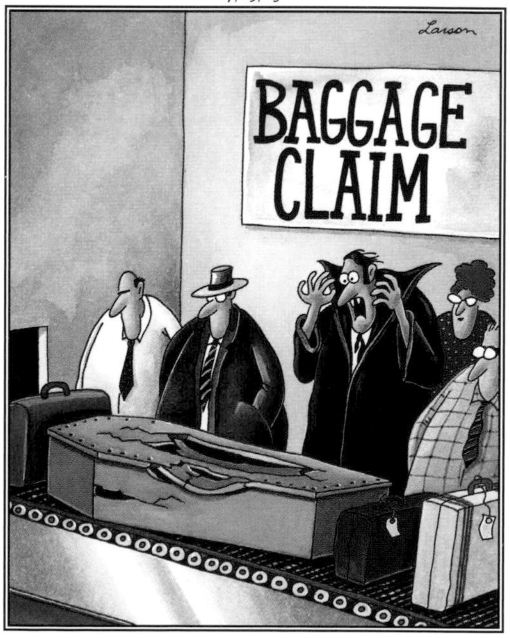
Larson
BAGGAGE
CLAIM

8/1/83

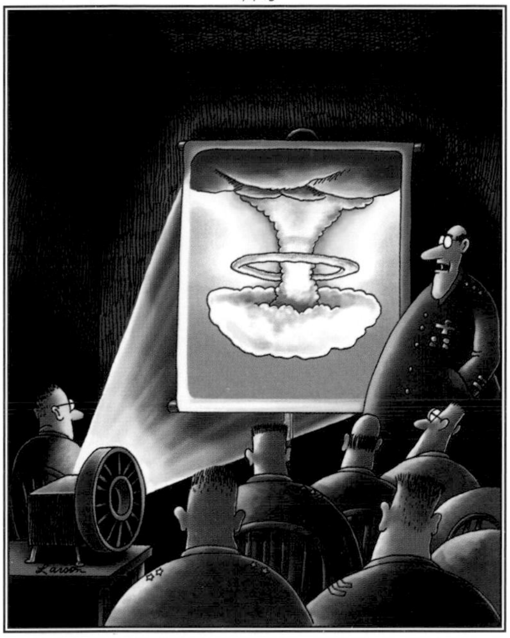

"Now this next slide, gentlemen, demonstrates the awesome power of our twenty megaton ... for crying out loud! Not again!"

8/3/83

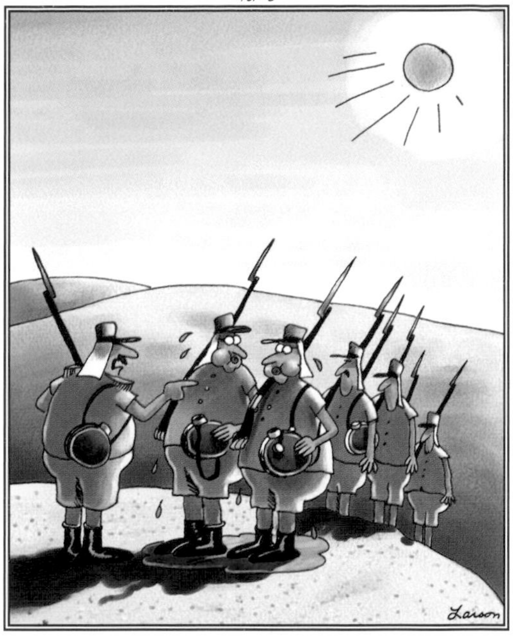

"HALT! ... Okay! Johnson! Higgins! ... You both just swallow what you've got and knock off these water fights once and for all!"

8/6/83

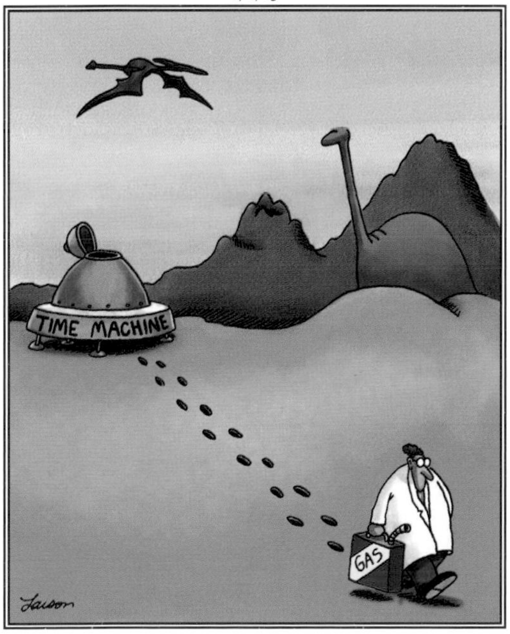
TIME MACHINE
GAS

8/9/83

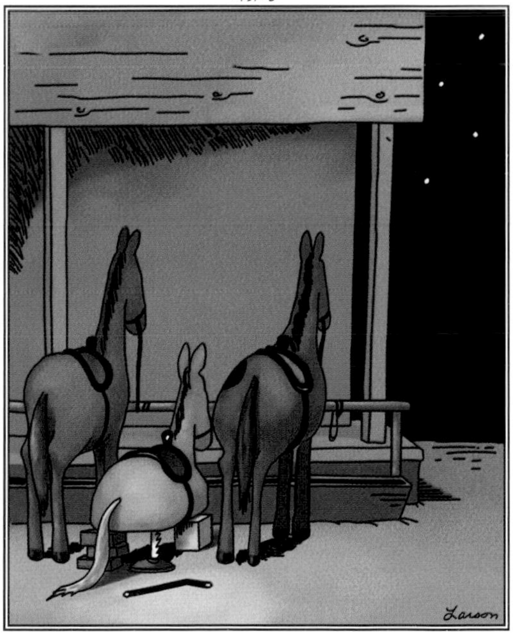

Never park your horse in a bad part of town.

8/2/83

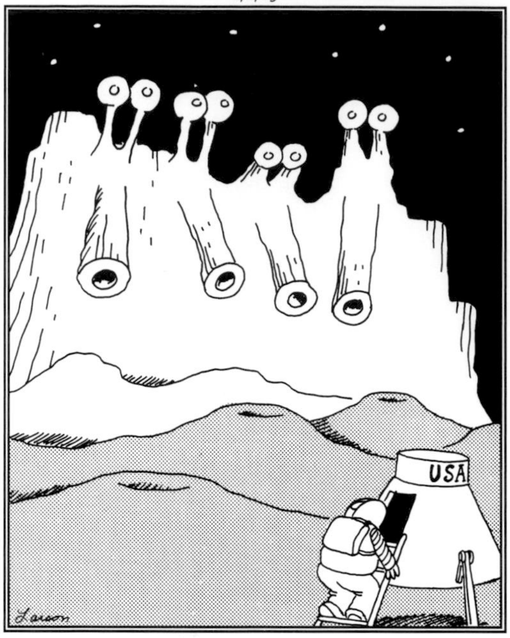
USA

8/4/83

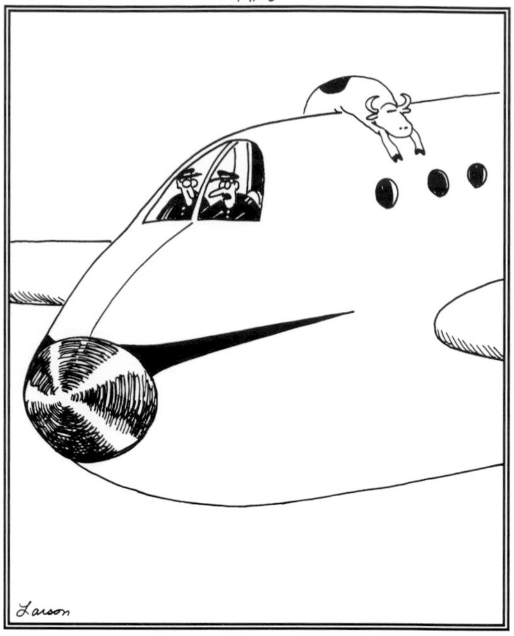

"Fool! ... Give me those controls! ... You're just dang lucky both barn doors were open!"

8/8/83

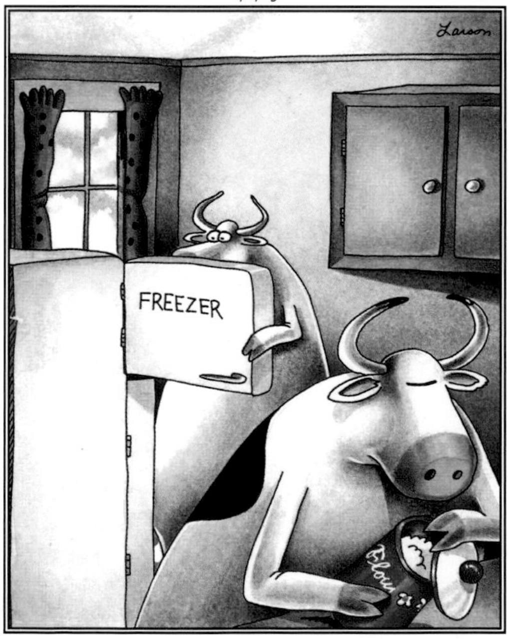
FREEZER

While Farmer Brown was away, the cows got into the kitchen and were having the time of their lives—until Betsy's unwitting discovery.

August 8, 1983

Gary Larson
Chronicle Features
c/o Washington Post
1150 15th St. NW
Washington, DC 20071

Dear Mr. Larson:

Please help us settle this minor family dispute. My son maintains that Betsy's unwitting discovery was finding steaks in the freezer. My husband and I believe that Betsy found Farmer Browns supply of frozen bull semen.

Which of the above is the right answer - or, are they both wrong? Did you have something more delightful in mind? What? We can hardly bear to wait for your answer.

Thank you for making our mornings a real pleasure. Your cartoons are weird, but deliscious.

Sincerely,

Janet A. Dinerman

8/10/83

Larson

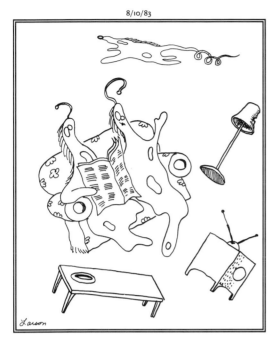

Things that live in a drop of water, and some of their furniture.

8/5/83

Yeeeeeeehaaaaaaaaaa
ACME
INSECTICIDE
INC.
Larson

8/17/83

Larson

"Hey! Look at Red Bear! ... Waaaaaait ... *that* not real!"

8/22/83

Larson

"And you call yourself an Indian!"

8/11/83

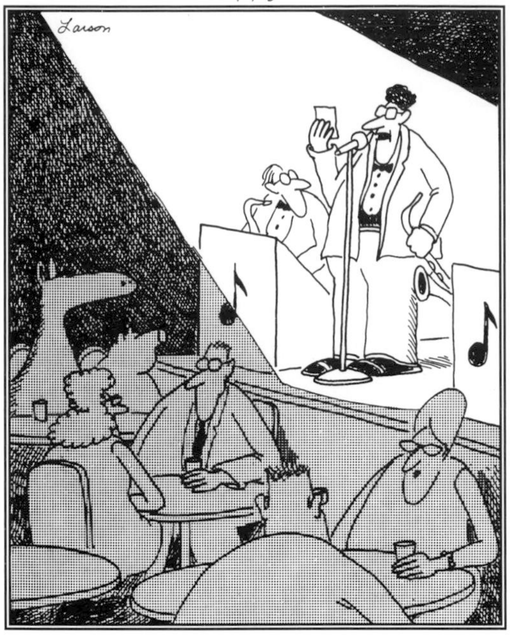

"What? ... *Another* request for 'Old McDonald'?"

8/12/83

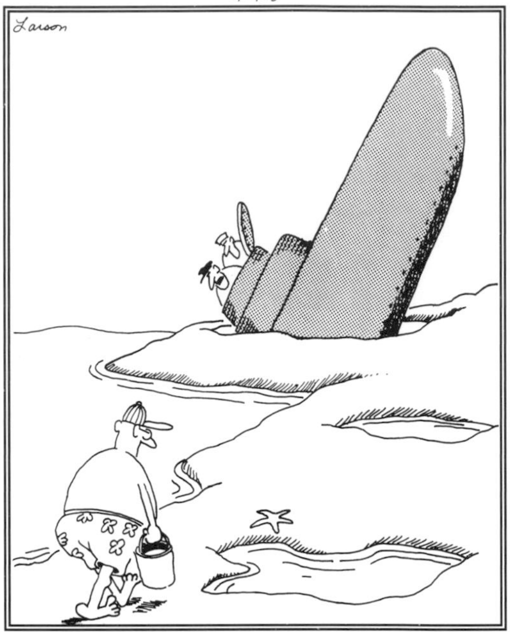

"Blast! Caught in another tide pool! ... And here comes some damn beachcomber!"

8/13/83

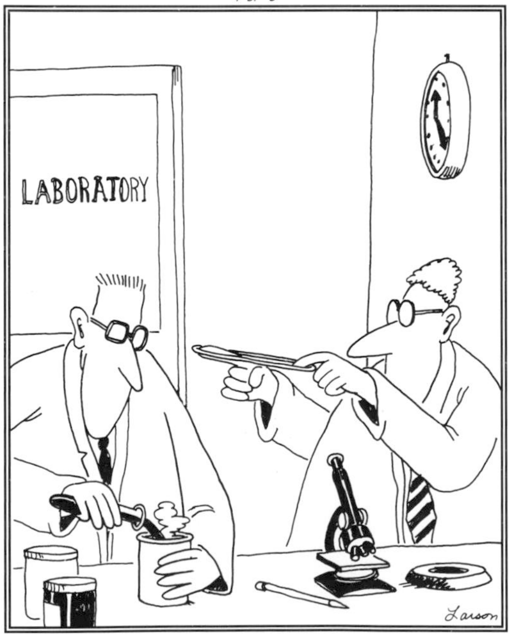
LABORATORY

On Oct. 23, 1927, three days after its invention, the first rubber band is tested.

8/15/83

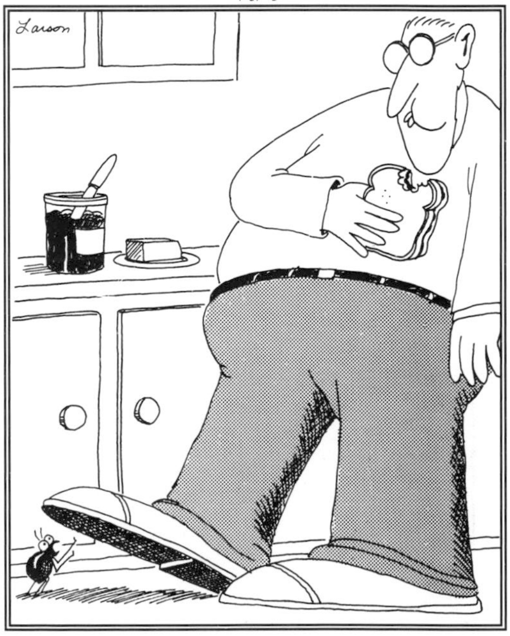

"Wait! Spare me! ... I've got a wife, a home, and over a thousand eggs laid in the jelly!"

8/16/83

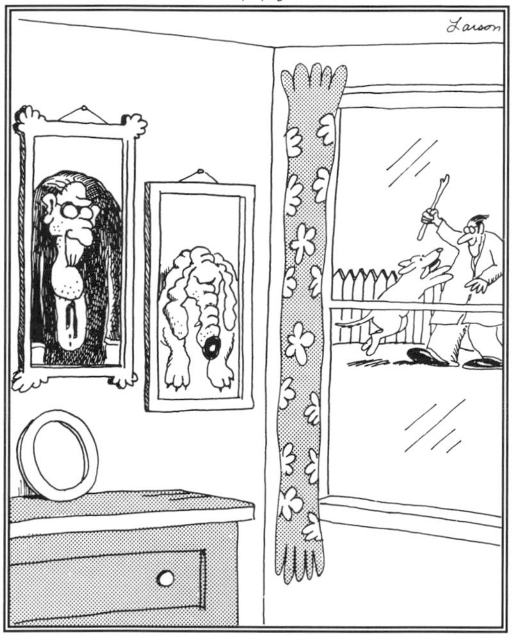
Larson

The Portrait of Dorian Gray and his dog

8/18/83

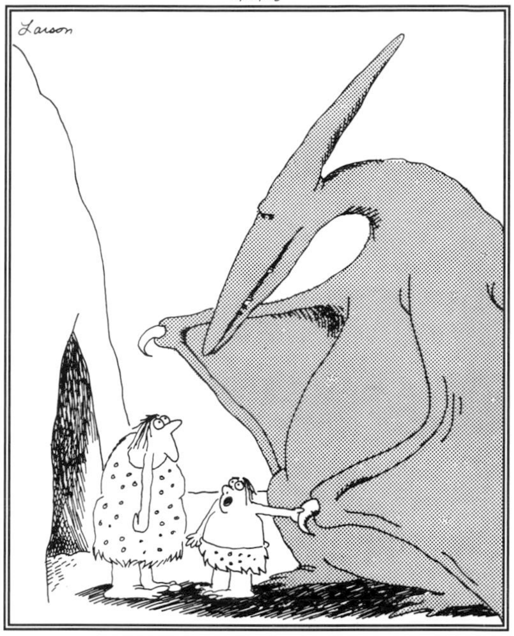
Larson

"Oh please, Mom! ... I've already handled him and now the mother won't take him back."

8/19/83

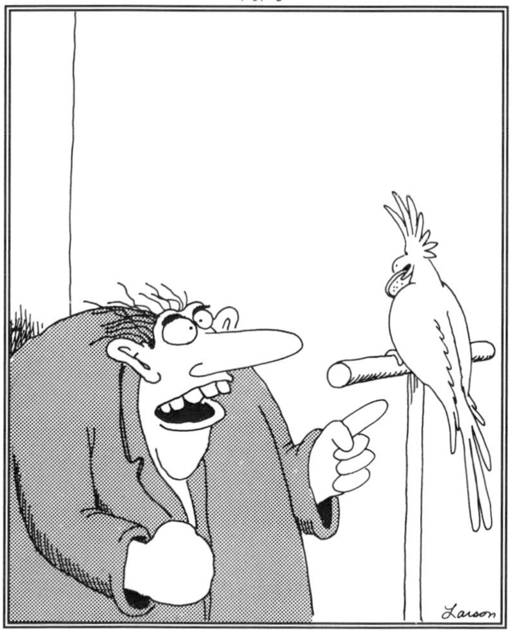
Larson

"Okay, now it's my turn. ... Bob want the cracker ... Bob want the cracker ... "

8/20/83

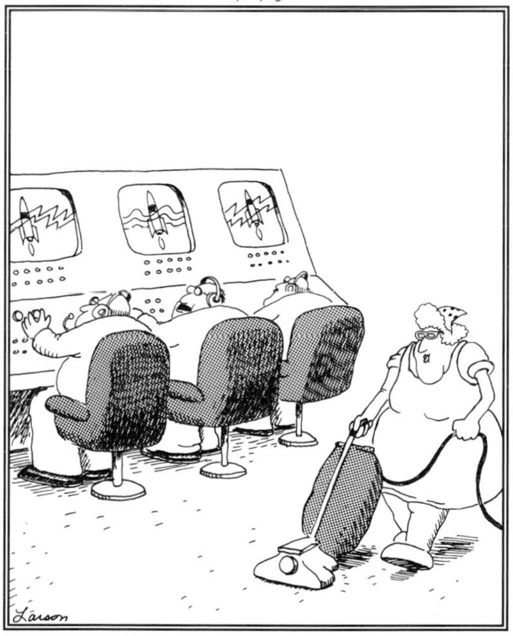
Larson

"Hey! What's going on here? ... We're losing the visual!"

8/23/83

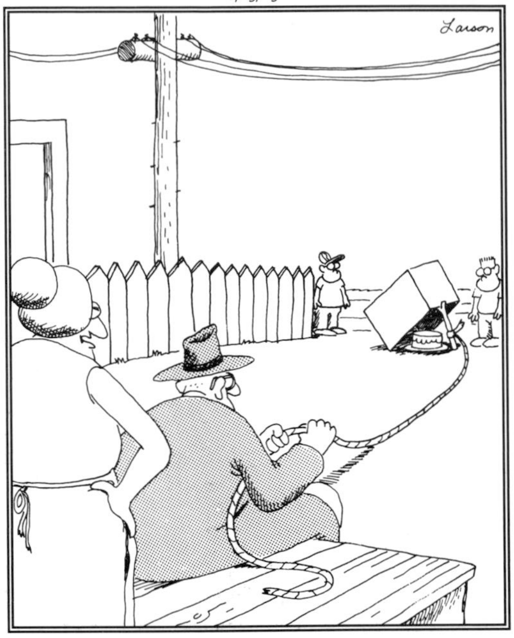
Larson

"Good heavens, Charles! You're at it again! ...
And with my fresh sponge cake, I see!"

8/24/83

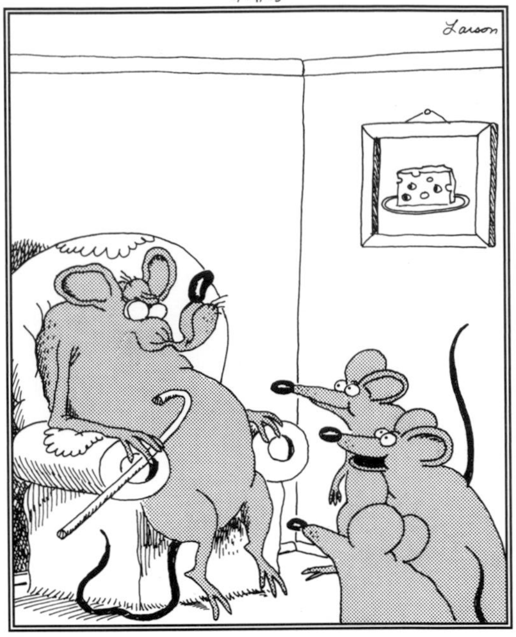
Larson

"Wow! Well, what happened next, Gramps—
after you found the cheese sitting on the
little block of wood?"

8/25/83

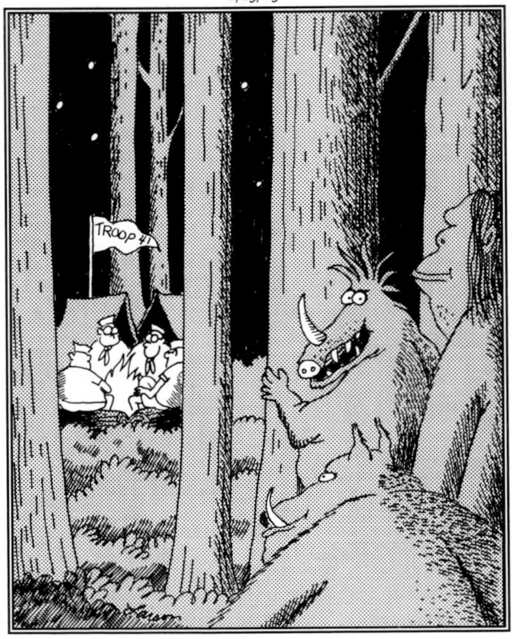
TROOP 41
Larson

"Oh no! They're telling the story of
'The Hooked Hand'! ... I'll *never* get
to sleep tonight!"

8/26/83

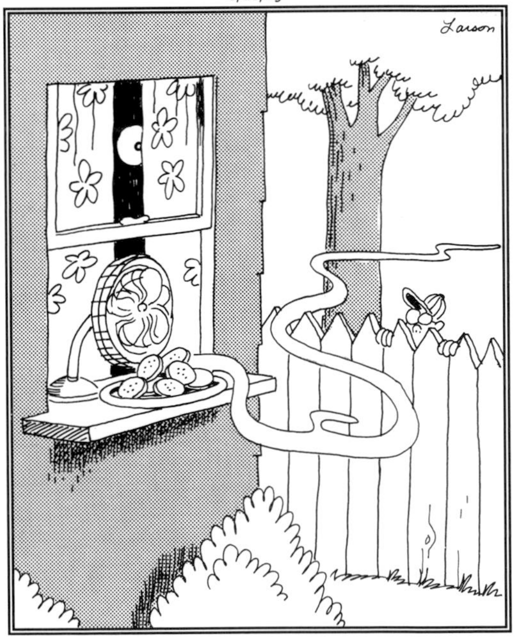
Larson

8/27/83

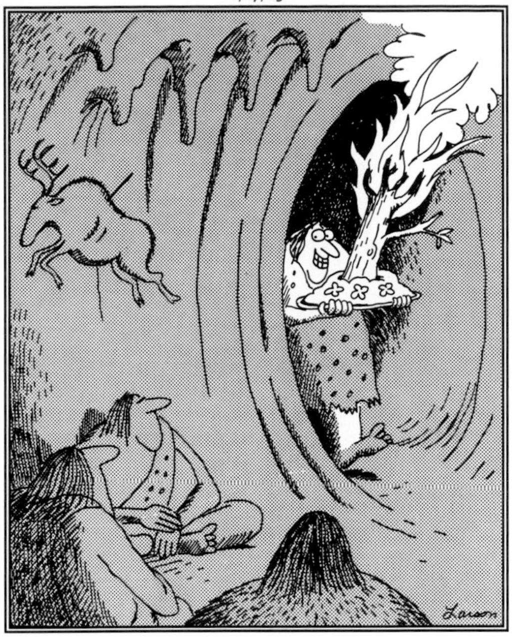
Larson

8/29/83

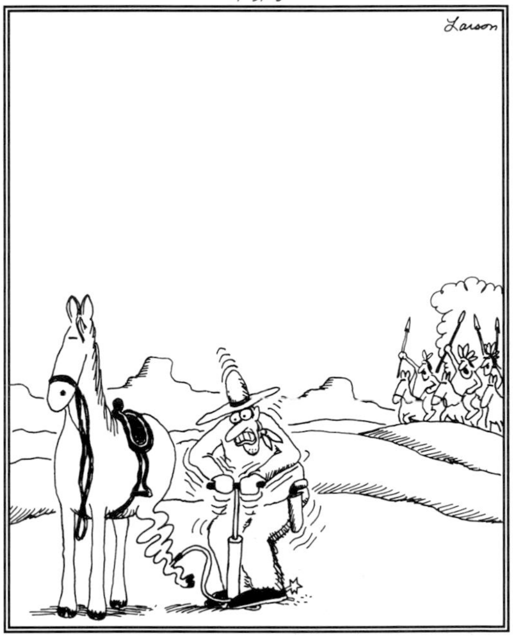
Larson

8/30/83

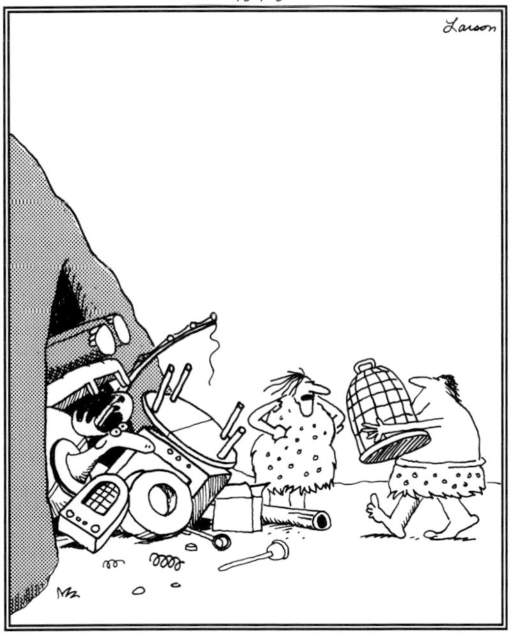
Larson

"Well, here comes Mr. Hunter and Gatherer with another useless treasure."

8/31/83

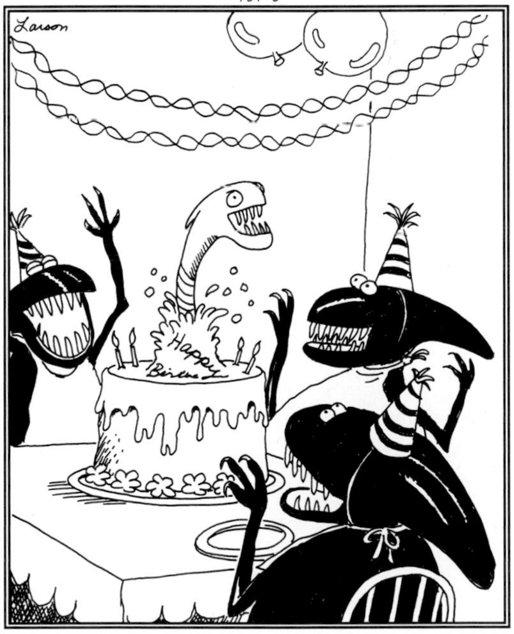
Larson

9/1/83

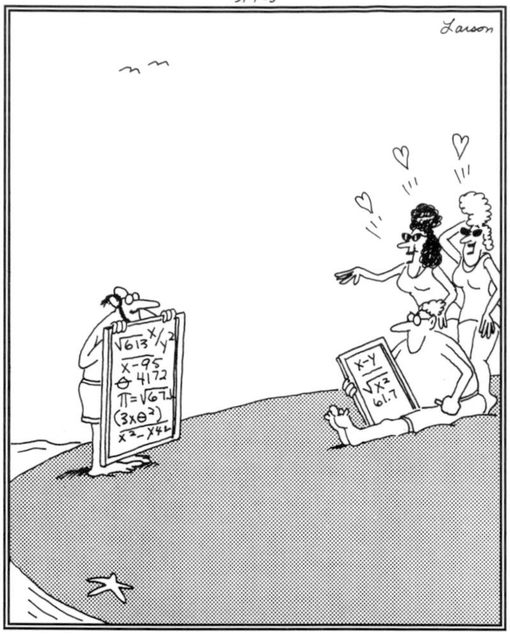
Larson
√613 X/y²
X-95
4172
π=√67
(3xθ²)
x²-x42
X-Y
√X²
61.7

9/2/83

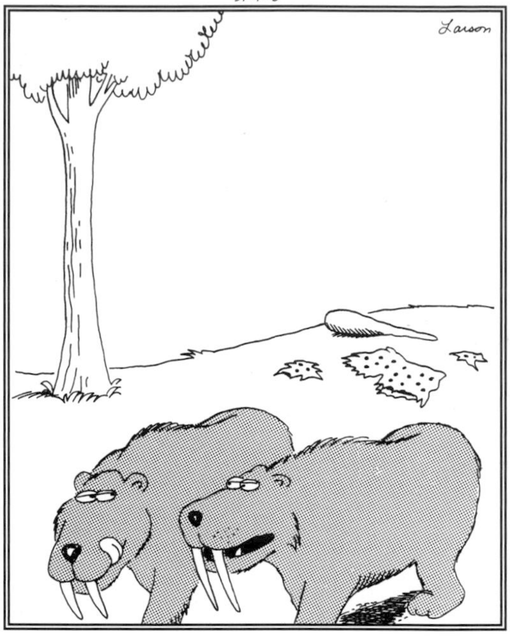
Larson

"I've heard all kinds of sounds from these things, but 'yabba dabba doo' was a new one to me."

9/5/83

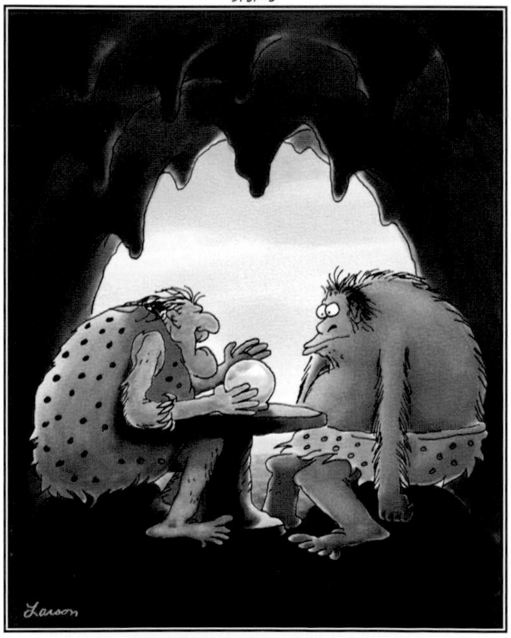
Larson

"I see your little, petrified skull ... labeled and resting on a shelf somewhere."

9/6/83

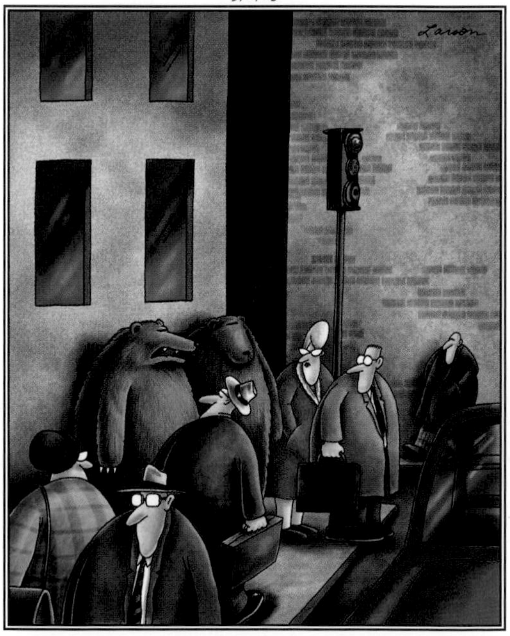
Larson

"Well, we're lost ... and it's probably just a matter of time before someone decides to shoot us."

9/3/83

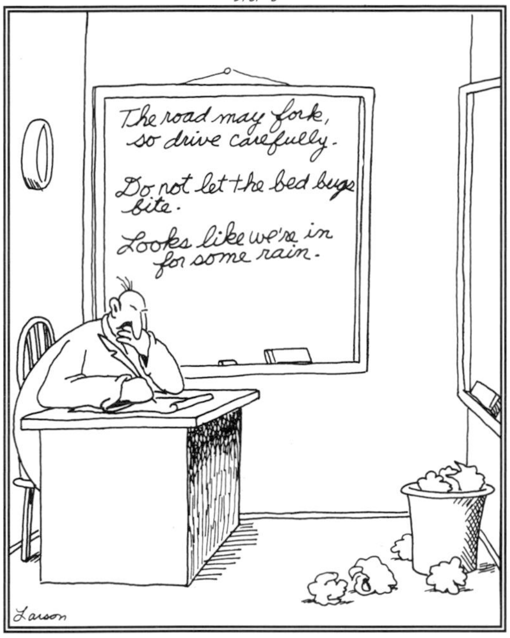
The road may fork,
so drive carefully.
Do not let the bed bugs bite.
Looks like we're in for some rain.
Larson

Confucius at the office

9/7/83

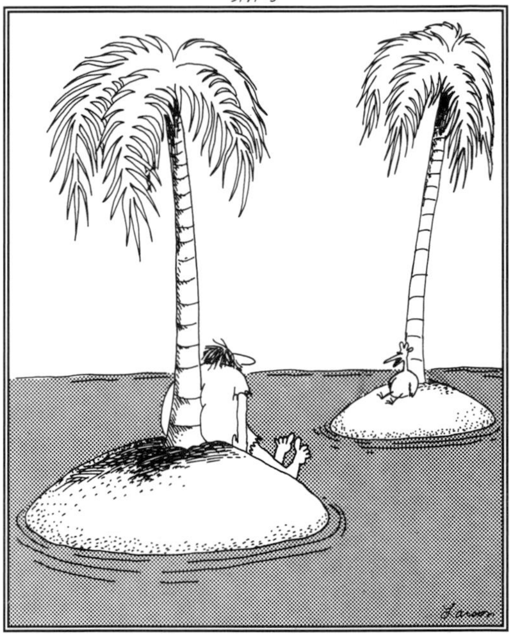

"Boy, there's sure a lot of sharks around here, aren't there? ... Circling and circling. ... THERE GOES ANOTHER ONE! ... Killers of the sea ... yes siree ..."

9/9/83

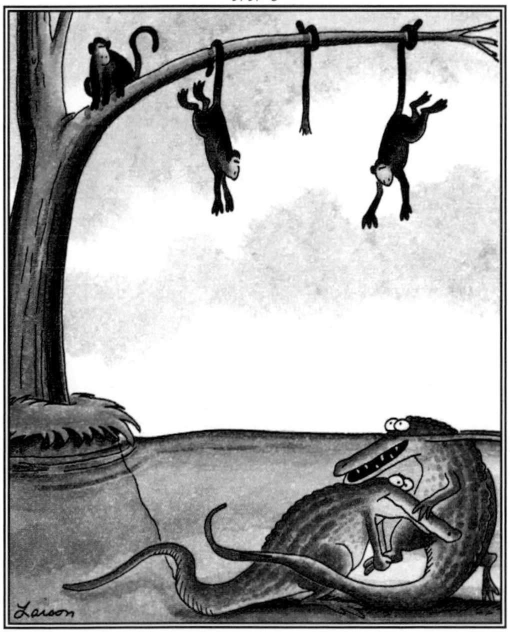

"Okay, here we go again ... one ... two ..."

9/14/83

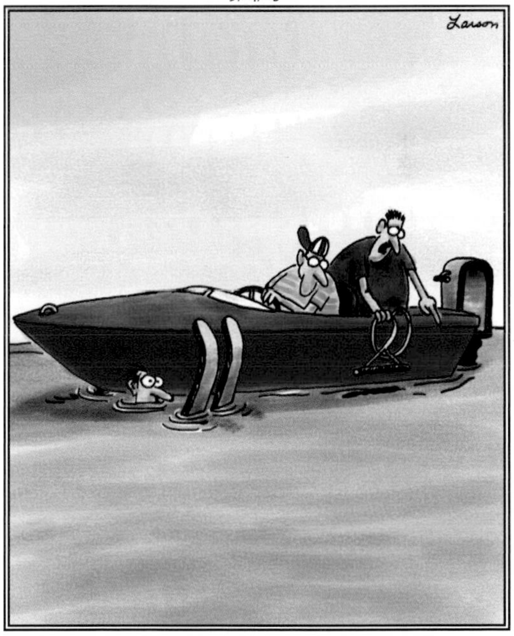

"There! Quick, Larry! Look! ... Was I kidding? ... That sucker's longer than the boat!"

9/8/83

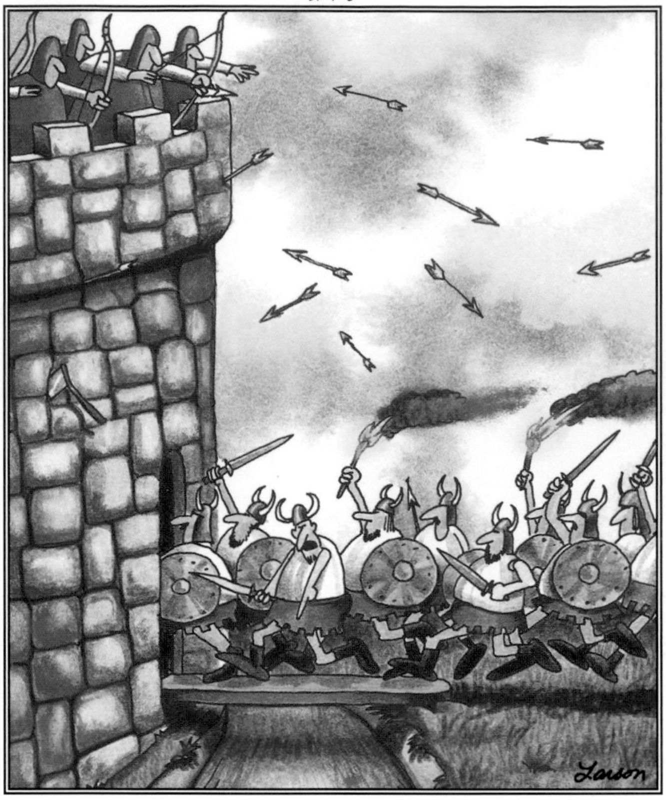

"Oo! Goldfish, everyone! Goldfish!"

9/12/83

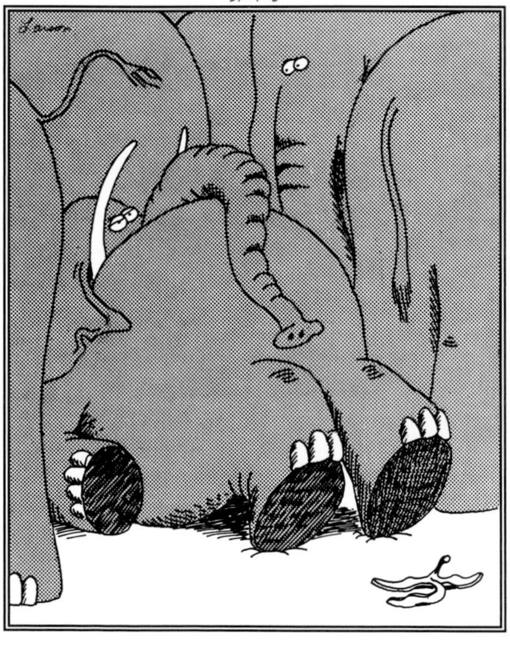

9/13/83

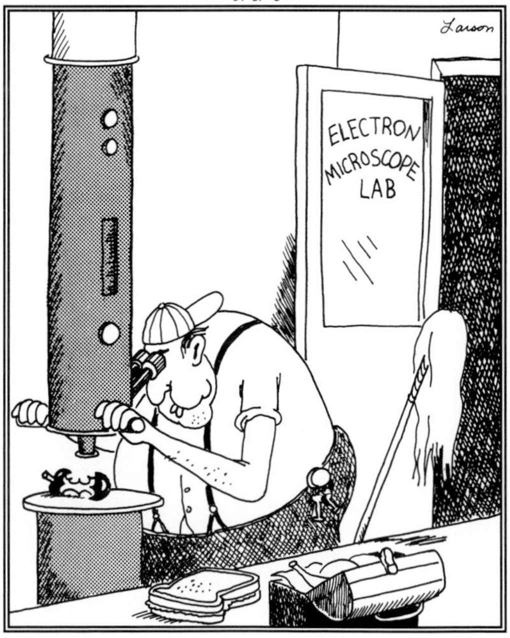
ELECTRON
MICROSCOPE
LAB

9/15/83

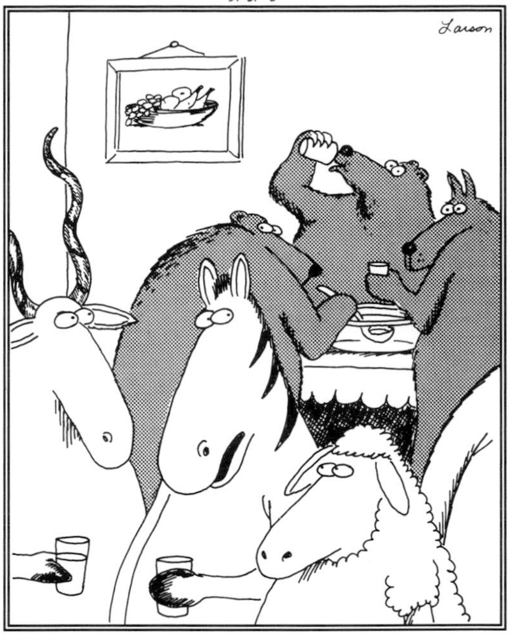
Larson

"I don't like this. ... The carnivores have been boozing it up at the punchbowl all night—drinking, looking around, drinking, looking around ..."

9/16/83

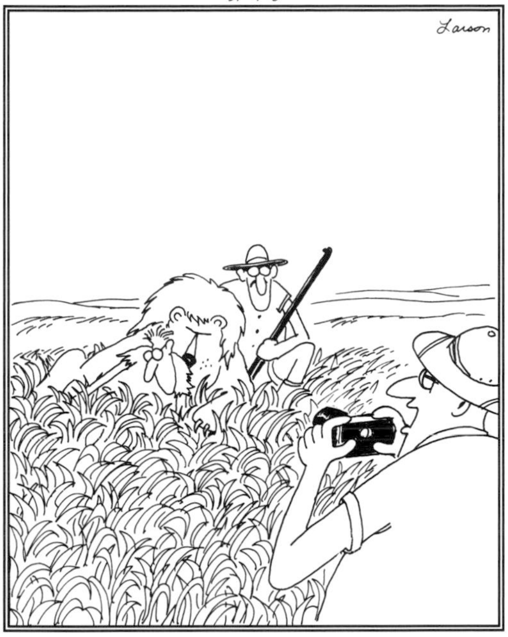
Larson

"Andrew! Fix Edgar's head! ... It's not facing the camera!"

9/10/83

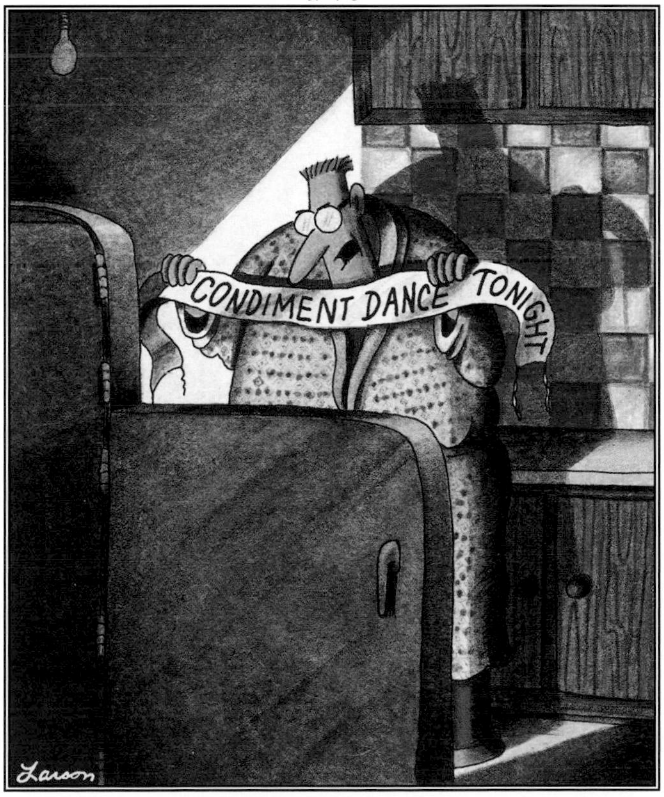
CONDIMENT DANCE TONIGHT
Larson

"I'll just take *this*, thank you! ... And knock off that music!"

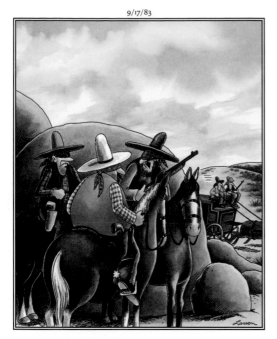

"Dang! This can't be right. ... I can *hear* the
stage, but I can't see a blamed thing!"

The frogs at home

9/26/83

Larson

"Tick-tock, tick-tock, tick-tock, tick-tock ..."

9/27/83

Larson

"Say ... *you're* not Bob! ... You look like him, but you're certainly not him!"

9/20/83

Larson

"Yes, with the amazing new 'knife,' you only have to wear the *skin* of those dead animals."

9/29/83

Larson

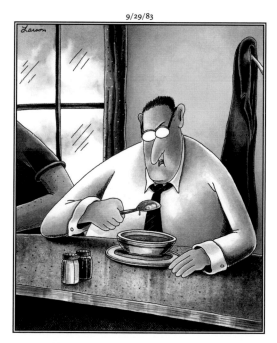

Darrell suspected someone had once again slipped him a trick spoon with the concave side reversed.

9/21/83

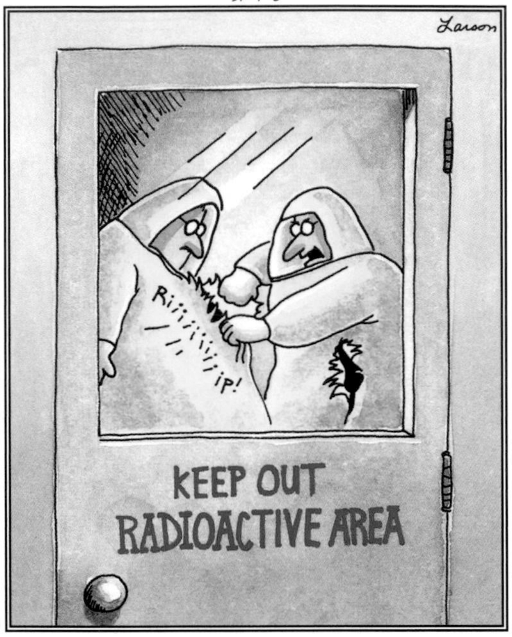
KEEP OUT
RADIOACTIVE AREA

"So, Foster! That's how you want it, huh? ...
Then take THIS!"

9/23/83

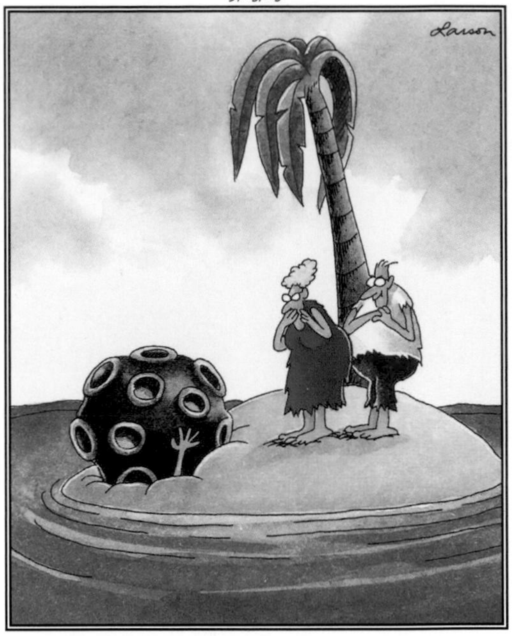

With Roger out of the way, it was Sidney's big chance.

9/28/83

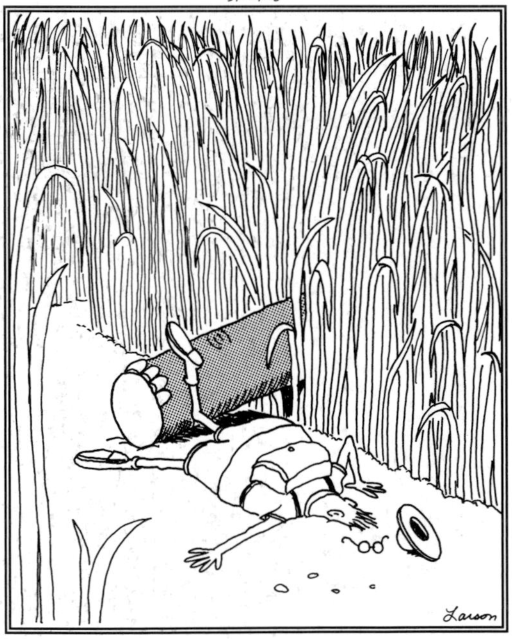

Beware the elephant in tall grass.

9/30/83

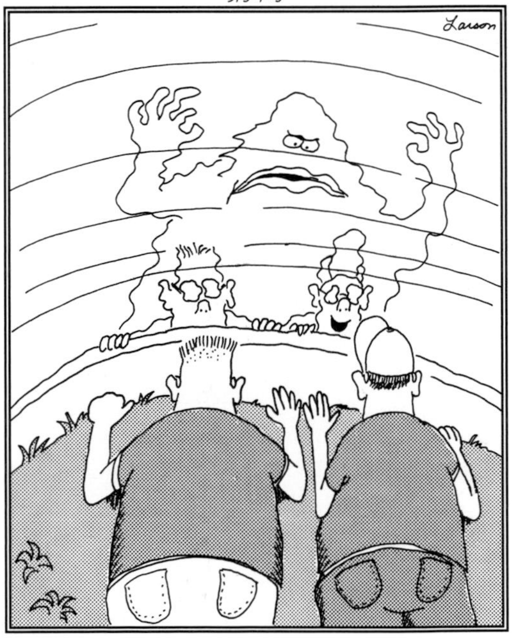

"*My* reflection? Look at *yours,* Randy. ...
You look like some big, fat swamp thing."

10/7/83

Larson

"You call that mowin' the lawn? ... Bad dog! ...
No biscuit! ... Bad dog!"

10/6/83

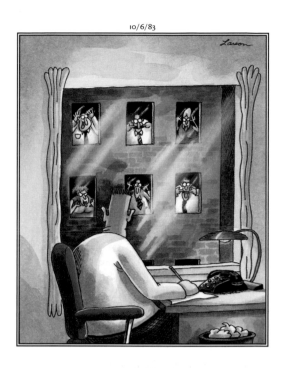

Larson

10/1/83

Larson

Charles wanders into a herd of dirt buffaloes.

10/3/83

Larson

"My turn? ... Well, I'm originally from the
shores of the upper Nile and ... saaaaaaay ...
did anyone ever tell you your pupils are *round*?"

10/4/83

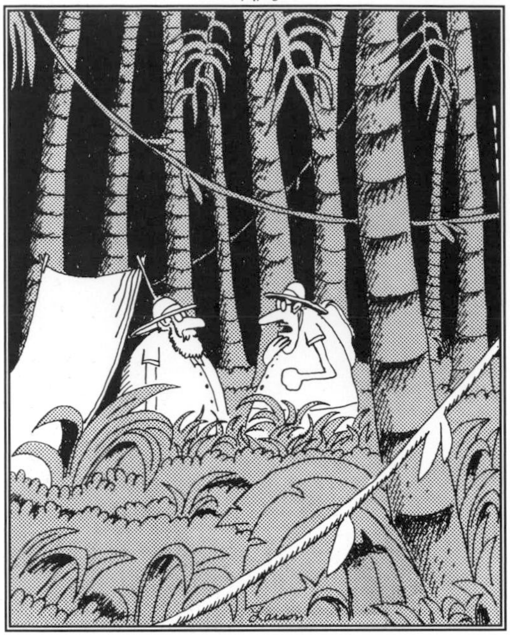
Larson

"I presume you're Dr. Livingstone. ... I mean ... presumably, you're Dr. Livingstone. ... No wait. ... Dang! I've screwed it up!"

10/5/83

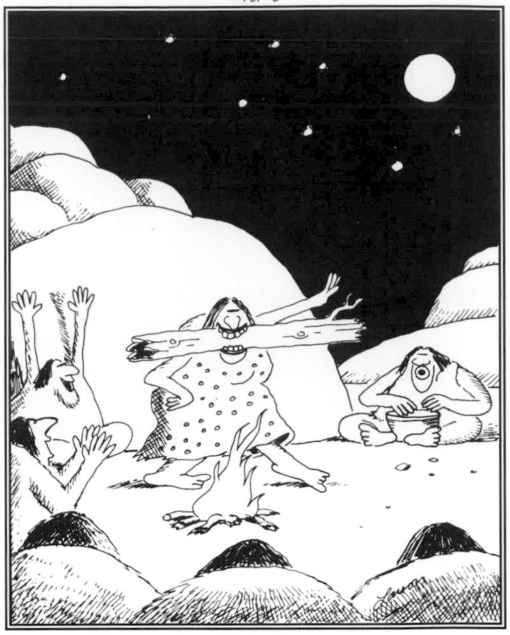

Primitive fandango

10/10/83

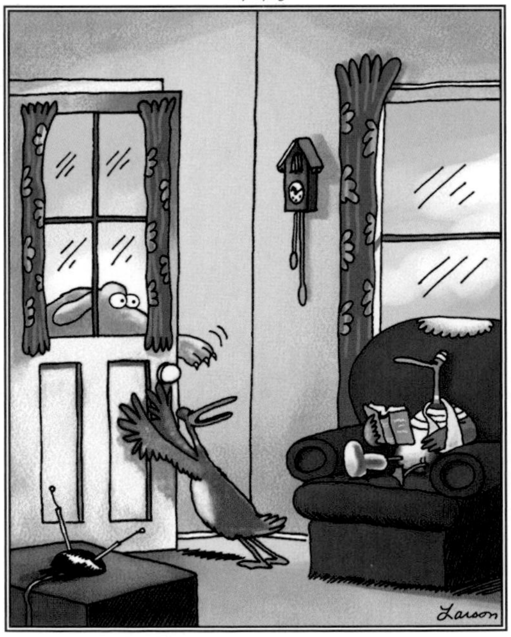
Larson

"Look out, Larry! ... That retriever has finally found you!"

10/11/83

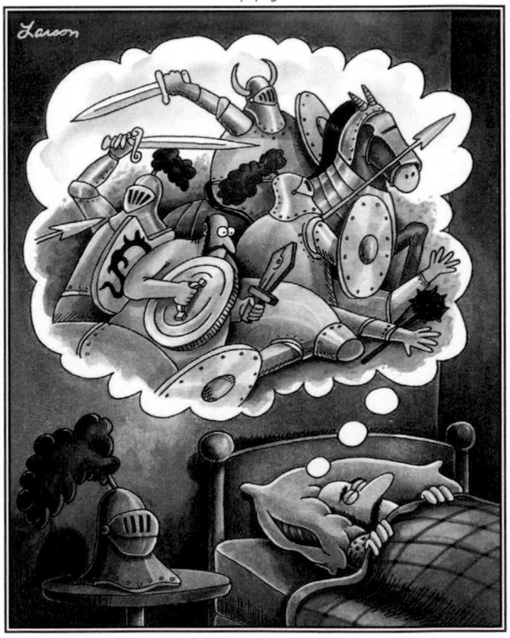
Larson

Common medieval nightmare

10/8/83

"Saaaaay. ... I think I smell *perfume!* ...
You haven't been over at the
Leopard Woman's, have you?"

10/12/83

Clayton frequently watched the monsters, until
the night he knocked over the garbage can
and was subsequently eaten.

10/14/83

10/22/83

"So now tell the court, if you will, Mrs. Potato
Head, exactly what transpired on the night your
husband chased you with the Veg-o-matic."

335

"Well, Captain Grunfield, it says here you were expelled from the belly of a large squid after ... ha ... after your boat ... ha ha ... after ... ha ha ha ha ha ha ha! ..."

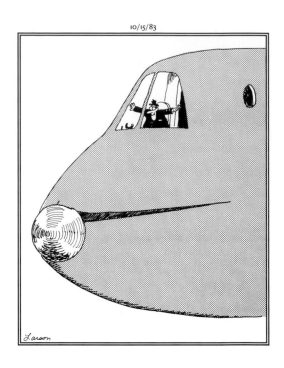

"Dang! ... Who ate the middle out of the daddy longlegs?"

"Well, I'll be darned. ... I guess he does have a license to do that."

10/19/83

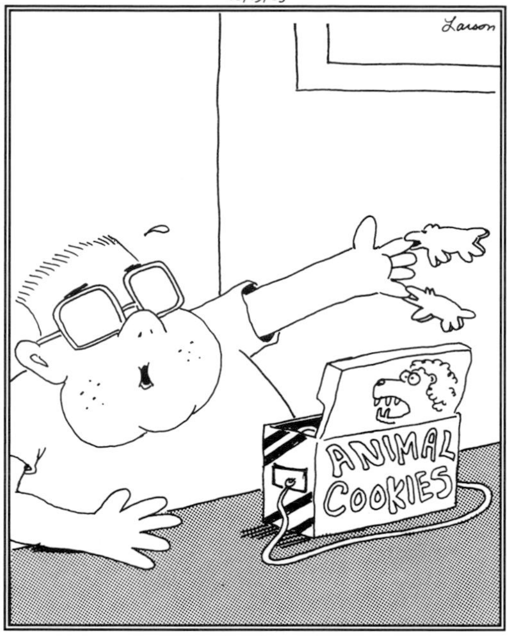
Larson
ANIMAL COOKIES

10/20/83

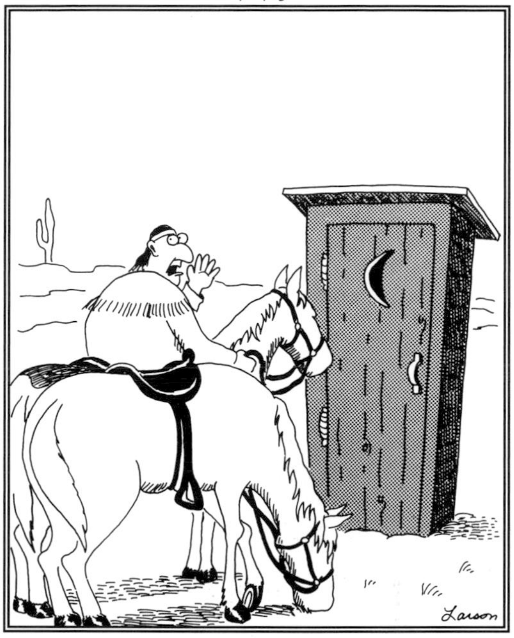
Larson

"Kemosabe! ... The music's starting! The music's starting!"

10/21/83

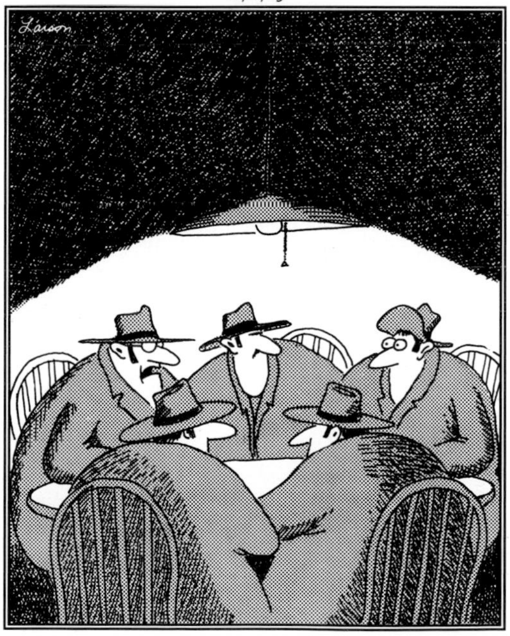
Larson

"So then, when the bank doors open, we ... Louie! You jerk! ... Your hat brim is up!"

10/26/83

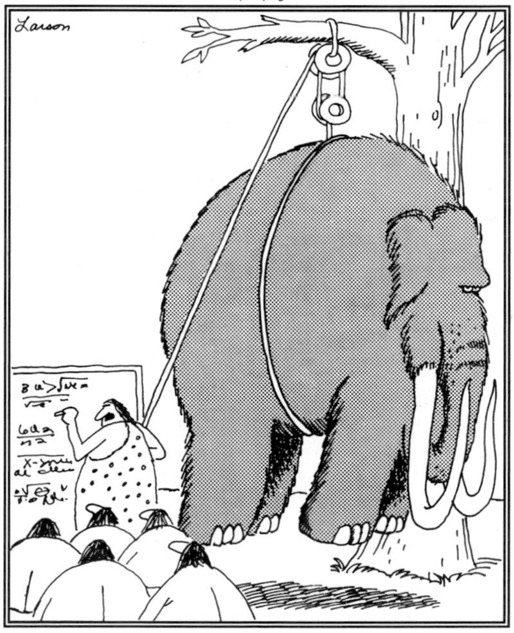
Larson

Early physics

10/27/83

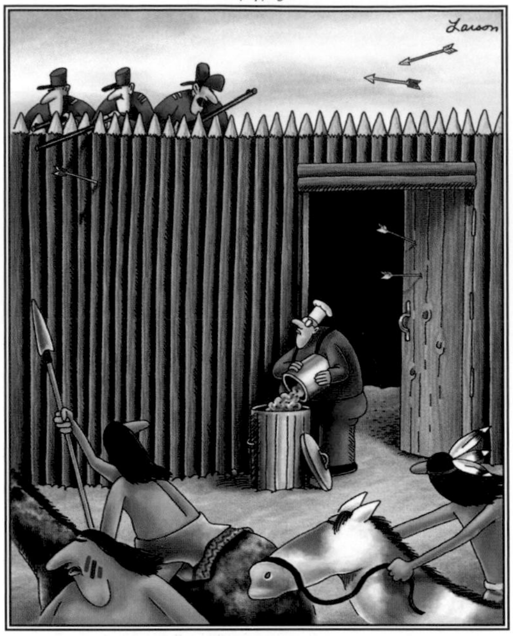
Larson

"FLETCHER, YOU FOOL! ...
THE GATE! THE GATE!"

10/25/83

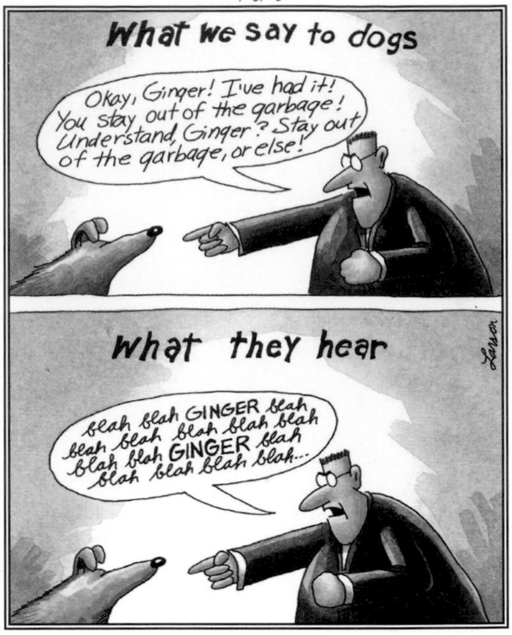
What we say to dogs
Okay, Ginger! I've had it! You stay out of the garbage! Understand, Ginger? Stay out of the garbage, or else!
What they hear
blah blah GINGER blah blah blah blah blah blah blah blah GINGER blah blah blah blah blah...
Larson

10/24/83

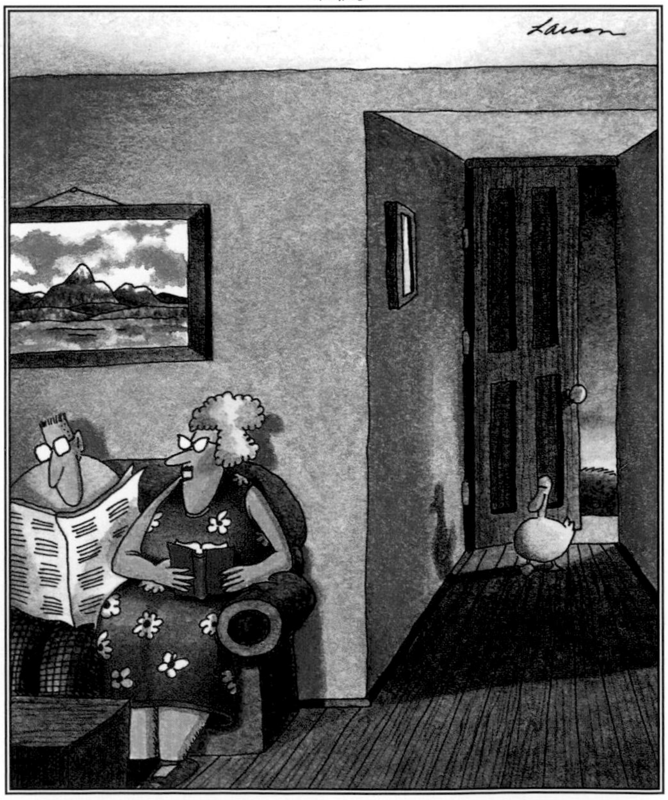
Larson

"Here he comes, Earl. ... Remember, be gentle but
firm ... we are absolutely, positively, NOT
driving him south this winter."

10/31/83

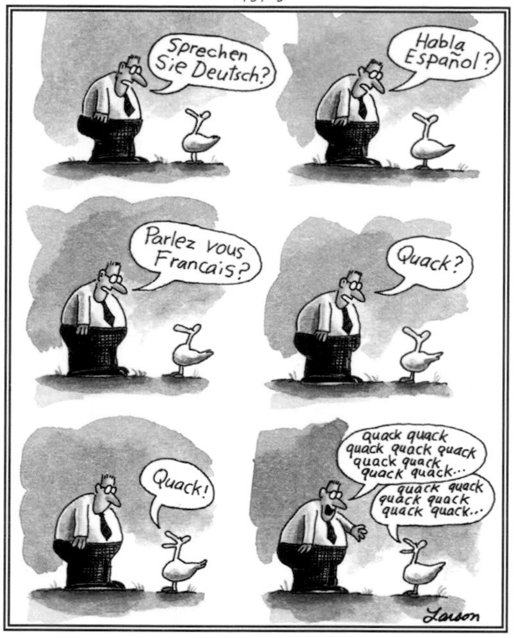
Sprechen Sie Deutsch?
Habla Español?
Parlez vous Francais?
Quack?
Quack!
quack quack quack quack quack quack quack quack quack...
quack quack quack quack quack quack...
Larson

10/28/83

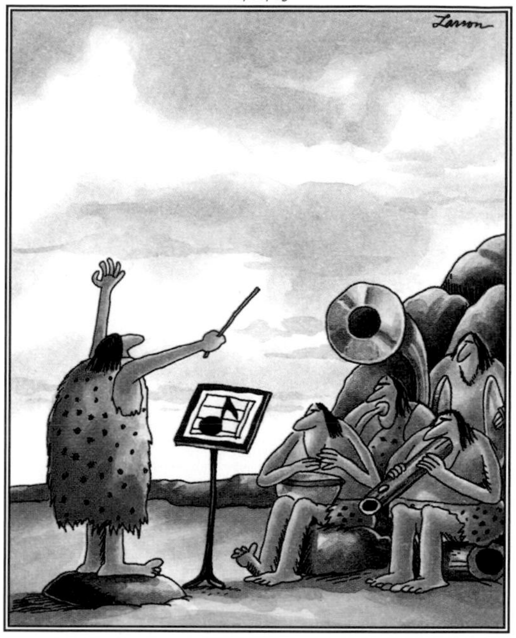
Larson

10/29/83

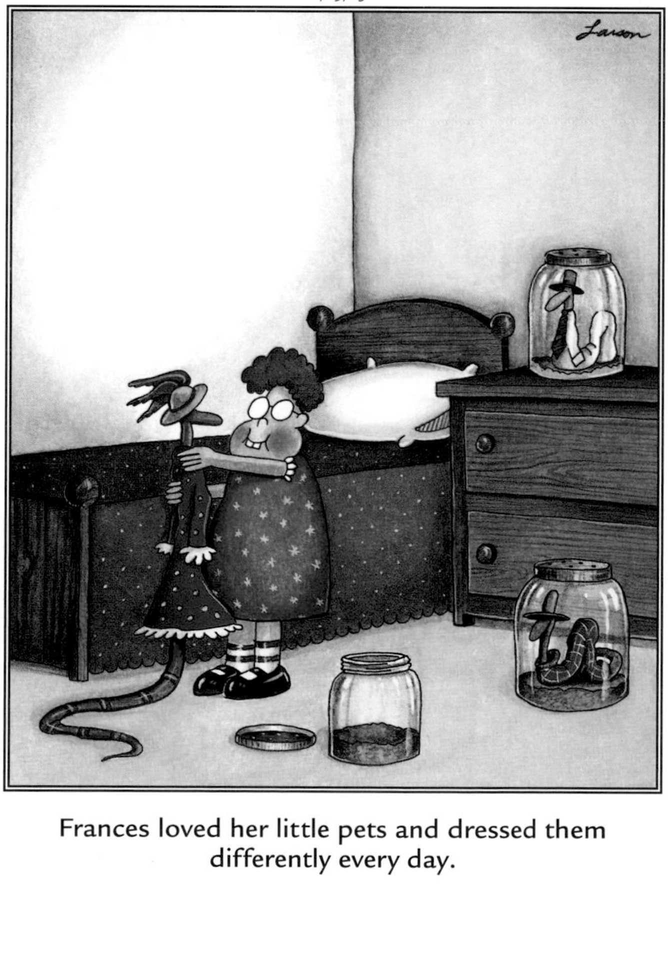
Larson

Frances loved her little pets and dressed them differently every day.

11/2/83

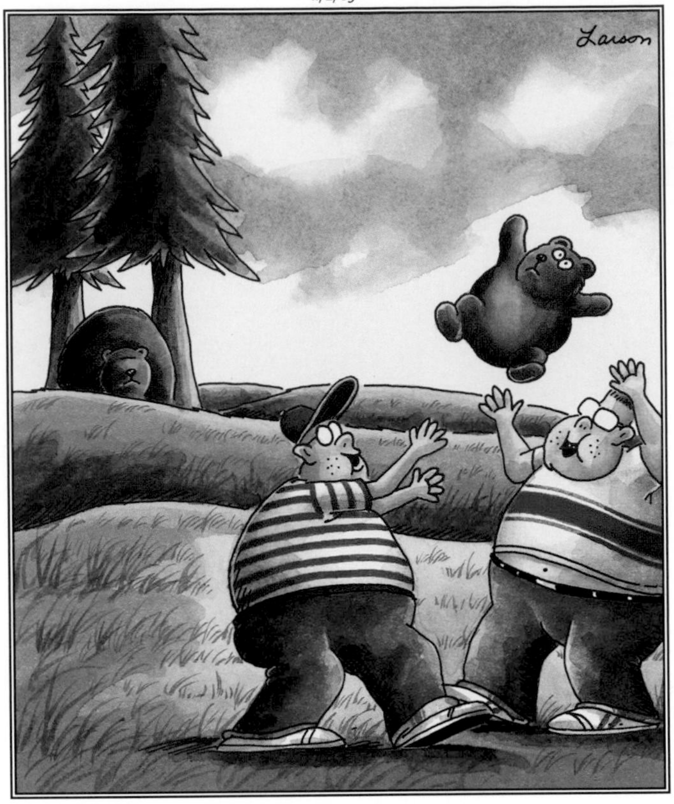
Larson

And no one ever heard from the
Anderson brothers again.

11/1/83

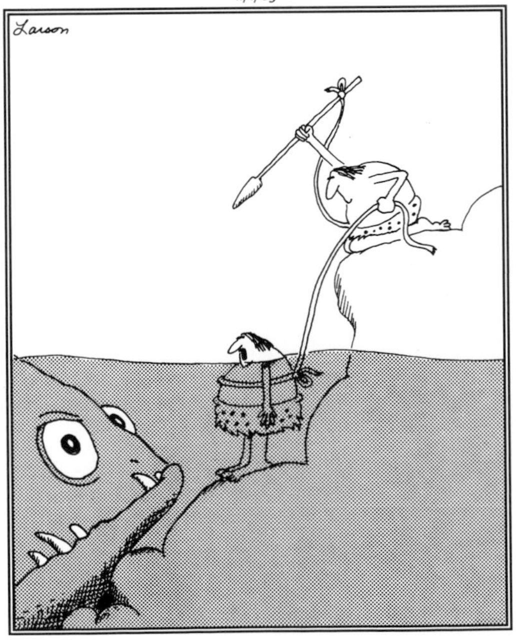
Larson

"Now, Grog! Throw! ... Throoooooow! ...
Throw throw throw throw throw throw! ..."

11/5/83

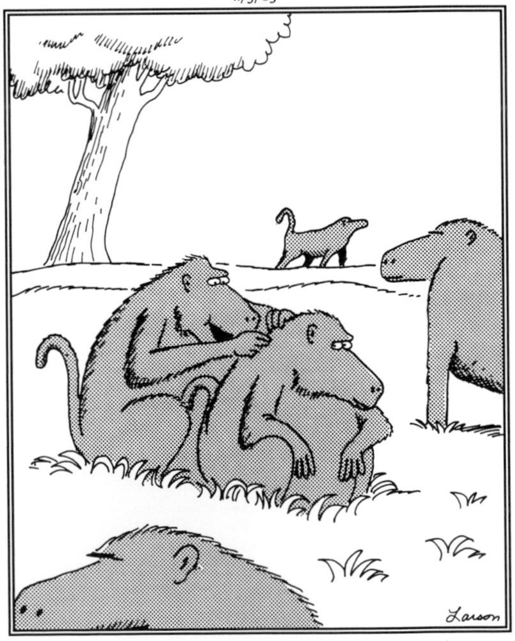
Larson

"So then Sheila says to Betty that Arnold
told her what Harry was up to, but Betty
told me she already heard it from
Blanche, don't you know ..."

11/10/83

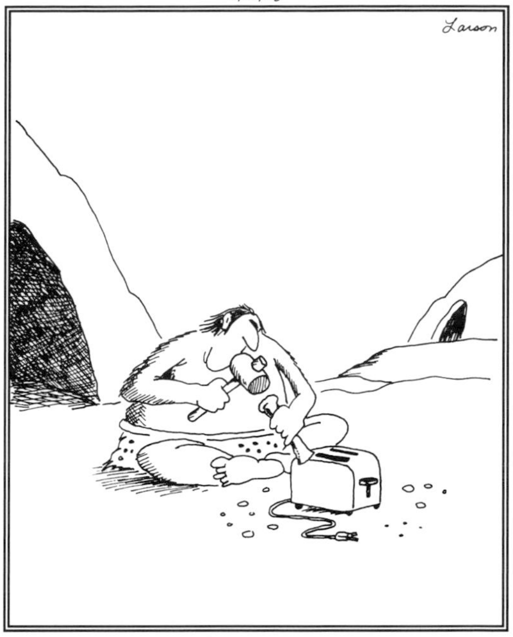
Larson

11/4/83

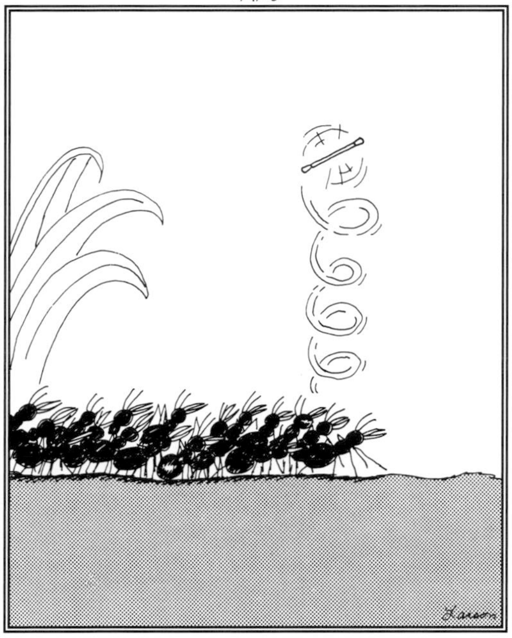
Larson

11/3/83

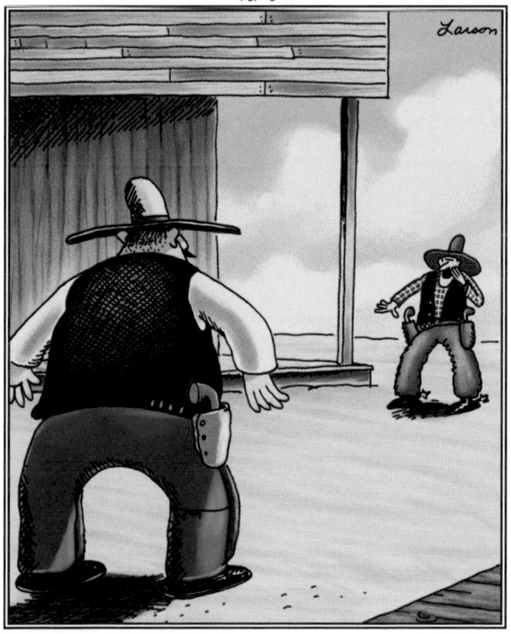
Larson

"SHOE'S UNTIED!"

11/7/83

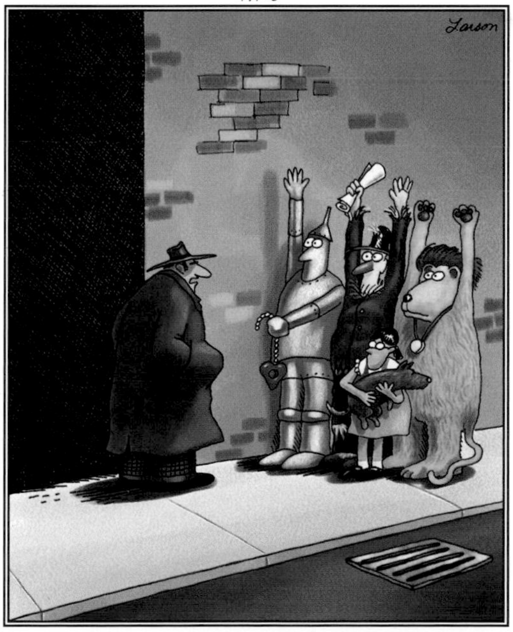
Larson

"C'mon, c'mon, buddy! The heart! Hand over the heart! ... And you with the brains! ... Let's have 'em!"

11/11/83

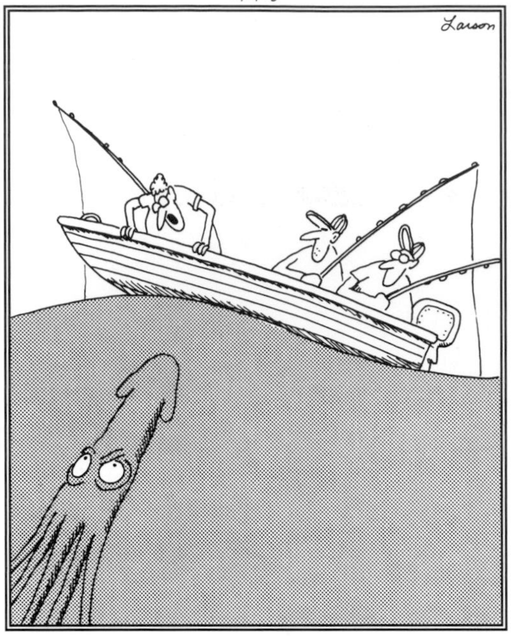
Larson

"Look out, everyone! ... We're being attacked by a giant sq ... well, no ... I'd say medium squid!"

11/12/83

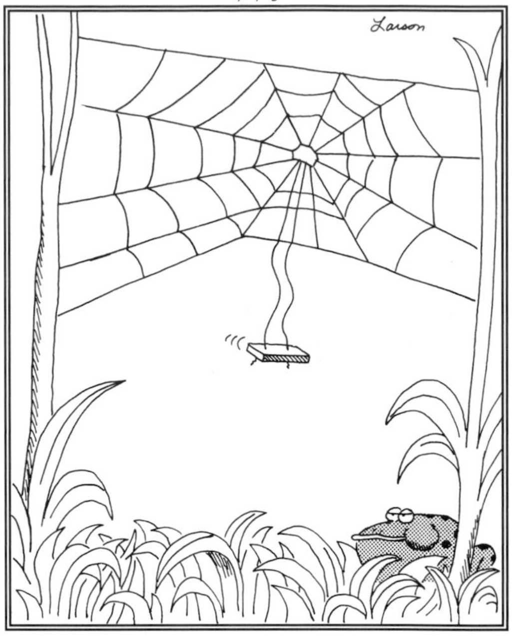
Larson

11/8/83

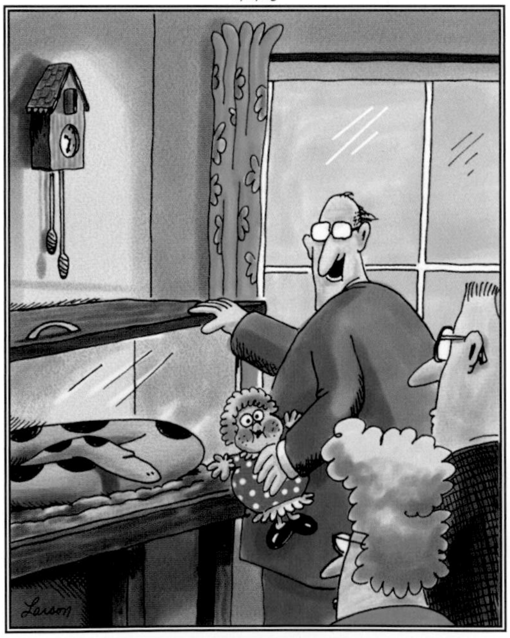
Larson

"Hey! You'll get a kick out of this, Bill and Ruth! ... Watch what Lola here does with her new squeeze doll!"

11/9/83

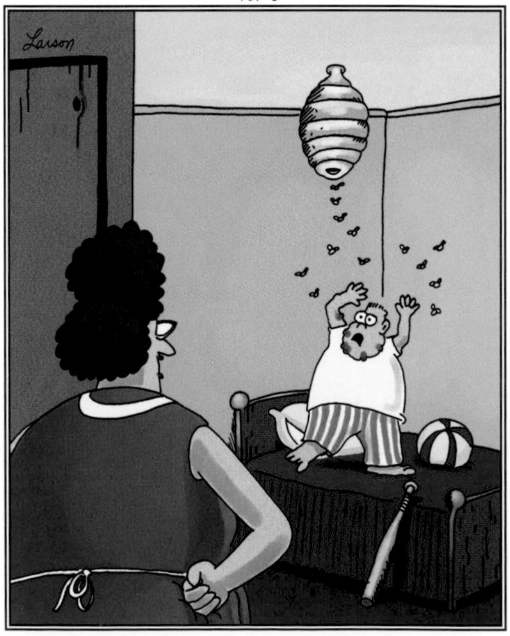
Larson

"Well, Bobby, it's not like you haven't been warned. ... *No roughhousing under the hornets' nest!*"

11/14/83

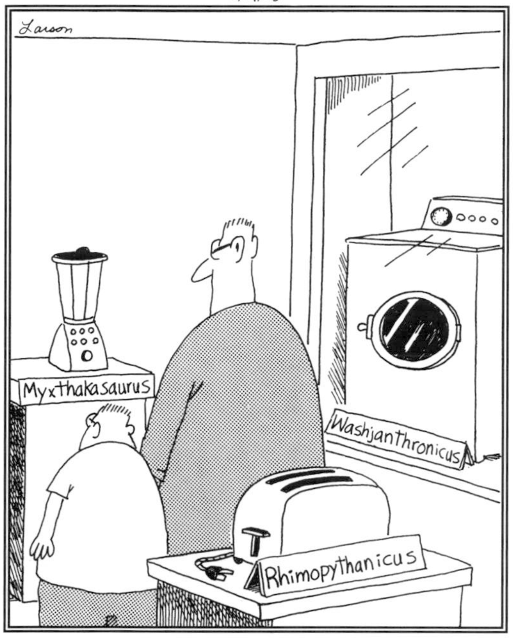
Larson
Myxthakasaurus
Washjanthronicus
Rhimopythanicus

Museums of the future

11/15/83

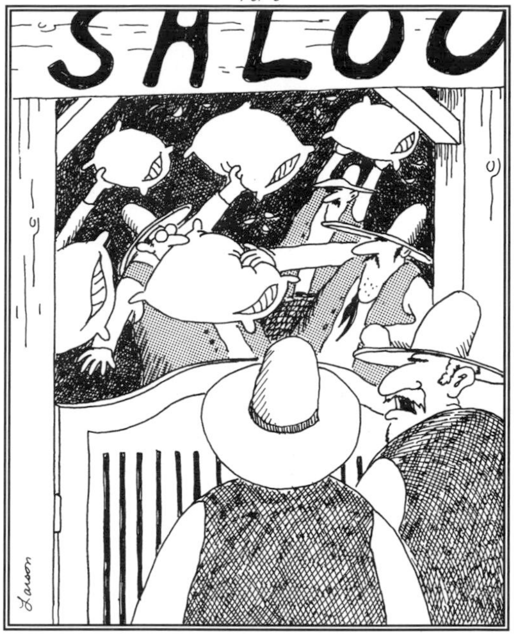
Larson

"Somebody better run fetch the sheriff."

11/17/83

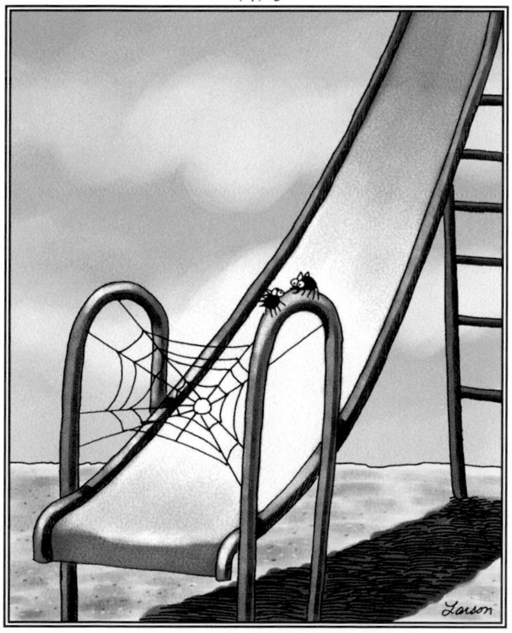
Larson

"If we pull this off, we'll eat like kings."

11/18/83

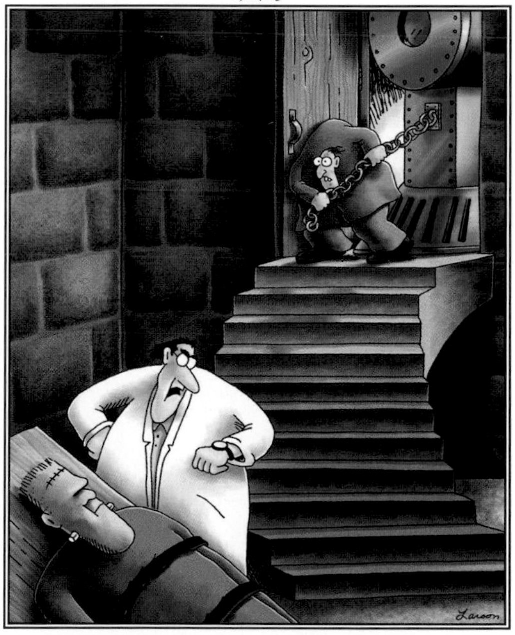
Larson

"Curses! ... How long does it take Igor to go out and bring back a simple little brain, anyway?"

11/16/83

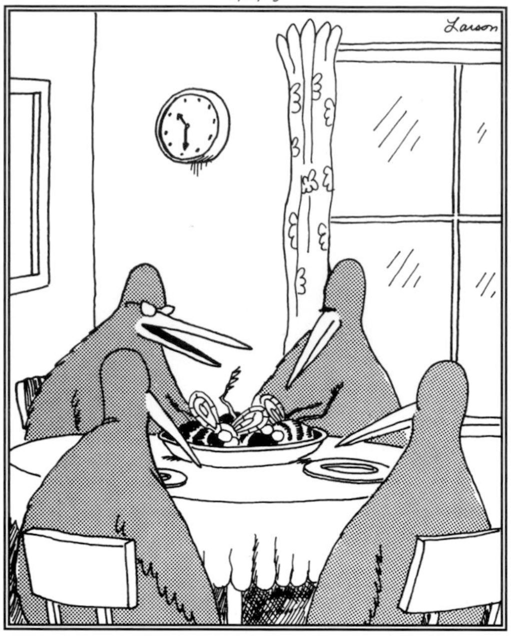
Larson

"Okay, everyone, dig in ... and you kids watch for stingers."

11/19/83

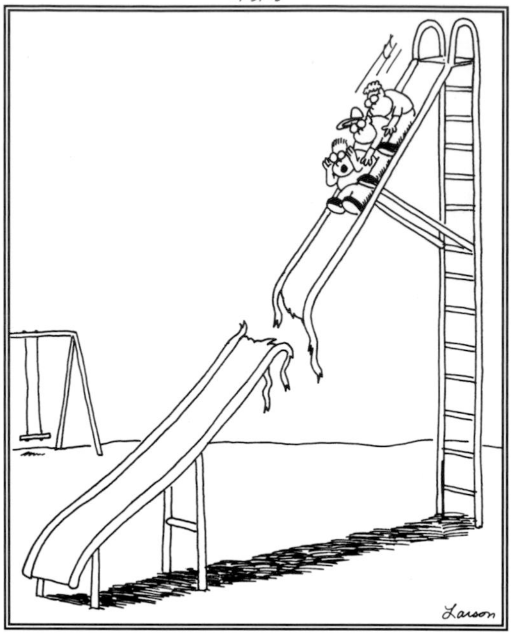
Larson

At the head of the train, Russell was first to notice the slide was out.

11/21/83

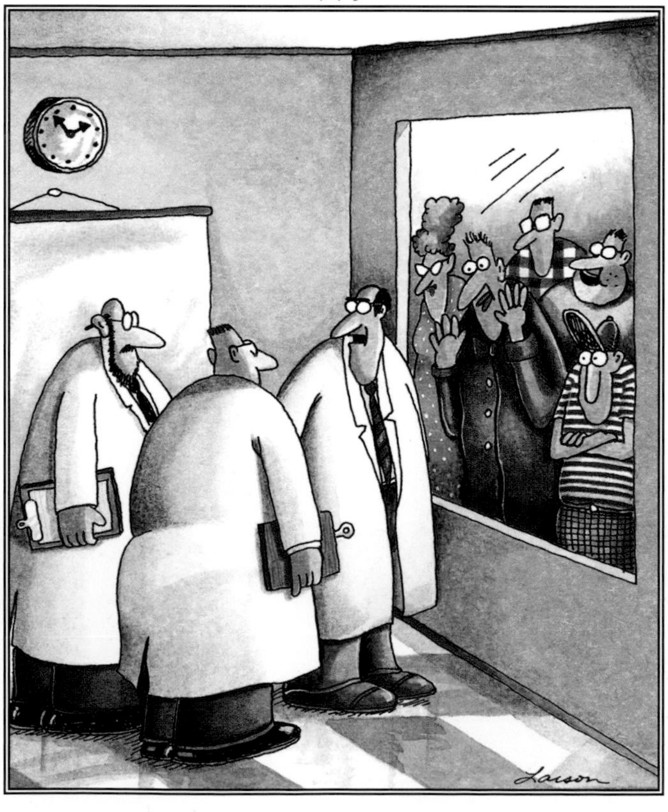
Larson

"Yes, they're all fools, gentlemen ... but the question remains, 'What *kind* of fools are they?'"

11/24/83

It's a mammoth.

Early microscope

11/25/83

KISSING FISH

11/22/83

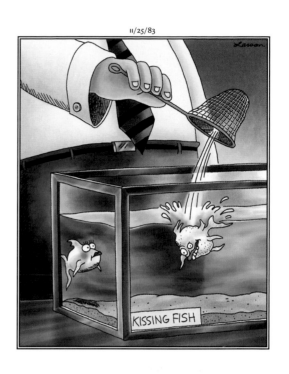

"So, there we were! ... Locked into this life and death tug-o'-war! ... Your grandma had one end of me, the bird had the other, but everyone went away satisfied."

11/28/83

"My word! ... That one came just too close for comfort, if you ask me."

11/23/83

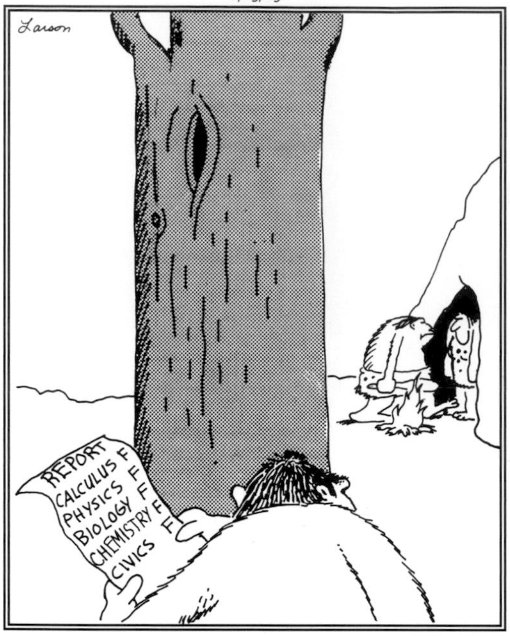
REPORT
CALCULUS F
PHYSICS F
BIOLOGY F
CHEMISTRY F
CIVICS F

Grog hesitated, not wanting to face his parents.

11/26/83

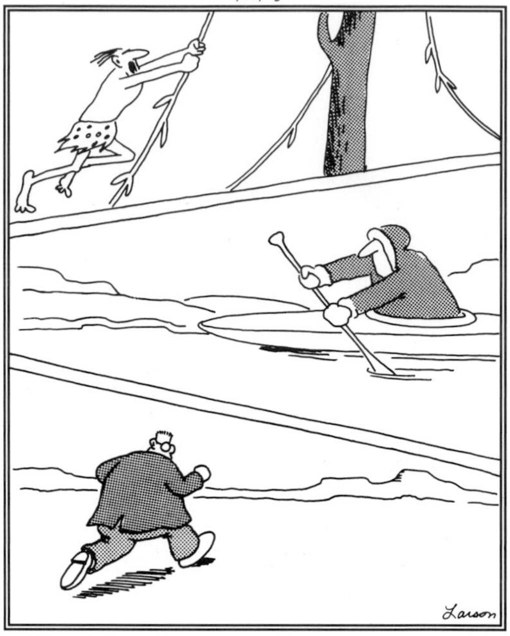

Tarzan of the Jungle, Nanook of the North, and Warren of the Wasteland

11/29/83

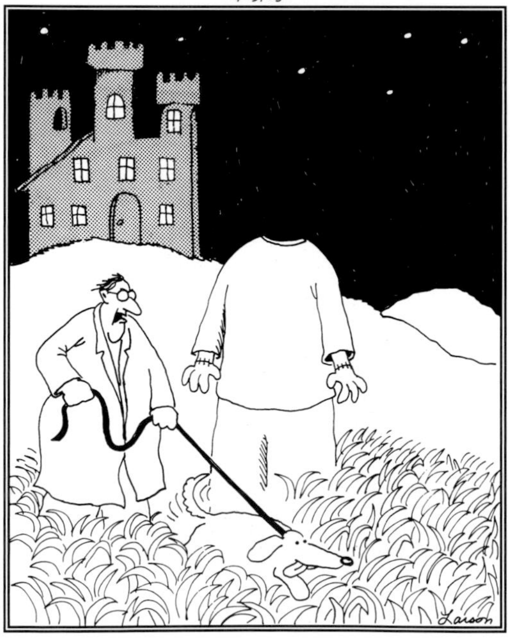

"Blast! This cinches it! ... If we ever find it again, I'm gonna bolt the sucker on!"

11/30/83

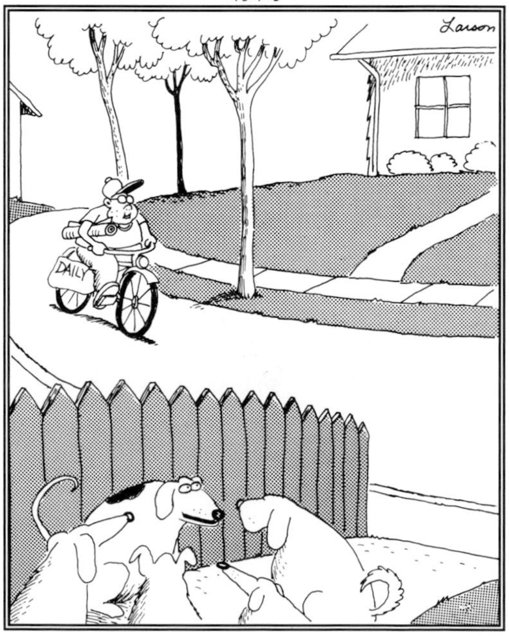
DAILY

"Okay, this time Rex and Zeke will be the wolves, Fifi and Muffin will be the coyotes, and ... Listen! ... Here comes the deer!"

12/1/83

"I've had it, Doc! I've come all the way from Alabama with this danged thing on my knee!"

12/2/83

MUSEUM
INFORMATION
ping!
MING DYNASTY
VASE
CIRCA 1500 A.D.
ANCIENT
1450-17

12/3/83

Little Beaver? Red Eagle?..
Where is everyone? Okay...
Joke's over!

Last of the Mohicans

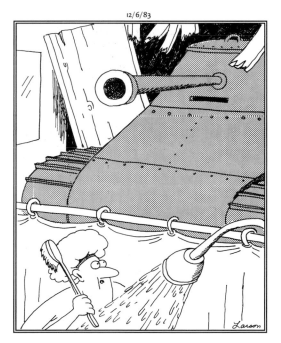

12/6/83

Psycho III

12/7/83

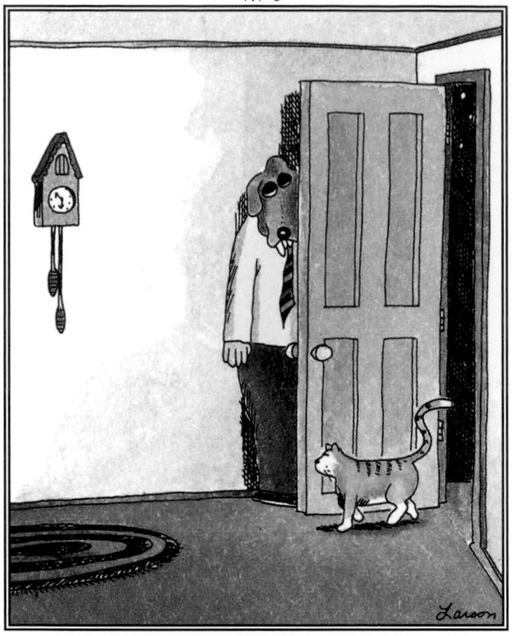

Games you can play with your cat.

12/8/83

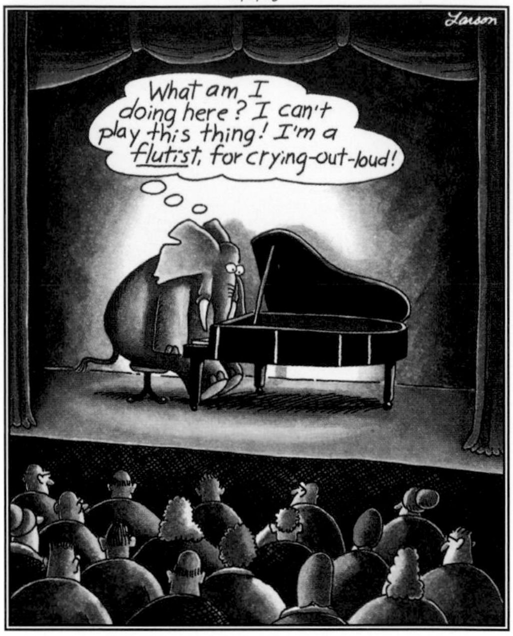
What am I doing here? I can't play this thing! I'm a flutist, for crying-out-loud!

The elephant's nightmare

12/5/83

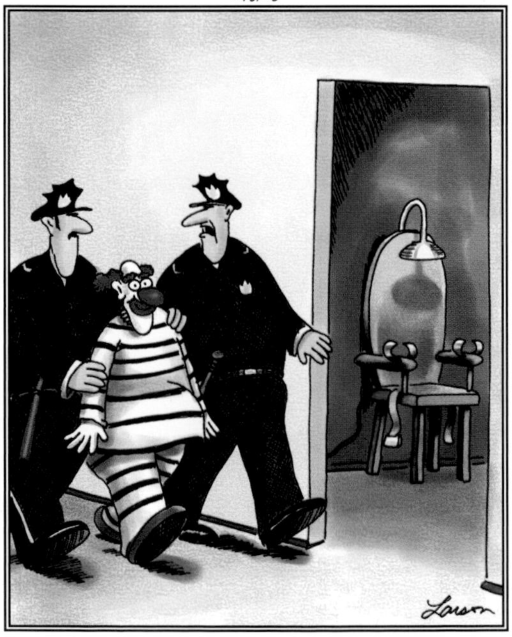

"I don't think I'll be able to tell the kids about this one."

12/9/83

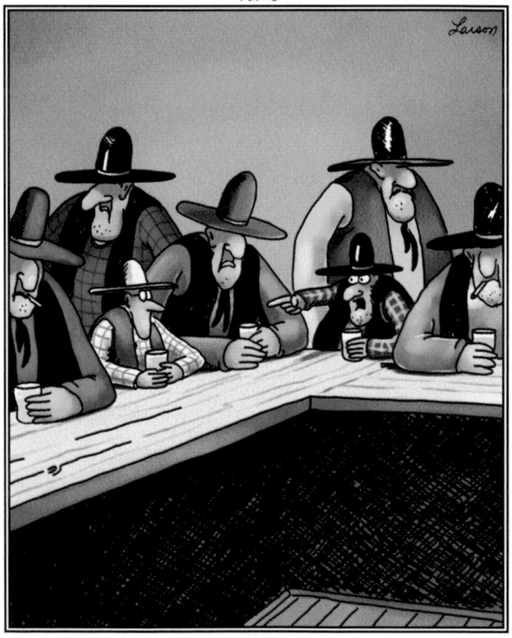

"Hey! You! ... Yeah, that's right! I'm talkin' to YOU!"

12/10/83

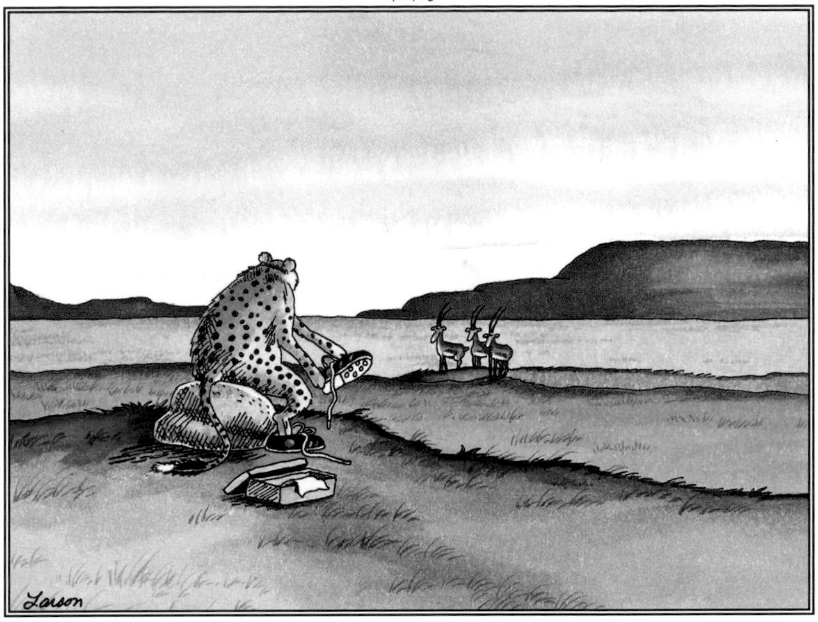
Larson

12/12/83

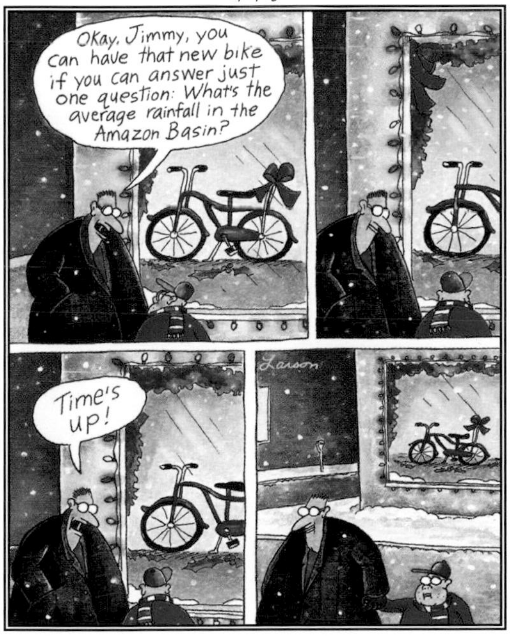
Okay, Jimmy, you can have that new bike if you can answer just one question: What's the average rainfall in the Amazon Basin?
Time's up!
Larson

12/14/83

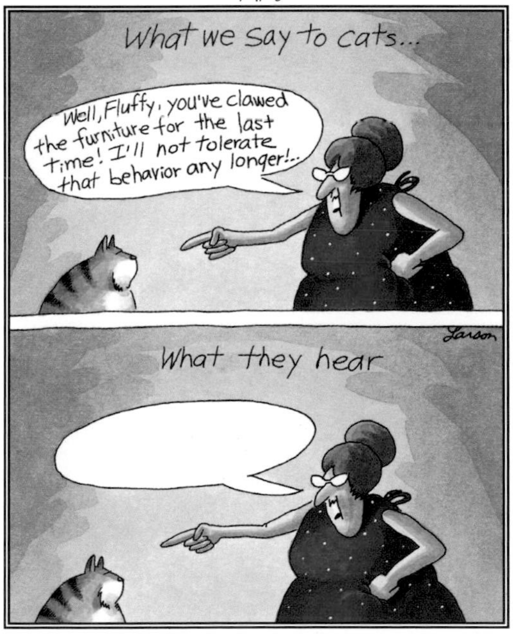
What we say to cats...
Well, Fluffy, you've clawed the furniture for the last time! I'll not tolerate that behavior any longer!..
Larson
What they hear

12/13/83

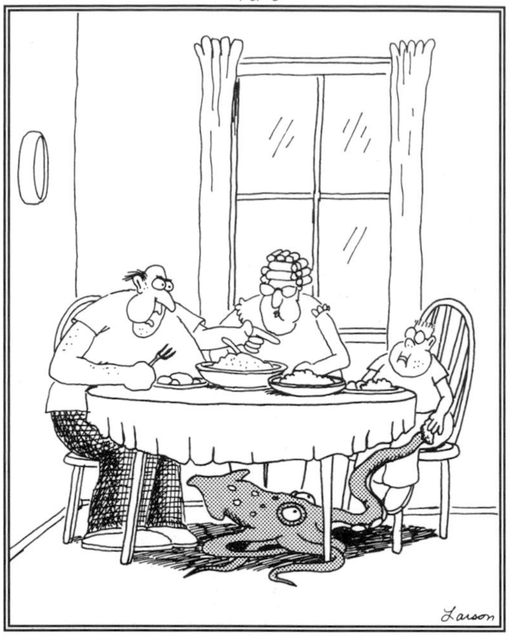
Larson

"Hold it right there, young man! ... Are you feeding the squid under the table again?"

12/15/83

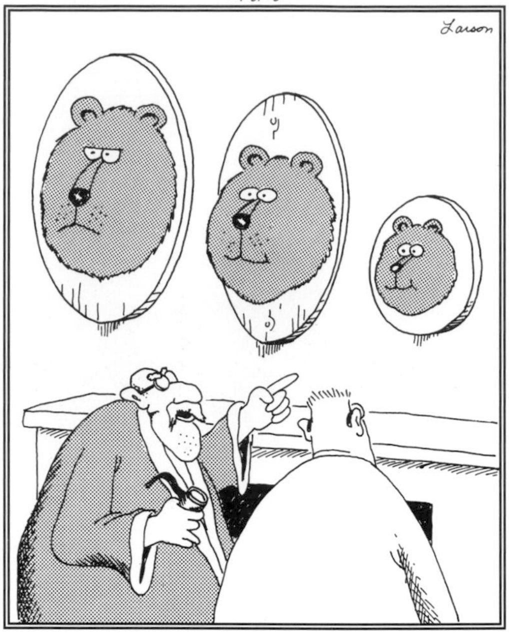
Larson

"The first two gave me trouble, but not that little bear. ... I bagged him juuuuuuuuust right."

12/17/83

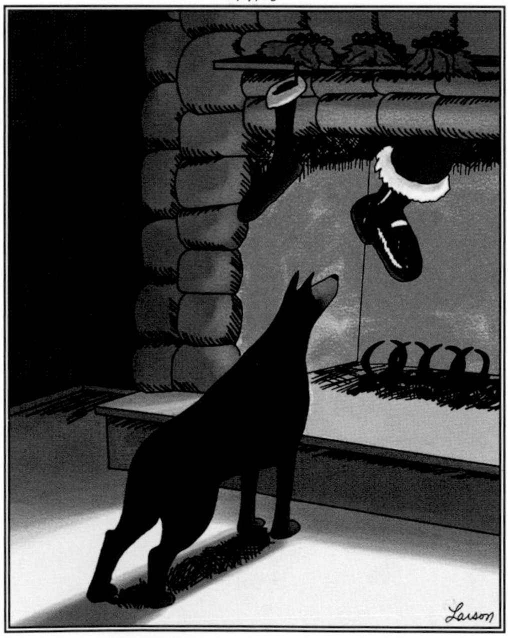
Larson

12/19/83

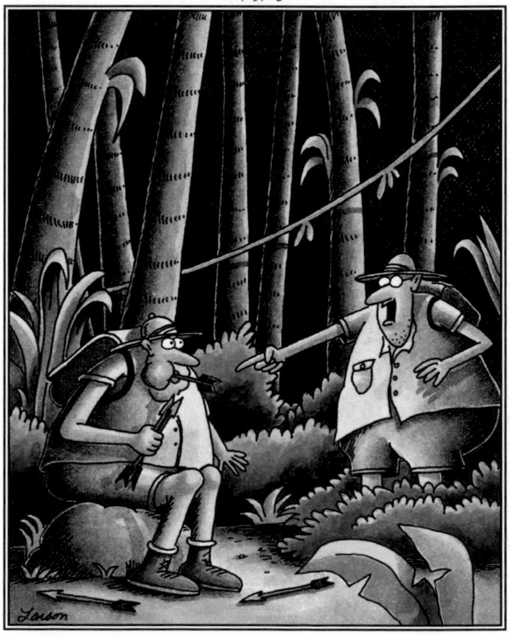
Larson

"Oh my gosh, Andrew! Don't eat those! ... Those are *poison* arrows!"

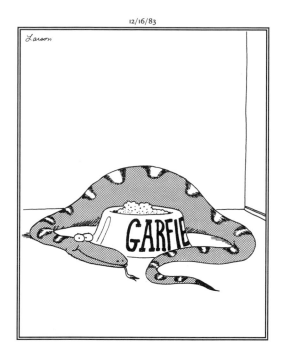

12/16/83

GARFIE

12/20/83

INSECT AWAY

12/21/83

TAXI
TAXI

12/22/83

Murray is caught desecrating the secret appliance burial grounds.

12/27/83

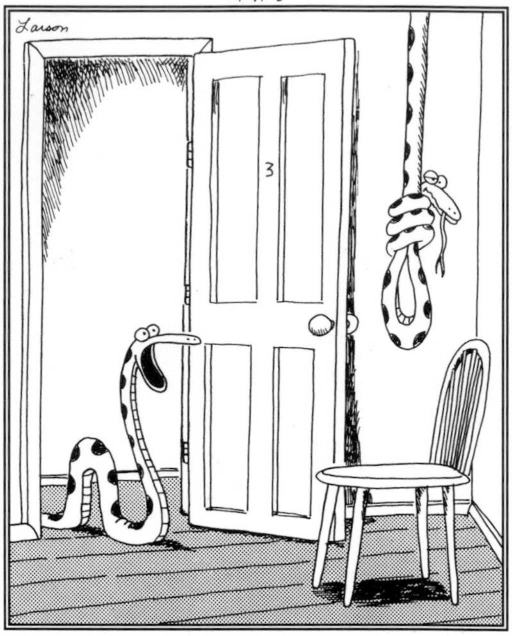
3

"Oh no, Elliott! Why? ... Why? ..."

12/23/83

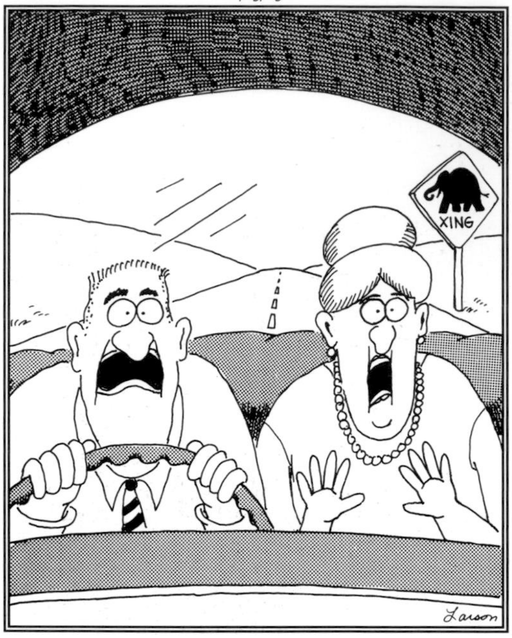
XING

12/26/83

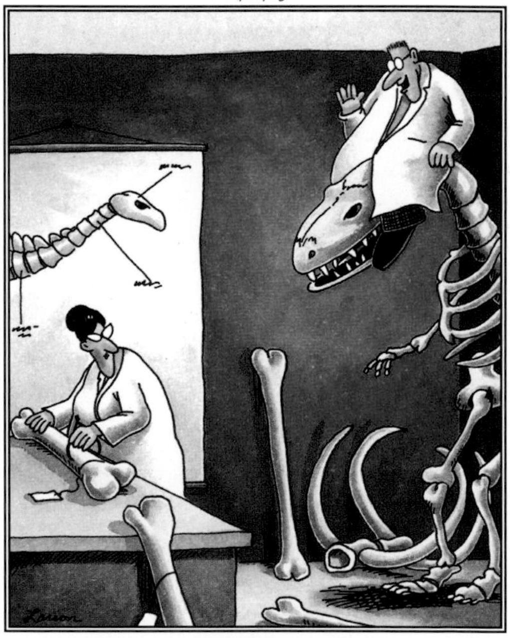

"Hi ... Hi, Miss Collins."

12/24/83

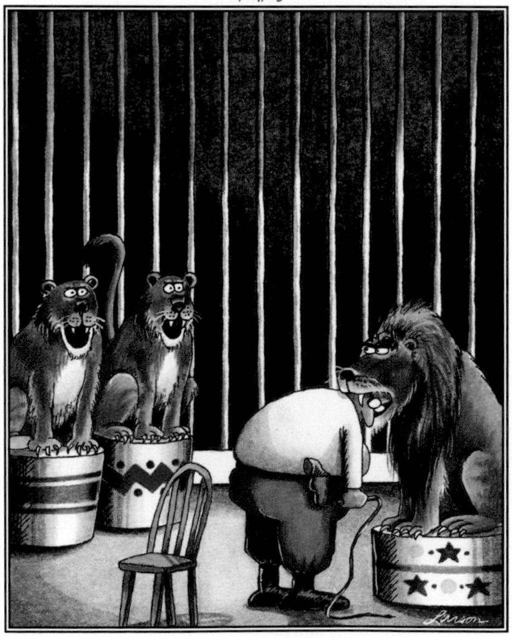

"Ernie's a chicken, Ernie's a chicken ..."

12/29/83

"A one more time! ... HEY! *I've been workin'*
on the railroad, all the live-long day,
HEY! *I've been ...*"

12/30/83

Elephant skyways

12/28/83

"Wonderful! Just wonderful! ... So much for
instilling them with a sense of awe."

12/31/83

"Mom! Edgar's making that clicking
sound again!"

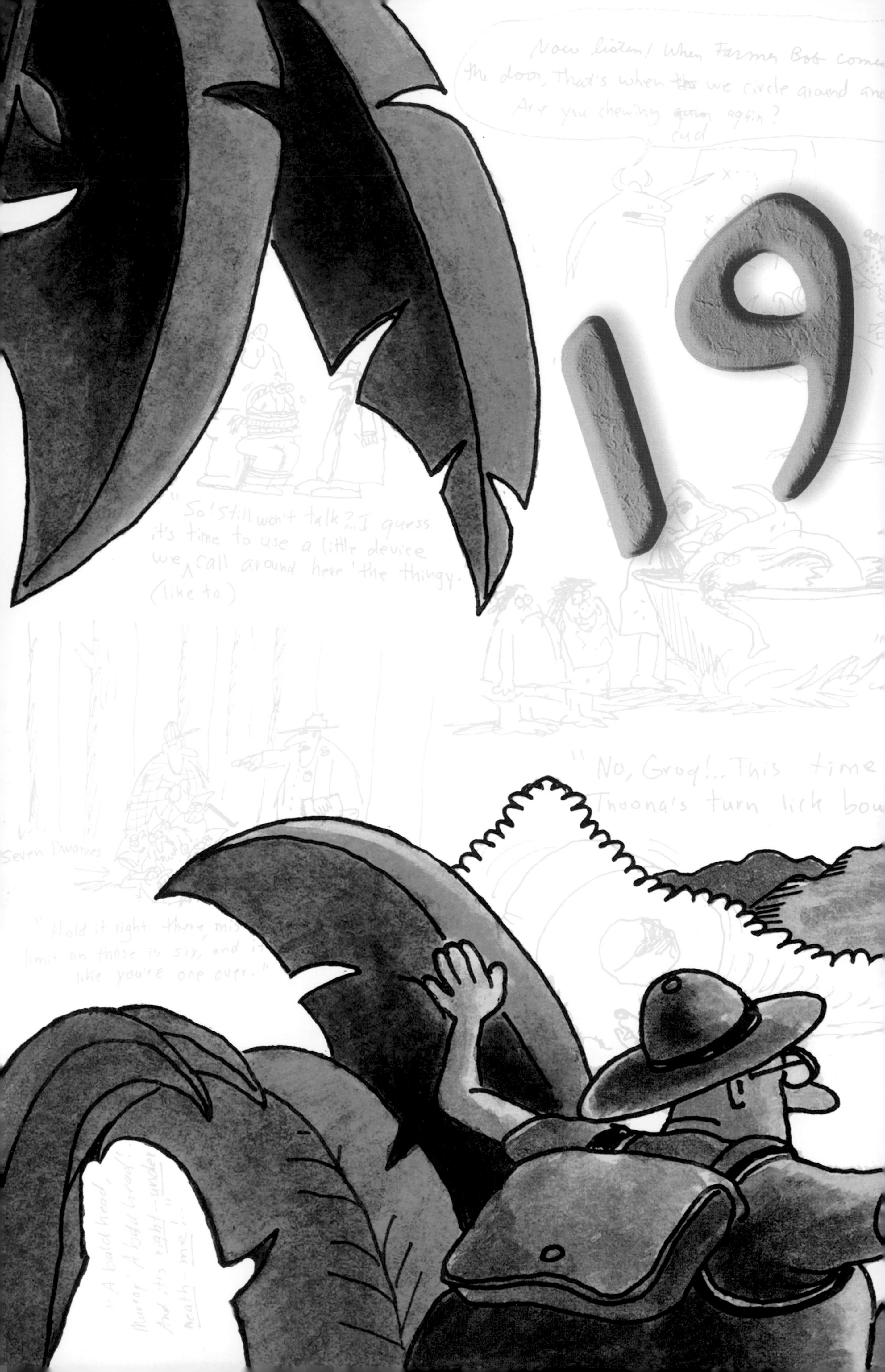

19
Now listen! When Farmer Bob comes
the door, that's when we circle around and
Are you chewing agin?
cud
"So! Still won't talk?... I guess it's time to use a little device we call around here 'the thingy.'
(like to)
Seven Dwarves
"No, Grog!... This time
Thuona's turn lick bow
"Hold it right there, mis
limit on those is six, and it
like you're one over."
"A bald head, Murray! A bald head! And it's right under neath me!"

84

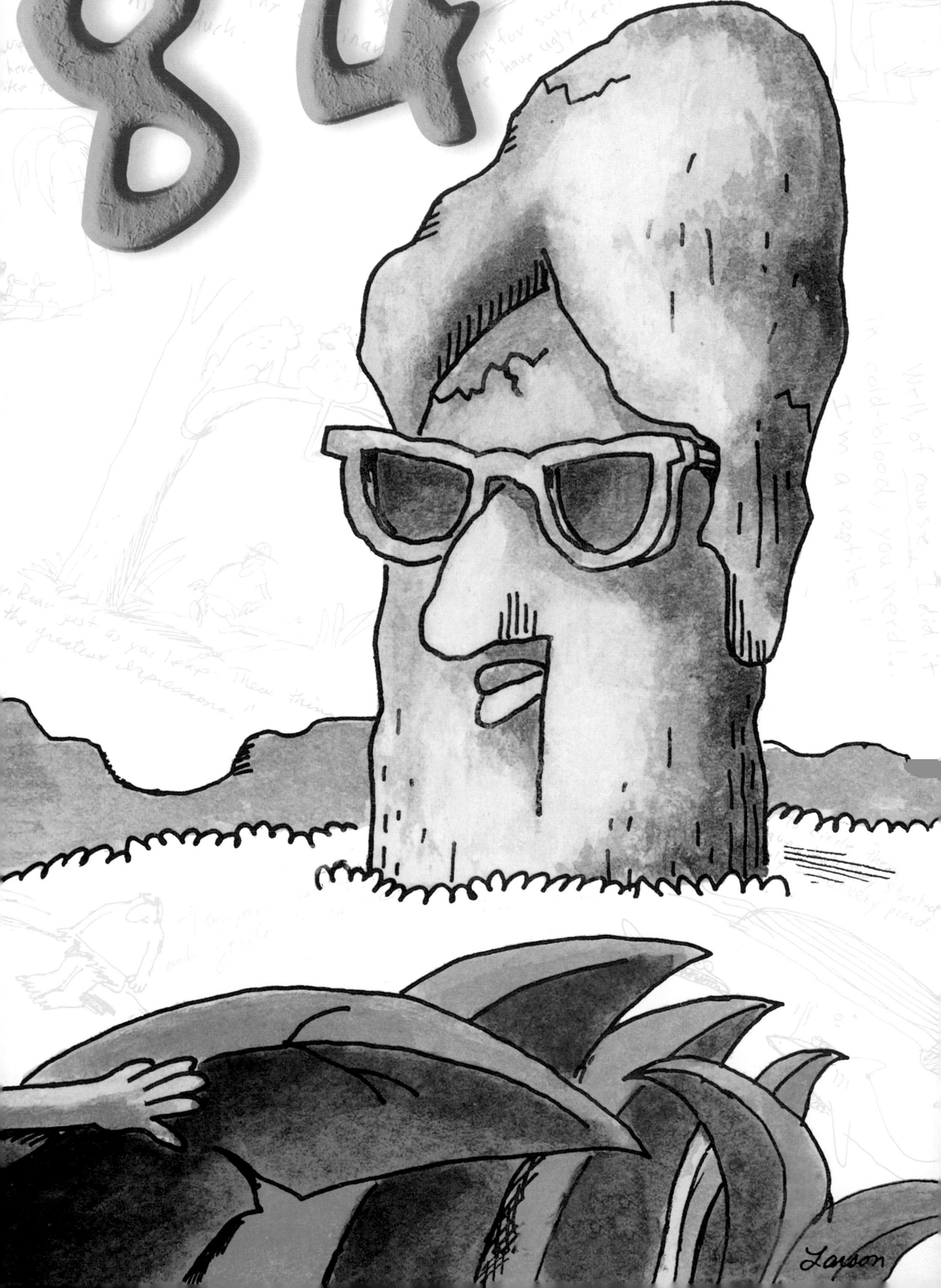
Larson

A Bad Day in Cartoon Land

This is something I swore I would never reveal—ever. It was the worst day of my cartooning career—a day when I curled up into a fetal position on the floor of my studio (my usual reaction to adversity) and stayed there until the urge to die had passed.

I had promised myself I would never talk about this to anyone unless someone else brought it up. And no one ever did. (Actually, that's not true. A 12-year-old kid did ask me about it at a book signing, but he was easy to blow off.) In essence, I made it to the end of my career without ever being asked about the thing I had once thought would be my undoing. And oddly enough, 24 hours after my panic had been triggered, my book editor, with a single word, made my worst day ancient history.

It was 1984, and my publisher had been pumping out *Far Side* books with a who-knows-how-long-this-will-last fervor. I was never very keen on this process, as folks there were well aware, but they were the experts, not me. ("Momentum" was one of those words that got bandied around a lot.)

But the more tangible downside to this rush-to-print was the parallel rush to come up with new book titles and covers. I literally could get a phone call on Monday from someone in the production department telling me she needed a book title and a cover on Friday. And complicating the usual frenzy, once you've come out with a book called *The Far Side*, what's next? Hello to the following: *Beyond The Far Side, Valley of The Far Side, In Search of The Far Side, Hound of The Far Side, It Came from The Far Side,* and *Bride of The Far Side.* (Have I left any out?)

Somewhat better titles followed, I think, but for a while things were in a rut. My own idea of just numbering the books—*The Far Side #1, The Far Side #2,* and so on—horrified everyone and didn't get very far.

And so we come to *In Search of The Far Side.* Not a difficult cover and title to conceive, really. Just draw a couple of explorers who have hacked their way through the jungle and are gazing upon a giant stone carving in the image of a woman I often draw. Done.

A couple of months later, the book was printed, and I got a few advance copies. Always exciting. And the cover looked nice. (I drew it, an artist painted it, and you can see it on the previous page.) Then one evening a few friends came over, and there's my latest book to show off. It got passed around, until one person stopped, looked at the cover, and then sort of strangely looked up at me, and said, "Isn't this woman sort of, uh ... phallic-looking?" (DON'T LOOK AT IT!)

My God, that was a horrible evening. I grabbed the book and just stared at the cover. I'm thinking, I'm a dead man. I, Gary Larson, in my rush to meet a deadline, have drawn a gigantic penis on the cover of a book. (I SAID DON'T LOOK!)

I'm telling you, officially, *this was an accident!* Once the stone woman was painted in a contiguous gray, all her usual features blended into a single, uh, element. (Should I be blaming this on the artist?) It was just like I had imagined it, but here was a time when my imagination didn't quite get to the next level. The level of doom.

Enter Donna Martin, my main book editor. I called her the very next morning (early, and from my fetal position on the floor), letting her know the sky was about to fall. At the time, Donna was maybe in her early 50s, conservative-looking, professional, born and raised in America's heartland. Not what you'd call a flamboyant, devil-may-care kind of person. In fact, I wasn't even sure how to tell her what I had done, but somehow I got it out. *In Search of The Far Side*, I told her, had something on the cover that might be "mistaken" for something else. Specifically, Donna—a penis.

Donna was quiet. (I remember this very well.) I knew she was studying the cover. And then she said the one word I never expected, and its impact on me was unbelievable.

"So?"

That was it. In fact, she didn't even try to reassure me by saying something like, "Oh, Gary, people see what they wanna see." That response would probably have convinced me I *was* doomed. But Donna didn't veer from the issue in the slightest. With absolute calm in her voice, she matter-of-factly stated how cultures all over the world are rife with phallic imagery. Big deal, was her calm assessment. It was like, *C'mon, Gary—I thought you had some major concern to discuss. … I got an office to run here!*

And that's the last time it was ever brought up, by me or anybody else. (Except for that 12-year-old kid.) Over the years, I sometimes wondered what was going on out there among the other people who bought the book, but I never worried about it again. I had my response ready. "Soooooo?" Man, what a great word.

On that day, the worst day of my cartooning life, that single word made every concern just vanish. And, to tell you the truth, I even like that cover. (BUT DON'T LOOK AT IT!)

1/3/84

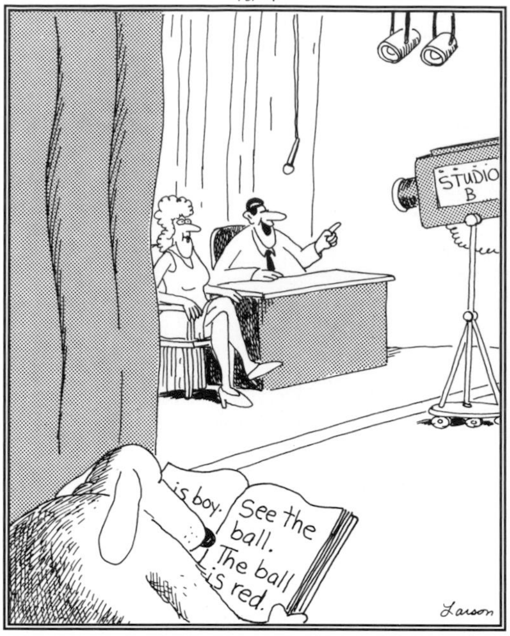
STUDIO B
is boy. See the ball. The ball is red.
Larson

"And now—can dogs really talk? ... We found one who's willing to try, right after this message."

1/10/84

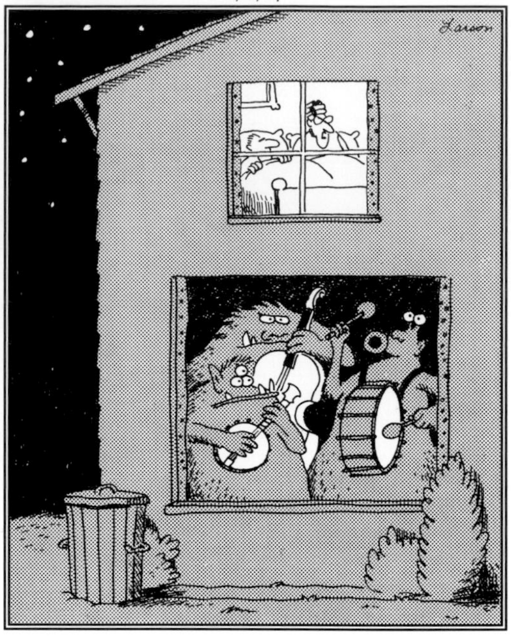
Larson

"Well, okay, Frank. ... Maybe it *is* just the wind."

1/2/84

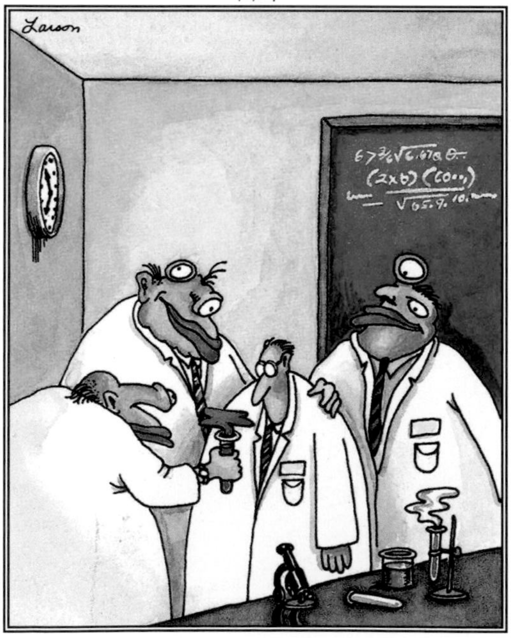
Larson

Laboratory peer pressure

1/4/84

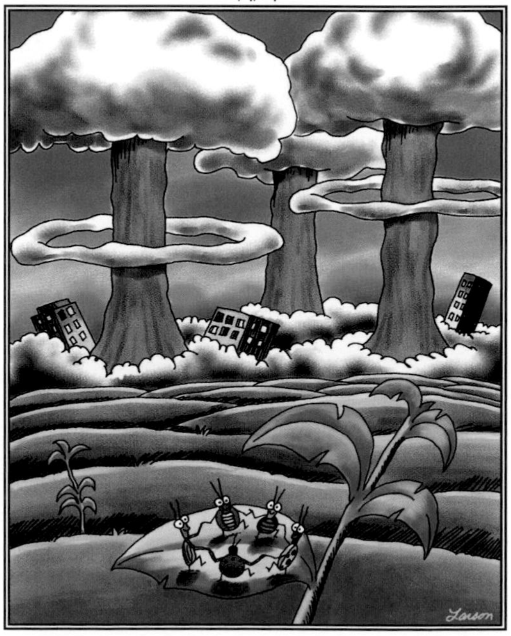
Larson

1/13/84

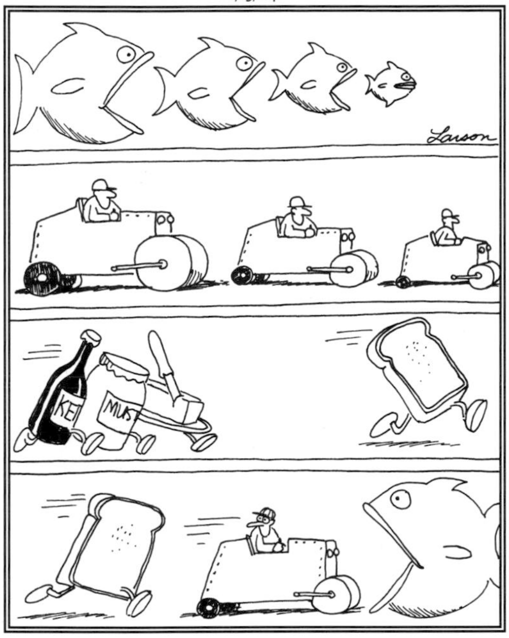
KE
MUS

Various philosophies

1/12/84

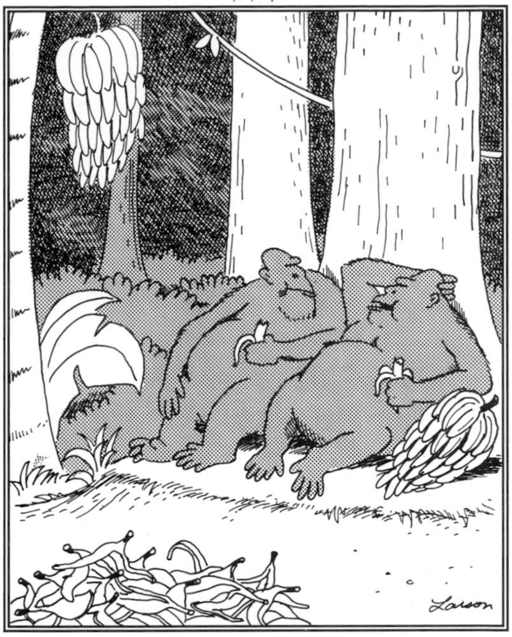

"You know, Sid, I really like bananas. ... I mean, I know that's not profound or nothin'. ... Heck! We *all* do. ... But for me, I think it goes far beyond that."

1/5/84

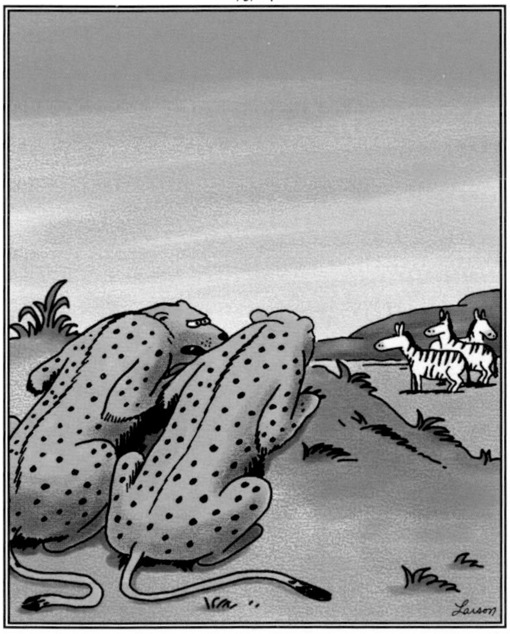

"Listen ... I'm fed up with this 'weeding out the sick and the old' business. ... I want something in its prime."

1/9/84

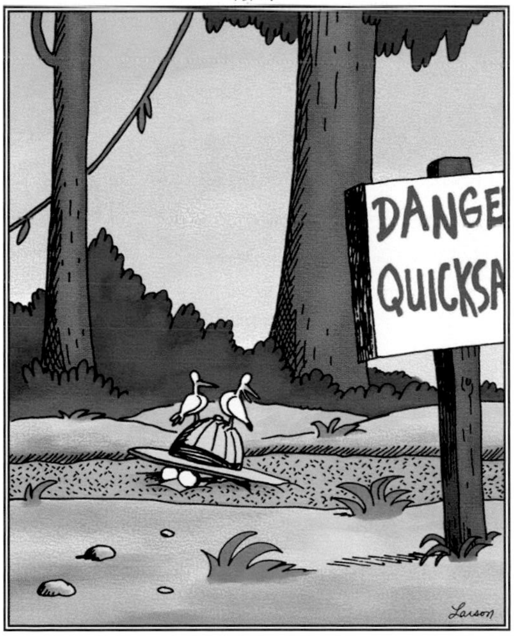
DANGE
QUICKSA

"Say, there's something wrong here. ... We may have to move shortly."

1/6/84

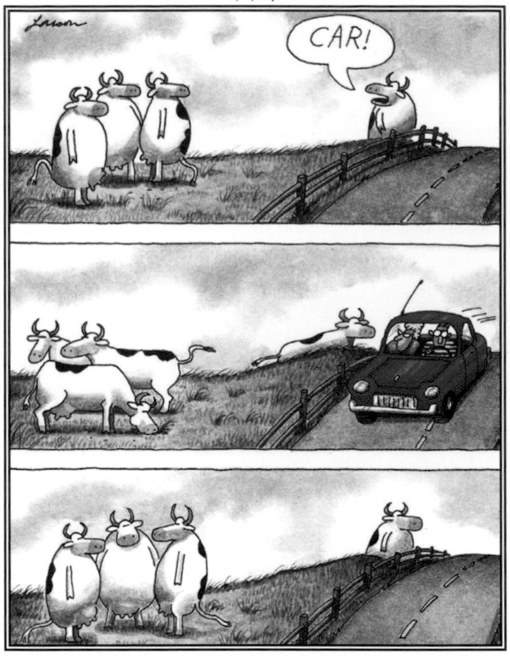
CAR!

1/7/84

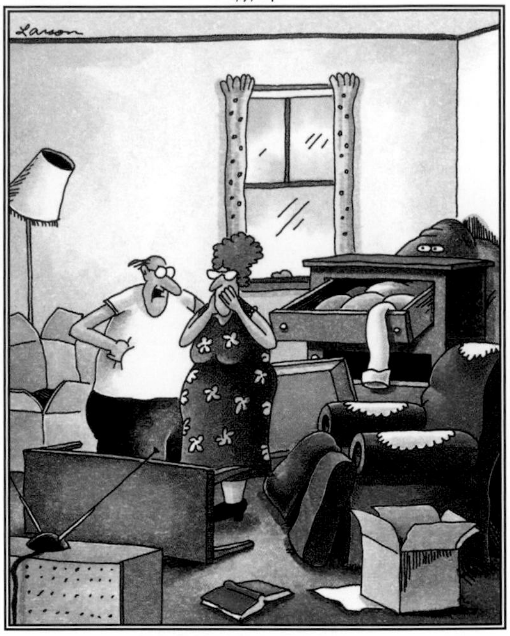

"Now calm down, Barbara. ... We haven't looked everywhere yet, and an elephant can't hide in here forever."

1/16/84

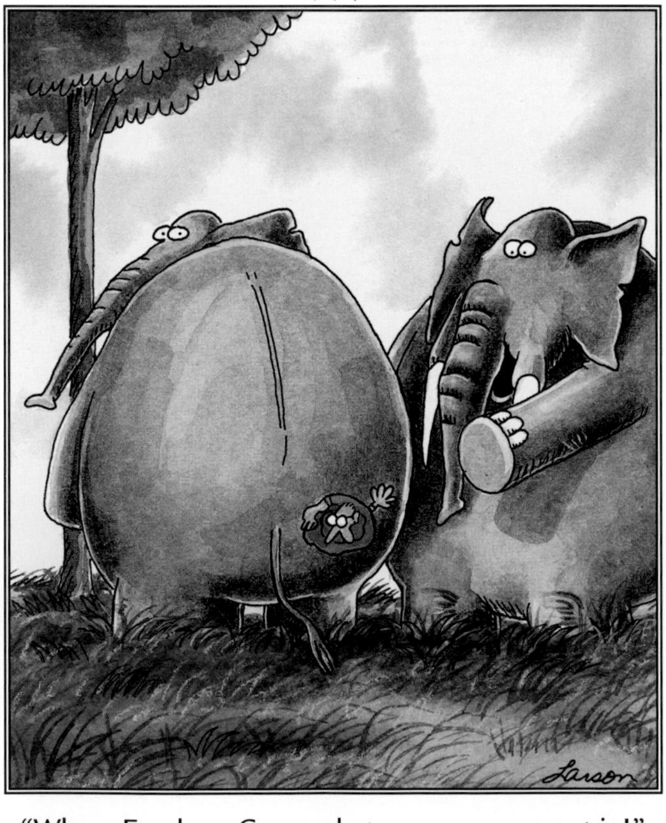

"Whoa, Frank. ... Guess what youuuuuuuuu sat in!"

1/17/84

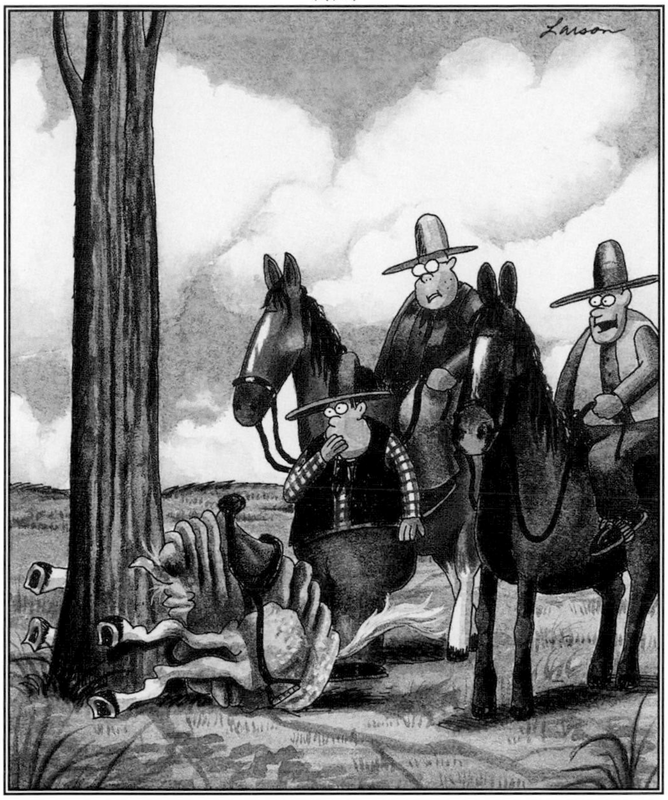

"What are you gonna tell your dad, Chuck?"

1/11/84

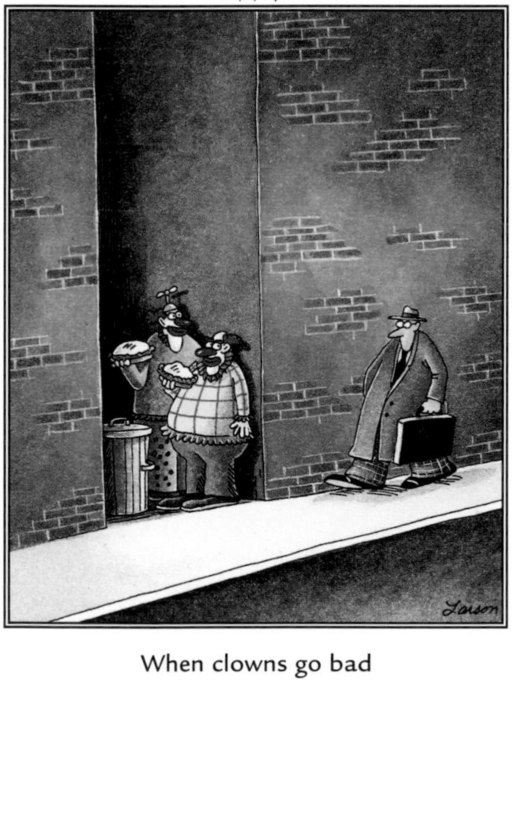

When clowns go bad

1/14/84

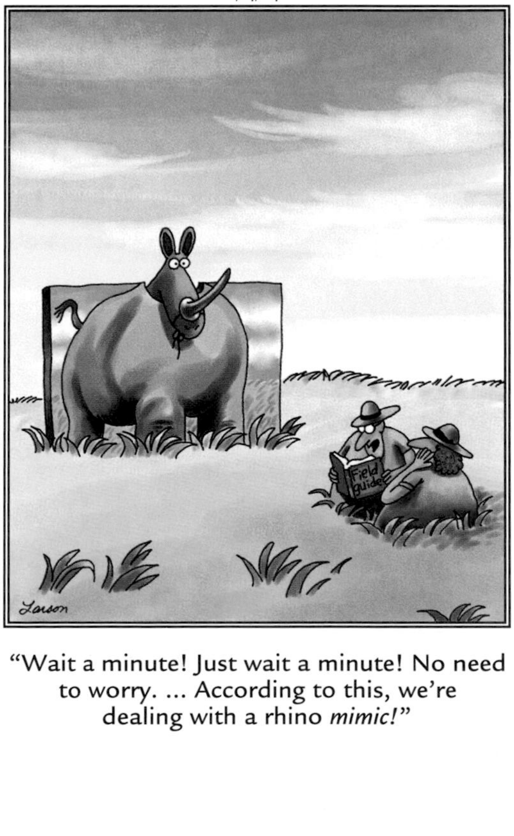
Field guide

"Wait a minute! Just wait a minute! No need to worry. ... According to this, we're dealing with a rhino *mimic!*"

1/20/84

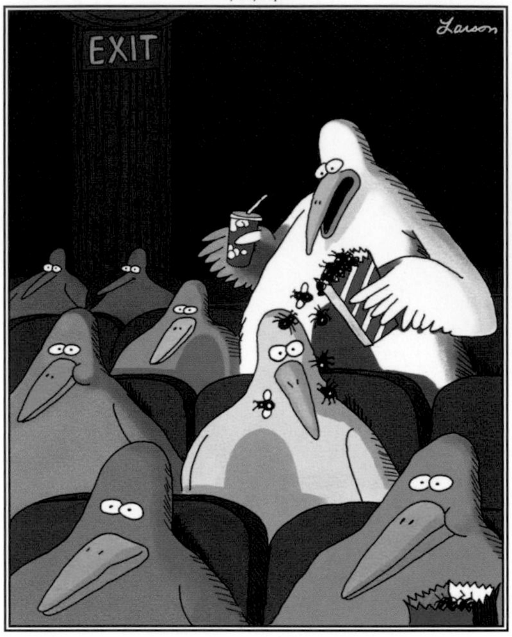
EXIT
Larson

"Dang! ... Sorry, buddy."

1/19/84

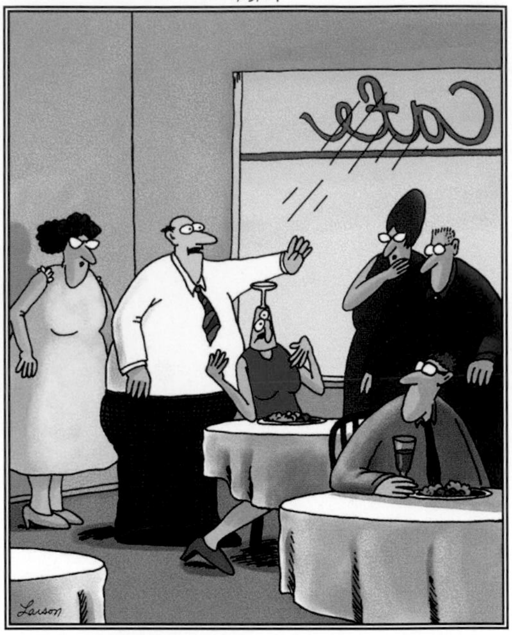
Larson

"Calm down, everyone! I've had experience with this sort of thing before. ... Does someone have a hammer?"

1/18/84

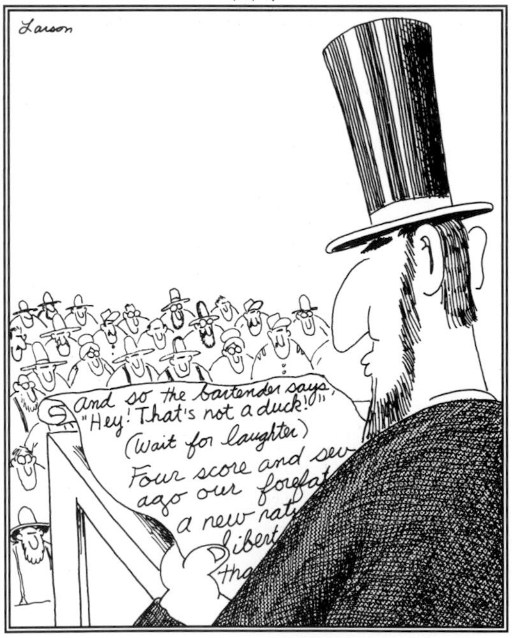
Larson
and so the bartender says,
"Hey! That's not a duck!"
(Wait for laughter)
Four score and sev
ago our forefat
a new nati
Libert
tha

1/21/84

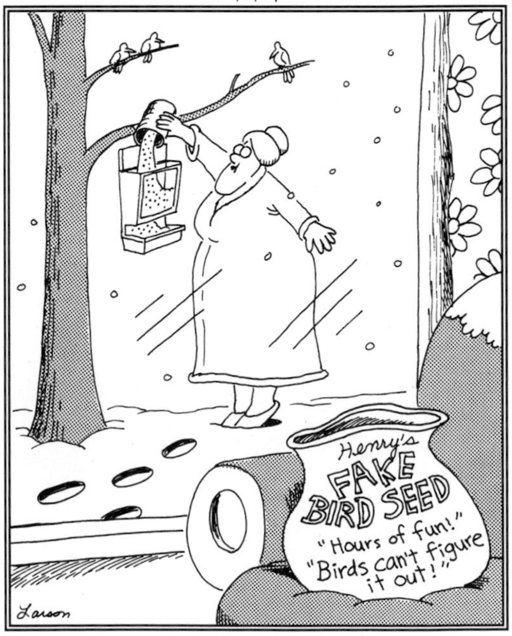
Henry's
FAKE
BIRD SEED
"Hours of fun!"
"Birds can't figure it out!"
Larson

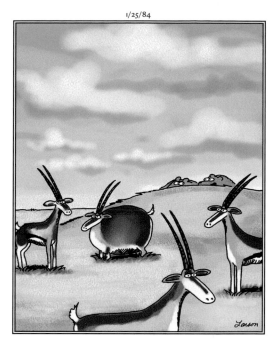

"Dibs."

Confused by the loud drums, Roy is flushed into the net.

Water buffaloes

1/23/84

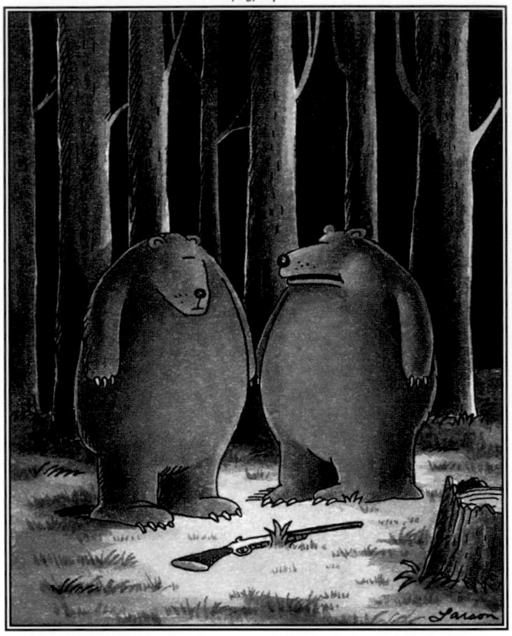

"Thunderstick? ... You actually said, 'Thunderstick'? ... That, my friend, is a Winchester thirty-aught-six."

1/27/84

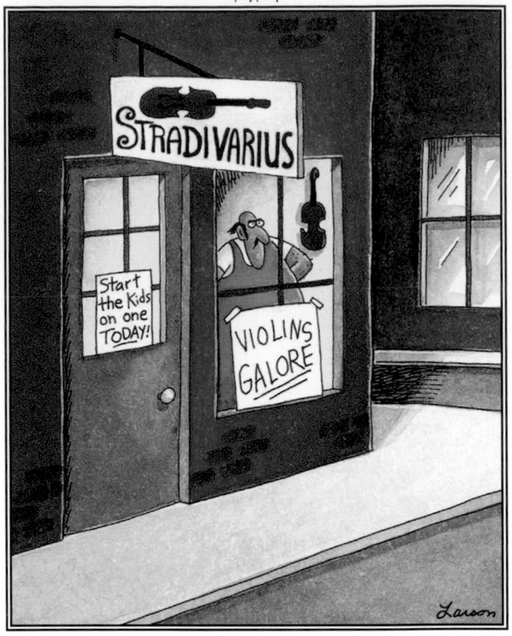
STRADIVARIUS
Start the Kids on one TODAY!
VIOLINS GALORE

1/26/84

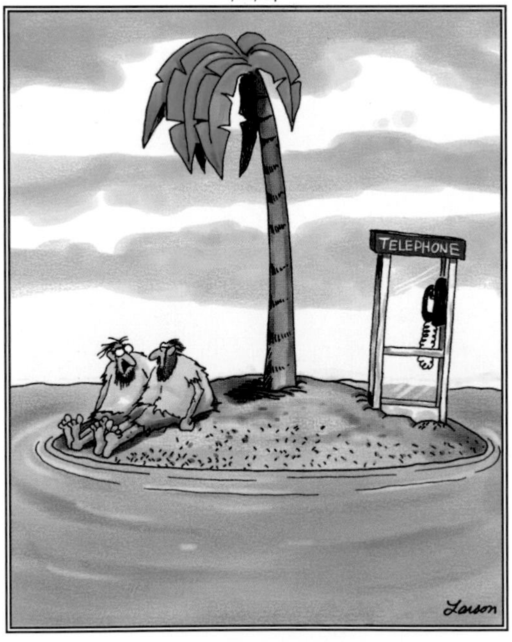
TELEPHONE

"For the one-hundredth time in as many days—I HAVEN'T GOT A QUARTER!"

1/30/84

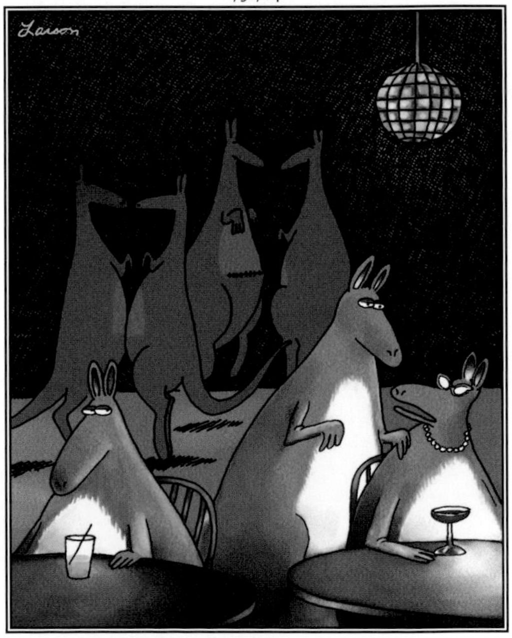

"No, thank you ... I don't jump."

2/2/84

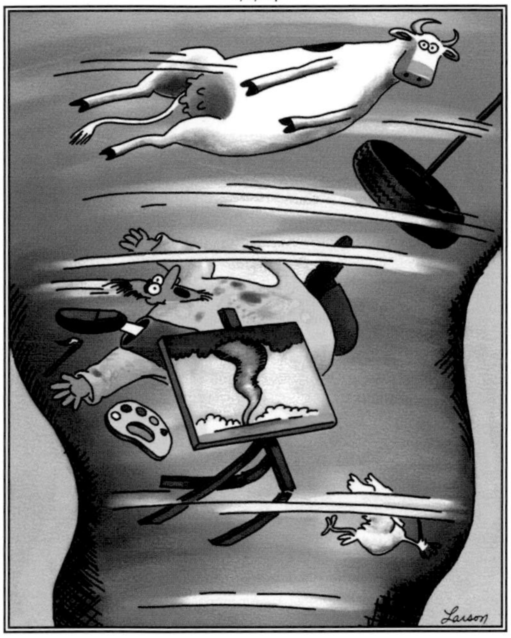

2/3/84

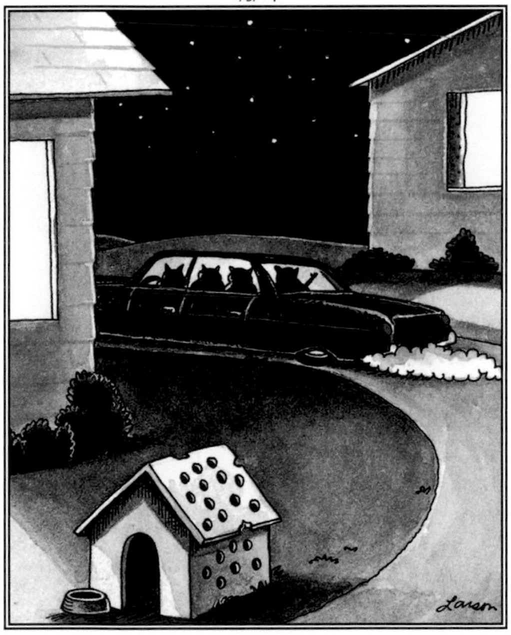

2/4/84

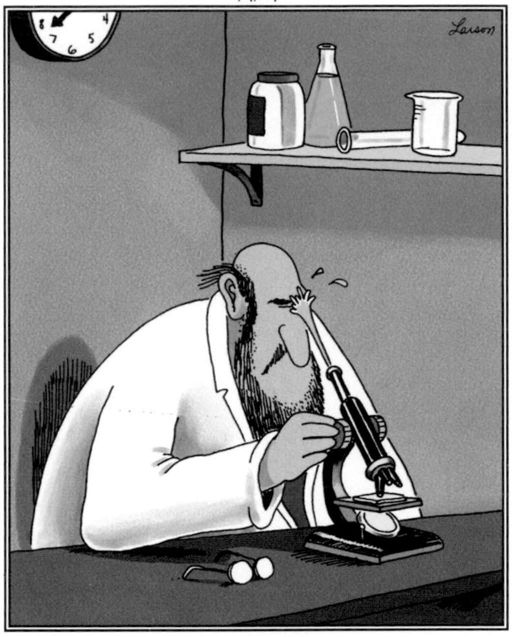

Paramecium humor

2/6/84

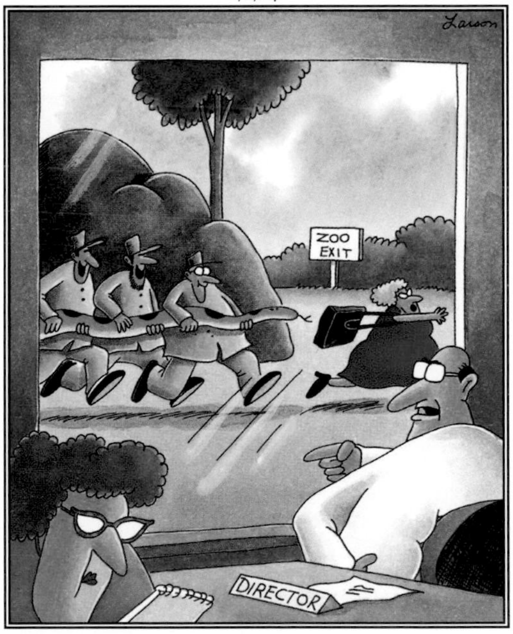
ZOO
EXIT
DIRECTOR

"Take another memo, Miss Wilkens. ... I want to see all reptile personnel in my office first thing tomorrow morning!"

2/1/84

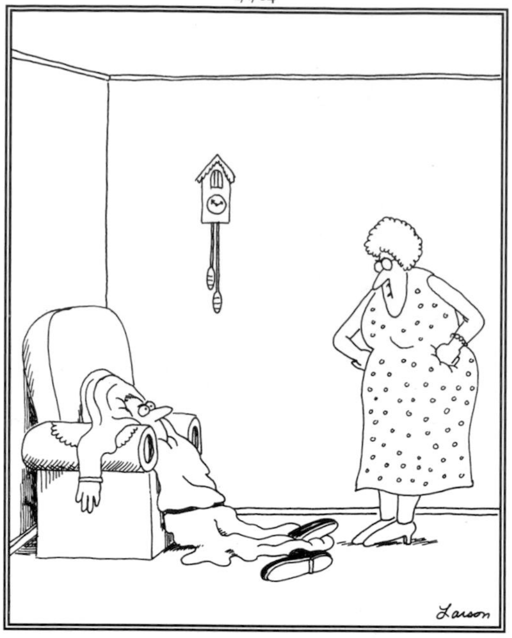

"Irwin, you're nothing but a spineless, slimy, gelatinous blob. ... There, I've finally said it."

2/11/84

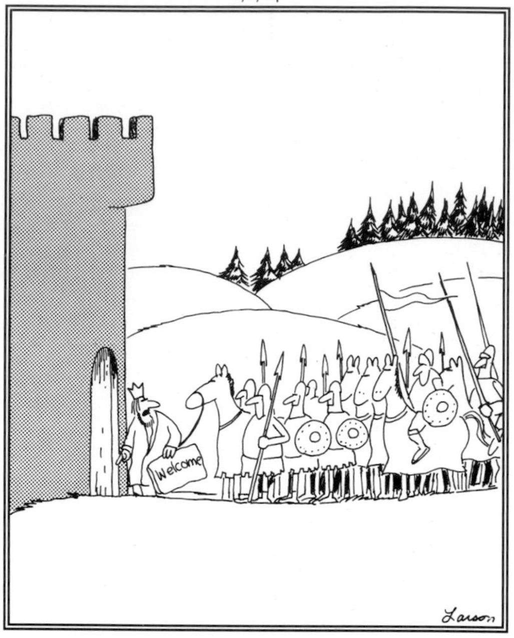
Welcome

"Well, this is great. ... Some imbecile has taken the key from under the mat!"

2/7/84

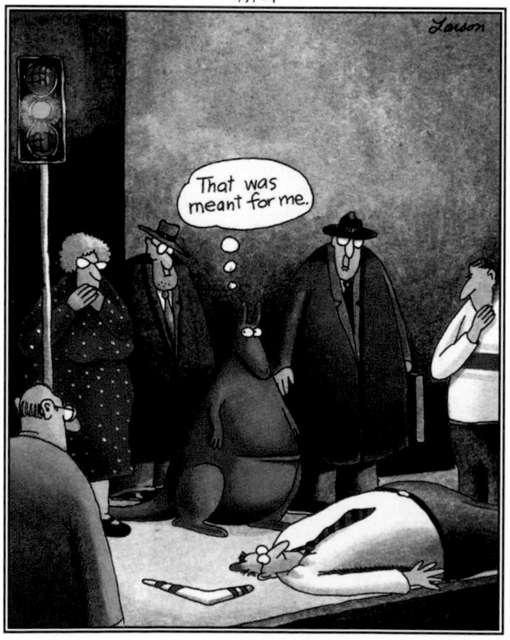
That was meant for me.

2/8/84

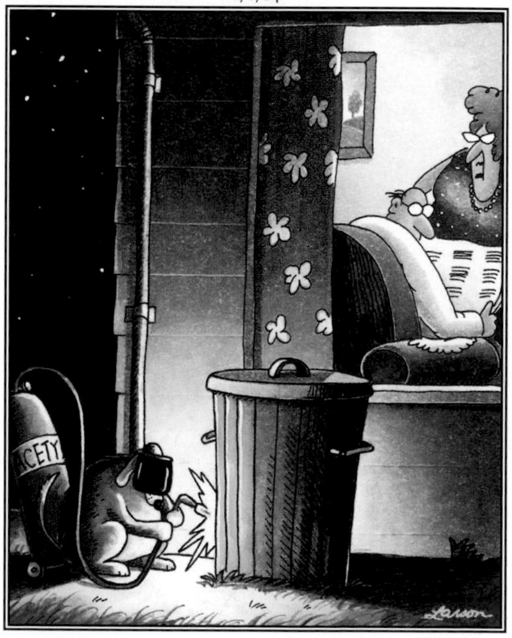

"Vernon! That light! ... The Jeffersons' dog is back!"

2/13/84

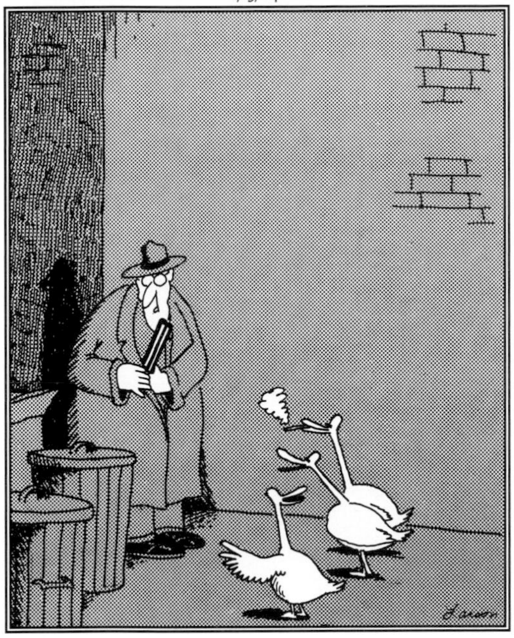

Cornered by the street ducks, Phil wasn't exactly sure what to do—and then he remembered his 12 gauge.

2/9/84

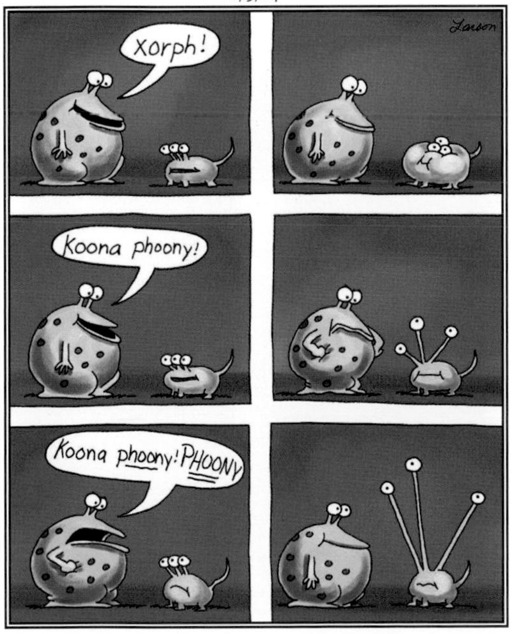
Xorph!
Koona phoony!
Koona phoony! PHOONY

Pet tricks on other planets

2/17/84

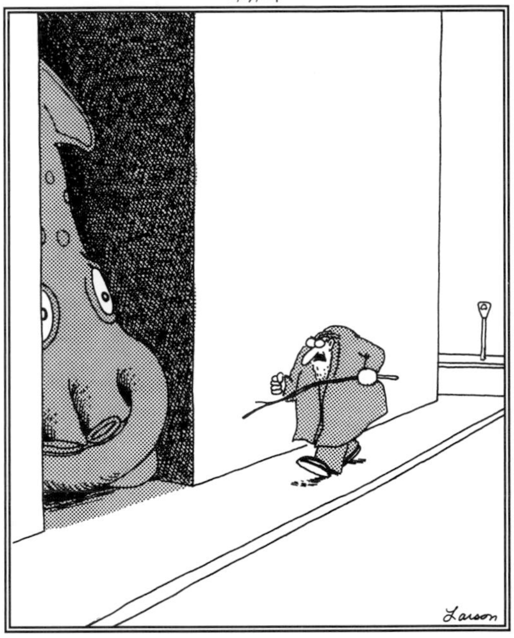

"I've had it! This time I've really had it! ... Jump the fence again, will he? ... Dang!"

2/10/84

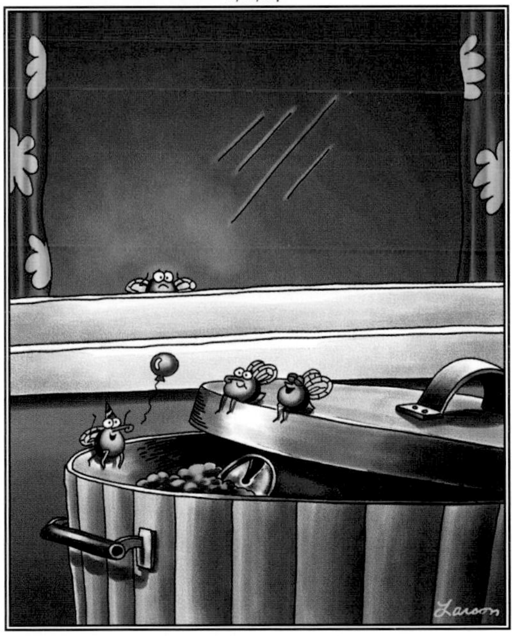

2/14/84

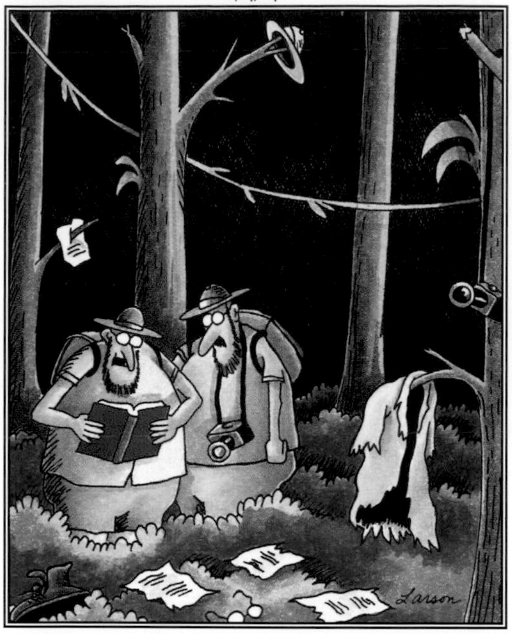
Larson

"Here's the last entry in Carlson's journal: 'Having won their confidence, tomorrow I shall test the humor of these giant but gentle primates with a simple joy-buzzer handshake.'"

2/16/84

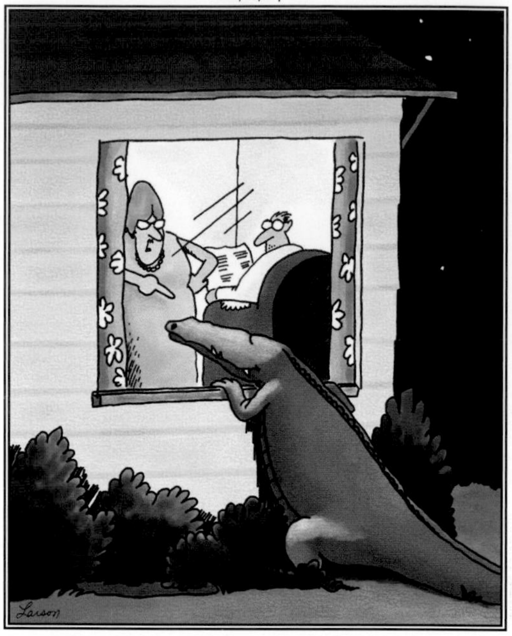
Larson

"It's back, Arnie! Okay—get the book! ... We're gonna settle whether it's an alligator or a crocodile once and for all!"

2/15/84

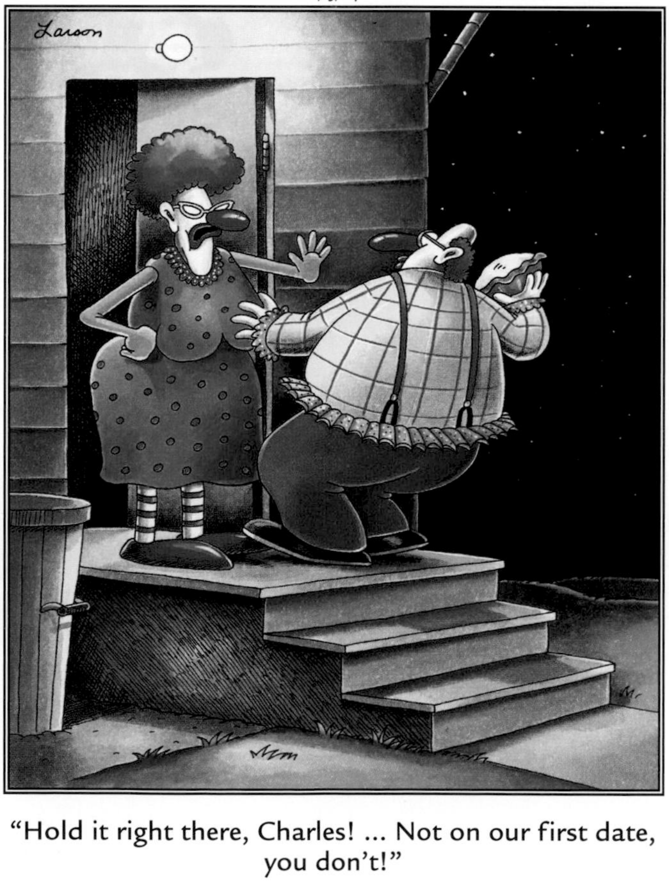
Larson

"Hold it right there, Charles! ... Not on our first date, you don't!"

2/18/84

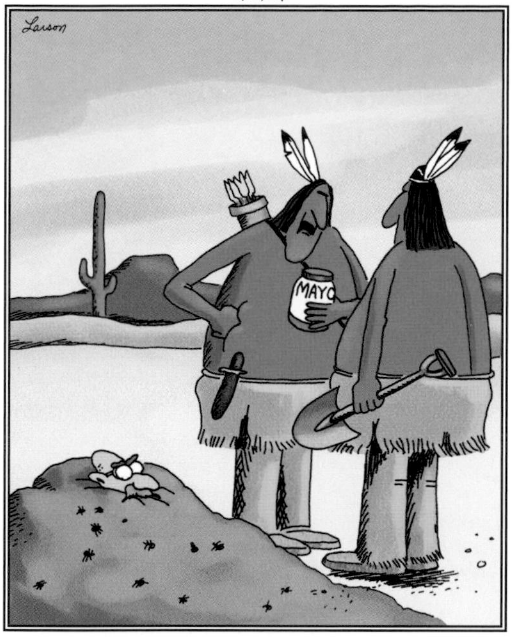
Larson
MAYO

“You fool! ‘Bring the honey,’ I said. …
This isn’t the same thing!”

2/20/84

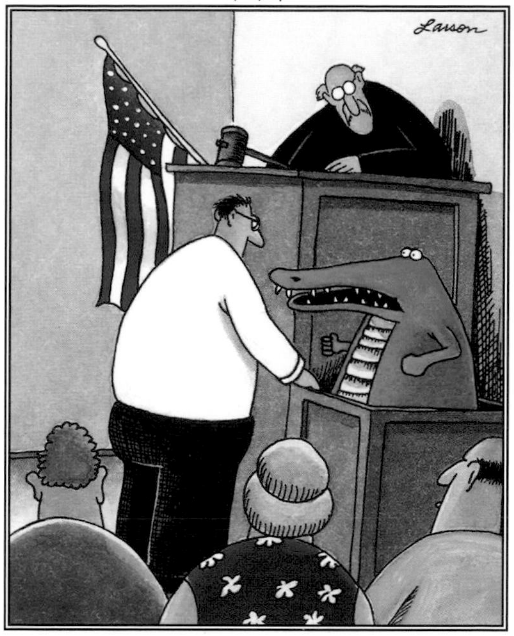
Larson

“Well, of *course* I did it in cold blood,
you idiot! … I’m a reptile!”

2/24/84

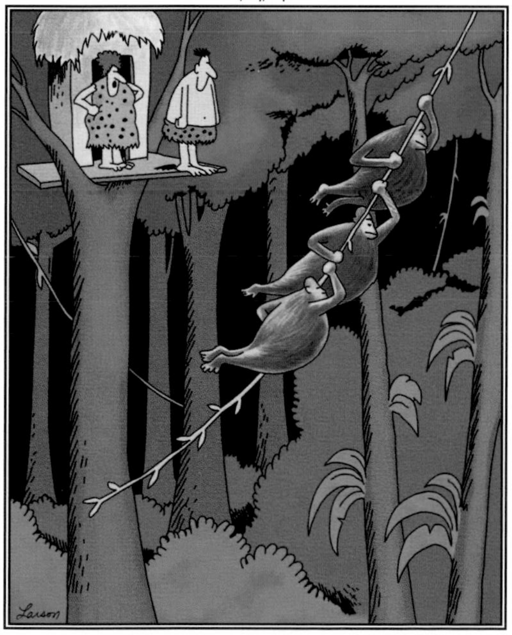
Larson

“Well, you’ve overslept and missed your
vine again.”

2/29/84

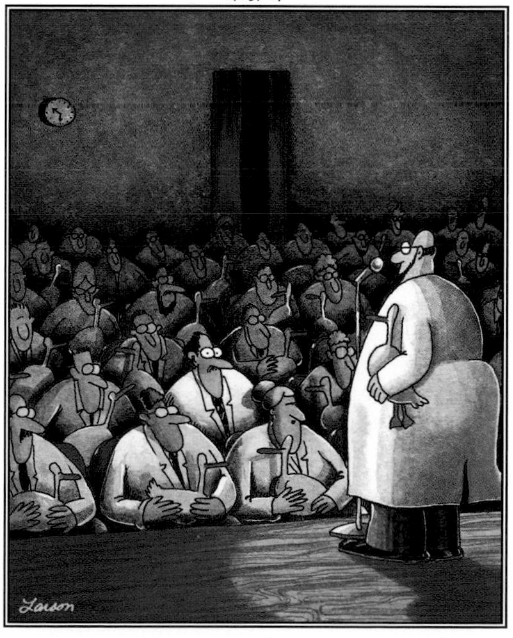
Larson

Suddenly, Professor Liebowitz realizes he has
come to the seminar without his duck.

2/21/84

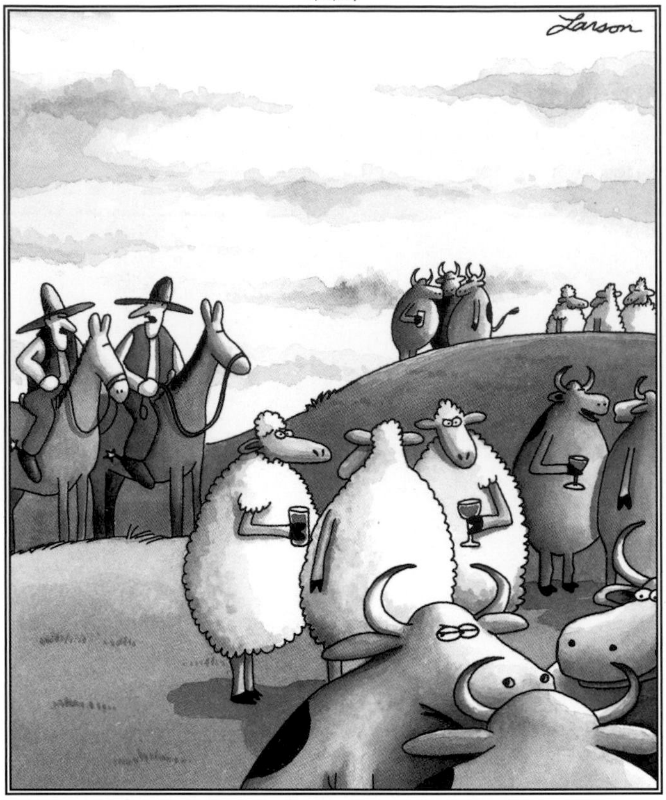
Larson

"Well, what have I always said? ... Sheep and cattle just don't mix."

2/22/84

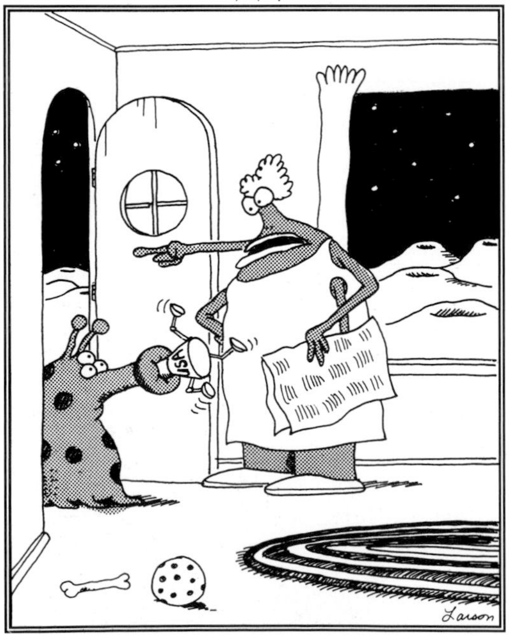
USA
Larson

"Aaaaaaa! ... No, Zooky! Grok et bok! ... Shoosh! Shoosh! ..."

2/23/84

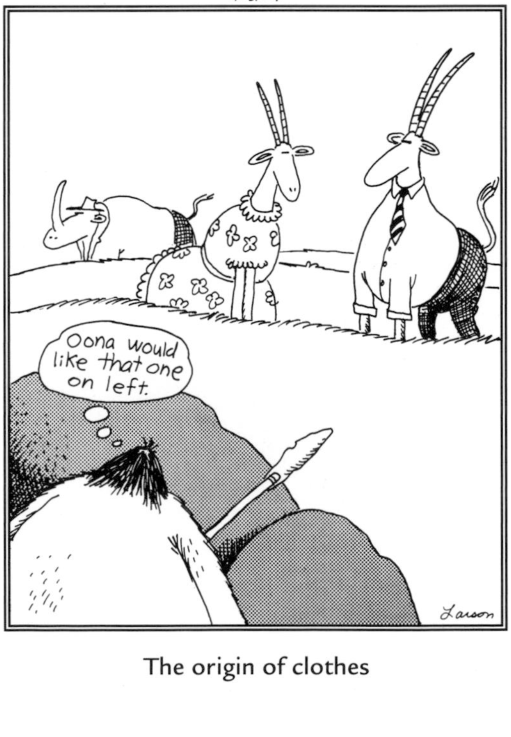
Oona would like that one on left.
Larson

The origin of clothes

2/27/84

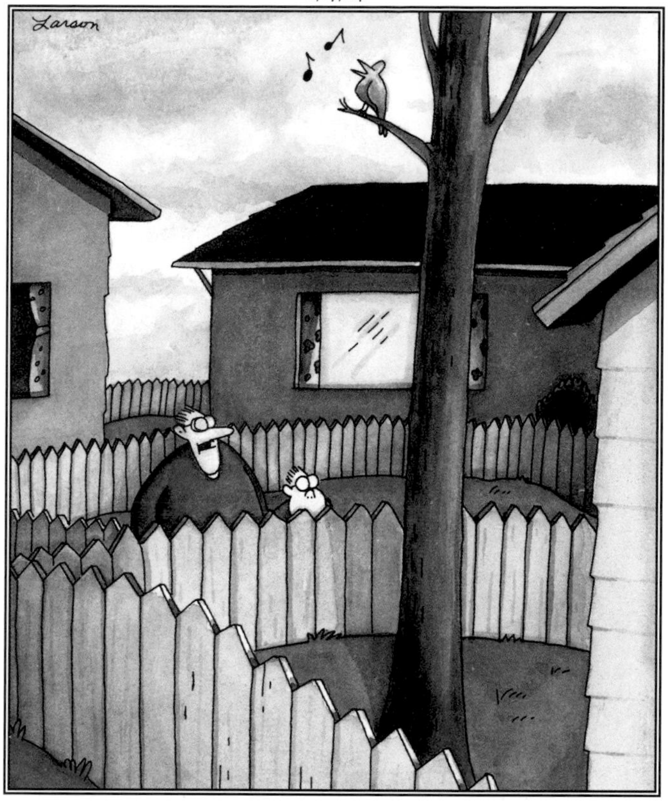
Larson

"And now, Randy, by use of song, the male sparrow will stake out his territory ... an instinct common in the lower animals."

2/25/84

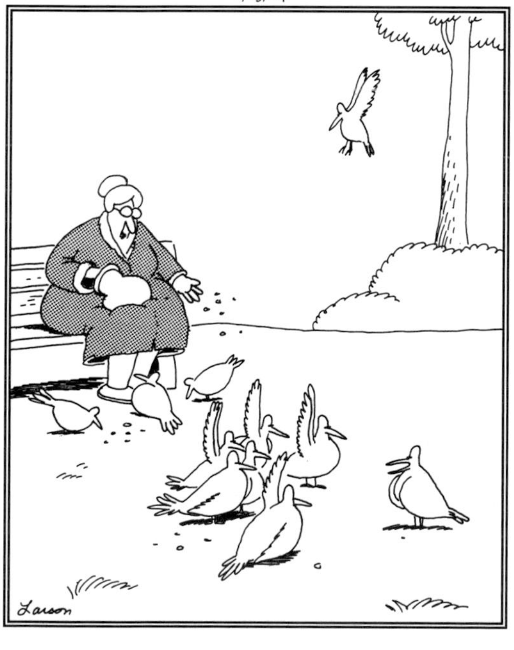
Larson

"I've got an idea. ... How many here have ever seen Alfred Hitchcock's *The Birds*?"

2/28/84

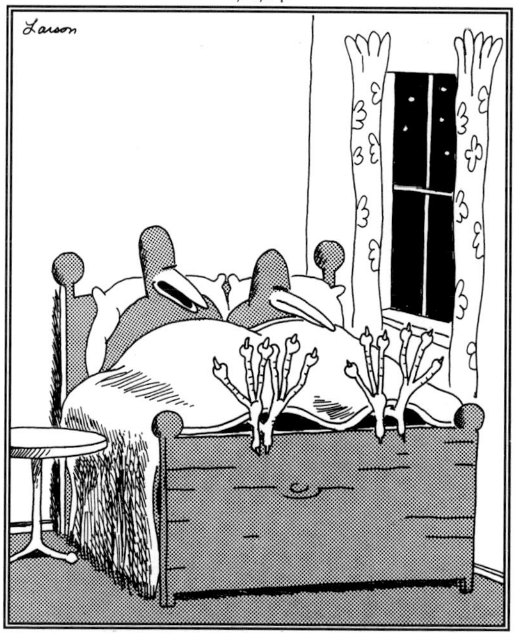
Larson

"Well, I dunno, Warren ... I think your feet may be uglier than mine."

3/1/84

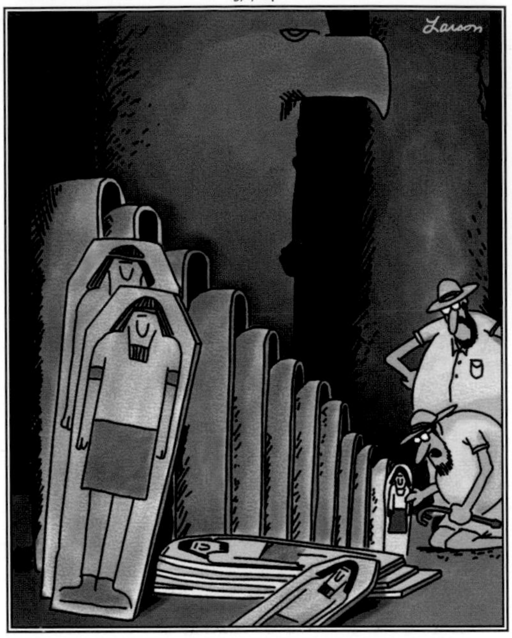

"What the? ... *Another* little casket?"

3/2/84

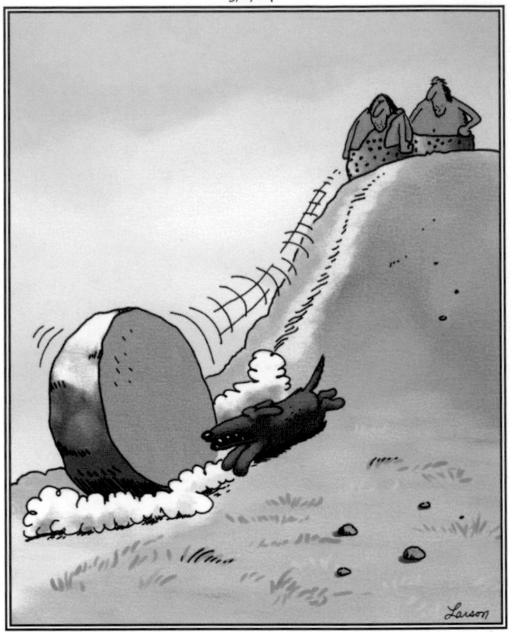

3/3/84

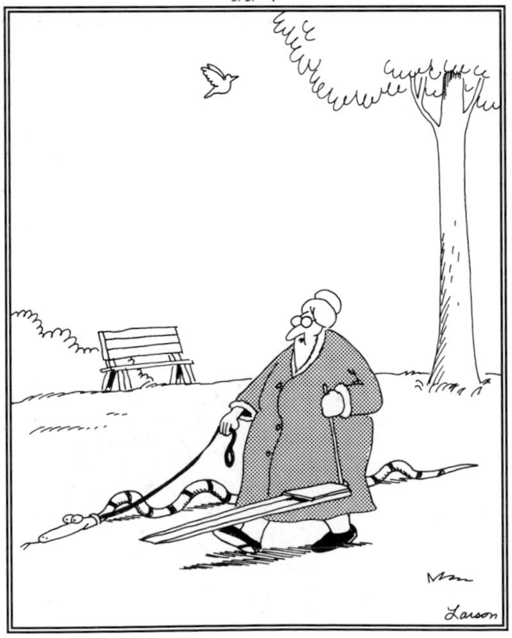

3/7/84

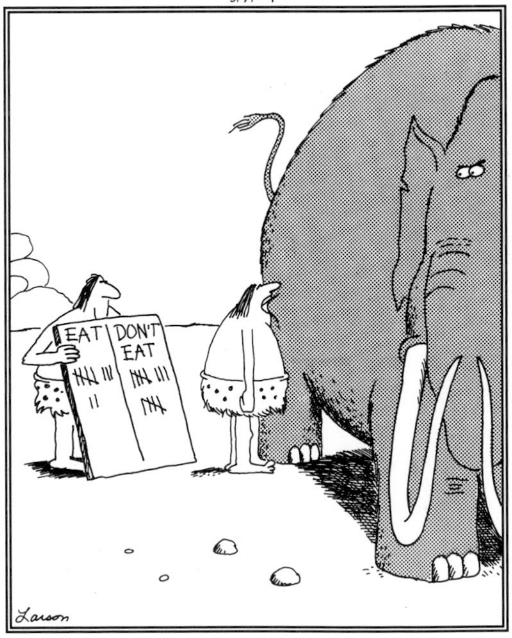
EAT
DON'T EAT

3/9/84

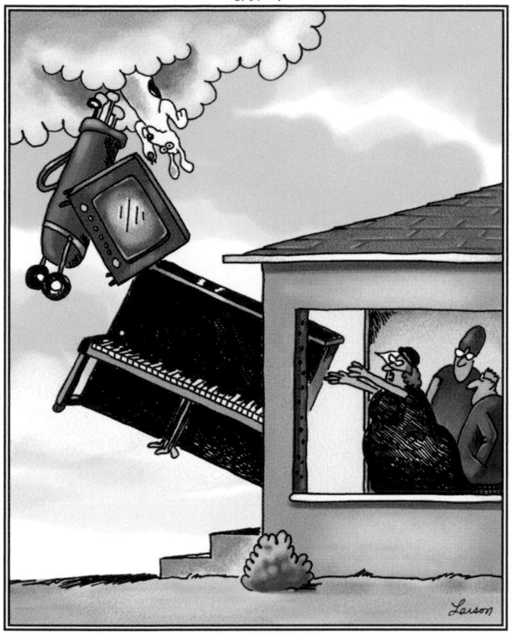
Larson

"Aaaaaaa! ... It's George! He's taking it with him!"

3/5/84

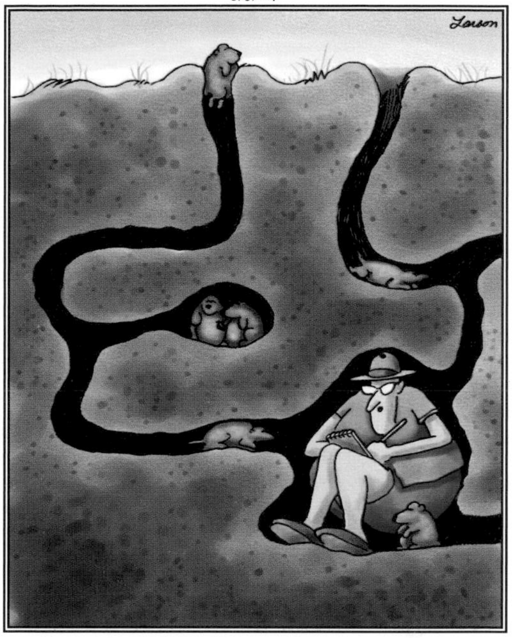
Larson

"March 5, 1984: After several months, I now feel that these strange little rodents have finally accepted me as one of their own."

3/8/84

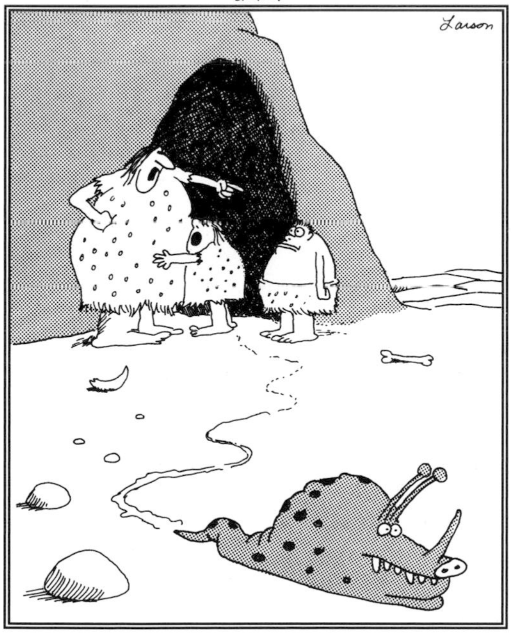
Larson

"Grobby! Bad! ... Not put things down Oona's back no more!"

3/10/84

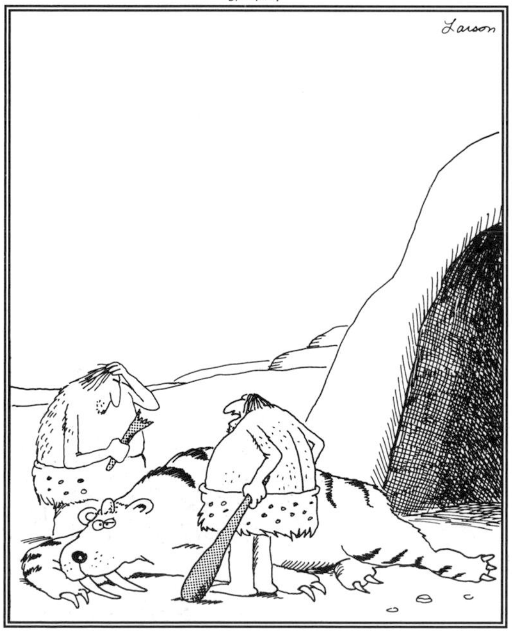
Larson

"Always keep label up, Dag."

3/6/84

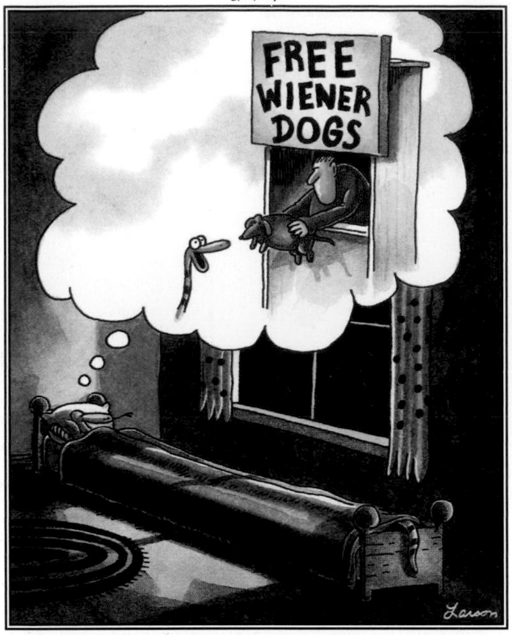
FREE
WIENER
DOGS
Larson

Snake dreams

3/12/84

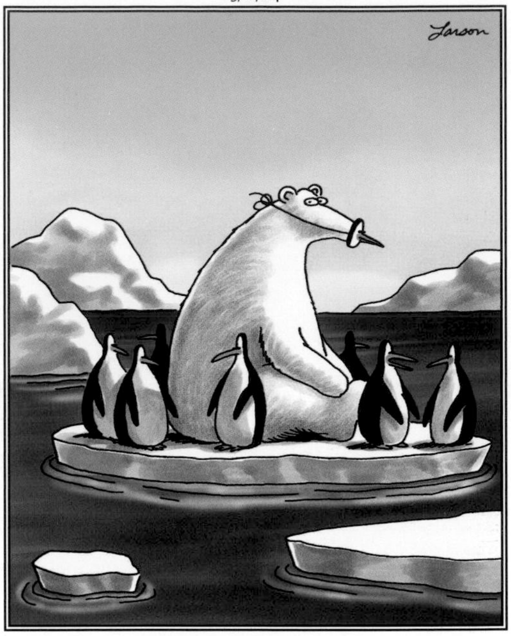
Larson

"And now Edgar's gone. ... Something's going on around here."

3/13/84

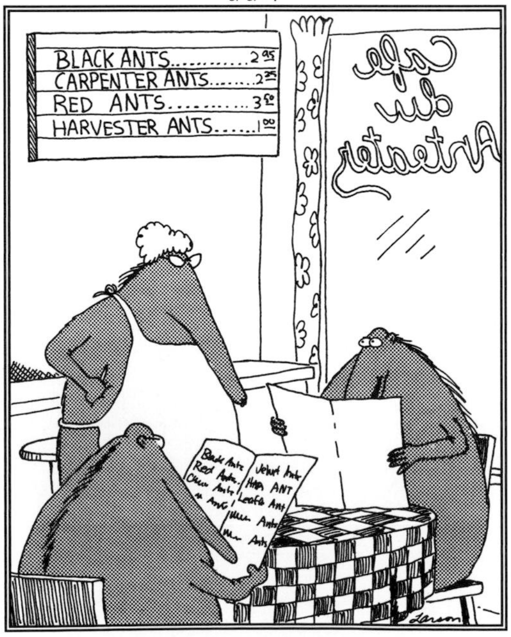
BLACK ANTS..........2.95
CARPENTER ANTS.......2.25
RED ANTS..........3.50
HARVESTER ANTS......1.00
Larson

"Hmmmm. ... Are the red ants right off the hill?"

3/15/84

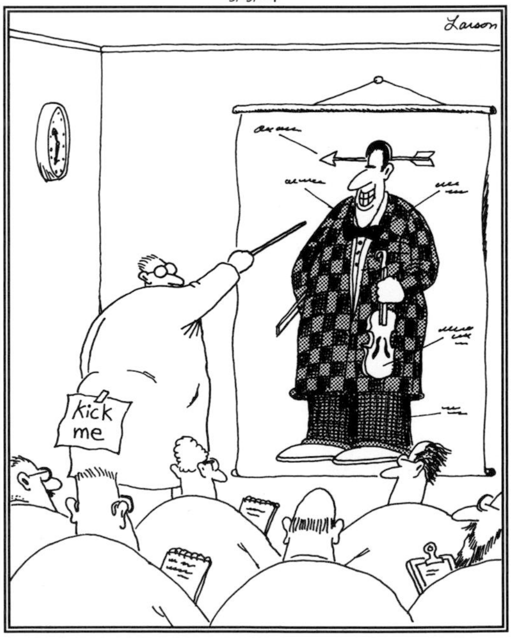
Larson
kick me

Analyzing humor

Stimulus-response behavior in dogs

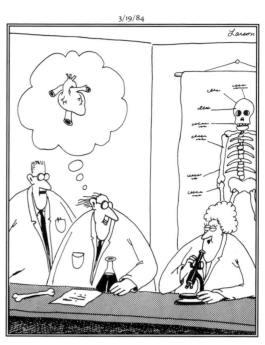

"I believe, Farnsworth, that the data from the previous tissue sample was ... Farnsworth! Are you listening to me?"

"Oh, that's right! You *did* have a hat. ... I believe you'll find it in the other room."

"Guess who!"

Nature scenes we rarely see

"That time was just too close, George! ...
Jimmy was headed straight for the
snake-pit when I grabbed him!"

"Listen ... you've got to relax. ... The more you
think about changing colors, the less chance
you'll succeed. ... Shall we try the green
background again?"

3/27/84

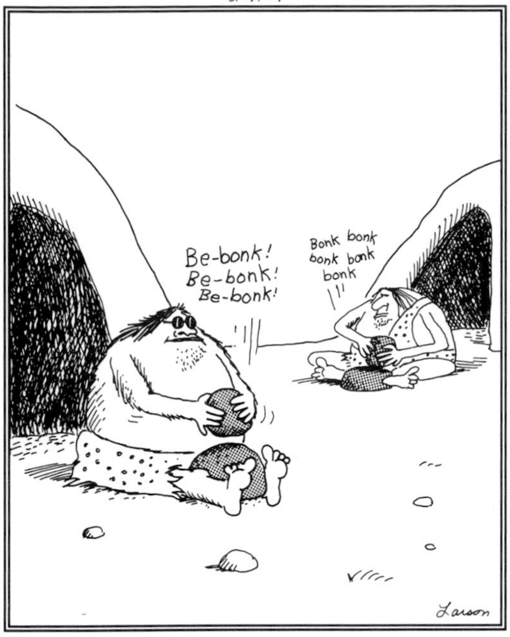
Be-bonk!
Be-bonk!
Be-bonk!
Bonk bonk
bonk bonk
bonk
Larson

The birth of jazz

3/28/84

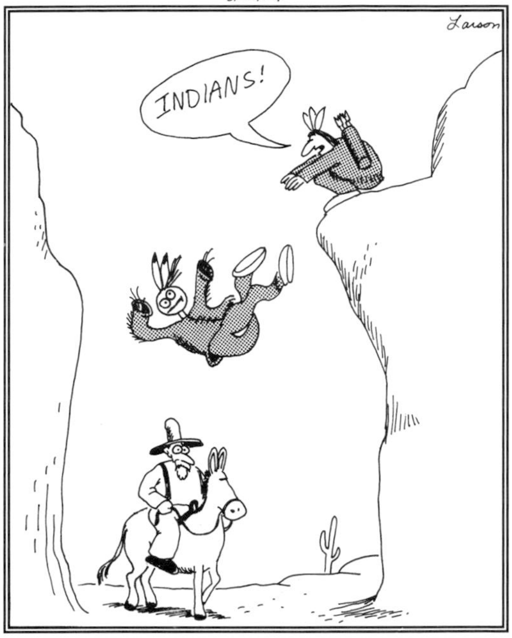
Larson
INDIANS!

Humor in the Old West

3/30/84

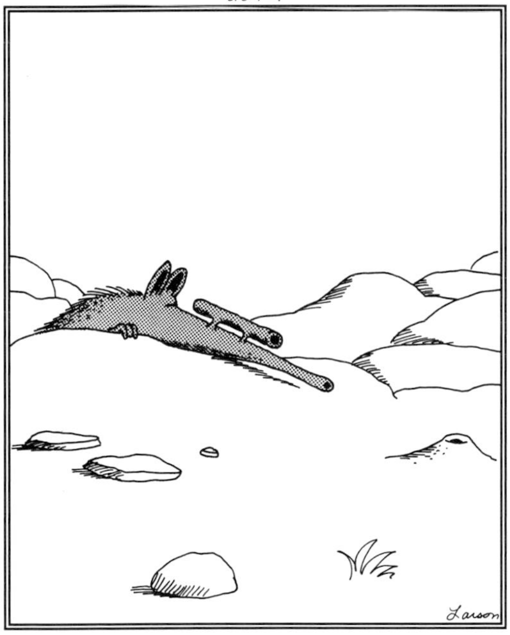
Larson

Anteaters of the future

3/31/84

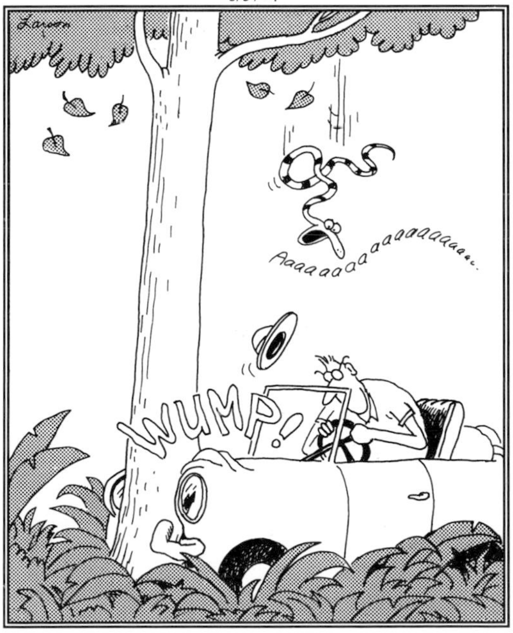
Larson
Aaaaaaaaaaaaaaaaaaaaa...
WUMP!

3/23/84

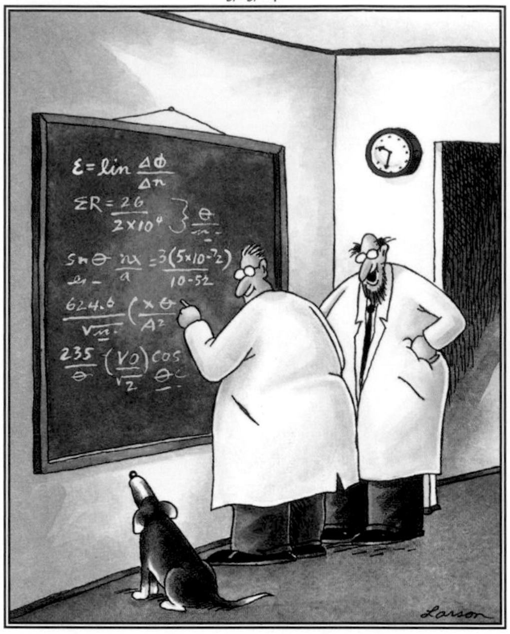
Larson

"Ohhhhhhh. ... Look at that, Schuster. ... Dogs are so cute when they try to comprehend quantum mechanics."

3/29/84

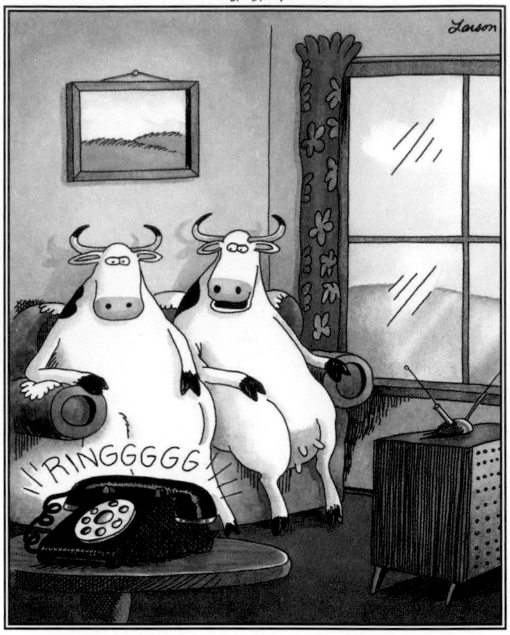
Larson
RINGGGGG

"Well, there it goes again. ... And we just sit here without opposable thumbs."

3/26/84

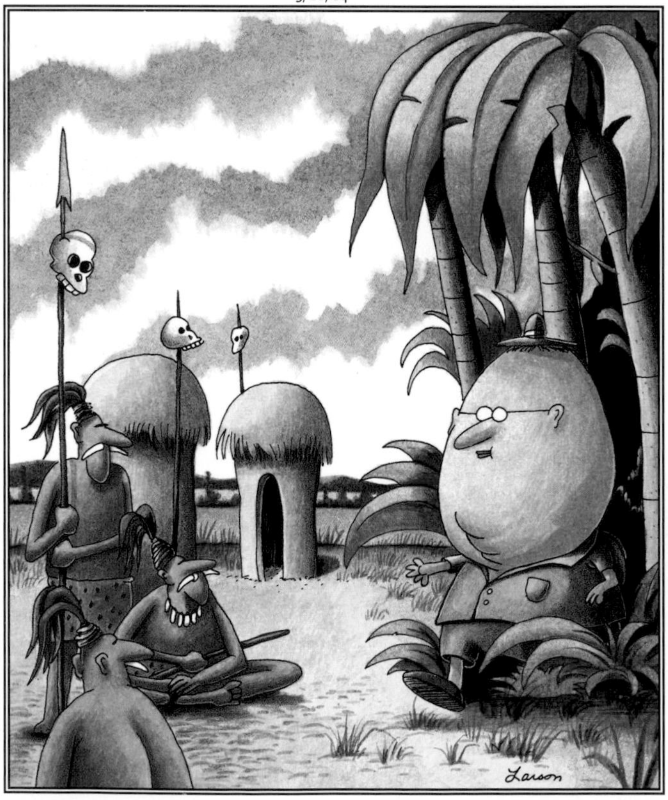
Larson

Unwittingly, Palmer stepped out of the jungle and into headhunter folklore forever.

4/6/84

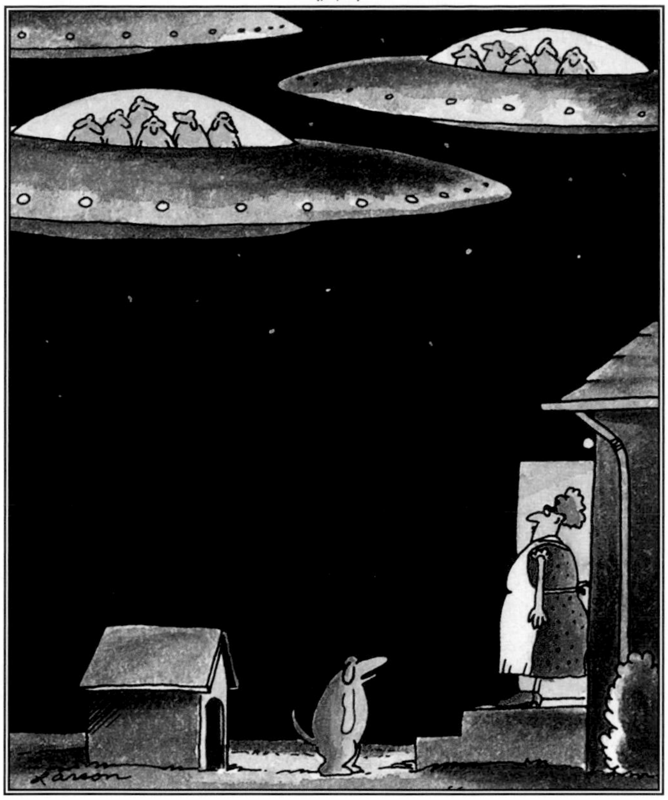

"Well, they finally came ... but before I go, let's see you roll over a couple times."

4/4/84

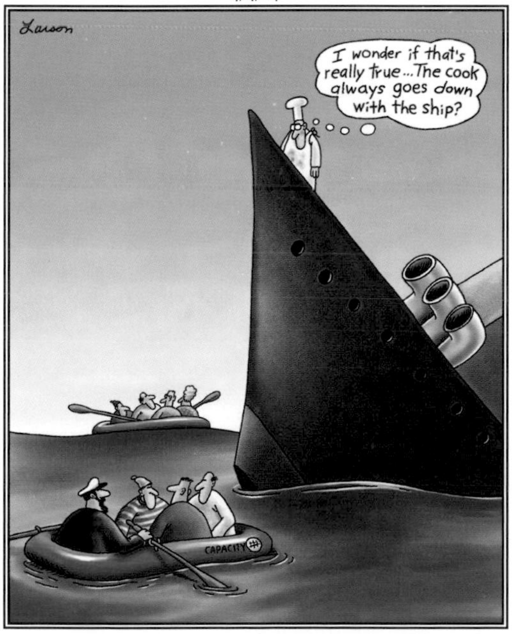
I wonder if that's really true...The cook always goes down with the ship?
CAPACITY

4/3/84

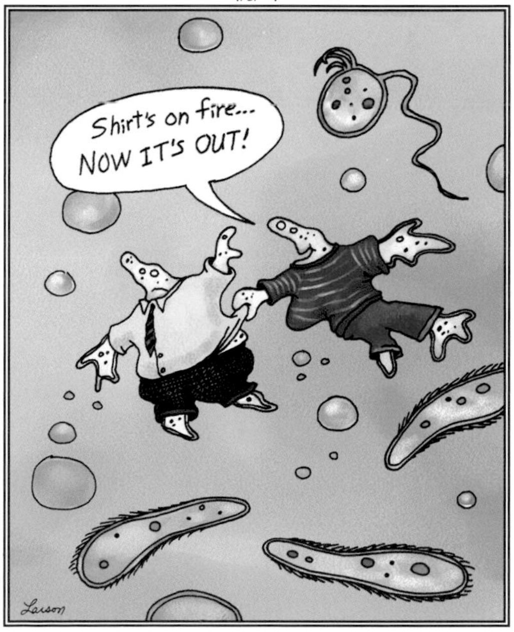
Shirt's on fire... NOW IT'S OUT!

Humor at its lowest form

4/2/84

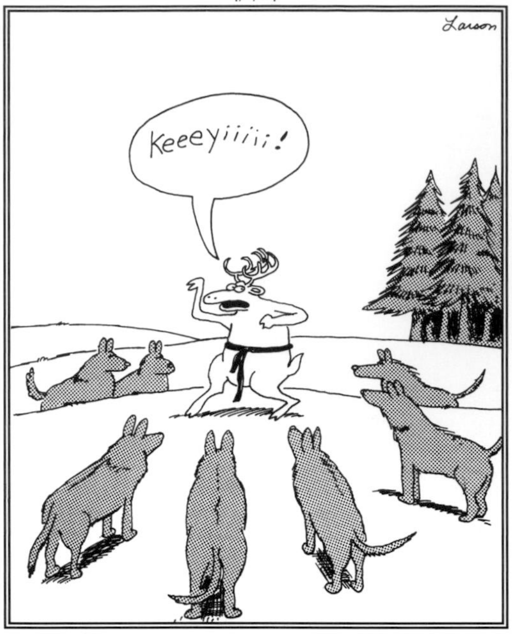
Keeeyiiiii!

4/11/84

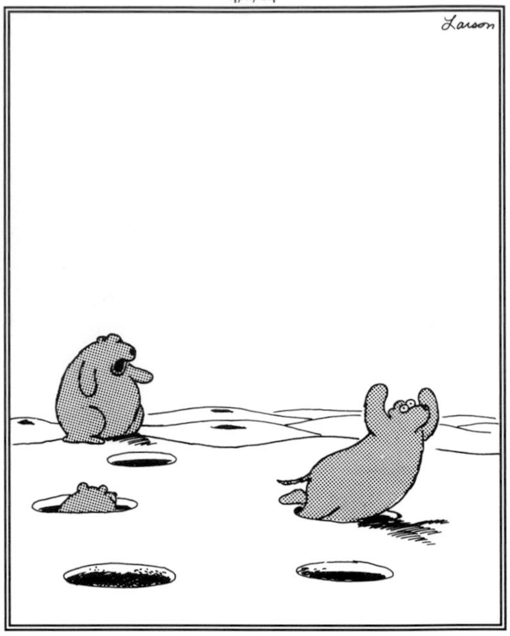

"Carl! Watch for holes!"

4/12/84

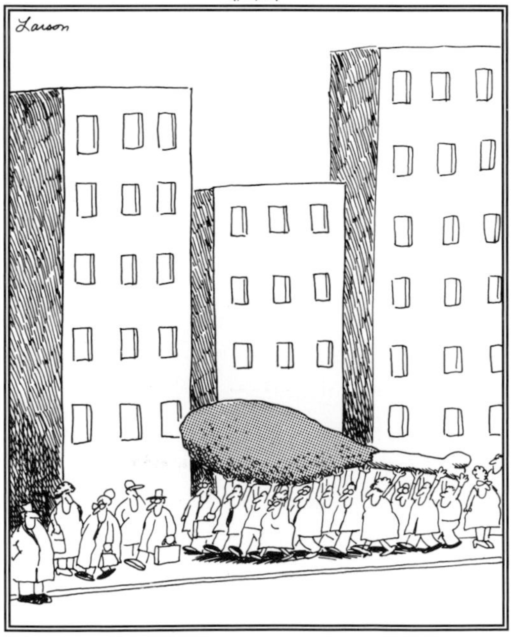

How social animals work together

4/13/84

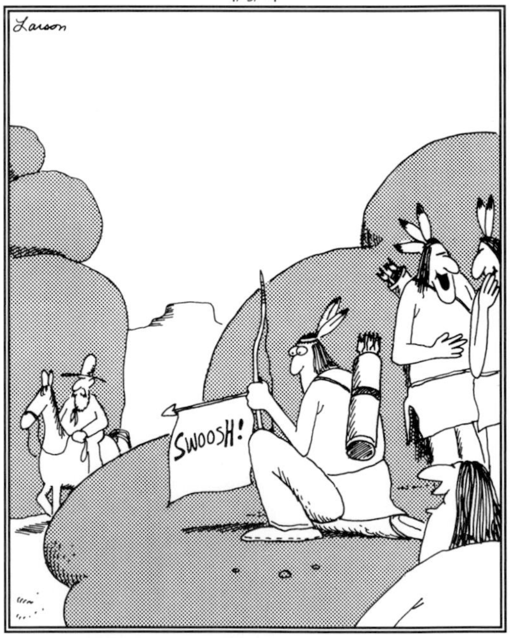
SWOOSH!

Releasing the shaft, Red Bear falls victim to the old fake-bow-and-arrow trick.

4/7/84

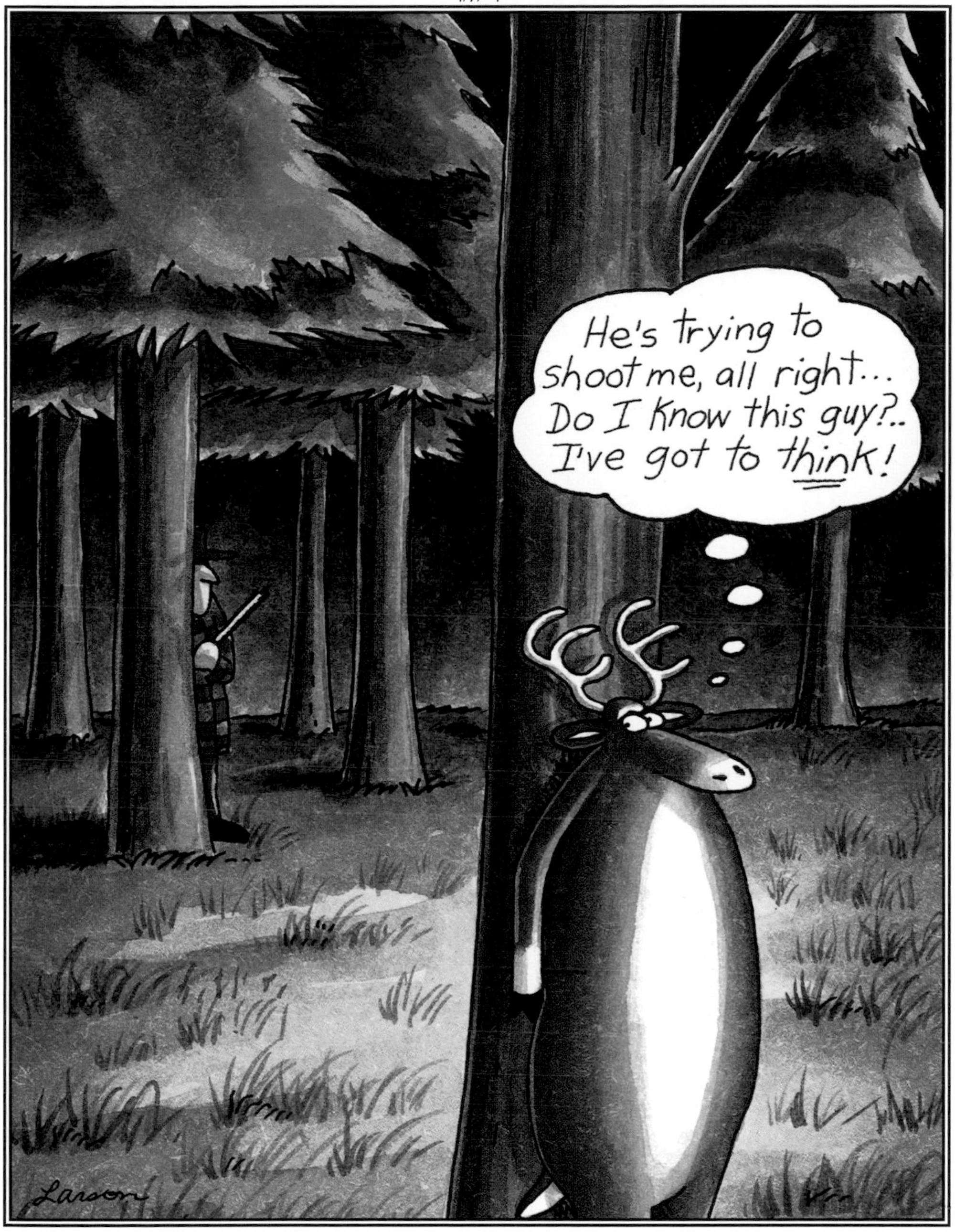
He's trying to shoot me, all right... Do I know this guy?.. I've got to think!
Larson

4/5/84

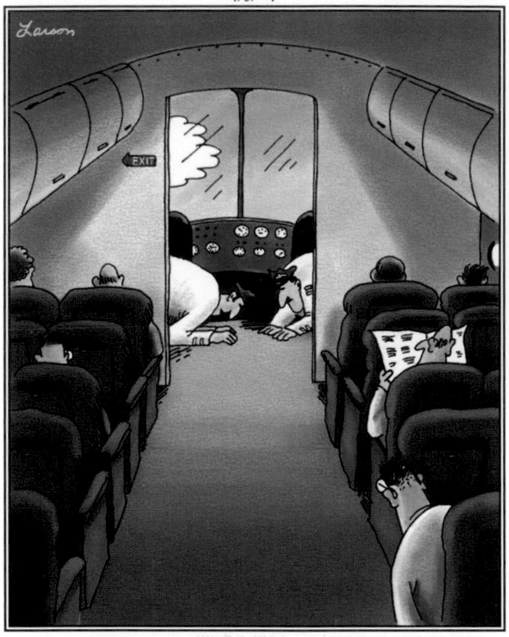
Larson
EXIT

"Well, there is some irony in all this, you know. ... I mean, we *both* lose a contact at the same time?!"

4/9/84

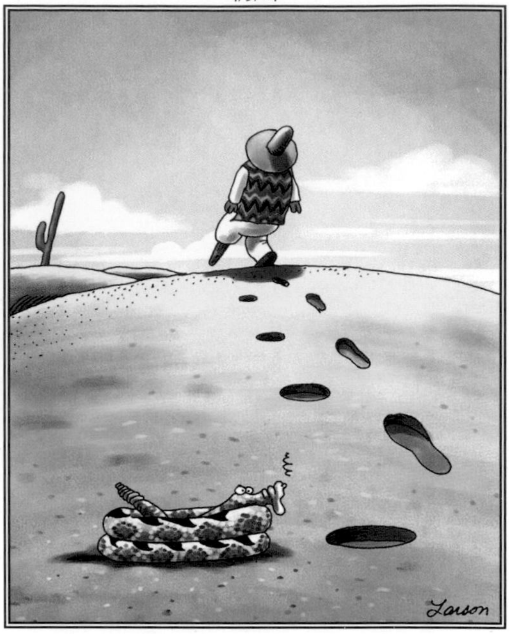
Larson

4/10/84

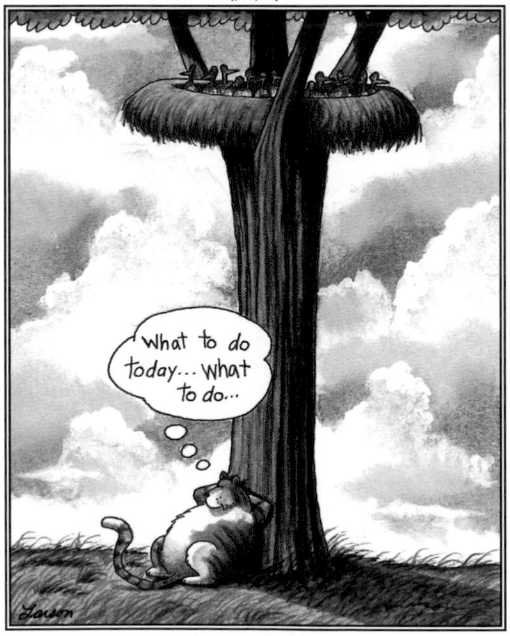
What to do today... what to do...
Larson

4/14/84

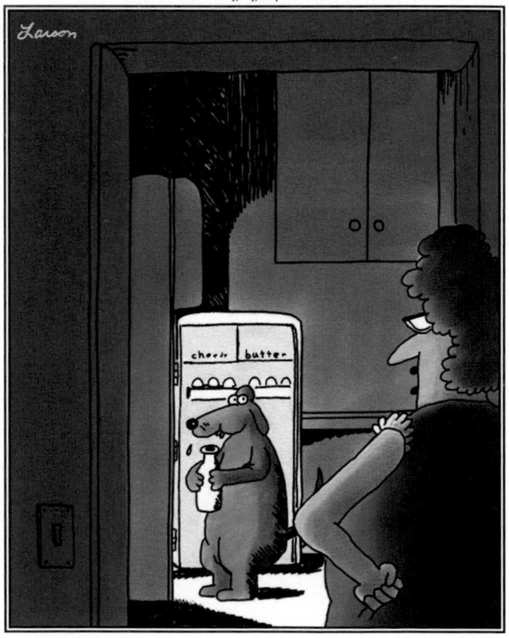
Larson
butter

"Aha! As I always suspected! ... I better not ever catch you drinking right from the bottle *again!*"

4/18/84

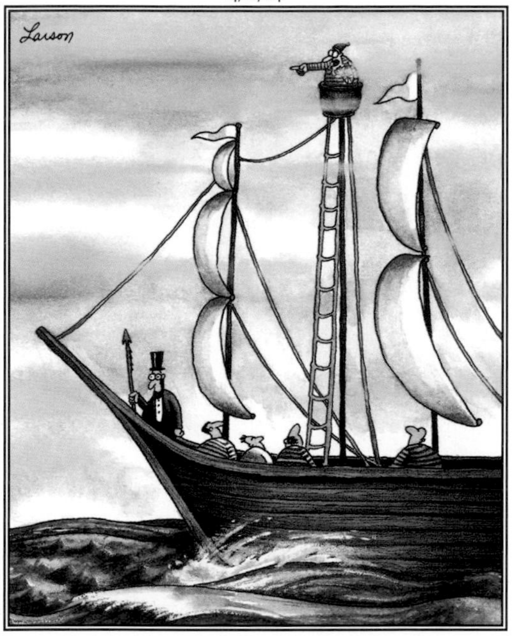
Larson

"The white whale! The whiiiiiiite wh ... no, no ... my mistake! ... A black whale! A regular, blaaaaaack whale!"

4/17/84

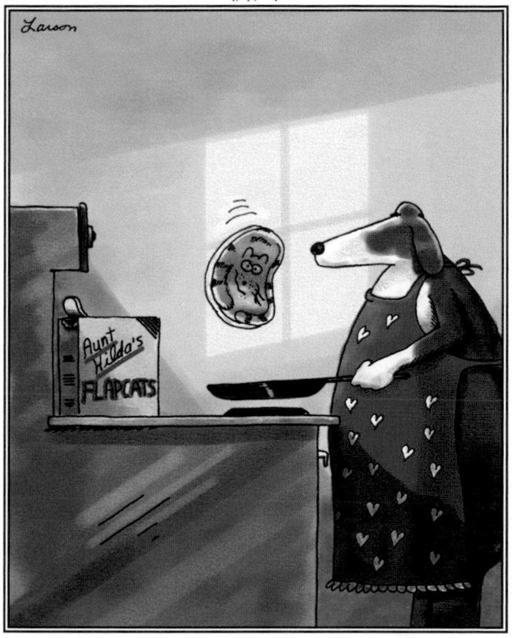
Larson
Aunt Hilda's
FLAPCATS

4/19/84

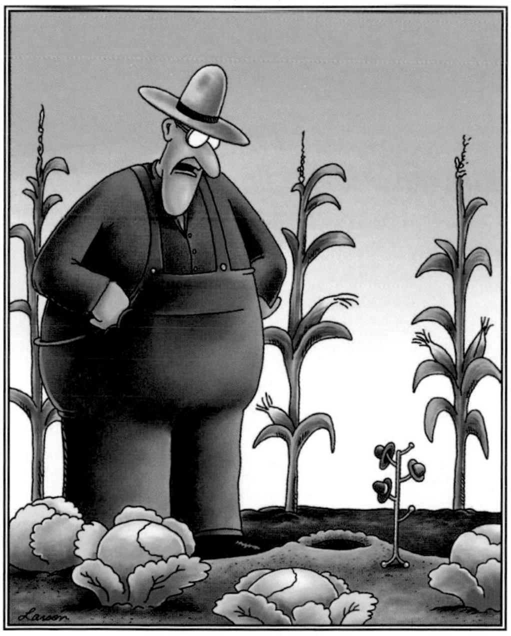
Larson

"So! They're back, are they?"

4/21/84

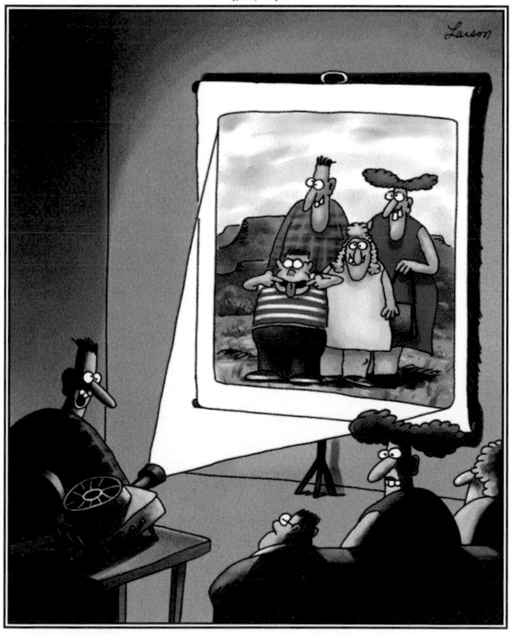
Larson

"Well, here we all are at the Grand Canyon ... but, as usual, Johnny just had to ruin the picture for everyone else."

4/16/84

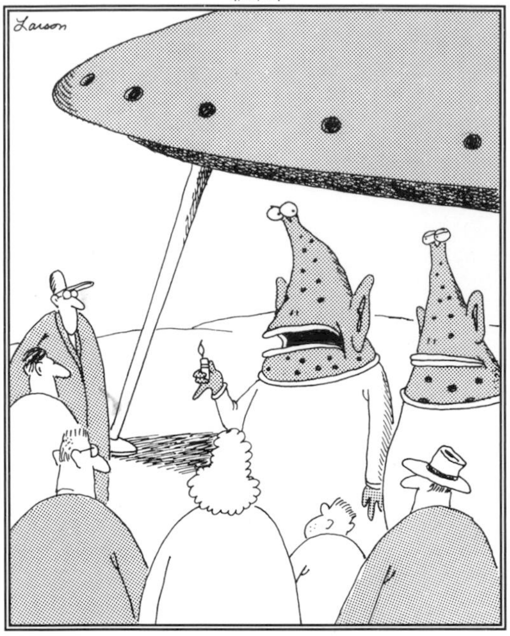

"Well, they're unimpressed. ... And now what are *we* going to do with fifty cases of butane lighters?"

4/24/84

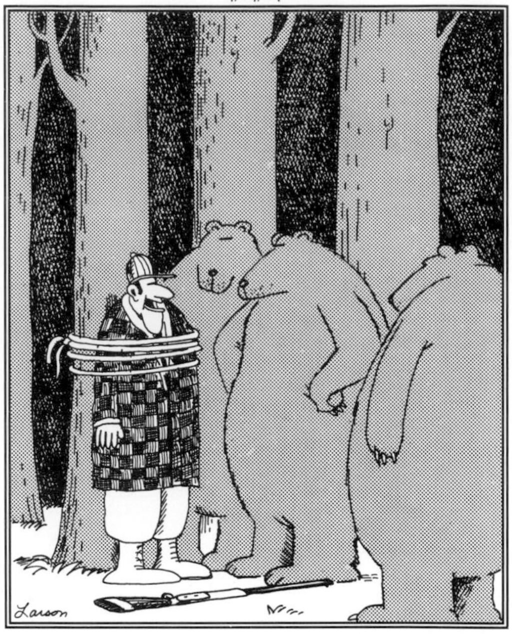

"Do what you will to me, but I'll never talk! ... NEVER! And, after me, there'll come others—and others—and others! Ha ha ha!"

4/20/84

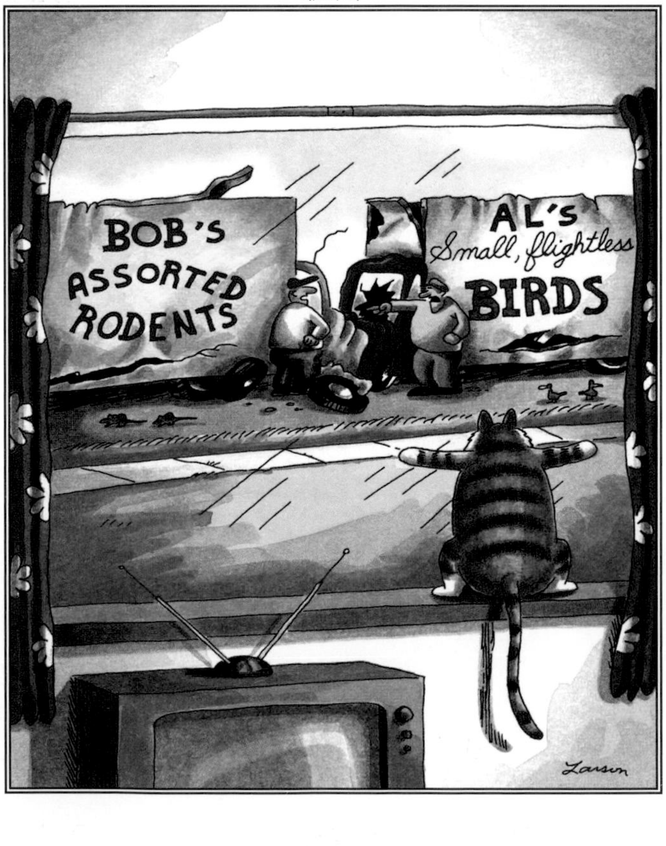
BOB'S ASSORTED RODENTS
AL'S Small, flightless BIRDS

4/25/84

"Oo! I know, Doris! ... Drape one of his
arms over your shoulder!"

4/28/84

"No, Zak. ... It Wilga's turn lick bowl."

4/23/84

Trying to calm the herd, Jake himself was suddenly
awestruck by the image of beauty and unbridled
fury on the cliff above. Pink Shadow had returned.

4/26/84

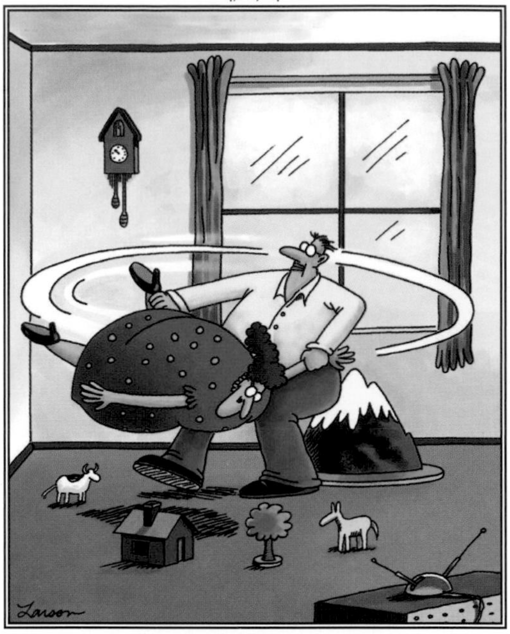

On the next pass, however, Helen failed to clear the mountains.

4/30/84

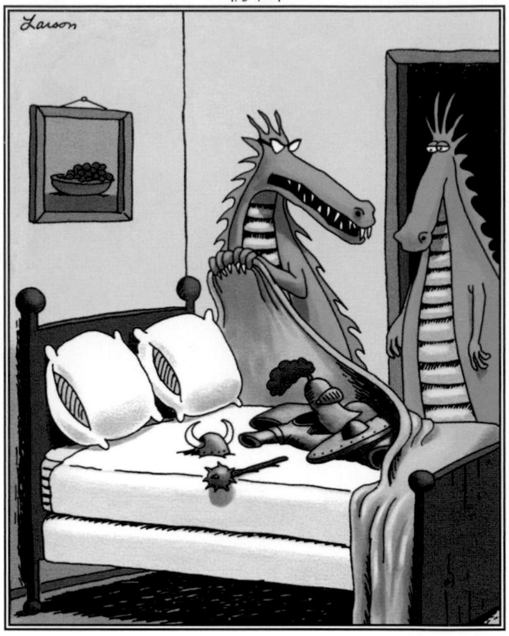

"What have I told you about eating in bed?"

4/27/84

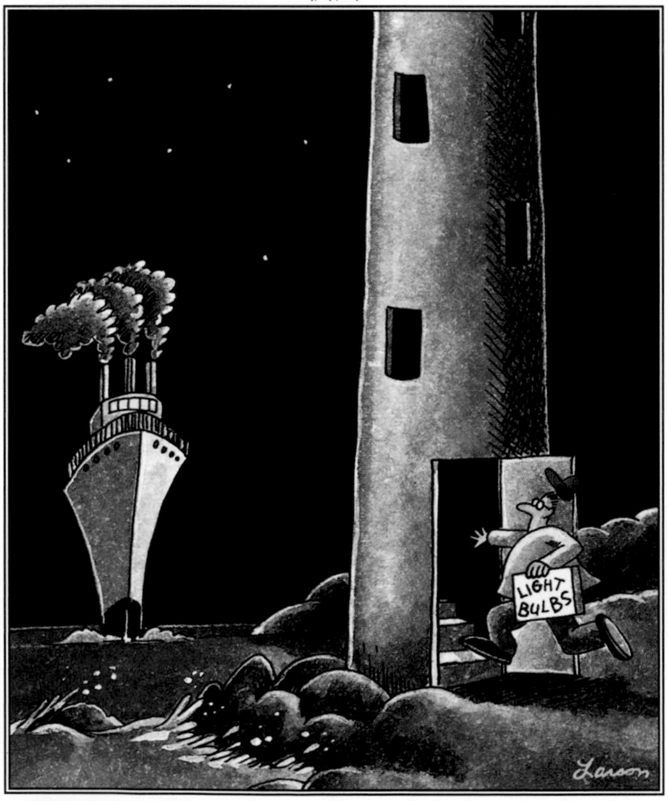
LIGHT BULBS

5/3/84

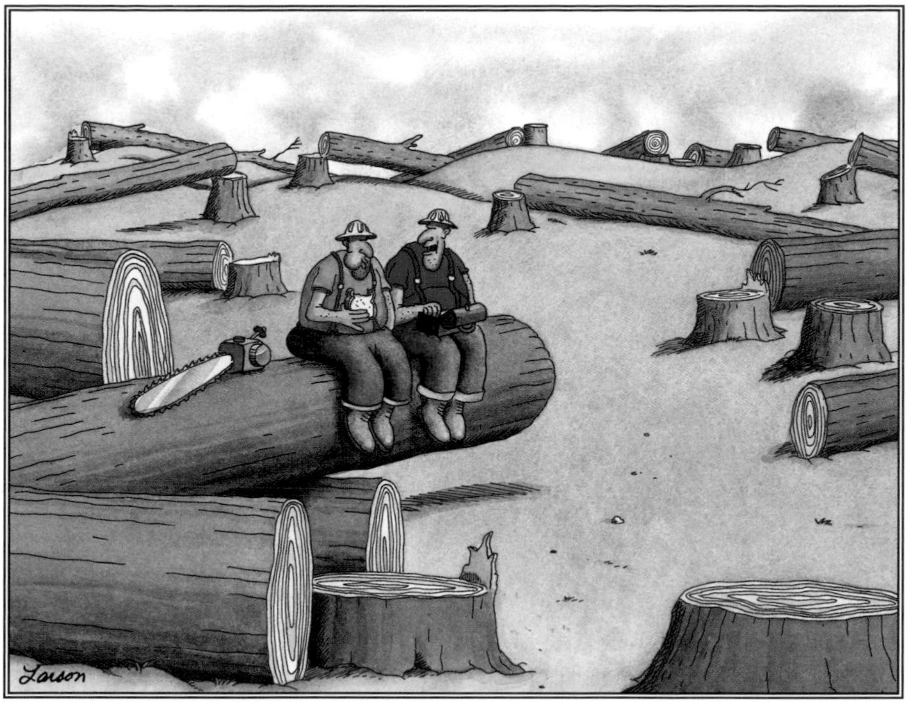
Larson

"You know what I'm sayin'? ... Me, for example. I couldn't work in some stuffy little office. ... The outdoors just calls to me."

5/1/84

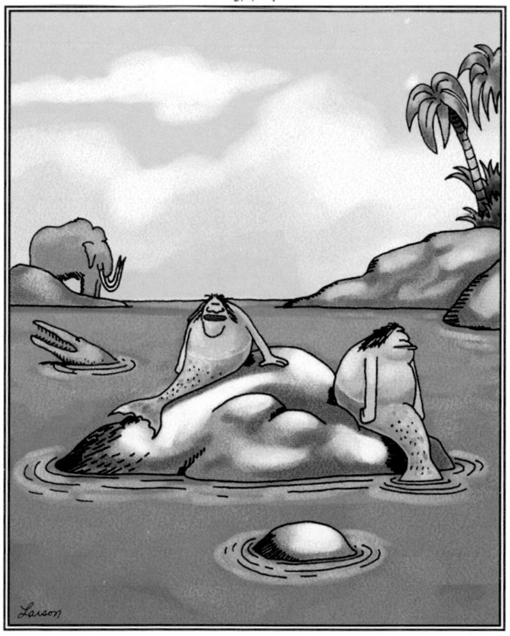
Larson

Early Pleistocene mermaids

5/2/84

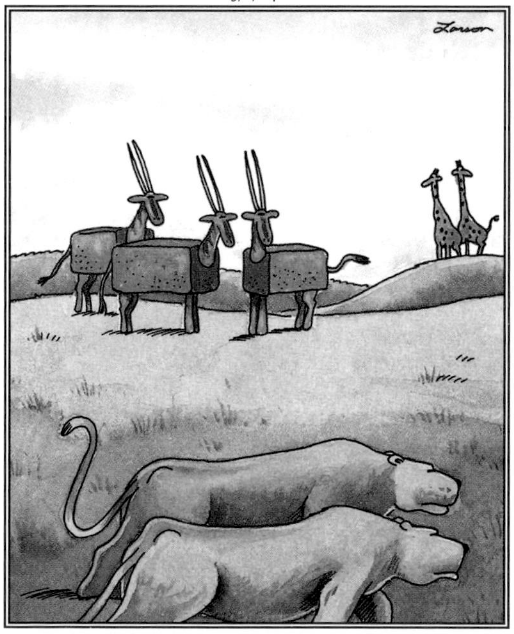
Larson

Knowing the lion's preference for red meat, the spamalopes remained calm but wary.

5/4/84

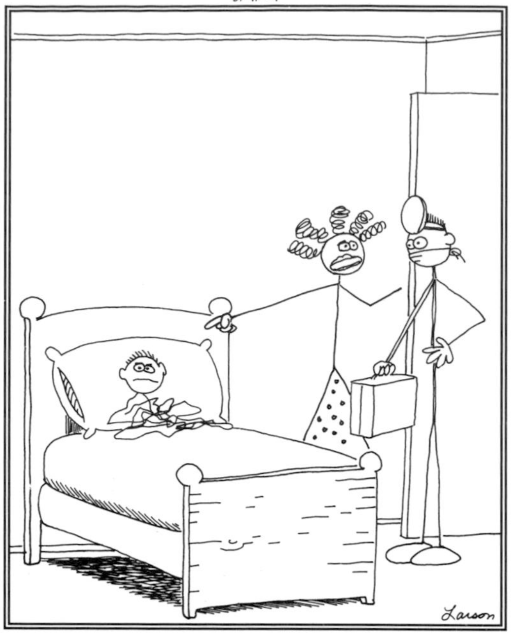

"Thank goodness you're here, Doctor! ... I came in this morning and found Billy just all scribbled like this!"

5/5/84

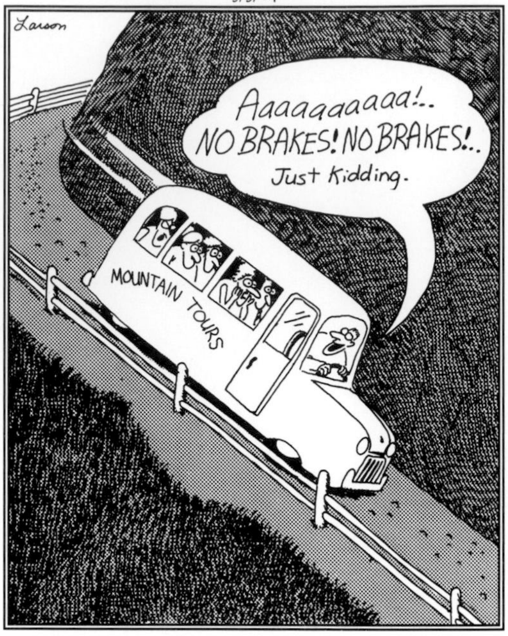
Aaaaaaaaaa!..
NO BRAKES! NO BRAKES!..
Just Kidding.
MOUNTAIN TOURS

The Boy Who Cried "No Brakes"

5/7/84

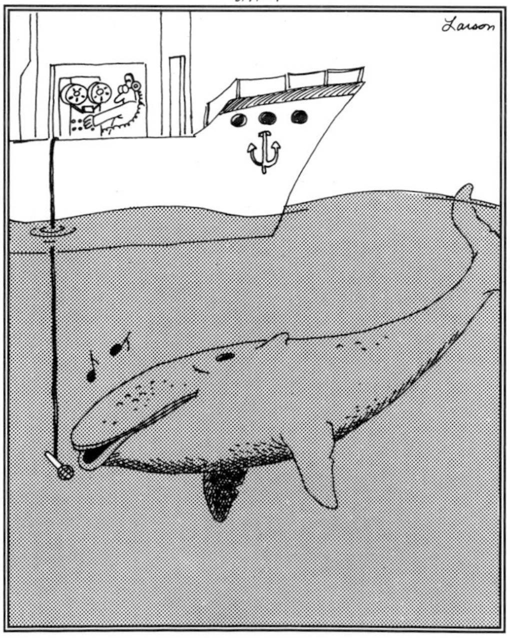

"A Louie, Louie ... wowoooo ... we gotta go now ..."

5/9/84

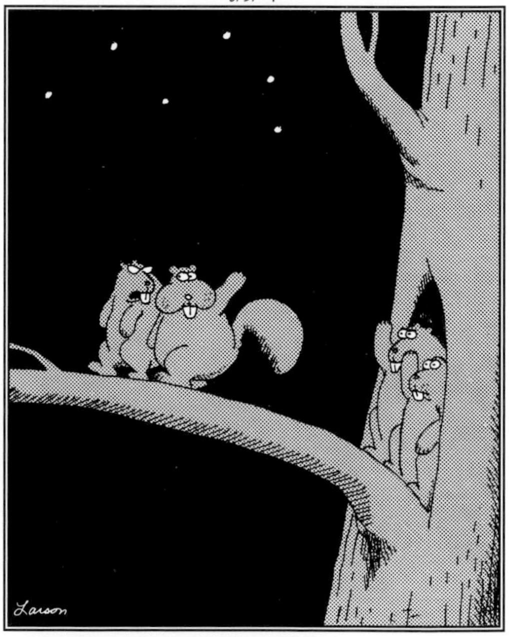

"I've never been so embarrassed. ... After dinner, you just never gave up trying to cram the world into your cheek pouches!"

5/11/84

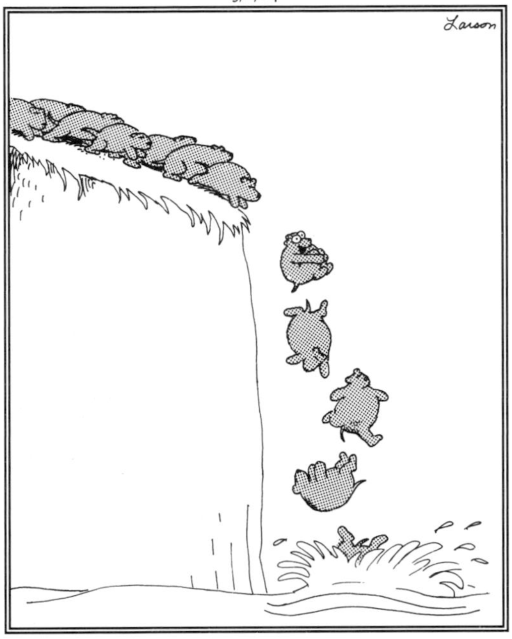
Larson

"CANNONBAAAAAAAALLLLLLLLL!"

5/12/84

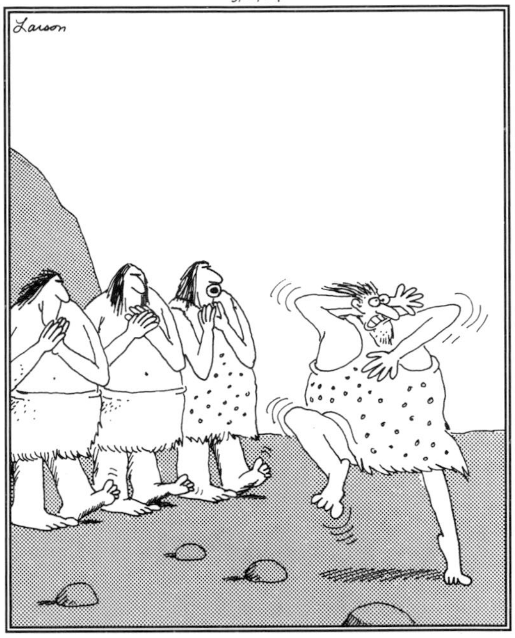
Larson

Grog Schwartz eats some bad beetle grubs, and the art of dance is born.

5/15/84

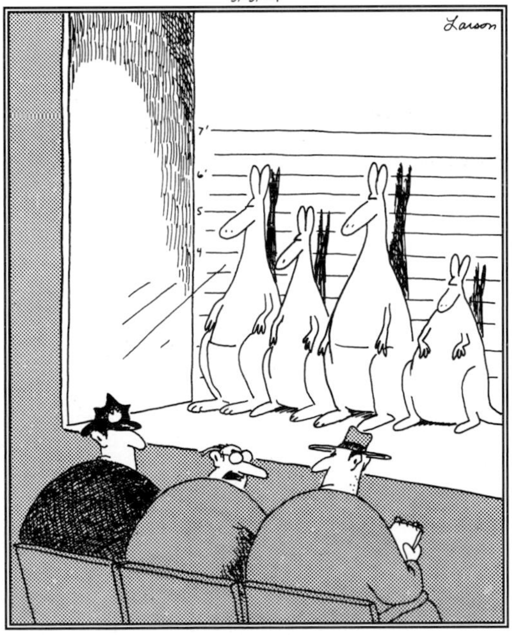
Larson
7'
6'
5'
4'

"Don't rush me! Don't rush me! ... I've *always* gotten my kangaroos and wallabies confused!"

5/17/84

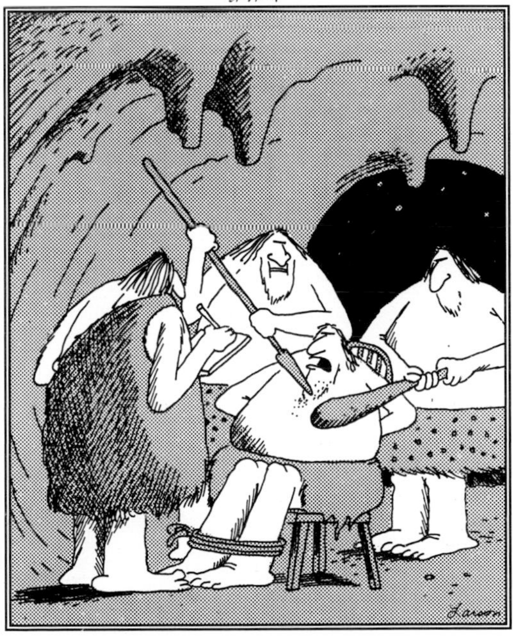
Larson

"Okay! I'll talk! I'll talk! ... Take two sticks of approximately equal size and weight—rub them together at opposing angles using short, brisk strokes ..."

5/8/84

Early vegetarians returning from the kill

5/10/84

"Ladies! Ladies! He's back! ... Our mystery man
who does the Donald Duck impression!"

5/18/84

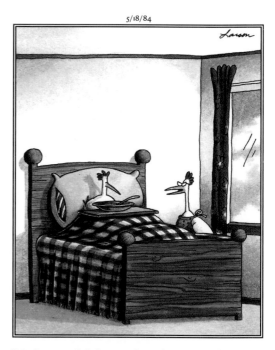

"Quit complaining and eat it! ... Number one,
chicken soup is good for the flu, and
number two, it's nobody we know."

5/14/84

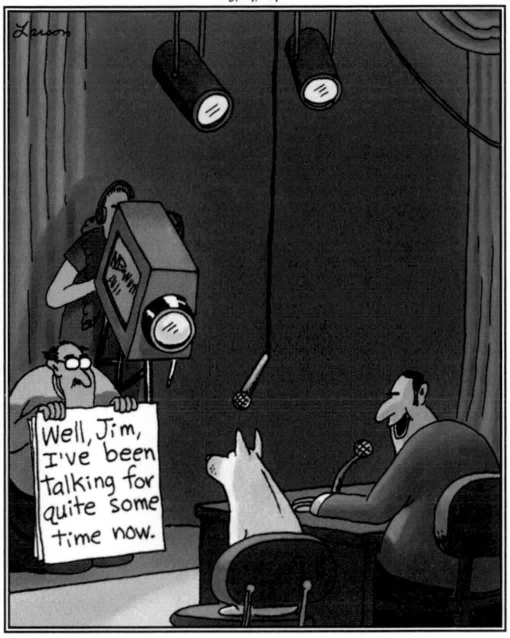
Well, Jim, I've been talking for quite some time now.

"So tell us, Buffy—for how long have you been a talking dog?"

5/21/84

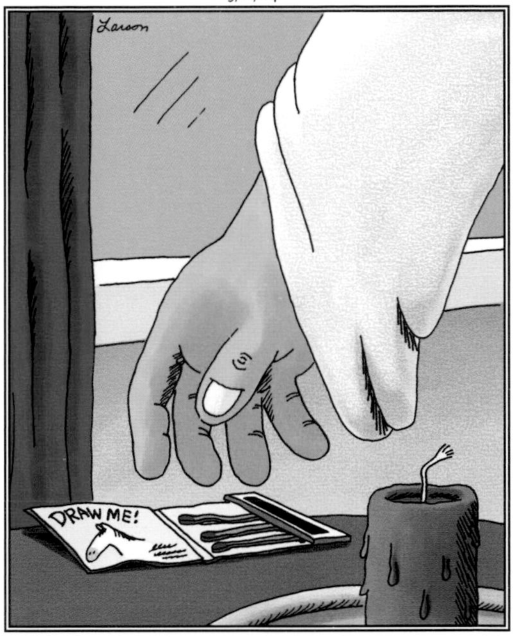
DRAW ME!

One day, as he nonchalantly reaches for a match, Leonardo da Vinci's life is suddenly transformed.

5/16/84

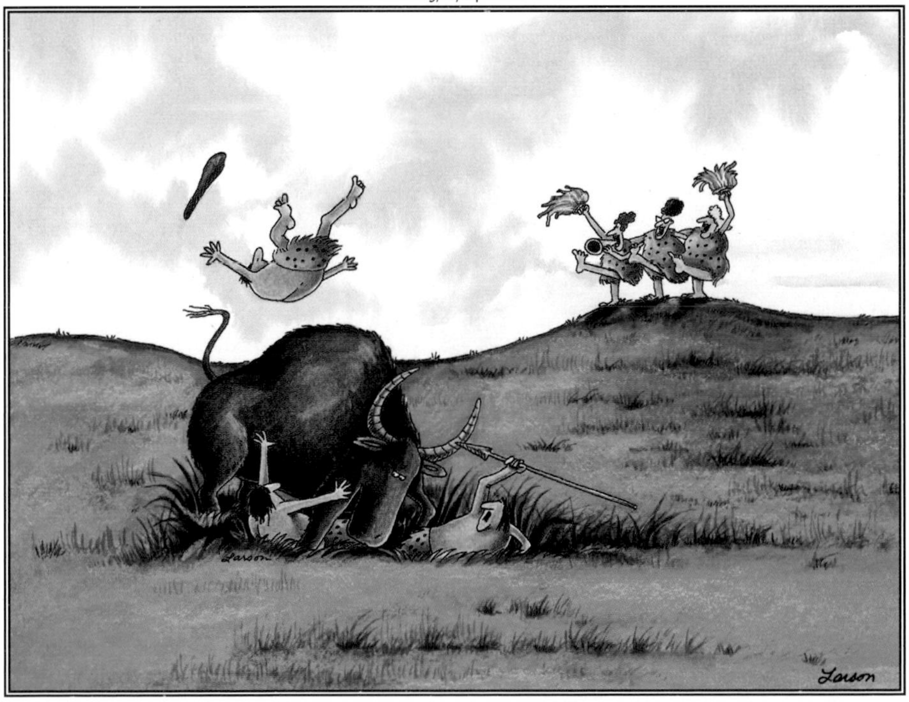

5/19/84

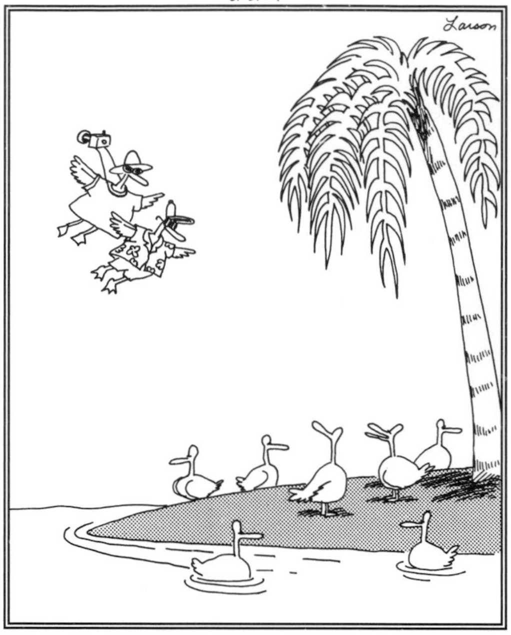

"Well, more arrivals from the States, I see."

5/25/84

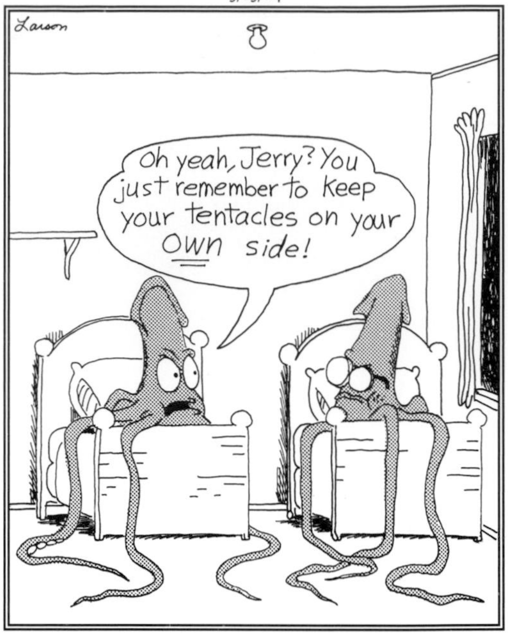
Oh yeah, Jerry? You just remember to keep your tentacles on your OWN side!

The Squid kids at home

5/22/84

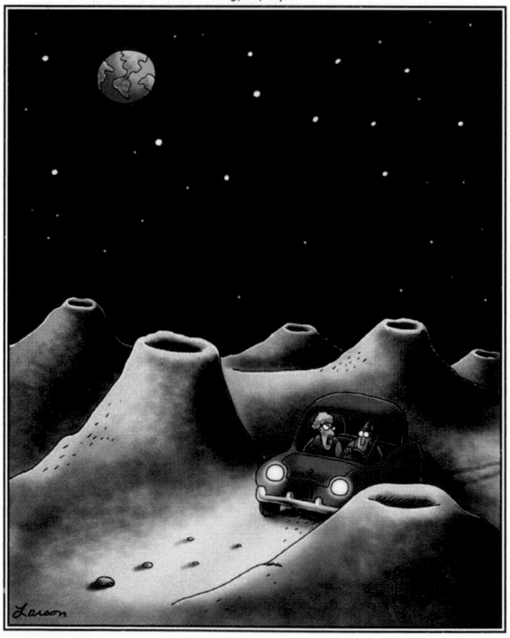

"For heaven's sake, Elroy! *Now* look where the earth is! ... Move over and let me drive!"

5/23/84

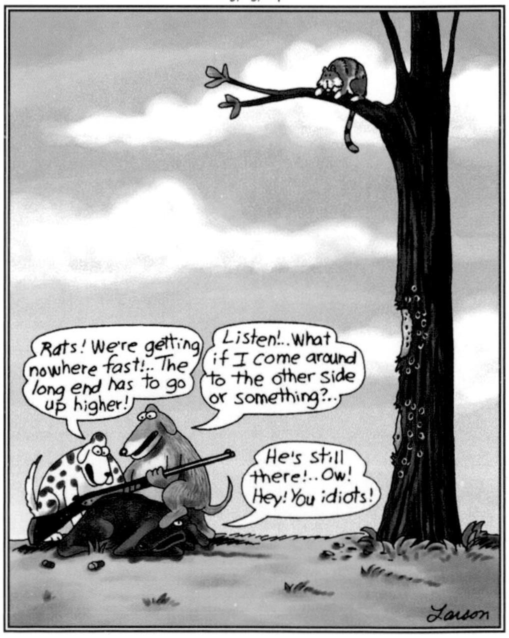
Rats! We're getting nowhere fast!.. The long end has to go up higher!
Listen!.. What if I come around to the other side or something?..
He's still there!.. Ow! Hey! You idiots!

Dog Stooges

5/29/84

Hank knew this place well. He need only wait. ...
The deer would come, the deer would come.

5/28/84

"I don't know about this. ... The red ants
never gave us anything before."

5/31/84

"Well, I'll be danged! ... I'm okay!"

5/30/84

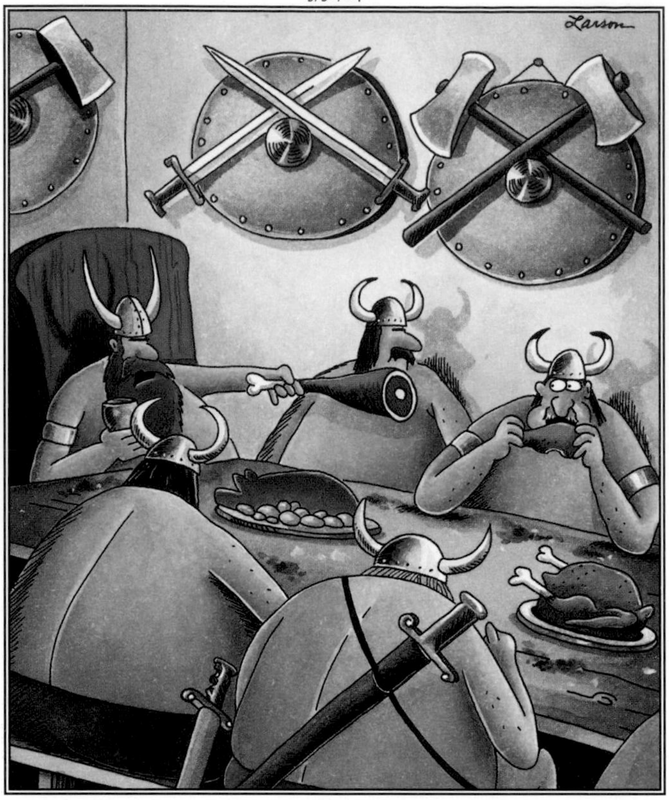
Larson

"Uh-uh-uh-uh-uh. ... Question. Can anyone here tell me what Hanson there is doing wrong with his elbows?"

5/24/84

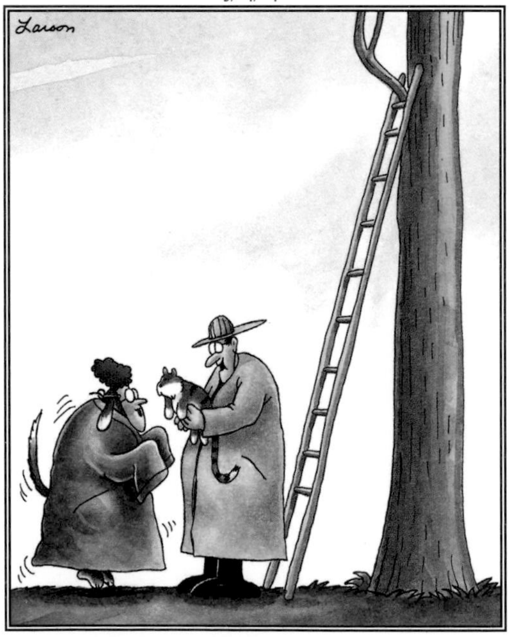
Larson

"Now calm down there ma'am ... your cat's gonna be fine ... just fine."

5/26/84

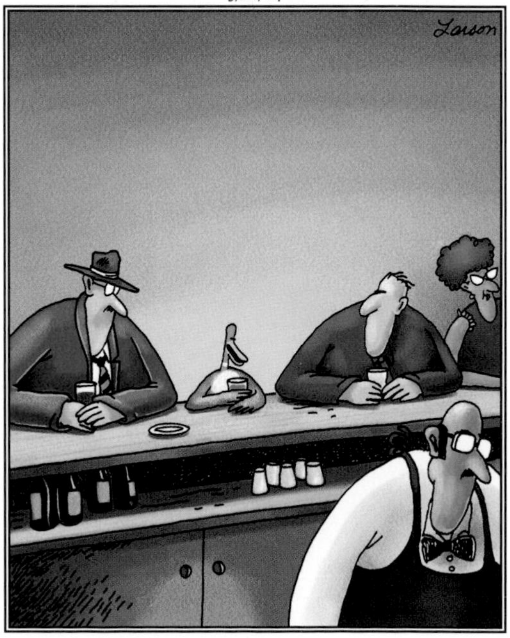
Larson

"I tell you she's drivin' me nuts! ... I come home at night and it's 'quack quack quack'... I get up in the morning and it's 'quack quack quack.'"

6/1/84

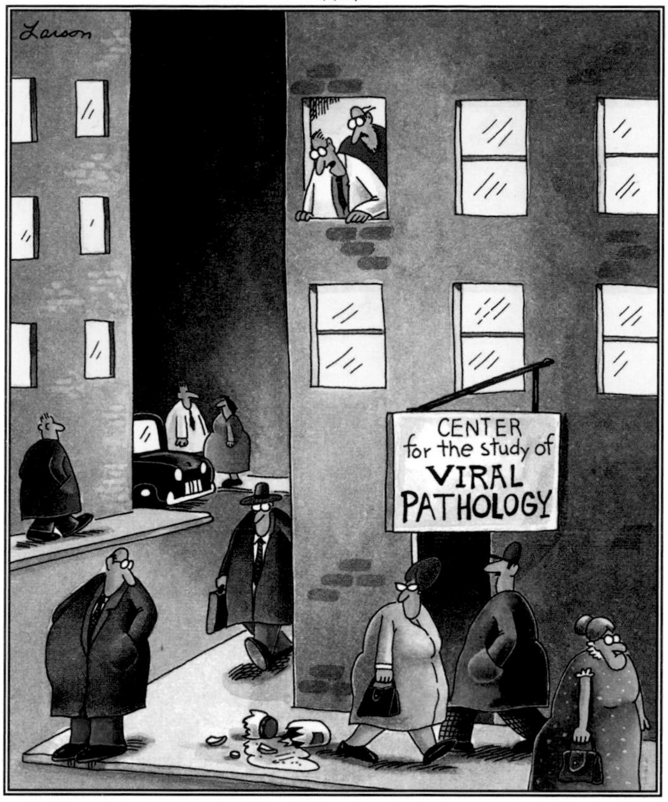
CENTER
for the study of
VIRAL
PATHOLOGY

"Uh-oh."

6/4/84

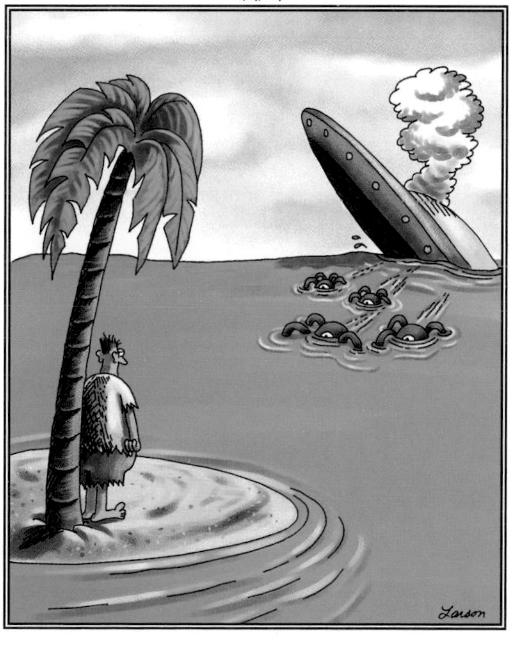

6/5/84

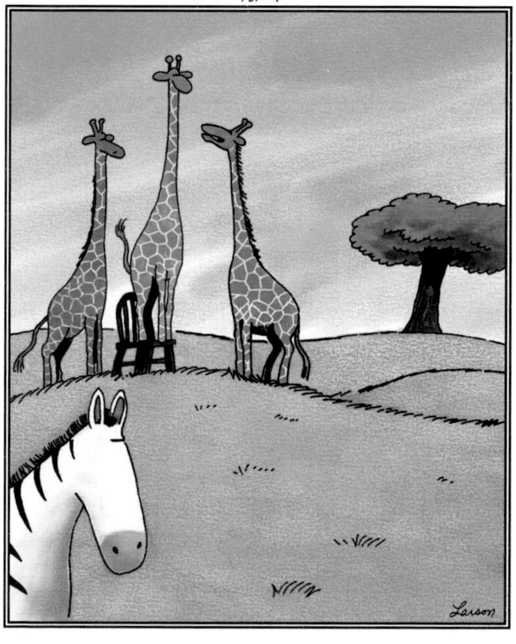

"No lions anywhere? ... Let me have the chair."

6/6/84

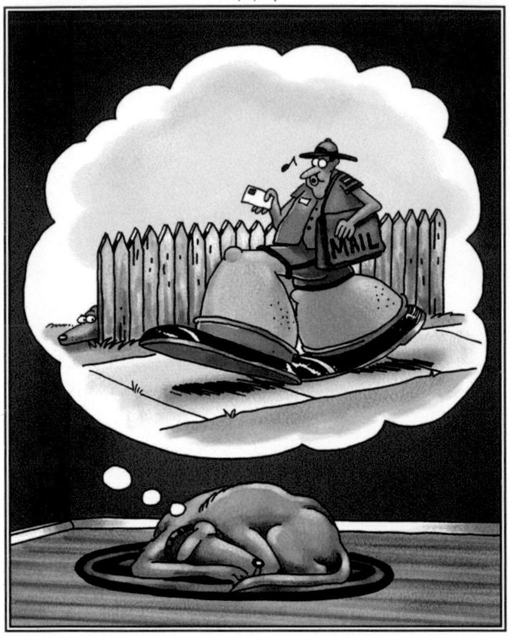
MAIL

What dogs dream about

6/13/84

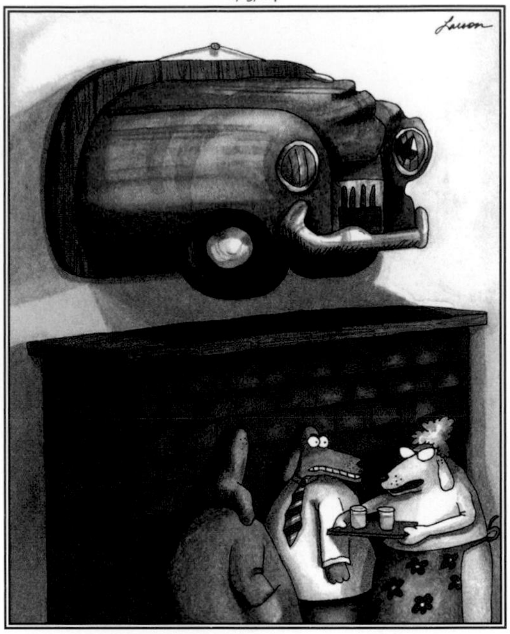
Larson

"Don't listen to him, George. He didn't catch it ... the stupid thing swerved to miss him and ran into a tree."

6/2/84

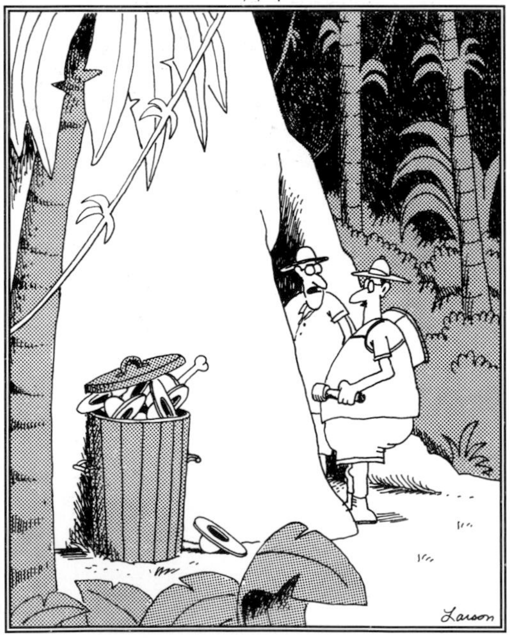
Larson

"Relax, Worthington. ... As the warm, moist air from the jungle enters the cave, the cool, denser air inside forces it to rise, resulting in turbulence that sounds not unlike heavy breathing."

6/8/84

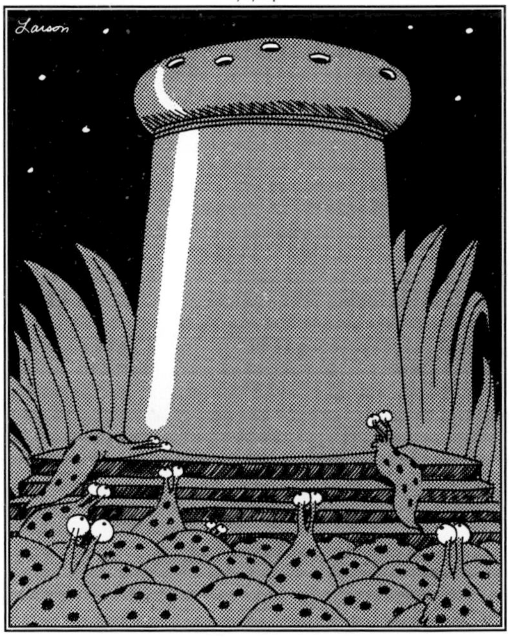
Larson

Of course, the slugs worshipped their god out of fear, not love.

6/14/84

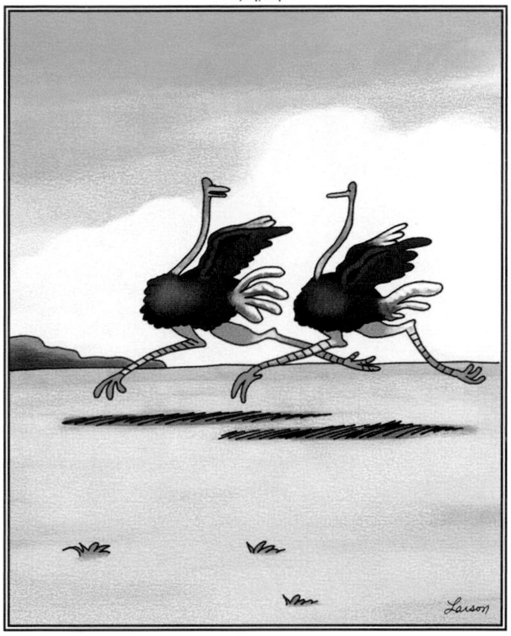
Larson

"For crying out loud, Norm. Look at you ... I hope I don't look half as goony when I run."

6/15/84

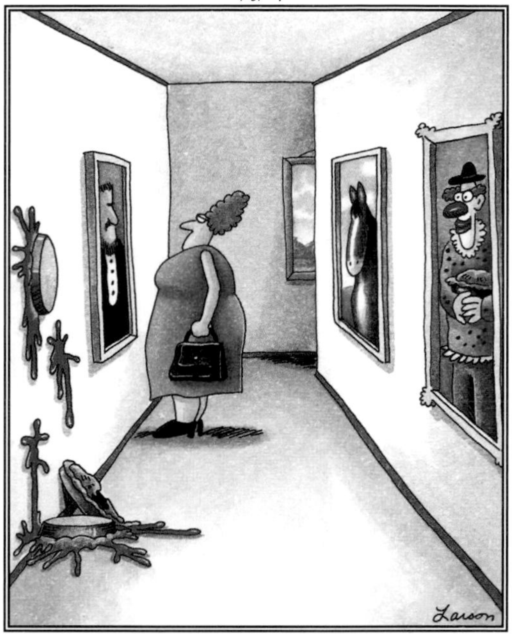
Larson

6/7/84

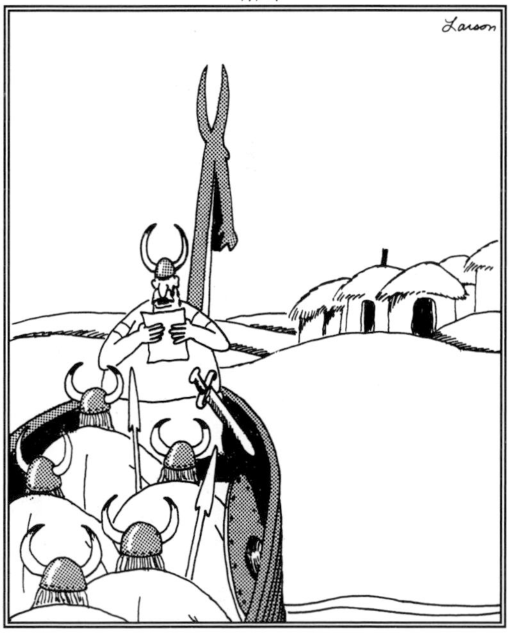
Larson

"Okay, before you go, let me read this one more time: 'Burn the houses, eliminate the townsfolk, destroy the crops, plunder their gold!'... You knuckleheads think you can handle all that?"

6/9/84

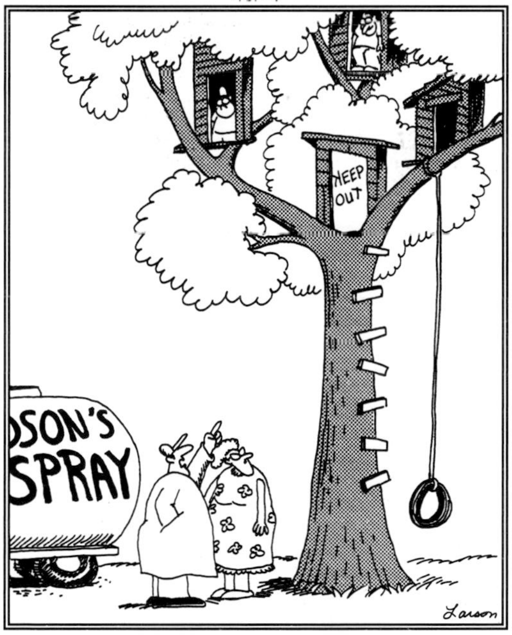
KEEP OUT
DSON'S
SPRAY
Larson

"Well, you've got quite an infestation here, ma'am. ... I can't promise anything, but I imagine I can knock out some of the bigger nests."

6/11/84

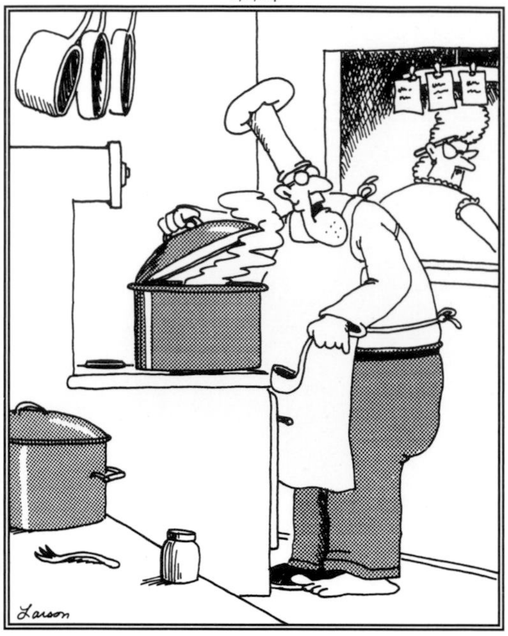
Larson

"Soup of the day is ready!"

6/12/84

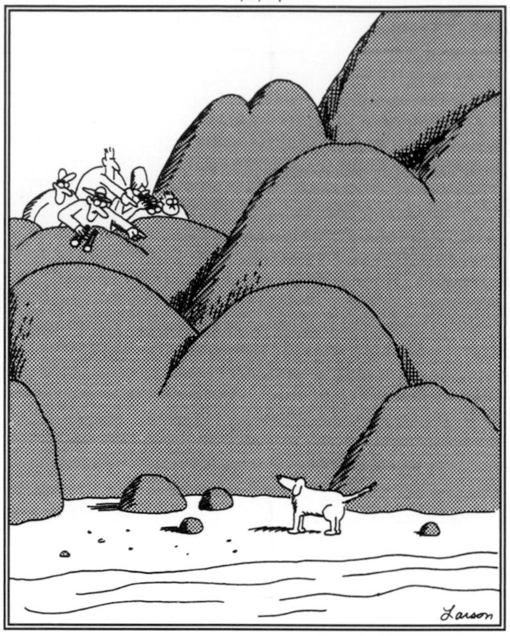
Larson

Another sighting of the Loch Ness dog

6/16/84

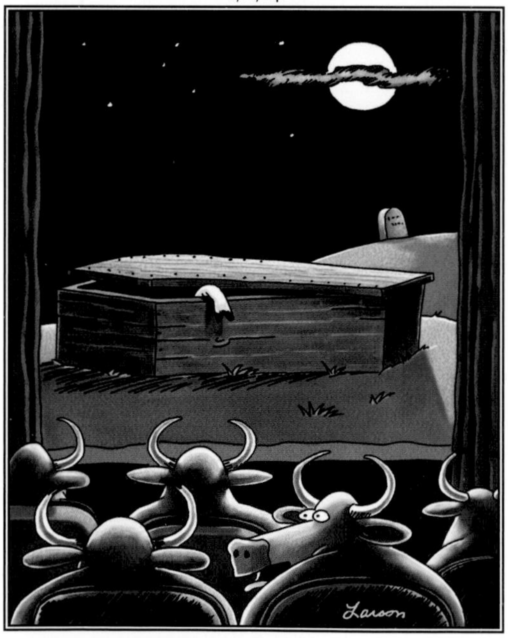
Larson

"Oo! ... Here he comes to feed on the milk of the living."

6/22/84

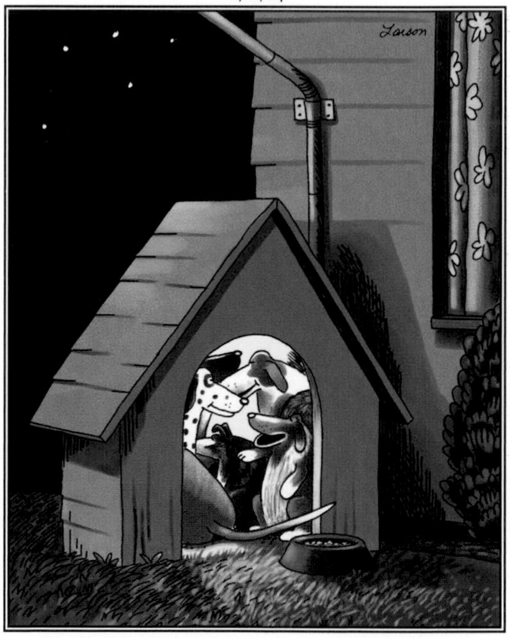
Larson

"Oh, hey! Fantastic party, Tricksy! Fantastic! ... Say, do you mind telling me which way to the yard?"

6/25/84

"FIRE!"

6/18/84

Larson

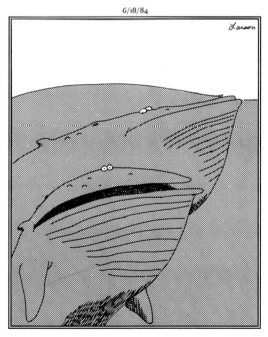

"Oo! Icky icky! ... Something just went down
that surrrrrrre wasn't plankton!"

6/19/84

Larson

Lost in the suburbs, Tonga and Zootho
wander for days—plagued by dogs,
kids, and protective mothers.

6/20/84

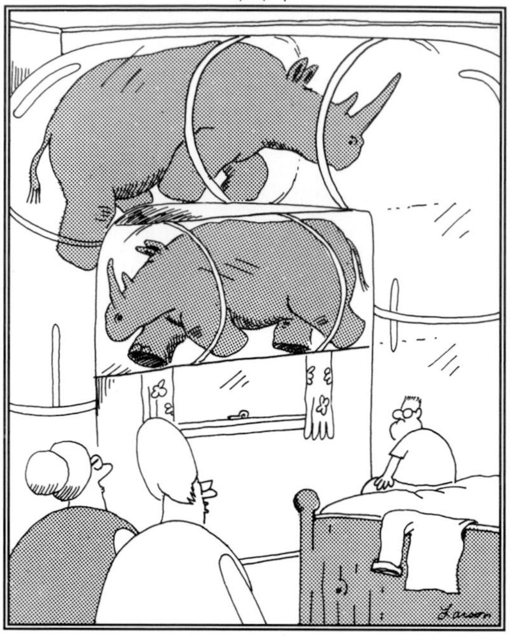

"Dennis, do you mind if Mrs. Carlisle comes in and sees your rhino tube-farm?"

6/21/84

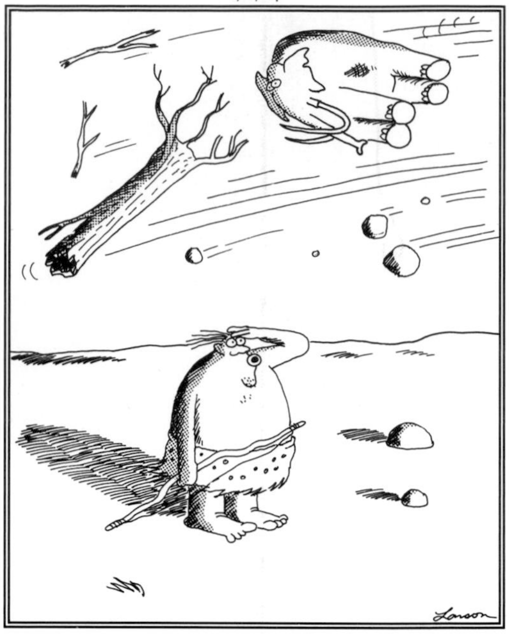

The first cruise arrow is tested.

6/23/84

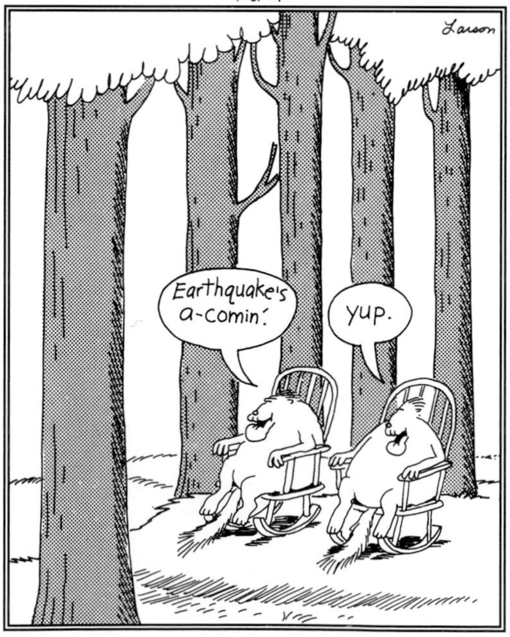
Earthquake's a-comin'.
yup.

The mysterious intuition of some animals

6/26/84

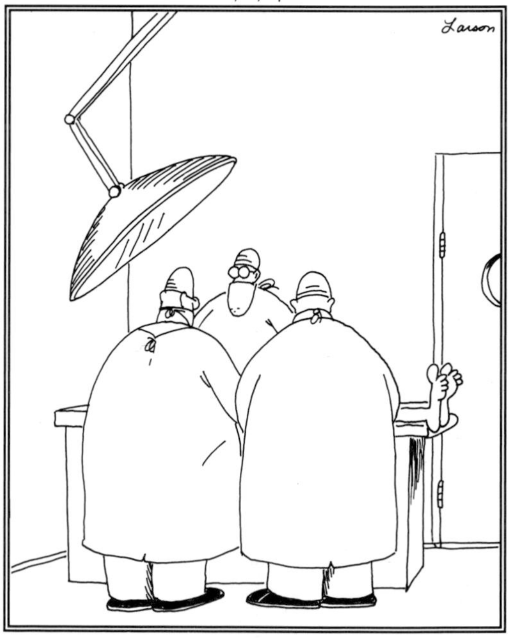

"Okay, Wellington. I'm comfortable with my grip if you are. ... Have you made a wish?"

6/27/84

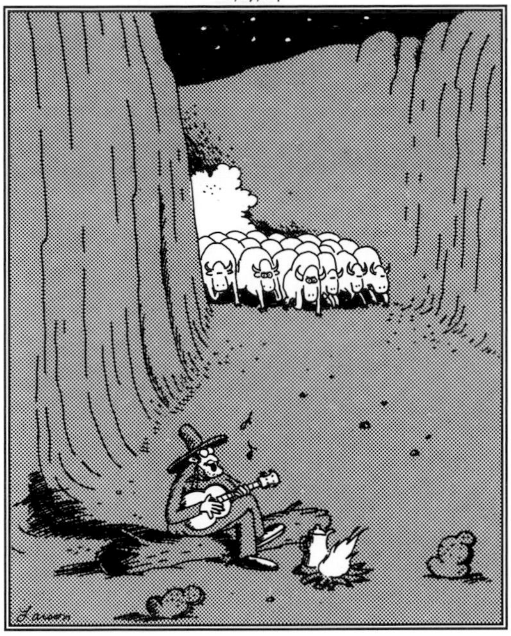

"Oh, give me a home, where the buffalo roam ..."

6/28/84

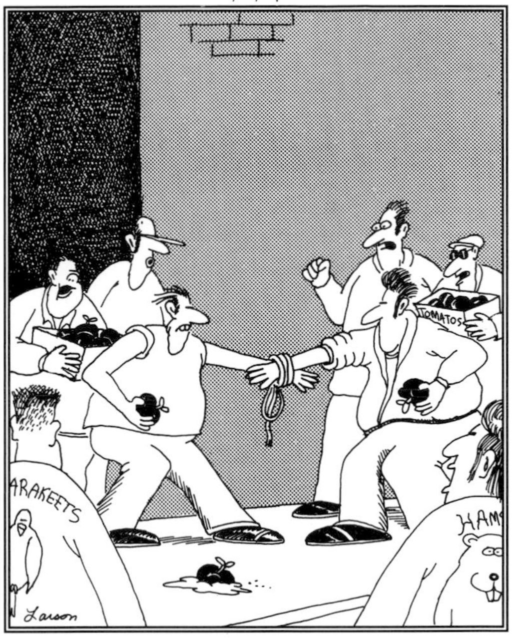

Goaded on by their respective gangs, the leaders of the Hamster Demons and the Parakeet Devils square off.

6/29/84

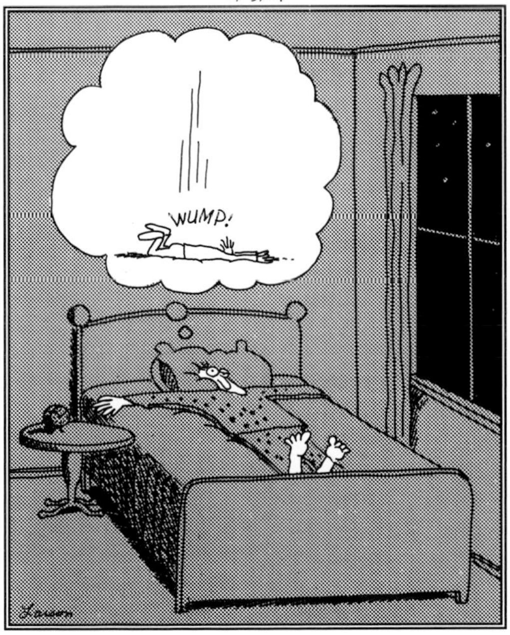
WUMP!

Dreaming he's falling, Jerry forgets the well-known "always-wake-up-before-you-land" rule.

6/30/84

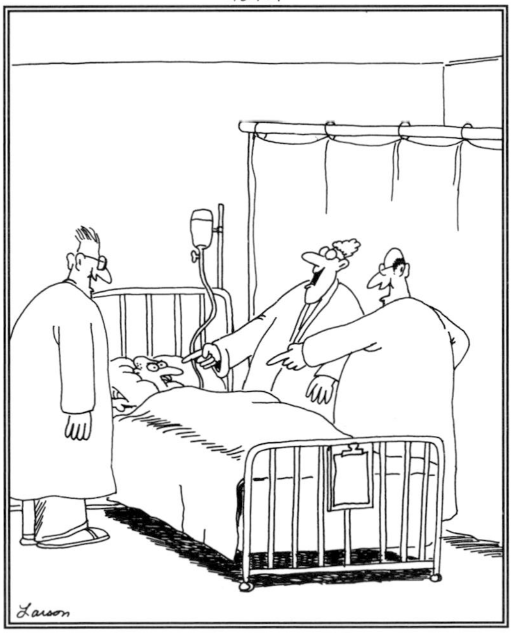

Testing whether laughter *is* the best medicine.